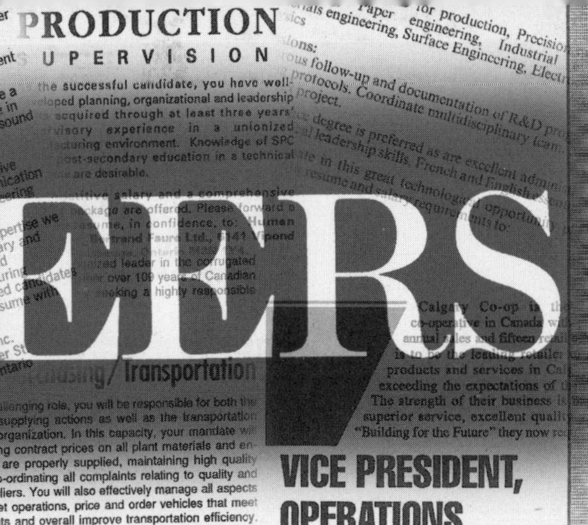

A major Toronto-area manufacturer is seeking ... management team. With existing contracts ... rewrite the company's materials management ...

If you are comfortable working in an extremely ... you have a track record of proven success in ... turing... if you are excited by the challenge ... contribution in one of these leadership roles:

MATERIALS MANAGER

- 15-plus years of experience with university ...
- CAPICS or CPP designation
- Strong pace-setting and team-building skill ...
- Functional expertise in all aspects of M/M: production scheduling, forecasting, distribution, inventory control, material flow, Kan-Ban, MRP, etc.
- Automotive or electronics industry background

PRODUCTION CONTROL MANAGER

- 5 to 10 years of experience including 2 to 3 years as supervisor
- CAPICS certification
- Expertise in EDI, forecasting, master production scheduling, MRP, related disciplines
- Automotive parts/OEM industry background

DISTRIBUTION MANAGER

- 10-plus years of experience including 5 years ...

NAFTA

WAREHOUSE SUPERVISOR

- 5-plus years of experience including 2-plus years as supervisor
- Expertise in receiving, shipping, bar coding/locator and other automated systems
- Automotive, packaged goods, or electronics sector background

ENGINEERING PROG... MANAGER

You will apply your well developed problem solving and risk assessment ab... cross functional (engineering, design, q... manufacturing) team leadership ... Engineering graduate, preferably M... Engineering, you have a minimum of f... engineering program management experi... thorough working knowledge of q... procedures, product design, tooling and a... manufacturing systems. This position re... spreadsheet skills and overnight travel. ... systems experience is an asset.

Attractive salaries and comprehensive be... offered. Please forward a detailed res... confidence, indicating the position of inte... **Human Resources, Bertrand Faure Ltd ... Vipond Drive, Mississauga, Ontario L5T...**

An Equal Opportunity Employer

TOOLING ENGIN...

REQUIRED FOR BRAMALEA ASSEMBLY P...

Qualifications:

- Bachelors degree in Mechanical Engineering
- ...ars experience in the automotive indus...
- ...nce in Process Design and Tooling

Pride in our products and the efforts of some truly valuable people have made Nu•Pharm an international success in the development and marketing of generic pharmaceuticals. We invite you to contribute to our vision of excellence in the key role of:

QUALITY CONTROL MANAGER

Reporting to the Vice President, Scientific Affairs, your goal will be to plan, implement and administer all Quality Control functions and standards across all areas of our business. This highly responsible position requires a strong communicator with the knowledge and expertise gained from completion of a B.Sc. in Chemistry and a minimum of five years of progressive supervisory experience in a pharmaceutical Quality Control laboratory. Knowledge of US cGMP, and experience with FDA auditing procedures are definite assets.

Operation

...lour of Canada

...of one of the world's top chemical manufacturers serves a ...50MM capital program is underway to enhance the capacity ...change, innovation and employee involvement dominate the

...anager

...lity, safety and productivity. You'll provide the financial, ...ive record of championing change, team building and cost ...re to respond to demanding customers and business plans ... not just managers. Comfortable on the shop floor or in ...al climate, decision tools and communication channels to

...e with entrepreneurial prowess. You think ... ativity in your people, but you know ...

QE/QA Managers

Major Automotive Component and Systems Supplier operating under global market opportunities is seeking qualified individuals in the field of Quality Engineering and Management.

As a successful candidate, you will be well organized, have excellent communication skills and enjoy working in a fast-paced, progressive environment. A self motivated, team ...

Plant Manager

Barrie

Northern Telecom, a leading global manufactu... telecommunications systems, is ahead of the technolo... Our incredible success and position of leadership in ... today's most advanced technologies has led to this ... for a Plant Manager our Barrie operations.

PLANT MANAGER

Galsteel processes and distributes flat rolled carbon steel to the automotive, manufacturing and construction sectors. We are seeking a team oriented individual to join our management team as

The ideal candidate should possess the following qualifications:

- Minimum of 5 year's supervisory experience in a steel service centre
- Knowledge of slitting, shearing and cutting-to-length of flat rolled carbon steel
- Hands-on approach with strong mechanical aptitude and ability to complete mechanical maintenance/repairs
- Strong interpersonal and communication skills to motivate others to achieve high goals of quality and customer service.

We offer a unique environment with competitive salary, full benefits and an opportunity to join an organization dedicated to excellence in Customer Service. If you are interested in joining our team, please forward your resume to:

OPERATIONS MANAGER

Our client, a leading provider of community based health care currently has an opportunity for an Operations Manager who will enhance their ability to provide customer service excellence.

Reporting to the Director, Operations, you will work directly with staff in the warehouse and distribution areas. You will also manage the physical plant and be involved in special projects to develop operational procedures and systems to support the growing business.

As an energetic, flexible self-starter with a long-term strategic outlook towards operations, you must possess excellent organizational and problem solving capabilities, together with strong communication, interpersonal, and people management skills. Advanced PC knowledge with experience in delivery/distribution logistics is essential. Recognized certification in business/materials management is ideal, and experience gained in the health care field is a definite asset.

Our client offers a competitive salary and comprehensive benefits package together with opportunities for personal and career development in an exciting new industry with tremendous potential. Please send your resume, accompanied by a letter of introduction describing relevant skills/experience, in confidence, to: **Tony Power, Hayward, Fretz, Power and Associates, 145 King Street, West, Suite 1002, Toronto, Ontario M5H 3X6.** *We appreciate your response and will be in touch if a meeting is required.*

A.O. Smith in Stratford is ISO 9002 registered, and a growing manufacturer of waterheaters, boilers and hydropneumatic tanks. We currently have the following openings:

PRODUCTION SUPERVISOR

The ideal candidate will have to rotate shifts and supervise approximately 20 employees. Must have experience with production fabrication including assembly, welding and painting. ... interpersonal skills and problem solving ability, preferably ... unionized environment, is a requirement. Must have minimum ... with 5 years supervisory experience.

QUALITY CONTROL COODINATOR/ PRODUCTION SCHEDULER

Reporting to the Quality Control Manager, this position ... responsible for auditing of manufacturing processes, failure ... performance evaluation testing and production scheduling. ... must be able to work independently, have strong computer skills, good problem solving and communication skills. Additionally, ... should possess assembly line Q.C. experience as well as know... various measurement techniques. Must have a minimum of ... a college technical diploma preferred.

SALES COORDINATOR

We have an opening in our Canadian head office that ... handling orders, follow-up warranty administration, quota... technical assistance. ...

One of the world's leading manufacturers specializing in the design of high-technology seats to the automotive industry has opportunities in:

PRODUCTION

SUPERVISION

As the successful candidate, you have well-developed planning, organizational and leadership skills acquired through at least three years' supervisory experience in a unionized manufacturing environment. Knowledge of SPC and a post-secondary education in a technical discipline are desirable.

PURCHASING TEAM L...

SUPPLY AND SERVICES B...

$52,371 - $63,749 per an...

Reporting to the Director of Supply and Service... will lead a team of professionals responsible fo... cost-effective acquisition of supplies and se... Legislative Assembly of Ontario. Specific d... assisting and providing procurement leadership ... staff in the development of diverse functional ... specifications; optimizing methods of sup... evaluation criteria; determination of appropr... negotiation strategies; advice on negotiation ... development and presentation of award recom... and contract administration quality control. Thi... monitor and report on progress against Supply ... goals and objectives and be responsible for ide... maintaining current knowledge of broad an... procurement issues such as environmentally ... procurement practices, employment equity, pro... agreements, and will develop and communicate p... staff for effectively and uniformly addressing the... acquisition projects.

LOCATION: Toronto.

QUALIFICATIONS: Extensive knowledge of p... techniques and practices ideally gained by a combin... appropriate University degree/PMAC professional ... designation and senior purchasing assignments in b... and private sector purchasing environments. Dem... strengths in contract law, and the skills to coach a... team of seasoned procurement professionals in me... exceeding the challenging needs and the expecta... highly sophisticated client population. Excellent ne... communication/interpersonal/organizational skills ... ability to manage competing priorities/deadlines. Ex... in the acquisition of construction, printing and IT ... an asset.

Please submit your résumé with a covering lette... received no later than May 12, 1995 by 4:30 p.m., and ... **File LA-95-12, to: The Legislative Assembly of O... Human Resources Branch, Room 2540, Whitney ... Queen's Park, Toronto, Ontario M7A 1A2.**

While we appreciate all applica...

...You will execute and maintain ... products are meeting both internal and external ... provide statistical information for yield improvement and liaiso... on all testing related aspects. You will also be required to contin... equipment and methods to improve yield and efficiency, provi... troubleshoot guides and training to support subcontractors a... staff. You have a degree in electronics engineering or equivalent ... 4-5 years' of relevant experience in a high tech electronic and high volum... environment. Experience with computer graphics cards, PC softwar... applications is preferred.

Production Scheduler... In this position, you will ... increasing activities of subcontractors and strengthen the product... function. You will also be responsible for the following: production scheduling for subcontractors, expedite materials to meet with scheduling ... versus plan, monitor WIP level and clear any outstandi... work with other internal departments. You have a post s... with experience in PMC. Good computer skills are requ...

Manufacturing Engineering T... positions, you will oversee the technical aspects of ... repair the equipment and provide technical process ... surface mount line. You have a degree or diploma in M...

Novopharm Limited, an establishe... rapidly growing Canadian pharmace... company dedicated to "Quality... Compromise", is widely recognize... excellent products and state-of-the-... facilities. Our progressive organization ... has a unique opportunity for a:

Planner

Reporting to the Planning Manager, ... position will translate marketing forecasts ... production requirements, smooth pla... capacities, balance inventory levels and liai... between Materials Management, Custome... Service and Quality Control.

...u must have 3-5 years' scheduling experien... MRP II environment, a professional Materia... agement-related certification (or in progress)... understand pharmaceutical product flow... also demonstrate excellent interpersonal ... communication skills, and ideally, are ... puter literate with a specific knowledge of ... ing spreadsheets.

...eturn we offer ongoing opportunities for ... professional development as well as a ... petitive salary and benefits package. ... forward your resume, by June 2, 1995, ... nfidence, to: Employment Coordinat...

New Horizons New Opportunities

At deHavilland Inc., we have maintained our position of leadership through the manufacture of sophisticated commercial transport aircraft and products for markets around the world. Continued success has led to this opportunities for accomplished professionals.

Senior Quality Assurance Manager

...anager

OPERATIONS MANAGEMENT *in Canada*

OPERATIONS MANAGEMENT *in Canada*

Don Waters • Ragu Nayak

Addison-Wesley Publishers Limited

Don Mills, Ontario • Reading, Massachusetts
Menlo Park, California • New York • Wokingham, England
Amsterdam • Bonn • Sydney • Singapore • Tokyo • Madrid
San Juan • Paris • Seoul • Milan • Mexico City • Taipei

Executive Editor: Joseph Gladstone
Managing Editor: Linda Scott
Acquisitions Editor: John Clelland
Editor: Linda Collins
Design and Page Layout: Anthony Leung
Production Coordinator: Melanie van Rensburg
Manufacturing Coordinator: Sharon Latta Paterson
Cover Design and Illustrations: Anthony Leung

Reviewers: The authors and publishers are grateful to the following people for their insightful comments on the initial draft of this manuscript:
Abbey Cohen, *Dawson College*
Alex Donnelly, *Lambton College of Applied Arts and Technology*
Joe Ribic, *British Columbia Institute of Technology*
Les Miscampbell, *Centennial College of Applied Arts and Technology*
Jeff Mace, *Algonquin College*
Allan Garner, *Durham College*

Canadian Cataloguing in Publication Data

Waters, C.D.J. (C. Donald John), 1949–
Operations management in Canada

Includes index.
ISBN 0-201-82907-X

1. Production management - Canada. I. Nayak, Ragu. I. Title.

HD31.W37 1995 658.5'00971 C95-932564-6

ISBN 0-201-82907-X

Photo Credits

Chapter 1: *p.7* The Stock Solution (coal mine); Picture Perfect USA™ Image (brewery); Phototake (hospital); *p.18* Plitron Manufacturing Inc. / **Chapter 2:** *p.20* Tetra Pak Laval; *p.28* Magna International Inc.; *p.29* Magna International Inc.; *p.44* Plitron Manufacturing Inc. / **Chapter 3:** *p.49* Caradon Indalex / **Chapter 5:** *p.136* Dorothea Knitting Mills / **Chapter 6:** *p.153* Ferrari North America Inc.; *p.155* Honda of Canada Manufacturing; *p. 169* ©Bell Canada. Courtesy Bell Historical Collection; *p. 171* IPL Inc.; *p.173* Courtesy of Grand & Toy Ltd. / **Chapter 7:** *p.194* The Stroh Brewery Company; *p.198* Canadian Tool and Die / **Chapter 8:** *p.212* Disneyland, Paris; *p.237* Courtesy of Ontario Hydro / **Chapter 10:** *p.286* Anthony Leung / **Chapter 12:** *p.347* Honeywell Limited / **Chapter 14:** *p.387* Courtesy of Avon Canada Inc.; *p. 389* Yamaha Motor Canada Ltd.; *p. 391* The Woodbridge Group; *p. 405* Honeywell Limited / **Chapter 15:** *p.411* Courtesy of SkyDome Corporation; *p. 420* The Scotch Whisky Association / **Chapter 16:** *p.450* Domtar Inc.; *p.460* Ford Motor Company of Canada; *p. 463* Wal-Mart / **Chapter 17:** *p.469* Grand & Toy Ltd. / **Chapter 18:** *p.510* Hudson's Bay Company; p.514 McDonald's

A B C D E -BP- 99 98 97 96 95

Printed and bound in Canada.

PREFACE

The Subject

Every organization takes a number of inputs and converts them to outputs. Factories take components and raw materials and turn them into finished products; hospitals take sick patients and turn them into healthy ones; power stations convert fuel into electricity; restaurants take food and turn it into meals. All the activities needed for these conversions are called *operations.*

Every organization—manufacturers, services, governments, charities, and every other kind of organization—has a set of operations at its centre. *Operations management* is concerned with the way these operations are designed, planned, organized, and controlled.

Operations management is used in every organization, and at every level. This means it is sometimes difficult to describe very general principles. To simplify the terms, this book assumes that every organization makes a *product.* This product might be a good or a service, or a combination of the two—whatever an organization produces is called a product.

Approach of the Book

The book gives a broad introduction to operations management. It assumes little previous knowledge from the reader—so it can be used for many introductory courses. The book is especially designed for new students meeting operations management for the first time. For this, it takes a conceptual viewpoint. Ideas are introduced by discussion, examples, and real cases. Only the most important mathematical techniques have been included, and these have been kept deliberately simple.

One important feature of the book is its Canadian perspective. It describes operations management as practised in Canada—with many Canadian cases and examples. It describes the job actually done by Canadian operations managers—and the jobs Canadian students can expect to get when they finish their courses.

The book follows a logical path through the decisions made in an organization. It discusses the types of decisions made in operations in all organizations. This means that it is not limited to manufacturing or services. It discusses contemporary ideas, such as just-in-time and total quality management.

Contents

The book starts with a introduction to the subject. Then later chapters follow a path through specific types of decisions. These begin with the planning needed for a product, and then move on through planning the process, quality management, and a range of other important decisions.

The book is divided into 18 chapters. The first two chapters give an introduction to the subject—they define the subject, give examples of operations, and discuss the kinds of decisions needed in operations managements.

All organizations make product—which may be goods or services—so Chapter 3 gives some details of product planning and design. Every product is made by a process and we describe some options for this in Chapter 4. The layout of the process is discussed in Chapter 5, while Chapters 6 and 7 describe how to ensure the quality of products.

The next few chapters describe some aspects of planning and scheduling, beginning with a forecast of demand for the product—as described in Chapter 8. This forecast is used for capacity planning and production planning—as described in Chapters 9 and 10. More detailed scheduling of resources is described in Chapters 11 to 14. A special type of planning—used with projects— is described in Chapter 15.

The last three chapters describe some aspects of logistics, including inventory control and location decisions.

Two appendices review the principles of the Normal distribution, and give solutions to review questions.

Format of Each Chapter

Each chapter has a consistent format. This starts with a list of contents, an introduction, and the specific objectives of the chapter. Within each chapter there are summaries and review questions to ensure that students thoroughly understand the material. There are numerous example and case studies to illustrate points—often taken from Canadian organizations. Actual case studies have a coloured band at the edge of the page; fictional ones have a grey, screened background. At the end of each chapter is a review of the chapter, a set of key terms, problems, and discussion questions.

Some of the ideas introduced in this book are based on quantitative reasoning—but this does not mean that operations management is mathematical. We are mainly concerned with the concepts rather than the detailed arithmetic—we are looking at principles rather than calculations. So quantitative ideas are only included if they are useful—and then they are introduced by worked examples. Most people have access to computers. The book does not assume everyone has a computer, but the calculations can be done most easily using standard packages—particularly spreadsheets.

Harold Baerthel of Centennial College has prepared an instructor's manual, including a test item bank, to accompany the text.

If you have any comments or queries about this book, the authors would welcome your views.

C. D. J. Waters
Calgary, Alberta, September 1995

R. R. Nayak
Scarborough, Ontario, September 1995

ACKNOWLEDGEMENTS

The authors would like to acknowledge and thank the following persons for their help in developing some of the cases and career profiles included in the text.

Jim Giansopolous
Howard Gladstone
Edwin Joseph
John M. MacMillan
Larry Sanderson
Leonard smith
Patricia Steger
Vipin Suri
Donald Walker

TABLE OF CONTENTS

CHAPTER 3
PRODUCT PLANNING AND DESIGN

Making the right products 47

CHAPTER 4
PROCESS DESIGN

Deciding how to make the product 77

CHAPTER 5
LAYOUT OF FACILITIES

What is the best way to arrange equipment and buildings? 113

CHAPTER 6
QUALITY MANAGEMENT

Making products with perfect quality 149

CHAPTER 7
QUALITY CONTROL

CHAPTER 8
FORECASTING DEMAND

CHAPTER 9
CAPACITY PLANNING

CHAPTER 10
PRODUCTION PLANNING

CHAPTER 11
SCHEDULING RESOURCES

CHAPTER 12
JOB DESIGN AND WORK MEASUREMENT

CHAPTER 13
MATERIAL REQUIREMENTS PLANNING

CHAPTER 14
JUST-IN-TIME

CHAPTER 15
PROJECT MANAGEMENT

How to plan one-of-a-kind operations 407

CHAPTER 16
LOGISTICS MANAGEMENT

Moving materials from suppliers, through operations, and on to customers 447

CHAPTER 17
MANAGING INDEPENDENT DEMAND INVENTORY

CHAPTER 18
FACILITIES LOCATION

To Marjorie

– C. D. J. Waters –

To my parents,
my wife Veena,
and
my daughter Anita

– R. R. Nayak –

Chapter 1

WHAT IS OPERATIONS MANAGEMENT?

Introducing this important function

Contents

Introduction

This chapter introduces the key concepts of operations management. It shows how all organizations take a variety of **inputs**, and transform these to **outputs**. "Operations" are the activities whereby these transformations take place. "Operations management" ensures that the transformations are as efficient and effective as possible.

All organizations make goods or provide services of some kind. Operations management is concerned with the way goods are made or services provided. It is a primary function in all organizations.

This chapter describes how operations management has developed, the types of problems tackled in operations management, and some careers in the field. We shall see how operations management is used in every organization and in all types of industry.

Learning Objectives

After reading this chapter you should be able to answer questions such as:

- What exactly are "operations" and "operations management"?
- How has operations management developed in recent years?
- Why is operations management important?
- What are the primary functions in an organization?
- Are there differences between manufacturing and service organizations?
- What careers are available in operations management?

Case Study

UPS Emphasizes Operations

United Parcel Service Canada Ltd. employs over 5,000 people, made over $283 million in revenue in 1993, and enjoyed 9 percent market share. Its ground fleet consists of 1,350 delivery trucks, 68 tractors, and 354 trailers. It is a subsidiary of UPS America Inc., which had annual revenue of US$17.8 billion in 1993.

The reason behind "Big Brown's" success is its emphasis on operations. It has a well-trained, dependable, and productive workforce. The company pays attention to every detail of a driver's delivery motions such as how to step from the truck and how to carry packages. Such attention to detail helped UPS increase its productivity by 20 percent in 1994. The workers are also rewarded generously for their hard work and enjoy one of the highest wage rates in the industry.

The company knows that it has to be efficient and customer-oriented to survive in this fiercely competitive industry. It has introduced new services, and invested $2 billion in technology and a computerized tracking system to stay ahead of its competitors.

The management sees that a challenge lies ahead. It will have to make the operations even more efficient, while still treating its employees fairly.

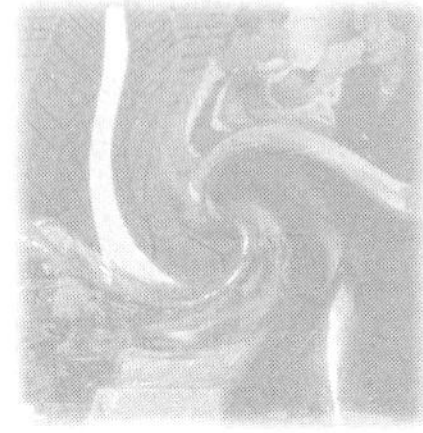

Historical View of Operations Management

Beginning around 1760 in Britain, a series of inventions—notably the steam engine of Scottish engineer James Watt—allowed manufacturers to increase their productivity dramatically. These increases were achieved by replacing manual labour and hand tools by machines and power tools, which allowed for large-scale industrial production. The resulting changes in Britain and elsewhere were so great that the period became known as the **Industrial Revolution**.

For the next century manufacturers relied on bigger and better machines to increase output. It was only around the turn of the twentieth century when people began to look beyond the technology to study the way it was managed. American engineer Frederick Winslow Taylor, for example, developed the principles of **scientific management** in the 1890s. His work clearly showed that a) the productivity of an organization depends on both the technology it uses and how well this technology is managed; and b) good managers use a variety of knowledge and skills in their decision making, and do not rely on guesswork and feelings.

Taylor's *Principles of Scientific Management*, published in 1911, laid the foundation for operations management. He showed that the performance of an organization depends on the quality of its managers. In particular, operations managers are directly responsible for making an organization's products and play a key role in its performance. This role is described in more detail later in the chapter.

Once its importance had been recognized, operations management developed quickly. American companies saw the benefits of good operations management, and, largely because of this, they soon dominated many areas of business. IBM became the world's largest computer manufacturer, General Motors the largest car manufacturer, ESSO the largest oil company.

By the 1970s, however, such leading companies had become complacent and did not adapt to changing circumstances. American car manufacturers ignored early demands for smaller, more economical cars, and allowed imports to take a major share of their market. IBM ignored personal computers for several years and continued to work with the shrinking mainframe market. In 1960, seven of the world's ten largest banks were American; by 1991 Citicorp was the only U.S. bank in the top ten. PanAm and TWA used to be the world's leading airlines, but neither survived massive reorganizations of the industry.

By the 1980s Japanese companies had taken the lead in operations management. They concentrated on high quality, customer service, and high productivity, and soon dominated the market for products such as motorcycles, consumer electronics, photocopiers, cameras, machine tools, steel, computer chips, ships, and cars, and for services such as banking.

The Japanese achieved this success by using good operations management. For example, car manufacturers used to hold large stocks of raw materials to make sure their production lines worked without interruption. Toyota considered these stocks a waste of resources. They spent 20 years developing a just-in-time (JIT) inventory system, which kept production lines busy but virtually eliminated stocks of raw materials (this approach is described in Chapter 14). Similarly, Yokogawa-Hewlett-Packard spent five years improving the quality of their goods to meet the high standards demanded by customers. As a result, they tripled their market share and profit, while halving their manufacturing costs.

There is more evidence that the Japanese success is founded on good operations management when they take over existing factories. In 1977 Motorola employed 1,000 hourly paid employees and produced about 1,000 TV sets per day at its Quasar plant in Chicago. Later that year Matsushita bought the plant. Within two years it had cut the indirect staff from 600 to 300, reduced assembly repairs by 95 percent, reduced annual warranty costs from $16 million to $2 million, and doubled the production rate to 2,000 sets per day, with the same 1,000 hourly paid staff.

Other countries learned from Japan's economic success and are now following its lead, particularly the Pacific Rim countries of South Korea, Taiwan, Singapore, and Hong Kong. At the same time companies in America and Europe are improving their own operations to regain their competitive edge. This has led to a dramatic increase in world trade and international competition. To meet this global competition, Canadian companies need skilled managers who recognize the importance of operations management.

In Summary

The performance of an organization depends on the quality of its managers. Operations managers are responsible for making an organization's goods or providing its services, and directly affect its performance. North America used to be a leader in operations management, but has been overtaken by Japan and other countries. This has led to a sharp increase in international competition, which a company can only meet by using good operations management.

Review Questions

1. List the factors that affect the productivity of an organization.
2. What happens if an organization ignores operations management? Provide examples.

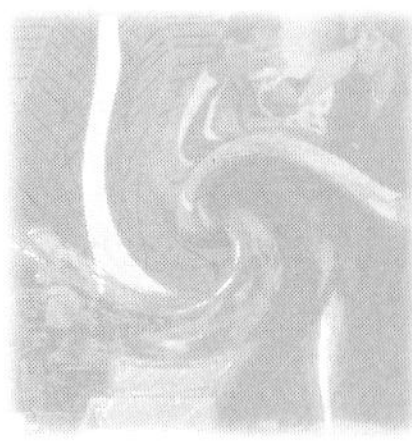

Defining Operations Management

The **operations** in an organization consist of all the activities that are directly concerned with making a product or providing a service. They give the answer to the question, "What does the organization do?" For example, hospitals treat sick people; schools teach children; banks borrow and lend money; and farms grow food.

> **Operations management** is concerned with all activities involved in making a product or providing a service: it is responsible for gathering various kinds of inputs and transforming them into desired outputs.

You can see from this definition that operations managers see organizations as transforming inputs to desired outputs. They take various *inputs* (raw materials, money, people, machines) and perform operations (manufacturing, assembly, packing, serving), which produce *outputs* (goods and services). For example:

- General Motors Canada's Oshawa plant takes inputs such as components, energy, robots, and people; it performs operations such as welding, assembly, painting, finishing; the outputs are cars, spare parts, and wages.
- La Caille Restaurant takes inputs such as a kitchen, customers, waiters, food, and drinks; it performs operations of food preparation, cooking, and serving; outputs include prepared food and satisfied customers.
- Centennial College takes inputs of students, books, buildings, and staff; it performs operations of teaching, administration, and service; outputs are better educated people.

The examples in Table 1.1 show how operations management is concerned with all kinds of organization from agriculture and manufacturing to services. It is important to emphasize, therefore, that **products** can be either goods or services, and operations are the processes which make either of these.

As you can see from Figure 1.1 on page 8, operations are at the heart of an organization. The diagram shows how managers make the decisions that keep an organization working. These decisions affect inputs, operations, and outputs. Feedback on performance and other relevant information is then used to update future decisions.

Three other elements can be added to this diagram:

- *Customers* who receive the outputs, give comments and opinions, and create demand
- An *external environment* in which the organization works, including competitors, government, and national priorities
- The separation of "operations" into a series of connected processes rather than a single step

Table 1.1 *Systems View of Some Typical Organizations*

Organization	Inputs	Operations	Desired Outputs
Farm	Seeds, fertilizer, fields, animals, machinery	Planting, growing, harvesting, milking	Grains, milk, meat
Coal mine	Miners, coal, tools, explosives, transport	Extraction, removing waste, cleaning, delivery	Coal, wages
Oil refinery	Crude oil, chemicals, energy	Refining, distribution, processing	Gasoline, oil, plastics
Computer manufacturer	Components, computer chips, energy, robots, people	Assembly, finishing, testing, packing	Computers, spare parts
House building	Land, bricks, woods, cement, people, capital, equipment, plans	Brick laying, carpentry, plastering, plumbing, electrical wiring	House, investment, garden
Brewery	Hops, water, cans, grain, bottles, skills, experience	Preparing, mixing, brewing, canning, bottling	Bottled and canned beer
Hospital	Patients, staff, beds, medicines, equipment	Surgical operations, treatment, monitoring	Healthy patients, information
Retail shop	Goods, customers, space, servers	Selling, marketing, advising, packing	Purchases, satisfied customers
Airline	Planes, terminals, passengers, agents	Booking tickets, flying, entertaining	Satisfied passengers, goods moved

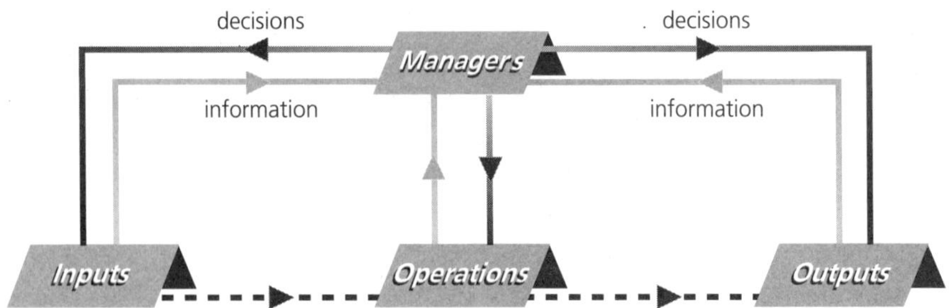

Figure 1.1 Schematic of Operations Management

Adding these elements gives the overall picture of operations management shown in Figure 1.2.

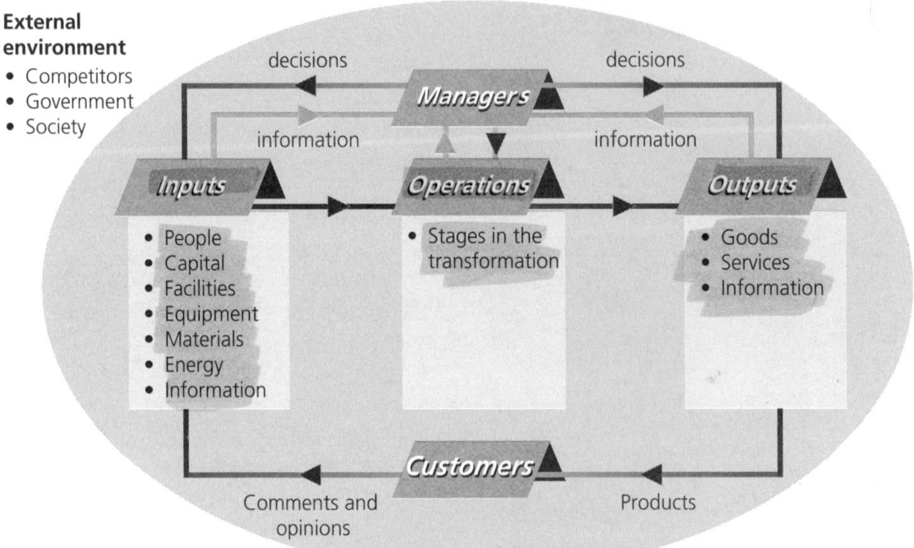

Figure 1.2 Overall Schematic of Operations Management

In Summary

The operations in an organization are directly concerned with making a product; they transform a variety of inputs to the desired outputs. Operations management is responsible for all the activities involved in such transformations. It is an important function which is used in all types of organizations.

Case Study – Peerless Plastic Products Inc.

Peerless Plastic Products Inc. (3P) is a large manufacturing company with operations throughout Canada. Its Industrial Plastics Division makes a range of plastic parts for other companies. These are generally sold to other manufacturers who use them as components in automobiles, electronic products, and various types of business equipment.

The Industrial Plastics Division was founded in 1960, and now occupies a specially designed 2500-square-metre building. Fifty people work here, with another 25 people employed at other locations.

The Division has 25 state-of-the-art injection moulding machines. To make a typical product, like a knob or gear, a precisely weighed amount of raw plastic is poured into a mould cavity. This is heated to a high temperature and pressure is applied to close the mould. When the pressure is released, the moulded part is removed and any further work is done to finish the part.

Questions

- What are the inputs, operations, and outputs at the Industrial Plastics Division?
- Draw an overall schematic diagram of operations management at the Industrial Plastics Division.

Review Questions

1. What is meant by "operations"?
2. Define "operations management."
3. List the inputs, operations, and outputs for an organization with which you are familiar.

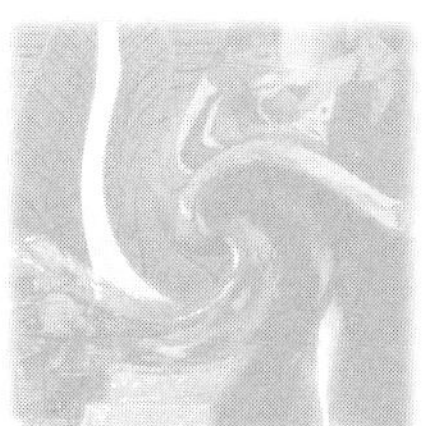

Operations Management as a Primary Function

An organization's success is dependent upon its customers. It must, therefore, supply the kinds of products its customers want.

The main purpose of an organization is to meet customer demand. This is a simplified view but it shows the three primary functions that occur in all organizations are:

1. **Sales/marketing** identifies customer demand, generates new demand, collects information on customer demand and passes this back to the organization, organizes advertising, takes orders, ensures products are delivered to customers, and gives after-sales service.
2. **Operations management** is responsible for actually making the product.
3. **Accounting/finance** raises funds, records financial transactions, collects money, pays bills, collects cost information, and maintains accounts.

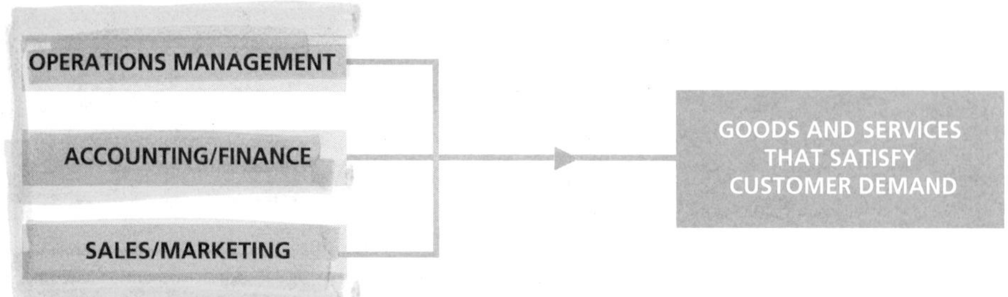

Figure 1.3 Primary Functions in an Organization

These primary functions are *directly* concerned with the product. You might say that an organization needs many other functions, such as human resources, research and development, catering, computer services, administration, and public relations. Usually, however, these can either be included in one of the primary functions or they are not *directly* concerned with the product. Table 1.2 shows some examples of the primary functions in different organizations.

The three primary functions—which need not be separate departments—work together to achieve the goals of the organization. They exist in all organizations, but the emphasis put on each will vary. A manufacturing company such as Magna might emphasize operations but must still market its products and control its finances; Sleeman's brewery may emphasize sales and marketing but must still have efficient operations and control its accounts. It would be fair to say that during the 1970s organizations emphasized marketing, while the 1980s saw a move toward stronger financial management, including mergers and takeovers. More recently, organizations have realized that they can only survive in the long term if they continue to satisfy customer demand with efficiently made high-quality products. This means that they must emphasize operations management. Some evidence for this comes from surveys of Chief Executives in Canada, which suggest that promotions are being made from the following backgrounds:

Operations	35%
Finance	25%
Marketing	20%
Research	10%
Law, etc.	10%

In Summary

Operations management is a primary function in organizations, along with sales/marketing and accounting/finance. There is a growing trend to put more emphasis on operations management.

Table 1.2 *Primary Functions in Different Organizations*

Organization	Sales and Marketing	Operations	Accounting and Finance
Brewery	Advertising, marketing, distribution	Brewing, packaging, delivery	Attracting investment, recording costs
Car assembly plant	Advertising, marketing, dealerships	Assemble cars, provide spare parts	Control investments, pay suppliers
Hospital	Publicity, public relations	Treatment, research, training	Pay staff, check running costs, donations
Retail shop	Sales, advertising, purchasing	Selling, stockholding, delivering	Record costs, pay suppliers, collect cash
Airline	Sales, advertising, franchises	Flight operations, ground operations, engineering	Collect fares, pay expenses, buy planes
College	Marketing, publicity, recruitment	Teaching, writing	Pay staff, collect fees

Review Questions

1. Describe the primary functions in an organization with which you are familiar.
2. Why is personnel management not considered a primary function?

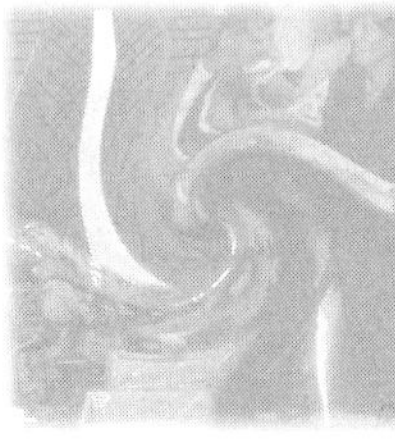

Operations Management in Services

Operations management is concerned with *all* operations, not just manufacturing.

When we discuss product design, it is probably easier to imagine a car being built than a type of insurance policy being developed. Nonetheless, the discussion applies to all kinds of products, whether they are goods or services.

- **Goods** are tangible, physical items, such as cars, usually made by manufacturers.
- **Services** are intangible products supplied by service industries, such as insurance industries.
- **Products** are both goods and services supplied by an organization.

Most people in Canada work in the service sector. There are several ways in which service organizations differ from manufacturers, as shown in Table 1.3.

Table 1.3 *Differences Between Service and Manufacturing Organizations*

Service Organization	Manufacturing Organization
• The product is intangible.	• The product is tangible.
• Services cannot be kept in stock.	• Goods can be kept in stock until needed.
• Production occurs at the same time as consumption.	• There is a delay between production and use.
• Products are more likely to be unique and cannot be mass-produced.	• Products are usually similar and can be mass-produced.
• There is direct customer contact.	• There is little contact between manufacturers and customers.
• Customers participate in the service.	• Customers do not help with manufacturing.
• Facilities are located near customers.	• Factories are located away from customers.
• Services are labour-intensive.	• Manufacturing is largely automated.
• Quality is difficult to measure.	• Quality is easier to measure.
• Quality depends largely on the server.	• Quality does not depend upon one person.
• It is difficult to measure the output.	• The output can usually be counted.

After reading this list you might think that services are all the same. This is not true. There is, for example, a range of organization size from one-person firms to the United Nations, and a range of activities from churches to armies. The term "services" covers a broad range of activities, and it is useful to classify them as follows:

- *Public services,* such as defence, social services, health, and education, provided by all levels of government
- *Retail and wholesale stores*
- *Distribution services* for both goods and information, including transport, mail, libraries, and newspapers
- *Nonprofit services* such as charities and churches
- *Other services for industry,* including finance, legal, and a variety of professional services

- *Other services for individuals,* including leisure, banking, and domestic services

Although the preceding list illustrates some important differences between services and goods, many people believe that these differences are becoming less noticeable. They say that all products are really a combination of goods and services. Consider, for example, a restaurant, which provides a service in preparing and serving meals, and goods in manufacturing meals. A television broadcasting company both makes goods—such as videotapes of programs—and provides services—with transmissions of programs. A company that makes washing machines is clearly a manufacturer, but it also provides an after-sales service.

As there is sometimes no clear distinction between goods and services, a spectrum of organizations should be considered. At one end are organizations that primarily supply goods, such as Inglis, which makes appliances. At the other end are organizations that primarily give services, such as Canada Life, which provides insurance. A fast-food restaurant would fall in the middle of the spectrum.

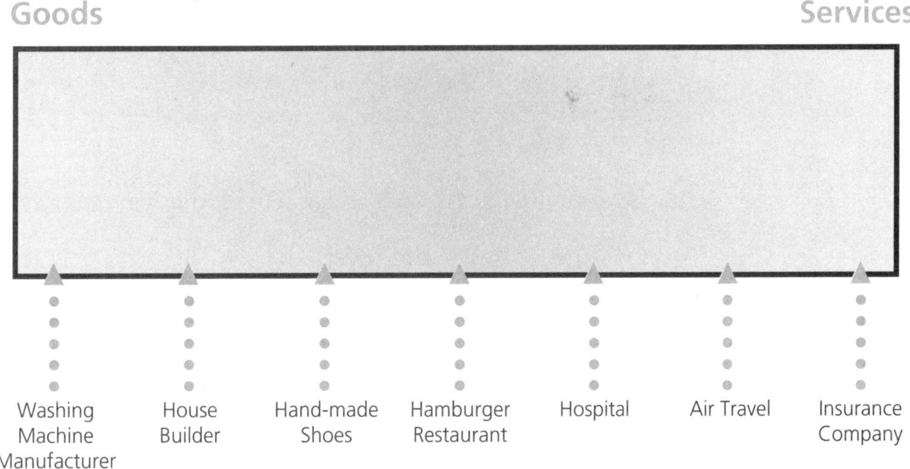

Figure 1.4 A Spectrum of Goods and Services

Since products are usually a combination of services and goods, managers in all organizations face similar problems. Regardless of their industry, they have to plan products, forecast demand, check quality, schedule activities, and motivate staff. The problem of locating facilities, for example, is essentially the same whether the organization is Toyota Canada or The Royal Bank of Canada.

In Summary

Although there are some differences between service and manufacturing organizations, there are many similarities. Operations management tackles problems in a wide range of organizations.

Review Questions

1. In what ways are service industries fundamentally different from manufacturing ones?
2. How can services be classified?
3. "Operations management is another name for production management". Do you think this is true? Why or why not? Explain your answer.

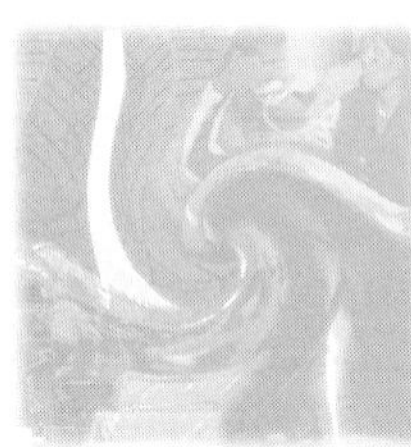

Why Study Operations Management?

Because of its vital role, the operations function in a typical organization accounts for 60 percent of its employees and over half of its budget. But operations management has a wider impact on our national wealth. The wealth of a country is measured by its **Gross Domestic Product** (GDP), which is the total amount the country produces in a year. The GDP of Canada is around $700 billion, or $25,000 per person. This GDP comes from three types of industry:

1. *Extractive industries,* such as agriculture, mining, quarrying, and forestry
2. *Manufacturing and construction*
3. *Service industries,* including government, education, health, retailing, and catering

Most countries' economies rely on extractive industries—particularly agriculture—and are developing by encouraging manufacturing. Developed countries, like Canada, already have strong manufacturing industries and are moving into service industries. This means that very few people work in extractive industries (perhaps 5 percent of the workforce), and a decreasing number in manufacturing (perhaps 20 percent). The remaining 75 percent work in service industries.

As more countries develop, there is an increase in world trade and international competition. For many industrialized countries, this means a decline in their share of the world market. Canada currently has half of one percent of the world's population, but produces almost 3 percent of its goods and services. In the long run, Canada's proportion of trade will decline as other countries become relatively more prosperous. Some see this as a threat and suggest putting tariffs or quotas on imported goods. This might work in the short term, but in the longer term Canadian companies must become more productive to meet the competition—they must concentrate on good operations management. This means good planning, effective control of operations, working with customers to meet their precise demands, ensuring high-quality products, responding quickly to changing circumstances, motivating the workforce, encouraging flexibility in operations, improving communications, using teamwork, increasing productivity, reducing the amount of bureaucracy, using appropriate technologies, and looking for ways to improve performance.

In Summary

Operations management is important as a primary function in all organizations. It also has a wider impact on our national wealth. International competition is increasing and Canadian companies must have well-designed operations to compete.

Review Questions

1. "Most people living in industrialized countries work in the manufacturing industry." True or false?
2. Why has interest in operations management increased in recent years?

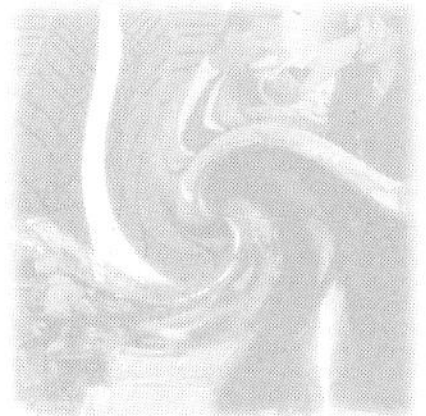

Careers in Operations Management

In most organizations, the majority of employees work in operations. These range from people directly making the product—perhaps hourly paid—to senior managers who control the operations. The people who work in operations have a wide range of titles.

Most early studies of management were conducted in factories. These studies led to a number of related disciplines, such as **industrial engineering**, **management science**, and, most popularly, **production management**. In the past, a typical manufacturing company would employ a production manager to look after its operations. Later studies of management looked at service companies, and the production manager's equivalent became known as an operations manager. The operations in a factory would be the responsibility of a production manager, while the operations in a transport fleet would be the responsibility of an operations manager. In recent years, all types of organizations have begun to use the general title **operations manager**.

This title is not universal. For every organization—whether a factory, bank, store, college, office complex, or hospital—there is someone in charge of the operations. This person may not be called an operations manager, but that is certainly the person's job. Table 1.4 lists a variety of operations-management titles.

Table 1.4 *Operations-Management Titles*

Production Manager	Plant Manager
Site Manager	Materials Controller
Operations Analyst	Inventory Controller
Scheduler	Shop Manager
Matron	Postmaster
Chef	Supervisor
Principal	Transport Manager
Factory Superintendent	Maintenance Manager
Production Engineer	Quality Assurance Engineer
Management Scientist	

You can see these different titles when you read job ads in a newspaper. The following terms were used in recent advertisements in a large daily newspaper:.

- *Operations Manager.* This person is in charge of the overall operations. Specific responsibilities include long-term planning, budgeting, and policy-making. Equivalent titles include Vice-president, Operations; Vice-president, Production; Vice-president of Manufacturing; Production Manager; Plant Manager; and Works Manager.
- *Line Manager.* This person has direct responsibility for people working in operations. Two examples are the manager of the painting department in a manufacturing company and the manager of the hardware section of a department store.

Entry-level position:	Supervisor or Foreman
Middle-level position:	Superintendent or Department Manager
Senior-level position:	Operations or Production Manager

- *Quality Controller.* This manager is responsible for the quality of the product. He develops policies and procedures for quality, trains people in fault prevention, and organizes the inspection of products.

Entry-level position:	Inspector
Middle-level position:	Quality Manager
Senior-level position:	Director or Vice-president of Product Quality

- *Materials Manager.* This manager is responsible for purchasing, storing, and transporting materials.

Entry-level position:	Buyer, Materials or Inventory Analyst
Middle-level position:	Purchasing, Transport, or Inventory Manager
Senior-level position:	Director of Purchasing or Vice-president, Materials Management

- *Work Study and Facilities Planning Manager.* This manager is responsible for planning and designing the plant and work place, and improving methods and procedures.

Entry-level position:	Methods or Time-study Analyst
Middle-level position:	Industrial Engineering Manager
Senior-level position:	Director of Plant Engineering

Operations occur in so many different circumstances that we might be tempted to say that *operations management is what operations managers do.* This seems an unhelpful remark, but it is justified by the wide range of jobs available. If someone tells you that they are a lawyer, you have a general idea of what they do, but you might find it difficult to give a precise definition of their job. Now, if someone tells you they are an operations manager, you know they are involved in managing the primary functions that make their organization's products.

Operations managers need a number of skills. They may need technical knowledge to understand the details of operations. They also need good interpersonal skills. In general, operations managers make all of the important decisions about their organization's operations, so their jobs will include the following:

- *Planning*—to establish the organization's goals and the means of achieving these
- *Organizing*—structuring the organization in the best way to achieve its goals
- *Staffing*—ensuring suitable employees are available for all jobs
- *Directing*—telling employees the tasks they should be doing
- *Motivating*—encouraging employees to do their jobs well
- *Monitoring*—checking progress toward the achievement of goals
- *Controlling*—taking action to ensure the organization keeps moving toward its goals

In Summary

Operations managers work in all organizations, but they are given different titles. Because the majority of people work in operations, there is a wide range of careers available.

Review Questions

1. List ten different titles for "operations managers."
2. What skills would you expect an operations manager to have?

Case Study

Plitron Manufacturing Inc.

Plitron Manufacturing Inc. is a manufacturer of state-of-the-art Toroidal transformers. It was established in 1983 by Howard Gladstone. Plitron is a successful small business with a steady growth record over the last 10 years.

The Product

A transformer is an electrical device which is used to alter the voltage of an electrical current. It is used in almost all electrical appliances. In Canada, the main electrical line is at 110 volts AC, but all electrical devices operate at a much lower DC voltage. So, they need transformers as part of the power supply.

Conventional laminated-type transformers are bulky and inefficient. Toroidal transformers use a doughnut-shaped solid metal core, with copper windings spread over the entire surface. Toroidals are smaller, lighter, operate at low temperature, make less noise, are more efficient, and easy to mount. At Plitron, advanced production techniques using high-speed winding equipment have made it possible to produce toroidal transformers at a low cost.

Product Line

Plitron makes transformers in a variety of sizes from 25 mm to 300 mm diameter, weighing up to 90 lbs. It makes a standard line of power transformer, as well as custom transformers for various industries such as computer peripherals, medical electronics, telecommunications, audio, and video. Most of the transformers (80 percent) are made to the customers' specifications, in various batch sizes. The remaining 20 percent of sales come from 12 standard sizes.

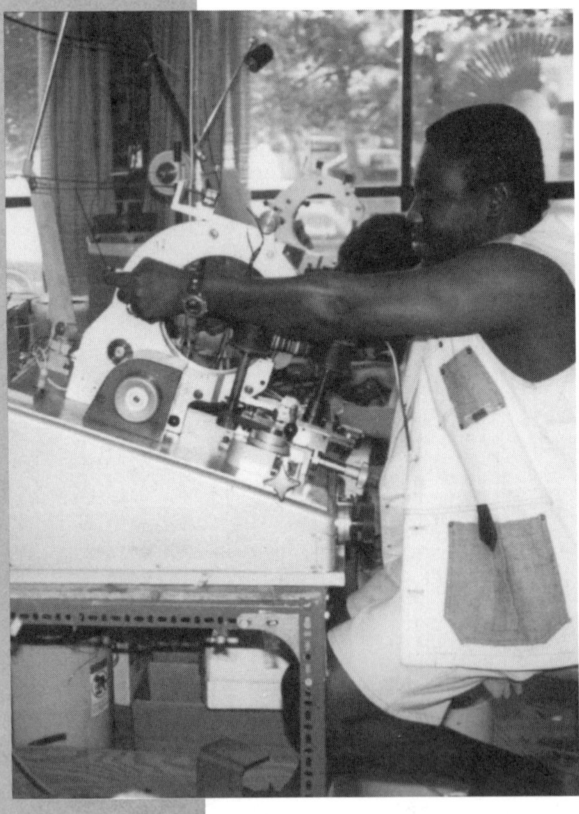

The Facility

Plitron has grown over the years. It started in an industrial plaza and as it grew, it acquired the adjacent unit. Further expansion made it necessary for Plitron to acquire space in a building across the street in the same industrial plaza. Now, it occupies a total floor area of 1,100 m^2. The plant is divided into two areas. The new plant makes the larger transformers (over 120 mm in diameter), and the original facility houses the offices and manufactures smaller transformers. The manufacturing process for the small and large transformers is essentially the same.

Plitron employs approximately 50 people. They use specialized, yet flexible equipment, capable of making various sizes of transformers.

The Plitron Process

a) Product Design

Normally, the customer supplies transformer specifications. But many times Plitron's sales representatives, customer service, and engineering staff work closely with customers to help develop the specifications. Plitron uses a sophisticated proprietary software program to develop the transformer design based on the specifications. During design, efforts are made to use the standard manufacturing process and materials, where possible. This helps to reduce costs. The customer is then quoted a price based on the cost of manufacturing the product.

Once the customer and Plitron have reached a general agreement on the specification and the price, prototypes are produced. These prototypes are made and shipped as soon as possible to the customer for testing.

When the customer is satisfied with the prototype, an acceptance form is completed. This form allows the engineering staff to formalize the product documentation. Plitron emphasizes product safety and its products meet the UL, CSA, or International Standards.

b) Materials Control

The buyers, engineers, and quality-control personnel all work together with vendors to develop a consistent base of raw materials. Some of the raw materials used in toroidal transformers are steel core, silicon steel, polyester tape, copper wire of various gauges, epoxy resin, and PVC sleeves. The company also buys hardware such as steel cups, nuts, bolts, and washers. Complete vendor histories are maintained by the quality department for analysis of supplier performance.

Plitron uses an MRPII program to determine the materials to be ordered. Once all the materials are in, the production scheduler releases the work to the plant. Each customer order has a manufacturing order, which contains the product description, product drawings, the bill of material, and routing instructions, as well as the product-testing instructions.

c) Production Steps

The product typically goes through the following steps:

1. Winding: Using the machines to wrap wires on the core in an engineered number of turns.
2. Taping: Electrical insulation between windings applied by machines.
3. Leadwork (Wire Finishing): Insulating and identifying exit wires from transformers, and applying connectors when required.
4. Product Testing: Testing voltage and current to ensure transformers meet specifications.
5. Potting: Encapsulating transformers in epoxy compound or cases, when this has been specified.
6. Inspection: Final physical examination of transformers before shipment.
7. Packing: The transformers are packed in specially engineered boxes to protect them during shipping and transportation.
8. Shipping: The product is shipped to the customer.

The manufacturing process uses the most up-to-date equipment available, and highly trained operators to produce the products. Plitron works closely with the equipment manufacturer to modify the machines to meet its needs. The workers undergo an extensive three-month training program in both the operation of their machines and quality in-process inspection techniques.

d) Quality Control

All transformers are 100 percent tested using calibrated equipment and trained test personnel. Electrical testing equipment includes turn counters, oscilloscopes, and dielectric strength tests. All shipments are final inspected by QA, which includes dimensional checks and visual inspection.

Plitron is working toward attaining ISO 9001 certification.

As you can see from this description of a job shop, Plitron is a well-managed, small manufacturing company.

Case Study

Tetra Pak Laval

Tetra Pak Laval is a Swedish company with a strong presence in the food-processing and packing industry. Tetra Pak, one of its four operating divisions, is involved in developing, manufacturing, and marketing of processing equipment, packaging machines, and packaging materials for liquid food products. Tetra Pak juice and milk cartons are a common sight in supermarkets. They are excellent packaging systems for liquids. The Tetra Brik Aseptic packaging system allows even perishable products such as milk to be packaged for extensive periods without refrigeration. In 1993 the company helped distribute 40.7 billion litres of liquid foods worldwide.

Tetra Pak's Aurora, Ontario, plant manufacures Tetra Brik Aseptic material. The packaging material is delivered in reels, which are easy and economical to transport and store.

Here is an excerpt of an interview, conducted by Ragu Nayak with Mr. Leonard Smith, Factory Manager of Tetra Pak's Aurora, Ontario, plant.

Q. What does your plant manufacture?

A. We produce reels of Tetra Brik Aseptic (more commonly referred to as "juice box") packaging material at this plant. This multilaminate material is made up of paper, aluminum foil, and polyethylene.

Q. What is the size of your plant?

A. The floor of the plant is 11,000 square metres. We have 204 employees at this location: 156 of them work in the plant. The plant operates on a three-shift, seven-day operation.

Q. What is the process of making your product?

A. It's a three-step process. The first step is printing. The wide (up to 39") paper rolls are printed with the customer's product information. Secondly, the printed paper is laminated with aluminum foil and polyethylene. And thirdly, the wide, laminated rolls are slit into individual reels.

Q. What is the plant's production capacity?

A. We have three printing presses that can run anywhere between 6,000-18,000 metres per hour. We have one lamination machine and two slitters.

Q. Is it a capital-intensive process?

A. Very much so. A 5-colour printing press costs in excess of $10 million and the lamination machine is still more expensive.

Q. What are your production lot sizes?

A. We make to customers' requirements. We are, essentially, a custom shop. Our lot sizes vary from 6,000 metres to 600,000 metres.

Q. What is your manufacturing lead time?

A. Usually, it is three weeks to produce and deliver, if we have the artwork. For new designs, additional time is required to prepare the artwork, film, and plates.

Q. Is your product labour- or material-intensive?

A. Definitely material. Our raw materials are paper, aluminium foil, polyethylene, and ink. The material cost could be 80 percent of our total cost.

Q. What is your inventory level?

A. We try to operate with low inventory levels. We do not have any finished goods inventory, since we make only to customer orders. There have been some raw material shortages lately. So, we try to keep one month's usage of raw materials on hand.

Q. How do you do your production planning?

A. We have a sophisticated, computer-based integrated planning system called the Production Administration Sytem (PAS). This is an inhouse-developed, customized planning system, used by all Tetra Pak plants worldwide. It develops a weekly production schedule, and the dispatch lists are revised twice daily.

Q. Are good employee relations important to you?

A. Absolutely. Tetra Pak believes that good employee relations are important for its success. We have employee suggestion boxes. We are processing an employee's suggestion right now, which has the potential to save us a large amount of money. We reward the employees for their efforts. All suggestions are evaluated by a committee. Tetra Pak tries very hard to improve communications. We hold the president's breakfasts several times a year where our president meets with all our employees. We have internal newsletters, annual meetings, department meetings, all in an effort to improve internal communication.

Q. Do you have employee training programs?

A. Yes, all employees receive the necessary training to do their daily job. We have a good orientation program for new employees. Employees are also taken for customer visits. We have weekly employee meetings, where employees talk about various work-related issues like quality, work-place safety, etc. We have an on-site computer trainer, and we are now undertaking many quality initiatives which will require significant training.

Q. Is quality important to you?

A. We will never compromise quality. Product specifications are set worldwide. Sixty percent of our production is exported. Hence our quality requirements are more stringent than the Canadian requirements. We are in the process of obtaining ISO 9002 certification, which will ensure consistent quality. Also, most of our customers use our machines to process and fill the products so we must ensure that the whole process which we provide to our customers is superior.

Q. How is quality controlled?

A. Our lab checks the raw materials. Also, finished products are analyzed by the lab. Every employee is responsible for his/her quality of the products produced. We use Statistical Process Control (SPC) technique.

Q. What type of skills do you look for in an employee?

A. We try to, as much as possible, promote internally. Suppose, if we were to hire a shift coordinator, then I would emphasize both technical skills as well as communication skills. The person should know something about printing technology and the process. Also, he or she should possess good people skills, be able to work with others. We provide good career paths to our employees.

Career Profile

Larry Sanderson

Manager of Manufacturing Operations

Bunn-O-Matic Canada, Aurora, Ontario

Education:

Diploma in Production and Operations Management

Centennial College, Scarborough, Ontario

Work Experience:

After graduating from Centennial College in 1986, Larry started work as a Master Scheduler in a packaging company, then moved to Motorola Canada as a Production Planner, and after a few years joined Crouse-Hinds as a Materials Manager. At Crouse-Hinds he was also involved in planning and implementing a Just-in-Time manufacturing cell, which continues to be the company's showcase in production lines.

Current Duties and Responsibilities:

Larry continued his career progression with a move to Bunn-O-Matic Canada, where he is currently employed as Manager of Manufacturing Operations. At 30, Larry runs a plant with 68 employees and 5 supervisors. He is responsible for purchasing, quality control, distribution, and manufacturing.

He also teaches production and operations courses at Centennial College's night school.

Professional Development:

Immediately after graduation, Larry began courses with CAPIC, until he obtained his CPIM designation. He is currently pursuing his B.A. at York University on a part-time basis.

Philosophy for Success:

Larry attributes his success to seeking additional responsibilities beyond his job description, and ongoing education. He believes people must continue to educate themselves for both today's and tomorrow's job.

Job Advertisment

The following job advertisement was recently published in a newspaper.

OPERATIONS MANAGER

Established downtown toy manufacturer requires a General Operations Manager. The successful candidate will manage the day-to-day functions of both the plant and administrative facilities employing approximately 75 people.

The ideal candidate must have a strong human resources/employee relations background.

In addition, this person should have experience in the toy manufacturing industry, be computer-literate, be experienced in equipment and physical plant management, and in financial analysis.

What are the responsibilities of the operations manager as outlined in this advertisement?

What qualifications do you think the candidate needs?

If you had the appropriate experience, would you be interested in the job? Why?

Chapter Review

- Operations are those activities directly concerned with making a product; they transform a variety of inputs into desired outputs.
- Operations management is the management function responsible for this transformation.
- Operations management is a primary function in all organizations, along with sales/marketing and accounting/finance.
- Although there are some differences between service and manufacturing organizations, there are many similarities. Operations management is important in all kinds of organizations.

- Developments in the past few years, particularly increased competition, have emphasized the need for organizations to have well-designed operations.
- All organizations have operations managers, but they are given a range of titles. The majority of people work in operations, so there is a wide range of careers available.

Key Terms

accounting/finance *(p.9)*
goods *(p.12)*
Gross Domestic Product (GDP) *(p.14)*
industrial engineering *(p.15)*
Industrial Revolution *(p.3)*
inputs *(p.2)*
management science *(p.15)*
operations *(p.6)*
operations management *(p.6)*
operations manager *(p.15)*
outputs *(p.2)*
production management *(p.15)*
products *(pp.6, 12)*
sales/marketing *(p.9)*
scientific management *(p.3)*
services *(p.12)*

Discussion Questions

1.1 Terms such as "accounting" and "marketing" are more easily understood than "operations management." Why do you think this is?

1.2 Discuss some of the problems a company may have if it does not pay enough attention to its operations.

1.3 An organization will always produce direct outputs (goods and services) and indirect ones (such as wages, taxes, improved technology, and waste materials). Discuss *all* of the outputs that might be found in a typical factory.

1.4 When a car dealership sells a car, is it producing a good or providing a service? What about the car manufacturer? Is there really a clear distinction between the suppliers of goods and services? Explain.

1.5 "The operations in different sectors of industry are similar enough to allow a common approach to their management." Do you agree or disagree with this statement? Explain.

1.6 There is often interdepartmental rivalry within an organization. Why do you think this is so? Should it be encouraged? Explain.

1.7 "As countries enter a "postindustrial" phase, they develop strong service sectors and no longer need to worry about their manufacturing industries." Do you think this is true? Explain.

1.8 Describe some different types of careers that are available in operations management.

Chapter 2

OPERATIONS MANAGEMENT DECISIONS

What types of decisions do operations managers make?

Contents

Introduction

Some decisions are very important to an organization—such as the location of its offices or the products it makes—with effects felt over many years. Other decisions are less important, with effects lasting just days or even hours. This chapter examines the relative importance of decisions and classifies them as strategic, tactical, or operational.

The most important decisions in an organization concern its overall aims and beliefs. These form its mission. This mission leads to other strategic decisions, which may concern the organization as a whole or may be within its primary functions.

Strategic decisions made by operations managers form the organization's operations strategy. This strategy leads to a series of decisions at all levels, ranging from long-term facility location to short-term production scheduling.

Learning Objectives

After reading this chapter you should be able to answer questions such as:

- What types of decisions do managers make?
- What are the differences among strategic, tactical, and operational decisions?
- What are the mission and business strategy of an organization?
- How do these lead to other strategic, tactical, and operational decisions?
- What are typical operations management decisions?

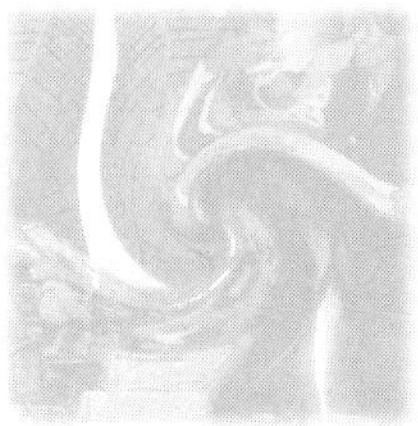

Decision-making in Organizations

Chapter 1 showed that managers make the decisions within an organization. This chapter examines the types of decisions they make: **strategic**, **tactical,** or **operational**.

Strategic decisions are made by senior managers; they are long term, use many resources, and involve high risk.
Tactical decisions are made by middle managers; they are medium term, use fewer resources, and involve less risk than strategic decisions.
Operational decisions are made by junior or supervisory managers; they are short term, use few resources, and involve low risk.

You can imagine these differences by considering a boat. The captain represents top management and examines charts to decide where the boat should go. The helmsman represents middle management, is directed by the captain, and steers the boat in the right direction. A crewman represents junior management and rows the boat to keep it moving.

Every organization makes decisions at all levels. You can see this in the following examples.

- For a manufacturer, such as Spar Aerospace, a decision to build a new factory five or ten years in the future is strategic; a decision to introduce a new product one or two years in the future is tactical; a decision about hiring occasional workers next week is operational.
- A research organization like Bell Northern could make a strategic decision to look for new advances in electronic technology, a tactical decision to develop a new microprocessor, and an operational decision about scheduling work over the next few weeks.
- For CN railway, deciding whether to continue a passenger service to a given area is strategic; whether to structure the fares to attract business or leisure passengers is tactical; finalizing short-term crew schedules is operational.
- For a farmer in Saskatchewan, a decision to continue growing grain is strategic; choosing the kind of grain and areas to sow next season is tactical; scheduling the planting of seed is operational.
- For a college or university, opening a new campus is strategic; whether to offer a particular course in one or two years is tactical; choosing someone to teach a course next week is operational.

Case Study

Magna International Inc.

Magna is a prime example of a successful Canadian business, started by an enterprising tool and die maker, Frank Stronach. Frank, through his astute management skills and by tapping the entrepreneurial zeal of his employees, turned Magna into a multibillion dollar company with 84 plants (business units or divisions) employing over 20,000 people in 1993. Magna is a leading global supplier of technologically advanced automotive systems, assemblies, and components. The company is divided into six major divisions, each of which is responsible for a particular group of auto parts and systems. For example, Atoma Interior Systems is responsible for the seating systems and interior panel systems, the Europa group is responsible for the safety systems (air-bags), and Tesma makes engine and transmission parts.

Mr. Don Walker, a young engineer and the President and CEO of Magna, is very optimistic about Magna's future. Magna's long-term strategy is based on simple and prudent business principles and practices: to make money, reward management for their performance, build the business for the long term, and provide long-term employment for the employees. Magna's corporate culture emphasizes a decentralized operating structure, small operating units, entrepreneurial managers, an employee charter, and employee ownership. (The details of the employee charter are described on page 335.)

Walker states, "If a general manager of a business unit keeps the customers, shareholders, and employees happy, then he can virtually run his division the way he wishes." According to him, to keep customers happy, a

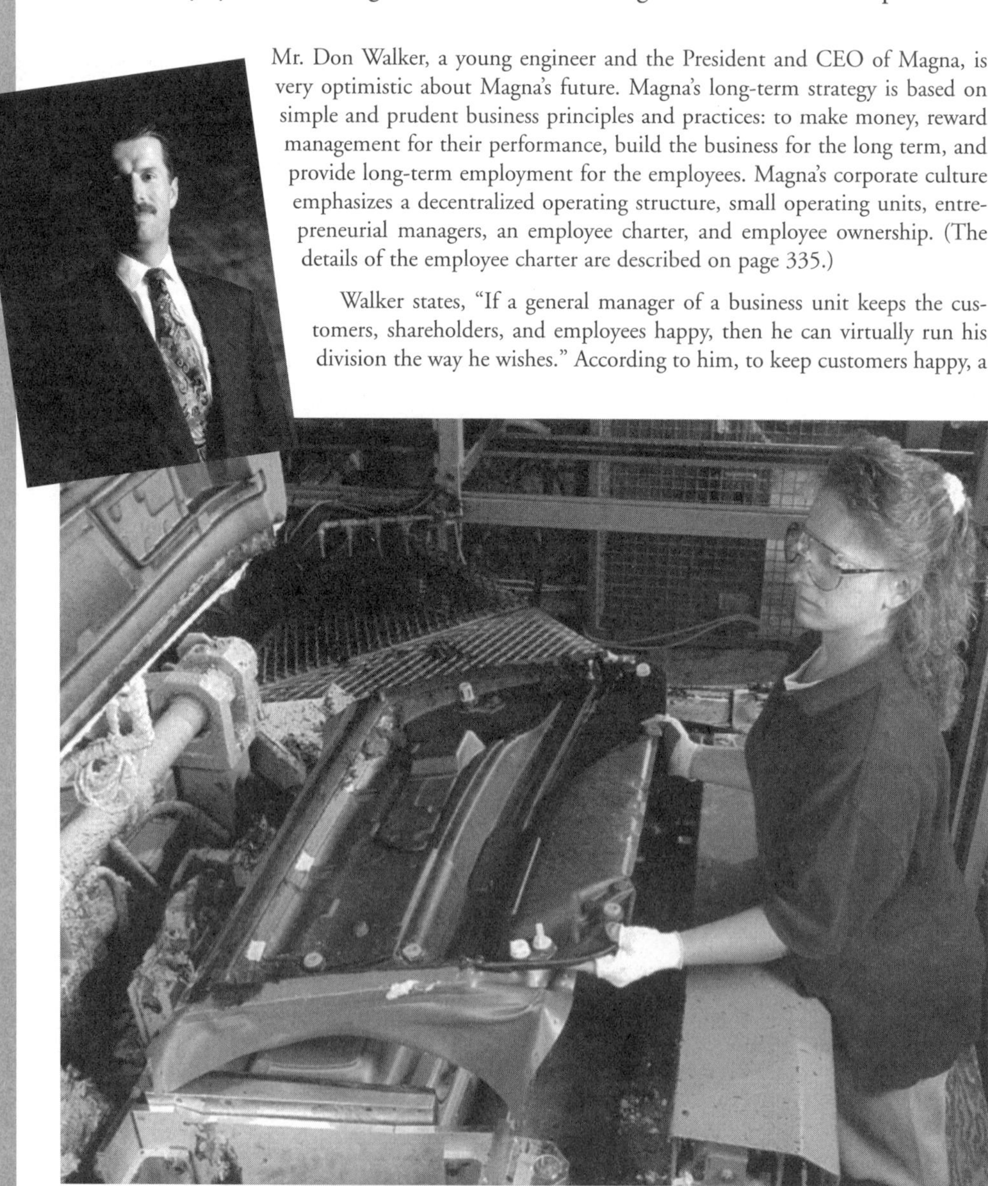

business unit will have to supply high-quality products, provide good and reliable service, and meet the changing needs of the customers. "You have to make profit to keep stockholders happy, and employees will be happy if you treat them with respect, listen to them, and provide them job security," adds Mr. Walker.

Magna is known for its innovative product designs and technologically advanced manufacturing capabilities which is evident from the fact that it employs 1,500 skilled tool and die makers and 1,000 engineers. All of its general managers have a strong operations and technical background. Don states, "A general manager must be knowledgeable about the product and process technology."

"The automotive sector is one of the toughest sectors to be in," comments Walker. Magna emphasizes providing value to its customers. It employs value analysis and value engineering techniques to reduce product cost and improve the product design. Magna also tries to provide the best management tools to its managers. The tools are developed by a team of experts at Magna, employees are given intensive training to use these tools, and then a standard procedure, called a business operating system, is developed to apply these tools on a regular, routine basis at the divisional level. For example, Magna has developed an extensive business operating system for quality improvement, which includes application of the important quality improvement concepts such as Design of Experiment (DOE), Quality Function Deployment (QFD), and Value Analysis/Value Engineering.

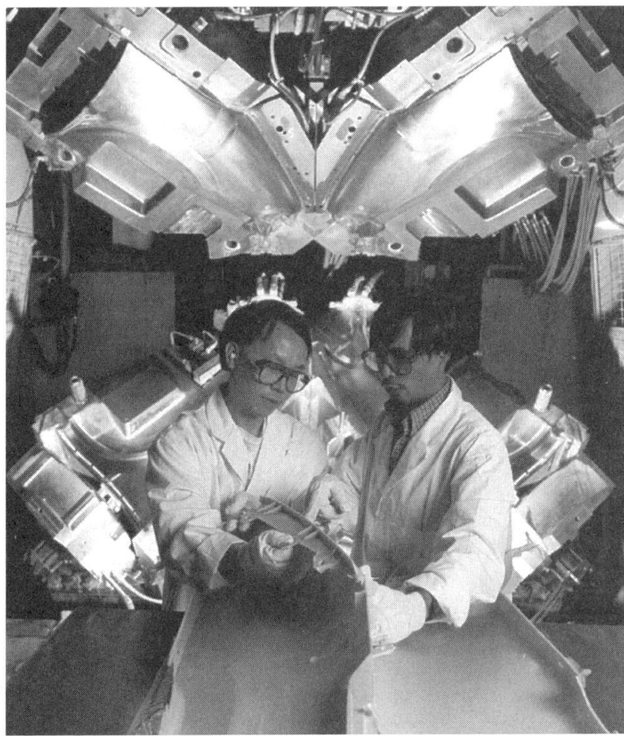

One of Magna's priorities has been to implement a human resource management system to ensure that the employees' needs are met and they are happy. Under this system, a hot line has been set-up for the employees to voice any concerns, fairness committees have been established in each plant, and confidential employee surveys are conducted annually at each plant. The human resource management system is a tremendous resource for all general managers to involve all employees.

Magna tries to hire young, educated, and entrepreneurial type people. Don feels that an ideal manager for his organization would be a trades person with a community college education and some university level courses.

In fiscal 1996, Magna expects to reach the $5 billion mark. Most of the future growth will be financed without any debt, comments Walker. Magna also expects to design and build complete body systems for auto makers in the future.

Source: Interview with Mr. D. Walker and Magna 1994 Annual report. With permission from Magna International Inc.

The timeframe of decisions varies widely among organizations. At BC Hydro, for example, a strategic decision might concern the building of new power stations, look 20 years or more into the future, and involve the expenditure of hundreds of millions of dollars. A strategic decision for a small retail store might look one or two years into the future and involve the expenditure of a few thousand dollars. Some other differences among these three types of decision are shown below in Table 2.1.

Table 2.1 *Types of Decisions*

	Strategic	Tactical	Operational
Level of Manager	Senior	Middle	Junior
Importance	High	Medium	Low
Resource Used	Many	Some	Few
Timeframe	Long	Medium	Short
Risk	High	Medium	Low
Uncertainty	High	Medium	Low
Amount of Detail	Very general	Moderate	Very detailed
Data Available	Uncertain	Some	Certain
Structure	Unstructured	Some	Structured
Focus	Whole organization	Divisions in the organization	Individual units

Senior managers make the strategic decisions that set an organization on its course. These strategic decisions are the beginning of a planning process that filters down through the entire organization. Once strategic decisions have been made, they are passed down to middle management and give the constraints and objectives for their more detailed tactical decisions. These, in turn, are passed down to give the constraints and objectives for the detailed operational decisions made by junior managers. The result is a hierarchy of decisions as shown in Figure 2.1.

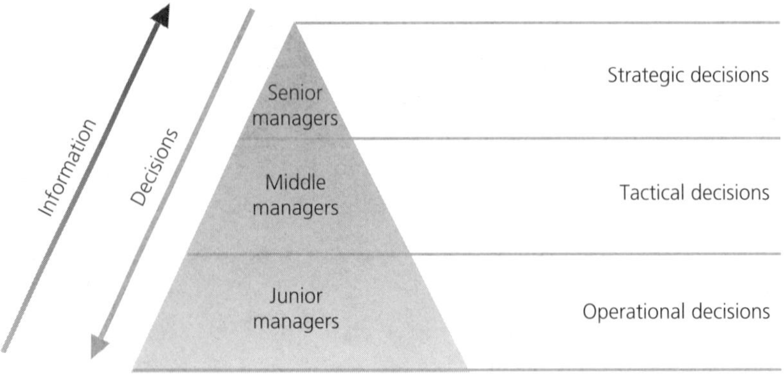

Figure 2.1 Hierarchy of Decisions in an Organization

While decisions are passed downward through the management hierarchy, information about actual performance and other feedback is passed upward. This information is filtered as it passes upward, so that top managers are not swamped by too much irrelevant detail. The filtering must be done carefully so that it allows enough detail to be useful but not so much that overall patterns are hidden.

In Summary

Managers in all organizations face decisions of different types. These can be described as strategic, tactical, or operational. Strategic decisions are made by senior management; tactical decisions are made by middle managers; and operational decisions are made by junior or supervisory managers.

Review Questions

1. Describe the different levels of decisions in an organization.
2. "Tactical decisions are most important to an organization because they concern its day-to-day operations." Do you agree with this? Explain.
3. What kind of decision is:
   a) finding the best location for a new factory?
   b) deciding how many hours of overtime are needed next week?
   c) deciding whether to start an air service to South America?
   d) deciding whether to publish a proposed textbook?

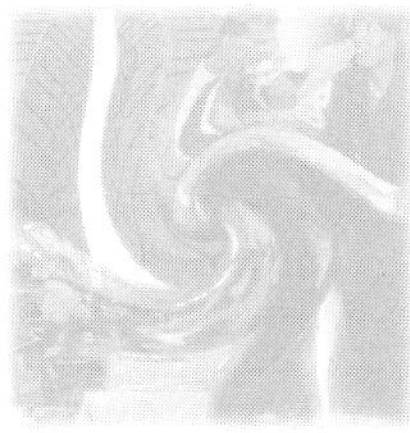

Setting Overall Goals

The last section examined the different types of decisions made in an organization. This section discusses the strategic decisions that set the overall course of an organization.

The Mission

Many organizations have a statement of their purpose. This defines their **mission**—it gives the purpose of the organization—its reason for existence. Some examples of missions are:

- *A hospital*—providing first-class health care
- *A bank*—safeguarding and increasing the value of customers' investments

- *A manufacturer*—supplying high-quality products to a wide market, while making a reasonable profit
- *A television network*—entertaining, informing, and educating the widest possible audience

The mission statement is sometimes very brief. A restaurant, for example, might simply say, "We aim to provide the best meals in Toronto." Often the statements are considerably longer and describe the aims and beliefs of the organization. They answer questions such as, What is our purpose? What business are we in? and What are our overall objectives? Sometimes they include the organization's responsibilities to its shareholders, employees, customers, and community.

In Summary

The mission is a statement about an organization's overall purpose. It gives the context for all other decisions within the organization.

Mission Statements

Mark's Work Warehouse has its headquarters in Calgary. It runs a nationwide chain of retail stores which sell workwear, casual clothing, and customized uniforms. Its mission statement is as follows:

"Our mission is to be a mature and stable enterprise known nationwide for being:

- the most customer-sensitive and responsive specialty retail organization in the markets we operate in
- a people-oriented work environment where employees are allowed the greatest possible freedom to carry out their responsibilities, own what they do, have fun and earn fair financial rewards
- a worthwhile financial return to investors and lenders through the successes that flow from being customer-driven and people-oriented."

Roland Inc is a Canadian manufacturer and distributor of fine papers. Its mission statement is:

"To ensure a reasonable rate of return on our shareholders' investment and enhance the value of their shares through the production and distribution of high-quality products that fulfil customer needs and bring satisfaction and well-being to our employees."

Even nonprofit organizations have mission statements. For example, the mission statement of the Purchasing Management Association of Canada is:

"The mission of the Purchasing Management Association of Canada is to provide national leadership in purchasing and supply management, with emphasis in the areas of education, research, standards of excellence and ethical conduct."

Business Strategy

Once the organization's mission has been defined, other strategic decisions can be made for the entire organization. These detail how the organization will achieve its mission. They can deal with the structure of the organization, its divisions, the responsibilities of each division, where the organization operates, its relationship with other organizations, and how it treats customers. Together, these strategic decisions, which affect the whole organization, form its **business strategy.**

A business strategy includes all long-term decisions about the business as a whole. These might typically include decisions about:

- Financial objectives
- Performance goals
- Organizational structure, which defines the number and type of divisions
- Competitive strategy, or how the organization deals with its competitors
- Level of diversification, or the range of products the organization makes
- Policies for buying or merging with other companies
- Geographical areas of operation
- Technology used
- Any other major decisions

When developing a business strategy, managers must consider two main factors: 1. the external environment in which the organization is working, and 2. the distinctive competence or internal environment which allows it to succeed in this environment.

The External Environment

The environment includes all factors that affect the organization but over which it has little or no control. When managers design the business strategy, they look at the environment and identify opportunities and threats to their organizations. They want to take advantage of opportunities and avoid the threats. The external environment includes:

- *Market conditions*—the market for the organization's products, its size, location, and stability
- *Competitors*—the organizations which make similar products. How many are there, how strong are they, how easy is it for others to enter the market?
- *Customers*—who buys the products? How old are they, what are their expectations, attitudes, demographics?

- *Social conditions*—what are people's lifestyles? How are these changing?
- *Economic conditions*—the local, national, and global economy, Gross Domestic Product, growth rates, inflation, exchange rates
- *Technology*—an organization is interested in any technological developments which might affect its products or processes
- *Political conditions*—how stable is the government, how does it view trade, how much control does the government want, how good are relations with other countries?
- *Legal restraints*—laws which restrict trade, or affect the organization in other ways, such as liability and employment laws
- *Shareholders*—who are they? What are their objectives? What profit margin do they want?
- *Outside interest groups*—these include anybody who is interested in the organization, such as environmental groups. What are their objectives, how strong are they, how much support do they have?

Distinctive Competence

Having studied the external environment, managers must now decide how the organization is going to succeed in it. In other words, what is its **distinctive competence?** This is defined by those factors which are under the control of the organization, and which set it apart from its competitors. A company that can design new products very quickly, and has the resources to market these, could say this ability to innovate is part of its distinctive competence. A financial institution such as Canada Trust may develop a very personal and friendly service as its distinctive competence; a hospital may specialize in treating specific illnesses; a store may offer expertise with specific types of goods such as imported CDs; a management consultant may offer help with a certain type of problem.

The distinctive competence of an organization depends on its assets. These assets include:

- *Customers*—their demands, loyalty, relationships
- *Employees*—skills, expertise, loyalty
- *Finances*—capital, debt, cash flow
- *Products*—quality, reputation, innovations
- *Facilities*—capacity, age, value
- *Technology*—those currently used, plans, special types
- *Suppliers*—reliability, service, flexibility

- *Marketing*—experience, reputation
- *Resources*—patents, ownership

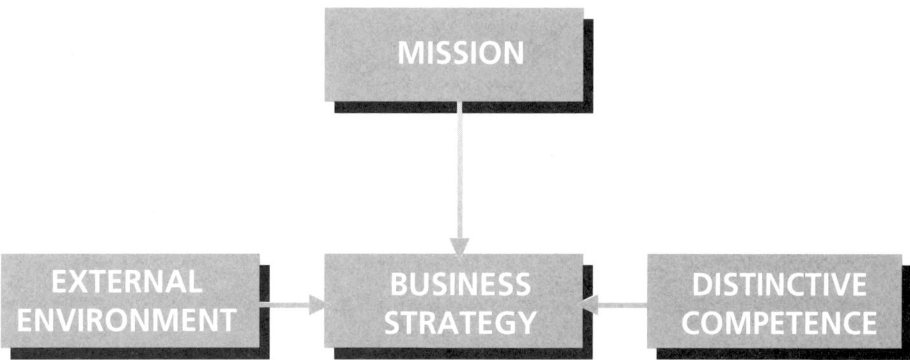

Figure 2.2 Inputs for Developing a Business Strategy

When an organization develops its business strategy, it must look at its own strengths and weaknesses in relation to those of its competitors. A **SWOT analysis** gives a useful way of summarizing these. It lists:

- **S**trengths: what the organization does well—features it should build on
- **W**eaknesses: what problems the organization has—areas it should improve
- **O**pportunities: that can help the organization—openings it should seize
- **T**hreats: that can damage the organization—hazards it should avoid

An important part of the business strategy concerns the way an organization deals with its competitors. This part is sometimes called the **competitive strategy**. Suppose, for example, a company is good at providing a high-quality product, while most of its competitors are aiming for lower quality. The competitive strategy is clear, as it should produce the best product available. This is the strategy of Rolls Royce cars. If there is a trend for very large supermarkets in large suburbs, one competitive strategy would be to build small corner stores like 7-eleven stores.

When managers develop a competitive strategy, they look for ways of overcoming their competition. Two ways of doing this are **cost leadership**, which provides the same products as competitors at lower prices; and **product differentiation**, which provides noticeably different products than competitors.

A computer manufacturer, such as Apple for example, must decide whether to make a standard personal computer at a low price—gaining cost leadership—or a computer with more features than the competition—gaining product differentiation. This is a rather simplified explanation; in practice an organization can develop its distinctive competence by competing with cost, quality, service, reliability, availability, flexibility, delivery speed, location, and a number of other features.

Other questions an organization should ask when designing its competitive strategy are the following:

- What is the structure of our industry?
- What changes are likely to occur in the future?
- Who are our customers?
- Who are the competitors?
- What are the competitors' strengths?
- How flexible are we?

The answers to these suggest a range of more detailed questions such as:

- What products should we concentrate on?
- What volumes should we make?
- What quality should we provide?
- Do we make low- or high-cost products?
- Are our products reliable?
- Do we give fast deliveries?
- Do we have adequate financing?

As you can see, these decisions are becoming more directly related to the primary functions of the organization. (Remember that Chapter 1 described the primary functions in all organizations as sales/marketing, operations, and accounting/finance.) These decisions do not directly concern the whole organization, but only parts of it. The next types of decision, then, are still strategic, but they are made within the primary functions.

Figure 2.3 Strategic Decisions in an Organization

Managers in the primary functions make these strategic decisions within the context of the overall business strategy. If, for example, a business strategy is to make large numbers of a product at low cost, this could lead to a strategic decision within operations to use an automated production line. This in turn affects other strategic decisions about the product, customers, production process, and costs.

However, there is a difference between operations—which is one of the primary functions in an organization—and decisions at an operational level—which are the lowest level of decisions. It is unfortunate that these two terms are so similar, and can be confusing. The discussion here has centred on the operations function—there are strategic, tactical, and operational decisions within this function.

In Summary

Strategic decisions that affect the organization as a whole form the business strategy. These decisions are based on the organization's environment and its distinct competence. An important part of the business strategy is the competitive strategy. The business strategy leads to a range of other decisions within the primary functions.

Case Study – Markland, Merrit, and Anderson

Markland, Merrit, and Anderson is a well-established company specializing in marine insurance. Their mission statement is as follows.

"We aim to be a leader in the international market for marine insurance. We shall achieve this by using the highest professional standards and integrity to provide our customers with the best possible service. This will allow us to form long- term, mutually beneficial partnerships with our customers, employees, and shareholders. "

This mission leads to the series of related decisions and values shown in the following summary.

"To fulfil this mission we must achieve the following objectives:

- The highest possible level of customer satisfaction
- Efficient and cost effective operations
- High profitability to reward shareholders
- Knowledgable, trained and motivated staff
- Long-term commitment to the industry."

"To achieve these objectives we must adopt the following key values:

- Responsiveness to customers
- Concern for people
- Teamwork and co-operation
- Professionalism and expertise
- Value for money"

Question

What types of decisions do you think are made at Markland, Merrit, and Anderson?

Review Questions

1. What is an organization's mission?
2. What is a business strategy?
3. What factors should be considered when designing a business strategy?
4. What questions are asked when designing a competitive strategy?

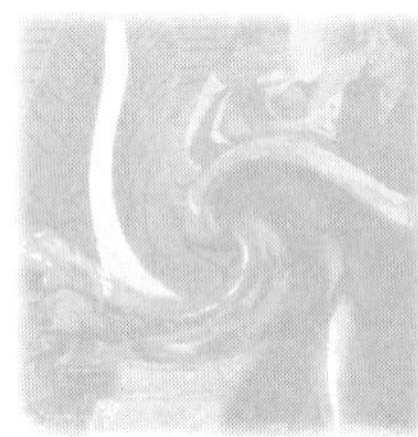

Decisions in Operations Management

Strategic decisions in the organization as a whole lead to strategic decisions within the primary functions. These in turn lead to tactical and operational decisions within the primary functions, as shown in Figure 2.4. This section looks at some of the decisions tackled by operations management. The strategic decisions within the operations function are known as the **operations strategy**.

The operations strategy is developed from the business strategy and is clearly linked to strategic decisions within the other functional areas. It is important that the strategies in each of the primary functions reinforce one another. Unfortunately, this is sometimes difficult. Consider, for example, a manufacturer whose business strategy requires high profits. The operations function might interpret this as an aim of reducing costs by concentrating on a narrow range of products. At the same time, sales and marketing might interpret it as a sign to increase sales by offering a wide range of products. These two are clearly contradictory, and the differences must be resolved. Each function has its own objectives, but these should not interfere with the organization's overall objectives.

Positioning

An operations strategy should make sure that there is no conflict with other departments. The operations strategy gives guidelines for the selection of appropriate machines, the hiring of employees, the use of new technology, the introduction of new products, and the selection of proper planning and control systems.

How should an organization go about developing the operations strategy? There are many approaches to this, but one method uses **positioning**. Positioning defines an organization's position or place in a competitive arena. It may be difficult for an organization to do all aspects of the operations function well (relative to its competitors), so it might focus on some aspects of its operations and so define its position.

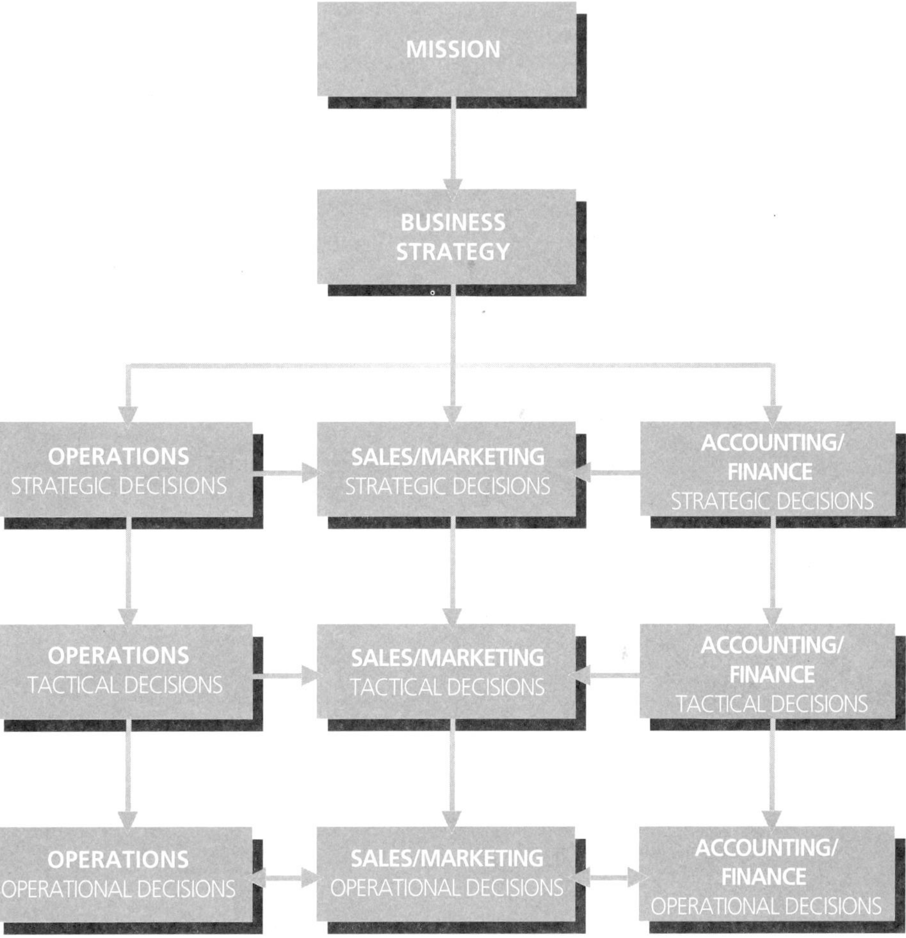

Figure 2.4 Decisions Within an Organization

Customers normally buy a product after looking at three main features: quality, price, and availability. It is difficult for a product to be superior in all three features. So the management should clearly define, through its business strategy, what products it will make and which market segments it will serve. Once those have been defined, the operations manager can translate that into an operations strategy using positioning. If the business strategy emphasizes quality, the operations people have to make a high-quality product. To make a high-quality product, the design must be good, the plant should have trained workers, high-quality raw materials should be used, and so on.

The price of the product is determined, to a large extent, by the cost of producing it. If you are a low-cost producer, you can set lower prices for your products. So a product at the lower end of the price scale needs cost-efficient production. Some ways of becoming cost efficient are to buy specialized machines, standardize the products, pay lower wages to the employees, and emphasize productivity.

Customers want products to be readily available, and they expect suppliers to be dependable and flexible.

Dependability refers to whether or not the organization can supply products on promised dates. For an organization to be dependable, it should have, among other things, good planning and scheduling systems, low absenteeism among its workers, and reliable and well-maintained machines.

Flexibility refers to how versatile the organization is in dealing with changes in product, demand level, and processes. To be flexible, a company must have versatile machines, cross-trained workers, and a good working relationship among all departments.

Positioning helps develop an operations strategy by assigning relative importance to the four performance characteristics: quality, cost efficiency, dependability, and flexibility.

A company might position itself as a top-quality producer, at the same time emphasizing flexibility, dependability, and cost efficiency in that order. This helps decision making for the operations function.

One way to visualize this is to use a pyramid. The four corners of the pyramid

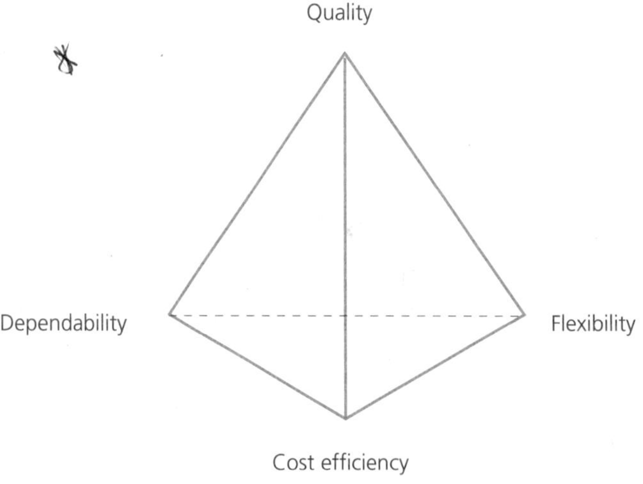

Figure 2.5 Positioning Pyramid

represent the four performance characteristics. If a company is the best in all four criteria, then it occupies the total space of this pyramid. In reality, a company cannot occupy all four corners of the pyramid, but it occupies some space within this pyramid. When you define your positioning, you are also revealing the empty space in the pyramid. Your competition might try to occupy the empty space.

In general, the operations strategy answers questions such as:

- What types of product does the organization supply?
- What types of processes does it use?
- How does it ensure high quality?
- In what geographic areas does it operate?
- How does it plan capacity?

The operations strategy sets the overall direction for operations. Then a series of shorter-term tactical decisions can be made about the layout of facilities, process design, capacity planning, make/buy decisions, quality assurance, maintenance plans, and recruiting. These tactical decisions, in turn, lead to short-term operational deci-

Case Study – Excello Canada Inc.

Excello Canada Inc. is a successful manufacturer of customized cutting tools for metal work. These tools are made by skilled workers, who take considerable pride in their products. They use state-of-the-art computer-controlled machines and make consistently high quality products. This is in line with their operations strategy which "emphasizes high quality and service to get above average profit margins."

A recent market survey showed that there is likely to be little growth in Excello's current market. Future growth is expected in sales of woodworking tools for use in home renovation. Excello decided to take advantage of this by making a range of competitively priced, lower quality, standard tools such as saws, drill bits, and chisels. This had the advantage of increasing utilization of Excello's equipment, as the new lines would complement their existing products. The production manager expected no problems in making the new products and expected increased sales and profits.

Unfortunately, one year after introducing the new line, things were not going well. Production costs had risen and inventory levels had grown alarmingly. For the first time, Excello had received a number of complaints about quality, with products being returned by established customers. The workers who took pride in their work were unhappy. Absenteeism and lateness were much more common.

Questions

- What was Excello's operations strategy before introducing the new line?
- Why did the company introduce the new line?
- Why do you think there were so many problems with the new line?
- What do you think the managers should do now? What are the alternatives?

sions about resource scheduling, inventory control, reliability, and expediting. Some illustrations of these decision areas are shown in Table 2.2.

Table 2.2 *Typical Decisions in Operations*

Strategic Decisions	
Business	What business are we in?
Product	What products do we make?
Process	How do we make products?
Location	Where do we make products?
Capacity	How large should facilities be?
Quality Management	How good are the products?
Tactical Decisions	
Layout	How should we arrange operations?
Planning	When should we introduce new products?
Quality Assurance	How do we maintain planned quality?
Logistics	How should we organize distribution; what transport should we use?
Maintenance	How often should equipment be maintained and replaced?
Staffing	How many people should we employ, with what skills?
Technology	What is the best level for planned production?
Make/Buy	Is it better to make or buy components?
Operational Decisions	
Scheduling	In what order should we make products?
Inventory	How much should we hold in stock?
Reliability	How often does equipment break down; what can be done to improve this?
Maintenance	When can maintenance periods be scheduled?
Quality Control	Are products reaching designed quality?

The distinctions among strategic, tactical, and operational decisions are not as clear as suggested by this table. Quality, for example, is a strategic issue when a company is planning its competitive strategy, perhaps aiming for a very high-quality product. However, it becomes a tactical issue when the organization is deciding how quality can be measured and what targets should be set. Then it becomes an operational decision when checking production to see if quality targets are being met. Similarly, inventory may be a strategic issue when deciding whether to build a warehouse for finished goods or to ship directly to customers, a tactical issue when deciding how much to invest in inventory, or an operational issue when deciding how many materials to buy this week.

All the decisions mentioned so far have the supply of a product as a key element. The long-term survival of any organization depends on its ability to supply products that satisfy customer demand. The organized supply of these products does not come by chance but depends on effective decisions made by operations managers. The rest of this book describes how such decisions are made.

Review Questions

1. "Operations managers only make decisions at operational levels." Do you think this is true? Explain.
2. What is the difference among business strategy, competitive strategy, and operations strategy?
3. Which level of operations decision should be made first? Why?

The Seven Deadly Diseases of Managers

Edwards Deming (whom we will meet again in Chapter 6) described "The Seven Deadly Diseases" of managers:

- *Lack of constancy of purpose.* The whole organization must know where it is heading and aim at improving its performance.
- *Emphasis on short-term profits.* Organizations are too often judged by their short-term performance, like annual profit and quarterly sales. They should take a longer view and aim for the best results over the long term.
- *Evaluation of performance, merit rating, or annual review.* Again, this tends to emphasize people's short-term performance instead of looking at the long term. Another problem occurs when people do poorly in these evaluations and are left bitter, dejected, and unfit for work.
- *Mobility of top management.* Managers move freely among companies, but such moves leave them with no knowledge or interest in the long-term success of a particular organization. They often appear more interested in improving their own "market value."
- *Running a company on visible figures alone.* Some of an organization's performance can be measured, such as income or profit. There are many aspects of performance that cannot be measured, bu they should not be ignored.

The last two of Deming's diseases are only relevant to the United States:

- *Excessive medical costs*
- *Excessive costs of lawsuits*

Case Study

Plitron Manufacturing Inc.

Howard Gladstone, president of Plitron Manufacturing Inc., is a visionary. His company has been experiencing growth for the last ten years, and much of it could be attributed to his astute strategic management. "We are embarking on fundamental research and development, product enhancement, and new product development to create new markets," says Gladstone. Plitron has introduced a new line of Packaged Power Products. These are whole power supply units rather than the transformers used in power units which account for most of Plitron's business.

Gladstone believes that for business strategy to succeed, the company's marketing, production, and financial plans have to be closely integrated. At Plitron, the mandate of the production department is to provide good customer service. "In our business, we have to provide the customer what he needs, and provide it fast," comments Gladstone. Quality, of course, is also important to their customers. Plitron has developed a reputation as a manufacturer of superior quality products.

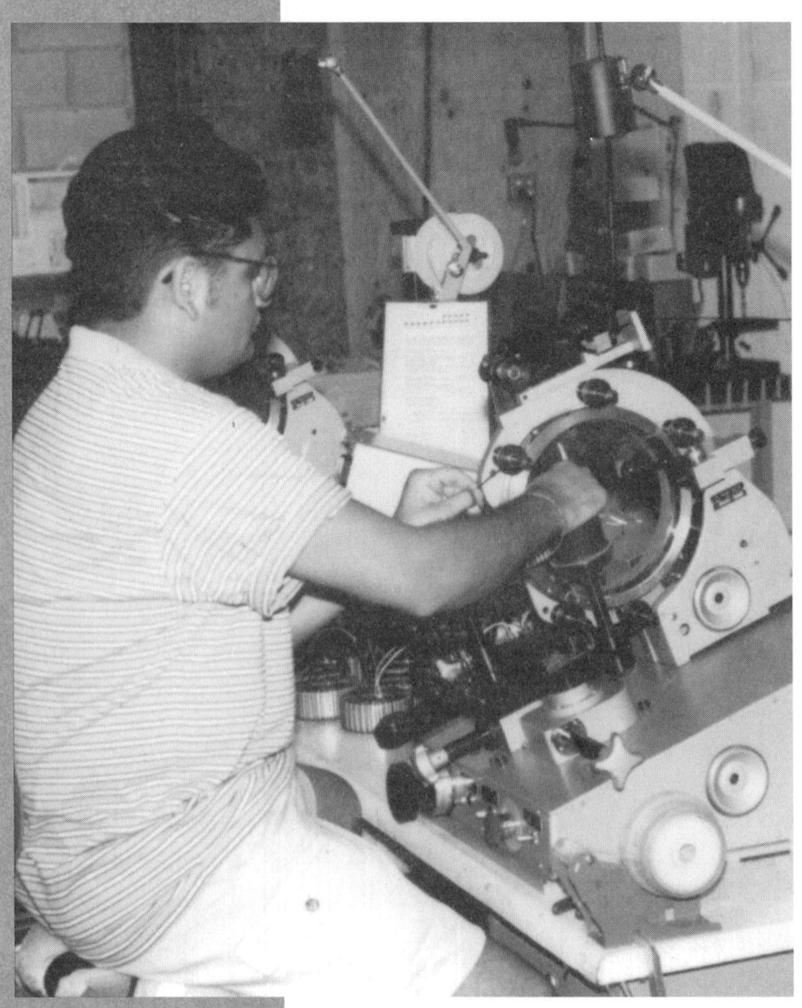

Lately, Plitron has been experiencing price pressures. Its customers would like the company to supply high-quality products, give fast and reliable service, and do all this at low prices. That, according to Gladstone, is very difficult, if not impossible. One of the strategic solutions to this challenge was found by exploring offshore sources. This led Gladstone to form a joint venture with a company in India. Plitron will work closely with the Indian company by providing the technical know-how, and by training the Indian company's employees to manufacture the price-sensitive, simpler products, whereas the high-quality, complex products will be produced at Plitron's existing Toronto facility.

Case Study – Nash's Service Station

Jim Nash, the owner of Nash's Service Station, was thinking about expanding the business he had bought five years ago. He had worked hard to make it a success. The service station has ten gas pumps, both self-serve and full service. His garage has four service bays, which specialize in tune-ups, brake jobs, and engine repairs. This service centre has developed a reputation for doing good work at reasonable prices, and has an increasing number of loyal customers.

At the back of the service station is an area of unused land. Jim was wondering what to do with this, and he came up with many ideas. The two he liked best were a) to open an automated car wash; and b) to set up a quick oil-change service, similar to the Pit Stop service of Canadian Tire.

Jim preferred the quick oil-change service because there were several other gas stations in the neighbourhood with car washes. He thought that many customers would like their oil changed quickly when they came in for gas. The mechanics could do the work in the oil-change area when they were not busy, or when there were long lineups for oil.

Six months after opening the oil-change station, Jim was wondering if he had made the right move. What surprised him most was that some of his regular customers had complained about the quality of work they got from his mechanics. They jokingly asked if the mechanics were trying to do the car repairs at the same speed as they did an oil change. Nash's reputation as a high-quality repair shop was slipping. One of the experienced mechanics decided to leave—largely because he was tired of moving between the two shops.

Jim also found that his quick oil-change service was not profitable. It never attracted the volume of customers that Jim expected.

Questions

- What was the operations strategy at the service centre?
- What is the strategy of the new, quick oil-change business?
- Why is Jim Nash facing so many problems?

Chapter Review

- The types of decisions made in an organization can be classified as strategic, tactical, or operational.
- Strategic decisions are made by senior managers, involve many resources, high risk, and a long timeframe; tactical decisions are made by middle managers, involve fewer resources, have less risk, and are medium term; operational decisions are made by junior management, involve few resources, little risk, and a short timeframe.
- An organization's mission describes its overall aims and beliefs, and sets the context for all other decisions.

- The mission allows a series of strategic decisions about the organization as a whole, which define the business strategy. An important part of this concerns competitive priorities. Other strategic decisions are made within functional areas.
- Strategic decisions within the operations function form the operations strategy. This sets the context for a range of operations decisions at tactical and operational levels.

Key Terms

business strategy *(p. 33)*
competitive strategy *(p. 35)*
cost leadership *(p. 35)*
distinctive competence *(p. 34)*
mission *(p. 31)*
operational decisions *(p. 27)*
operations strategy *(p. 38)*
positioning *(p. 39)*
product differentiation *(p. 35)*
strategic decisions *(p. 27)*
SWOT analysis *(p. 35)*
tactical decisions *(p. 27)*

Discussion Questions

2.1 What do we mean by saying that strategic decisions are less structured than tactical and operational ones?

2.2 Describe some decisions made at different levels in a specific organization.

2.3 Compare the mission statements published by five Canadian organizations, and state how these are affected by the type of organization. Why are some mission statements short and others very long?

2.4 Suppose you are about to start a company to manufacture rollerblades. Do a SWOT analysis of your business. What would be your business strategy?

2.5 Explain, giving suitable examples, the differences between business strategies and functional strategies.

2.6 How can a manufacturing company develop a competitive strategy?

2.7 How can a service industry develop a competitive strategy? What happens when the service has a near monopoly, such as health or education?

2.8 Consider a specific organization and design a business strategy for it. How does this lead to tactical and operational decisions?

2.9 There is often interdepartmental rivalry within an organization. Do you think this should be encouraged?

2.10 How would you develop an operations strategy using positioning?

Chapter 3

PRODUCT PLANNING AND DESIGN

Making the right products

Contents

Introduction

Every organization makes products for its customers. These products may be goods such as cars, computers, houses, or clothes. They may be services such as transportation, vacations, health care, or insurance. In practice, most organizations supply a combination of goods and services. When you buy a car, for example, you are given both goods (the car itself) and services (after-sales service, maintenance contract, delivery); when you eat in a restaurant, you are given goods (the food and drink) and services (given by the staff); when you use a bank, you are given goods (cheque books and cash cards) and services (the range of services offered by the bank).

Product planning ensures that an organization's products match customer demand. In particular, it plans new products that keep the range of products up to date. Before it is sold to customers, each new product must go through several stages of development. These include initial design, testing, and technical feasibility and commercial evaluations.

An organization will often be developing several products at the same time but will only have enough resources to market one of them. Then it must compare the products to find the best one.

After it is introduced, a product has a distinct life cycle. Each stage in this life cycle has different operational requirements, cost, revenue, and profit.

Learning Objectives

After reading this chapter you should be able to answer questions such as:

- What is product planning?
- What are its aims?
- How wide a range of products should an organization make?
- What factors are important in product design?
- How is a new product developed?
- How can different products be compared?
- When will a product begin to make a profit?
- What is a product life cycle?
- How do operations, costs, and profits vary during the life cycle?
- What are entry and exit strategies?

Case Study

Indalex

Indalex, a division of Caradon Ltd., is a world leader in aluminum extrusion, finishing, and fabrication. The state-of-the-art Mississauga plant makes products for the residential, construction, electrical, transportation, and consumer product markets.

To visualize the extrusion process, imagine the process of making pasta. Spaghetti, for example, is made by squeezing the pasta dough through a template which has small holes in it. Indalex's extrusion process consists of heating the aluminum billets and pressing them at 2,500 ton pressure through a die opening. The die opening is exactly the same as the cross-sectional shape of the product to be made. The product is extruded in a continuous, customer-specified form, which is cut to desired lengths.

Extrusion is a fast and economical way to mass-produce complex shaped, precision products. We often come across extruded products in our daily life, for example, window frames, step ladders, aluminum sidings, curtain rods, and storm doors.

Indalex uses high-grade aluminum bars or billets to make the extruded products. The billets are approximately 7 inches in diameter, 19 feet long, and weigh 900 pounds. The extrusion dies are forged from high-grade tool steel, so they maintain their shape and dimensions for a long time. A computer program is used to keep track of the usage history of all their dies. When a die does not conform exactly to the customer's specifications, it is sent to the die shop where skilled technicians repair it.

There are three extrusion presses at Indalex, four heat-treating furnaces, a paint line, and a fabrication department. All material handling is done by special overhead cranes. All processes are highly automated and computerized.

Indalex emphasizes quality and service. Currently, Indalex is implementing a total quality management program, which will further strengthen quality and service commitment to its customers.

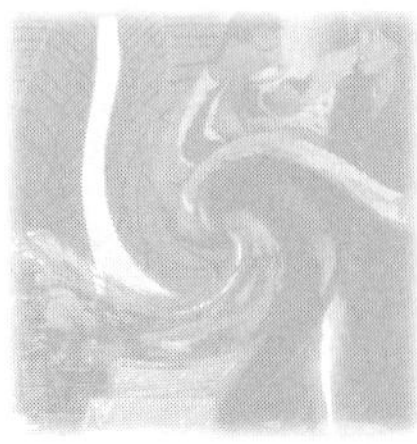

Product Planning

An organization can only be successful if it makes products that customers want. As customer demands change over time, the products offered must also change. In winter we want warm clothing, but in summer we want clothes that keep us cool; ten years ago we wanted cassette tapes and records, now we want CDs; we used to want FAX machines that connected to computers in our homes, but now we want portable FAX machines. This is where product planning is used.

Product planning is concerned with all decisions about the introduction of new products, changes to existing products, and the withdrawal of old products.

The purpose of product planning is to ensure that an organization continues to make products that customers want.

Organizations must respond to changes in demand by continually offering new products. Thus Northern Telecom will develop new digital-exchange equipment, or the CBC will replace a show whose ratings fall.

In Summary

Product planning ensures that an organization makes products that its customers want. This means it must supply a continually changing range of products.

Range of Products Offered

Ideally, organizations would like to make a single product, as this would simplify their operations. However, customers all have slightly different needs. We all buy clothes, for example, but we want different sizes, styles, and colours. Organizations allow for these differences by supplying variations of a basic product. Clothing manufacturers make different sizes, styles and colours; colleges give different courses; construction companies build different types of houses; management consultants offer different services; and so on. The result is that most organizations supply a **range of similar or related products.**

Most organizations concentrate on one kind of product. This means that any new product must both a) satisfy customer demand; and b) fit in with existing products. Toyota, for example, will introduce a new model of car but will not start making perfume.

Each organization must decide how wide a range of products to make. This decision must balance two factors: 1. if it makes a narrow range, the organization can use standard operations, but some customers will be lost to competitors who offer more products or different ones; 2. if it makes a wide range, the organization can satisfy varied customer demands, but it loses the efficiency that comes from standardization.

This means that there is always a compromise between producers who would like to make a narrow range of products and customers who would like a wide range. At present, more organizations are aiming for a narrower range of standard products. In the 1960s, car manufacturers made a wider range to cater for different tastes; now the trend is to make fewer models using standard parts and components. This standardization has the following advantages:

- Specialized production machinery and equipment
- Long production runs (the same product is made for a long time rather than having frequent changes of product)
- Reducing production set-up times (the time needed to prepare equipment before starting to make a product)
- Making production routine and well practised
- Increasing staff experience and expertise with the product
- Encouraging the allocation of resources to improve the product
- Making associated purchasing, inspections, and handling routine
- Reducing employee training time
- Smaller inventories of parts and materials

Despite these benefits, varying customer demands force almost all organizations to make a range of related products.

In Summary

Ideally, organizations would like to make a narrow range of products. This would bring many benefits to their operations. However, varying customer demand forces most organizations to make a range of related products.

Review Questions

1. What is a product?
2. What is the purpose of product planning?
3. Why do organizations make a range of products?
4. Why do organizations make a range of similar products rather than completely different ones?

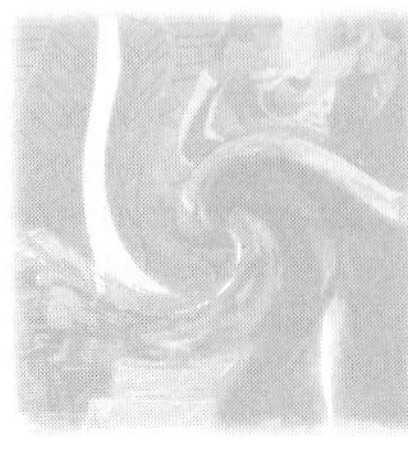

Developing New Products

Product planning is an ongoing process. New products are introduced to customers, while old ones are updated or withdrawn. In 1993, for example, Intel Corporation was the world's largest manufacturer of microprocessors. It had developed the highly successful 286 and 386 processors, but these were withdrawn when it marketed the 486. This was modified several times until it in turn was replaced by the Pentium. Competition from other manufacturers, particularly PowerPC, forced Intel to keep improving its products. Despite some problems with the Pentium chip, the original Pentium 60/66 was quickly modified to give the Pentium 90, then the Pentium 100, then the Pentium 150.

The introduction of a new product is expensive. The development of the Airbus Industrie A3XX, for example, cost $12 billion up to 1995. Ford spent $7 billion developing its Mondeo in 1993. This money is spent on a long development process that starts with some initial ideas and ends when the product is sold to customers. The details of this process depend on the organization and the product, but a common approach has six stages: 1. generation of ideas; 2. initial screening of ideas; 3. initial design and testing; 4. commercial analysis; 5. final product development; and 6. launch of product.

Generation of Ideas

Most organizations continuously search for new ideas that can be turned into successful products. Some of these ideas come from within the organization. Often, a research department will develop a new product. At other times, operations people suggest a change to an existing product, such as using more standard components to simplify production. Many ideas are found outside the organization. A competitor's product might be adapted to fit into the company's operations, customers may demand a product that is not currently available, or new government regulations may make a new product essential. There are many sources for initial ideas, including:

- Results from research and development
- Sales and marketing surveys and observations
- Other internal sources
- Competitors' products
- Customers' demands
- Changing government regulations
- Other external sources

New ideas are fairly easy to find. The difficult part is selecting the ones that will lead to successful products that customers want.

Initial Screening of Ideas

All ideas must go through an initial screening to reject those with obvious flaws. This screening can quickly reject ideas which:

- Are impossible or technically difficult to make
- Have been tried before
- Duplicate an existing product
- Use expertise or skills which are not available
- Do not fit into current operations

This screening can be done by a committee of people from marketing, finance, and operations. It typically removes 80 percent of the original ideas. The remaining 20 percent have no obvious flaws and can move to the next stages of development.

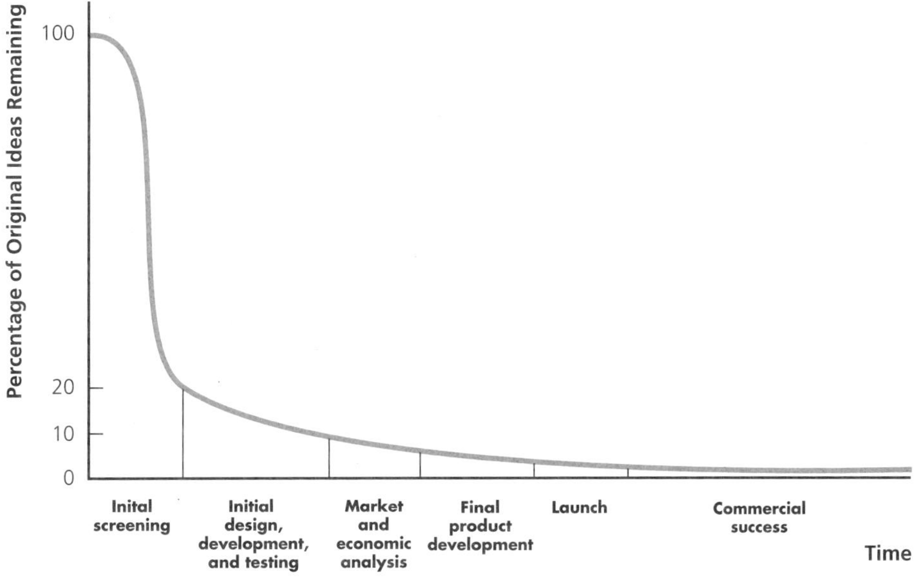

Figure 3.1 Proportion of Ideas Which Are Typically Lost at Each Stage of Development

Initial Design and Testing

This stage involves a technical evaluation of ideas to see if the product could be made by the organization. It typically asks two types of questions.

- Questions about the general idea for the product. Is the idea based on sound engineering principles? Could such a product be made? Is it entirely new, or a variation on old ideas? If it is an old idea, why has the organization not made it before? Are there problems with patents or competitors? Are new developments likely to make the product obsolete?

- More specific questions about the product. Is the proposed design technically feasible? Can it be made with available technology? Does it fit into current operations? Does the organization have the necessary skills and experience? To answer some of these questions a prototype might be developed and tested.

This stage removes about half of the remaining ideas.

Commercial Analysis

If the product passes the technical evaluation, it moves on to the commercial analysis. This determines whether the product is likely to be a commercial success. It studies the market and finances to see how it will sell, what competition exists, if it will make a profit, what investment is needed, and what return on investment can be expected. Market surveys to gauge customer reaction are often done at this stage.

Unfortunately, the commercial evaluation rejects many technically good ideas. It is sometimes difficult to accept that an idea that is technically viable may not get enough sales to make a profit.

The technical evaluation and commercial analysis together form the **feasibility study**.

Final Product Development

If the product passes the feasibility study, it moves to final design and testing. This is where the product changes from a prototype or concept model to the form which will be passed on to customers. Lessons from the technical and commercial evaluation are used, and the design is finalized. This design should be both functional (so that it meets the requirements of customers) and attractive (so that it appeals to customers).

The design can significantly affect the cost of production. A product should, therefore:

- Be easy to make
- Use the simplest and cheapest process
- Have a standard design, so there are few variations in the final products
- Use standardized, interchangeable components and parts wherever possible
- Use high-quality materials so that scrap and defects are minimized

After the final product designs, the process used to make it can be finalized. Then production can begin and the new product launched.

Launch of Product

The launch is the point where the product is sold to customers. This is the first chance to see if it will actually be a success. Many products which are launched turn out to be unsuccessful, often with considerable costs. The Ford Edsel lost $350 million in the late 1950s. In the 1970s, Joseph Schlitz Brewing Co. started "accelerated batch fermentation" for its beer. Customers did not like this, sales plummeted, and the company never recovered from its losses. IBM's PC Junior had lost $100 million by 1985. In the 1980s, Coca-Cola changed its recipe, but customers forced a return of the original "classic" range.

The success of a product often depends on the competition. Customers may consider a number of factors when making comparisons, but the most common are:

- *Price.* If similar products are competing, the one with the lowest price may be most successful, but not always. There are many examples ranging from perfumes to luxury cars where demand seems to rise with higher prices.
- *Availability.* The most obvious aspect of availability is a fast delivery. A piece of furniture that can be taken home from a store will sell better than an identical one that will be delivered in ten weeks. More people will use a bus service if there are regular arrivals every few minutes than if there are only one or two arrivals an hour.
- *Quality.* There are two important aspects to quality. The first is **designed quality**, which shows how good a product is meant to be. A silk shirt, for example, has a higher designed quality than a polyester one, and a luxury hotel has a higher designed quality than a boarding house. The second aspect of quality describes actual performance, with **achieved quality**. An airline might design its timetables so that 98 percent of flights arrive on time. If only 30 percent of flights actually arrive on time, the designed quality is high but achieved quality is low.
- *Flexibility.* The ability of an organization to meet specific customer requirements or react to changing circumstances is called flexibility. An organization with more flexibility can meet customer demands more precisely and therefore offers better products.

Very few of the initial ideas, perhaps one to two percent, complete all stages of this development process to the point where they are sold to customers. Even fewer become successful products.

In Summary

New products go through an extensive screening before they are marketed. This includes a technical evaluation and a commercial analysis. Even after this screening there is no guarantee that a product will be a success.

Review Questions

1. What are typical stages in the screening and introduction of a new product?
2. What criteria are used to judge a new product?
3. "The most difficult part of developing a new product is getting new ideas from the research team." Do you agree with this?

Product Design

The design of a product is crucial to its success. A poorly designed product will not sell well. However, there is such a wide range of products and so many different factors to consider in product design that it is impossible to say what makes a good design in all circumstances. There are three general requirements of **product design**. A product must be:

- *Functional.* The product must do the job it is designed for. You can probably think of many gadgets that look good, but do not work properly; these are not functional. The best way to make sure a design is functional is to ask potential customers what they want the product to do, and then ask a team of designers to meet these needs. The designs must then be tested and revised, perhaps using prototypes, before they are finalized.
- *Attractive.* The product must have an appearance which customers like. This is obviously more important for products such as clothes than industrial machines. Nonetheless, most products have some aesthetic needs which designers must consider.
- *Easy to make.* The cost of a product depends on many factors, but the design is probably the most important. You can imagine that a product which is made automatically on an assembly line will cost less to make than one requiring a lot of skilled manual work. Generally, higher costs come from:
    - Needing an expensive process to make the product
    - Using nonstandard parts and components
    - Using too many or expensive materials
    - Demanding too high quality
    - Interfering with the production of other items

You can see from these comments that the design of a product needs teamwork. There are artistic, technical, operational, financial, and other aspects to be considered, with important inputs from marketing and customers themselves.

From an operations point of view, an organization should simplify and standardize its products as a way of reducing the costs. It is easier to do this when the product is still being designed rather than after it has been introduced in the market.

Simplification means that unnecessary parts are removed so the product is easier to make. This could involve critical analysis and review of the product design by various people such as engineers, production managers, and quality inspectors. If a product has fewer components and moving parts, then it will be easier and cheaper to make, and it will have a longer life.

Standardization is another way to reduce product cost. Standardization means using common components in a range of different products. There are many types of standards—a company standard, the industry standard, national or international standards. In Canada, we have a national standard for electrical items such as sockets, plugs, and wires. This allows you, for example, to buy a bulb anywhere in Canada and use it anywhere else in the country.

There are many benefits to standardization. Standard items are significantly cheaper to buy and are readily available. By standardizing parts, one can reduce the number of items to be stocked and thus reduce the amount of inventory. It also helps reduce product design and development time and costs.

Standardization does not necessarily reduce the choice available to customers, as the standard parts can be used to produce a wide range of products. Car manufacturers, for example, use standard components, but juggle these to give a range of models.

In Summary

The design of a product is important to its success. Although it is difficult to give general guidelines on design, a product should be functional, attractive, and easy to make.

Review Questions

1. "The aim of product design is to create a product with artistic merit." Do you agree with this?
2. What factors are important in product design?

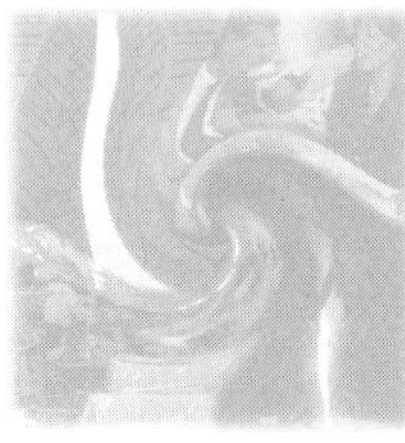

Comparing Products

Suppose an organization is looking for a new product and has several alternatives that finish the initial screening stage at the same time. Occasionally the organization will have enough resources to develop and market all of these alternatives. More commonly, the organization has limited resources and must choose one product in preference to the others. It needs some way of comparing products and selecting the best.

Two general methods of comparing products are scoring models and break-even analyses.

Scoring Models

Many factors must be considered when comparing products. Some of these factors are quantifiable, while others are subjective or qualitative. We could not, for example, quantify the design of competitors' products, the amount of innovation in a product, its colour, or our experience with similar products. A simple way of dealing with such comparisons is to list the important factors and decide whether a product gives satisfactory performance in each.

Example

Factor	Product A	Product B	Product C	Product D
Time to develop	✓	✓	✓	✓
Expected useful life	✓		✓	✓
Cost of developing	✓			✓
Fit with other products	✓		✓	✓
Equipment needed	✓			✓
Initial demand	✓	✓	✓	
Stability of demand	✓	✓	✓	
Marketing requirement	✓	✓	✓	
Competition	✓	✓	✓	
Expected profit	✓	✓	✓	✓

A company lists ten factors it considers important in a new product. Proposals for four new products are being considered, but the company has only enough resources to work on one of these. After intense discussions, managers have agreed on whether each product reaches a satisfactory standard for the ten factors. In the table to the left, a check mark shows that a product *has* performed well enough. Which product should the company develop? If this product is found to be technically infeasible, which product should the company develop?

Solution

The only product that satisfies all ten factors is A, so this one should be developed.

If product A is infeasible—perhaps because it needs some production process that the organization does not have—the company has several alternatives. It can say that no product satisfies all the factors, so none of them will be developed. In practice, it is unusual to find an ideal product which satisfies all criteria, so a compromise is needed and the best available one is chosen. In this case, the best is clearly not B, as C satisfies all the conditions that B does, as well as some additional ones. The choice is between C, which performs well in marketing, and D, which performs well in development.

One problem with simple checklists is that they cannot show the relative importance of factors. An organization might, for example, feel that ease of production is more important than marketing. It can show this using a **scoring model,** which gives different weights to each factor.

The first step in building a scoring model is to list the important factors. This time their relative importance is shown by giving a maximum possible score to each. Technical factors, for example, might be given a maximum score of 10; marketing considerations are half as important and are given a maximum score of 5; return on investment is twice as important and is given a maximum score of 20. When maximum scores have been given, each product is examined to see how it actually performs. A score is given for each factor, up to the maximum. The scores for each product are then added, and the product with the highest score is the one that should be developed.

This procedure for scoring models is summarized in Table 3.1.

Table 3.1 *Procedure for Scoring Models*

1. Decide the most important factors for a product.
2. Decide a maximum possible score for each factor.
3. Consider each product in turn and give a score for each factor.
4. Add the total scores for each product.
5. Identify the best product as the one with the highest total score.
6. Discuss the result, look at other factors, and make a final decision.

Example

Four alternative products are judged by five factors, as shown to the right. What is the relative importance of the factors? On this evidence, which product is best?

Factor	Maximum	A	B	C	D
Technological advance	20	11	15	18	15
Financial performance	30	28	16	26	12
Market	15	9	13	12	8
Ease of production	25	18	19	20	19
Competition	10	9	7	6	9

Solution

The most important criterion is financial performance, which is given the highest maximum score. Ease of production is considered slightly less important (25/30 times as important), then technological advance (20/30 times as important), then market, and finally competition.

Adding the scores for each product gives totals of

A = 75 B = 70 C = 82 D = 63

On this evidence, product C is clearly the best.

In Summary

There are several ways of comparing new products. Choosing the best from a number of alternatives can involve both qualitative and quantitative factors. Scoring models are useful in such comparisons.

Break-even Point

An important question for new products is whether the sales will be high enough to make a profit. The income generated must cover not only the cost of producing each unit, but it must also recover the money spent before the product was launched. This includes the cost of research, development, buying equipment to make the product, market surveys, and trial runs.

The profit from selling a product is defined as:

$$\text{Profit} = \text{income} - \text{total costs}$$

The income is found from:

$$\text{Income} = \text{number of units sold} \times \text{price charged per unit}$$

$$= n \times P = nP$$

where: n = number of units sold

P = price charged per unit

The total costs of making the product come from a number of sources and can be classified as:

- **Fixed costs,** which are constant regardless of the number of units made
- **Variable costs,** which depend on the number of units made

Research and development costs, for example, are fixed regardless of the number of units made. Other fixed costs include marketing, administration, lighting, heating, rent, debt payments, and a range of overheads that are unaffected by the output. On the other hand, the cost of raw materials, direct labour, maintenance, and some other overheads are variable and are affected by output. A doubling of output will double raw material costs, for example.

Consider the cost of running a car. This can be divided into a fixed cost of repaying the purchase loan, licence fee, and insurance, and a variable cost for each kilometre travelled for gas, oil, tires, and depreciation.

Total costs = fixed cost + variable cost

= fixed cost + number of units made × variable cost per unit

$= C_F + n \times C_U = C_F + nC_U$

C_F = fixed cost

C_U = variable unit cost

The income and total cost both rise linearly with the number of units made, as shown in Figure 3.2. The point where these lines cross is the break-even point.

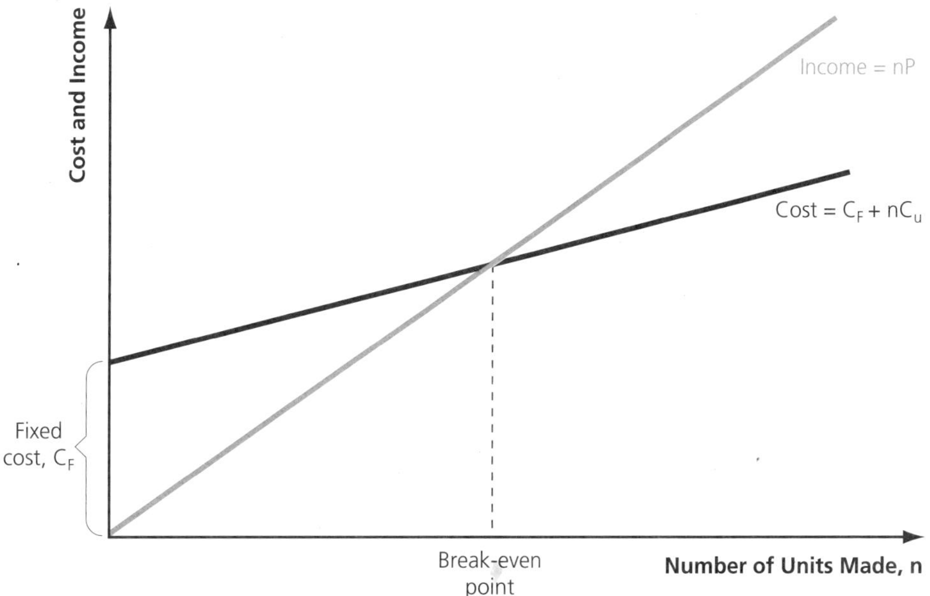

Figure 3.2 Defining the Break-even Point

The **break-even point** is the number of units which must be sold before an organization recovers fixed costs and starts to make a profit.

Suppose a new product has had $300,000 spent on research and development, buying equipment, and other preparations needed before production began. Other overheads cost $100,000, giving a total fixed cost of $400,000. During normal production, each unit has a variable cost of $600 and is sold for $800. The company will only start to make a profit on this product when the original $400,000 has been recovered. The point where this occurs is the break-even point.

Each unit sold contributes \$800 - 600 = \$200 to the company, so 400,000/200 = 2,000 units must be sold to cover the fixed cost. Then:

- The break-even point is 2,000 units
- If less than 2,000 units are sold, the company will make a loss on the product
- If more any than 2,000 units are sold, the company will make a profit on the product

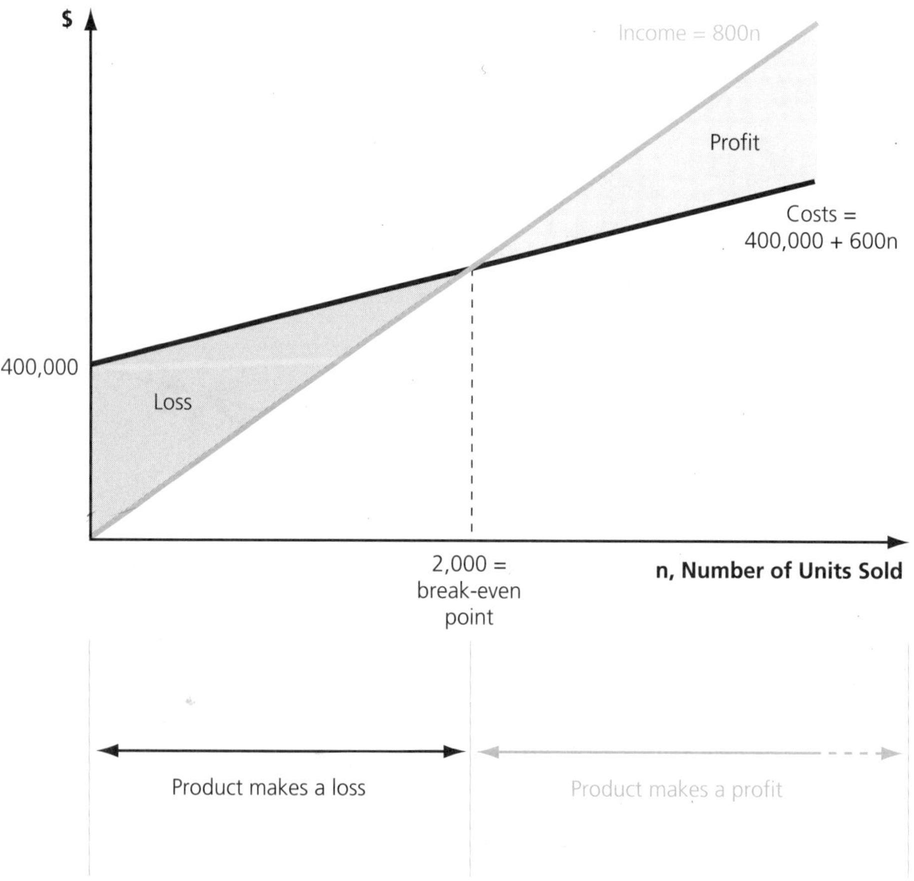

Figure 3.3 Break-even Point for Example

In general, the break-even point comes when:

$$\text{Income} = \text{total costs}$$

$$nP = C_F + nC_U$$

or break-even point,

$$n = \frac{C_F}{P - C_U}$$

$$n = C_F / CP - C_U$$

In our last example:

$$n = \frac{C_F}{P - C_U} = \frac{400,000}{800 - 600} = \frac{400,000}{200} = 2,000$$

Example

A company makes an average of 100 units of a product every month. The revenue generated has to cover fixed costs of \$63,000 a month. Each unit of the product has raw material and other variable costs of \$500.

a) Does the company make a net profit if the selling price is \$1,200 a unit?

b) If the selling price is reduced to \$1,000 and sales increase to 150 units a month, would the company make a profit?

Solution

a) The variables we are given are:

Fixed cost (C_F) = \$ 63,000
Variable cost per unit (C_U) = \$500
Selling price per unit (P) = \$1,200
Number of units sold (n) = 100

The break-even point is calculated from:

$n = C_F / (P - C_U)$ = \$ 63,000/(\$1,200 – 500) = 90

The company is actually selling 100 units per month. This is more than the break-even point, so it is making a profit. This profit can be calculated from:

Income = nP = 100 × 1200 = \$120,000 a month
Total costs = $C_F + nC_U$ = 63,000 + 100 × 500 = \$113,000 a month
Profit = income – total costs = 120,000 – 113,000 = \$7,000 a month

b) The new break-even point is:

$n = C_F/(P - C_U)$ = 63,000/(1,000 – 500) = 126

Actual sales are 150, so the product is making a profit. This profit can be calculated from:

Income = nP = 150 × 1,000 = \$150,000 a month

Total costs = $C_F + nC_U$ = \$63,000 + (150 × 500) = \$138,000 a month

Profit = income – total costs = \$150,000 – 138,000 = \$12,000 a month

In Summary

Break-even points give another method of comparing products. They describe the number of units that must be sold before costs are covered and a profit is made.

Review Questions

1. Why are scoring models used?
2. If a scoring model shows a particular product is the best available, would any further analysis be needed? Why or why not?
3. What does the "variable cost" vary with?
4. What costs might be included in "fixed cost"?
5. The break-even point for a product is 1,000 units. What does it mean if actual sales are 1,200 units?

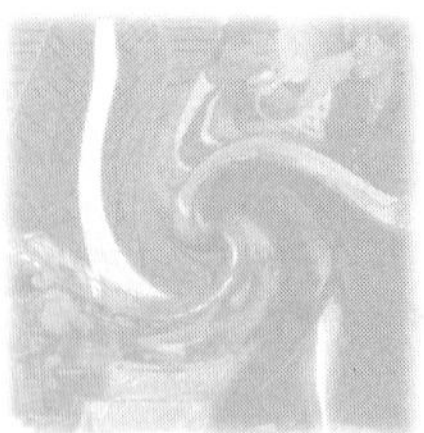

Product Life Cycle

Organizations continually develop new products to meet changing customer demands, but even these new products have a limited life span and will eventually need replacing. In other words, all products have a **life cycle**.

Stages in the Life Cycle

Life cycles can be divided into five stages, as shown in Figure 3.4.

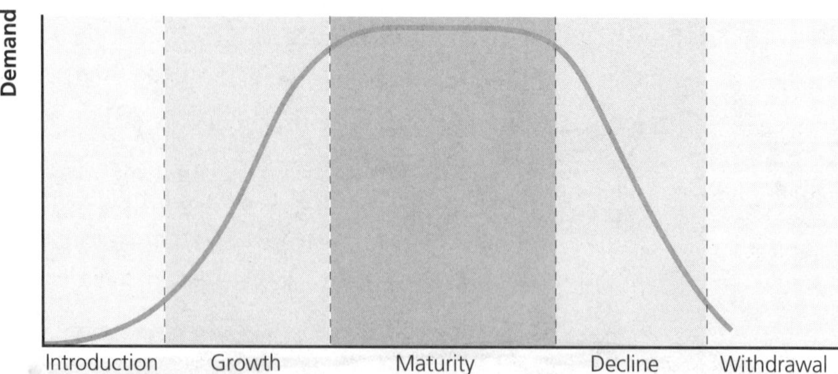

Figure 3.4 Life Cycle of a Product

1. *Introduction.* A new product is on the market and demand is low while people learn about it, try it, and see if they like it.
2. *Growth.* New customers buy the product and demand rises quickly.
3. *Maturity.* Most potential customers know about the product and are buying it in steady numbers. Demand stabilizes at a constant level.
4. *Decline.* Sales fall as new products, which customers prefer, become available.
5. *Withdrawal.* Demand falls to the point where it is no longer worth making the product.

For example, there are several different types of printers for personal computers. Some of these are based on fairly new ideas, such as colour laser printers, which are at the introductory stage; ordinary laser printers have become established and as their price falls, they are moving through a growth stage; ink jet printers are moving into a mature stage; dot-matrix printers are at the mature stage and starting to decline; and printers based on typewriters are no longer selling and are in the decline and withdrawal stage.

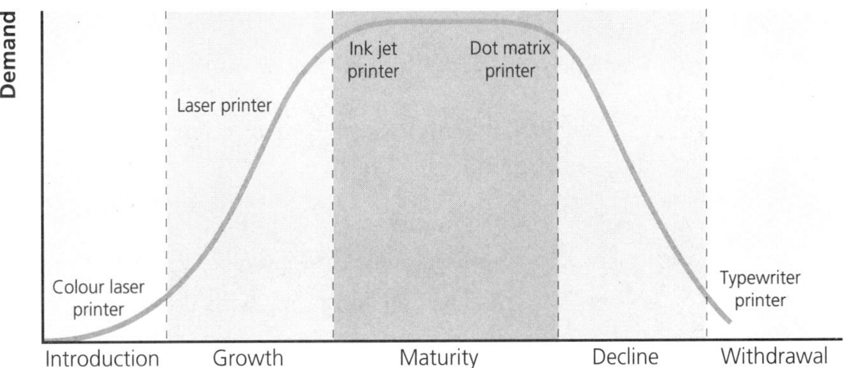

Figure 3.5 Life Cycle of a Product

The exact shape of the life cycle varies from product to product, but the most important variable is its length. Each edition of a newspaper has a life cycle of a few hours; clothing fashions and fad computer games have a life cycle of a few months or even weeks; types of washing machines have life cycles of five or ten years; some basic commodities such as soap and coffee remain in the mature stage for decades. Unfortunately, there are no real guidelines for the expected length of a life cycle. Some products have an unexpectedly short life and lead to commercial failure. Other products have been at the mature stage for a long time and suddenly start to decline. Sugar and full cream milk have been at the mature stage for a very long time, but health concerns now mean they are starting to decline.

It can take several years to develop a new product. This means that development must start some time before the product is actually needed. In practice, organizations have a range of products at different stages of their life cycle. This gives long-term stability of output, with new replacements for older products that are declining or being withdrawn. The overall output is smoothed, rather than widely fluctuating, as shown in Figure 3.6.

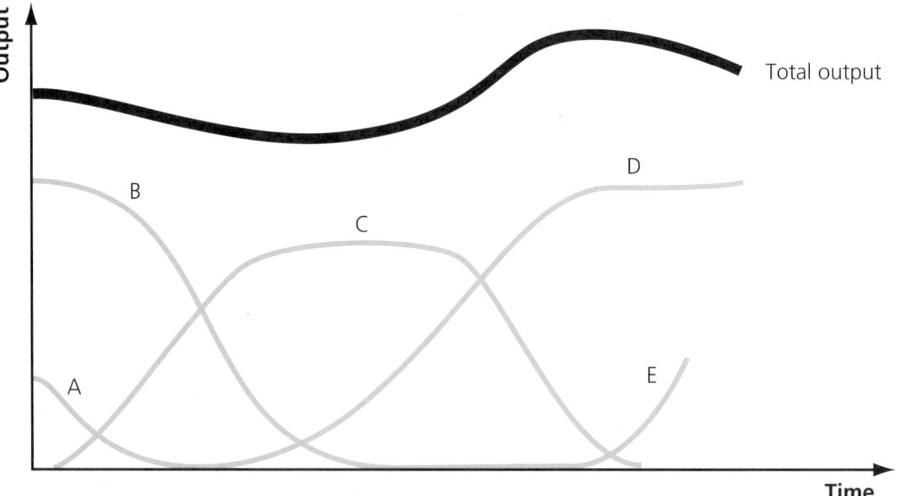

Figure 3.6 Introduction and Withdrawal of Products (A–E) to Maintain Stable Total Output

From an operations management point of view, there are three important consequences of product life cycles.

- The first concerns the different operational emphasis at each stage.
- The second has costs, revenues, and profits varying considerably at each stage.
- The third has organizations with different expertise starting (and later stopping) making products at different points in their life cycles.

These are discussed in the following sections.

In Summary

The demand for all products follows a standard life cycle. The length of this cycle varies considerably. To ensure stable output, an organization should have products at different stages in the cycle.

Emphasis of Operations in the Life Cycle

A new product needs much development work before it can be marketed. This means that operations centre on research and development. At the end of this, the product is launched and offered to customers. Initially, an organization will make small numbers of units, perhaps in a craft environment or with individual units made for specific orders. Operations emphasize the need to meet due dates and specifications, while refining the design and generally providing acceptable quality.

If customers like the new product, the organization will increase production. Then operations look for improvements in the production process. This often means a change from the low-volume craft process to a mass-production process, which may use some automation. The aim is to make more units while ensuring high quality and reducing the unit cost. This in turn puts more emphasis on supply and procurement systems, which must find reliable sources of parts and materials. At the same time, marketing and distribution networks are built to stimulate and meet customer demand.

If the product's success continues, it moves into the growth stage when demand increases rapidly. Operations are now concerned with forecasting future demand and making sure there is enough capacity to meet this. Products are no longer made for specific orders but are put into a stock of finished goods, from which customer demands are met with short lead times. Production planning becomes important as resources are scheduled to make sure production matches demand.

At some stage the product matures and reaches its steady demand. Forecasting, capacity, and planning are no longer difficult as production is stable and does not change. The process might have changed several times, perhaps ending with a high volume process such as an assembly line. The production process may be automated and use high technology. This implies an increase in standardization, reducing the number of options offered. Competition may increase and emphasis is, therefore, put on cost reduction and improved productivity.

During the decline stage, the product design may be changed in an attempt to extend the useful life. When this is no longer worthwhile, termination procedures are designed to stop production.

In Summary

As a product moves through its life cycle, the emphasis put on different types of operation will change.

Costs, Revenues, and Profits

When a new product is introduced, a lot of money has already been spent on research, development, design, planning, testing, buying equipment, and setting up facilities. These are part of the fixed costs which must be recovered from later sales. In the early stages of the life cycle, when small numbers are made, the unit costs are high. This is mainly because the low-volume production process is expensive, but the organization may also try to recover some of the fixed costs from early sales. At this stage, the **profit** on each unit may also be high, as customers are willing to pay a premium to get a new or novel product. Total revenue is, however, limited by small sales, as shown in Figure 3.7.

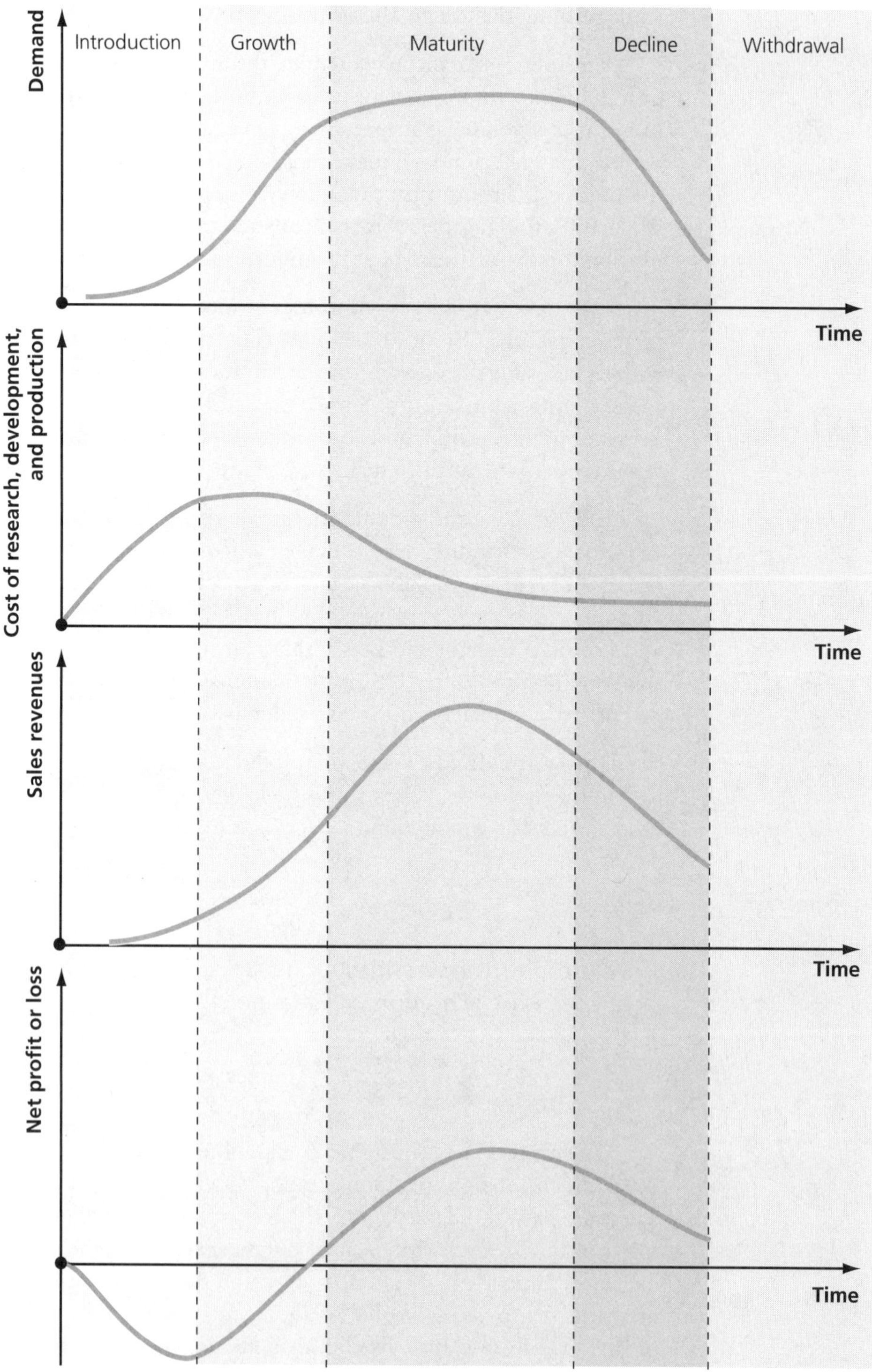

Figure 3.7 Revenue, Costs, Profits, and Loss During a Typical Life Cycle

Income will rise substantially when the product moves from introduction to the growth stage. This is when most of the fixed costs are recovered, and the product begins to make an overall profit. The profit per unit is high at this time, as customers view the product as new and may be willing to pay a high price, there is little competition, and new production equipment is working efficiently.

Increasing demand will allow the profit per unit to rise until sometime in the mature stage. Continually changing the production process to cater for higher volumes will reduce unit costs. This means that profits can remain high. There comes a time, however, when competitors start to make similar products and demand slackens. This leads to reductions in both price and profit.

As the product moves into a decline, profits fall as excess capacity leads to competition for the smaller demand. Sometimes, improved production methods, experience, and higher productivity can offset the decline, but the time of high profits has passed. At some stage, demand and profit fall to an unacceptably low level and the product is withdrawn.

It is usually less expensive to extend the life of an existing product than to introduce a new one. This means that there are benefits in delaying the withdrawal of a product. There are a number of ways of doing this, including the following.

- Increasing advertising and market support. Sales of Marlborough cigarettes are increasing despite a general decline in tobacco sales, largely because of the company's advertising campaigns.
- Finding new uses for the product and hence new markets. Microcomputers were originally developed for office use, but their sales increased enormously when they were used in the home.
- Modifying the product to make it appear new or different by redesign or additional features. The Boeing 747 was introduced in 1970 but was continually modified so that the 747-400 and 747-500 were still selling well in 1995.
- Changing the packaging with new sizes or different emphasis. Perfumes are often put into new containers to update their image.
- Selling the product in new geographic areas. McDonald's opened new restaurants around the world, most recently in China and Eastern Europe, to keep increasing sales.

The disadvantage of these methods is that they are usually short term and only really give cover until a new product is available.

Example

Month	Revenue	Cost
1	12.3	4.2
2	13.0	3.4
3	13.3	2.7
4	13.2	2.4
5	12.9	2.0
6	12.7	1.8
7	12.4	1.6
8	12.0	1.4
9	11.4	1.1
10	10.8	1.0
11	9.7	0.8
12	9.0	0.6
13	8.3	0.5

The revenue and costs of a product over the past 13 months have been recorded as shown to the left (values are in thousands of dollars). Where is the product in its life cycle, and what plans would you expect the supplier to be making?

Solution

Subtracting the cost from the revenue gives the following profits in each month:

Month	1	2	3	4	5	6	7	8	9	10	11	12	13
Profit	8.1	9.6	10.6	10.8	10.9	10.9	10.8	10.6	10.3	9.8	8.9	8.4	7.8

A graph of these is shown in Figure 3.8. Although we do not know the demand, it is clear that revenue and profit from the product have begun to decline in recent months. This suggests that the product has moved from maturity to decline. This decline is quite sharp, and the product is approaching the withdrawal stage. The company should have a replacement product either already introduced or very close to introduction.

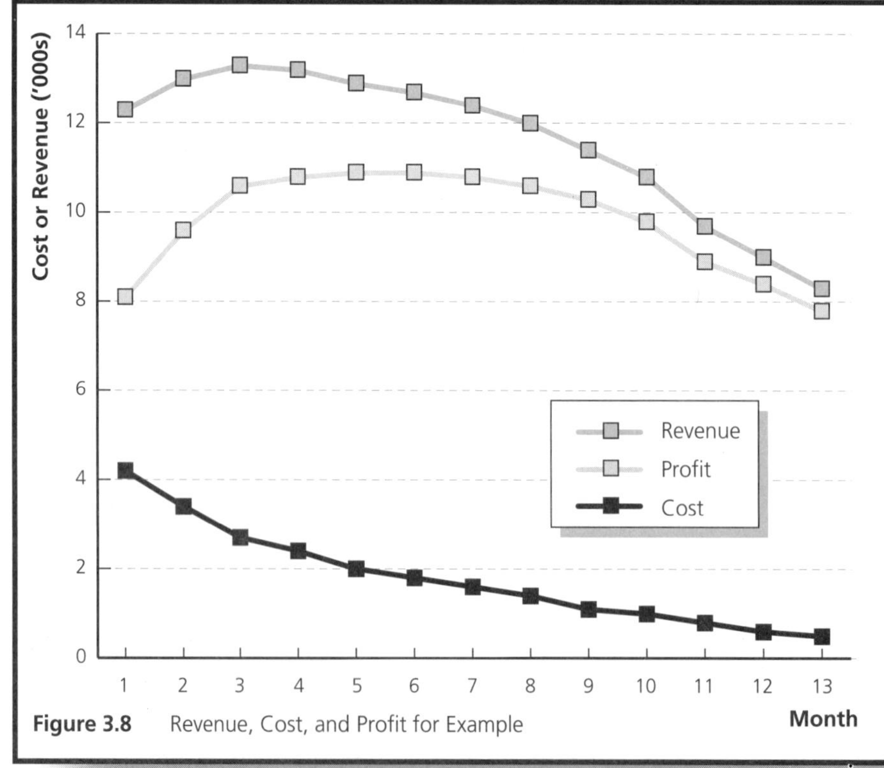

Figure 3.8 Revenue, Cost, and Profit for Example

Case Study – Making Roller Skates at 3P

The Recreational Marketing Division of Peerless Plastic Products (3P) had the largest share of the market for roller skates and skateboards. Nonetheless, Sally Bisset, the Marketing Manager, was rather nervous. 3P's sales had been steadily declining for some time. Its production costs had been rising, while competitors had been reducing their selling prices. This gave 3P lower sales and smaller profit margins.

Sally was particularly worried about the company's roller skates. 3P made three different models in a variety of sizes and colours. Sally wanted to reduce their selling price, and this meant reducing production costs.

Jose Valdez, the Production Manager, was now feeling the pressure to reduce his costs. He thought that cost increases over the past five years had been rather modest, especially with the current rates of inflation. He saw his main problems as falling production quantities and too many products and parts. There were virtually no common parts between the three models, and this gave high inventories and small production runs. Jose complained to Sally, suggesting that they should either reduce the product range, or increase sales to lower unit production costs.

Questions

- In what stage of the product life cycle are the roller skates?
- Is Sally correct in blaming most of the cost increases on the production department?
- What do you think should be done about the roller skates?

In Summary

Changing demand and operations through the product life cycle affect costs, income, and profit. Higher unit profits can generally be found near the beginning of the life cycle.

Entry and Exit Strategies

Some companies spend a great deal of money on research and development. This research looks for new knowledge and can be either a) *pure research*, which looks for new discoveries; or b) *applied research*, which looks for solutions to particular problems.

Most of this research looks for new products that can be marketed. Some pharmaceutical manufacturers, for example, conduct research to develop entirely new drugs; microprocessor manufacturers try to design more powerful computers; automobile makers look for new safety features. These companies seek the high profits which come from new products. The obvious disadvantage of this approach is the high cost of research and development. In pharmaceuticals, for example, both Roche and Ciba have annual research budgets of over two billion dollars, or 10–15 percent of their revenue.

Most companies, however, do not start with basic research to develop entirely new products; nor do they follow the product to the end of its life cycle when demand dies. Most companies start their product planning by looking at products already supplied by competitors. They look for existing products which would fit into their range and make modifications to create their own "new" product. In other words, they start supplying the market with an existing product that is already some way through its life cycle. The timing when an organization starts (and later stops) making a product defines its **entry and exit strategy**.

The entry and exit strategies used by an organization depend on its overall objectives. Some organizations do basic research and provide the ideas and technology for new developments, but they do not exploit them. They enter the market at the introduction stage and leave it before the growth stage. Typically, such organizations are very good at innovation but do not have the resources and production skills to manage a growing demand.

Other organizations look for research with commercial potential and then exploit it during the growth stage. These aim for the high prices which can be charged during growth, and exit when profit margins begin to fall. Other organizations are "cost reducers" who enter at the mature stage and produce large quantities efficiently enough to compete with organizations already in the market. These exit when the product declines and the volume is too low to maintain high production levels.

We can classify these different entry and exit strategies as follows.

- *Research driven*—such as Cray, which makes small numbers of very powerful computers
    - Good at research, design, and development
    - Innovative with constant changes in product
    - High quality and high cost
    - Low sales volumes
    - Slow delivery
- *New product exploiters*—such as Microsoft, which is the world's largest supplier of software
    - Identify new products with wide appeal
    - Good at developing new processes for production—strong in marketing to create demand
    - High quality with reducing cost
    - Moving to high volume
- *Cost reducers*—such as Packard-Bell, which is the second largest supplier of microcomputers in North America.
    - High volume, low-cost production
    - Low innovation, concentrating on established products
    - Low price and fast delivery
    - Often automated with production or assembly lines

In Summary

Organizations with different objectives and strengths adopt different entry and exit strategies.

Review Questions

1. What are the stages in a typical product life cycle?
2. What would be the typical lengths of life cycles for:
   a) a personal computer; b) a model of car; c) a particular insurance policy; d) a newspaper?
3. "As operations are performed throughout the life of a product, the main operational emphasis remains the same." Do you think this is true? Explain.
4. How do costs and profits vary over a product's life?
5. "Organizations do basic research for a product and then supply the product throughout its life cycle until demand ceases." Is this true? Explain with an example.
6. How could you classify organizations according to their entry and exit strategies?

Case Study – 3P Introduces a New Product

Peerless Plastic Products Inc. (3P) was worried by the declining sales of its roller skates and skateboards. It started making roller blades in the spring of 1994. This was a direct response to competitors who started making a range of roller blades around the same time. 3P justified its decision by saying that both roller skates and skateboards were in a decline, but its roller blades were in a period of growth. 3P's sales were forecast to increase from 20,000 pairs in 1994 to 150,000 pairs in 1995 and then peak at 250,000 pairs in 1996. The sales were then expected to decline from the year 2000.

3P's DX model of roller blades sell for $79.99 a pair. The more expensive LX line has leather uppers and hardened plastic rollers, which wear better, and sell for $99.99 a pair.

The company uses an old moulding machine to make the rollers used in its roller blades. It costs $2.50 to mould a set of ten rollers for each pair of roller blades. If 3P bought a new injection-moulding machine costing $50,000, the cost would drop to $2.00 per set of ten rollers.

Questions

- Do you think it was a good idea to introduce the roller blade line?
- Draw an expected life-cycle curve for the roller blades.
- What is the break-even point for the new injection machine?
- Should 3P buy the new injection-moulding machine? Would it give a saving over the four years 1995–1998?

Chapter Review

- Product planning is concerned with all decisions about new products or changes to existing products. It allows an organization to make products that customers want.
- Most organizations would like to make a narrow range of standard products. This allows for very efficient operations. However, differing customer demands force most organizations to make a range of related products.
- There are several stages in the development of a new product. These start with the generation of initial ideas and finish with sales to customers. Very few ideas go through all the stages and become successful products.
- Organizations need some way of comparing alternative products. These comparisons are usually based on a combination of quantitative measures and qualitative opinions. Scoring models give useful results here.
- Break-even analyses find the number of units which must be sold before all costs are recovered and a profit is made.
- Every product follows a standard life cycle. This has five distinct stages of introduction, growth, maturity, decline, and withdrawal.
- Each stage in the product life cycle has different characteristics in terms of emphasis of operations, costs, revenue, and profit.
- Most organizations do not develop entirely new products, but adapt existing ones. The organization's objectives and strengths will determine its entry and exit strategies.

Key Terms

achieved quality *(p. 55)*
break-even point *(p. 61)*
designed quality *(p. 55)*
entry and exit strategies *(p. 72)*
feasibility study *(p. 54)*
fixed cost *(p. 60)*
life cycle *(p. 64)*
product design *(p. 56)*
product planning *(p. 49)*
product range *(p. 49)*
profit *(p. 67)*
scoring models *(p. 59)*
simplification *(p. 57)*
standardization *(p. 57)*
variable costs *(p. 60)*

Problems

3.1 Quarterly revenue and costs of a product over the past three years have been as follows (values are in thousands of dollars):

Quarter	Revenue	Cost
1	7.2	16.2
2	10.1	17.5
3	14.9	21.0
4	19.2	21.0
5	20.4	20.1
6	23.3	17.8
7	25.7	15.7
8	26.7	13.8
9	27.4	10.5
10	27.5	7.7
11	27.4	6.2
12	27.4	6.0

Where is the product in its life cycle, and what plans would you expect the supplier to be making?

3.2 Ten factors are considered important in comparing four possible products. Points have been given to each factor, as shown below. What is the relative importance of the factors? On this evidence, which product is best?

Factor	Maximum	A	B	C	D
Resources	10	8	10	8	7
Finance	30	28	27	24	17
Market	35	17	33	22	18
Production	25	18	19	20	19
Competition	20	12	11	16	19
Technical	15	10	9	5	12
Skills	10	9	4	3	9
Compatibility	5	3	3	1	5
Location	10	6	10	7	6
Experience	15	8	6	4	12

3.3 A company makes 100 units of a product a week. These sell for $100 a unit, while variable costs are $50 a unit and fixed costs are $150,000 a year. What is the break-even point for the product, and what profit is the company making? What is the average cost per unit? By how much would production have to rise to reduce the average cost per unit by 25 percent?

3.4 An airline is considering a new service between Paris and Vancouver. Its existing airplanes, each of which has a capacity of 240 passengers, could be used for one flight per week with fixed costs of $60,000 and variable costs amounting to 50 percent of ticket price. If the airline plans to sell tickets at $400 each, how many passengers will be needed for the airline to break even on the proposed route? Does this seem a reasonable number?

Discussion Questions

3.1 What would happen if an organization decided to stop product planning?

3.2 Why do some organizations supply a wide range of products while others concentrate on a few? What are the benefits of each approach?

3.3 How can an organization guarantee a series of ideas for new products?

3.4 What are the benefits of using standard components and parts in products?

3.5 How could you compare a series of similar, competing products? Take specific examples of goods and services to illustrate your answer.

3.6 Find a small electrical appliance, like a drill. Look at its design. How could you change the design so that it is easier to make or more convenient to use?

3.7 Is there a difference between product design in services and in manufacturing? Explain.

3.8 Is it inevitable that a product will follow a life cycle? Explain.

3.9 Describe two different entry and exit strategies.

Chapter 4
PROCESS DESIGN

Deciding how to make the product

Contents

Introduction

The last chapter described some aspects of product planning and design. This chapter describes the next step: how to make a product. This involves the design of the **process**. In essence, the process describes the operations used to make a product.

The chapter describes the types of process available and the circumstances in which each is best. An important factor is the level of technology used. Process planning aims at making sure a product is made by the best possible process.

The chapter begins by describing different types of process. Each of these is used in different circumstances—each uses different types of equipment, different layouts, and so on.

Learning Objectives

After reading this chapter you should be able to answer questions such as:

- Why is process planning needed?
- How can processes be classified?
- What factors affect the choice of process?
- How can the productivity of intermittent processes be improved?
- What types of process technology are available?
- How can you choose the best level of automation?
- What processes are used in the service sector?
- How can you describe a process using a chart?

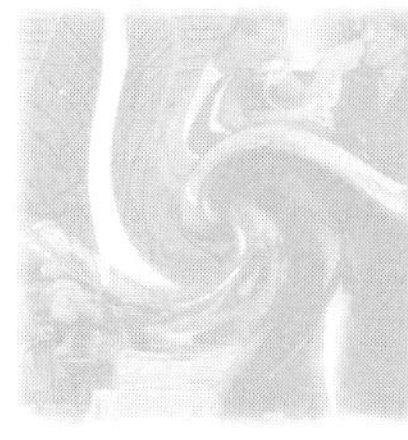

Planning for the Process

As stated in Chapter 1, an organization takes inputs and performs operations to produce outputs. The way these operations are organized defines the process. You may find it easier to imagine the process used in manufacturing. But processes used in services are similar and the same ideas apply.

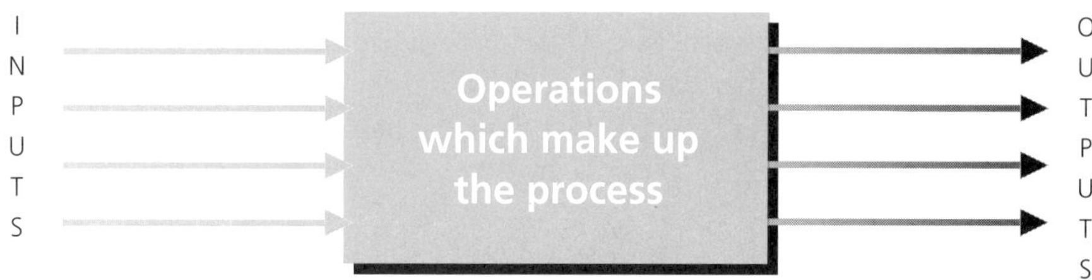

Figure 4.1 Defining the Process

The inputs for making a hamburger, for example, include a meat patty, a bun, dressings, a cook, a grill, and a toaster. The operations needed to make the hamburger include toasting the bun, grilling the patty, and preparing the hamburger with dressings. All of these operations form the process for making the hamburger. In planning the process, we look at the way in which the operations are organized.

Processes can be classified in several ways. For example, in the case of natural resources, the process could be classified as exploration, mining, refining, manufacturing, distribution, and service.

- *Exploration process.* This process looks for natural resources. Geologists and other specialists visit various sites, collect samples, and test and analyze the samples. Their tests indicate whether the site has any natural resources such as oil, nickel, or coal.
- *Mining process.* Exploration identifies sites containing resources. Then a mining process removes the material from the site. This material is moved to a place where it can be refined.
- *Refining process.* Refining is the process of extracting minerals from ore. This is a very expensive process which needs a large refinery, such as the nickel processing plant in Sudbury, Ontario.
- *Manufacturing process.* This takes primary metals and other materials and changes them into finished goods. Most of the products you see every day, such as toasters, computers, and cars, are made by manufacturing processes.
- *Distribution process.* This changes the location of the material, moving it on to the customers. As you can see, distribution is involved in all processes as material is always being moved.

- *Service process.* This type of process provides all the intangible services needed by people and organizations. For example, service processes give health care, education and entertainment to people—and banking, communications, and utilities to organizations.

Most products can be made by a number of different processes. A table, for example, can be hand built by craftsmen, it can be assembled in parts by semi-skilled labour, it can be made automatically on an assembly line, or it can be formed in one piece from plastic. The choice of process determines its efficiency and cost. Managers must, therefore, be careful when they plan a process. They should match the characteristics of the product with the best process for making it.

Process planning makes the decisions about a process. It gives a detailed description of the operations needed to make a product. The aim is to design a process which can make the product as efficiently as possible.

Decisions about the process are needed whenever there is a change in operations, such as the following:

- An entirely new product is introduced
- An old product is changed
- There is a major change in the pattern of demand
- Costs of inputs or operations change
- Competitors change their products or there are other changes in the market
- The current performance is found to be unsatisfactory

In Summary

The process describes the way in which a product is made. It looks at the way the operations are organized. Process planning and design make sure that each product is made in the most efficient way.

Review Questions

1. What is a "process"? Give an example of a process.
2. What is process planning and when is it used?

Case Study – Prairie Fabricators

Prairie Fabricators run a number of metal workshops in Central Canada. They take customers' designs and can make almost any product in metal. Most of their products can be made by one of five processes:

- Casting—where liquid metal is poured into a mould
- Hot forming—where metal is heated until it can be shaped under pressure
- Cold forming—where high pressure is used to shape metal without heating
- Machining—where machines remove metal by drilling, boring, turning, milling, shaping, planing, or grinding
- Assembly—where components are joined together

When customers submit a design, a production planning team meets to consider the best process for making the product. Often the team will suggest changes that will improve the quality or reduce the cost of the finished product.

Questions

- What processes can be used at Prairie Fabricators?
- Who plans the process? How might they do this?

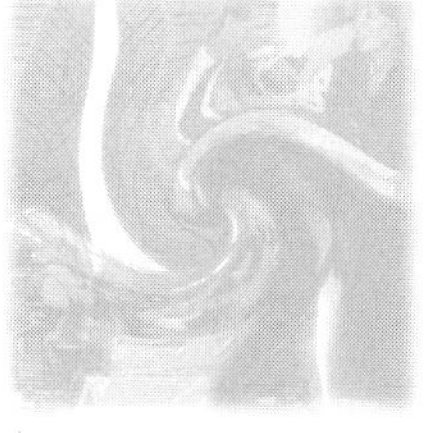

Process Design

This section describes different types of process, how to choose the best process, and how to improve the productivity of intermittent processes.

Types of Process

Processes can be classified in several ways. We have already described them in natural resources as exploration, mining, refining, manufacturing, distribution, or service. Another useful classification looks at the frequency that products change. At one extreme are continuous flows, such as with oil refineries which make the same product, without any change or interruption, in an endless flow. At the other extreme are single projects, like satellites where a series of distinct, one-of-a-kind products are made. We can use these differences to define five types of process: 1. project; 2. job shop; 3. batch; 4. mass production; and 5. continuous flow.

Each of these processes is suited to different circumstances, particularly the variety of products and the quantities to be made.

- **Project process.** This process makes single units, usually tailored to customers' specifications. Each product is a one-off, so the process makes a wide variety of products with little standardization. The process needs a lot of flexibility to deal with new situations and problems. The workforce must be skilled and may work in teams to tackle specific parts of the job. The process uses general purpose equipment. It is controlled by project management methods (discussed in Chapter 15).

Although the number of units made is low, each involves a good deal of work. This kind of process usually has very high unit costs.

Examples include building a ship, satellite assembly, construction of an office building, writing a book, and development of computer software.

- **Job shop**. This process makes small numbers of a wide variety of products. It is typically used in small engineering companies whose products are often made to customers' specifications. The range of products made by the organization is narrower than for project processes, but there is still a lot of variety. The process uses general purpose equipment which must be set up and changed every time a new product is started. Each product will go through a different sequence of operations on the equipment. This requires flexible equipment and a skilled workforce.

As each product uses only a part of the resources available—both human and equipment—utilization is generally low. At other times, there are bottlenecks as some resources are temporarily overloaded. The mix of different products makes scheduling and keeping track of work difficult. Job-shop processes usually have high unit costs.

Examples include makers of specialized vehicles, furniture manufacturers, printing firms, restaurants, and travel agents.

- **Batch processing**. This process occurs when batches of similar products are made on the same equipment. In a job shop, every time a new product is begun, the equipment must be set up, and there are associated disruptions and costs. These can be reduced by making a number of units in each run. Over time, a series of batches are made, with products held in stock until they are sold to customers.

This process is useful for medium volumes of products where customer requirements are known in advance. This means there is less product variety and little customizing. The equipment used is still fairly general, but there is room for some specialization. The process can have frequent set-ups and changes, so some skilled labour is needed.

Examples include book publishing, pharmaceutical and clothing manufacturers, bottling plants, colleges organizing courses, and insurance companies processing different types of policies.

- **Mass production**. This process is used in an assembly or production line that makes large numbers of a single product, such as computers, cars, or washing machines. There is little variety in the product—except for small changes during the finishing.

Mass production processes rely on a steady, high demand for a product that is known in advance. Specialized equipment can be used. As the product does not change, there are no disruptions to the process and few management problems. There is, for example, no need to schedule individual pieces of equipment or check the progress of individual units. Once the system has been set up, it needs a small workforce to keep it working, and in extreme cases may be completely automated. The people who work on mass-production processes often find the work monotonous. Unit costs for mass production are low.

Examples include cars, computers, consumer electronics such as televisions, domestic appliances, photographic processing, and newspaper publishing.

- **Continuous flow**. This process is used for high volumes of a single product or small groups of related products, such as bulk chemicals, oil, and paper. The process is different from assembly lines as the product emerges as a continuous flow rather than discrete units. Such processes use highly specialized equipment that can operate round the clock with virtually no changes or interruptions. The process is capital-intensive, but it needs a very small workforce and the high volume leads to low unit costs.

Examples include gasoline refineries, breweries, paper mills, sugar refineries, television broadcasts, and police service.

Each of these processes is used for different production quantities and product variety. Job shop and batch processes are called intermittent—as they make a variety of different products. Mass production is also called repetitive process. These are general terms which can be used equally to describe manufacturing and service operations.

Another important difference is that projects and job shops are **make-to-order systems,** which wait to receive an order from a customer and then make the product requested. Batch, mass production, and continuous flow are **make-to-stock systems,** which make the product according to a fixed schedule, and then keep it in stock until customers actually demand it. The main differences among processes are summarized in Table 4.1 on page 84.

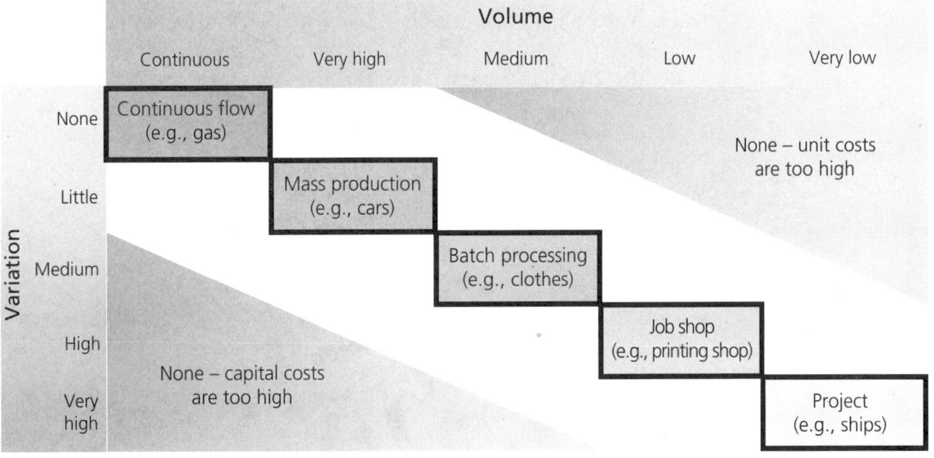

Figure 4.2 Types of Process and Their Product Quantities and Variation

Table 4.1 *Differences Among Processes*

Process Type	Volume	Product Variation	Frequency of Change	Equipment	Number of Operators	Skill Level	Capital Cost	Unit Cost
Project	One	One-off	Not applicable	General	Large	High	Low	High
Job Shop	Low	Considerable	Frequent	General	Large	High	Low	High
Batch Processing	Medium	Some	Some	Some specialized	Small	Medium	Medium	Medium
Mass Production	Very high	Little (minor modifications)	None	Specialized	Small	Low	High	Low
Continuous	Continuous	None	None	Specialized	Small	Low	Very high	Low

Case Study – Henry Cranshaw Watercolours

Henry Cranshaw lives in Niagara. Twenty years ago he began to paint watercolours of the Falls. These sold well to tourists, but Henry could only paint about five pictures a week. He sold the pictures for $100 each, but he found it difficult to make a comfortable living. To make more money, Henry's obvious alternatives were to charge higher prices or to paint more pictures. He ruled out the first option because tourists would not pay much more than his current prices for a souvenir. So he decided to paint more pictures.

Henry could not just paint faster, so he realized the best way to increase his output was to change the process he used. Originally he used a project process, where each picture was a unique product. This gave a series of unique products, but low productivity.

Although it meant a fundamental change to his products, Henry decided to aim for large sales of mass-produced pictures. This meant making standard products— typically a view of the Falls with forests around it—and having different people working very quickly on each painting. One person would prepare the canvas, a second person would paint the sky and cloud formations, a third would add the background forest, a fourth would paint the Falls, a fifth would add the river in the foreground, and so on. This was equivalent to a job-shop process.

Like all decisions about processes, this one needed to balance several factors. The final product is obviously very different to Henry's original paintings—but the output rose dramatically. Henry now produced 40 to 50 pictures a week, and still sold them for about $100 each. But he had to employ six part-time artists. As his aim was to increase his income, he had to monitor costs and sales very carefully. Eventually Henry refined the process so it became almost mass production, with paintings passed very quickly along a row of artists, each of whom added a small part to the picture. Using this method, Henry could get a finished painting in under an hour. The output of the gallery rose dramatically, and despite the lower price of each painting the income rose sharply.

Questions

- Describe the types of process that Henry Cranshaw used. What do you think would be the main benefits and problems with each process?
- Can you think of other examples where changing the process has had major effects on the organization?

In Summary

Processes can be classified as project, job shop, batch, mass production, or continuous flow. Each of these is suited to different types of product and production quantities.

Choosing the Best Type of Process

Decisions about the process can have long-term consequences on profitability, production, costs, and flexibility. When a car maker builds an assembly line, it can cost hundreds of millions of dollars. If the company then decides that it should have used a different approach, correcting the mistake will be very expensive. This example shows that there is often no process which is obviously best for a product. Ever since Henry Ford started building cars on assembly lines, it has been accepted that this is the best process for mass-produced cars. In recent years, however, several companies have come to doubt this, including Volvo whose plant at Uddevalla in Sweden has small groups of people assembling separate cars in workshops.

Managers must consider a number of factors before selecting the type of process, including the following.

- *Product design.* The product's design will determine the overall type of processes needed. If a tailor designs a very high quality suit to specifications given by a customer, it will be hand-made rather than use an automated process. However, the design will usually allow a variety of processes, and operations managers must select the best. A well-designed product allows an efficient process and gives low production costs.
- *Overall demand.* The production numbers clearly affect the best type of process. Portraits, for example, can either be painted or photographed—painters use a project process to produce very small numbers, while film processors use mass production to make very large numbers.
- *Changes in demand.* The choice of process can also be affected by changing patterns of demand. If production changes to meet a highly seasonal demand, it must use a more flexible process with enough capacity to meet peak demands and still be efficient during slacker times. This is called **demand flexibility.** Hotels, for example, must cater for large numbers of guests in holiday seasons, but still work efficiently with smaller numbers out of season.
- *Product flexibility.* This relates to the speed with which a process can stop making one product and start making another. The combination of demand and product flexibilities allows a process to respond quickly to changes in customer needs.
- *Human resources.* Another aspect of flexibility concerns the workforce. A flexible process relies on operators who are skilled enough to do a variety of jobs. Different processes require different abilities, so the process affects the workforce skills,

management skills, training needed, and labour productivity.

- *Automation.* Until recently, **automation** could only be used for high-volume processes, as it needed expensive, specialized equipment that gave little flexibility. However, low-volume processes used less expensive, more flexible, general purpose equipment. In the past few years this has changed; some aspects of flexible automation are discussed later in the chapter.
- *Customer involvement.* In most manufacturing processes, the customer is not involved. In services, however, customers play an active part in the process. Self-service gas stations, self-service restaurants, and automated banking machines use customers to take over much of the process previously done by employees. Those processes with high customer involvement generally give a personalized service.
- *Product quality.* As outlined in Chapter 6, organizations should aim at making products of perfect quality. The traditional means of ensuring high quality was to employ highly skilled craftsmen to make small numbers of a product. Such craft processes are still the best for some products, but automated processes give high quality in a wide range of other products. The most reliable computers, for example, are not handmade but come from completely automated assembly lines.
- *Finances.* Different processes have widely different costs. Thus, the choice of process can be affected by the capital available and installation cost. In turn, the process will affect the operating expenses, return on investment, and purchase price of the product.
- *Amount of vertical integration.* Logistics is the function which coordinates all the movement of products from initial suppliers through to final customer. Vertical integration refers to the amount of the logistics function—or the supply chain—which is owned by one organization. A manufacturer which buys all its components from suppliers and sells all finished products to wholesalers has little vertical integration. Another manufacturer which makes all its own components and sells to customers through its own distributors has a lot of vertical integration.

  There are two distinct types of vertical integration:

  1. **Backward integration** means an organization controls its sources of supplies of parts and raw materials. If a printing company owns a paper mill, this is backward integration which ensures the availability of raw materials, and reduces costs.
  2. **Forward integration** means that an organization controls its own distribution to customers. Most of the major oil companies use forward integration as they have their own retail gas stations.

     Petro Canada is an example of a fully vertically integrated company. Its main activity is refining crude oil. But it has backward integration since it does oil exploration and owns oil wells. It has forward integration since it owns or controls the Petro Canada gas stations used to distribute and sell the gasoline to consumers.

Vertical integration can affect the process in a number of ways. More vertical integration is usually associated with higher volumes. It also means that large investments are needed in production facilities—so the amount of flexibility in a process is reduced, but the organization has more control over suppliers and it can have lower inventories of materials.

Vertical integration can often appear as a make-or-buy decision, which asks whether it is better for an organization to make components or to buy them from suppliers. There are several reasons why an organization may prefer to buy a component, including:

- It does not have enough free capacity
- Demand for the product is variable—suppliers can cope with this because aggregate demand from many sources is likely to be more stable
- The component may be cheaper to buy than to make
- It cannot justify the research and development costs
- It lacks experience in making the component
- It may not be able to guarantee as high quality as specialist suppliers

In Summary

The choice of best process depends on a number of factors. Some of the most important include product design, overall demand, changes in demand, product flexibility, finance, automation, customer involvement, product quality, human resources, and vertical integration.

Case Study – Big John's Hamburger Place

Big John's Hamburger Place is a very popular fast-food restaurant. It claims its service is the fastest in town, and the hamburgers are the tastiest. Because of its popularity, Big John's can only deal with demand by using a repetitive process—similar to the assembly lines in other fast-food restaurants. Both the product and process are standard, and the diagram to the right shows the process.

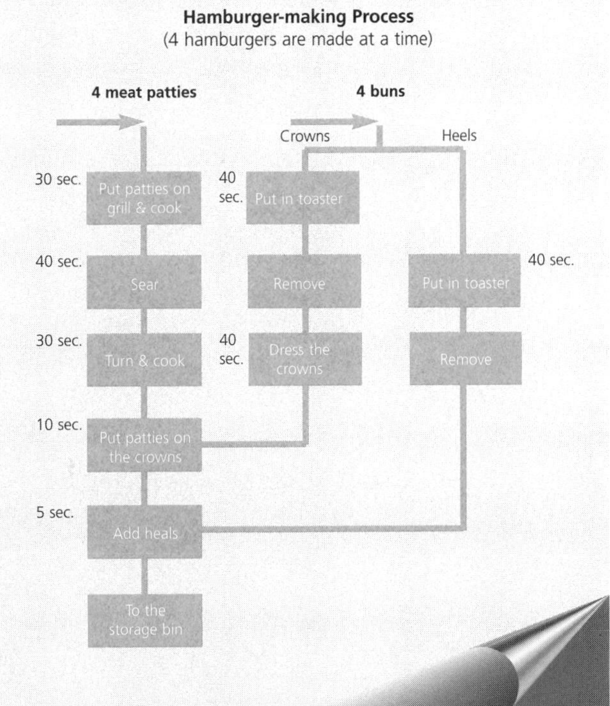

Questions

- How long does it take to make a hamburger?
- How many hamburgers can be made in one hour?
- Suggest ways to improve the process.

Improving the Productivity of Intermittent Processes

Mass-production and continuous-flow processes use specialized equipment which, once started, needs little supervision. These processes have high capital costs but low variable costs, and utilization of equipment can approach 100 percent. However, intermittent processes, such as job shops and batch, make a variety of products and the mix changes continually. Each job uses a different combination and sequence of equipment and operators. This variability makes it difficult to utilize resources fully. At times, much equipment will be idle, either because the current workload does not match equipment capacity or because of set-ups needed between changes of product. At other times, there will be bottlenecks as some resources are in heavy demand. The average utilization of resources is low, typically around 25 percent in a job shop, and often as low as 5–10 percent. The result is that intermittent processes generally have low capital costs, but high variable costs.

If an organization wants to increase the utilization of its resources, it should move away from intermittent processes toward higher volume processes. Unfortunately, the demand for many products is neither high enough nor stable enough to justify the cost of a mass-production process. These products must continue to use intermittent processes. There are, however, several ways of improving their productivity. Some of the most widely used are the following.

- *Reorganize machine operators.* Supervisors of intermittent processes often assign one operator to a piece of equipment. The utilization of equipment is low, so the operator spends a good deal of time waiting for something to do. Productivity can be improved by assigning one operator to a number of machines. This is most useful when machines can work for some time without direct operator involvement, so the operator is kept busy loading and unloading several machines that actually work by themselves. A multiscreen cinema, for example, does not need a projectionist for each theatre.

- *Increase batch size with group technology.* A more imaginative approach to the problem is group technology. A number of distinct products with some common characteristics are grouped together to form a single batch. Several different products may, for example, each need a 5-cm hole drilled. These products can all be combined into a single batch for the drilling. The equipment set-up time is then reduced, and more efficient, automated equipment may be justified by the larger batches.

- *Use flexible automation.* Flexible automation uses high-technology equipment to reduce the set-up time needed between different products. Numerically controlled machines, for example, can be reprogrammed very quickly between batches, and industrial robots can make a variety of products with very little set-up time. This idea is discussed later in the chapter.

Example

A manufacturing company is planning the process for a new product. Related costs are:

Process	Annual Fixed Cost	Unit Variable Cost
Job Shop	$100,000	$50
Batch	$250,000	$40
Mass Production	$1,000,000	$15

When is each type of process best? If the company has forecast a demand of 25,000 units per year, which process should it use?

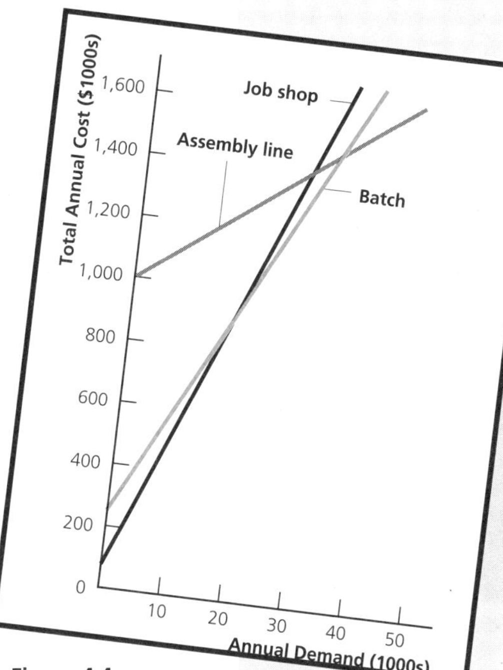

Figure 4.4
Break-even Points for Example

Solution

This is an example of a break-even analysis, described in Chapter 3. The costs are shown in Figure 4.4.

You can see from this graph that:

- A job-shop process is best for demand, D, from zero until:

  100,000 + 50D = 250,000 + 40D or D = 15,000

- A batch process is best for demand from 15,000 until:

  250,000 + 40D = 1,000,000 + 15D or D = 30,000

- After this, a mass-production process is best.

With a forecast demand of 25,000 units a year, the company should look at a batch process.

In Summary

Intermittent processes, like projects, job shops, or batch, generally have lower utilization of equipment and people than higher volume processes. There are several ways that utilization can be increased, including reorganization of equipment operators, increasing batch sizes by group technology, and using flexible automation.

Computer Example

Whenever you have such calculations, try to use a computer. When the choice of process depends on the costs, for example, you can use a break-even analysis. This can be done easily using a spreadsheet. The following example shows a printout for comparing the costs of three processes.

Break-even - Unit Cost Calculations

Production	Process		
	Manual	Flexible Automation	Hard Automation
0	20	80	100
5	20	64.4	90
10	20	50.6	80
15	20	38.6	70
20	20	28.4	60
25	20	20	50
30	20	13.4	40
35	20	8.6	30
40	20	5.6	20
45	20	4.4	10
50	20	5	0
Cheapest	**0 to 25**	**25 to 47.75**	**Over 47.75**

Printout 4.1 Spreadsheet Showing Break-even Analysis

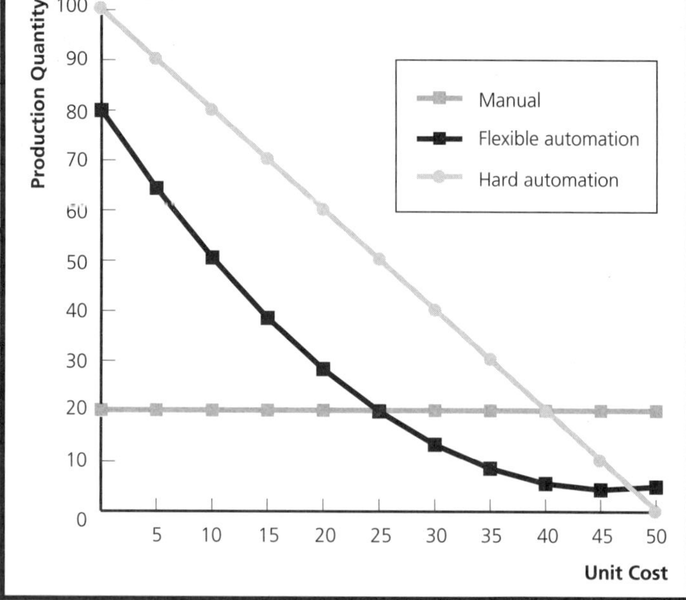

Review Questions

1. List the factors in process design from most important to least important.
2. What types of process are available?
3. Which type of process would be best for making:
   - a. washing machines
   - b. liquid fertilizer
   - c. "home-baked" cakes
   - d. specialized limousines
   - e. printed T-shirts
   - f. airplanes
4. What types of process have the highest productivity? Why?
5. How can the productivity of intermittent processes be increased?

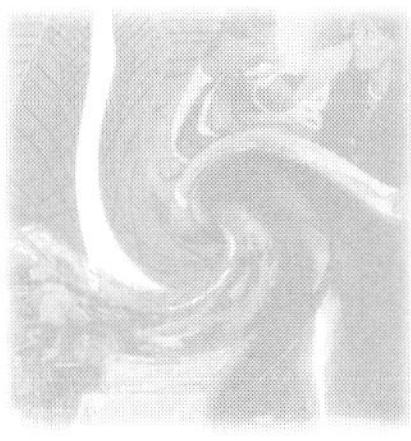

Process Technologies

When we described the different types of process, we often mentioned the amount of technology used. In this section we are going to look at this technology in a bit more detail.

Classification of Technologies

The level of technology used in processes is described as:

1. Manual
2. Mechanized
3. Automated

Manual systems

With manual systems, an operator has full control over the equipment, which needs continuous attention. The operator loads the equipment, works with it, and then unloads it. Driving a bus is an example of a manual process.

Historically, manual processes were developed first, and they are still widely used. They have the benefits of flexibility, low capital costs, and, consequently, low risk. Their disadvantages are high unit cost, need for skilled operators, variable quality, and low output. If an organization wants to increase production with a manual process, it employs more people and equipment. There comes a point, however, when it is cheaper to invest in some mechanized process.

Mechanized systems

An operator loads the equipment, but this can work without further intervention until the task is finished, when the operator unloads it. Using a VCR is an example of a mechanized process.

Mechanized processes were developed during the Industrial Revolution, and were the most advanced technology available until fairly recently. Initially, mechanization was based on general purpose machines such as lathes, grinders, and drills. Later, more specialized machines were dedicated to one product, and the reduction in set-up time greatly increased productivity.

Mechanized processes still need operators to load the machines, do some of the operations, and help with problems. As available technology improved, it became clear that human operators often slow down the process, add variability to the quality, and increase unit costs. These problems can be overcome by using automated processes.

Automated systems

This is a broad category, in which equipment can perform a number of tasks without any operator involvement. Some details of different types of automation are given later in the chapter.

These different levels of automation can be illustrated with the example of a post office: a manual system for sorting letters needs people to put letters in appropriate bags; a mechanized system has operators directing equipment to route letters; an automated system has scanners to read the postal code and automatically move letters.

This classification of technologies is clearly linked to the choice of process. Higher levels of automation are used for higher volumes of output. Therefore, low-volume processes are usually manual, medium-volume processes are mechanized, and high volumes use automation, as shown in Figure 4.5. You might imagine projects and jobs shops with manual processes; batches made with mechanized processes; and mass production and continuous flows using automation.

As shown later in the chapter, this is generally true, but there is some variation, especially as developments in computing have allowed automation for lower volume processes.

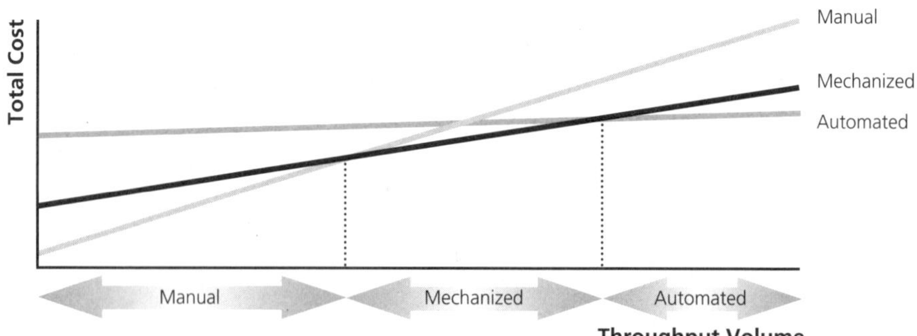

Figure 4.5 Costs of Different Types of Automation

In Summary

Levels of automation can be classified as manual, mechanized, or automated. Each of these has different characteristics which are best suited to different circumstances.

Types of Automation

Traditionally, automation meant using equipment that was specially designed to make a single product, such as the machines on a factory assembly line. Unfortunately, this kind of automation is very expensive, and organizations can only justify its use for making large numbers of a single product. Systems of this kind are now called **fixed** or **hard automation**. They typically consist of a conveyor moving units along a fixed path between single-purpose, specialized machines. As the conveyor moves units along the path, they are worked on in turn by the various machines. The result can be a highly specialized, efficient operation, but with no flexibility.

More recently, there has been much progress in using high technology for lower volume processes. These systems aim at combining flexibility with efficiency and are called **flexible** or **programmable automation.**

Flexible automation for intermittent processes first became possible with **numerically controlled (NC) machines.** Originally these were simple, general-purpose machines which were designed to run without the immediate control of humans. In other words, they allowed mechanization rather than automation. Paper tapes were used to control the machines, and they could be reprogrammed by simply replacing the control tape.

NC machines developed into large machine tools that could follow a series of preprogrammed instructions, perhaps drilling, planing, milling, boring, and turning products of different shapes and sizes. These have the advantages of requiring no human operator except to change the program or load the machine, and give consistently high quality at low unit cost.

Magnetic tapes replaced paper tapes to control NC machines and these in turn were replaced by microcomputers. Essentially, each machine is now programmed and controlled by a microcomputer dedicated to its operation. These **computerized numerically controlled (CNC) machines** do a series of operations without interruption. Readily available programs allow even low production quantities to be made reliably and at low cost. Such systems, where computers assist in the actual manufacturing processes, are called **computer-aided manufacturing (CAM).**

Computer-aided manufacturing often uses robots. These were developed in the 1960s but only became common in the 1980s. In essence, they are stationary machines with reprogrammable "manipulators" to move materials through a variety of tasks and perform a limited range of activities. A robot can move a spray gun to paint a car or a welding torch to assemble panels into car bodies. As technology has improved, so too has the range of jobs robots can perform. Typically, they are used for spot welding, spray painting, testing, automatic inspection, and limited assembly. They have obvious uses in reaching places that are difficult for humans to get at, or handling dangerous substances, like explosives, hot steel ingots, or radioactive materials.

The next stage in automated production is **flexible manufacturing systems (FMS).** These combine all of the computers controlling each piece of equipment (CNC or robot) so that a number of separate machines are under the control of a central computer. This central computer can coordinate all the operations to give high utilization of equipment and fast throughput. It can also control the flow of goods with an automated transport system, with wire-guided trucks (Automatically Guided Vehicles—AGV) moving between machines. This transport system carries products, components, materials, and tools as needed. The link between the transport system and the manufacturing machines is made with automatic loading and unloading stations at each point of transfer.

The essential parts of FMS are: 1. a central computer to schedule, route, load, and control operations; 2. a number of production machines under the control of the central computer; 3. a computer-controlled transport system between machines; and 4. computer-controlled loading and unloading equipment.

Once a FMS is programmed, the system can work with very little human intervention. It has the following advantages:

- Allows faster and cheaper changes between different products
- Reduces labour costs to a minimum
- A computer takes over scheduling and routing
- Achieves very high utilization of machines—up to three times that of conventional machines
- The computer controls inventories so that stocks of raw materials and work-in-process are reduced
- Achieves consistently high quality, without the variation found in less automated processes

Some disadvantages of FMS are:

- Equipment is expensive to buy and set up
- Although the systems can be programmed to make many different products, there are limitations and they lack the flexibility of some other processes
- The system must match current production, so there can be problems if major changes are made to products
- The technology is still being developed, and there are often "teething" problems
- FMS works best with families of similar products which require small changes, rather than radically different products
- The machines still have fixed capacities, tolerances, and other limitations so they cannot deal with unusual products

In Summary

There are many types of automation. These range from numerically controlled machines to flexible manufacturing systems.

Computer-aided Design

Automation is used directly in the production process, but it can also be used in associated operations, such as product design. For many years, designers have used the graphics capabilities of computers to design products on screen. They can design, test, and change plans very quickly. Initial designing time is also reduced by using computers to store designs of similar products. Then, rather than designing from scratch, similar designs are recovered and modified as necessary. This approach is called **computer-assisted design (CAD).**

The computer can also check the design for obvious faults, do related calculations, print the results, produce sets of blueprints, and transmit results to distant sites. Thus CAD reduces the initial design time; allows very rapid changes to existing designs; enhances basic drawings, showing how the actual product will look; does calculations for stresses, strengths, and other engineering needs; produces all necessary drawings and blueprints from the master set; stores a library of designs; estimates product cost as it is being designed; generates a list of the materials needed to make a product; and communicates with other computer systems.

In the past, even when designs were drawn with the aid of computers, there was a lag between the design stage and the manufacturing stage. It soon became obvious that if computers were designing the products (CAD) and controlling the machines (CAM), the two systems could be linked to make a single CAD/CAM system. In these systems, designs are worked on and finalized in the CAD part and are then automatically transferred to the CAM part, which generates the programs to control machines and actually make the products.

This kind of FMS is often described as **computer-integrated manufacturing (CIM),** but terms in this area are often used rather vaguely and there is some disagreement about their precise meaning. Most people view CIM as a further extension of FMS—so that FMS consists of the actual production machine, while CIM includes design and related systems. Thus CIM would include product design and production control, and it would also use information from marketing, procurement, maintenance, accounting, and logistics. The system now provides a common database and allows all functions to work together as an integrated unit.

Integrated systems are now common, and there seems little to prevent the development of an **automated factory.** This would involve a product designed with computer assistance; computers would then take over all the subsequent stages automatically. Manufacturing would be planned and controlled, materials and components would be ordered, final products delivered, and bank accounts updated, without any human intervention.

Another type of technology concerns the processing of information. Computers are now almost universally used for processing information, but there are particularly interesting developments in **artificial intelligence (AI).** This is the branch of computer science that attempts to give computers the ability to understand language, apply reasoning, make assumptions, learn and solve problems; in other words, to create computers that can make reasoned decisions in the same way as humans.

One part of AI concerns **expert systems,** which help in making decisions by recording the skills of experts in the field. Engineers collect experts' knowledge, skills, opinions, decisions, and rules in a knowledge base. A person using this knowledge base describes his or her problem to an inference engine. This is the control mechanism that looks at the problem and the knowledge base and decides which rules to apply to get a solution.

In Summary

Automated systems can be used in actual operations, and they can also be used for associated activities. Computer-assisted design allows integrated systems, which can lead to automated factories.

Choosing the Level of Technology

High technology can give a process with very high productivity. But this does not mean that every organization should replace its current processes by a high technology alternative. A number of other factors must be considered. The most obvious of these is the high capital costs of high-technology systems.

Example

The current manual process for a product has fixed costs of $300,000 per year and variable costs of $80 per unit. The company is considering an automated process with fixed costs, including capital repayment, of $900,000 per year and variable costs of $40 per unit. What production level would justify this system?

Solution

This is a variation of the break-even analysis discussed in Chapter 3. The automated process would be justified when it lowers cost. With an annual production of P, this means:

$$900{,}000 + 40P < 300{,}000 + 80P \text{ or } P > 15{,}000$$

With annual production up to 15,000 units, the manual system would be less expensive, but above this, the automated system would be better.

Apart from cost, there are a number of other trade-offs to consider in choosing the appropriate technology. As stated, higher levels of automation reduce the flexibility of a system. Another problem may be the barriers created between customers and the final product—when a bank replaces its human tellers by automated teller machines, it saves money but its personal service is reduced. Perhaps the major criticism of automated systems is that they ignore the skills people can bring to the job, including:

- Pattern recognition
- Creativity
- Drawing upon varied experiences
- Intelligent use of all available information
- Use of subjectivity and judgement
- Flexibility
- Ability to adapt to new and unusual circumstances
- Generation of entirely new solutions

Conversely, machines have the advantages of:

- Working with consistent precision
- Being very fast and powerful
- Performing many tasks simultaneously
- Storing large amounts of information
- Doing calculations quickly
- Working continuously without tiring
- Being reliable
- Being good at monitoring and reacting to signals

People and machines are better at different jobs. Because automation is better in some circumstances, it should not be assumed that it is better in *all* circumstances. Nonetheless, continuous improvements of high-technology processes mean they can be used for an increasing range of activities. In many libraries, for example, books and journals are being replaced by CD-ROMs.

In Summary

The choice of the best technology to use depends on a number of factors. The most obvious is cost, but automation can bring a number of other advantages. Nonetheless, the best process for making a product is not always the one with most automation.

Review Questions

1. How could you classify the technologies available for processes?
2. What types of automation might you see in a factory?
3. What do the following abbreviations stand for?

   a. NC b. CNC c. CAM
   d. CAD e. FMS f. CIM
4. What are the main aims of automated production?
5. Rank the following in terms of increasing levels of automation:

   a. CIM b. NC c.FMS d. CAM e. CNC

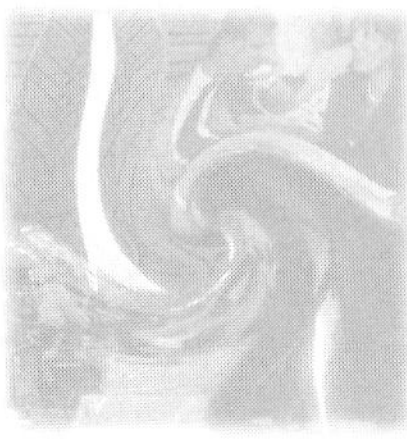

Processes in Service Industries

Although much of the last section referred to processes in manufacturing, exactly the same principles apply to services. For example, processes are still classified as project, job shop, batch, mass production, or continuous. Consider the service provided by a restaurant. Some specialized restaurants allow customers to phone in their orders in advance and the restaurant prepares the meal requested. This is a project. Expensive restaurants have an extensive menu, so the preparation of any meal is like a job shop. Canteens and cafeterias have set meals, which are produced in batches. Fast-food restaurants function like mass-production assembly lines. Meals are discrete, so it is difficult to describe a continuous flow process, but the supply of coffee or beer approaches a continuous flow.

Again there is the familiar pattern with intermittent processes having more flexibility, but higher unit costs; mass production has less flexibility but lower unit costs. Unfortunately, many services such as those provided by dentists, lawyers, doctors, accountants, hairdressers, and cab companies, are produced either singly or in very small numbers. Each customer demands a different end product from the service, so services use a project process, with considerable flexibility but high costs.

In recent years, however, services have started to use more automation. Again, the technology used can be classified as manual, mechanized, or automated. The only problem is that services vary so much that it is difficult to describe automation in the same general terms as for manufacturing. The service offered by a lawyer, for example, has little in common with a postal service, so the principles behind automation in services can best be illustrated by some specific examples.

- *Offices.* The operations done in offices include typing, copying, filing, and handling messages. Until recently, all of these were done manually, with an electric typewriter as the most sophisticated technology available. Clerical jobs have now been transformed by technology. Word processors and desktop publishers have significantly increased the productivity of typists; copying is done by automatic photocopiers or networked word processors; filing is done on computerized databases; messages are handled by electronic mail and FAX machines. Longer term developments aim for the paperless office and the virtual elimination of manual clerical jobs.
- *Banks.* Customers in banks used to be served exclusively by tellers. These provided a flexible service, but line-ups seemed inevitable at busy times. To shorten these lineups and reduce costs, banks introduced plastic cards and automated banking machines. Then, a manual operation was replaced by an automated one, cheques were replaced by machine-readable cards, paperwork was reduced, the customers did some of the work themselves, and banking operations became less expensive. In the future, cards and machines will become much more sophisticated, with coins and notes being replaced by smart cards containing microprocessors.

- *Supermarkets.* Store customers used to tell a store employee what they wanted to buy. The employee would then fetch the goods, weigh and wrap them, and present the customer with a bill. Supermarkets introduced a mechanized system, where customers did most of the work by collecting what they wanted, and checkout operators added up the costs and presented a bill. The next stage in automation will be computer-readable shopping lists, automatic-materials handling equipment to fetch and deliver goods to a customer, and automatic debiting of bank accounts. Beyond this, there will be no need to visit the supermarket, as communications through telephone and television will allow automatic ordering, delivery, and accounting.
- *Postal services.* Sorting letters used to be a labour-intensive manual process. It is now largely automated through the use of postal codes. More recently the need to send letters has been reduced by electronic mail and FAX machines.
- *Warehousing.* Traditionally, warehouses had people moving goods to and from racks, with inventory movement recorded on cards. Such systems could not cope with high volumes or rapid movements, so mechanized systems were introduced. Later, automated warehouses were developed. In these, computers not only record stock movements but also control the handling of goods.
- *Reservation systems.* Airlines started using on-line reservation systems in the 1960s. They are now considered essential, and similar systems are used for such things as buses and trains, theatres, sporting events, and taxis.

There are many examples of service organizations moving to automated processes. As with manufacturing, the aim is to bring the efficiency of high-volume processes to smaller batches. As the average productivity of service industries is low, this area has a great deal of potential for future development.

In Summary

The processes used for services can be considered in the same way as the processes for manufacturing. Many services use a project process and have high associated costs. An increasing number of services are using greater automation.

Review Questions

1. How can you classify the types of process used in services?
2. "Services are expensive because the batch size is small and each job is considered as a project." Do you agree with this? Explain your answer.

Multimedia Education

Education has traditionally used a batch process, where a classroom of children are taught the same things at the same time. The aim of many educators is to move toward a project process, where each child is taught as an individual. At the moment this is too expensive, but multimedia CD-ROMs can revolutionize the way children learn. They give students access to vast amounts of information, which is presented through sound, text, pictures, and videos. Perhaps most importantly, they allow interaction so that students can control the pace, depth, and direction of their learning.

Over two million CD-ROM drives will be sold in Europe this year, and surveys suggest that 80 percent of parents think they are a good idea for enhancing learning. Traditional teaching methods can appear dull, but CD-ROMs can be so entertaining that the market for "edutainment" or "infotainment" discs is likely to expand dramatically.

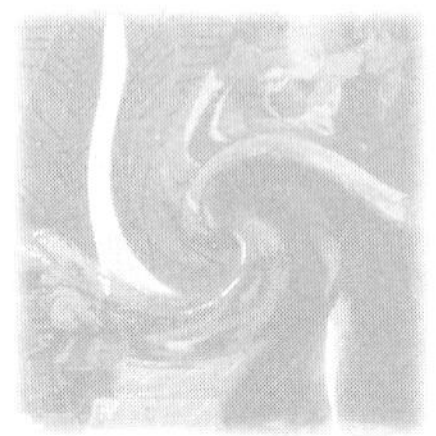

Analyzing a Process

So far we have talked in general terms about processes. Suppose, though, that you want to describe the details of a process and show the sequence of individual operations. The easiest way of doing so is to use a process chart.

Process Charts

There are several different types of process charts, but they all start by breaking down the entire process into a number of distinct operations. Consider, for example, the process of a patient visiting a doctor's office. The operations might be described as follows: 1. enter the office and talk to the receptionist; 2. sit down and wait until called; 3. when called, go to the examination room; 4. discuss problems with the doctor; 5. when finished, leave the examination room; 6. talk to the receptionist and leave.

This process is illustrated in the informal process chart shown in Figure 4.6.

Process charts show the details of the relationship between the operations in a process.

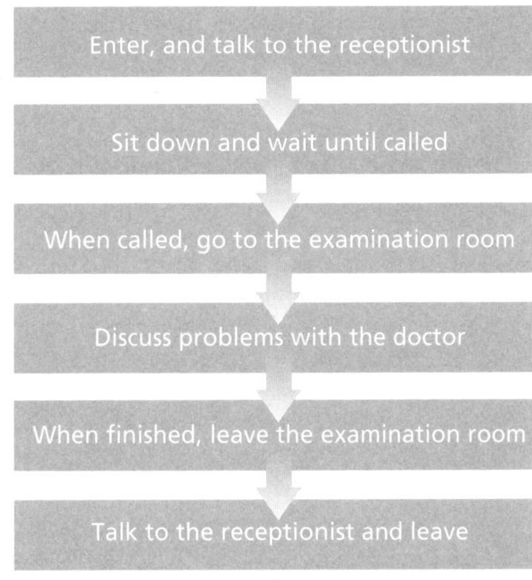

Figure 4.6 Informal Process Chart

This informal chart gives a general view of the process, but it does not give many details. We really want answers to questions such as:

- What types of operations are being done?
- What is the sequence of these operations?
- Which operations cannot begin until others have finished?
- How long does each take?
- Is there any idle time?
- Are products being moved?

When these are answered, we have a clear picture of the process and can start looking for improvements. One approach to process charts starts by looking at each operation and classifying it according to:

- *Operation*—something is actually done—this is the only productive activity
- *Movement*—objects are moved
- *Storage*—objects are put away until needed
- *Delay*—products are temporarily held up
- *Inspection*—tests the quality of the product

Now we look at a process and start to describe it in a chart. The procedure for this is as follows.

1. Observe the process and list all the operations in their proper sequence from the start to finish.
2. Classify each step according to operation, movement, inspection, delay, and storage. Find the time taken and distance moved in each step.

3. Summarize the process by adding the number of each type of operation, the total time for the process, the rate of doing each operation, and any other relevant information.

   These three steps give a detailed description of a process, and an example of the resulting chart is shown in Figure 4.7. Steps 1 and 2 are probably done by observation, while Step 3 is a calculation. The next part of the analysis looks for improvements to the process.

4. Critically analyze each operation. Ask questions such as: Can we eliminate this activity? How can we improve this operation? Can we combine operations?

5. Based on this analysis, revise the process. This should result in fewer operations, shorter times, and less distance travelled. Make sure that each operation can still achieve the output necessary for the process. If there are bottlenecks in the process or equipment that is being used inefficiently, adjust the process.

6. Check the new process, prepare the organization for changes, train staff, and implement changes.

Figure 4.7 shows a typical process chart. Now the maximum output of each operation can be found. Operation 1 takes 2.5 minutes, so the maximum number of units that can be processed is 60/2.5 = 24 per hour. Operation 2 takes 2 minutes, so the maximum output is 30 per hour, and so on. The maximum output of the whole

Process Chart: Part 421/302

Step Number	Description	Operation	Movement	Inspection	Delay	Storage	Time (min.)	Distance (metres)	Comment
1	Fetch components		X				2.5	50	
2	Put components on machine	X					2.0		
3	Start machine	X					1.2		
4	Fetch subassembly		X				3.0	40	
5	Wait for machine to stop				X		5.2		
6	Unload machine	X					2.0		
7	Inspect result			X			1.5		
8	Join subassembly	X					5.0		
9	Move unit to machine		X				2.5	25	
10	Load machine and start	X					2.0		
11	Wait for machine to stop				X		5.0		
12	Unload machine	X					1.4		
13	Carry unit to inspection area		X				2.0	25	
14	Inspect and test			X			5.2		
15	Carry unit to finish area		X				1.4	20	
16	Finish unit	X					5.5		
17	Finish inspection			X			3.5		
18	Carry unit to store		X				5.3	45	

Summary		No.	Time		
	Operations	7	19.1	Time:	56.2 min
	Movements	6	16.7	Distance:	205 metres
	Inspections	3	10.2		
	Delays	2	10.2		
	Storage	0	0		
		18	15.2		

Figure 4.7 Example of a Typical Process Chart

process is given by the operation with the smallest output—this is the bottleneck. Finishing the product takes 5.5 minutes, so the output from this process cannot be more than 60/5.5 = 10.9 units per hour. If forecast demand is higher than this, the process must be changed, perhaps adding more finishers or changing the way the finishing is done.

The process chart in Figure 4.7 can also suggest areas for improvements. In operations 5 and 11, the machine operator has to wait a total of 10.2 minutes. This might be reduced by better planning. In operations 1, 4, 9, 13, 15, and 18, the product is moved a total of 205 metres, which takes 16.7 minutes. This might be reduced by better layouts.

In Summary

Process charts are used to describe the relationship between individual operations in a process. There are several types of process charts. Each starts by breaking the whole process into its separate operations. A useful process chart can answer a variety of questions about the process, and show where improvements can be made.

Figure 4.8 shows an example of a process chart for someone visiting a bank to secure a personal loan.

Process Chart: Personal bank loan

Step Number	Description	Operation	Movement	Inspection	Delay	Storage	Time (min.)	Distance (metres)	Comment
1	Customer selects bank and visits		X						
2	Initial screening	X					5		
3	Move to loans office		X				2	15	
4	Wait				X		10		
5	Discuss with loans officer	X					15		
6	Complete application forms	X					15		
7	Carry forms to verifier		X				2	10	
8	Forms are checked			X			2		
9	Wait as credit analysis and verification are done				X		25		
10	Supply further information	X					5		
11	Move back to loans office		X				2	15	
12	Wait				X		20		
13	Forms are checked			X			5		
14	Complete arrangements	X					15		
15	Leave		X						

Summary

	No.	Time
Operations	5	55
Movements	5	6
Inspections	2	7
Delays	3	55
Storage	0	0
	15	123

Time: 123 min
Distance: 40 metres

Figure 4.8 Process Chart for Securing a Personal Loan

Case Study – The Registration Nightmare

Student registration at the Canadian Business and Computer Institute is as follows. Students pick up registration forms at the information booth. They fill out the forms, walk 50 feet to the registrar's office, and line up in front of the registrar's window. Here a clerk reviews applications for accuracy. Then the students see an academic counsellor in the business or computer department. Both of these departments are 300 feet from the registrar's office. The academic counsellor reviews the students' academic records to determine which courses they should take for the semester. Then students walk back to the registrar's office. Here a clerk calculates students' tuition fees based on the number of courses taken. Then they go to a cashier's window, which is 50 feet away, to pay their fees. If students have to pay for parking, they must go to the parking department, which is 500 feet from the cashier. On average, the wait at any one of the departments is about 10 minutes and the actual processing time is 2 minutes.

Questions

- Draw a process chart for students who want to register for the semester and pay for their parking.
- Calculate the average time it takes a student to go through the whole process.
- Suggest improvements to this process.

Precedence Diagrams

An alternative form of process chart is a **precedence diagram.** This uses a series of circles and arrows to show the relationship of operations in a process. Suppose a simple process consists of two operations, A and B, where A must be finished before B can start. The operations can be illustrated with circles and the relationship between them with an arrow, as shown in Figure 4.9. The arrow shows that the product moves from operation A to operation B.

Figure 4.9 Relationship Between Operations A and B

This approach can be extended to more complex processes, as shown in the following example.

Example

The process in a bottling plant has the following five operations:

1. Clean and inspect the bottle
2. Fill the bottle
3. Put a cap on the bottle
4. Stick a printed label on the bottle
5. Put the bottle in a box and move it away

Draw a precedence diagram of this process.

Solution

Some operations must clearly be done before others, so, for example, the bottle must be filled before the cap is put on.We must start by defining all these relationships. Operation 1(cleaning and inspecting the bottle) can be done first. Operations 2 (filling) and 4 (labelling) can both be done immediately after Operation 1. Operation 3 (capping) can be done after Operation 2, while Operation 5 (putting the bottle in a box) must wait until Operations 3 and 4 are both finished. This gives the following results:

Operation	Must Be Done After
1	-
2	1
3	2
4	1
5	3, 4

These relationships can be drawn as a precedence diagram. This starts with the earliest operations and moves systematically through the process. So, we start by drawing Operation 1 at the left, and then add Operations 2 and 4. Operation 3 is added after 2. Finally, Operation 5 is added, after both 3 and 4 are finished. The complete precedence diagram is shown in Figure 4.10.

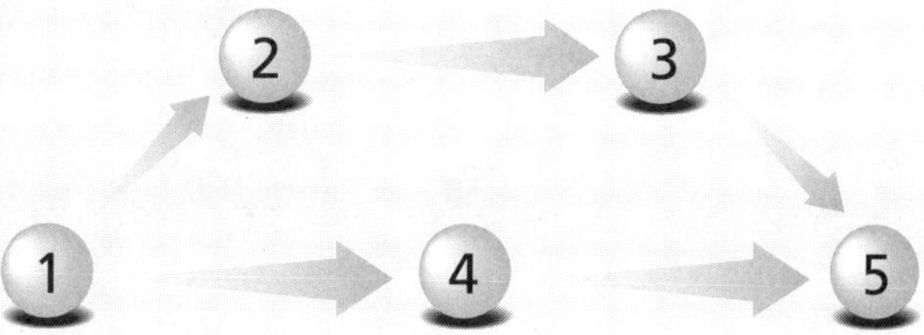

Figure 4.10 Precedence Diagram for Example

Example

A product must go through 11 operations, with the relationships shown in the following table. Draw a precedence diagram of the process.

Operation	Must Be Done After
1	-
2	1
3	1
4	2, 3
5	4
6	4
7	4
8	5
9	6, 7
10	6, 9
11	10

Solution

To draw the precedence diagram, begin with the earliest operations and then systematically work through all other operations. Operation 1 can be done right at the start. When 1 is finished, both Operations 2 and 3 can start. Operation 4 can be done after both 2 and 3, and so on. This precedence diagram is shown in Figure 4.11.

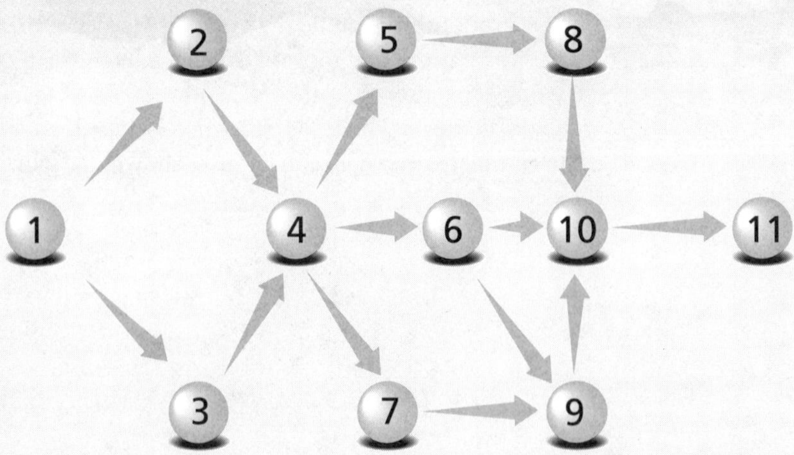

Figure 4.11 Precedence Diagram

In Summary

Precedence diagrams are a useful way of showing the relationships among operations in a process. These diagrams have operations represented by circles and relationships by arrows.

Multiple Activity Charts

Process charts and precedence diagrams show the relationships among the operations in a process. They are useful in describing and analyzing a process, but they do not show clearly what each participant in the process is doing at any given time. We may, for example, not only be interested in the total time that an operator is busy during a process, but also how this time is distributed. An operator who is idle for long periods could be assigned to other jobs, but not if the operator is idle for a number of short periods. This kind of analysis can be done using a **multiple activity chart.**

A multiple activity chart has a time scale down the side of the diagram, with all the participants listed across the top. The time each participant works on the process is blocked off. Suppose two typists work on word processors that are connected to a single high-quality printer. The participants in the process are the typists, the word processors, and the printer. Suppose each typist has a series of documents to type, each of which takes 15 minutes to type and 5 minutes to print. A multiple activity chart for their operations during the first hour of a day is shown in Figure 4.12. This assumes that the two typists start at the same time, that the printer can print only one document at a time, that a word processor cannot be used while a document is being printed, and that each document is printed before the next is typed.

This chart shows at a glance what each participant is doing at any time in the process. At the start of the day, both typists use their word processors to type documents. After 15 minutes, they both finish. Word processor 1 is connected to the printer, while

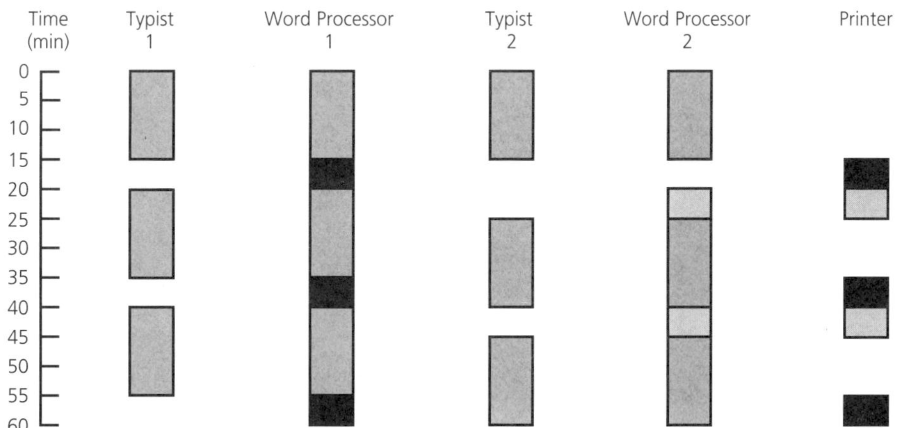

Figure 4.12 Multiple Activity Chart for Typists

both typists and word processor 2 wait for the printer to finish. After 20 minutes, Typist 1 starts typing his or her second document, while word processor 2 is connected to the printer. The chart shows that at the end of the hour, both typists have been idle for 15 minutes, the word processors are in use all the time after the initial 5 minute wait, and the printer has been used for 25 minutes.

Example

One person is currently assigned to operate each of three machines. The machines work a cycle with 6 minutes for loading, 6 minutes of operating, and 4 minutes for unloading. An operator is needed for the loading and unloading, but the machine can then work without any intervention. The operations manager proposes to make savings by using two people to operate the three machines. Draw a multiple activity chart to see if this is possible. What would be the resulting utilizations?

Solution

A multiple activity chart for three machines and two operators is shown in Figure 4.13. In this chart all people and machines are assumed to be idle at the start. The process for the first hour of operation is shown.

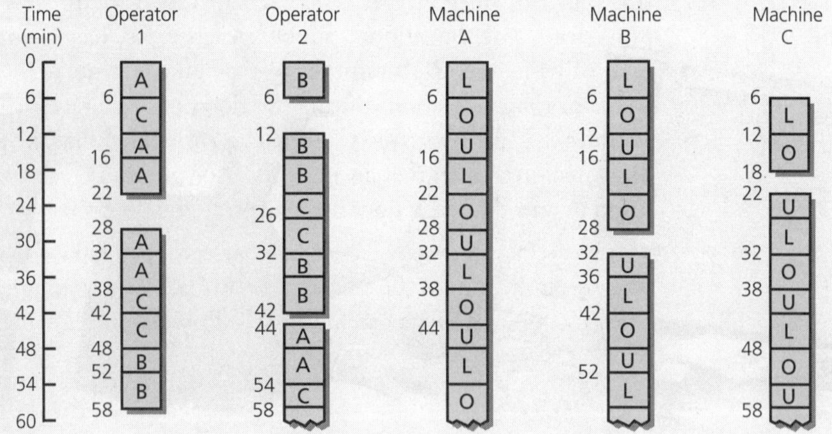

Figure 4.13 Multiple Activity Chart for Example

The process starts with Operators 1 and 2 loading machines A and B respectively. These machines start operating, while Operator 1 loads machine C. Machines A and B are unloaded as soon as they are finished, and are then reloaded. Machine C has to wait to be unloaded until an operator is free. This process continues for 60 minutes. At the end of this time, both operators have been idle for 8 minutes and the three machines have been idle for 0, 4, and 10 minutes respectively. Utilizations are 87 percent for operators and an average of 92 percent for machines. Because some of this idle time was needed at the start of the day, the average utilization of machines would increase if the chart was drawn later in the day. Overall, the new arrangement seems to work reasonably well.

In Summary

Multiple activity charts are a form of process chart that show what each of the participants in a process is doing at any given time.

Review Questions

1. What is the purpose of process charts?
2. What are precedence diagrams, and when are they used?
3. What exactly is meant by "operation A precedes operation B"?
4. When are multiple activity charts used?

Chapter Review

- The process describes the detailed operations needed to make a product. This chapter looked at process planning and design. Process planning finds the best possible type of process for making a product.
- Processes can be classified as project, job shop, batch, mass production, or continuous flow. Each of these has different characteristics and is best suited to different types and quantities of products.
- The best process is determined by a number of factors including demand, variation in demand, product mix, capital available, and workforce skills.
- Intermittent processes have lower productivity than higher volume processes. Productivity can be improved by reorganizing equipment operators, using group technology, or flexible automation.
- Different levels of automation are classified as manual, mechanized, or automated. Higher levels of technology usually have higher productivity.
- Although many ideas in the chapter were introduced by reference to manufacturing, the same principles apply to services. Much of the service sector uses project processes, and these tend to be expensive. However, some services are highly automated.
- Process charts describe the details of an existing process and highlight areas where improvements can be made. Several types of charts were described, including process charts, precedence diagrams, and multiple activity charts.

Key Terms

artificial intelligence (AI) *(p. 95)*
automated factory *(p. 95)*
automation *(p. 86)*
backward integration *(p. 86)*
batch processing *(p. 82)*
computer-aided manufacturing (CAM) *(p. 93)*
computer-assisted design *(p. 95)*
computer-integrated manufacturing *(p. 95)*
computerized numerically controlled (CNC) machines *(p. 93)*
continuous flow *(p. 83)*
demand flexibility *(p. 85)*
expert systems *(p. 95)*
fixed or hard automation *(p. 93)*
flexible automation *(p. 93)*
flexible manufacturing systems (FMS) *(p. 93)*
forward integration *(p. 86)*
job shop *(p. 82)*
make-to-order systems *(p. 83)*
make-to-stock systems *(p. 83)*
mass production *(p. 82)*
multiple activity chart *(p. 107)*
numerically controlled (NC) machines *(p. 93)*
precedence diagram *(p. 104)*
process *(p. 78)*
process chart *(p. 100)*
process planning *(p. 80)*
programmable automation *(p. 93)*
project process *(p. 81)*
vertical integration *(p. 86)*

Problems

4.1 A manufacturing company is considering a new product but has not yet forecast demand. Experience suggests costs will depend on the type of process used, as follows.

	Annual Fixed Cost	Variable Cost
Project	100,000	2,000
Job Shop	150,000	250
Batch	450,000	150
Mass Production	1,500,000	100

Within what range of production quantities is each process best?

4.2 A factory works two eight-hour shifts per day, five days a week, 50 weeks a year. Welders have the unpleasant job of getting into an awkward, enclosed space to spot-weld two parts. They are paid $21 per hour directly, with a further $9 per hour to cover other costs. The operations manager has suggested that a robot for this job would cost $450,000. It would work virtually nonstop for an expected life of 7 - 10 years, and have operating costs of $6 per hour. Do you think this is a reasonable investment? Explain.

4.3 A company can use three different processes to make a product, with total unit costs as follows:

a) Manual process: fixed at $40 a unit
b) Hard automation: $200 - 4D
c) Flexible automation: $10,000 - 25D
where D is the annual demand in hundreds of units

Over what range would each type of process give the lowest unit cost?

4.4 A factory works three eight-hour shifts per day, five days a week. It could save $40 per hour in labour costs by using an industrial robot which costs $500,000 to buy. If the factory pays 15 percent interest on a debt with the bank, and the robot has a life expectancy of 7 years, is this a good investment? Explain.

4.5 Draw two alternative process charts for the process of getting a mortgage from a trust company.

4.6 A product is made using eight operations. Draw a precedence diagram of the process using the following information.

Operation	Must Be Done After
1	-
2	1
3	2
4	1
5	4
6	3, 5
7	3, 6
8	5, 6

4.7 A unit of product comes off a production line, and a random sample is taken for inspection. The inspection of each unit has three separate elements, each of which uses a different type of machine. There are two machines of each type in the inspection area. Each unit of product takes three minutes on each machine for inspection, and then two minutes on each machine for final adjustment. There are three inspectors working in the area. Draw a process chart for the inspection area. How many units can be inspected in an hour?

Discussion Questions

4.1 What technological developments do you think will affect operations over the next decade or so?

4.2 "It is not the process that matters but the final product." Do you agree with this view? Explain.

4.3 Describe the process used to make a number of products you are familiar with. Why are these types of process used?

4.4 Some people suggest that operations can only be automated at the expense of the people working in them. Do you agree with this? Explain.

4.5 What is meant by the flexibility of a process? What factors would increase the flexibility?

4.6 "Automation increases productivity and should be introduced as widely as possible." Do you agree with this? How do you think automation will develop in the future?

4.7 When people think about automation, they often imagine factories and automobile assembly lines. Most people work in services. Describe some specific areas where automation has affected services. What do you think will happen in the future?

4.8 What information should you be able to get from a process chart? What kinds of chart can be used to get this information ? (Do not restrict yourself to the charts described in this chapter.)

Chapter 5
LAYOUT OF FACILITIES

What is the best way to arrange equipment and buildings?

Contents

Introduction

Chapter 4 described the different types of processes that can be used for making products. This chapter looks in more detail at how the process is laid out—or how the parts of the process are physically arranged.

Two important types of layout are process layout and product layout. Process layouts group together similar types of equipment. Product layouts group together all the equipment needed to make a specific product.

There are several other types of layout. Hybrid layouts, for example, are a combination of process and product layouts. Fixed position layouts are often used for projects. There is also a range of other layouts for specific types of organizations, such as warehouses, offices, and retail shops.

Learning Objectives

After reading this chapter you should be able to answer questions such as:

- What is facility layout, and why is it important?
- How can different layouts be classified?
- What is a process layout?
- How can one reduce movements between operations?
- What is a product layout?
- How is mass production organized?
- What are hybrid layouts?
- When are fixed position layouts used?
- How can one design layouts for warehouses, offices, and retail shops?

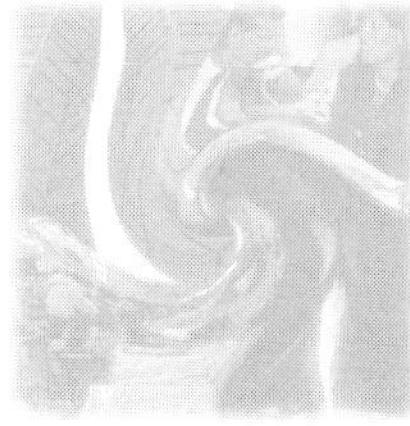

Layouts for Different Types of Process

Facility layout is the physical arrangement of equipment, offices, and rooms within an organization. It describes the location of resources and their relationship to each other.

When you go into a Canada Safeway store, you see that goods are arranged in parallel aisles. Much thought has gone into this layout. It is especially designed to encourage customers to buy more goods. Every organization, whether a store, a manufacturer, a warehouse, or an office, must consider the layout of its operations.

Some organizations have good layouts, and their operations run smoothly—others have poor layouts which cause problems. One video store, for example, may be convenient and easy to use, while another is confusing and difficult to use. In the same way, some airports handle large numbers of people very efficiently, while others have long lineups, crowds milling around, and people wandering around looking lost. So we can say that one aim of facility layout is to allow the operations to run smoothly.

The aim of layout design is to organize the physical arrangement of equipment, offices, and departments so that operations are as efficient as possible.

The overall aim of layout design can lead to a number of related objectives. An obvious one is the efficient use of available space. Another objective is a safe working environment. Other objectives are to reduce the distance travelled between operations, and to allow a smooth flow of products through the process. An organization must design its layout to achieve a number of these objectives.

At the same time, it must consider the constraints on layouts. There is, for example, only a certain amount of space into which all the operations must be fitted. Other constraints depend on:

- The product design
- Type of process used
- The planned capacity of the process
- Total space available
- Design of the buildings
- Material handling equipment used
- Space needed by employees
- Safety needs, including space around equipment
- Quality of the environment

There are five standard types of layout:

- *Process layout,* or job shop layout
- *Product layout,* or assembly line layout
- *Hybrid layout*

- *Fixed position layout,* or project layout
- *Other layouts,* such as retail shops and warehouses

Table 5.1 *Types of Layout*

Type of Layout	Usual Type of Process	Examples
Process	Job shop	Job shops, hospitals, kitchens
Product	Mass production	Electronic assembly lines, bottling, production lines
Hybrid	Batch	Fast-food restaurants, airport terminals
Fixed Position	Project	Ship building, road laying, bridge building
Other	Any	Warehouses, offices, retail shops

In Summary

The layout describes the physical arrangement of the process. The overall aim of facility layout is to arrange operations so they are as efficient as possible. There may be a number of objectives and constraints on the layout. Alternative layouts can be classified as process, product, hybrid, fixed position, or other.

Review Questions

1. What is meant by "layout", and why is it important?
2. What are the objectives of good layouts?
3. What constraints might there be on a layout?

Process Layouts

In a **process layout,** all similar pieces of equipment are grouped together. Drilling machines are put in one area, grinders in another, sanding machines in a third, milling machines in a fourth. Hospitals use a process layout and put all equipment for emergencies in one ward, surgical patients in another, paediatrics in another, and so on. Every product uses a different sequence of operations, so each product will follow a different route through the facilities. This is shown in Figure 5.1.

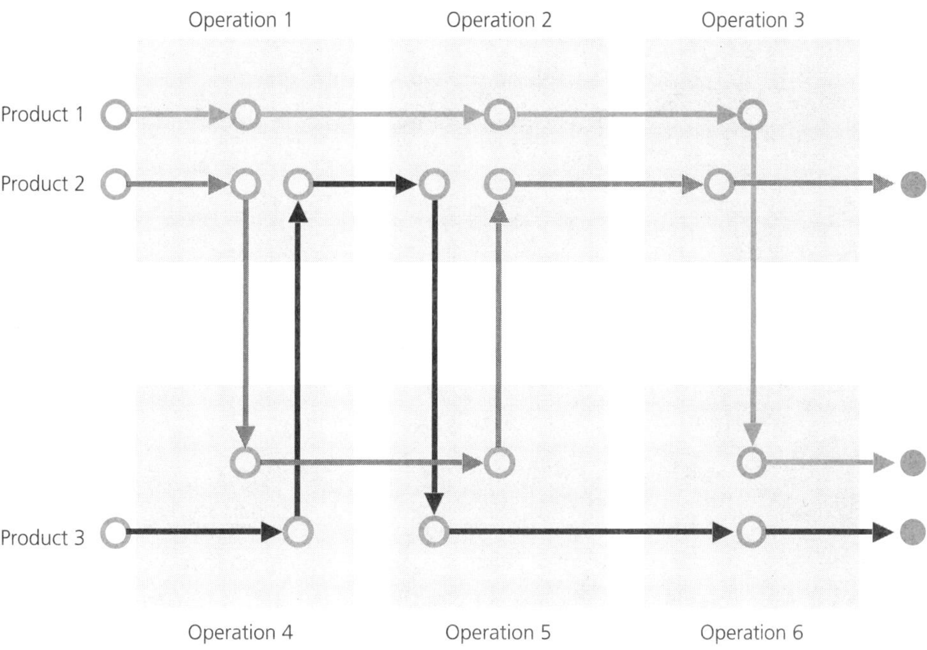

Figure 5.1 Products Following Different Paths Through a Process Layout

This layout works best when many different products are made on the same equipment. You can imagine this as a job shop that makes small batch sizes of different products. Process layouts have the following advantages and disadvantages.

Advantages of Process Layout

- A variety of products can be made on the same equipment
- General purpose equipment is used, and this is usually less expensive than specialized equipment used in mass production
- Operations can continue if some equipment is not available—because of breakdown or planned maintenance
- It is suited to low volumes and variable demand
- Products can be made for specific orders

Disadvantages of Process Layout

- It is used for small batches, which give lower utilization of equipment and higher unit costs

- There are larger stocks of work-in-process
- Scheduling work on equipment is complicated, and it must be done continually
- More skillful operators are needed for the general purpose equipment
- Controlling the work is difficult, needing good supervision
- There is much movement of products and materials between operations

In Summary

Process layouts group together all equipment with similar functions. This is typical of job shops. There are both advantages and disadvantages to this type of layout.

Movement Between Operations

In process layouts, a product must be physically moved between operations. It must be moved *from* the area with equipment for the last operation *to* the area with equipment for the next operation. If there are, say, ten operations in a process, every unit must be moved ten times. This means there can be a good deal of movement during a process. A reasonable layout would try to reduce this movement.

There are several ways of reducing the amount of movement between operations. The most widely used are simple rules of thumb. Suppose, for example, there is a lot of movement between two operations, say drilling and milling. It would be sensible to put these operations as close together as possible. However, operations with no movement can be put farther apart.

A common way of designing process layouts is to draw a plan of the available space and then add arrows to show the most frequent movements. The thickness of the arrows shows the number of movements. People look at these plans and can quickly get some ideas for layouts.

In Summary

Process layouts put operations with a lot of movements between them close together. Rules of thumb and experience can give reasonable layouts for reducing the amount of movement.

Example

A museum has seven main galleries. These have recently been renovated and more people are visiting. A questionnaire was given to visitors as they left the museum to see how they liked the new arrangements. Most comments were favourable, but some people felt they passed the same exhibits several times. To see if this was true, the routes taken by visitors during a typical morning were recorded. These are summarized in Figure 5.2. How could the layout of the galleries be improved?

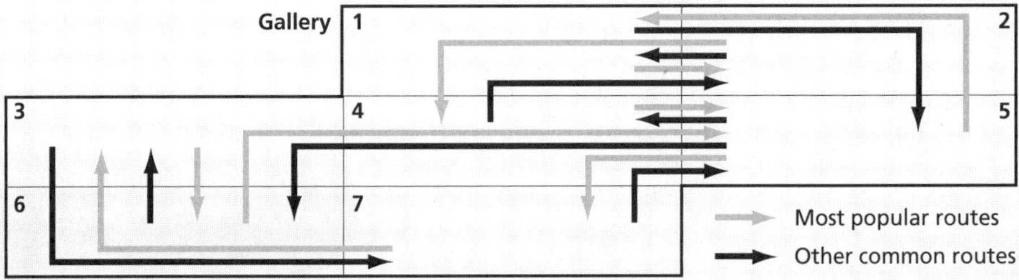

Figure 5.2 Original Layout of Seven Galleries in Museum

Solution

If you look at the dominant flows in Figure 5.2, you can see that the criticisms are true. Some improvements to the layout can be made as follows.

- Most people walk through Gallery 4 as they move from Gallery 5 to Gallery 6. They also visit Gallery 5 twice—after both Galleries 1 and 7—but it does not have a central position. An obvious improvement would be to exchange Galleries 4 and 5, so Gallery 5 moves to the centre and Gallery 4 moves out of the way.
- Most people walk through Gallery 3 to get to Gallery 6 and then return to Gallery 3. These two could also be exchanged.

These simple adjustments give the improved movements shown in Figure 5.3.

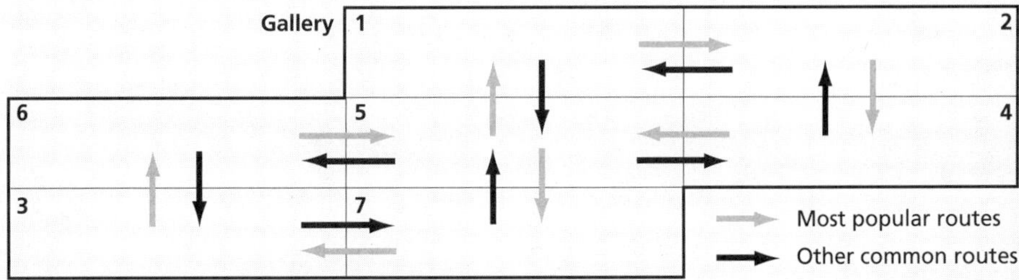

Figure 5.3 Improved Layout That Reduces Movement

Designing Process Layouts

The informal approach described for the museum example works well for small problems, but a more formal approach is required for larger problems. The formal method has three steps.

- First, collect relevant information about space needed for each operation; quantities moved between operations; and number of trips between operations.
- Second, build a general block plan and try to minimize the total movements.
- Third, add details to the block plan to give a final layout after talking to architects, engineers, consultants, and other experts.

The key step of this process is the second one. This builds a general layout in terms of blocks. A useful method of doing this has the following six steps.

1. List the separate operations or departments to be located and find the space needed by each one.
2. Build a "from-to" matrix. This shows the number of trips directly between each pair of operations, and can usually be found by observation over some typical period.
3. Use common sense to design an initial diagram for the layout—perhaps based on the existing layout or layout of a similar process.
4. Find a cost for this layout. This can be calculated from the total distance moved (= $\sum$ movements × distance), weight-distance moved (= $\sum$ movements × distance × weight), or any other convenient measure. If this solution is acceptable, go to Step 6, otherwise continue to Step 5.
5. Improve the initial layout. This can be done using trial and error, an algorithm, or experience. Go back to Step 4.
6. Complete the block plan by including details of cost, additional constraints, preferred features, and problems.

The most obvious difficulty with this approach is finding improvements for Step 5. In practice, there are several ways of doing this, usually with a computer evaluating a large number of alternatives.

Example

A process consists of six areas of equal size to be fitted into a rectangular building. The following movements were recorded during a typical period.

		To a	b	c	d	e	f
	a	-	30	10	0	12	0
	b	0	-	10	40	5	0
From	c	0	5	-	60	0	20
	d	0	10	15	-	0	10
	e	60	20	0	0	-	10
	f	0	0	30	5	10	-

These figures include both the number of journeys and the amount of goods carried. Draw a block diagram of a good layout for the process.

Solution

Following the method described on page 120:

- Step 1 has already been done, with six areas, a to f, each needing the same amount of space.
- Step 2 builds a from-to matrix. Assuming that a journey from a to b is effectively the same as a journey from b to a, we can combine the top and bottom halves of this matrix to give a revised from-to matrix.

		To a	b	c	d	e	f
	a	-	30	10	0	72	0
	b		-	15	50	25	0
From	c			-	75	0	50
	d				-	0	15
	e					-	20
	f						

Step 3 uses common sense to develop an initial plan. One approach is to rank the links according to the number of movements. Then, the busiest link is c to d with a value of 75, next comes a to e with a value of 72, and so on. The number of movements across each link, and their ranking, are:

(Continued)

Example - Continued

Rank	Link	Number of Movements
1	c-d	75
2	a-e	72
3	b-d	50
4	c-f	50
5	a-b	30
6	b-e	25
7	e-f	20
8	b-c	15
9	d-f	15
10	a-c	10
11	a-d, a-f, b-f, c-e, d-e	0

Common sense suggests that areas c and d should be close together as they have the most movement, while a and d have no movement and can be a long way apart. If we concentrate on those areas which should be close together, and move down the ranking above, we could draw the trial layout shown in Figure 5.4b.

(a) Rectangular Building with Six Areas

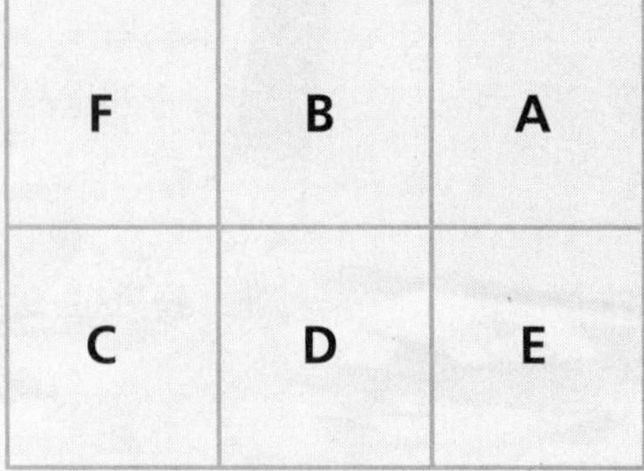

(b) Trial layout

Figure 5.4 Layout for Example

Step 4 finds a cost for this layout. A simple way to do this is by multiplying the numbers in the from-to table by the distance on each journey. We can simplify the calculations by assuming the areas are squares with sides one unit long, and use rectilinear distances—which are simply the horizontal distance moved added to the vertical distance. Then f is one unit from c, two units from d, and three units from e. The distances are given in the following table. The actual units are not important, provided they are consistent.

Example - Continued

		To					
		a	b	c	d	e	f
	a	-	1	3	2	1	2
	b		-	2	1	2	1
From	c			-	1	2	1
	d				-	1	2
	e					-	3
	f						-

Multiplying the number of movements by the distance gives the cost of movement between areas as follows.

		To					
		a	b	c	d	e	f
	a	-	30×1	10×3	0	72×1	0
	b		-	15×2	50×1	25×2	0
From	c			-	75×1	0	50×1
	d				-	0	15×2
	e					-	20×3
	f						-

The total cost for this layout is the sum of these costs, which is 477. If this is unacceptable, the layout can be adjusted and an alternative tested.

- Step 5 looks for improvements to this layout. One weakness is the distance between e and f, which contributes 60 to the total cost. This can be reduced by rearranging the areas as shown in Figure 5.5.

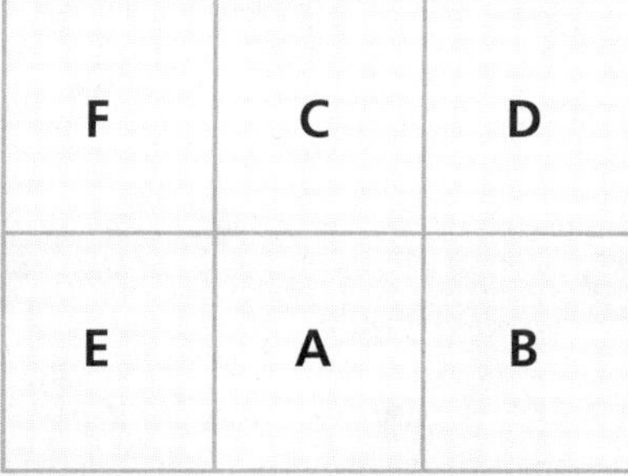

Figure 5.5 Improved Layout

(Continued)

Example - Continued

Using the same method of costing, the total cost is 417. This is a considerable improvement, but if we wanted to reduce costs even more, we could continue looking for other solutions.

		To					
		a	b	c	d	e	f
	a	-	30×1	10×1	0	72×1	0
	b		-	15×2	50×1	25×2	0
From	c			-	75×1	0	50×1
	d				-	0	15×2
	e					-	20×3
	f						-

- Step 6 adds details to this block plan. These details could include the exact size and shape of each area, as well as layout of aisles, stairs, offices, and other general purpose areas. Later, details of individual pieces of equipment, furniture, and partitions can be added.

As you can imagine, this approach to layout design can become complicated, especially when there are many operations. In practice, it is much easier to use a computer. There are many packages for process layouts. The following example shows the result from one of these.

In Summary

We described a simple method for designing good process layouts. Unfortunately, this can become complicated for large processes. Real process layouts are usually designed by computer.

Systematic Layout Planning

Sometimes the movements between different operations cannot be counted—for example, a layout for a completely new process. At other times, it may be difficult to collect the data, or the amount of movement may not be a good measure for layout.

A useful method of designing layouts in these cases is **systematic layout planning.** This replaces the from-to matrix by managers' opinions of how close operations should be. Suppose, for example, a large office block has a Security Group. There may be little movement between this group and the main entrance. But the group should be put near the entrance so it can control access to the building. However, a noisy or dangerous piece of equipment or machinery should be put as far as possible from quiet office areas. A number of distinct categories can be used, with letters to show the importance of the two areas being close together.

- A—Absolutely essential
- E—Especially important
- I—Important
- O—Ordinary importance
- U—Unimportant
- X—Undesirable

We can also add a note about the reason for a decision. The most usual reasons for decisions are as follows:

1. Sharing the same facilities
2. Sharing the same staff
3. Ease of supervision
4. Ease of communications
5. Sequence of operations in a process
6. Customer contact
7. Safety
8. Unpleasant conditions

Then, A/5 means it is absolutely essential that two operations be adjacent because of the sequence of operations in the process. These can be put into a matrix which shows both the importance of the operations' close proximity and the reason, as shown below. This shows that operations b and d must be close together because they share the same facilities, while c and e must not be close together because of unpleasant conditions, for example.

		Operation					
		a	b	c	d	e	....
Operation	a	-	U/-	O/3	O/3	X/8	....
	b		-	A/5	E/1	U/-	....
	c			-	U/-	X/8	......
	d				-	I/2	....
	e					-	..
	.	.	.	.	.		
	.	.	.				

Methods of designing layouts with this kind of information are rather informal. The usual approach takes connections in the order of importance. The first step is to look at the matrix and find all the Xs. These operations are put as far apart as possible. Then find all the As in the matrix and put these operations as close together as possible. Next find all the Es and put these operations as close together as possible, and so on.

Example

A new office is about to be opened, with six equally sized areas as shown in Figure 5.6a. The importance of the closeness of these areas is shown in the following matrix.

		Area					
		a	b	c	d	e	f
	a	-	E/2	U/3	U/2	A/1	I/2
Area	b		-	X/8	O/3	U/-	U/-
	c			-	X/8	I/8	U/-
	d				-	O/5	E/2
	e					-	E/1
	f						-

Suggest a layout for the office.

Solution

There are two Xs for areas b-c and c-d. So, these are put as far apart as possible. Then there is one A for areas a-e. These are put as close together as possible. One trial layout for this office is shown in Figure 5.6b.

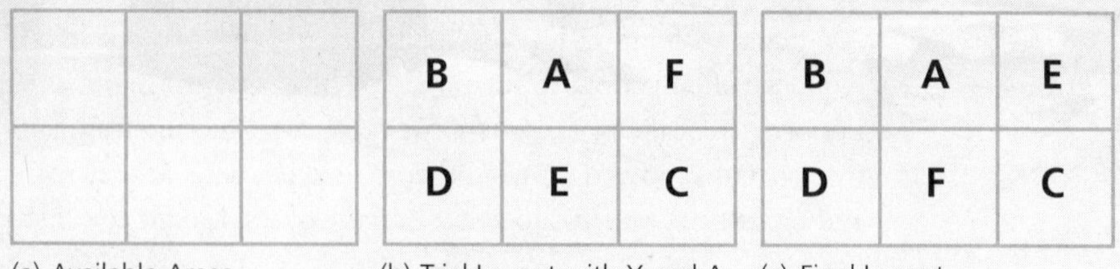

Figure 5.6 Example of Systematic Layout Planning

There are three Es for areas a-b, d-f, and e-f. This trial layout only has one of these pairs together. An obvious improvement is to exchange e and f, as shown in Figure 5.6c. This still satisfies the A and X conditions, but also satisfies two of the E conditions. This solution seems reasonable, but if necessary other adjustments can be made.

In Summary

Sometimes it is not possible to build a matrix which shows the movements between operations. At other times movements between areas are not important in layout decisions. In these cases systematic layout planning can be used. This uses managers' opinions about how close together operations should be.

Review Questions

1. "Product layouts are only used in job shops." Do you think this is true?
2. "Good process layouts can be found by looking at the pattern of movements." Do you agree with this?
3. Why might examining the number of movements between areas be a poor way of judging a layout?
4. What do the letters A, E, I, O, U, and X mean in systenatic layout planning decisions?

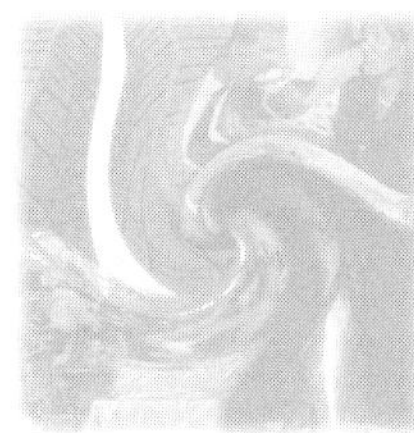

Product Layouts

A **product layout** groups together all the equipment used to make a particular product. A common form of product layout lines up equipment in the order it is needed, and passes each unit of the product straight down the line. In manufacturing, this is the basis of production or assembly lines, as shown in Figure 5.7.

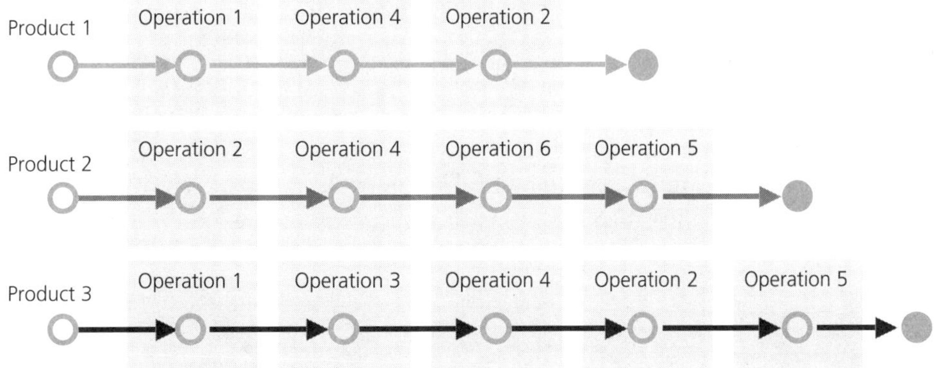

Figure 5.7 Product Layouts Are Like Assembly Lines

The process uses dedicated equipment which is laid out so the product can move through in a steady flow. There is an obvious link between product layouts and mass-production processes, and this gives the following advantages and disadvantages.

Advantages of Product Layout

- They can give high outputs
- High equipment utilization leads to low unit costs
- Automation can be used with few operators
- Material handling is easy, often using conveyors
- There are low inventories of work-in-process
- Scheduling facilities is easy

Disadvantages of Process Layout

- Operations are inflexible—it is difficult to change the output rate, product, or process
- Equipment failure and routine maintenance can disrupt the whole process
- Equipment may be specialized and expensive
- Operators find the work dull
- There is often high initial investment

In Summary

Product layouts cluster together the equipment needed to make a specific product. They can be viewed as assembly lines.

Work Stations

In principle, a product layout is simpler than process layout—it consists of a sequence of equipment through which the product moves. The equipment is essentially put into a line, and the main problem is to ensure that products move down this line as smoothly as possible. Equipment on the line can be divided into a number of distinct **work stations**. At each work station, a number of related operations are done at the same time. For example, on an automobile assembly line one work station may put all the doors on the body; another work station might add the wheels. Then, the line consists of a series of discrete work stations, each of which does a number of operations. This arrangement is shown in Figure 5.8.

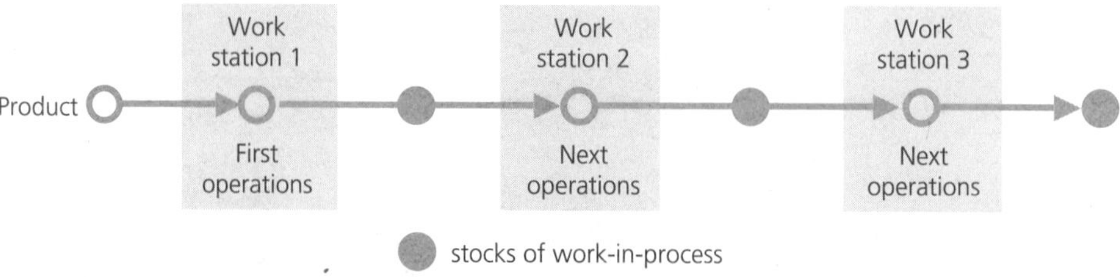

Figure 5.8 A Product Layout with Discrete Work Stations

Each unit moves from one work station to the next on its journey down the line. The aim of product layout design is to make this flow as smooth as possible, and to get high utilization of all stations. The amount of time spent at each station must be about the same—and the line is then described as *balanced.* If a line is unbalanced, some stations will work on products quickly and stocks of work-in-process will build up in front of the next station, which is working more slowly. This creates bottlenecks, which cause delays and low utilization of equipment farther down the line.

Imagine a simple line with two work stations, with operations taking one minute in the first and three minutes in the second, as shown in Figure 5.9a. The maximum output of the line is one unit every three minutes, set by the second work station. Unfortunately, this gives the first work station a utilization of only 33 percent, and the line is unbalanced. An obvious improvement is to put three sets of equipment for the second work station in parallel. This triples output and gives full utilization. The line is then perfectly balanced. The aim of line balancing is the highest possible utilization of all parts of the line.

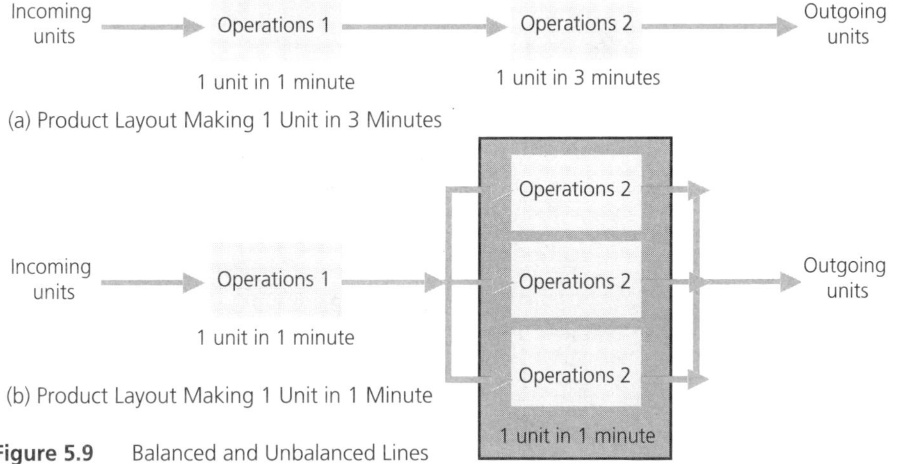

Figure 5.9 Balanced and Unbalanced Lines

As you can see from Figure 5.9, there is an inventory of work-in-process between each work station. If one work station breaks down for a short time, the next can carry on working normally. Unfortunately, there are costs of holding these extra units, and they need storage space near the line. It is usually much better to have low stocks of work-in-process and a balanced line.

In Summary

Product layouts can be viewed as production lines. Units move through a series of work stations. The main problem is to get a smooth flow of products. A balanced line has all work stations working at about the same speed, with high utilizations.

Line Balancing

> **Line balancing** assigns operations to each work station so that the line is balanced, there is a steady flow of products, and equipment has high utilization.

There is a standard procedure for line balancing, which has three parts.

- First, find the **cycle time,** which is the maximum time a station can work on each unit. This is calculated by dividing the planned number of units by the time available. If, for example, planned production is 60 units per hour, then each operation in the line can last one minute at most. If the operations at any work station take longer than one minute, there is a bottleneck and the planned output cannot be reached.
- Second, calculate the theoretical minimum number of work stations needed for the whole process. This is found by taking the total time needed for all operations on a unit and dividing by the cycle time. If, for example, it takes a total of five minutes to make a product and the cycle time is one minute, the minimum number of work stations along the line is five. In practice, this minimum can almost never be achieved because of the unevenness of work times, calculations that give fractions of a machine, and the fixed order in which operations must be done.
- Third, do the actual line balancing and allocation of operations to each work station. The total time taken for operations in each work station should be as close as possible to the cycle time. A method for this is described below.

The procedure for the third step, actually balancing the line, is best done using a precedence diagram. Precedence diagrams were described in the last chapter. The steps are then as follows.

1. Draw a precedence diagram for the process.
2. Take the next operation and put it on a new work station.
3. Now look at the list of operations and ignore all operations that have already been put on work stations; ignore all operations whose preceding operations have not yet been finished; and ignore all operations that are too long to fit into the time left on the current work station.
4. We now have a list of operations that could be added to the current work station. Put these operations in order of their importance. This is often the same as taking the longest operations first.
5. Add operations in this order to the work station until: there are no more operations in the list found in Step 4 (if there are still operations that have not been

put in work stations, go back to Step 2); or no more jobs in the list found in Step 4 can be added to the current work station without exceeding the cycle time. If there are any operations remaining, go back to Step 2; or all operations have been put on work stations, so the initial layout has been completed. Go to Step 6.

6. Calculate the utilization of each work station and make small adjustments to improve the final line.

Example

The operations in a product layout are shown in the following table of precedences.

Operation	Time (minutes)	Operation Must Follow
A	5	-
B	10	A
C	4	B
D	6	B
E	4	C, D
F	2	E
G	4	F
H	5	G
I	3	H
J	2	G
K	5	J
L	8	G
M	4	L
N	2	I, K, M
O	6	N
P	1	O
Q	5	P

The line works an eight-hour day during which target output is 48 units. Design a balanced layout for the process.

Solution

To solve this, follow the procedure given above.

First, calculate the cycle time.

$$\text{Cycle time} = \frac{\text{time available}}{\text{number of units to be made}} = \frac{8 \times 60}{48} = 10 \text{ minutes}$$

If a work station spends more than ten minutes on a unit, the target of 48 units per day cannot be reached.

(Continued)

Example – Continued

Second, calculate the theoretical minimum number of work stations. This is found by dividing the total time to make one unit of the product by the cycle time. The time to complete all operations on a unit is 76 minutes, so:

$$\text{Theoretical minimum number of work stations} = \frac{\text{total time for a unit}}{\text{cycle time}}$$

$$= \frac{76}{10} = 7.6$$

Each work station would thus be fully occupied, and work flows perfectly smoothly through the line. As a fraction of a work station is impossible, at least eight work stations are required.

Third, use the algorithm for assigning operations to work stations.

- Step 1 draws the precedence diagram shown in Figure 5.10.

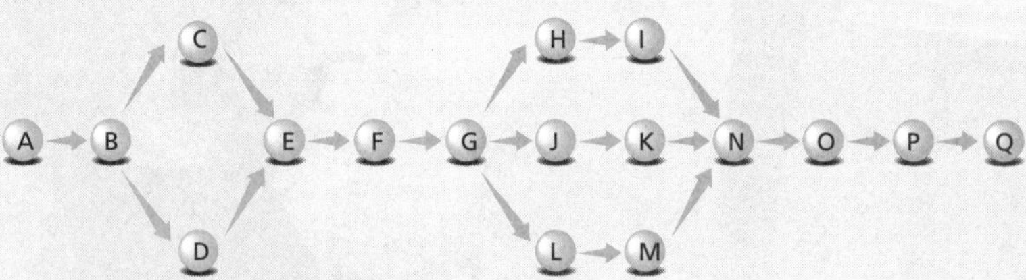

Figure 5.10 Precedence Diagram

- Step 2 assigns operation A to Work Station 1.
- Step 3 ignores all activities except B as their preceding activities have not yet been finished. But B cannot be added to Work Station 1, as the time needed (5 + 10 minutes) is longer than the cycle time.
- Step 4 then has no operations that can be added to the current work station.
- Step 5 returns to Step 2.
- Step 2 starts Work Station 2 with Operation B.
- Step 3 ignores all activities except C and D, as their preceding activities have not yet been finished. But neither of these can be added to Work Station 2, as they give times longer than the cycle time.
- Step 4, then, has no operations that can be added to the current work station.
- Step 5 returns to Step 2.

Example – Continued

Returning to Step 2, the algorithm assigns Operation C to Work Station 3. Then it adds D, and so on. The procedure continues to give the following results.

Work Station	Activities	Used Time	Spare Time	Utilization
1	A	5	5	50%
2	B	10	-	100%
3	C,D	10	-	100%
4	E,F,G	10	-	100%
5	L,J	10	-	100%
6	H,K	10	-	100%
7	M,I,N	9	1	90%
8	O,P	7	3	70%
9	Q	5	5	50%

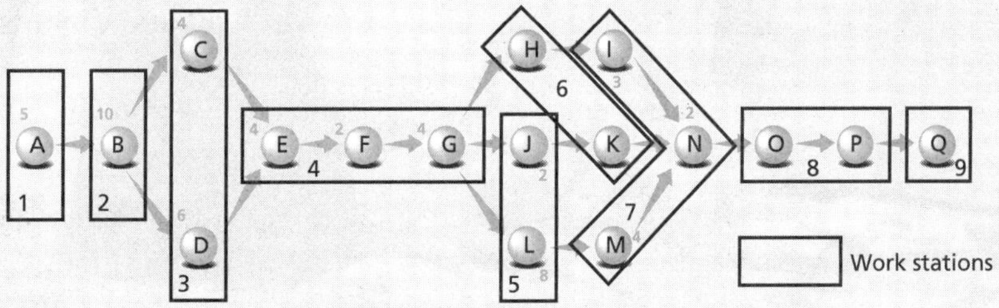

Figure 5.11 Assigning Operations to Work Stations

Step 6 calculates the overall utilization of the process as:

$$\text{Utilization} = \frac{\text{time used in a day}}{\text{number of stations} \times \text{time on each}} = \frac{76 \times 48}{9 \times 480} = 0.844 \text{ or } 84.4\%$$

This approach gives good product results, but it can be rather messy by hand. In practice, computers are always used for this type of analysis.

In Summary

The aim of line balancing is to ensure a smooth flow of products through the layout, with all resources used as fully as possible. A simple algorithm can be used to design balanced layouts. In practice, line balancing is always done by computer.

Review Questions

1. "Product layouts are generally more capital-intensive than process layouts, but give lower unit costs." Do you think this is true? Explain.
2. What is the purpose of stocks of work-in-process between work stations?
3. What sets the maximum output of a product layout?
4. What is a perfectly balanced line, and do you think this is often achieved?
5. What is the cycle time, and why is it important?

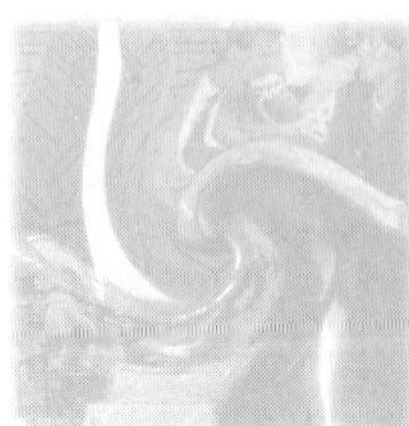

Hybrid Layouts

Many organizations use neither a pure process layout nor a pure product one. They use some combination of the two, which is called a **hybrid layout.** One product may, for example, be assembled from two components. One of these is made in a job shop, which has a process layout, and the other is made on a production line, which has a product layout. The overall layout is a hybrid.

One common hybrid arrangement is a **work cell.** Suppose a process has a dominant process layout, but with some operations set aside in a product layout. For example, a manufacturing plant may have most machines laid out in a process layout but a certain series of operations is repeated so often that a special area is set aside as an assembly line. This special area is a work cell. Such cells can be seen as islands of product layout in a sea of process layout, as shown in Figure 5.12.

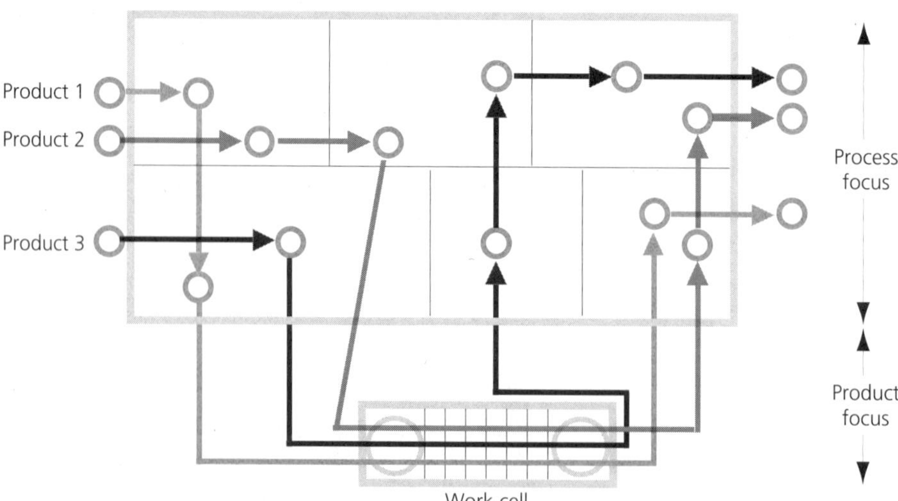

Figure 5.12 Example of a Work Cell

The purpose of work cells is to get the high utilizations and other benefits of product layouts in a process environment. This type of layout has become more popular with **group technology** and **flexible manufacturing.** Group technology combines families of products with common characteristics so that they can be processed in larger batches. Several products might, for example, each need a series of 5-cm holes drilled. These products could be combined into single batches for the drilling machines. If the batches become large, it would make sense to do the common operations using a product layout, even though most other operations use a process layout.

Examples of work cells:

- A job shop gets an order to make a large number of a particular product. It might maintain its overall process layout but will set aside a separate work cell as an assembly line to meet the order.
- An airport passenger terminal has a process layout with separate ticket purchase area, check-in area, food mall, and duty free shops. Despite this, there are some product layouts, such as customs clearance.
- A fast-food restaurant has areas of the kitchen set aside for different purposes, but a line which prepares all hamburgers.
- A hospital has wards set aside for different types of illness, but the patient-admissions area has a product layout.

Some people suggest that there is an important difference between the first of these examples and the others. The arrangement in the job shop is temporary to meet a specific order, while the others are all designed as permanent arrangements. If this distinction is important, the term **work cell** can be used to describe a temporary arrangement and **focused work centre to** describe a permanent arrangement. Then work cells are flexible arrangements which can easily be changed, while focused work centres are more expensive and need more dedicated resources. An automobile repair workshop, for example, might use a process layout. If the bulk of its work is to replace tires and exhausts, it may move some equipment to a separate area specifically to do these on an assembly line. If this arrangement is permanent, it would be a focused work centre.

The idea of a focused work centre can be extended to **focused factories.** Here the focused work centre is moved to another building. Then a focused factory uses a product layout to make a product, which becomes a component in a following process. A factory which uses an assembly line to make windshield-wiper motors for automobiles is an example of a focused factory.

Case Study

Dalmuir Knitwear

Dalmuir Knitwear makes fairly small numbers of fashion garments. It weaves, knits, dyes, sews, assembles, and finishes a range of clothes mainly for women, but with some sportswear for men. Because of the fairly small quantities involved, it uses a process layout, with a weaving room, knitting room, finishing room, and so on.

Two years ago, it won a large order to supply garments to Sears. This was a major success for the company, which was pleased that it could meet the high standards demanded by Sears. Because these standards were higher than their normal operations, Dalmuir set aside a specific area of their factory to make the Sears order. This area was completely refurbished and they moved in their latest machines. In effect, they created a production line to meet this one contract.

This is an example of a work cell. If the arrangement becomes permanent, it is a focused work centre.

In Summary

Hybrid layouts have some operations with a product layout and others with a process layout. Work cells are examples of this arrangement. These have mostly a process layout, but some areas have a product layout. Focused work centres and focused factories extend this idea.

Review Questions

1. What are hybrid layouts? Give some examples of hybrid layouts.
2. What are work cells and why are they used?

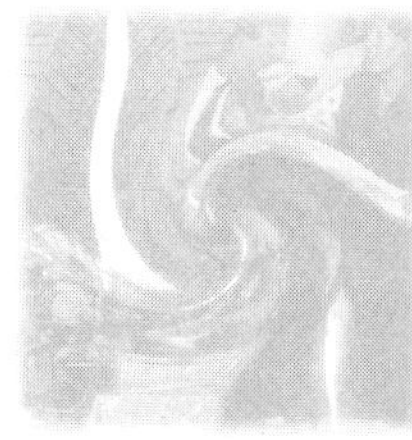

Fixed Position and Other Layouts

The layouts described thus far cover many operations, but there are several other types of layouts. Some of these are designed for specific operations, and can be illustrated by four common examples: fixed position layouts, warehouses, offices, and retail shops.

Fixed Position Layouts

In **fixed position layouts,** each unit of product stays in the same place, and all operations are done at this site. This typically happens when a product is too big or heavy to move around. Common examples are shipbuilding, airplane assembly, and construction sites. The approach is also used when special environments are needed, such as dust-free rooms.

Fixed-position layouts have many disadvantages, including:

- All materials and components must be moved to the site
- All people involved with operations must move to the site
- There is often limited space at the site
- A reliable timetable of operations must be kept
- Disruptions to this timetable can cause delays in completion
- The intensity of work varies
- External factors, such as weather conditions, may affect operations

Because of these disadvantages, fixed position layouts are only used when there is no alternative, that is, when moving the product is either impossible or very difficult. One way to reduce the difficulties of fixed position layouts is to do as much work as possible offsite. A road bridge, for example, must be completed onsite, but many of the parts can be prefabricated offsite and moved for erection.

In Summary

Fixed position layouts keep the product in the same place. All operations are done at this site. There are several drawbacks to this arrangement, and it should only be used if there are no alternatives.

Warehouses

The purpose of a warehouse is to store goods at some point on their journey between suppliers and customers. The essential elements in a warehouse are:

- *Arrival bay,* where goods coming from suppliers are delivered and checked
- *Storage area,* where the goods are kept as inventory
- *Departure bay,* where customers' orders are assembled and shipped out
- *Material handling system,* for moving goods around as necessary
- *Information system,* which records the location of all goods, arrivals from suppliers, departures to customers, and all other relevant information

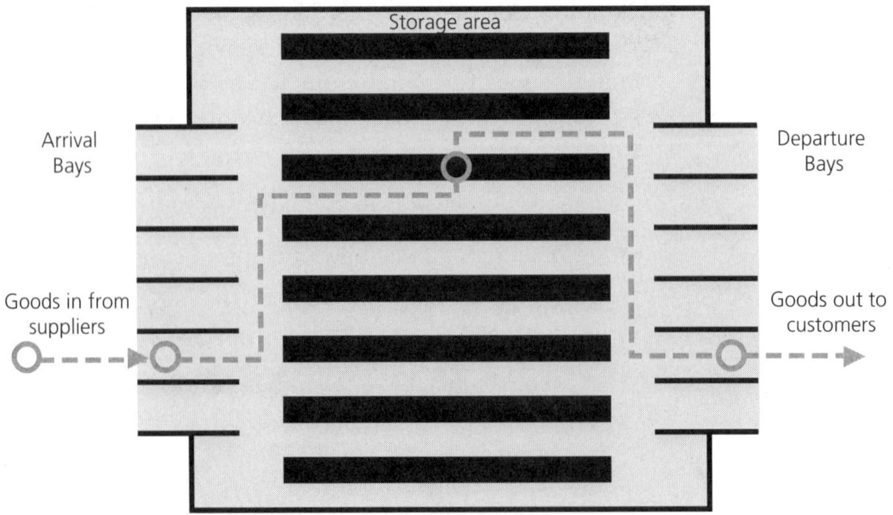

Figure 5.13 Layout of a Typical Warehouse

When designing the layout of a warehouse, the objective is to minimize the total costs. Many of the costs are fixed, such as rent and utilities. Others depend on management policies, such as the amount of inventory held. The main costs which depend on layout come from the time spent locating items, and either adding them to stock or removing them from stock.

The layout of a warehouse will depend on the type of goods being stored and the handling equipment used. Suppose the goods are small and light, such as boxes of pills. Material handling can be done by hand, so the warehouse must be small enough to walk around, and have everything stored within easy reach. But for large and heavy goods, such as engines, material handling will use fork-lift trucks, and the warehouse must be big enough for these to manoeuvre. These two examples show different approaches to warehousing—one is manual and the other is mechanized. The third level of technology is automated, where materials-handling equipment does not require human control.

- *Manual warehouses.* These store light items which are easy to lift. Storage is on shelves which are close together. They can be no higher than two metres. The warehouse must be heated, well lit, and allow people to work comfortably.
- *Mechanized warehouses.* These use fork-lift trucks, conveyors, and tow lines. Some equipment needs wide aisles to manoeuvre, but goods can be stored higher—perhaps up to 12 metres with a fork-lift truck and higher with conveyors. Fork-lift trucks have high costs and are best suited to short journeys around loading and unloading bays. Conveyor systems are less expensive for small items and need less space.
- *Automated warehouses.* These use vehicles, robots, and automated handling for moving units to and from storage areas. The equipment uses narrow aisles and can be very high, so that computer-controlled cranes can reach all items very quickly. As people do not work in the storage areas, money can be saved on heating and lighting.

The layout of a warehouse also depends on the way goods are taken from storage shelves to departure bays. This is called **picking.** There are four distinct ways of picking.

- *Out-and-back.* A single unit is picked at a time. This is used when demand is low, or with heavy and bulky goods that can only be moved one at a time.
- *Batch picking.* Units are picked to satisfy a number of customers.
- *Customer picking.* A variety of different products are picked to satisfy an order from a given customer
- *Zone picking.* A picker stays in one area of the warehouse and loads units, as needed, onto passing conveyors.

There are many other factors in warehouse layout. There is an almost limitless range of warehouse designs, each of which is best suited to particular circumstances.

Example

A store has a rack with nine colours of paint in five-litre cans. At one end of the rack is an issue area where the storekeeper works. Weekly demand for the paint is as follows.

Colour	Red	Blue	White	Black	Brown	Green	Yellow	Grey	Pink
Cans	100	140	860	640	320	120	240	40	60

If all paint is stored in identical sized bins, design a reasonable layout for the rack.

Solution

The objective here is to minimize the distance walked by the storekeeper, assuming that each can of paint needs a separate journey. The paint should be laid out so that colours with highest demand are nearest the issue area. The best layout then has paint in the order white, black, brown, yellow, blue, green, red, pink, and grey. If each bin is one unit wide, this has a total travel distance for the storekeeper of:

$$2 \times (1 \times 860 + 2 \times 640 + 3 \times 320 + 4 \times 240 + 5 \times 140 + 6 \times 120 + 7 \times 100 + 8 \times 60 + 9 \times 40) = 2 \times 7{,}020 = 14{,}040$$

The factor of two allows for return journeys.

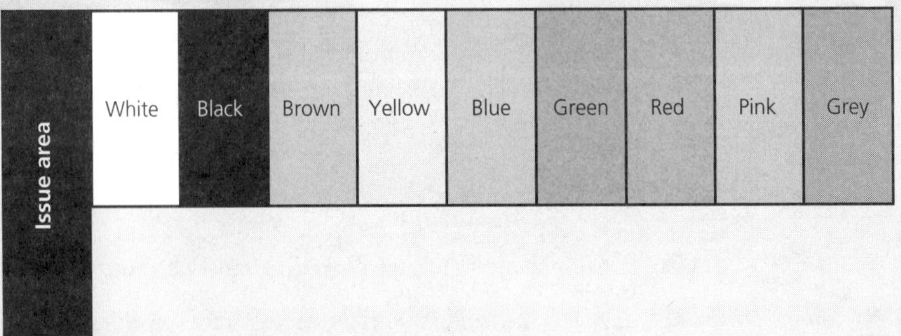

Figure 5.14 The Best Layout for Paint Store

In Summary

Warehouses store goods on their journey between suppliers and customers. There are many possible warehouse layouts. These depend on the products stored and handling equipment used. Some guidelines can be given for good layout.

Offices

Factories and warehouses are concerned with the movement of physical goods, but offices are concerned with the movement of information. This can be done:

- By people talking face to face
- In meetings or groups
- By telephone, intercom, or simultaneous computer link
- On paper
- By electronic mail or computer link

If all communications were indirect, using telephones or some other equipment, the amount of movement in offices could be small. In practice, most efficient communications are done face to face. This needs more planning for the layout. Those areas with most personal contacts should clearly be placed close to each other, while those with less personal contact can be separated—even if they have a lot of indirect contact.

Despite advancing technology, most offices are filled with people, who must have conditions in which they are comfortable and can work efficiently. Some tasks, such as discussing financial arrangements with customers, are best done in private offices. Other tasks, such as processing high volumes of routine paper work, are best done in open areas. Alternative layouts for offices are:

- Desks arranged in rows in an open area
- Desks arranged less formally in open areas, with filing cabinets, plants, and bookcases separating areas
- Desks in open areas separated by moveable partitions, which are typically about 2 metres high
- Areas divided into separate offices by semi-permanent floor-to-ceiling partitions
- Permanent separate offices

A number of other factors must be taken into account when designing offices. These include:

- The amount of face-to-face contact needed in the office will determine the total amount of movement (employees within groups usually have a lot of face-to-face contact)
- The type of work determines the best type of office
- Individual offices have different facilities, size, and location—depending on the job and status of the occupant
- Areas to be visited by customers often have different needs from areas used strictly for work
- Some special facilities may be needed, such as conference or committee rooms, lecture theatres, and boardrooms
- Areas must be set aside for lounges, rest rooms, cloakrooms, storage areas, cleaning equipment
- Aisles should allow people to reach all areas quickly, but no one should have too much traffic passing their work place
- Shared facilities, such as photocopiers, files, and coffee machines, should be convenient for everyone

In Summary

The purpose of offices is to process information. There may be a lot of automation, but many operations rely on people. The layout used should allow office staff to work comfortably and efficiently.

Retail Stores

The layout of retail stores is related to that of warehouses. They both bring in goods, store them, and then take them out to satisfy customer demand. There is, however, an important difference. A good warehouse design minimizes the total distance travelled to collect goods—so those goods with highest demands are kept near the issue area. A store realizes that the longer customers are in the store, the more they will buy—so a good layout increases the distance travelled between purchases. You can see this clearly in supermarkets, which spread basic food items like bread and milk around the store. This forces customers to pass lots of other goods before finding all the basic items they always buy.

Several guidelines have been suggested for store layouts, including:

- Spread basic goods around the store, preferably around the outside aisles

- Do not have crossover aisles, as customers should be encouraged to walk the full length of each aisle
- Use the first and last aisle for products that customers buy on impulse, and that have high profit margins
- Set the image for the store near the door—if customers see a lot of special sales here, they will assume all prices are low
- Put magazines and candy near the checkouts
- The end of aisles are highly visible and should be used, perhaps for special promotions
- Put goods which are attractive to children within their reach
- Circulate customers clockwise

In Summary

Retail stores have similarities with warehouses. But their layout has entirely different objectives. Experience and space limitations are often key factors in designing store layouts.

Review Questions

1. "Fixed position layouts keep all equipment in fixed locations and move products through these in a specified sequence." Do you think this is true? Explain.
2. What are the disadvantages of fixed position layouts?
3. "The layout of supermarkets should allow customers to collect their goods as quickly as possible." Do you think this is true? Explain.
4. Overall, how many different types of layout are there?
5. What type of layout do you think would be used for:
   a. bottling beer
   b. a library
   c. assembling communication satellites
   d. assembling washing machines
   e. a college campus
   f. making specialized sports cars?

Chapter Review

- Layout is concerned with the way equipment, offices, and other resources are physically arranged. The objective of layout design is to find the best arrangement for a process. A good layout will make sure operations are efficient and run smoothly.
- There are many different types of layout. These can be classified as process, product, hybrid, fixed position, or other.
- Process layouts group together similar types of equipment. This is typical of the layout in a job shop. The main problem in designing process layouts is to minimize the movements between areas. For small problems this can be done using an informal method. Larger problems are solved with a computer.
- Product layouts group together the equipment needed to make a product. They can be viewed as assembly lines and consist of a series of work stations. Each work station does a number of operations in a prescribed order. The main problem is to ensure each work station in the line has the same throughput, giving a balanced flow of products.
- Many processes use a mixture of product and process layouts. These are called hybrid layouts. Work cells are a common type of hybrid layout, where some areas use a product layout, but overall there is a process layout.
- Many layouts cannot be described as process, product, or hybrid. Fixed position layouts, for example, keep the product in a single location where all work is done.
- There are many other types of layout including warehouses, offices, and retail stores.

Key Terms

cycle time *(p. 130)*
facility layout *(p. 115)*
fixed position layout *(p. 137)*
flexible manufacturing *(p. 135)*
focused factories *(p. 135)*
focused work centre *(p. 135)*
group technology *(p. 135)*
hybrid layout *(p. 134)*
line balancing *(p. 130)*
picking *(p. 139)*
process layout *(p. 116)*
product layout *(p. 127)*
systematic layout planning *(p. 125)*
work cell *(p. 134)*
work station *(p. 128)*

Problems

5.1 A process layout has five identically sized areas in a straight line. The following movements are made between the areas during a typical day.

	a	b	c	d	e
a	0	17	12	42	2
b	12	0	1	22	6
c	0	22	0	17	7
d	47	11	3	0	12
e	53	5	6	25	0

What is the best layout for the process?

5.2 One floor of a building has six office areas, which are all the same size. The current layout is shown in Figure 5.15, but this seems to give a lot of movement between areas.

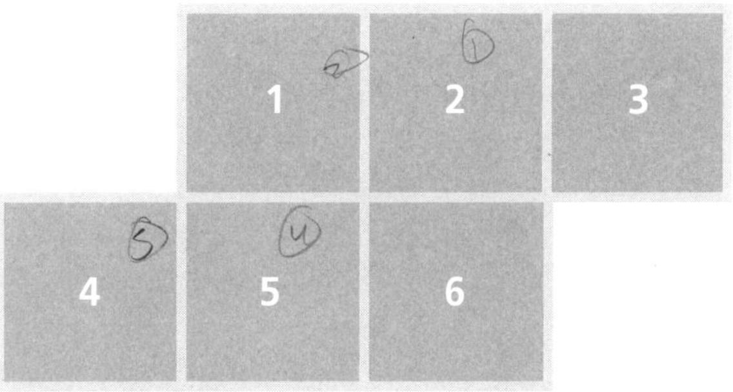

Figure 5.15 Office Layout

During a typical period, the following movements were counted between areas. How could you improve the layout of areas?

	1	2	3	4	5	6
1	-	-	100	-	35	-
2	120	-	10	20	15	10
3	-	15	-	80	-	75
4	-	55	-	-	75	-
5	-	10	-	125	-	-
6	80	20	-	-	-	-

5.3 A process consists of a sequence of 15 operations with the following times.

Operation	1	2	3	4	5	6	7	8	9	10	11	12	13	14	15
Time in Minutes	2	6	8	4	10	2	1	15	11	8	2	4	10	7	5

Find the best allocation of operations to work stations for different levels of production.

5.4 An assembly line has seven activities, with times and precedences shown below.

Activity	Description	Time (seconds)	Activity Must Follow
A	Clean bottle	20	-
B	Inspect bottle	5	A
C	Fill bottle with liquid	20	B
D	Put top on filled bottle	5	C
E	Put label on bottle	5	B
F	Put bottles into boxes	10	D,E
G	Seal boxes and move	5	F

The forecast demand for bottles is 120 per hour. Calculate the cycle time and minimum number of work stations needed. Balance the line by assigning operations to work stations.

5.5 Each operation described in Figure 5.16 takes four minutes. Design a line that will process six units an hour.

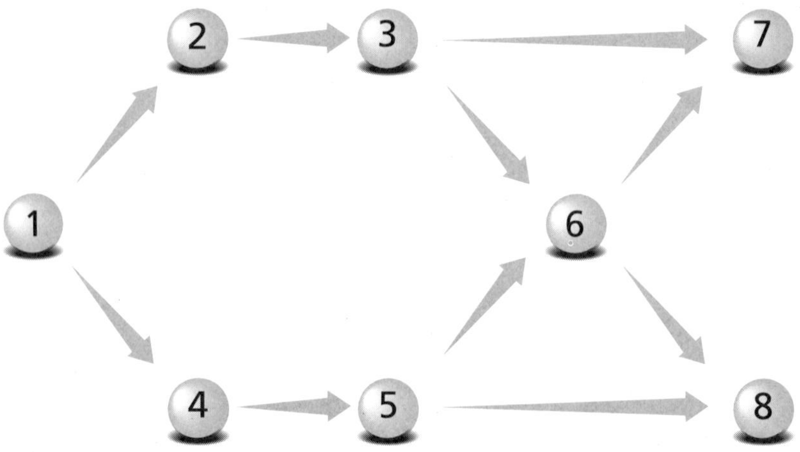

Figure 5.16 Precedence Diagram

5.6 A warehouse has a single aisle with 12 bins as shown in Figure 5.17. It stores six products with the following characteristics. Design a good layout for the warehouse.

Product	Withdrawals	Bins Needed
1	150	1
2	700	3
3	50	1
4	900	3
5	450	2
6	300	2

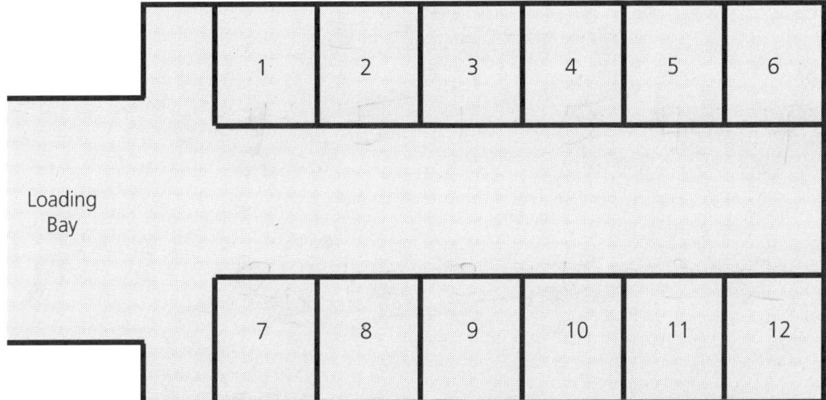

Figure 5.17

5.7 If the design in Problem 5.6 referred to a supermarket, how would the design differ?

Discussion Questions

5.1 Do you think that layout design can be a strategic issue for an organization, or is it purely tactical? Explain.

5.2 Describe some successful layouts that you have seen. What makes these successful? Compare them with some unsuccessful layouts for similar operations.

5.3 "Layout design should be left to architects and planners." Do you think this would give good results? Explain.

5.4 Do you think there is such a thing as an optimal process layout? Do computer packages give optimal solutions?

5.5 Many computer programs help design layouts. What do you think these should do? Give some examples of software you have seen.

5.6 Many people are now writing about focused factories. Why do you think they are writing so much about an old idea? Explain.

5.7 Describe the features you would expect to see on a production line. What are the major questions to be considered in product layout designs?

5.8 The layout of a supermarket has to be convenient for customers. At the same time, managers want to keep customers in the shop as long as possible so they buy more. Give examples of other services that need a similar compromise in their layout.

5.9 Do you think that some offices customers visit should be more luxurious than others? If so, give examples.

Chapter 6

QUALITY MANAGEMENT

Making products with perfect quality

Contents

Introduction

In recent times, there has been a good deal of talk about quality. You have probably seen Ford's advertisement, "Quality is Job 1." Nabob coffee commercials say, "Quality goes in before the name goes on." These are not just slogans but are signs that companies are serious about the quality of their products.

Although it is difficult to define quality, it is clear that the quality of an organization's products is vital to its survival. An organization can reap many benefits from making high-quality products. These benefits, which include reduced costs, have led most organizations to aim for perfect quality in their products, or "zero defects." This can be achieved with Total Quality Management (TQM), whereby the whole organization focuses on the quality of its products.

Learning Objectives

After reading this chapter you should be able to answer questions such as:

- Why is product quality important?
- How can quality be defined?
- What costs are associated with high quality?
- What is Total Quality Management?
- How can quality management be introduced to an organization?
- How is quality managed in services?

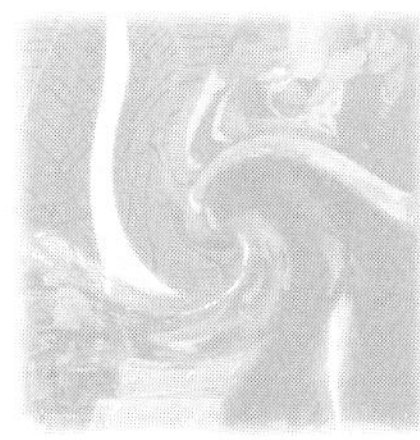

Definitions of Quality

Canadian businesses are becoming very quality conscious. Is this because Canadian consumers are demanding higher quality? Or, is it to prevent Japanese and other foreign companies taking a bigger share of the market? Whatever the reason, quality is important for every organization.

But what is meant by quality? How can it be defined? In some cases, quality can be measured quantitatively, but in others, it is a subjective matter. You might, for example, find it difficult to judge the quality of a video game or a CD.

But suppose you were asked about the quality of a ball-point pen. You might say it has high quality when it writes clearly, without smearing ink. You might say that the quality of a computer is high because it is easy to operate and functions quickly. A general view, then, is that a product has high quality if it can do the job it was bought to do.

In its broadest sense, **quality** is the ability of a product to meet—and preferably exceed—customer expectations.

If quality is such an important aspect of a product, then surely the top management of a company should be concerned about it. This seems obvious, but historically managers have viewed quality as a minor technical matter. They believed it could be controlled through inspections that could be handled by technicians. Only recently have managers come to realize the strategic importance of quality; if their product's quality is not high enough, they will lose market share and profits. This realization has led to the growth of quality management.

Quality management is the management function that is concerned with all aspects of a product's quality.

Quality management is an area that is still evolving. In the past few years, there has been a whole range of new developments, which some people call the **quality revolution**. These developments occurred for three main reasons: 1. improved processes for making products can guarantee consistently high quality; 2. organizations began to use high quality as a means of gaining an advantage over competitors; and 3. consumers have come to expect high-quality products and will not accept anything less.

Thus, organizations *must* emphasize product quality. Competition ensures that any organization whose products do not meet the high quality demanded by customers will lose out to those that do. Although high quality does not ensure the success of a product, low quality will certainly ensure its failure. Survival, then, is the main reason for organizations to use quality management. Some other benefits of high-quality products are shown in Table 6.1 on page 152.

Table 6.1 *Benefits of High-Quality Products*

- Enhanced reputation
- Increased competitiveness
- Need for less marketing
- Better sales and market share
- Increased productivity
- Higher profits
- Reduced liability for defective products
- Reduced costs

Most of these benefits are fairly obvious—if an organization increases the quality of its products, it can expect people to recognize this quality, to buy its products instead of the competitors', and thereby to contribute to its success. But the idea that increasing quality can reduce costs is particularly interesting. This contradicts the traditional view that higher quality can only be achieved at higher cost. It seems obvious that making a higher quality product uses more time, more careful operations, a more skilful workforce, and better materials. However, some costs are actually reduced with increasing quality.

Suppose a bicycle is sold with a faulty part. Customers will complain, and the manufacturer must arrange for the bike to be repaired. The manufacturer could have saved money by finding the fault before the bike left the factory—and it could have saved even more by making a bicycle that did not have a fault in the first place.

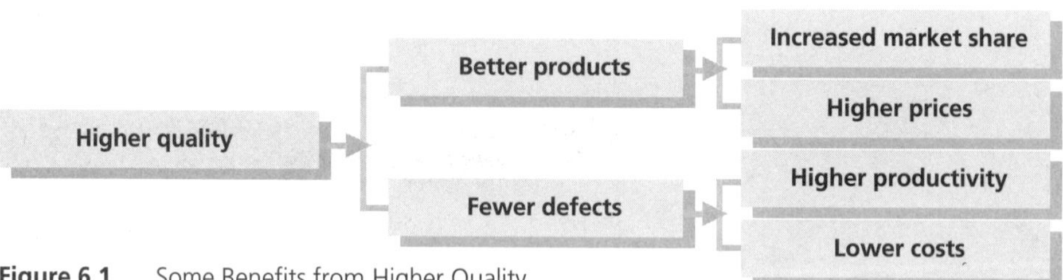

Figure 6.1 Some Benefits from Higher Quality

In Summary

It is often difficult to define the quality of a product. A general view is that quality measures how well a product meets customer expectations. All organizations are concerned about the quality of their products. In recent years, there has been a strong movement towards higher quality.

Different Views of Quality

So far we have looked at the consumers' view of quality—a product should do the job for which it was bought, and it must meet customer expectations. But quality can be very personal and each customer may have a different view. How can a producer satisfy everyone?

Certain products are generally perceived as having high quality. A Ferrari is a high-quality car; a Wedgwood dinner set has a higher quality than a plastic one; *Hamlet* is a higher quality play than a TV soap opera. But it is difficult to be more specific. For example, if the purpose of a car is to provide transportation from point A to point B, then an inexpensive car may do this just as well as a Ferrari; if the purpose of a dinner set is to provide a surface to rest food on while we eat, a cheap plastic one works just as well as an expensive china one; audience figures show that far more people watch TV soap operas than see plays such as *Hamlet*.

Faced with these problems, some people may simply give up when asked to define quality and simply say, "We don't know how to define quality, but we recognize it when we see it." Quality depends on many factors, only some of which can be measured. Any reasonable view of quality must take into account many factors—and it would be foolish to judge a product or service on the basis of some factors and ignore others. For example, the quality of a medical clinic cannot be judged by the number of patients without considering the treatment patients receive. A common practice, then, is to consider a "cocktail" or mix of factors that, taken together, define high quality. Unfortunately, this mix of criteria still relies on opinion. The judgement of quality for almost any product would require a list of criteria such as the following:

- Innate excellence
- Fitness for intended use
- Performance
- Reliability
- Durability
- Specific features, perhaps for safety or convenience
- Convenience of use
- Attractive appearance and style
- Ratio of performance to cost
- On-time deliveries
- After-sales service

We have emphasized the importance of customers' views of quality, but there are many other viewpoints. We can summarize these as: 1. the *external* view of the customer, who defines quality by how well a product does the job for which it was bought; and 2. the *internal* view of the producer, who defines quality as how well the product performs to its designed specifications.

The customers' view of quality is most important, but producers often have different views. A producer must have a clear view of quality, so that it can design operations to make the product efficiently. Using qualitative terms for quality is not good enough. Describing a car as long lasting, reliable, and fuel-efficient will not help a designer or production department make a high-quality car. All of its features must be clearly defined in measurable terms. In other words, the product must have a complete set of **specifications**. Then a smooth ride can be defined in terms of the amount of vibration when driving the car at 60 km/h; the fuel consumption can be defined as the amount of fuel used to travel 100 km. The organization can then test its products to see whether they meet these specifications.

In the past, organizations tended to emphasize the internal view, suggesting that a product that met the producer's specifications should be acceptable to the customers. People who complained to companies were often surprised to get letters back saying, "We have considered your complaint, but have found that our product was perfectly satisfactory." More recently, organizations have recognized the obvious fact that customers' opinions about a product's quality are important. This perception is based on a number of factors, so customers will not always demand products that have the highest technical quality. They demand some balance of features that give an acceptable overall picture. A Ferrari, for example, has high-quality engineering, but most people include the price factor in their judgement and buy a less expensive make. Bearing this in mind, three components of quality should be considered.

First is the **designed quality**, which looks at the product design and specifications. If you want a wristwatch that will not lose more than a few seconds per month, you may want a high-quality Swiss watch that uses high-quality materials and very high specifications. This watch would have high designed quality. An inexpensive plastic watch would have low designed quality.

But a high designed quality does not mean that the product will actually meet these specifications. So the second component of quality is **achieved quality**, which shows how closely a product meets its designed specifications. An airline that plans to have 98 percent of its flights arrive on time has a high designed quality; if only 30 percent of flights are actually on time, its achieved quality is much lower.

After a customer has bought a product, the supplier's job is not finished. Customers also judge quality by the product's warranty, help available with any problems, and so on. Features of this kind form the third component of quality, the **quality of after-sales service**.

Honda

Honda believes that customer satisfaction is the ultimate goal of the company, and to achieve this it aims for exceptional products. Honda believes that it cannot make exceptional products by using the same manufacturing processes as other companies, so almost all of its manufacturing systems are designed and built by Honda.

These manufacturing systems are designed for two customers: 1. external customers who buy Honda products; 2. internal customers who use the systems to make these products. These customers have different views and consider different factors important. The most important factors for each type of customer are given below.

External customers consider products:

- Attractiveness—appearance, new technology, variety of options, flexibility, improvements over previous models
- Quality—well made, durable, reliable, easy to maintain
- Price—low purchase price and running costs, long warranty
- Delivery—short lead time, easily available, many options

Internal users consider use of the system:

- Safety—preventing accidents, meeting safety standards
- Reliability—consistent, durable, does not break down
- Environment—clean, pleasant work, machinery easy to operate
- Maintenance—product well designed and laid out, easy to maintain
- Communications—get customer feedback, listen to everyone, avoid bureaucracy
- Good service—technical support, manuals

In Summary

There are many possible views of quality. Some of these can be measured, but many are opinions. Producers of goods and services need some aspects of quality defined in measurable terms so they can give specifications. Overall quality of a product is composed of designed quality, achieved quality, and quality of after-sales service.

Review Questions

1. "If the price is right, people will buy a product regardless of its quality." Do you think this is true? Explain.
2. Why is quality management important to an organization?
3. Why is it difficult to define "quality"?

Costs of Quality Management

Costs of Quality

As stated, costs can be reduced by increasing the quality of a product. Suppose a manufacturer sells products with a 5 percent defect rate. When these defects are reported by customers, the manufacturer replaces them under its warranty. This kind of operation is clearly inefficient. The manufacturer has to increase production by 5 percent to cover the defects. It must also maintain a system for dealing with customer complaints, and another system for collecting defective units, inspecting, repairing or replacing them, and returning them to customers. If the defects are eliminated, productivity will rise by 5 percent, unit costs will fall, there will be no customer complaints, so the cost of dealing with them is eliminated, and the whole system for correcting faults is not needed.

Another consequence of poor quality was the once common practice of **overage**. If a factory needed 100 components, it would buy 110 on the assumption that 10 would be defective. This overage was often doubled, as suppliers who were asked for 110 units would send 120 to make sure 110 were satisfactory. The use of overage is obviously wasteful and has become increasingly unacceptable.

In general, making a product without defects has the following benefits:

- Increased productivity
- Reduced unit cost
- Reduced administration costs for dealing with customer complaints
- Elimination of procedures for correcting defects
- Reduced warranty costs

- A range of indirect benefits, such as increased customer goodwill and improved company reputation

Organizations can save money by making higher quality products.

While our discussion has emphasized the savings that can be made by higher quality products, common sense dictates that there must be some additional costs involved. In the past, even though the company did not manage quality properly, it was assumed that the cost of quality control was typically around 5–10 percent of sales. In reality the figure is closer to 20–30 percent of sales. What are these costs, and why are they so high? There are four types of costs associated with quality:

1. Prevention costs
2. Appraisal costs
3. Internal failure costs
4. External failure costs

The first two of these rise with increasing product quality, while the failure costs decline.

Table 6.2 *Types of Quality Costs*

Type of Cost	Cause	Change with Increasing Quality
1. Prevention	Preventing defects being made	Rises
2. Appraisal	Checking designed quality is actually being achieved	Rises
3. Internal Failure	Defects found within the organization	Falls
4. External Failure	Defects found by customers	Falls

Prevention Costs

These costs are incurred to prevent defects from occurring. The quality of a product is usually set at the design stage, so the best way of achieving high quality in a product is not by inspecting it during the production process but by designing a good product in the first place. In part, this means that the design should allow high quality despite small, unavoidable variations during the production process. It can also include product simplification, which reduces the number of parts in a product.

Prevention costs include all aspects of designed quality. They include direct costs for the product itself, such as the choice of materials, inclusion of certain features, and amount of time needed to make the product. They also include indirect costs, like the ease of production, amount of automation that can be used, skill level required of the workforce, type of process used, procurement activities, and the amount of training needed. In essence, the prevention costs are incurred for the planning and design of the product and for the production process to ensure that products achieve high quality.

All things being equal, prevention costs rise with the quality of the product, largely because of the direct costs. But customers will not pay an unlimited sum to get products of the highest possible quality. This is a ceiling on the price they will not pass regardless of the quality offered, and this sets the practical limit for designed quality.

Appraisal Costs

These are the costs of ensuring the designed quality is actually achieved. As products move through their process, they are inspected to make sure they reach the quality specified in the design. Related costs include sampling, inspecting, testing, and all the other elements of quality control. Generally speaking, the more effort put into quality control, the higher the end quality of the product, and the higher the costs needed to achieve this quality.

Internal Failure Costs

As a product goes through the various operations in its production, it may be inspected several times. Any units that do not meet the specified quality are scrapped, returned to an earlier point in the line, repaired, or allowed to continue along the line in the hope that the fault is not important enough to affect the product's value. With the exception of the last, these alternatives involve extra work to bring a unit up to satisfactory quality. There is also the implication that some work already done has been wasted.

The farther a product goes through the process, the more money will have been spent on it, and the more expensive it will be to scrap or rework. Ideally, then, defects should be found as early as possible in the process. Companies should avoid allowing a defective unit to continue in the process. More money is spent on a unit that is known to be defective, and later detection and scrapping will increase the total waste.

Some of the internal failure costs arise directly from the loss of material, wasted labour effort, and wasted machine time in making the defective item; others arise from the indirect costs of higher inventory levels, longer lead times, and additional capacity to allow for scrap and rejections.

External Failure Costs

Suppose a product goes through the entire production process, is delivered to a customer, and is then found to be defective. The producer will usually give some kind of performance guarantee and is responsible for correcting any faults. The product must be brought back from the customer and replaced, reworked, or repaired as necessary. The cost of this work forms part of the external failure cost, which is the total cost of making defective products that are not detected within the process but are recognized as faulty by customers.

These costs can be very high. In 1982, for example, General Motors found a fault in some of its cars and had to recall 2.1 million vehicles at a cost of over $100 million. Not surprisingly, GM has since become one of the leaders in quality management. Such costs can be even higher if, say, a defective part in an airplane causes a crash which leaves the manufacturer liable for damages.

In Summary

The costs associated with product quality can be classified as prevention, appraisal, and internal and external failure. The first two of these rise with increasing product quality, while the failure costs decline.

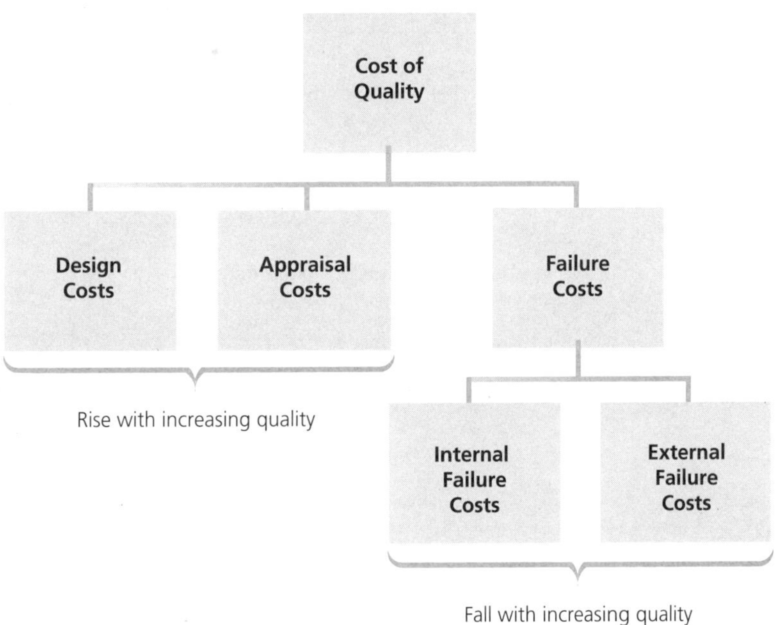

Figure 6.2 The Costs of Quality

Minimizing the Total Cost of Quality

The total cost of quality is found by adding together the four separate components: prevention, appraisal, internal failure, and external failure. This cost can often be 20–30 percent of sales. Traditionally, organizations have tried to minimize this by identifying an optimal level of quality, as shown in Figure 6.3 on page 160, which shows that the design and appraisal costs increase with quality, while the failure costs decrease.

Case Study – American Home Appliance Co.

American Home Appliance Co. manufactures a full range of home appliances such as stoves, dishwashers, and refrigerators. Its Ohio plant makes dishwashers. Maytag may have the best name in the industry, but the dishwashers made by American Home Appliances are recognized as having above average quality. But recently the company has been having some problems, particularly with its Model 550. Because of these problems, the company's market share and profits are declining.

The Model 550 was introduced in 1990, and it used high-pressure jets to clean dishes. Unfortunately, the company soon had a lot of complaints and warranty claims. The Service Department was swamped with calls. The company was understandably worried that its reputation would be badly damaged if it failed to solve the problem quickly.

An analysis of complaints showed that the majority of the problems were caused by three parts:

1. The pump motor, where poor workmanship caused it to jam
2. The lower sprayer, which was poorly designed
3. The selector switch, which used poor materials

The Model 550 had obviously been introduced too quickly, without proper design reviews, process planning, and worker training.

The quality manager estimated that 3 percent of all Model 550 dishwashers sold will have to be replaced with a new model of equivalent value. Another 5 percent will need service calls. The total cost of fixing or replacing faulty machines will be around $2.5 million. The company feels this is a small price to pay for avoiding a bad name, which would adversely affect the sales of its other products.

Questions

- What are the possible reasons for the quality problem?
- What should the company do both immediately and in the long term to solve this problem?

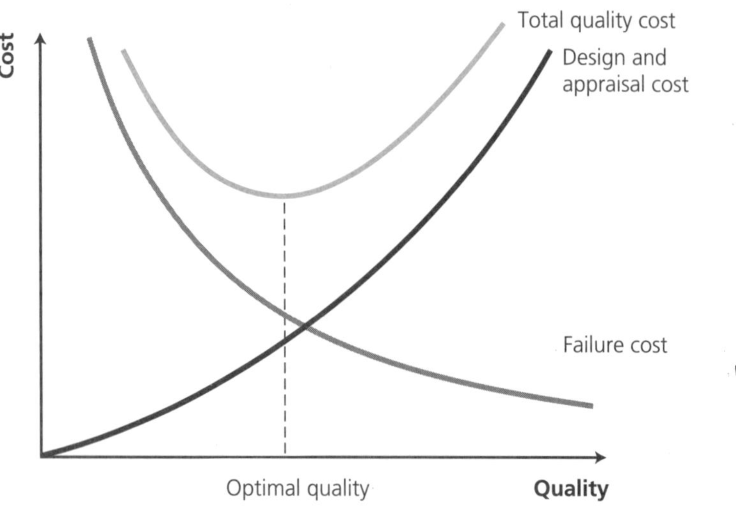

Figure 6.3 Finding the Optimal Quality

Unfortunately, this analysis is now recognized as faulty. In particular, the true costs of external failures are considerably higher than shown. Customers are increasingly reluctant to accept *any* defects in products, so low quality usually results in low sales. In addition, producers are becoming more responsible for the consequences of defects in their products—surgeons are liable if their negligence during an operation injures a patient; pharmaceutical manufacturers are responsible for faults in their drugs; management consultants are liable for bad advice. The resulting high costs of external failure mean that the optimal quality for a product is generally "perfect quality", where every unit is completely free of defects.

Example

Rocky Mountain Fabricators recorded costs (in thousands of dollars per year) for two years immediately before it changed its quality management program and two years immediately after. Based on the following data, how effective do you think this program has been?

Year	-2	-1	+1	+2
Sales Value	1,247	1,186	1,456	1,775
Costs				
Design	8	9	30	32
Appraisal	17	20	64	65
Internal Failure	72	75	24	20
External Failure	60	66	23	17

Solution

The easiest way to judge the quality management program is to calculate the total cost as a percentage of sales. Dividing the costs by sales value and showing this as a percentage gives:

Year	-2	-1	+1	+2
Costs				
Design	0.64	0.76	2.06	1.80
Appraisal	1.36	1.69	4.40	3.66
Internal Failure	5.77	6.32	1.65	1.13
External Failure	4.81	5.56	1.58	0.96
Total	12.58	14.33	9.69	7.55

The new quality management program has clearly put more emphasis on design and appraisal, so there have been reductions in failures. The overall costs decline and sales increase, so the program can be judged a success.

This aim of perfect quality, or **zero defects**, contrasts with the traditional view that sets a target number of faults. It assumes—and even encourages—some defects, and allows these to pass through the process until they are detected at some point, when all previous work on them has been wasted.

In Summary

The lowest cost of quality is usually found with zero defects. Every unit produced has perfect quality.

Review Questions

1. "Higher quality inevitably comes at a higher cost." Do you think this is true?
2. What is the total cost of quality?
3. Why do internal failure costs fall with increasing quality?
4. How would you find the optimal level of quality for a product?

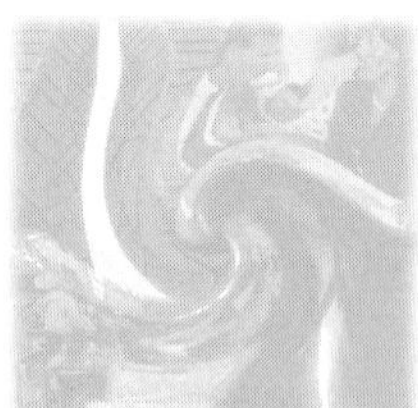

Managing for Perfect Quality

Total Quality Management

For many years, statistical quality control, which inspects units as they pass through the production process, was the main tool for ensuring product quality. Sometimes quality-control people tested every unit, with defects being identified and corrected—but often they only tested a sample. This allowed defective units to go undetected and be sold to customers. Although statistical quality control is still widely used, there has recently been a change of emphasis, shown by the phrase "you can't inspect quality into a product." Quality managers have realized that the best way to improve quality is not to inspect production and discard defective units, but to ensure that no defective units are made in the first place. The term **quality control** is now applied to sampling and inspection—the broader function for ensuring quality is known as **quality assurance** or **quality management**.

Quality management is a broad function that includes all work concerned with ensuring the quality of an organization's products.
Quality control is a more limited function that involves statistical sampling and testing to check the quality of a product.

The important point about quality management is that it is not a separate, isolated function, but an integral part of all operations. Suppose you go to a tailor and order a suit. You will only be satisfied if the suit is well designed, if it is well made, if there are no faults in the material used, if the price is reasonable, if the salesperson is helpful, if the store is pleasant, and so on. This means that everyone in the organization—from the person who designs the suit to the person who sells it, from the person who owns the organization to the person who keeps it clean—is directly involved in the quality of their product. This is the view taken by **Total Quality Management** (TQM).

Total Quality Management involves the whole organization working together and systematically improving product quality.

TQM was developed by Japanese manufacturers. In the 1940s, Japanese industry had been disrupted by wars, its plants and equipment were out of date, productivity was low, and products suitable for the wartime economy were no longer needed. To get its industries working again, Japan made cheap, low-quality imitations of products from other countries. As industry developed, living standards rose and so did operating costs. It became more difficult to make cheap products, so Japanese manufacturers began to concentrate on higher quality, more expensive ones. They were obviously successful, and by the 1970s dominated world markets for products such as motorcycles, consumer electronics, automobiles, machine tools, steel, and computer equipment.

The key element in Japan's success was recognizing that it could compete in the world market by offering consistently high quality. This emphasis on quality was illustrated by studies in the early 1980s that found that air conditioners made in North America had 70 times as many defects on the assembly line as those made in Japan, and had 17 times as many breakdowns in the first year of operation. A North American manufacturer of television sets had more than 150 defects per 100 completed sets, and was trying to compete with Japanese companies which averaged 0.5 defects per 100 completed sets. North American manufacturers of car components had warranty costs ten times higher than their Japanese counterparts.

An ironic feature of Japan's success is that much of the early work in implementing quality management was done by Edwards Deming, an American who visited Japan in the late 1940s to help improve productivity and quality.

In Summary

Total quality management aims at getting the whole organization involved with the continuous improvement of product quality. Much of the development work for this was done by Japanese manufacturers.

Effects on the Organization

Traditionally, organizations used a separate quality control department to inspect the work of production departments. These two functions had different objectives. Production would try to make products as quickly as possible, while quality control inspected products to make sure they met specifications, possibly by slowing down production. This inevitably led to conflicts, with one department benefiting only at the expense of the other.

When it became clear that processes could be designed that would guarantee high-quality products, quality control changed its emphasis from inspections at the end of production to focus on operations during the process itself, to ensure no defects were made. It even moved into the planning stages to make sure the product designs allowed for high quality. Quality control then became an integral part of the process. In effect, production departments took responsibility for their own quality.

The transfer of quality management from a separate department to part of the production function does not simply mean that different people do the same inspections—it is part of a fundamental change in an organization's attitude toward quality. This is the basis of Total Quality Management, which realizes that quality must be a part of every function—everyone in the organization must work for quality, from top management downward.

Consider the people who work directly on the production process. With TQM, each person becomes responsible for passing on only products that are of perfect quality. This is often called **quality at source**—with **job enlargement** for each person, who is now responsible for both his or her previous job and an inherent quality management function.

As each person is responsible for passing on products of Perfect quality, if a fault is found it shows that something has gone wrong. Quality at source programs give anyone authority to stop the production process and investigate a fault. The reason for the fault is found, and suggestions made for avoiding any more faults in the future. This contrasts to traditional practices that only stop the production process as a last resort, with the cause of the fault perhaps left unnoticed until it causes more severe problems. Moving responsibility down to the workforce means that fewer supervisors are needed and the organization becomes "flatter."

Consider, also, the way employees are rewarded. Traditionally, people working on the production process were rewarded for making high volumes, often regardless of quality. Many people were paid by "piece work" where their job was simply to make as many units as possible. TQM states that employees should be paid for the quality of their products, so they become interested in how well the products are made, and are willing to make suggestions for improvement.

Managers can collect suggestions for improvements through informal progress meetings or through suggestion boxes. More regular meetings can be arranged through **quality circles**. These are informal, voluntary groups of about ten people from all levels of the process. A typical quality circle meets for an hour once or twice a month to discuss ways in which their operations might be improved. They might identify a problem which is affecting the quality of their product, discuss alternatives for improvements, examine comments put into a suggestion box, suggest modifications to designs, and so on. Their aim is simply to discuss the operation and to try to find improvements.

Many companies that use quality circles have found immense benefits to these, but they can only be used when a number of conditions are met. These include:

1. A well-educated workforce capable of recognizing, analyzing, and solving problems
2. People who are able and willing to exchange ideas
3. People who see themselves as working for the good of the organization
4. A management that is willing to share information on costs and operations

Table 6.3 *New Attitude with TQM*

Criteria	Traditional Attitude	New Attitude with TQM
Cost	High quality costs money	High quality saves money
Inspection	Inspection is needed	Inspection is a waste
Responsibility	Quality assurance department	Everyone
Importance	Quality is a technical issue	Quality is a strategic issue
Defect Level	Based on average quality level	Zero defects
Attitude	Inspect quality in product	Build quality into product
Target	Meet specifications	Continuous improvement
Emphasis	Detecting defects	Preventing defects
Defined By	Organization	Customers

In Summary

Total quality management causes a number of changes within an organization. These changes include quality at source, job enlargement, and changes in rewards.

Implementing Total Quality Management

Aiming for total quality creates a reorganized quality-management function, lower costs, higher productivity, an involved workforce, and quality at source. Unfortunately, implementing TQM can take several years and a great deal of effort from the organization. Edwards Deming spent 40 years developing TQM in Japan, and he compiled a list of 14 principles which give guidelines for the implementation of TQM.

Case Study

Total Quality Management

There are many stories about companies that have introduced TQM and have found considerable benefits. Most of these are anecdotal, as shown in the following examples.

- The Hiroshima Plant of Japan Steel Works began work on TQM in 1977. Between 1978 and 1981, production rose 50 percent; the number of employees fell from 2,400 to 1,900; the accident rate fell from 15.7 per million man-hours to 2.3; the cost of defects fell from 1.57 percent of sales to 0.4 percent; and the number of suggestions per employee rose from 5.6 per year to 17.6.
- In 1984, Ford of America had been running its "Quality is job one" program for five years. During this period, the number of warranty repairs dropped 45 percent; faults reported by new owners fell 50 percent; Ford's share of the U.S. market rose to 19.2 percent; sales rose 700,000 units in a year to 5.7 million units; pretax profits rose to $4.3 billion; annual operating costs fell by $4.5 billion.
- Within one year, Hewlett-Packard's Computer Systems Division increased direct labour productivity by 40 percent; faults with integrated circuits fell from 1950 parts per million to 210; faults with soldering fell from 5,200 parts per million to 100; and faults in the final assembly fell from 145 parts per million to 10.

Case Study

TQM at Standard Aero Ltd.

Standard Aero Ltd. is an engine repair company based in Winnipeg. When Bob Hamaberg became its president in 1988, the company was inefficient and heavily dependent on government contracts. By 1991, Hamaberg realized that if Standard Aero was going to survive it had to change the way it operated. In particular, he saw an urgent need to implement TQM.

To implement TQM, a nine-member team was chosen from various departments. The team decided that TQM should be gradually phased into the organization, so it started with the T56 Allison turboprop engine line. The team's first job was to find out what customers really wanted. They spent two months and $100,000 doing this. To their surprise, customers' major concerns were not cost and quality but lead times and ease of doing business. Standard Aero decided that it wanted to be twice as good as the next best company, so it set a target of overhauling a T56 in 15 days compared to the industry average of 75 days and the industry best of 35 days.

The team simplified and improved the engine overhauling process. For this they studied the process, critically analyzed it, cut out 93 percent of nonchargeable steps, and reduced the distance travelled between operations by 80 percent. The process was reduced from 213 steps to 51.

When Standard Aero bid for a US$ 10 million contract to overhaul some of the military's gear boxes, they were 50 percent below the competition with a much shorter delivery time. The Pentagon would not believe the bid, so they sent a team of 13 senior officers to inspect the company. The team liked what they saw and Standard Aero was awarded the contract. Hamaberg firmly believes that the company won the contract only because of TQM, and says, "We are making more money than ever."

Source: Ted Wakefield, "No Pain, No Gain," Canadian Business, January 1993.

Table 6.4 *Deming's 14 Points*

1. Create constancy of purpose toward product quality.
2. Refuse to accept customary levels of mistakes, delays, defects, and errors.
3. Stop depending on mass inspection, but build quality into the product in the first place.
4. Stop awarding business on the basis of price only—reduce the number of suppliers and insist on meaningful measures of quality.
5. Develop programs for continuous improvement of costs, quality, productivity, and service.
6. Institute training for all employees.
7. Focus supervision on helping employees to do a better job.
8. Drive out fear in the organization by encouraging two-way communication.
9. Break down barriers between departments and encourage problem solving through teamwork.
10. Eliminate numerical goals, posters, and slogans that demand improvements without saying how these should be achieved.
11. Eliminate arbitrary quotas that interfere with quality.
12. Remove barriers that stop people having pride in their work.
13. Institute vigorous programs of lifelong education, training, and self-improvement.
14. Put everyone to work on implementing these 14 points.

Deming's 14 points emphasize that managers are in control of the organization and are responsible for improving its performance. If an organization is performing poorly, it is the fault of managers. Many people blame workers for poor quality, but Deming suggests that this is unfair. A production process can be divided into two parts:

1. The system over which managers have control and which contributes 85 percent of the variation in quality
2. The workers who are under their own control and contribute 15 percent to variation in quality

Major improvements in quality come from managers improving the system rather than workers improving their own performance. The best way to improve productivity is not to make people work harder but to improve the design of the process. A person digging a hole with a shovel can work very hard but may still have a lower productivity rate than a lazy person with an electric hole digger. Similarly, a person working very conscientiously to get good quality in a poor system will get worse results than a less conscientious person in a better system.

Another interesting point in Deming's list is that everyone in the organization should be properly trained for their job. In America, Ford sent over 6,000 people to training courses in two years. They also recognized that they could only make good products if they could buy good components, so they also trained over 1,000 suppliers. They made a clear statement that Ford would only consider suppliers whose feelings toward quality matched their own. This approach has become common. So, organizations needed some way of ensuring supplier reliability. Larger organizations could follow the example of Ford and give their suppliers the necessary training. Other organizations who would routinely inspect purchases as they were delivered could move these inspections to the suppliers' premises, so that faulty units were not delivered. In many circumstances, however, neither of these options was realistic. It became clear that some form of qualification was needed to show that a supplier could give consistently high quality. This is the purpose of the **ISO 9000** family of standards.

Several countries developed their own quality standards, and these were brought together in the International Standards Organization's (ISO) certification program. Organizations which achieve certain quality standards can apply for ISO 9000 certification. There are actually five separate standards in the ISO 9000 family:

1. ISO 9000 defines quality, describes how an organization can achieve TQM, and gives a series of quality standards an organization might aim for
2. ISO 9001 deals with the whole range of TQM, from initial product design and development through to standards for testing final products
3. ISO 9002 concerns the actual production process and how quality can be documented for ISO certification
4. ISO 9003 deals with final product inspection and testing
5. ISO 9004 states what should be done within the operations to develop and maintain quality

ISO 9000 and 9004 are guides for setting up quality-management programs, while ISO 9001, 9002, and 9003 define quality standards.

ISO certification gives an organization a competitive advantage, as a growing number of organizations, particularly those who already have certification themselves, will only deal with suppliers who have the qualification. In the long term, it will be increasingly difficult for organizations without certification to compete.

In practical terms, an organization needs seven steps to implement TQM.

1. *Get commitment from top management.* As managers have control of the organization, they must be convinced that this is not another management fad but a way of thinking that genuinely improves the performance of their organization.
2. *Find out what customers want.* This goes beyond simply asking for their opinions, and gets them involved in the process, perhaps discussing designs in focus groups.

Case Study

Bell Canada

Bell Canada wants to implement TQM and has been working with the union for the past four years. It would like to improve customer service, corporate efficiency, and job security. A union-management team has been touring various facilities that have implemented TQM. One of these was General Motor's Saturn Plant, which is widely viewed as a showpiece of TQM.

The union representatives said that the outcome of TQM would be the restructuring of jobs so that 1. workers will be given more authority—since they are the ones who are in direct contact with the customers, they know what customers want; 2. managers will be more team leaders or coaches; 3. there will be better cooperation among departments and cross-functional teams.

The union representative said that not all problems have been resolved but the work will start in those areas where there is agreement. The workers' job security will not be affected.

Source: "Bell Canada laying groundwork for TQM," *The Financial Post,* July 5, 1994.

3. *Design products with quality in mind.* The aim is for products which meet or exceed customer expectations.
4. *Design the production process with quality in mind.* Quality must be considered at all points in the process so that high-quality products can be made.
5. *Build teams of empowered employees.* Recognize that employees really are an organization's most valuable asset, and make sure they are trained, motivated, and able to produce high-quality products.
6. *Keep track of results.* Measure progress, benchmark to compare performance with other organizations, and strive for continual improvements.
7. *Extend these ideas to suppliers and distributors.*

These stages may seem straightforward, but they need a lot of effort. Implementing TQM might take five or more years of continuous effort, so it is not surprising that many organizations fail somewhere on this road.

In Summary

Deming suggested 14 points needed for achieving total quality. These emphasize the view that quality is achieved by management using suitable processes. TQM can take a lot of effort to implement, but the rewards will justify this. An increasing number of organizations will deal only with companies who have ISO 9000 qualifications.

Review Questions

1. What is the difference between quality control and quality management?
2. What is meant by "quality at source"?
3. What is a quality circle?
4. What are the benefits of TQM?

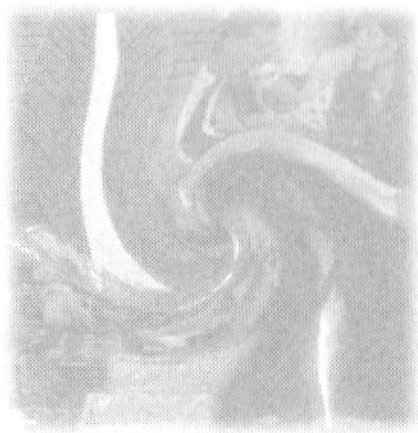

Quality in Services

Many products have some specific features which can be measured to judge their quality. We can measure the weight of a bar of chocolate, or the volume of a bottle of detergent. It is relatively simple to ensure that each unit satisfies this measure of quality, but the overall quality of the product still relies on subjective judgement. How good does the chocolate taste, or how clean does the detergent wash?

ISO 9001: The Ultimate Quality Standard

IPL Inc. is a medium-sized plastic fabricator located in St. Damien, Quebec. It has always emphasized the high quality of its products. It earned Ford's coveted Q-1 quality certification in 1984 and the Quebec Chamber of Commerce's Total Quality Mercury award in 1988. So why did IPL spend two years and $350,000 to get ISO 9001 certification?

IPL saw the ISO certification as a means of telling its customers that it produces consistently high-quality products. After getting ISO 9001 certification, IPL won new contracts with General Motors, Bell Canada, and Bombardier. IPL is in the final stages of implementing the QS9000 Standard. QS9000, based on ISO 9001, is a standard specifically for the automotive industry.

Stephen Van Houten, head of the Canadian Manufacturers Association, said in a recent news conference that Canadian firms that do not adopt ISO 9000 standards will be shut out of big markets in Europe and elsewhere. The Ontario government has set up a new program to help small and mid-size firms adopt ISO 9000 standards.

Sources: John Southerst, "The Gold Standard," The New Industrial Revolution, *Canadian Business,* December 1993.

"Quality Standards Vital, Group Says." *Toronto Star,* September 29, 1994.

Services do not have as many measurable qualities as goods, and judgements about their quality are largely a matter of opinion. It is, for example, difficult to measure the quality of a haircut, but people generally know when they get a bad one. But services do have some measurable features, such as the proportion of trains that arrive on time, or the time it takes to process a mortgage application. The quality of service offered by a bank will include both quantitative measures—such as ratio of loans to deposits, interest rates, charges, total deposits—and features that cannot be measured quantitatively—such as how secure any investment is, how courteously customers are treated, how competently transactions are processed, and how well the offices are decorated. In general, the quality of a service is measured by:

- Its reliability
- Availability
- Competence of servers
- Courtesy of service
- The organization's understanding of customers' needs
- Credibility
- Security
- Comfort of customer surroundings
- Communication

But how can an organization see if it is meeting customer expectations in these areas? The most common way is to question customers after they have received the service, usually with a questionnaire. The questionnaire usually asks for a score between 1 (for excellent) through 3 (for average) to 5 (for very poor) for each feature. The responses show how closely customer expectations are being met and what areas need improvement.

Customers are particularly sensitive to the quality of services. Many services are tailored to individual needs and are expensive—you can, for example, buy a computer relatively inexpensively, but it costs a lot to get someone to repair it. These high costs raise customer expectations—but these expectations are often not met. Many people think that the inability to define a good service is used as an excuse for providing a poor one. Unfortunately, we can examine goods before buying them, but services can only be judged after they have been purchased. To be fair, there are a number of reasons why the quality of services may be lower than goods. These include the following:

- Services are intangible, so it is inherently difficult to define and measure satisfactory quality.
- Services depend on personal contact between customer and supplier, which may involve more disagreements and perceptions of poor service.
- People working in services often see them as short-term jobs. This leads to poor training and lack of dedication.
- Customer expectation is lower for services than for goods (based largely on experience).
- Some products are largely customized to individual requirements, so there is more opportunity for error.

Case Study

Grand & Toy

Grand & Toy (G&T) was founded in 1882 and now runs 121 stores across Canada that sell office supplies, business furniture, and printed forms. It provides a service package that consists of four parts—goods supplied, facilities, explicit services, and implicit services. The quality of service offered by G&T can be judged by its performance in these four areas.

Goods. G&T sell a range of over 3,000 items in each store, but 10,000 items are kept in central stores and can be delivered within a short time. The company only keeps high-quality goods in stock, and low-quality or damaged goods are immediately discarded. If a customer wants a product that is not available, the staff will trace the product and arrange its delivery as soon as possible. This also helps with inventory control, which is the responsibility of all staff.

Facilities. The shops are conveniently located in city centres, often within shopping malls. They are well-designed and laid out in a standard pattern with no annoying lights, sights, or noises. To get customers' attention, three display units are put at the front with special offers, and other shelves are obviously well stocked. The stores are clean, well-carpeted, attractive, and welcoming, with cleaning done continuously by all staff during quiet periods.

Explicit services. The explicit service offered by G&T is the offer for sale of a variety of products. However, the company believes that its staff are the most important part of its service package. All staff have on-the-job training, weekly meetings to discuss products, concerns, and plans, and are encouraged to study product development and sales techniques. G&T aims for a consistent service across its stores, and part of the training describes the service that staff must give to customers. This goes beyond selling, and includes giving information and advice. Staff times are scheduled so that no customer has long to wait for service, even at busy times.

Implicit services. G&T attracts the best employees by offering competitive wages, benefits, opportunities for promotion, and an attractive work place. Because of the good working conditions, the staff are friendly to customers, proud of their company, and enthusiastic about their jobs. Surveys have found a very high level of customer satisfaction with the staff and stores in general.

Implementing Continuous Improvement

Every manager realizes that continuous improvement is a good idea for improving quality and reducing costs. But managers often have difficulties knowing where to start. Many managers say they lack resources to implement continuous improvement. In reality, the most important resource is readily available and obvious. It is the workers who are involved in the operations. To implement continuous improvement, one does not need people with a great deal of engineering experience—a good place to start is to train machine operators to do set-ups. This has many positive effects: it makes their jobs more interesting; it teaches them new skills; they can start with simple tasks, such as cleaning and lubricating equipment, and move on to do preventive maintenance; they become members of quality improvement teams.

Source: "Continuous Improvement in Manufacturing," *Business Quarterly*, Spring, 1994.

Case Study – Rose Cosmetics

Susan Rosenthal, the president of Rose Cosmetics, was concerned about the quality of her company's products, which were mainly hair and deodorant sprays. The company also produced aerosol cans for other companies on a contract basis. Susan recently hired Victor Mathias as a director of quality assurance, with clear instructions to do whatever is necessary to improve the company's quality.

Victor spent much of his first weeks talking to employees and trying to understand the real quality problems at the company. He noticed that the company lacked policies about quality. He also saw that the production department's main objective was to meet output quotas.

He was presented with one quality problem that concerned overpressurized cans. An inspector had tagged some cans that were overfilled and asked the operator to set them aside until he could find the extent of the problem. The line supervisor wanted to keep his production schedule and told the operator to release a little pressure from the cans by squeezing the nozzles. Then they could be shipped out to customers.

The quality inspector, while trying to find the cause of overfilling, found that the pressure gauge on the filling machine was not working properly, the nozzles shipped by the supplier were not up to standard, and the operator was new and not fully trained to work on the line. When the inspector mentioned the incident to Victor, the products were already packed and ready to ship.

Questions

- What are some of the quality problems at the company?
- Do you think the supervisor was right in trying to ship the defective cans?
- What should Victor do to solve the immediate quality problems? What should he do in the long term?

In Summary

Quality of services is more difficult to measure than quality of goods, as it relies more directly on personal opinion. The usual way of measuring quality is to ask customers for their opinion of the service offered.

Review Questions

1. "Measuring the quality of services is totally different from measuring the quality of goods." Do you agree with this? Explain.
2. How might you measure the quality of a hairdresser?

Chapter Review

- Organizations must supply the kind of products that their customers want. As customers are no longer willing to accept poor quality products, organizations must ensure their products are of consistently high quality. This is the function of quality management.
- It is difficult to define quality precisely. A general view states that quality is the ability to meet customer expectations; a more specific view judges quality by a number of factors and viewpoints.
- The total cost of quality is found by adding the prevention, appraisal, internal failure, and external failure costs. These last two can be particularly high, but decline with increasing quality. This suggests that organizations should aim for perfect quality in their products.
- Quality affects every part of an organization. Quality management has, therefore, moved away from its traditional role of quality control—doing the inspections to find defects—to a wider role encompassing all aspects of quality.
- Total Quality Management focuses the effort of the entire organization on quality. It encourages features like quality at source and quality circles. Deming has described a number of features needed by organizations using TQM.
- Assuring the quality of services can be particularly difficult, as it relies on views of customer satisfaction. This is usually measured using questionnaires.

Key Terms

achieved quality *(p. 154)*
designed quality *(p. 154)*
ISO 9000 *(p. 168)*
job enlargement *(p. 164)*
overage *(p. 156)*
quality *(p. 151)*
quality assurance *(p. 162)*
quality at source *(p. 164)*
quality circles *(p. 164)*
quality control *(p. 162)*
quality management *(p. 151, 162)*
quality of after-sales service *(p. 154)*
quality revolution *(p. 151)*
specifications *(p. 154)*
Total Quality Management (TQM) *(p. 163)*
zero defects *(p. 162)*

Problems

6.1 A company has had the following costs (in thousands of dollars) over the past six years. Describe what has been happening.

Year	1	2	3	4	5	6
Sales Value	623	625	626	635	677	810
Costs						
Design	6	8	18	24	37	43
Appraisal	15	17	22	37	45	64
Internal Failure	91	77	32	36	17	10
External Failure	105	101	83	51	27	16

Discussion Questions

6.1 What are the possible consequences of poor quality products? Is it ever really possible to make products of perfect quality?

6.2 How would you explain the shape of the graphs in Figure 6.3?

6.3 Do you think it is reasonable for organizations to aim for perfect quality? Are there some cases where the costs of achieving this are too high?

6.4 Explain, giving suitable examples, the difference between designed quality and achieved quality. Which of these is more important?

6.5 It is generally felt that the quality of services now causes more concerns than the quality of goods. Why do you think this is? What can be done to alter this?

6.6 Describe the development of quality in a specific product you are familiar with, such as computers, education, health, cars, or houses.

6.7 What incentive is there for a monopoly to improve the quality of its products?

Chapter 7

QUALITY CONTROL

Achieving planned quality

Contents

Introduction

Chapter 6 showed how Total Quality Management (TQM) involves the entire organization focusing its efforts on making products of the consistently high quality demanded by customers. TQM is based on the principle that the best way to improve quality is not to inspect products and discard defective ones but to ensure that no defects are made in the first place. But this does not mean that we do not need any inspections. They are still important for giving independent evidence that quality is, in fact, being maintained—that planned quality is being achieved. This process of independent inspection and testing is known as quality control.

Learning Objectives

After reading this chapter you should be able to answer questions such as:

- What is quality control and how does it fit into quality management?
- When are inspections needed?
- Why take samples?
- How large should a sample be?
- When should a batch be rejected?
- How are charts used for process control?
- What are p-charts?
- When are $\bar{X}$ and R charts used?

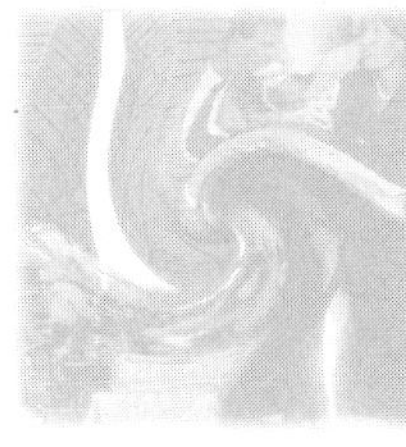

Quality Control

Most quality control processes use inspectors to take random samples of products. The inspectors test these samples to see if the quality reaches designed standards. If the samples reach the quality defined in the specifications, the whole output of the process is assumed to be acceptable. If a sample does not have such high quality, then something is wrong and it must be corrected. Sometimes an occasional unit is defective because of random faults or errors. At other times, the process has gone awry and needs adjusting.

The sampling done in quality control is based on statistical analyses, which concentrate on two types of sampling. Acceptance sampling checks that products are reaching their designed quality, while process control checks that the process is working properly.

Quality control uses a series of inspections and tests to see that planned quality is actually being achieved.

In Summary

Quality management is concerned with all the work needed to make sure products have high quality. An important aspect of this is quality control, which is responsible for sampling, inspecting and testing products.

Review Questions

1. "The best way to ensure the quality of a product is to have a lot of inspections to find faults." Do you agree with this?
2. What is the difference between quality control and quality management?

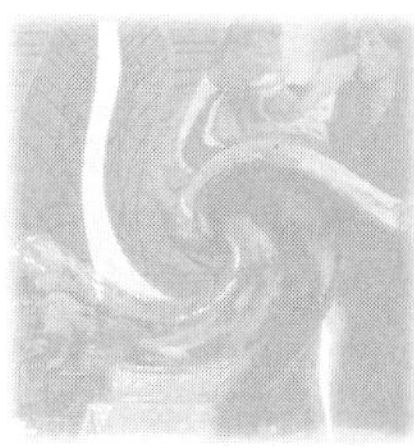

Statistical Quality Control

When to Inspect

In general, there are three types of inspections.

1. *Raw materials inspection*

   This inspects the raw materials and parts received from suppliers. Some organizations try to save money by inspecting only critical raw materials, materials received from a new supplier, or materials sent by a supplier with a poor record of quality. These inspections can be done a) at the suppliers' before delivery of materials; or b) when materials arrive at the organization.

2. *In-process inspection*

   This is done during the process to check the outputs from operations. Since there can be many operations in a process, many organizations try to save money by only inspecting after critical operations. Usually inspections are done a) at regular intervals during the process; b) before high-cost operations; c) before irreversible operations, such as firing pottery; or d) before operations which might hide defects, such as painting.

3. *Final inspection*

   This is the last inspection to ensure that the finished product has high overall quality. It is done a) when production is complete; or b) before the product is shipped to customers.

Organizations have traditionally put most effort into quality control in the latter stages of the production process. Main inspections were often done just before finished products were delivered to customers. But it is clear that the farther a unit goes through the process, the more money is spent on it. It would make more sense, then, to detect faults as early as possible, before any more money is wasted. It would, for example, be cheaper for a baker to find bad eggs when they arrive at the bakery, than to use the eggs and then scrap the cakes they were made with. The major effort in quality control should, clearly, be put at the beginning of the process. This should start by routinely testing materials sent by suppliers, and there is a strong case for conducting inspections before this, within suppliers' own operations. Inspections should then be continued all the way from the production of raw materials through to the completion of the final product and its delivery to customers.

If the main effort of inspection is done early enough, very few defects should be found at later stages. Certainly, by the time the product gets to the customer it should be as nearly free from defects as possible (see Figure 7.1).

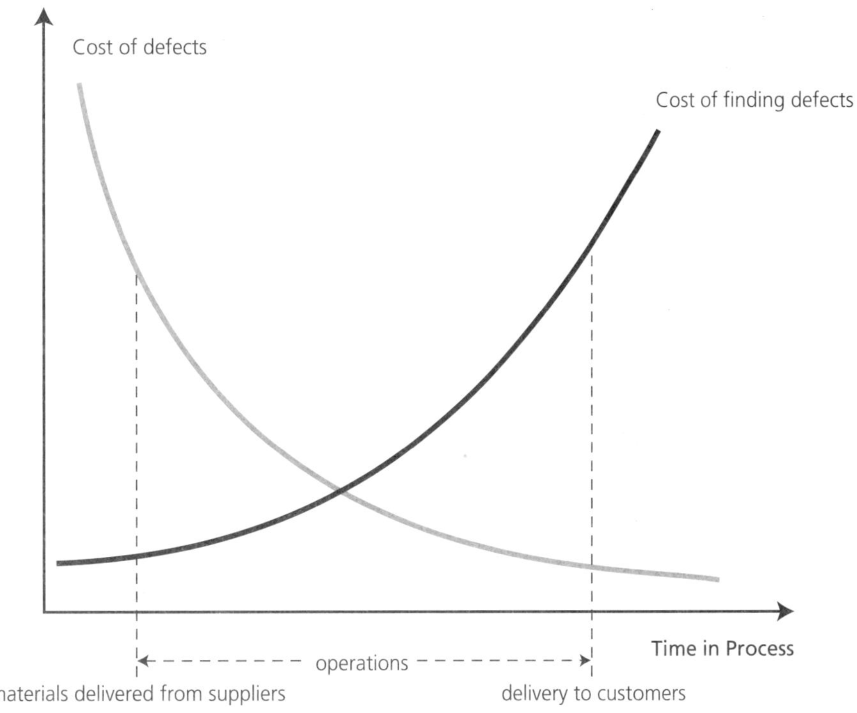

Figure 7.1 Cost of Finding Defects and Cost of Defects

There is always some variation in the output of a process. It is simply not possible to control all the variables in the process. An organization must accept this, and design products and processes which reduce the variation as much as possible. This means that "perfect" quality is defined as having all products within an acceptable range of performance, so their actual performance is close to specifications. Only when the performance goes outside these limits do units become defective.

Typical causes of faults are:

- Human errors in the operations
- Machine faults, e.g., caused by poor maintenance
- Poor materials
- Faults in operations, such as speed or temperature changes
- Changes in the environment, such as humidity or dust
- Errors in monitoring equipment, such as measuring tools

When there are faults, it may not be clear what caused them. Cause-and-effect diagrams and Pareto charts can help determine cause.

Cause-and-Effect Diagrams

A **cause-and-effect diagram** is a simple way of presenting the possible causes of a fault. Figure 7.2 shows a cause-and-effect diagram of a customer complaint reported at a hamburger restaurant. Managers may feel that the fault is caused by the raw materials, the cooking, the staff, or the facilities. Problems with the raw materials may, in turn, be caused by suppliers, storage, or other factors. A cause-and-effect diagram illustrates these relationships as coming from spines, like a fish bone. This is why the diagrams are often called fish-bone diagrams.

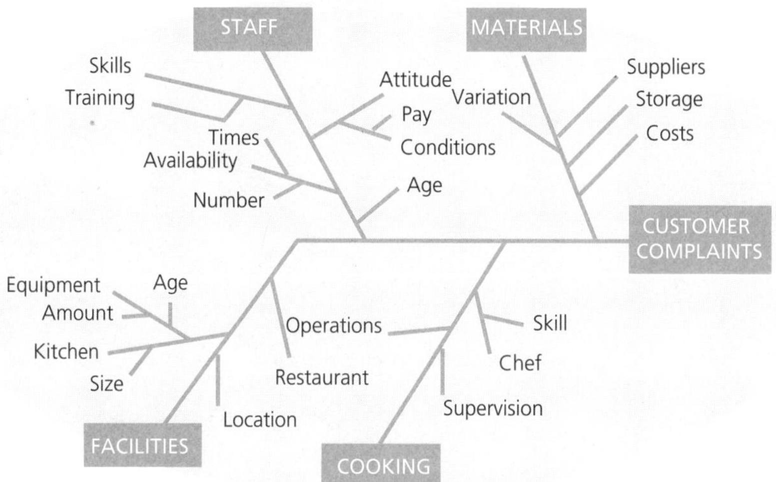

Figure 7.2 A Fish-bone Diagram for Complaints at a Hamburger Restaurant

The main spine of the diagram connects the box describing the defect with the major possible causes. The lines connecting these major causes are then joined by lines describing the possible detailed causes. These diagrams are usually drawn by a team of people who are familiar with the problem, and can agree on the causes; this team is typically a quality circle. When the alternatives have been laid out in this way, possible causes can be investigated and action taken to improve the process.

Pareto Charts

These charts are a variation of the Pareto Principle, an economic theory that holds that 80 percent of the wealth is held by 20 percent of the population. **Pareto charts** are based on the observation that 80 percent of problems come from 20 percent of causes. So the Hudsons Bay Company, for example, might find that 80 percent of customer complaints come from 20 percent of their products. A Pareto chart simply adds the number of defects for each of the possible causes. By listing the defects and their causes, the areas that need special attention are highlighted. If the few main causes of defects are removed, this will have a major effect on quality.

Case Study

Fremantle Restaurant

The Fremantle Restaurant is a well-established business near the centre of Halifax. It serves a lot of business lunches, and there is a healthy demand for its high-quality—and expensive—dinners. Paul Samson is the owner of Fremantle and looks after all the administration personally. Although there are very few complaints from customers, Paul always keeps a record of them. To identify problem areas, Paul collected the following figures over the past three years.

Cause	Number of Complaints	Percentage of Complaints
Faults in the bill	80	51
Slow service	31	20
Smokers seated too near nonsmokers	19	12
Comfort of the chairs	11	7
Wine	5	3
Temperature of the restaurant	5	3
Wait for a table	2	1
Too limited menu	2	1
Food—ingredients used	2	1
Food—cooking	1	1

From this analysis, Paul drew the Pareto Chart shown in Figure 7.3.

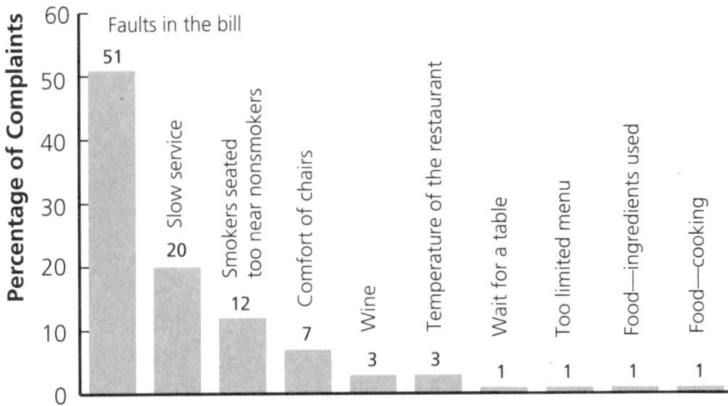

Figure 7.3 Pareto Chart for Fremantle Restaurant

This clearly shows the main causes of faults. There were almost no complaints about the food, so customers were clearly pleased with what they were eating. Over half of the complaints came from faults in the bill. Paul decided that he could correct these by installing a new computerized cash register. Sometimes the service was slow—usually at busy times when one of the staff was away. Paul contacted an agency who could provide someone to wait at the tables on very short notice. These two measures alone would deal with almost three-quarters of complaints. When the restaurant needs refurbishment, Paul decided he would get some more comfortable chairs and would increase the size of the nonsmoking area. This would deal with another 19 percent of complaints. By these simple procedures, Paul had dealt with 90 percent of the complaints.

In Summary

Inspections should be made throughout a process, starting as early as possible. When faults are found, it is a sign that something has gone wrong in the process. Cause-and-effect diagrams and Pareto charts can help identify the source of the problem.

Statistical Sampling

Quality control involves the independent checks that make sure products are achieving their designed quality. These inspections need to be carefully designed to specify the type, size, and frequency of testing, and to define what is acceptable performance. Such procedures are defined by **statistical quality control.**

There are two types of statistical quality control:

1. **Acceptance sampling** takes a sample of units from a batch and tests them for quality. If the sample reaches acceptable standards, it is assumed that the whole batch is good and it is accepted. If the sample has poor quality, it is assumed that the whole batch is unsatisfactory and it is rejected;
2. **Process control** takes samples during the operations to see if the process is working well or if it needs adjusting. If the process is working well, it will be making high-quality products. But if the process needs adjusting, there will be some patterns of defects.

Essentially, acceptance sampling identifies existing defect; process control tries to prevent defects occurring. Although the term "batches" has been used here, this does not mean that quality control is only concerned with batch production; the output during any suitable period may be considered as a batch.

Figure 7.4 Types of Statistical Quality Control

An obvious question is: Why use a sample instead of testing every unit made? There are several reasons for this:

- *Expense.* The cost of testing each unit may be high; and if the proportion of defects found is small, it would be very expensive to test every unit to find the few defects.

  The cost of inspection rises with the number of units tested, but the number of defective units found will also rise. There is a point when the total cost of inspections and missing defective units is minimized, as shown in Figure 7.5.

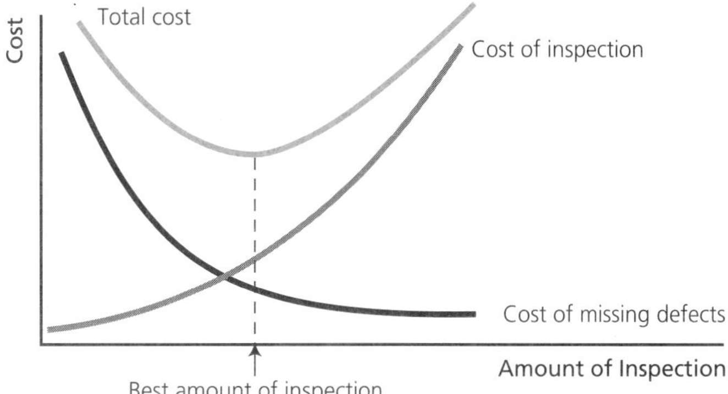

Figure 7.5
Finding the Best Amount of Inspection

- *Time.* Some tests are so long and complicated that they could not be fitted into normal operations—the time taken to test all units would simply be prohibitive.

- *Destructive testing.* Sometimes tests are destructive. If we want to find out how long lightbulbs last, we could test all the units to find the average life, but there would be no bulbs left to sell.

- *Reliability.* Testing all units can give results that are no more reliable than inspecting a sample. No inspection is completely reliable, as inspectors become tired or bored, people simply make mistakes, equipment breaks down, automatic tests develop faults, and subjective judgements are made.

- *Feasibility.* In some cases, there is an infinite number of tests that could be done. To test completely the effectiveness of a medicine, for example, it must be given to everybody who might take it, in all possible circumstance. This would give an almost infinite number of possible combinations.

Unfortunately, sampling is never entirely accurate. For example, suppose a process makes a batch of 1,000 units, and each batch has 100 defective units. If we inspected samples of 100 units, most would have about ten defective ones. But there will be some random variations, and in the extremes we could have a sample with either 100 defective units or none. It is these variations that introduce errors to the sampling. Statistical sampling looks for ways of reducing the effects of these errors, as described in the following sections.

In Summary

Statistical quality control uses tests to see if the performance of products is satisfactory. It generally takes random samples of products to test whether the quality of the output is within acceptable limits. These tests might be for acceptance sampling of products or process control.

Example

Canada Light makes light fixtures on an assembly line. At one point the electric wiring is fitted, and experience suggests that faults are introduced to 4 percent of units. An inspection at this point would find 80 percent of the faults. The test would cost $0.60 to inspect each light and $1 to correct faults. Any fault not found will continue down the line and be detected and corrected later at a cost of $10. Without the inspection after wiring, this latter test costs an extra $0.40 per unit and each fault corrected costs $10. Is it worth inspecting all light fixtures when the wiring is fitted?

Solution

We can answer this by calculating the expected costs of doing a 100 percent inspection and of not doing one.

- With 100 percent inspection after wiring, the expected costs per unit are:
  - — cost of inspection = $0.60
  - — faults detected and corrected after wiring = proportion of faults detected × cost of repair = 0.04 × 0.8 × 1.00 = $0.032
  - — faults not found until later = proportion not detected × cost of later repair = 0.04 × (1-0.8) × 10 = $0.08

  This gives a total of $0.712.
- Without a 100 percent inspection after wiring, the expected costs per unit are:
  - — additional cost of inspection = $0.40
  - — faults detected and corrected = proportion with faults × cost of repair = 0.04 × 10 = $0.40

  This gives a total of $0.80 per unit.

It is clearly cheaper to do a 100 percent inspection when the wire is fitted and correct faults as soon as they are found.

Sampling Distributions

For this section you will need to remember the Normal Distribution (see the summary of this in Appendix A).

Larger samples inevitably have higher costs than smaller ones. However, they generally give more reliable results. The sample should be large enough to be representative of all units in the batch and yet small enough to be reasonable and cost effective.

In statistical terms, all of the production is called the **population**; therefore, samples are taken from a population. Some variation from sample to sample is expected. If, for example, boxes of fruit are packed with an average weight of 25 kg, it would not be surprising to find a series of four samples with average weights of 25.2 kg, 24.8 kg, 25.1 kg, and 25.0 kg. With a longer series of samples, the mean weight would follow a distribution. This is called the **sampling distribution of the mean.**

The sampling distribution of the mean has three useful properties:

1. If the population is Normally distributed, or if a sample of more than about 30 units is used, the sampling distribution of the mean is Normally distributed.
2. The mean of the sampling distribution of the mean equals the mean of the population, μ.
3. The standard deviation of the sampling distribution of the mean is calculated from $\sigma/\sqrt{n}$, where σ is the standard deviation of the population and n is the sample size.

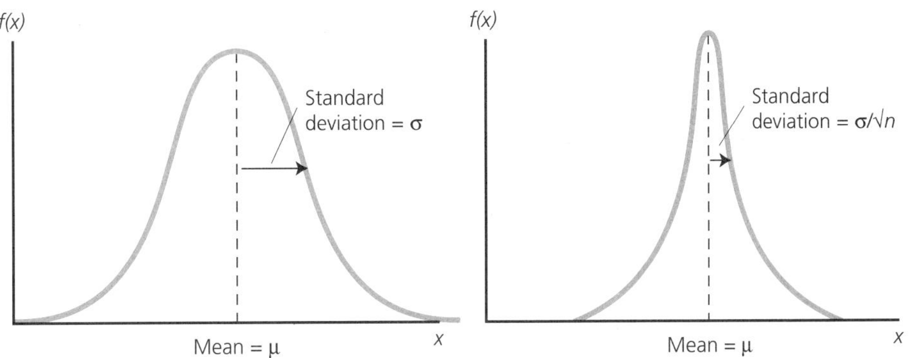

(a) Distribution of population

(b) Sampling distribution of the mean

Figure 7.6 Comparing the Population Distribution with the Sampling Distribution of the Mean

Example

Acme Tubes has a production line that makes tubes with a mean length of 100 cm and a standard deviation of 1 cm. What is the probability that a random sample of 35 tubes has a mean length of less than 99.6 cm?

Solution

With a sample size of 35, the sampling distribution of the mean is Normally distributed with a mean of 100 cm and a standard deviation of $\sigma/\sqrt{n} = 1/\sqrt{35} = 0.169$ cm. So the sampling distribution of the mean is Normally distributed with mean 100 cm and standard deviation 0.169 cm.

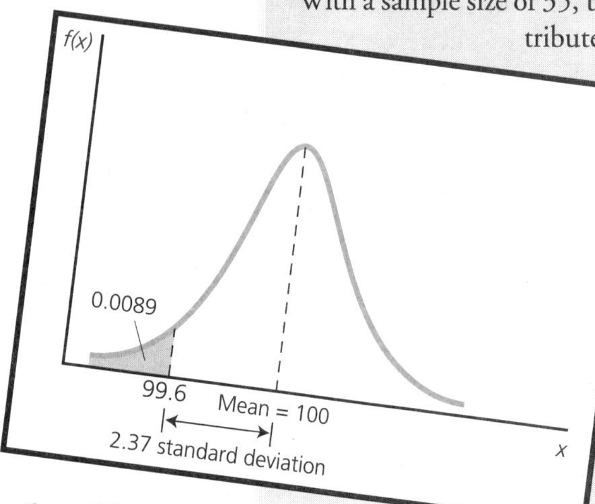

Figure 7.7
Sampling Distribution of the Mean

The number of standard deviations 99.6 cm from the mean is:

$$Z = (100 - 99.6)/0.169 = 2.37$$

Normal tables (in Appendix A) show that this corresponds to a probability of 0.0089, as shown in Figure 7.7.

Hence, 0.89 percent of samples will have a mean length of less than 99.6 cm.

In Summary

When a sample is taken from a population, we can measure some property, like mean weight. With many samples, the mean weights follow a sampling distribution of the mean. For large samples, this is Normally distributed with the same mean as the population and standard deviation of $\sigma/\sqrt{n}$.

Review Questions

1. When should checks for quality be started in a process?
2. What is the difference between acceptance sampling and process control?
3. Why are samples used?
4. Are the results from statistical sampling completely accurate? Why or why not?
5. What is the sampling distribution of the mean?

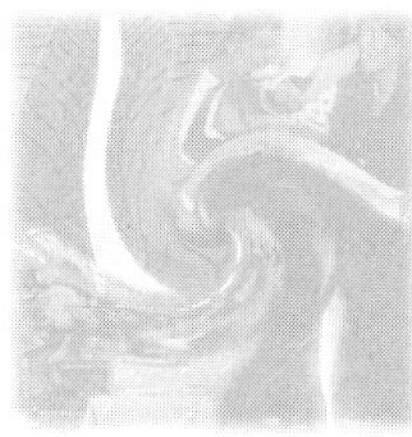

Acceptance Sampling

Sampling by Attributes and Variables

As stated earlier, acceptance sampling takes a sample of units from a batch and checks their quality. Based on the results from this sample, the whole batch is either accepted or rejected.

We can use the results for the sampling distribution of the mean to see if a batch should be rejected. This is called **sampling by variables** and involves measuring some continuous property, such as the weight, length, or power output of an engine. The average performance of the variable is then compared with a specified acceptable level to see if the batch should be accepted.

Remember the standard result given earlier that a population with mean value for the variable μ, and standard deviation σ, has a mean value for samples which is Normally distributed with mean μ and standard deviation of $\sigma/\sqrt{n}$.

> Acceptance sampling tests the quality of a product. It uses a number of units taken from a batch to check that the whole batch meets designed quality.

Example

Batches of raw materials are delivered with a guaranteed average weight of 25 kg per unit and a standard deviation of 1 kg. A sample of 20 units is taken to test each delivery, and the company wants to be 95 percent sure that its rejected batches are in fact defective. What range of mean weights is acceptable in the sample?

Solution

The mean weight of samples will be Normally distributed with mean 25 kg and standard deviation = $\sigma/\sqrt{n} = 1/\sqrt{20} = 0.224$ kg.

95 percent of samples will be within 1.96 standard deviations of the mean, so the range of acceptable sample means is:

$\mu + Z\sigma$	to	$\mu - Z\sigma$
$25 + 1.96 \times 0.224 = 25.44$ kg	to	$25 - 1.96 \times 0.224 = 24.56$ kg

If the company rejects batches with weights outside this range, it will be making the right decision 95 percent of the time.

The alternative to sampling by variables is called **sampling by attributes.** This needs some criterion of quality which defines a unit as either "acceptable" or "defective." Sometimes this criterion is obvious. A lightbulb is "acceptable" if it works and "defective" if it does not work. Sometimes the criterion relies less on measurement than on judgement. A piece of furniture made with polished wood, for example, may be rejected because its finish does not look good to an experienced inspector.

A standard result shows that if the proportion of defective units in a population is p:

- The proportion of defects in samples of size n is Normally distributed
- With mean p
- And standard deviation $\sqrt{p(1 - p)/n}$.

Example

A company has said that it will not accept materials with more than 4 percent of units defective. It receives a large shipment and takes a sample of 200 units. What criterion should the company use to reject a batch if it wants to be 97.5 percent sure of not making a mistake?

Solution

The proportion of defective units, p, is 0.04. In samples of size n, the proportion of defective units is Normally distributed with mean 0.04 and standard deviation = $\sqrt{p(1 - p)/n} = \sqrt{0.04 \times 0.96/200} = 0.014$.

95 percent of sample proportions are within 1.96 standard deviations of the mean, so 95 percent of samples will have proportions of defects between:

$\mu + Z\sigma$ and $\mu - Z\sigma$

$0.04 + 1.96 \times 0.014 = 0.067$ and $0.04 - 1.96 \times 0.014 = 0.013$

With a sample of 200, this means that 95 percent of batches will have between $200 \times 0.067 = 13.4$ and $200 \times 0.013 = 2.6$ defective units. This means that only 2.5 percent of batches will have more than 13.4 defects by chance, so if the company rejects batches with more than this it will be 97.5 percent sure of making the right decision.

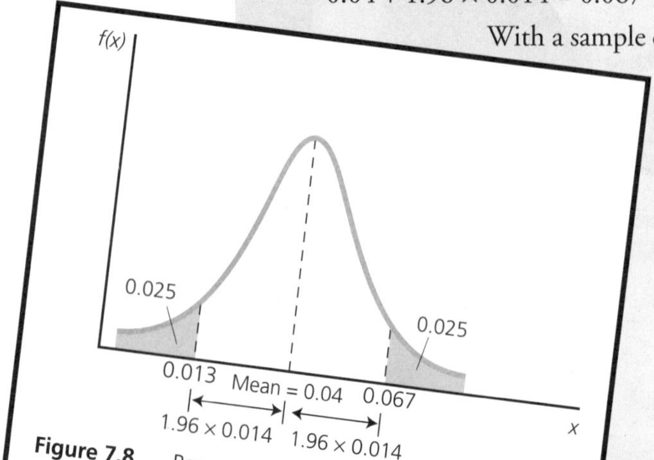

Figure 7.8 Range of Accepting a Batch

In Summary

Acceptance sampling uses a sample of products to see if the whole batch is reaching designed quality. The testing can use either sampling by attribute or sampling by variable

Designing an Acceptance Sampling Plan

The last section showed how a batch can be accepted or rejected based on the quality of a random sample. These results can be formalized in an **acceptance sampling plan.** The general procedure for using such plans is as follows:

- Specify a sample size, n
- Take a random sample of this size from a batch
- Specify a maximum allowed number of defects in the sample, c
- Test the sample to find the numbers that are actually defective
- If the number of defects is greater than the allowed maximum number, c, reject the batch
- If the number of defects is less than the allowed maximum number, c, accept the batch

The value of c, the maximum allowed number of defects in a sample, must be largely a matter of policy —it relies on opinions about the acceptable level of quality. Two important measures related to this decision are the acceptance quality level and the lot tolerance percent defective.

- **Acceptance quality level (AQL)** is the overall percentage of defects considered acceptable to customers. Figures around 2 percent are often quoted for this, but recent views suggest that the real target should be zero.
- **Lot tolerance percent defective (LTPD)** is the upper limit on the percentage of defective units that customers are willing to accept in a single batch. Any batches with more than this percentage of defects are unacceptable.

These definitions are based on the idea that customers are willing to accept an overall level of quality equal to AQL. As customers are demanding higher quality, this figure is inevitably approaching zero. It can be assumed that customers are willing to accept an occasional batch which is as poor as the LTPD, but they will not accept any batches with a higher proportion of defects.

These measures can be used to calculate appropriate values for n, the sample size, and c, the maximum number of allowed defects. In practice, the easiest way of finding these values is to use standard tables. An excerpt from one table is given below.

LTPD/AQL	c	n × AQL
44.89	0	0.05
10.95	1	0.36
6.51	2	0.82
4.89	3	1.37
4.06	4	1.97
3.55	5	2.61
3.21	6	3.29
2.96	7	3.98
2.77	8	4.70
2.62	9	5.43
2.50	10	6.17

To use these tables, calculate the ratio of LTPD/AQL and find the entry in the table which is equal to, or just greater than, this value. The next column shows a value for c, and the implied sample size is given in the last column.

Example

Mendip Minerals buys components in batches from a supplier. It wants the acceptance quality level to be 2 percent defective, and will accept batches with a maximum of 6 percent defective. What are appropriate values of n and c?

Solution

The values given are:

- Acceptance quality level, AQL = 0.02
- Lot tolerance percent defective, LTPD = 0.06

Then LTPD/AQL = 0.06/0.02 = 3. The value in the table which is equal to or slightly larger than this is 3.21, which corresponds to c = 6. The associated value of n × AQL is 3.29. AQL = 0.02, so n × 0.02 = 3.29, or n = 3.29/0.02 = 164.5.

This gives the sampling plan:

- Take samples of 165 units
- If 6 or less units are defective, accept the batch
- If more than 6 units are defective, reject the batch

Computer Example

There are many standard programs for designing acceptance sampling plans. Figure 7.9 shows one view of the last example. Notice that this gives four alternative plans based on slightly different values of variables called ALPHA and BETA. These are defined as:

- α, the **producer's risk,** is the probability of rejecting a good batch
- β, the **consumer's risk,** is the probability of accepting a bad batch

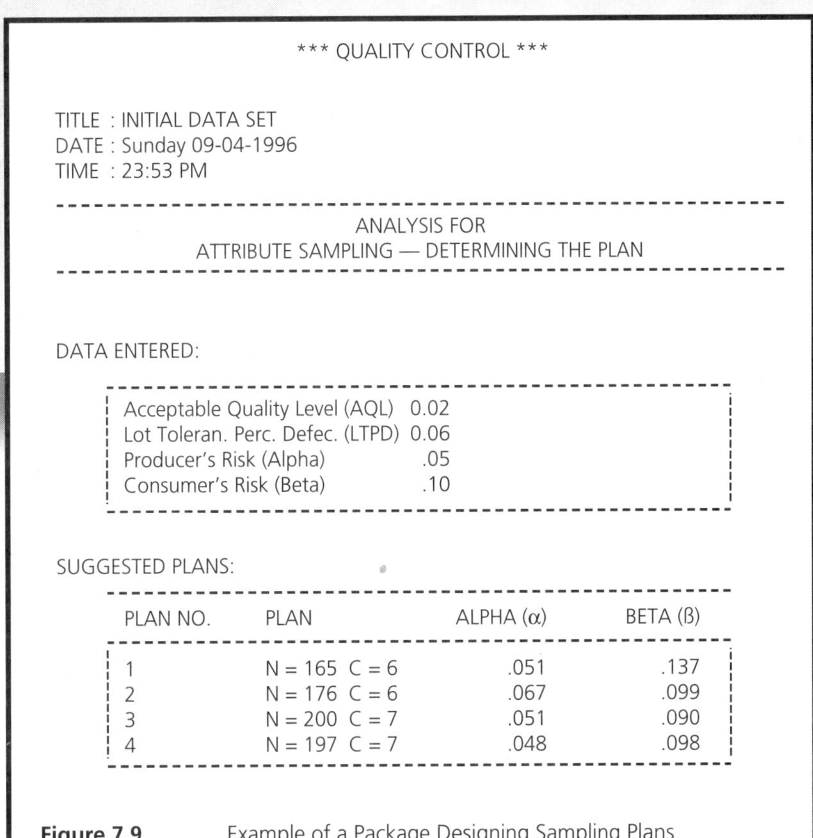
*** QUALITY CONTROL ***

TITLE : INITIAL DATA SET
DATE : Sunday 09-04-1996
TIME : 23:53 PM

ANALYSIS FOR
ATTRIBUTE SAMPLING — DETERMINING THE PLAN

DATA ENTERED:

Acceptable Quality Level (AQL)	0.02
Lot Toleran. Perc. Defec. (LTPD)	0.06
Producer's Risk (Alpha)	.05
Consumer's Risk (Beta)	.10

SUGGESTED PLANS:

PLAN NO.	PLAN	ALPHA (α)	BETA (β)
1	N = 165 C = 6	.051	.137
2	N = 176 C = 6	.067	.099
3	N = 200 C = 7	.051	.090
4	N = 197 C = 7	.048	.098

Figure 7.9 Example of a Package Designing Sampling Plans

In Summary

An acceptance sampling plan needs values for n, the sample size, and c, the maximum number of acceptable defects. Given an acceptance quality level and lot tolerance percent defective, we can use tables to find appropriate values for these.

Case Study

Stroh Brewery Company

This case study shows the amount of effort that is needed to test the quality of even a relatively simple product.

The Stroh Brewery Company of Detroit is a major producer of American beer. One of it plants is the Winston-Salem brewery which occupies over 100,000 square metres and makes almost 200 million gallons of beer a year.

The quality control of beer checks a number of factors ranging from taste to quantity in each can. To do these checks, the Winston-Salem brewery employs 38 people in separate laboratories for microbiology, brewing, and packaging. These people do 1,100 separate tests on each batch of beer. If any problems are found, the quality control department can stop production at any time and investigate the problem.

A typical test in the brewing laboratory checks the number of yeast cells during fermentation. Beer must have a standard 16 million yeast cells (± 2 million) per millilitre. For this test a small sample of beer is taken during fermentation, diluted, and the cells are counted through a microscope.

A typical test in the packaging laboratory checks the amount of air in a beer can. Because air can affect the taste, the company allows a maximum of 1 cc of air in a can. This is checked by testing three cans from the production line five times a shift. If a sample is found with more than 1 cc of air, the entire batch is put in "quarantine" and systematically tested to find the point where the canning goes wrong. This may involve a large number of cans, as each line fills 1,600 cans per minute.

Review Questions

1. What is the difference between sampling by attribute and sampling by variable?
2. What is meant by AQL and LTPD?

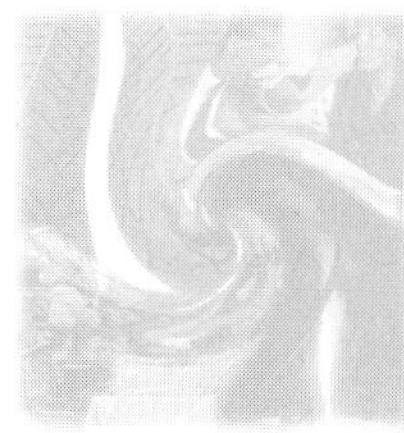

Process Control

Control Charts for Attributes

Acceptance sampling checks the quality of products, while process control checks that the process is working as planned.

A machine never makes two products that are exactly the same. The differences are often obvious. Sometimes products may look similar to the naked eye, but closer inspection will reveal some differences. This is always true regardless of the process—whether it is cutting steel rods, filling bags with potato chips, or serving meals. This variation is caused in two ways.

Firstly, every process has some built-in variation which cannot be eliminated. This is called common variation, which arises from a number of factors, each of which introduces a small, random variation. Even when a machine is operating perfectly, there is some play between various parts of the machine, vibrations, and changes in the environment. These factors will introduce variations in the final product.

Secondly, there are the avoidable or assignable causes. Cutting tools become dull, operators make mistakes, bolts become loose, materials are of poor quality. These factors introduce variations that are not random and that can be avoided.

So there is inevitably some variation in the performance of a process. Process control checks that a process continues to work within acceptable limits by taking samples of products over time to see if there are any noticeable trends. If there is a clear trend, the process might need adjusting. This can be shown most clearly in a **process control chart.**

We will start by describing process control charts for attributes, so we are again considering outcomes which are either acceptable or defective. A process control chart takes a series of samples over time, and plots the proportion of defective units in each sample. This is sometimes called a **p-chart.**

The proportion of defective units in a sample is usually around the mean value of the population. Provided it does not vary far from the mean, the process is said to be *in control.* If there is a trend, the proportion of defects moves away from the mean, and when it reaches some specified limit the process is said to be *out of control.* Then the process needs some adjustment. To see when a process is out of control, we need two control limits: an upper limit (UCL) and a lower limit (LCL). Provided the output remains between these two limits, the process is in control, but if it moves outside the limits, it is out of control (as shown in Figure 7.10).

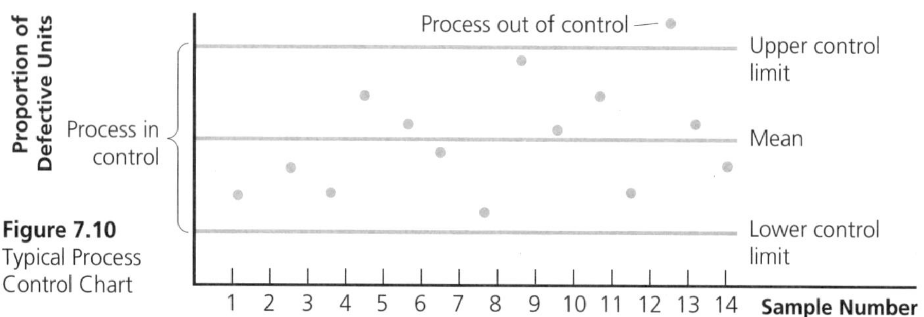

Figure 7.10
Typical Process Control Chart

The important point in process control is to define appropriate limits. This relies on the result stated earlier, that if the proportion of defects in a population is p, the proportion of defective units in a sample of size n is Normally distributed with mean, p, and standard deviation of $\sqrt{p(1 - p)/n}$. This is a standard result which allows us to calculate control limits as:

$$\text{Upper control limit} = \text{UCL} = \mu + Z \times \text{standard deviation}$$

$$\text{Lower control limit} = \text{LCL} = \mu - Z \times \text{standard deviation}$$

Here, Z is the number of standard deviations corresponding to the specified confidence limit. This confidence limit is chosen as part of the designed quality. It gives the proportion of samples that would normally be within a range if the process is in control. Thus, a 95 percent confidence interval (corresponding to $Z = 1.96$) finds the range within which 95 percent of samples lie if the process is in control.

Process control charts will have some observations that lie outside the control limits purely by chance. With a 95 percent confidence interval, random variations will leave 5 percent of samples outside the control limits. This means that every observation outside the control limits should be investigated to see if the process is really out of control or whether it is actually working normally.

The charts can show a number of other patterns that should be investigated. If, for example, there is a trend, even though the process is in control, it is a sign that further investigation is needed. Some patterns that need further investigation include:

- A single reading outside the control limits
- A clear trend
- Several consecutive readings close to a control limit
- Several consecutive readings on the same side of the mean
- A sudden change in apparent mean levels
- Erratic observations

Example

Jane Tanis took a sample of 500 units from the output of a process for each of 30 working days when it was working normally. She recorded the number of defective units each day as follows.

Day	Number of Defects	Day	Number of Defects	Day	Number of Defects
1	70	11	45	21	61
2	48	12	40	22	57
3	66	13	53	23	65
4	55	14	51	24	48
5	50	15	60	25	42
6	42	16	57	26	40
7	64	17	55	27	67
8	47	18	62	28	70
9	51	19	45	29	63
10	68	20	48	30	60

Draw a control chart with 95 percent confidence limits.

Solution

The average proportion of defects is:

$$p = \frac{\text{total number of defects}}{\text{number of observations}} = \frac{1{,}650}{30 \times 500} = 0.11$$

$$\text{standard deviation} = \sqrt{p(1-p)/n} = \sqrt{0.11 \times 0.89/500} = 0.014$$

The 95 percent confidence limits has Z = 1.96, therefore:

$$\text{UCL} = p + Z \times \text{standard deviation} = 0.11 + 1.96 \times 0.014 = 0.137$$

$$\text{LCL} = p - Z \times \text{standard deviation} = 0.11 - 1.96 \times 0.014 = 0.083$$

If the proportion of defects is between 0.083 and 0.137, the process is in control and differences are simply random variations. If the proportion of defects is outside this range, the process is out of control and adjustments are needed. With samples of 500, the process is under control when the number of defects is between 0.083 × 500 = 41.5 and 0.137 × 500 = 68.5.

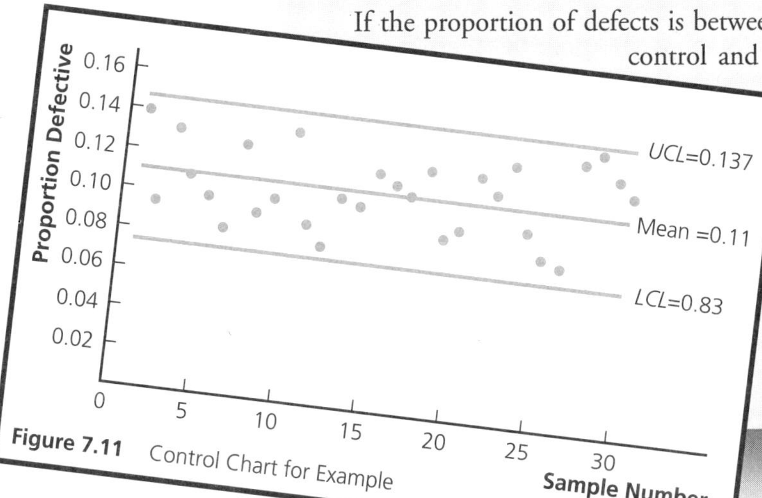

Figure 7.11 Control Chart for Example

Case Study

Making Process Control Work

It is not easy to introduce rigorous quality control to any organization. This is particularly true of statistical process control (SPC). Many suppliers are forced by their customers to adopt SPC. This happens in the automobile industry, for example, where the "Big 3" American car makers (General Motors, Ford, and Chrysler) demand that their suppliers use SPC. The suppliers may not really see the benefits of SPC, and the managers in these companies may not understand SPC, so they will not gain the real benefits of it. "SPC charts and graphs will be no more effective in reducing waste than a stethoscope in curing colds," according to Doug Burn. The real benefit comes when everyone in an organization is fully trained in SPC, can interpret the charts, and can make adjustments to the process.

Canadian Tool and Die in Winnipeg is one company whose management is fully committed to making SPC work. It recently finished a five week in-house training course for its 100 employees. Now the operators are responsible for the quality of what they produce. They take measurements of the parts produced, do the necessary calculations, plot the control charts, and take corrective actions when needed.

Any successful training for SPC must do two things. Firstly, it must overcome the mental blocks that many people have against statistics. Secondly, it must teach the statistical concepts of SPC. The training program should involve all levels of management within the company.

Source: 1. Doug Burn, "SPC Good Science, Bad Religion," *Canadian Machinery and Metalworking,* November 1989.

2. "Quality Is Key to Global Market for Winnipeg Co.", *Canadian Machinery and Metalworking,* November 1991.

3. "Statistical Training for Quality Control," *Canadian Chemical News,* July/August, 1993.

In Summary

Process control charts are used to see if a process is in control, or whether it has gone out of control and needs adjusting. Samples are taken over time, and the results should remain between upper and lower control limits. Some other patterns can also indicate problems over time.

Control Charts for Variables

Control charts can also be used for variable sampling. The approach is essentially the same as described earlier, with upper and lower control limits specified by a number of standard deviations away from the mean. We again use the sampling distribution of the mean which is Normally distributed with mean being the same as the process mean and standard deviation equal to $\sigma/\sqrt{n}$, where σ is the process standard deviation.

The approach used in the example below relies on the mean, μ, and standard deviation, σ, of all the output—that is the population—being known. As sampling removes the need for testing all the output, these values will probably not be known. There is no way of solving this problem, but one way of avoiding it is to add another check for the range of observations. This gives two charts, which are called $\bar{X}$ and

Example

Allstate Food Processors make packaged food with a mean weight of 1 kg and standard deviation of 0.05 kg. Samples of 10 are taken to make sure the process is still in control. Find the control limits that include 99 percent of sample means if the process is working normally.

Solution

The means of samples will be Normally distributed with

$$\text{Mean} = 1 \text{ kg and standard deviation} = \sigma/\sqrt{n} = 0.05/\sqrt{10}$$

A confidence interval of 99 percent corresponds to 2.58 standard deviation. Then:

$$\text{LCL} = \mu - Z \times \sigma/\sqrt{n} = 1 - 2.58 \times 0.05/\sqrt{10} = 0.959$$

$$\text{UCL} = \mu + Z \times \sigma/\sqrt{n} = 1 + 2.58 \times 0.05/\sqrt{10} = 1.041$$

Provided that the mean of samples stays within this range, the process is in control. If it moves outside the range, it is out of control and needs adjusting.

R charts. Then plot:

1. The series of sample means on an $\bar{X}$ chart
2. The series of sample ranges on an R chart

The range is simply the difference between the largest observation and the smallest in a sample.

$\bar{X}$ and R charts are drawn in exactly the same way as p-charts for attributes. To help find the control limits, we will also define:

$\bar{X}$ = mean value of a sample
$\bar{X}_o$ = overall mean of the sample means
R = range of a sample
R_o = overall mean of the sample ranges

With m samples $\bar{X}_o$ and R_o are found from:

$$\bar{X}_o = \frac{\sum^{m} \bar{X}}{m} \qquad R_o = \frac{\sum^{m} R}{m}$$

The upper and lower control limits must now be found. These could be calculated, but it is easier to use standard tables. Then the control limits are found as follows:

For means: $LCL = X_o - A \times R_o$ $\quad UCL = X_o + A \times R_o$

For ranges: $LCL = D_1 \times R_o$ $\quad UCL = D_2 + R_o$

Values for A, D_1 and D_2, are given in the tables, an extract of which is shown below.

Sample Size	Factor for $\bar{X}$ Chart A	Factors for R Chart D_1	D_2
2	1.88	0	3.27
3	1.02	0	2.57
4	0.73	0	2.28
5	0.58	0	2.11
6	0.48	0	2.00
7	0.42	0.08	1.92
8	0.37	0.14	1.86
9	0.34	0.18	1.82
10	0.31	0.22	1.78
12	0.27	0.28	1.72
15	0.22	0.35	1.65
17	0.20	0.38	1.62
20	0.18	0.41	1.59
25	0.15	0.50	1.54

These values relate to 99.7 percent confidence intervals and are sometimes known as three-sigma control limit factors.

Example

Samples of ten units have been taken from a process in each of the past 20 days. Each unit in the sample was weighed. The mean weight in each sample and the range were as follows.

Sample	Mean	Range	Sample	Mean	Range
1	12.2	4.2	11	12.5	3.3
2	13.1	4.6	12	12.3	4.0
3	12.5	3.0	13	12.5	2.9
4	13.3	5.1	14	12.6	2.7
5	12.7	2.9	15	12.8	3.9
6	12.6	3.1	16	12.1	4.2
7	12.5	3.2	17	13.2	4.8
8	13.0	4.6	18	13.0	4.6
9	12.2	4.3	19	13.2	5.0
10	12.0	5.0	20	12.6	3.8

Draw $\overline{X}$ and R charts for the process.

Solution

The overall mean values for weight and ranges are:

$\overline{X}_o = 252.9/20 = 12.65$ and $R_o = 79.2/20 = 3.96$

Then look up the factors for samples of size 10 and find:

$A = 0.31$ $D_1 = 0.22$ and $D_2 = 1.78$

Then for means:

$$LCL = \overline{X}_o - A \times R_o = 12.65 - 0.31 \times 3.96 = 11.42$$
$$UCL = \overline{X}_o + A \times R_o = 12.65 + 0.31 \times 3.96 = 13.88$$

and for ranges:

$$LCL = D_1 \times R_o = 0.22 \times 3.96 = 0.87$$
$$UCL = D_2 \times R_o = 1.78 \times 3.96 = 7.08$$

Provided future samples stay within these ranges, the process is in control. If future samples move outside these ranges, the process is out of control.

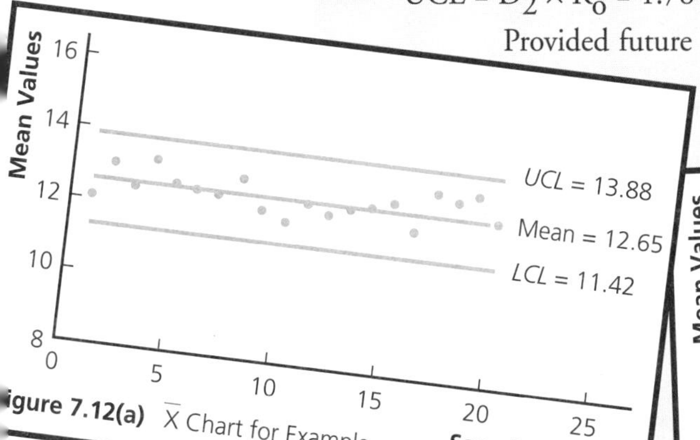

Figure 7.12(a) $\overline{X}$ Chart for Example

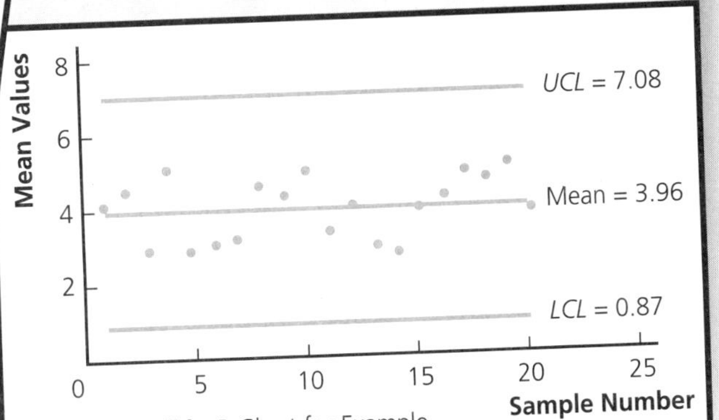

Figure 7.12(b) R Chart for Example

Computer Example

The following printout shows the result from using a standard package for drawing process control charts. As you can see, this gives an analysis for process control, and saves a lot of calculation.

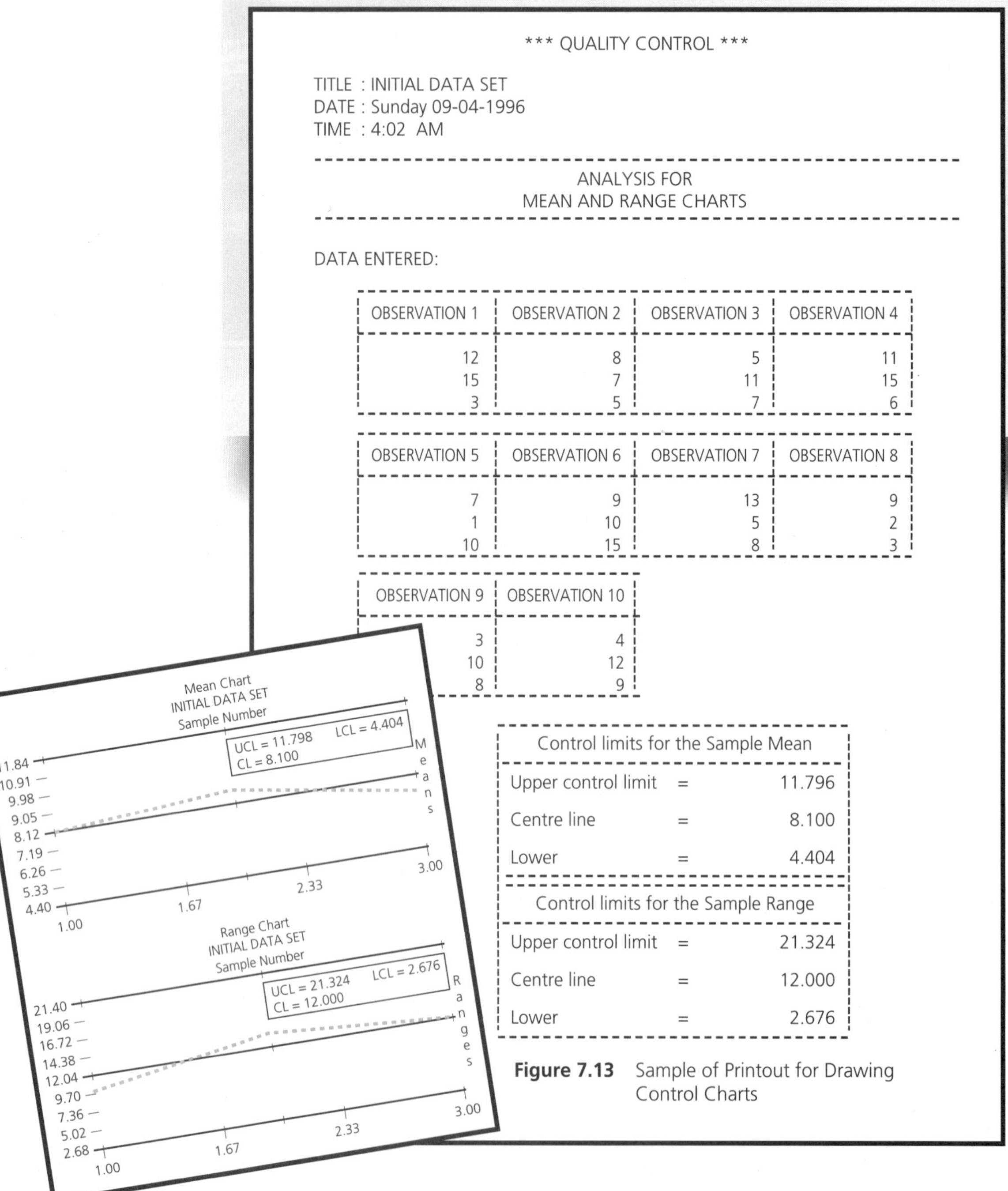

*** QUALITY CONTROL ***

TITLE : INITIAL DATA SET
DATE : Sunday 09-04-1996
TIME : 4:02 AM

ANALYSIS FOR
MEAN AND RANGE CHARTS

DATA ENTERED:

OBSERVATION 1	OBSERVATION 2	OBSERVATION 3	OBSERVATION 4
12	8	5	11
15	7	11	15
3	5	7	6

OBSERVATION 5	OBSERVATION 6	OBSERVATION 7	OBSERVATION 8
7	9	13	9
1	10	5	2
10	15	8	3

OBSERVATION 9	OBSERVATION 10
3	4
10	12
8	9

Control limits for the Sample Mean		
Upper control limit	=	11.796
Centre line	=	8.100
Lower	=	4.404

Control limits for the Sample Range		
Upper control limit	=	21.324
Centre line	=	12.000
Lower	=	2.676

Figure 7.13 Sample of Printout for Drawing Control Charts

In Summary

Control charts for variables are similar in principle to those for attributes. But the mean and standard deviation of the population variable are not generally known. So we plot separate charts for the sample means—giving $\bar{X}$ charts—and ranges—giving R charts.

Review Questions

1. With p-charts, would a larger confidence interval be nearer or farther away from the mean than a smaller one?
2. What does it mean if an observation is outside the control limits in a process control chart?
3. What patterns should be investigated in a control chart?
4. Why are R charts used?

Case Study – The Problem of Underfilled Bags

The National Flour Mill is a wheat and corn flour producer. It has two lines which fill bags with flour. Line number 1 fills 25-kg and 50-kg bags. These are sold to industrial and commercial customers such as bakeries, restaurants, and cafeterias.

The company was recently sent a couple of complaints from customers. These both said they had bought bags of flour that were underweight. One bakery had bought 100 25-kg bags. A sample of 10 bags weighed only 24.55 kg, whereas the sample should normally weigh between 24.8 and 25.2 kg. A similar problem was also noticed by another customer who had bought a shipment from the same batch.

Ken Lam, the quality control manager at National, asked the inspector about the checks on the line. The inspector told him that samples were taken at the beginning of a run to adjust the machine. Once the operator feels that the machine is filling bags properly, no more samples are taken. Visual checks are done occasionally during the run to check seams and stitching on the bags. If the operator thinks that bags are not being filled properly, he would take samples to check their weights.

Ken could easily see the weakness of the quality control procedure. He decided to develop and implement a better quality control procedure for the line.

Questions

- Why did Ken think that the current quality control procedure was inadequate?
- What kind of statistical process control would you implement on the line?
- How should Ken go about implementing statistical process control?

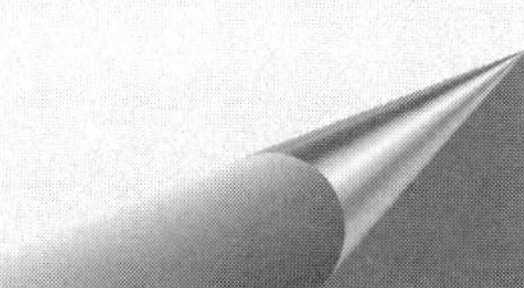

Chapter Review

- Quality control is an important part of the broader quality management function. It is concerned with the sampling, inspection, and testing needed to make sure planned quality is actually being achieved.
- These inspections are usually based on random samples which try to find the characteristics of a whole population by looking at a sample. Such inspections and testing should be started early in the process, preferably at the suppliers.
- Statistical quality control uses samples to test either the quality of products—in acceptance sampling—or the performance of the process—in process control.
- In acceptance sampling, statistical quality control finds the sample size and the maximum acceptable number of defects in the sample. Tables of appropriate values can be used, based on acceptable quality level and lot tolerance percent defective.
- The other purpose of sampling is process control. The most effective way of doing this uses process control charts. These plot the results from a series of samples taken over time. The process is in control when the output remains between two control limits.
- p-charts plot the progress of attributes, while variables can be checked using $\bar{X}$ and R charts.

Key Terms

acceptance quality level (AQL) *(p.191)*
acceptance sampling *(p.184)*
acceptance sampling plan *(p.191)*
cause-and-effect diagram *(p.182)*
consumer's risk *(p.193)*
lot tolerance percent defective (LTPD) *(p.191)*
Pareto charts *(p.182)*
p-chart *(p.195)*
population *(p.187)*
process control *(p.184)*
process control chart *(p.195)*
producer's risk *(p.193)*
quality control *(p.179)*
R chart *(p.200)*
sampling by attributes *(p.190)*
sampling by variables *(p.189)*
sampling distribution of the mean *(p.187)*
statistical quality control *(p.184)*
$\bar{X}$ chart *(p.199)*

Problems

7.1 A part is made on an assembly line. At one point, an average of 2 percent of units are defective. It costs \$1.00 to inspect each unit at this point, and the inspection would only find 70 percent of faults. If the faults are left, all parts will be found and corrected farther down the line at a cost of \$8. Would it be worthwhile inspecting all units at this point in the line?

7.2 A machine produces parts with a standard deviation in length of 2 cm. A sample of 40 units is taken and found to have a mean length of 148.7 cm. What are the 95 percent and 99 percent confidence intervals for the true length of the parts?

7.3 Soft drinks are put into cans which hold a nominal 200 mL, but the filling machines introduce a standard deviation of 10 mL. The cans are put into cartons of 25 and exported to a market which requires the mean weight of cartons to be at least the quantity specified by the manufacturer. To make sure this happens, the canner set the machines to fill cans to 205 mL. What is the probability that a carton chosen at random will not pass the quantity test?

7.4 A company says that its suppliers should send at most 2 percent defective units. It receives a large shipment and takes a sample of 100 units. The company wants to be 95 percent sure that a rejected batch is really unsatisfactory. What criteria should it use to reject a batch?

7.5 Batches of raw materials are delivered with a guaranteed average length of 100 cm and standard deviation of 1 cm. A sample of 100 units is taken to test each delivery, and the company want to be 95 percent sure that its rejected batches are in fact defective. What range of mean weights is acceptable in the sample?

7.6 A component is made in batches and transferred from one part of a plant to another. When it is made, an acceptance quality level of 1 percent of defective is used, but transferred batches are allowed to have a maximum of 4 percent defective. What would be a suitable sampling plan for the component?

7.7 A process makes products with a mean length of 75.42 cm and standard deviation of 2.01 cm. Samples of eight are taken to make sure the process is still in control. Find the control limits which will include 99 percent of sample means if the process is working normally.

7.8 Thirty samples of size 15 have been taken from a process. The average sample range for the 30 samples is 1.025 kg and the average mean is 19.872 kg. Draw $\overline{X}$ and R control charts for the process.

Discussion Questions

7.1 Discuss the differences between quality management and quality control.

7.2 How do you think the role of quality control has changed in recent years?

7.3 How does acceptance sampling differ from process control?

7.4 What are the advantages and problems of using samples rather than complete inspections?

7.5 Is it true that statistical sampling assumes that a certain number of units are defective, and provided that there are not too many defects in a particular batch, the operations are said to be satisfactory?

7.6 What is the purpose of control charts? Are there other means of achieving the same results?

7.7 Discuss some applications of statistical sampling in service industries.

Chapter 8
FORECASTING DEMAND

How much of a product should we make?

Contents

Introduction

Forecasts are needed for almost every decision in an organization. Most decisions affect the future of an organization, and should be based on circumstances not as they are now but as they will be when the decision comes into effect. For example, when Boeing decides how many airplanes to build, it does not simply make enough planes to meet current demand, but enough to meet forecast demand when the airplanes are ready for sale. In the same way, many other decisions must be based on forecasts of future circumstances. Forecasting is therefore one of the most important functions in an organization.

There are several ways of making forecasts. Some of these rely on judgement, or expert opinion, while others use quantitative analyses. Quantitative methods are generally more reliable than qualitative or judgemental methods.

This chapter describes a number of methods for quantitative forecasts. These methods are either causal—which look for cause-and-effect relationships—or projective—which extend past demand patterns into the future.

Learning Objectives

After reading this chapter you should be able to answer questions such as:

- Why is forecasting important?
- What types of forecasting method are used?
- What is judgemental forecasting?
- What are time series?
- What are causal forecasts?
- How can linear regression be used for forecasting?
- What is projective forecasting?
- How can one forecast using actual averages, moving averages, and exponential smoothing?

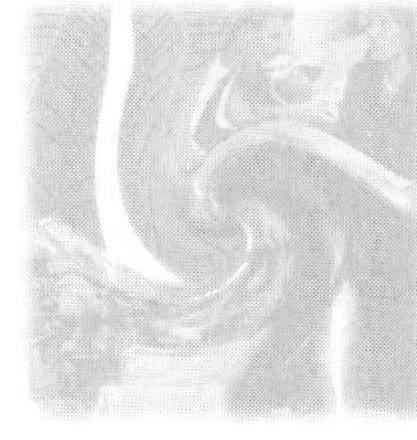

Importance of Forecasting

Forecasting is one of the most important functions in an organization. As it is so important, forecasting should be used throughout an organization. It should certainly not be seen as the work of an isolated group of specialists. Neither should forecasting be viewed as a job which is done once and finished. Forecasting is continuous; there is no point at which it is ever finished. Over time, forecasts are compared with actual demand, updates made, plans modified, decisions revised, and so on. This process is shown in Figure 8.1.

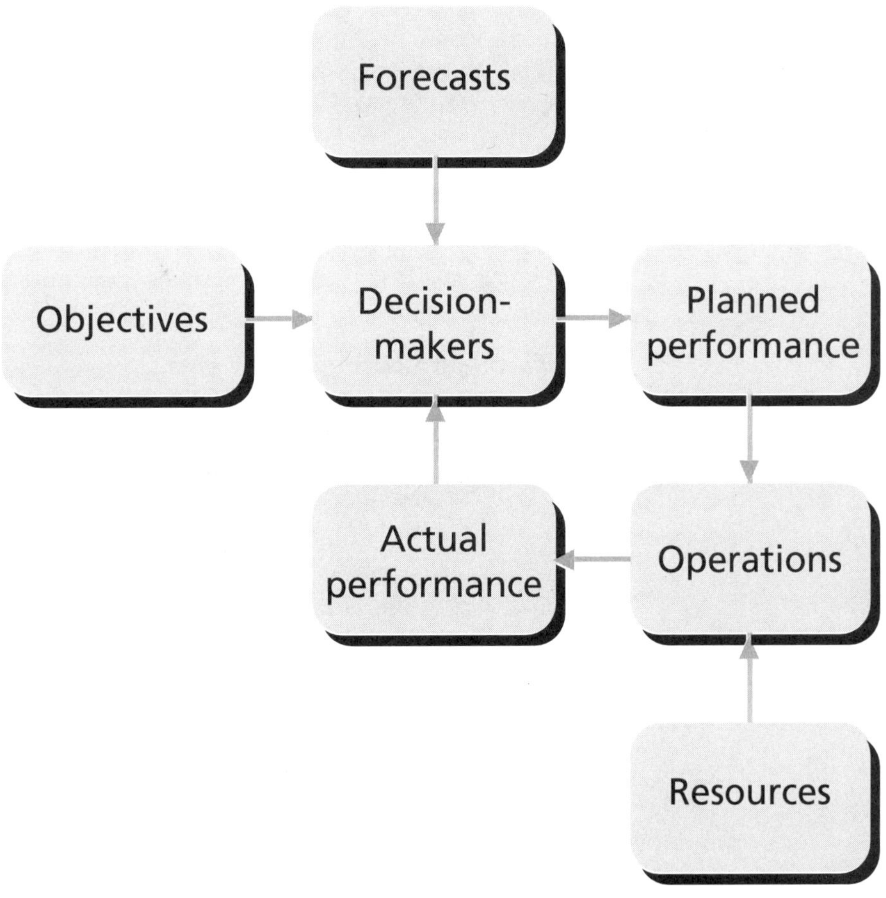

Figure 8.1 The Place of Forecasting in Decisions

Although we talk about "demand" being forecast, this is just for convenience. Many things can be forecast, and "demand" is just a useful general term.

Case Study – Jim Brown of Midway Construction

Jim Brown was in a bad mood. Business had been slack for the past few months, so he had too many workers on his construction sites. He had just fired 25 people. Unless things picked up, he would have to fire another 40 people before the end of the month.

"This is crazy!" Jim thought. "This is the sixth time in two years that I've laid off good, reliable workers. What usually happens next is that business picks up. Then I desperately look for people with the right skills that I can hire. If I could forecast the amount of work some time in advance, I could smooth the workload and not have to go through these peaks and troughs."

Jim is right. If he did some forecasting, he could plan his workload properly. He could smooth the work and avoid his current "hire and fire" approach.

Question

- What benefits could Jim derive from forecasting his future workload?

Forecasting methods can be classified in several ways. The first concerns the time horizon covered by forecasts.

- *Long-term* forecasts look ahead several years—the time typically needed to build a new facility, for example.
- *Medium-term* forecasts look ahead between three months and two years—the time typically needed to replace an old product with a new one. They are also used for buying materials with long lead times.
- *Short-term* forecasts cover a few week—describing the continuing demand for a product. They are used for such things as purchasing raw materials and scheduling work.

The time horizon affects the choice of forecasting method for several reasons. There may be no historical data of the right type, or the data may not be relevant. The time horizon also sets the time available to make the forecast, the time involved, how serious are the consequences of errors, and so on.

There is a clear link here with the different levels of decision making described in Chapter 2. Essentially, long-term forecasts are concerned with strategic decisions, medium-term forecasts with tactical decisions, and short-term forecasts with operational decisions.

As stated, forecasting methods can also be described as either **qualitative** or **quantitative**, as shown in Figure 8.2.

If an organization is already making a product, it will probably have records of past demand and know the factors that affect this demand. Then the organization can use a quantitative method for forecasting future demand. There are two alternatives for this:

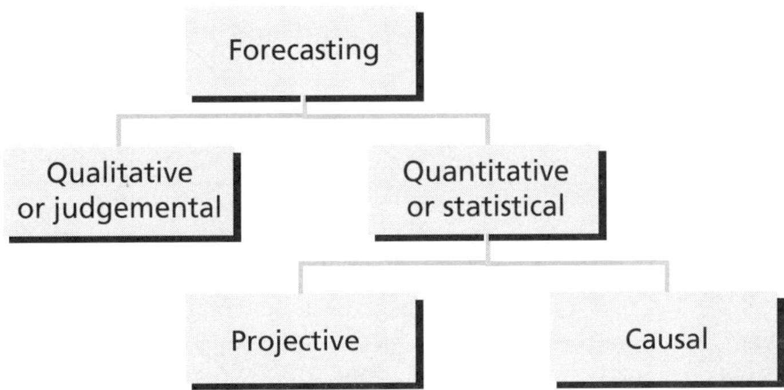

Figure 8.2 Qualitative and Quantitative Forecasting Methods

1. **Projective forecasts** look at the pattern of past demand and extend this into the future. If demand in the past four weeks has been 10, 20, 30, and 40 units, it seems reasonable to project this pattern and suggest that demand in the next week will be around 50.
2. **Causal forecasts** consider the effects of outside influences on demand. The productivity of a factory might depend on the bonus rates paid to employees. Then it would be more reliable to use the current bonus rate to forecast productivity than to project past figures.

Both of these approaches need accurate, numerical data. Suppose, though, that a company is developing an entirely new product. There are obviously no past demand figures that can be projected forward, and the factors that affect demand are not known. There is no numerical data, so a qualitative method must be used. This method relies on opinions, views, and subjective assessments.

This classification of methods does not mean that each must be used in isolation. Managers should look at all the available information before making the decisions they feel are best. This means that any forecasts should be looked at and discussed before the results are used.

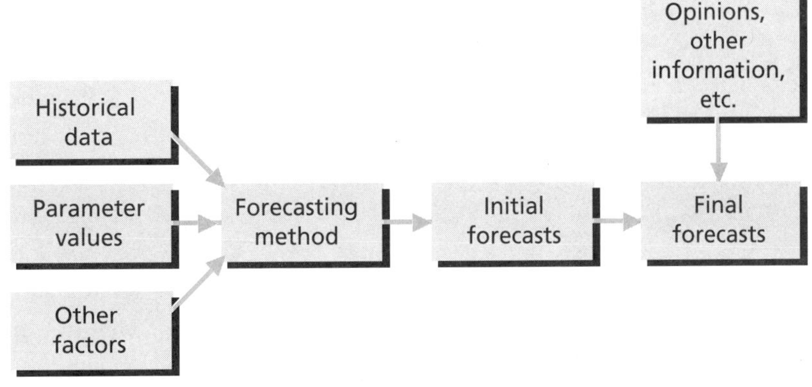

Figure 8.3 Use of Managers' Views to Update Forecasts

Case Study

Disneyland Paris

Disneyland Paris is a major theme park outside Paris. In its early years, this park had continuous financial problems, and faced closure in March 1994. At this point, its owners, 61 bankers, and other investors agreed to a rescue package valued at $3.5 billion.

The basic problem was that Disneyland Paris's income was not meeting its costs. A number of changes were made with the aim of attracting more visitors. These changes included cutting prices in the park; reducing hotel costs; seasonal pricing in the fall and winter when only 30 percent of visitors came; special deals for pensioners, school groups, and "kids-free" packages; more emphasis on short-term packages; and more promotion in Britain. Several other measures were agreed with Disney Enterprises, who own 49 percent of Disneyland Paris. These included $300 million of extra credit; selling $400 million of assets to Disney who leased them back at favourable terms; waiving of royalties on entry fees, food, and merchandise; and suspending management fees. Other plans included greater cost control, a new shopping mall, a multiplex cinema, new restaurants, more convention facilities, a high-speed rail link, and improved access. These measures aimed to make the park financially secure by 1997.

This rescue package was needed because of errors in forecasts. In 1993, Disneyland Paris attracted 9.8 million visitors. Despite the considerable effort put into forecasting demand before the park was opened, this was 13 percent fewer than expected. At the same time, each visitor spent at least 10 percent less than forecast. The result was an annual loss of $1.5 billion, which grew worse when 1994 saw less than 9 million visitors.

The errors in forecasts were largely the result of transferring experiences within the U.S.A. to a European setting. The operators clearly had no relevant European data to work with, so they adopted data from the U.S.A.—and underestimated the differences.

In Summary

Forecasting is needed for almost every decision. It is an important function in every organization. There are many methods of forecasting. A useful classification of these considers judgemental, causal, and projective forecasts. None of these is best in all circumstances.

Review Questions

1. Why is forecasting used in operations management?
2. "Forecasting is a specialized function which uses mathematical techniques to project historical data." Do you think this is true? Explain.
3. List three fundamentally different approaches to forecasting.

Judgemental Forecasting

Judgemental forecasting uses subjective assessments, often based on the opinions of experts. Judgemental forecasts are sometimes called qualitative or subjective forecasts.

Suppose a company is about to market an entirely new product, or a medical team is considering a new type of organ transplant, or a board of directors is considering plans for 25 years in the future. None of these has any historical data that can be used for a quantitative forecast. Sometimes there is a complete absence of data, and at other times the available data is unreliable or irrelevant to the future. As quantitative forecasts cannot be used, a judgemental method is the only alternative. Five widely used judgemental methods are:

- Personal insight
- Panel consensus
- Market surveys
- Historical analogy
- The Delphi method

Personal Insight

This method uses a single expert who is familiar with the situation to produce a forecast based on his or her own judgement. This is the most widely used forecasting method, and is the one that managers should try to avoid. It relies entirely on one person's judgement (including his or her opinions, prejudices, and biases). It can give good forecasts, but often gives bad ones, and there are countless examples of experts being totally wrong. The major weakness of the method is its unreliability. Comparisons of forecasting methods clearly show that someone who is familiar with a situation, using experience and subjective opinions to forecast, will produce *worse* forecasts than someone who knows nothing about the situation but uses a more formal method.

Panel Consensus

A single expert can easily make a mistake, but grouping together several experts and allowing them to talk freely should lead to a consensus that is more reliable. If there is no secrecy and if the panel is encouraged to talk openly, a genuine consensus may be found. However, there can be difficulties in combining the views of different experts when a consensus cannot be found.

Although it is more reliable than one person's insight, panel consensus still has the major weakness that all experts can make mistakes. There are also problems of group work, where "he who shouts loudest gets his way," everyone tries to please the boss, and some people do not speak well in groups. Overall, panel consensus is an improvement on personal insight, but results from either method should be viewed with caution.

Market Surveys

Sometimes, even groups of experts do not have sufficient knowledge to make a reasonable forecast. This happens, for example, with the planned launch of a new product. Experts may offer their views, but you can get more useful information by talking to potential customers.

Market surveys can give useful information, but they tend to be expensive and take a long time to organize. They can also have errors as they rely on:

- A sample of customers who accurately represent the whole population
- Useful, unbiased questions
- Fair and honest answers to questions
- Reliable analyses of the replies
- Valid conclusions drawn from the analyses

Historical Analogy

Chapter 3 described how the life cycle of a product follows a characteristic pattern with introduction, growth, maturity, decline, and withdrawal. If a new product is being introduced, it may be possible to find a similar product which was launched recently, and assume that demand for the new product will follow the same pattern. If, for example, a publisher is producing a new book, it could forecast likely demand from the actual demand for the last, similar book it published

Historical analogy can only be used if there is a similar product which was introduced earlier. In practice, it is often difficult to find products that are similar enough, and to fit the characteristic life-cycle curve.

The Delphi Method

The **Delphi Method** is the most formal of the judgemental methods and has a well-defined procedure. A number of experts are mailed questionnaires, the replies from these questionnaires are analyzed, and summaries are passed back to the experts. Each expert is then asked to reconsider his or her original reply in the light of the summarized replies from others. Each reply is anonymous so that the status of respondents does not influence people, and there is no pressure of face-to-face talks. This process of modifying replies in the light of responses made by the rest of the group is repeated several times—usually between three and six. By this time, the range of opinions should be narrow enough to help with decisions.

We can illustrate this procedure with an example from offshore oil fields. A company may want to know when underwater inspections of platforms will be done entirely by robots rather than divers. A number of experts are contacted to start the Delphi forecast. These experts come from various backgrounds, including divers, technical staff from oil companies, ships' captains, maintenance engineers, and robot designers. The problem is explained, and each of the experts is asked when he or she thinks robots will replace divers. The initial returns probably give a wide range of dates from, say, 1998 to 2050. These are summarized and passed back to the experts. Each person is now asked if he or she would like to change his or her answer in the light of other replies. After repeating this procedure several times, views might converge so that 80 percent of replies suggest a date between 2005 and 2015, and this is close enough to help the company with planning.

Comparison of Judgemental Forecasts

Each of these judgemental methods is best in different circumstances. If a quick reply is needed, personal insight is the fastest and cheapest method. If reliable forecasts are needed, it might be worth organizing a market survey or Delphi method. A general comparison of methods is shown in Table 8.1 on page 216.

Table 8.1 *Comparison of Forecasting Methods*

Method	Accuracy in Term: Short	Medium	Long	Cost
Personal Insight	Poor	Poor	Poor	Low
Panel Consensus	Poor to fair	Poor to fair	Poor	Low
Market Survey	Very good	Good	Fair	High
Historical Analogy	Poor	Fair to good	Fair to good	Medium
Delphi Method	Fair to very good	Fair to very good	Fair to very good	Medium to high

In Summary

Judgemental forecasts rely on subjective views and opinions. They are typically used when there are no relevant historical data. Five widely used methods are personal insight, panel consensus, market surveys, historical analogy, and the Delphi method.

Review Questions

1. What are "judgemental forecasts"?
2. List five types of judgemental forecast.
3. What are the main problems with judgemental forecasts?

Causal Forecasting

Time Series

Much data occur as **time series,** which are series of observations taken at regular time intervals. Monthly sales figures, daily absences, weekly demand, and annual profits are examples of time series.

If you have data for a time series, the most useful way of analyzing them is to draw a graph. This will show clearly any underlying patterns. The three most common patterns in time series are shown in Figure 8.4 as:

- *Constant series,* in which values take roughly the same value over time, such as annual rainfall

- *Series with a trend*, which either rise or fall steadily, such as a country's Gross National Product
- *Seasonal series*, which have a regular cycle, such as the annual sales of ice cream

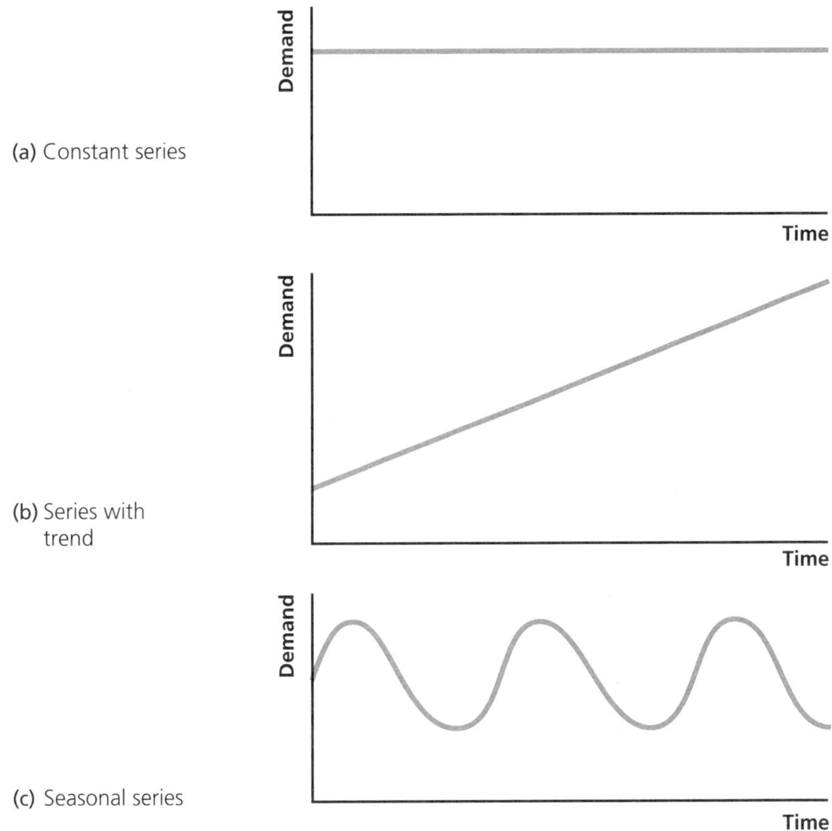

Figure 8.4 Common Patterns in Time Series

If all observations followed such simple patterns, there would be no problems with forecasting. Unfortunately, there are almost always differences between the underlying pattern and actual observations. A random **noise** is superimposed on the underlying pattern—so a constant series, for example, does not always take exactly the same value, but is somewhere close. For example; *200, 205, 194, 195, 208, 203, 200, 193, 201, 198* is a constant series of 200 with superimposed noise.

Actual value = underlying pattern + random noise

Noise is caused by all the unaccountable, random factors that affect demand. It is the noise that makes forecasting difficult. If the noise is relatively small, it is easy to make good forecasts—but if there is a lot of noise, it hides the underlying pattern and forecasting becomes more difficult.

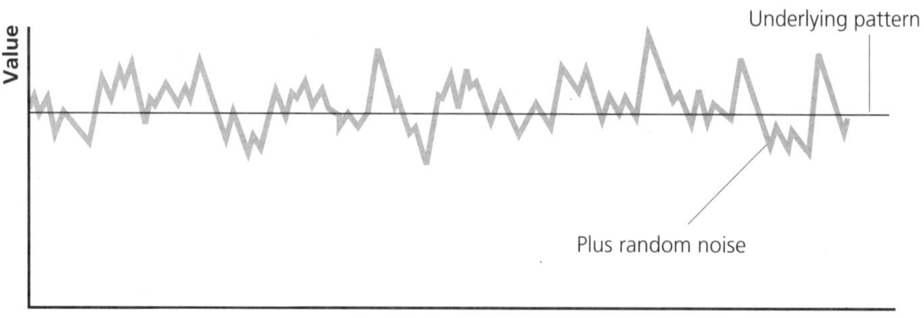

Figure 8.5 Random Noise Superimposed on an Underlying Pattern

Because of noise, forecasts almost always contain errors—there is a difference between the forecast and actual values. The aim of forecasting is to make these errors as small as possible.

In Summary

Time series consist of a number of observations taken at regular periods of time. These observations have an underlying pattern with superimposed noise. Because of the random noise, almost all forecasts contain errors.

Linear Regression

Linear regression is the most widely used method of causal forecasting. It looks at cause-and-effect relationships between factors.

Causal forecasting looks for a cause or relationship which can be used to forecast.

The sales of an item, for example, might depend on the price being charged. Then, we could find the relationship between price and sales, and use this to forecast sales at any particular price. Similar relationships can be found between advertising expenditure and demand, bonus payments and productivity, interest rates and borrowing, and amount of fertilizer and crop size. These are examples of true relationships where changes in the first, independent variable actually cause changes in the second, dependent variable.

Figure 8.6 illustrates causal forecasting by linear regression; it assumes the dependent variable is linearly related to the independent one.

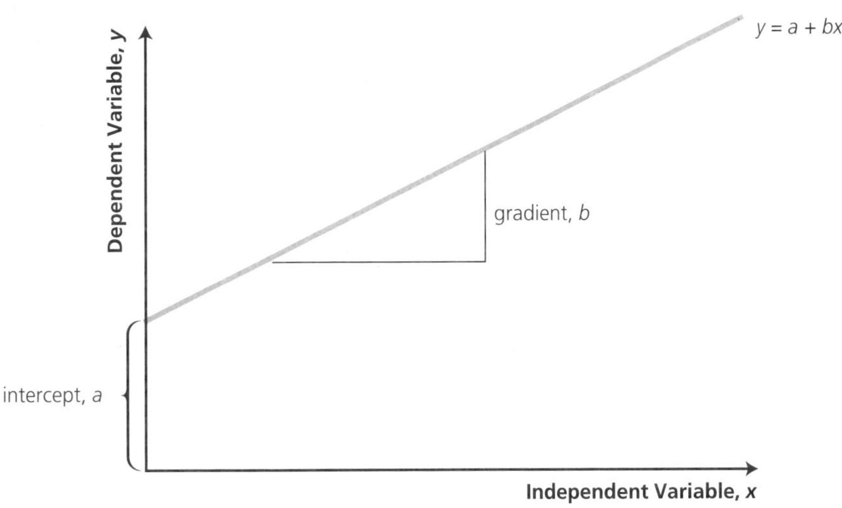

Figure 8.6 A Linear Relationship Between Variables

Example

At Colwith Service Centre, the total number of shifts worked each month and the number of people served is shown in the following table. If the Centre needs to serve 400 people next month, how many shifts should it work?

Month	1	2	3	4	5	6	7	8	9
Shifts Worked	50	70	25	55	20	60	40	25	35
People Served	352	555	207	508	48	498	310	153	264

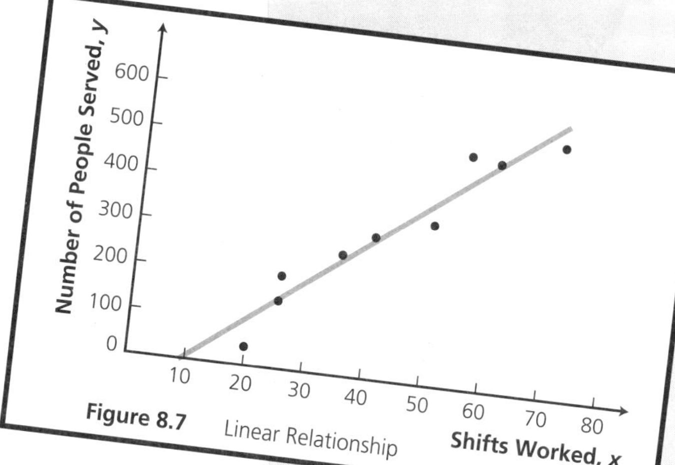

Figure 8.7 Linear Relationship

Solution

The best thing to do with a set of data like this is to draw a graph. A scatter diagram of shifts worked (the independent variable) and people served (the dependent variable) shows a clear linear relationship.

A reasonable straight line can be drawn through the data. This line shows that the Centre needs to work about 50 shifts to serve 400 people.

In this example, we drew a scatter diagram, noticed a linear relationship, and then drew by hand a line of best fit through the data. Although this informal approach can work quite well, it would be useful to have a more reliable method. In particular, it would be useful to find the equation of the line of best fit. For this you need to find values for the constants a and b in the equation:

Dependent variable = a + b × independent variable

or $y = a + bx$

Where: x = value of independent variable

y = value of dependent variable

a = point at which the line intersects the y axis

b = gradient or slope of the line

Because of random noise, even the best line through the data will not be a perfect fit, so there is an error in each observation. The line of best fit will minimize this error. You need not worry about the details of these calculations as, in practice, they are always done by computer. If you are interested in the equations—which are rather messy—they are given below.

For linear regression :

$$y = a + bx$$

$$b = \frac{n\sum xy - \sum x \sum y}{n\sum x^2 - \left(\sum x\right)^2}$$

$$a = \frac{\sum y}{n} - b\frac{\sum x}{n} = \bar{y} - b\bar{x}$$

Where : $\bar{x}$ and $\bar{y}$ are the mean values of x and y

n = the number of observations

Figure 8.8
Computer Printout for Regression

Linear Regression

	x	y	xy	x^2
	0	92	0	0
	1	86	86	1
	2	81	162	4
	3	72	216	9
	4	67	268	16
	5	59	295	25
	6	53	318	36
	7	43	301	49
	8	32	256	64
	9	24	216	81
	10	12	120	100
Totals	55	621	2238	385

Regression Output:

Constant	95.86
Std Err of Y Est	3.08
Correlation	0.99
No. of Observations	11
Degrees of Freedom	9
X Coefficient(s)	-7.88
Std Err of Coef.	0.29

Equation y = 95.867 - 7.88x

Computer Example

In practice, computers are always used for doing regression calculations. The printout to the left shows the results from a typical package for the following example.

Example

A company is about to change the way it inspects one of its products. It has conducted some experiments with differing numbers of inspections, and found the corresponding average number of defects:

Inspections	0	1	2	3	4	5	6	7	8	9	10
Defects	92	86	81	72	67	59	53	43	32	24	12

If the company plans to use 6 inspections, how many defects would it expect? What would be the effect of conducting 20 inspections?

Solution

The independent variable, x, is the number of inspections and the dependent variable, y, is the corresponding number of defects. A graph of these shows a clear linear relationship. You could do the calculations shown in the following table, but you should use a computer whenever possible.

												Totals
x	0	1	2	3	4	5	6	7	8	9	10	55
y	92	86	81	72	67	59	53	43	32	24	12	621
xy	0	86	162	216	268	295	318	301	256	216	120	2,238
x^2	0	1	4	9	16	25	36	49	64	81	100	385

With n=11, substitution gives:

$$b = (n\Sigma xy - \Sigma x\Sigma y)/(n\Sigma x^2 - [\Sigma x]^2)$$
$$= (11 \times 2238 - 55 \times 621)/(11 \times 385 - 55 \times 55) = -7.88$$
$$a = \Sigma y/n - b\Sigma x/n$$
$$= 621/11 + 7.88 \times 55/11 = 95.85$$

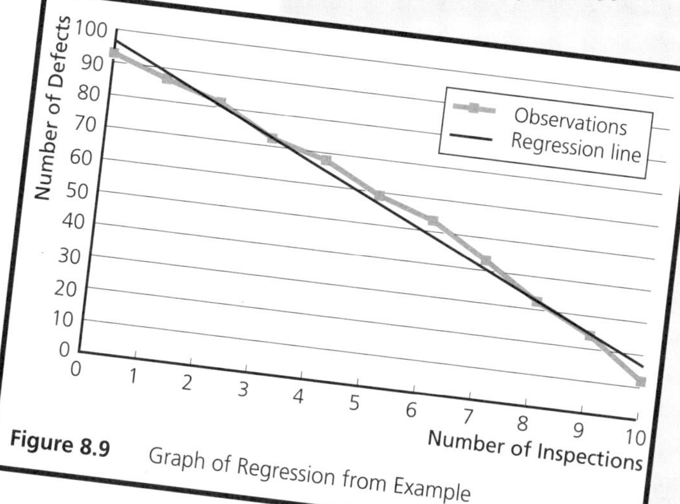

Figure 8.9 Graph of Regression from Example

The line of best fit is:

$y = 95.85 - 7.88x$

or Defects = 95.85 – 7.88 × Number of inspections

With 6 inspections, the company could forecast 95.85 – 7.88 × 6 = 48.57 defects.

With 20 inspections, a little more care is required. Substitution gives 95.85 - 7.88 × 20 = -61.75. A negative number of defects is obviously impossible, so one should simply forecast zero defects.

In Summary

Linear regression is a type of causal forecast. It finds the line of best fit through a set of observations. Because the arithmetic is so messy, these calculations are always done using a computer.

Coefficient of Correlation

You can now calculate the line of best fit through a set of data, but you really need some way of measuring how good this line is. If the errors are small, the line is a good fit, but if the errors are large even the best line is not very good.

A useful measure is the **coefficient of correlation**, which asks the question: How closely are x and y linearly related? You can see from the computer example (Figure 8.8) that packages always calculate the coefficient of correlation, r, which has a value between +1 and -1.

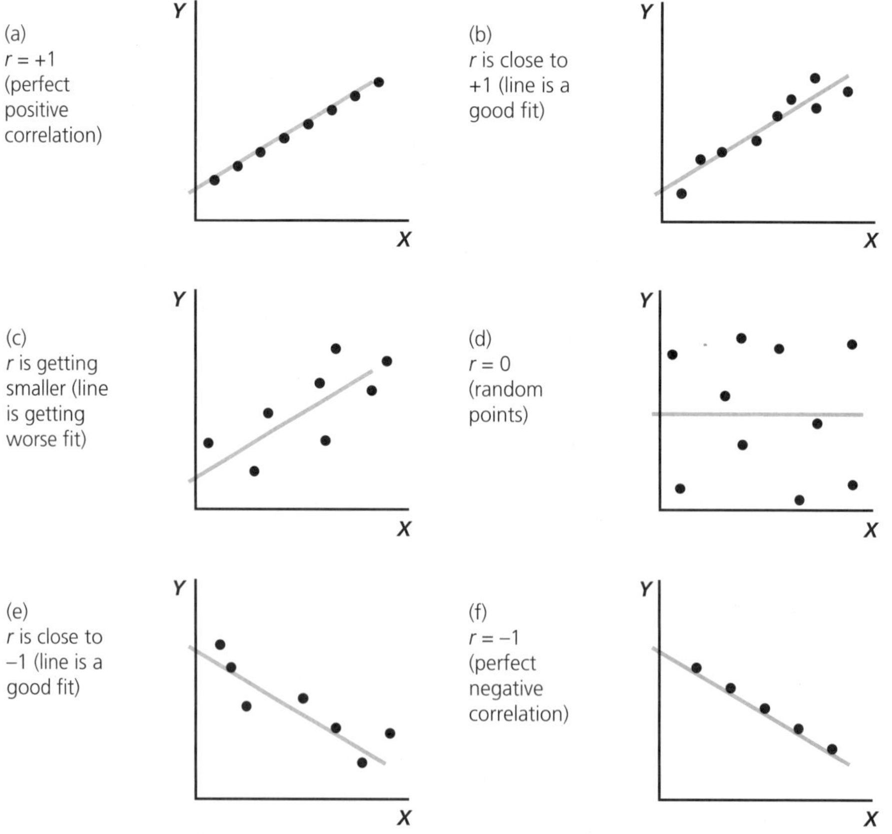

Figure 8.10 Coefficient of Correlation

- A value of r = 1 shows the two variables have a perfect linear relationship with no noise at all, and as one increases so does the other
- A low positive value of r shows a weak linear relationship
- A value of r = 0 shows that there is no correlation at all between the two variables and no linear relationship
- A low negative value of r shows a weak linear relationship
- A value of r= -1 shows the two variables have a perfect linear relationship and as one increases the other decreases

When the coefficient of correlation is between 0.7 and -0.7, even the line of best fit is not very good. This means there is a lot of random variation in the observations, and using these results would not give very reliable forecasts.

Example

Calculate the coefficients of correlation for the following data. What conclusions can you draw from these? What is the line of best fit?

x	4	17	3	21	10	8	4	9	13	12	2	6	15	8	19
y	13	47	24	41	29	33	28	38	46	32	14	22	26	21	50

Solution

There are many packages that calculate regression. Figure 8.11 shows the result from a spreadsheet. As you can see, the line of best fit is:

$$y = 15.38 + 1.55x$$

The coefficient of correlation is 0.79, which shows a good fit.

Product Changes, x	Time Lost, y	Regression Value
4	13	21.556
17	47	41.641
3	24	20.011
21	41	47.821
10	29	30.826
8	33	27.736
4	28	21.556
9	38	29.281
13	46	35.461
12	32	33.916
2	14	18.466
6	22	24.68
15	26	38.551
8	21	27.736
19	50	44.731

Regression Output:		
Constant		15.376
Std Err of Y Est		7.260555
Coeff of Correlation		0.796794
Coeff of Determination		0.634881
No. of Observations		15
Degrees of Freedom		13
X Coefficient(s)	1.54543	
Std Err of Coef.	0.325049	
Equation	$y = 15.376 + 1.545x$	

Figure 8.11
Spreadsheet Showing Regression Example

There are several extensions to the basic linear regression model. One considers multiple linear regression, with a linear relationship between a dependent variable and several independent ones:

$$y = a + b_1x_1 + b_2x_2 + b_3x_3 + b_4x_4 \ldots\ldots$$

The sales of a product, for example, might depend on its price, the advertising budget, number of suppliers, and local unemployment rate. The arithmetic in multiple regression is tedious, and it should only be tackled with a computer.

In Summary

The coefficient of correlation shows how strong the linear relationship is between two variables. This has a value between -1 and +1. Values close to -1 and +1 show a strong relationship, and values closer to zero (say between - 0.7 and + 0.7) show a weak relationship.

Review Questions

1. Why do forecasts almost always contain errors?
2. What is "linear regression"?
3. What is measured by the coefficient of correlation?

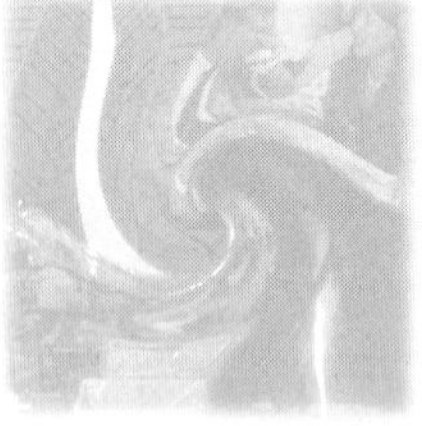

Projective Forecasting

Causal forecasting is *extrinsic*, as it tries to forecast demand by looking at other variables. Projective forecasting is *intrinsic*, as it examines historical values for demand and uses these to forecast future demand. Projective forecasting ignores any external influences and only looks at past values of demand to suggest future values. Four methods of projective forecasting are:

1. Simple averages
2. Moving averages
3. Exponential smoothing
4. Model for seasonality and trend

Simple Averages

Suppose you are planning a trip to Jamaica and want to know the expected temperature during your stay. The easiest way is to look up records for previous years and take an average. With a holiday due to start on July 1st, you could find the average temperature on July 1st over, say, the past ten years.

This is an example of forecasting using **simple averages**, where in general:

Forecasting with simple averages: $$F_{t+1} = \frac{\sum D_t}{n}$$

where: n = number of periods of historical data

t = time period

D_t = demand at time t

F_{t+1} = forecast for time t + 1 (*not* the forecast made at time t)

Example

Use simple averages to forecast demand for period six of the following time series. How accurate are the forecasts? What are the forecasts for period 24?

Period	t	1	2	3	4	5
Series 1	D_t	98	100	98	104	100
Series 2	D_t	140	66	152	58	84

Solution

- For series 1: $F_6 = \frac{\sum D_t}{n} = \frac{(98 + 100 + 98 + 104 + 100)}{5} = 100$
- For series 2: $F_6 = \frac{\sum D_t}{n} = \frac{(140 + 66 + 152 + 58 + 84)}{5} = 100$

Although the forecasts are the same, there is clearly less noise in the first series than the second. You would, therefore, be more confident in the first forecast and expect the error to be less.

Simple averages assume the demand is constant, so the forecasts for period 24 are the same as the forecasts for period 6—that is, 100.

Using simple averages to forecast demand is easy and can work well for constant demands. Unfortunately, it does not work as well if the pattern of demand changes. Older data tend to swamp the latest figures and the forecast is very unresponsive to the change. Suppose demand for an item has been constant at 100 units a week for the past two years. Simple averages would give a forecast demand for week 105 of 104 × 100/104 = 100 units. If the demand in week 105 suddenly rises to 200 units, simple averages would give a forecast for week 106 of:

$$F_{106} = (104 \times 100 + 200)/105 = 100.95$$

A rise in demand of 100 gives an increase of 0.95 in the forecast. If demand continued at 200 units a week, the following forecasts are:

$$F_{107} = 101.89 \quad F_{108} = 102.80 \quad F_{109} = 103.70, \text{ etc.}$$

The forecasts are rising, but the response is very slow.

Very few time series are stable over long periods. So the restriction that simple averages can only be used for constant series makes them of limited value.

In Summary

Projective forecasting uses past demand figures to find values for the future. Simple averages can be used for this, but they only work well for stable demands.

Moving Averages

Demand often varies over time, and only a certain amount of historical data is relevant to future forecasts. The implication is that all observations older than some specified age can be ignored. This suggests a forecasting method where the average demand over the past, say, six weeks is used as a forecast, and any data older than this are ignored. This is the basis of **moving averages.** Instead of taking the average of all historical data, only the latest n periods of data are used. As new data become available, the oldest data are ignored. Moving average forecasts are found from:

$$\begin{aligned} F_{t+1} &= \text{average of n most recent demands} \\ &= \frac{\text{latest demand} + \text{next latest} + \ldots + \text{n}^{\text{th}} \text{ latest}}{\text{n}} \\ &= \frac{D_t + D_{t-1} + \ldots D_{t-n+1}}{n} \end{aligned}$$

Example

The demand for an item over the past eight months is as follows:

t	1	2	3	4	5	6	7	8
D_t	135	130	125	135	115	80	105	100

The market for this item is unstable, and any data over three months old are no longer useful. Use a moving average to forecast demand for the item.

Solution

Only data more recent than three months are valid, so you can use a three-month moving average for the forecast. If you consider the situation at the end of period 3, the forecast for period 4 is:

$$F_4 = [D_1+D_2+D_3]/3 = (135+130+125)/3 = 130$$

At the end of period 4, when actual demand is known to be 135, this forecast can be updated to give:

$$F_5 = [D_2+D_3+D_4]/3 = (130+125+135)/3 = 130$$

Similarly,

$$F_6 = [D_3+D_4+D_5]/3 = (125+135+115)/3 = 125$$

$$F_7 = [D_4+D_5+D_6]/3 = (135+115+80)/3 = 110$$

$$F_8 = [D_5+D_6+D_7]/3 = (115+80+105)/3 = 100$$

$$F_9 = [D_6+D_7+D_8]/3 = (80+105+100)/3 = 95$$

The sensitivity of moving average forecasts to changing demand can be adjusted by using a suitable value of n. A high value for n takes the average of a large number of observations and the forecast is unresponsive: the forecast will smooth out random variations but may not follow genuine changes in demand. However, a small value for n will give a responsive forecast that will follow genuine changes in demand but may be too sensitive to random variations. A compromise value of n is needed to give reasonable results. Typically, a value around six periods is used.

Example

The following table shows monthly demand for a product over the past year. Use moving averages with n = 3, n = 6, and n = 9 to find one period ahead forecasts.

Month	1	2	3	4	5	6	7	8	9	10	11	12
Demand	16	14	12	15	18	21	23	24	25	26	37	38

Solution

The earliest forecast that can be made using a three-period moving average (i.e., n=3) is $F_4 = (D_1 + D_2 + D_3)/3 = (16 + 14 + 12)/3 = 14$

Similarly, the earliest forecasts for a six- and nine-period moving average are F_7 and F_{10} respectively. A computer printout of the results is shown in Figure 8.12.

Month	Observation	Moving Average with Period		
		Three	Six	Nine
1	16			
2	14			
3	12			
4	15	14.00		
5	18	13.67		
6	21	15.00		
7	23	18.00	16.00	
8	24	20.67	17.17	
9	25	22.67	18.83	
10	26	24.00	21.00	18.67
11	37	25.00	22.83	19.78
12	38	29.33	26.00	22.33
13		33.67	28.83	25.22

Figure 8.12 Calculation of Moving Average in a Spreadsheet

Plotting a graph of these forecasts shows how the three-month moving average is most responsive to change and the nine-month moving average is least responsive.

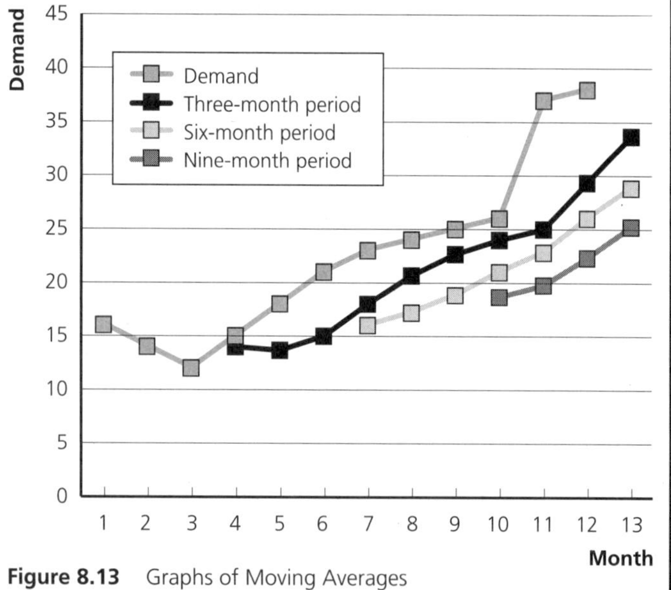

Figure 8.13 Graphs of Moving Averages

In this example, you can begin to see one of the useful properties of moving averages. This appears with demands which have strong seasonal variations. If n is set to equal the number of periods in a season, a moving average will completely "deseasonalize" the data. In other words, it will remove the peaks and troughs to find the underlying pattern.

Example

Use a moving average with 2, 4, and 6 periods to calculate the one-month-ahead forecasts for the following data.

Month	1	2	3	4	5	6	7	8	9	10	11	12
D_t	100	50	20	150	110	55	25	140	95	45	30	145

Month	Price	Moving Average with Period		
		Two	Four	Six
1	100			
2	50			
3	20			
4	150	75.00		
5	110	35.00		
6	55	85.00	80.00	
7	25	130.00	82.50	
8	140	82.50	83.75	80.83
9	95	40.00	85.00	68.33
10	45	82.50	82.50	83.33
11	30	117.50	78.75	95.83
12	145	70.00	76.25	78.33
13		37.50	77.50	65.00
		87.50	78.75	80.00

Figure 8.14 Calculation of Moving Averages

Solution

These data have a clear seasonal pattern, with a peak every fourth months. Calculating the moving averages gives the results shown in Figure 8.14.

The patterns can be seen clearly in a graph, shown in Figure 8.15.

The moving average with both n = 2 and n = 6 has followed the peaks and troughs of demand, but neither has the timing right: both forecasts lag behind demand. As expected, the two-period moving average is much more responsive than the six-period one. The most interesting result is the four-period moving average which has completely "deseasonalized" the data.

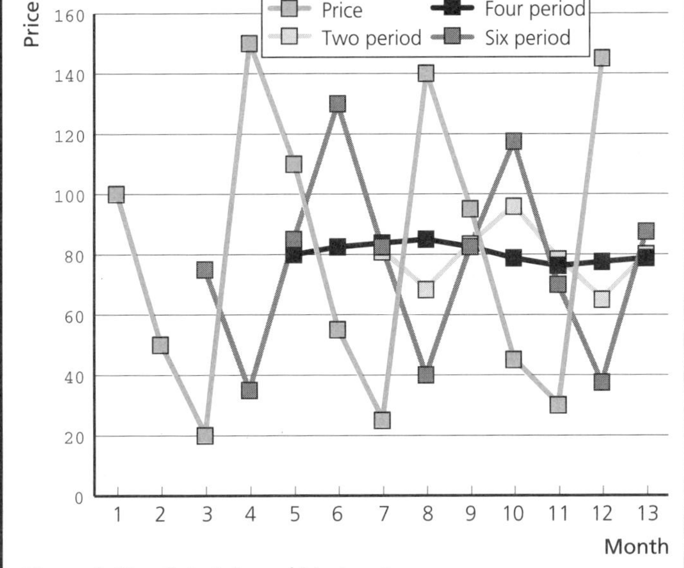

Figure 8.15 Calculation of Moving Averages

Although moving averages overcome some of the problems with simple averages, they still have three major defects:

1. All observations used are given the same weight
2. The method only works well with constant demand—it either removes seasonal factors or gets the timing wrong
3. A large amount of historical data must be stored to allow forecast updates

Exponential smoothing overcomes these defects.

In Summary

Moving averages give forecasts based on the latest n demand figures, and ignore any older values. The sensitivity can be changed by altering the value of n. Time series can be deseasonalized by setting n to the number of periods in a season.

Exponential Smoothing

Exponential smoothing is the most widely used forecasting method. It is based on the idea that as data become older, they become less relevant and should be given less weight. Specifically, exponential smoothing gives a declining weight to older data, as shown in Figure 8.16.

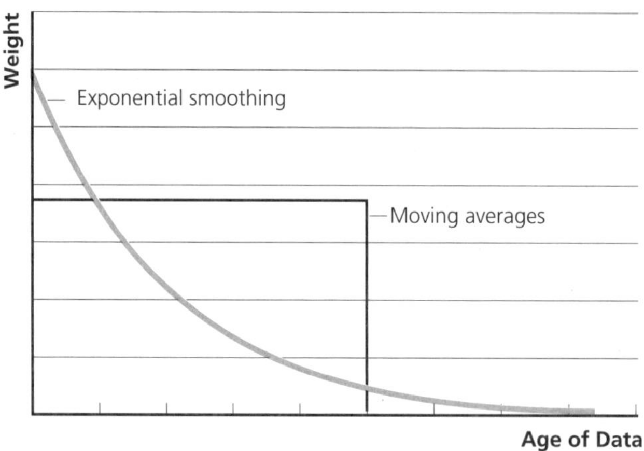

Figure 8.16 Weight Given to Data

This declining weight can be determined by using only the latest demand figure and the previous forecast. To be specific, a new forecast is calculated from a proportion, α, of the latest demand and a proportion, $1-\alpha$, of the previous forecast.

New Forecast = α × latest demand + $(1 - \alpha)$ × last forecast
$F_{t+1} = \alpha D_t + (1 - \alpha)F_t$

In this equation, α is the **smoothing constant,** which usually takes a value between 0.1 and 0.2.

A simple example shows how exponential smoothing adapts to changes in demand. Suppose a forecast was optimistic and suggested a value of 200 for a demand that actually turns out to be 180. Taking a value of $\alpha = 0.2$, the forecast for the next period is:

$$F_{t+1} = \alpha D_t + (1 - \alpha)F_t = 0.2 \times 180 + (1 - 0.2) \times 200 = 196$$

The difference between the optimistic forecast and actual demand moves the forecast for the next period downward.

Example

James Hardware has the following sales (in thousands of dollars). Use exponential smoothing with $\alpha = 0.2$ and an initial value of F_1=170 to find one-period-ahead forecasts for future sales.

Month	1	2	3	4	5	6	7	8
Demand	178	180	156	150	162	158	154	132

Solution

We know F_1 = 170 and α=0.2. Substituting values then gives:

$$F_2 = \alpha D_1 + (1 - \alpha)F_1 = 0.2 \times 178 + 0.8 \times 170 = 171.6$$
$$F_3 = \alpha D_2 + (1 - \alpha)F_2 = 0.2 \times 180 + 0.8 \times 171.6 = 173.3$$
$$F_4 = \alpha D_3 + (1 - \alpha)F_3 = 0.2 \times 156 + 0.8 \times 173.3 = 169.82$$

and so on, as shown in the spreadsheet below.

Figure 8.17 Forecasts Using Exponential Smoothing

Month	Demand	Forecast
1	178	170.00
2	180	171.60
3	156	173.28
4	150	169.82
5	162	165.86
6	158	165.09
7	154	163.67
8	132	161.74
9		155.79

The value given to the smoothing constant, α, sets the sensitivity of the forecasts. α determines the balance between the last forecast and the latest demand. A high value of α—say 0.3 to 0.35—gives a responsive forecast; a lower value—say 0.1 to 0.15—gives a less responsive forecast. A compromise is needed between a responsive forecast which might follow random variations, and an unresponsive one which might not follow real patterns.

Example

The following time series shows the number of people working in an office building. There is a clear step upward in month 3 when new facilities were opened. Use an initial forecast of 500 to compare exponential smoothing forecasts with varying values of α.

Period	1	2	3	4	5	6	7	8	9	10	11
Demand	480	500	1,500	1,450	1,550	1,500	1,480	1,520	1,500	1,490	1,500

Solution

Taking values of $\alpha = 0.1$, 0.2, 0.3, and 0.4 gives the results shown in Figure 8.18.

All these forecasts would eventually follow the sharp step and raise forecasts to around 1,500. Higher values of α make this adjustment more quickly and give a more responsive forecast, as shown in Figure 8.19.

Forecasts with Varying Alpha

Period	Demand	α = 0.1	α = 0.2	α = 0.3	α = 0.4
1	480	500.00	500.00	500.00	500.00
2	500	498.00	496.00	494.00	492.00
3	1,500	498.20	496.80	495.80	495.20
4	1,450	598.38	697.44	797.06	897.12
5	1,550	683.54	847.95	992.94	1,118.27
6	1,500	770.19	988.36	1,160.06	1,290.96
7	1,480	843.17	1,090.69	1,262.04	1,374.58
8	1,520	906.85	1,168.55	1,327.43	1,416.75
9	1,500	968.17	1,238.84	1,385.20	1,458.05
10	1,490	1,021.35	1,291.07	1,419.64	1,474.83
11	1,500	1,068.22	1,330.86	1,440.75	1,480.90
12		1,111.39	1,364.69	1,458.52	1,488.54

Figure 8.18 Forecasts Using Exponential Smoothing

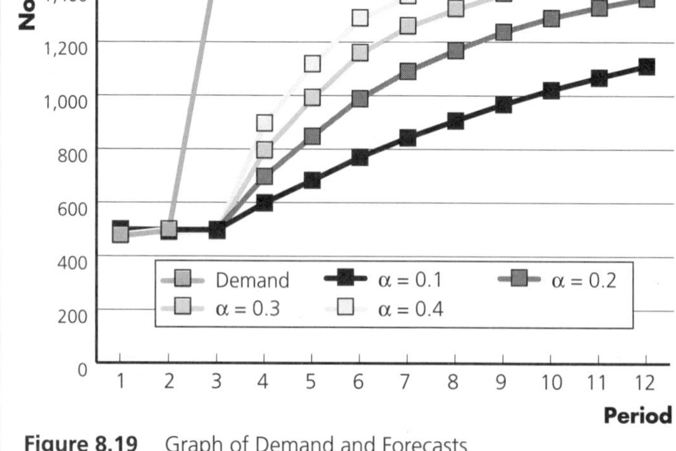

Figure 8.19 Graph of Demand and Forecasts

Although higher values of α give more responsive forecasts, they do not necessarily give more accurate ones. Demand always contains random noise, and very sensitive forecasts tend to follow these random variations. One way of choosing a value for α is to test several values using a trial period of historical data. The value that gives the best results is then used for all future forecasts.

Example

Use a smoothing constant of 0.2 and an initial forecast of 15 to calculate the one-period-ahead forecast for the following time series. What conclusions can you draw from these results?

Period	1	2	3	4	5	6	7	8	9	10	11	12	13	14	15	16
Demand	16	13	18	14	20	16	14	18	22	30	41	48	59	67	75	80

Solution

Substituting the values gives the results shown in Figure 8.20.

The forecast works reasonably well for the first half of the data, but obviously gets worse in the second half. If you draw a graph of the demand, there is a clear upward trend in the second half. Exponential smoothing works well for relatively stable time series, but does not work well if there is some other pattern.

Period	Demand	Forecast	Error
1	16	15.00	−1.00
2	13	15.20	2.20
3	18	14.76	−3.24
4	14	15.41	1.41
5	20	15.13	−4.87
6	16	16.10	0.10
7	14	16.08	2.08
8	18	15.66	−2.34
9	22	16.13	−5.87
10	30	17.31	−12.69
11	41	19.84	−21.16
12	48	24.08	−23.92
13	59	28.86	−30.14
14	67	34.89	−32.11
15	75	41.31	−33.69
16	80	48.05	−31.95

Figure 8.20 Showing the Increasing Errors in Forecasts

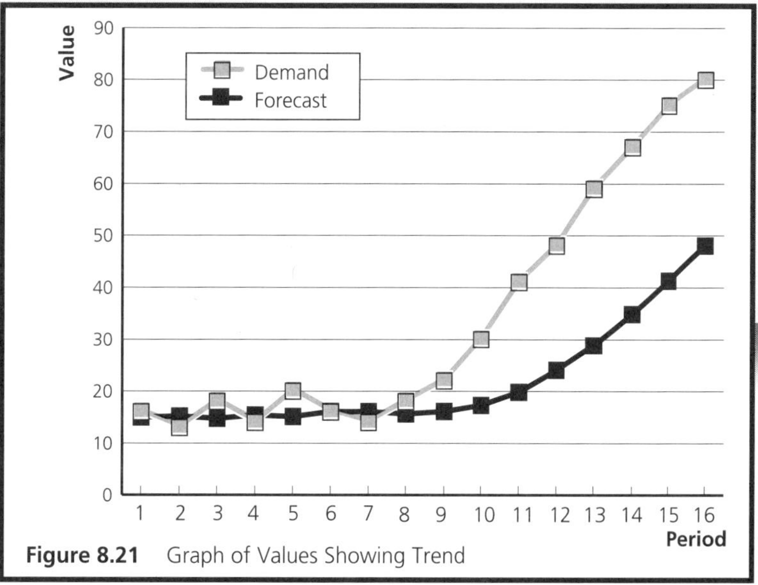

Figure 8.21 Graph of Values Showing Trend

In Summary

Exponential smoothing gives forecasts by adding portions of the last forecast to the latest observation. This reduces the weight given to data as their age increases. The smoothing constant sets the sensitivity of the forecast.

Model for Seasonality and Trend

The forecasting methods described so far give good results for constant time series, but they cannot deal with other patterns. This section outlines a model that can be used for data which has both *seasonality* and *trend*. In this sense, trend is the amount that demand grows between two consecutive periods. So if two consecutive periods have demands of 100 and 120, the trend is 20. If two consecutive periods have demands of 100 and 80, the trend is -20. Seasonality is a regular cyclical pattern, which is not necessarily annual. It is measured by seasonal indices, which are defined as the amounts deseasonalized values must be multiplied by to get seasonal values. Then:

$$\text{Seasonal index} = \frac{\text{seasonal value}}{\text{deseasonalized value}}$$

Suppose a newspaper has average daily sales of 1,000 copies in a particular area, but this rises to 2,000 copies on Saturday and falls to 500 copies on Monday and Tuesday. The deseasonalized value is 1000 - the average sales. The seasonal index for Saturday is 2,000/1,000 = 2.0; the seasonal indices for Monday and Tuesday are 500/1,000 = 0.5; and seasonal indices for other days are 1,000/1,000 = 1.0.

There are several ways of forecasting complex time series, but the easiest is to split the demand into separate components, and then forecast each component separately. The overall forecast is found by recombining the separate components. To be specific, demand is assumed to be made up of three components:

- **Trend** (T) is the long-term direction of a time series. It is typically a steady upward or downward movement.
- **Seasonal index** (S) is the regular variation around the trend. Typically, this shows the variations over a year.
- **Residual** (R) is the random noise or error whose effects cannot be explained.

Demand should really be forecast by adding the trend to the underlying value and multiplying this by the seasonal index. But it is easier to combine the underlying value and trend into a single figure. So that forecasts come from:

$$F = TS$$

Now to forecast, you must:

- Deseasonalize the data and find the underlying trend, T
- Find the seasonal indices, S
- Use the trend and seasonal indices to forecast:

  $F = TS$

There are two ways of finding the trend, T, both of which have already been discussed:

1. Linear regression with time as the independent variable
2. Moving averages with a period equal to the length of a season

You can use either of these, but if the trend is clearly linear, regression is usually better. It gives more information and an equation to work with. If the trend is not linear, moving averages are better.

As you can imagine, more complicated forecasting models involve a lot more arithmetic. In practice, computers are always used for this. The following example shows a printout for a problem with seasonality and trend.

Example

In Highway Sellers Inc., the demand for a product over the past 12 periods is:

Period	1	2	3	4	5	6	7	8	9	10	11	12
Demand	291	320	142	198	389	412	271	305	492	518	363	388

Forecast demand over the next few periods.

Period	Demand	Deseason-alized	Seasonal Index	Forecast
1	291	241.46	1.21	
2	320	259.51	1.23	
3	142	277.57	0.51	
4	198	295.62	0.67	
5	389	313.67	1.24	
6	412	331.72	1.24	
7	271	349.78	0.77	
8	305	367.83	0.83	
9	492	385.88	1.28	
10	518	403.93	1.28	
11	363	421.99	0.86	
12	388	440.04	0.88	
13		458.09	1.24	568.08
14		476.14	1.25	596.36
15		494.20	0.72	353.61
16		512.25	0.79	406.51

Figure 8.22a Forecasting with Seasonality and Trend

Solution

Figure 8.22 printout shows the solution.

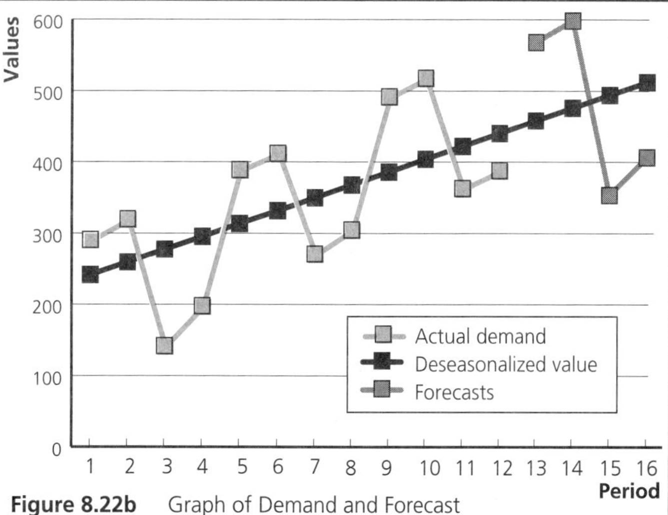

Figure 8.22b Graph of Demand and Forecast

In Summary

Forecasts for time series with seasonality and trend are made by considering each component separately, and combining them into an overall forecast. There are several ways of doing this, but we used a model where:

$$\text{forecast} = \text{underlying trend} \times \text{seasonal index}$$

How to Make a Forecast

Each forecasting method is best in different circumstances.The following is a summary of the whole procedure for making a forecast. This has the following steps.

1. Define the purpose of the forecast. This will show what you are trying to forecast, how the forecast will be used, when you need the forecast, and how much detail it should have.

2. Find the time horizon the forecast must cover—such as forecast demand for the next six months.

3. Choose a suitable forecasting method—such as exponential smoothing with a smoothing constant of 0.1.

4. Collect any historical data needed and test the forecasting method.

5. If the tests give good results, implement the forecasting method.

6. See how the forecast works in practice by comparing the forecast with actual demand. If the error is too large, change the method or parameters used.

Not all forecasts work well. Sometimes obvious mistakes are made, such as using the wrong method, the wrong parameters, or poor data. Four other common causes of problems are listed below.

1. Forecasters do not involve other people. Remember that a good forecast depends on many internal and external factors, so it is always best to involve people who understand the circumstances.

2. Sometimes people's expectations of a forecast are too high. Then if it turns out to be wrong, they become disillusioned with all forecasts.

3. Sometimes forecasts are done in too much detail. This happens when, for example, forecasts are made for individual items when it would make more sense to forecast for groups of items.

4. Failure to recognize people's needs. For example, salespeople often like to be optimistic in their approach, whereas finance people are more likely to be conservative.

Case Study

Generating Electricity

Like forecasting the weather, forecasting the demand for electricity can be very difficult. The problem is that electricity cannot be stored—except in very small quantities in batteries—so the supply from power stations must exactly match the demand from customers.

The long-term demand for electricity is expected to rise steadily. So enough power stations must be built to meet this long-term growth. Planning and building a nuclear power station can take 20 years and cost billions of dollars. Conventional stations can be built faster and probably cheaper, but they are still based on forecast demand a decade or more in the future.

In the shorter term, demand for electricity follows an annual cycle—generally demand is heavier in winter when more heating systems are switched on. There are also short irregular periods when demand is particularly high, perhaps during very cold periods. Demand also follows shorter cycles. Demand is lower at the weekends when industry is not working so intensely. On top of this are cycles during the day, with lighter demand during the night when most of us are asleep. Finally, there are irregular peaks during the day, often corresponding to breaks in television programs when people turn on other appliances.

Power stations need "warming up" before they can start supplying electricity. So all these effects must be forecast—long-term trend, annual cycle, short periods with changes, weekly cycles, daily cycles, and short-term variations. Electricity generators must then match their supply to this ever-changing demand.

Review Questions

1. Why are actual averages of limited use for forecasting?
2. How can moving average forecasts be made more responsive?
3. How can data be deseasonalized using moving averages?
4. Why is the forecasting method called "exponential smoothing"?
5. How can you make exponential smoothing forecast more sensitive?
6. What is a seasonal index?

Chapter Review

- All decisions become effective at some point in the future. This means that managers must make decisions that are not based on present circumstances but on circumstances as they will be when the decisions become effective. These circumstances must be forecast. Therefore forecasting is an important function in every organization.
- Despite its importance, there has been limited progress in many areas of forecasting. There are many different methods of forecasting, but none of these is best in all circumstances.
- There are three basic approaches to forecasting—judgemental, causal, and projective.
- When there are no relevant quantitative data, judgemental methods must be used. These collect opinions from groups of experts, and range from personal insight to the more formal Delphi method.
- Most quantitative forecasts are concerned with time series, where demand is measured at regular intervals of time. Demand can usually be described by an underlying pattern with a superimposed random noise. This noise cannot be forecast and is the reason why forecasts almost always contain errors.
- Causal forecasts look for cause and effect relationships between variables. Linear regression is widely used in causal forecasting. This draws the line of best fit through a set of data. The quality of the results can be judged by the coefficient of correlation.
- Projective forecasts look at the patterns in historical data and project these into the future. There are many ways of doing this, and we considered simple averages, moving averages, exponential smoothing, and a model for seasonality and trend.

Key Terms

causal forecast *(p.211)*
coefficient of correlation *(p.222)*
Delphi method *(p.215)*
exponential smoothing *(p.230)*
judgemental forecasting *(p.213)*
linear regression *(p.218)*
moving average *(p.226)*
noise *(p.217)*
projective forecast *(p.211)*
qualitative methods *(p.210)*
quantitative methods *(p.210)*
residual *(p.234)*
seasonal index *(p.234)*
simple averages *(p.225)*
smoothing constant *(p.231)*
trend *(p.234)*
time series *(p.216)*

Problems

8.1 A local amateur dramatic society is staging a play and wants to know how much to spend on advertising. Its objective is to attract as many people as possible, up to the limit of the hall's capacity. The spending on advertising (in thousands of dollars) and the audience size for the past 11 productions is shown in the following table. If the hall's capacity is now 300 people, how much would you spend on advertising?

Spending	3	5	1	7	2	4	4	2	6	6	4
Audience	200	250	75	425	125	300	225	200	300	400	275

8.2 Ten experiments were done to see if the bonus rates paid to salesmen affected sales. The following results were found.

% Bonus	0	1	2	3	4	5	6	7	8	9
Sales ('00s)	3	4	8	10	15	18	20	22	27	28

What is the line of best fit through this data?

8.3 Sales of a product for the past ten months are shown below. Use linear regression to forecast sales for the next six months. How reliable are these figures?

Month	1	2	3	4	5	6	7	8	9	10
Sales	6	21	41	75	98	132	153	189	211	243

8.4 Find the 2, 3, and 4 period moving average for the following time series, and state which gives the best results.

t	1	2	3	4	5	6	7	8
D_t	280	240	360	340	300	220	200	360

8.5 Find deseasonalized forecasts for the following time series. What is the underlying trend?

t	1	2	3	4	5	6	7	8	9	10
D_t	75	30	52	88	32	53	90	30	56	96

8.6 Use exponential smoothing with smoothing constant equal to 0.1, 0.2, 0.3, and 0.4 to give one-period-ahead forecasts for the following time series. Use an initial value of $F_1 = 208$ and state which value of α is best.

t	1	2	3	4	5	6	7	8
D_t	212	216	424	486	212	208	208	204

8.7 The following demand has seasonality, but no trend. Forecast values for periods 7 to 12.

t	1	2	3	4	5	6
D_t	100	160	95	140	115	170

8.8 The demand for a product is shown below. What forecasts would you give for demand in the following year?

Month	Jan	Feb	Mar	Apr	May	June	July	Aug	Sept	Oct	Nov	Dec
Year 1	100	87	86	75	92	107	115	131	120	118	120	142
Year 2	123	101	105	93	121	136	130	155	158	142	147	181

Discussion Questions

8.1 Is forecasting really essential for all decisions? Can you give examples where it is not needed?

8.2 What factors would you consider when choosing a forecasting method?

8.3 Discuss the way that forecasting systems can be integrated with other operations.

8.4 What are the assumptions of linear regression? Are these generally realistic?

8.5 Much forecasting can be done with spreadsheets. Design spreadsheets for linear regression and compare your results with standard statistical programs.

8.6 How could linear regression be extended? What programs do you have for this?

8.7 Design spreadsheets which can be used for forecasting with simple averages, moving averages, and exponential smoothing. Compare the results with standard forecasting programs.

8.8 Can you think of other methods for forecasting demand which has both seasonality and trend? How, for example, could you extend the basic exponential smoothing model?

8.9 Why do forecasts use smoothing? How could you find the best amount of responsiveness in a forecast?

Chapter 9
CAPACITY PLANNING

Making sure there is enough capacity to meet demand

Contents

Introduction

The last chapter discussed how to forecast demand for products. In the next few chapters, the discussion centres on how an organization can meet this demand by planning its production.

We shall start by looking at capacity planning. The capacity of a process sets the amount of a product that can be made in a specified time. Capacity planning involves the long-term decisions that ensure there is enough capacity for an organization to meet the forecast demand for its products.

Learning Objectives

After reading this chapter you should be able to answer questions such as:

- How can one measure the performance of an organization?
- What is meant by productivity?
- How can one measure capacity?
- Why is capacity planning used?
- How can one make short-term changes to capacity?
- How does capacity change over time?
- What is a learning curve?
- When should equipment be maintained and replaced?

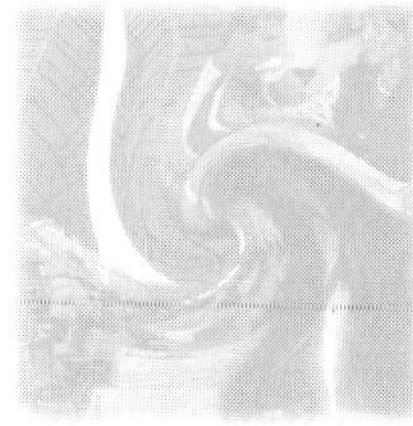

Measures of Performance

What Is Capacity?

An organization should be able to look at its forecast demand for a product, and use this to find the capacity it needs. But the amount made in a complex process can change quickly. People may alter the speed at which they work, problems may appear in the process, equipment may break down, raw materials may vary in quality, and so on. This means that when planning the capacity of a process, an organization must also consider how efficiently the process is working. In other words, before capacity planning can begin, measures of performance must be considered.

Chapter 4 discussed how higher levels of automation are generally used to meet higher demand because the equipment is more efficient and productivity is higher. But what is meant by "efficiency", and is high productivity necessarily good?

The basic measure of performance is **capacity**.

> The capacity of a process sets the maximum amount of a product that can be made in a given time.

Organizations should aim to match the capacity of a process to the forecast demand for products. Any mismatch between supply and demand will result in either unsatisfied customers or underused equipment.

- If capacity is less than demand, some demand is not met and the organization loses potential customers.
- If capacity is greater than demand, all demand is met but the process has underused resources.

Sometimes when you go into a store, there are not enough people serving and you have to wait. The capacity of the store is less than demand—and you will probably go to a competitor where the lines are shorter. In other stores, there are lots of people waiting to serve you. You do not have to wait, but the cost of paying these underused staff is added to your bill.

In Summary

Capacity sets the maximum output of a process. Organizations should try to match available capacity to forecast demand.

Other Measures

Two other measures are directly related to capacity—utilization and productivity. **Utilization** measures the proportion of available capacity that is actually used. **Productivity** measures the amount of output achieved for each unit of a resource. Suppose a process has a capacity of 100 units per week. This is the maximum number of units that can be made. If the process is idle for half the time and actually processes 50 units per week, its utilization is 50 percent. If it uses 25 hours of machine time to make these 50 units the productivity is two units per machine-hour.

One problem with these measures is that some people use the terms very loosely. Many assume that productivity is the number of units made by each employee. As discussed later, this is only one aspect of productivity. Sometimes the term **production**, or the total output from a process, is confused with productivity, which measures the output achieved for a unit of resource. So 100 units may be the production while 100 units per machine-hour is the productivity.

Another term that is confusing is **efficiency**. This is a widely used measure, but it means different things to different people. Here we define efficiency as the percentage of possible output that is actually achieved. Suppose office workers can process five forms per hour, but one worker has just spent an hour processing four forms. The workers' overall efficiency is 4/5 = 0.8 or 80 percent.

There is also confusion between **efficiency**, which measures how well an organization uses its resources, and **effectiveness**, which measures how well it sets and achieves its goals. This is the difference between "doing the right job and doing the job right." Opening a walnut with a sledge hammer would be very effective, but it would not be very efficient; building a wall without using cement would be very efficient as the builder could work very quickly, but it would not be very effective.

- *Capacity* is the maximum amount of a product that can be made in a given time.
- *Utilization* measures the proportion of available capacity that is actually used.
- *Production* is the total amount of the product made.
- *Productivity* is the amount produced in relation to one or more of the resources used.
- *Efficiency* is the ratio of actual output to possible output.
- *Effectiveness* shows how well an organization sets and achieves its goals.

An organization can use many other measures of performance, including:

- Flexibility
- Quality of product
- Profitability
- Return on investment
- Market share
- Conformance to industry standards
- Employee morale
- Innovation

Example

Two machines are designed to make 100 units each in a ten-hour shift. During one shift, the machines were actually used for eight hours, and made a total of 140 units. What measures of performance can you give?

Solution

- Capacity is the maximum amount which could be produced in a given time. This is 2 × 100 or 200 units a shift, or 20 units an hour.
- Utilization is the proportion of capacity actually used. This is 140/200 = 0.7 or 70 percent.
- Production is the amount actually made, which is 140 units.
- Productivity is the amount produced in relation to resources used. We can define this as 140/(2 × 8) = 8.75 units a machine-hour.
- Efficiency is the ratio of actual output to possible output. In the eight hours, this is 140/(8 × 20) = 0.875 or 87.5 percent.

Example

Albion Mail Order employed ten people to process 1,000 order forms each month. The direct costs of employing these people was $125,000. After a small reorganization 11 people processed 1,200 orders per month with direct costs of $156,000. How could you measure the performance of the process? Do you think the reorganization has improved operations?

Solution

There is enough information for two useful measures:

1. Number of forms processed per person
2. Direct costs per form processed

Calculating these before the reorganization gives:

- Number of forms per person = 1,000/10 = 100
- Direct costs per form = 125,000/1,000 = $125

After the reorganization:

- Number of forms per person = 1,200/11 = 109
- Direct costs per form = 156,000/1,200 = $130

The number of forms per person has increased with the reorganization, but the direct cost per form has also risen. Whether the reorganization improved operations depends on Albion's goals.

This last example shows how measures of performance can give conflicting views. This is simply because different things are being measured. When you drive faster than usual, it takes less time to complete the journey but the fuel consumption increases. If an organization reduces the selling price of a product, the demand may increase but the profit goes down. If a company reduces its hourly rates of pay, the payroll goes down but so might productivity. All organizations must be careful to use suitable measures of performance, that is, ones that show how well it is achieving its goals.

In Summary

An organization can use many measures of performance. These include capacity, utilization, production, productivity, efficiency, and several other measures. A range of these should be used to give an overall view of performance.

Review Questions

1. What measures can be used to show how well a process is working?
2. What are the differences among capacity, utilization, productivity, and efficiency?
3. Is it possible for the utilization of a process to rise while the productivity goes down? Explain.

Productivity

Many people assume that increasing the productivity of a process is relatively simple. Using a high-technology, automated process can increase productivity dramatically. But this is a simplified view. "Getting people to work harder" has very little to do with increasing productivity. A hard-working person with a shovel will be far less productive than a lazy person with a bulldozer. But productivity does not only measure the output per employee. We could define productivity as the output achieved for every dollar invested and get a completely different picture. Then higher levels of technology could give lower productivity. At this point we should define exactly what we mean by productivity.

As stated earlier, productivity is the amount produced in relation to one or more of the resources used. This definition can now be expanded by saying that the **total productivity** of an operation is the total output divided by the total input.

$$\text{Total productivity} = \frac{\text{total output}}{\text{total input}}$$

However, this definition has a number of drawbacks. To start with, the input and output must be in the same units, and this usually means that they are translated into dollars. These costs depend on the accounting conventions used—so that the measure is not objective. Another problem is taking account of all the inputs and outputs. Some inputs may be difficult to value—such as water and sunlight—as will some outputs—such as waste and pollution. Yet all inputs and outputs *should* be included in total productivity.

Because of these difficulties, organizations normally use other measures of productivity. These measure **partial productivity**, which considers the total output divided by one input. So the amount produced per machine-hour, or the amount produced per kilowatt-hour of electricity, or the amount produced per dollar of investment are examples of partial productivity.

$$\text{Partial productivity} = \frac{\text{total output}}{\text{single input}}$$

A few examples of partial productivity measures are:

- *Equipment productivity:* units of output per machine-hour, tonnes made per operating hour, units made per day of equipment use, etc.
- *Labour productivity:* units made per person-hour, tonnes of output per employee, shipments made for each dollar spent on labour, etc.
- *Capital productivity:* units made per dollar of investment, value of outputs per dollar of input, etc.
- *Energy productivity:* units made per kilowatt-hour, units of output for each cubic metre of gas, value of output per barrel of oil used, etc.

One may assume that increasing productivity is a good thing, but the definitions above show that this is a simplified view. Increasing levels of technology, for example, may increase the labour productivity but may reduce the capital productivity. Adding "energy savers" to machines may increase energy productivity but reduce equipment productivity. Any single measure of productivity gives only one, limited view of the organization. To get a broader, more useful view of an organization, several measures must be taken, which describe different aspects of operations.

In Summary

Total productivity is a useful measure, but it is difficult to measure in practice. Partial productivities can give more focused views of a process. These generally refer to the output for each unit of equipment, labour, capital, or energy. A range of performance measures is needed to give an overall view of an organization's performance.

Example

Sandra Lee is a financial analyst. Most of her work is in the operations area of Singer (Industrial) Inc. In two years she collected the following information.

	1994	1995
Number of Units Made	1,000	1,200
Selling Price	$100	$100
Raw Materials Used	5,100 kg	5,800 kg
Cost of Raw Materials	$20,500	$25,500
Hours Worked	4,300	4,500
Direct Labour Costs	$52,000	$58,000
Energy Used	10,000 kWh	14,000 kWh
Energy Cost	$1,000	$1,500
Other Costs	$10,000	$10,000

How could Sandra describe the productivity in Singer?

Solution

There are several measures of productivity she could use.

- Total productivity in 1994 is found from the costs:

$$\frac{\text{Total output}}{\text{Total input}} = \frac{100 \times 1,000}{20,500 + 52,000 + 1,000 + 10,000} = 1.20$$

  By 1995, this had risen to 120,000/95,000 = 1.26, which is a rise of 5 percent.
- Units of output per kilogram of raw material in 1994 was 1,000/5,100 = 0.196. In 1995, this was 1,200/5,800 = 0.207, which is a rise of 5 percent.
- Some other measures are as follows:

	1994	1995	Percentage Increase
Total Productivity	1.20	1.26	5
Units/kg of Raw Material	0.196	0.207	5.6
Units/$ of Raw Material	0.049	0.047	-4.1
Units/Hour	0.233	0.267	14.6
Units/$ of Labour	0.019	0.021	10.5
Units/kWh	0.100	0.086	-14.0
Units/$ of Energy	1.000	0.800	-20

In general, labour productivity has risen, raw materials productivity has stayed about the same, but energy productivity has fallen.

Review Questions

1. What is the difference between total and partial productivity?
2. Is it possible for some measures of productivity to rise while others fall?
3. "Labour productivity is the best measure of an organization's performance." Explain why you agree or disagree with this statement.

Process Capacity

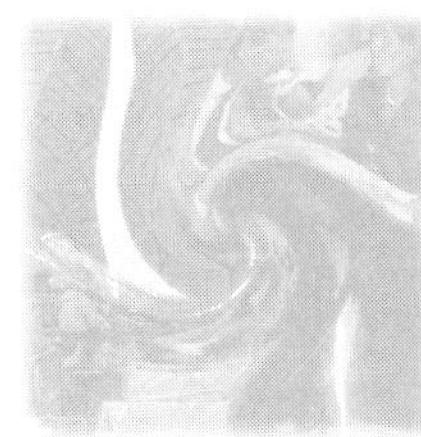

Measuring Capacity

All operations have some limit on their capacity: a factory has a maximum output per week, a machine has a maximum throughput per hour, an airplane has a maximum number of seats, a hotel has a maximum number of rooms, a truck has a maximum weight it can carry. The first two examples have a direct reference to time, but the last three also have an indirect reference to time. The number of seats on an airplane gives the capacity as a maximum number of passengers on a particular flight; the number of rooms in a hotel sets the maximum number of guests per night; the maximum weight of a truck sets the most it can carry on a single journey. The capacity measures the rate of output, and must always be phrased in terms of the output in a given time period. Some measures of capacity are shown in Table 9.1.

Table 9.1 *Measuring Capacity*

Organization	Measure
Car Manufacturers	Number of cars produced per year
Refinery	Gallons of oil produced per day
Hydroelectric Company	Megawatts of electricity
College	Number of students per term
Restaurant	Number of seats
Consulting Firm	Number of projects

Sometimes the capacity of an operation is obvious—the number of seats in a theatre, of beds in a hospital, or of tables in a restaurant. At other times, the capacity is less clear. How, for example, can the capacity of a supermarket, warehouse, or bank be determined? This difficulty is particularly obvious in the area of services. There is often some measure to set capacity, such as the number of customers per square metre of floor space. These measures are usually found by discussion and agreement rather than calculation. The maximum size of classes in schools, for example, is an agreed number of students rather than some limit set by the building; the maximum number of spectators in a football stadium is set by agreed safety regulations rather than physical limitations of space.

Even the capacity of manufacturing operations can be difficult to find. Could the capacity of an assembly line be increased simply by speeding up the flow of goods? Could the capacity of a pipeline be raised by increasing the rate of pumping? Could the capacity of an office be increased by having the employees work longer hours, perhaps at weekends or during an extra shift? In practice, it is often difficult to set a specific figure for the capacity of a process, and an agreed value must be used that is based on experience and judgement.

In Summary

The capacity of a process is the maximum number of units that can be made in a given time. This is often surprisingly difficult to find and relies on judgement and agreement.

Calculation of Capacity

Suppose a process uses N machines, each working H hours, on each of S shifts per day, for D days per year. The total available machine time is NHSD hours per year. If each unit of product takes T hours to make, the total annual capacity of the machines is:

$$\text{Capacity} = \frac{\text{time available in year}}{\text{time to make one unit}} = \frac{NHSD}{T}$$

where: N = number of machines

H = hours worked in each shift

S = number of shifts per day

D = days worked per year

T = time taken to make one unit in hours

This measure is the maximum output of the machines under ideal conditions, which is called the **designed capacity**. As operations rarely work under ideal conditions, a more realistic measure is the **effective capacity**. This is the maximum output that can be expected under normal conditions. The difference between designed capacity and effective capacity allows for such things as set-up times, breakdowns, stoppages, and maintenance periods. Most organizations do not work at designed capacity as they get better results in the long term when equipment is not stretched to its limit.

Example

Maxcorp has two pieces of equipment, each of which is designed to work for one eight-hour shift per day, five days per week, 50 weeks per year. When working, each piece of equipment can process 10 units per hour, but 10 percent of the machine time is needed for maintenance and set-ups. During one particular year, breakdowns, defective output, shortage of materials, and other problems meant the equipment only produced 30,000 units. What measures can be used to describe these figures?

Solution

- The designed capacity of the machine is the maximum output which could, ideally, be achieved in a year. This ignores the time needed for maintenance and set-ups.

  Designed capacity = NHSD/T = 2 × 8 × 1 × 250/0.1 = 40,000 units per year

- The effective capacity is the maximum output that could reasonably be expected. This takes into account the time needed for maintenance and set-ups.

  Effective capacity = 0.9 × NHSD/T = 36,000 units per year

  The actual output was 30,000 units per year.

  Efficiency is the ratio of actual output to possible output.

  Efficiency = 30,000/36,000 = 0.833 or 83.3 percent

  Utilization is the proportion of the available capacity that is actually used.

  Utilization = 30,000/40,000 = 0.75 or 75 percent

In Summary

The capacity of a process can often be calculated. There is a difference between the designed capacity and the effective capacity.

Review Questions

1. Why is the capacity always related to some period of time?
2. What is the difference between designed capacity and effective capacity?
3. What units could you use to measure the capacity of:
   a) a train
   b) a movie theatre
   c) a squash club
   d) a social work department
   e) a fire station?
4. Which is largest of actual output, designed capacity, and effective capacity?

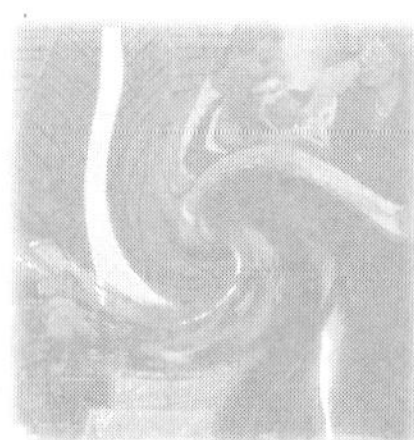

Capacity Planning

Aims of Capacity Planning

Capacity planning is largely a strategic issue because it involves decisions with a long time horizon. The capacity of a process might be increased by building another facility, introducing higher technology, employing more people, or buying more equipment. Capacity can be reduced by closing down facilities, selling equipment, or firing employees. These are serious questions of management policy—which require strategic decisions.

But there are also shorter-term aspects of capacity planning. Capacity could be increased by leasing additional space, working overtime, adding an extra shift, or using subcontractors. These are tactical and operational decisions. The objectives of capacity planning can be summarized as making capacity match forecast demand in the long term, while making adjustments to correct short-term mismatches.

The aim of **capacity planning** is to match available capacity to forecast demand over the long, medium, and short terms.

In Summary

Capacity planning is usually a strategic problem with long-term consequences. But organizations also need to match capacity to demand in the shorter term.

Case Study – Capacity Planning at Northern Publishers

The management of Northern Publishers Canada is faced with a major capacity planning decision. At the company's existing location in Don Mills, Ontario, there are 50,000 square feet of storage space. The company has been growing at approximately 10 percent per year. So in 1993 it needed to lease another 20,000 square feet of warehouse space in Scarborough. By 1995, this had grown to 35,000 square feet, which was leased on a short- term basis.

The operations manager estimates that to meet the company's long-term plan the company will need a total of 100,000 square feet of storage. It is not possible to add the extra 50,000 square feet of storage at the Don Mills location, so the management is thinking about signing a long-term lease for storage space at Scarborough and moving part of its operation there.

Questions

- How could you define the capacity of a warehouse?
- What factors should Northern Publishers consider in their decisions about capacity?

Short-term Capacity Planning

Short-term mismatches between supply and demand can be corrected in two ways:

1. By adjusting demand to match available capacity
2. By adjusting capacity to match demand

Demand can be adjusted in a number of ways, including the following:

- Varying the price, with increases for products with shortage of capacity and decreases for products with spare capacity
- Changing the marketing effort, with increases for products with spare capacity and decreases for products with shortages
- Offering incentives to customers buying products with spare capacity, such as free samples, bonus quantities, or price discounts (such as off-peak hour telephone calls or travel)
- Making changes to related products, so that substitutes can be given for products in short supply
- Keeping spare output in stock to be used later
- Varying the lead time, making customers wait for products in short supply
- Using a reservation or appointment system

It may seem strange, but such **demand management** often discourages customers from buying at times of high demand. In practice, this is quite common. Professional institutions, for example, put up barriers against newcomers wanting to enter; restaurants have lines outside at busy times which discourage people from going there; expensive cars offer long delivery times; artists produce limited editions of prints; the price of perfume is very high.

The alternative to demand management is **capacity management**, which looks for short-term adjustments to available capacity. The obvious way of doing this is to change the total operating time, by working overtime to increase capacity, or by working less time to reduce capacity. Ways of adjusting capacity include:

- Changing the total hours worked in any period, by changing the number of shifts or other work patterns
- Employing part-time staff to cover peak demand periods
- Scheduling work patterns so that the total workforce available at any time varies to match fluctuating demand
- Adjusting equipment and processes to work faster or slower
- Rescheduling maintenance periods
- Using outside contractors
- Leasing extra space
- Adjusting the process, perhaps using larger batches to reduce set-up times
- Making customers do some of the work, like using automatic banking machines or packing their own bags in supermarkets

These adjustments cannot be made too frequently or too severely. The workforce schedules, for example, cannot be changed every few days; extra space cannot be rented for a few hours at a time. Capacity cannot be changed quickly, so it really is a strategic issue. This means that capacity planning should aim for stable output over the long term. Wide fluctuations in production are very disruptive and give low productivity. This idea is considered in more detail in Chapter 10.

In Summary

Capacity management aims to match available supply of a product to forecast demand in the long, medium, and short term. This can be achieved by either changing the capacity of a process, or demand management.

Discrete Increases in Capacity

Utilization has already been defined as the ratio of actual output to designed capacity. Therefore, for a set of machines:

$$\text{Designed capacity} = \frac{\text{machine time available}}{\text{time to make a unit}} = \frac{\text{NHSD}}{\text{T}}$$

where: N = number of machines

H = hours per shift

S = number of shifts worked per day

D = days worked in a given period

T = time to make one unit in hours

You can turn this equation around to see how many machines are needed to make a certain number of units. If P is the annual production target, the total machine time available must be greater than, or at least equal to, the total time needed. With calculations in hours, this gives:

$$\text{time available} \geq \text{time required}$$

$$\text{NHSD} \geq \text{PT}$$

$$\text{so, number of machines, N} \geq \frac{\text{PT}}{\text{HSD}}$$

If the organization's original plans were to use less than N machines, they must either change production plans or use more machines. If there are more than N machines available, they will be working at an average utilization of:

$$\text{Utilization, U} = \frac{\text{machine time used}}{\text{machine time available}} = \frac{\text{PT}}{\text{NHSD}}$$

This can then be used to give an overall approach to capacity planning. This approach sets the production target—which is based on forecast demand—and calculates the resources needed. This process is sometimes called **resource requirement planning.** The detailed procedure has the steps shown in Table 9.2

Table 9.2 *Capacity Planning*

- Examines forecast demand and translates this into a capacity requirement
- Calculates the available capacity of present facilities
- Finds any mismatches between required capacity and available capacity
- Lists alternative plans for overcoming these mismatches
- Looks at the alternative plans and selects the best

Example

Sam Pradash forecast average demand for his latest CD-ROM at 1,000 units per week. His equipment has been designed to produce and test 8 CD-ROMs per hour. Sam's company works a single eight-hour shift five days a week, but could move to double shifts or work at weekends. How much equipment does Sam need?

Solution

Using consistent units, we have values for:

- Production, P = 1,000 units per week
- Time to make a unit, T = 1/8 hours
- Hours worked per shift, H = 8 hours

We can substitute these into the equation:

$$\text{Number of machines, } N \geq \frac{PT}{HSD} \geq \frac{1,000 \times 1/8}{8 \times SD} \geq \frac{1,000}{64 \times SD}$$

- Working a single shift on weekdays has S=1 and D=5, so:

  $N \geq 1,000 / 64 \times 1 \times 5 \geq 1,000 / 320 \geq 3.125$

As equipment comes in discrete quantities, this number must be rounded up to 4. The utilization of these will be:

$$\text{Utilization} = \frac{PT}{NHSD} = \frac{1,000 \times 1/8}{4 \times 8 \times 1 \times 5} = 0.78 \text{ or 78 percent}$$

This low utilization comes from buying 4 sets of equipment when only 3.125 sets are actually needed. Sam could increase utilization by buying only 3 sets of equipment and making short-term adjustments to make up the difference.

- If Sam moved to a double shift, S=2 and D=5 to give:

  $N \geq 1,000/64 \times 2 \times 5 \geq 1,000/640 \geq 1.56$

  He would need two sets of equipment, but utilization would again be 78 percent.

- If Sam stayed with a single shift but worked at weekends, S=1 and D=7 to give:

  $N \geq 1,000/64 \times 1 \times 7 \geq 1,000/448 \geq 2.23$

  He would need three set of equipment and utilization would be:

  $U = 1,000 \times 1/8/3 \times 8 \times 1 \times 7 = 0.744$ or 74.4 percent

The capacity planning would be finished when Sam has examined these alternatives and implemented the best.

The example on page 256 illustrates one of the difficulties of matching capacity to demand. Demand usually comes in small quantities and can take almost any value. But capacity is increased by using an additional machine, opening another shop, employing another person, or using another vehicle. It only comes in large, discrete amounts. Therefore organizations must effectively try to match a discrete capacity to a continuous demand.

Suppose that demand for a product rises steadily over time. Capacity must be increased at some point, but the increase will come as a discrete step. This problem cannot be avoided, but there are three basic strategies for dealing with it. These are shown in Figure 9.1.

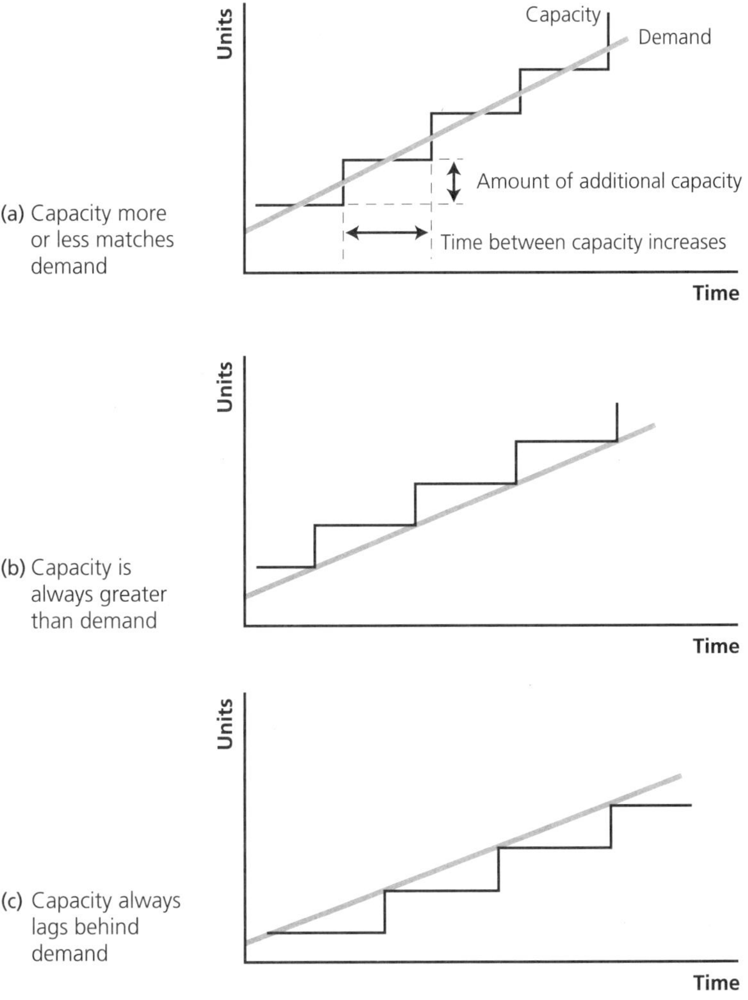

Figure 9.1 Options for Increasing Capacity

1. More or less can be used to match capacity demand, so that sometimes there is spare capacity and sometimes a shortage.
2. Capacity can at least equal demand at all times. This requires more equipment and results in lower utilization of equipment.
3. Capacity can be added only when the additional facilities would be fully used. This requires less equipment and gives high utilizations but limits output and sales.

Each of these strategies is best in different circumstances, but there is seldom an ideal solution where all resources are fully used. Factors that generally encourage capacity to be increased early (as shown in Figure 9.1b) are:

- Uneven or variable demand
- High profits, perhaps for a new product
- High cost of unmet demand, possibly resulting in lost sales
- Continuously changing product mix
- Uncertainty in capacity
- Variable efficiency
- Capacity increases that are relatively small
- Low cost of spare capacity, which may be used for other work

However, the main factor that encourages delaying an increase in capacity until the last possible moment (as shown in Figure 9.1c) is the capital cost.

There is another problem with capacity when planning an expansion. Whenever there is a change of capacity, operations will be disrupted by construction, staff training, and movement of equipment. So it may be better to have a few large increases in capacity, rather than several smaller ones, as shown in Figure 9.2. When an organization extends its offices, for example, it is often better to build more space than it currently needs to avoid more disruptions in the future.

The benefits of a few large increases are:

- Capacity stays ahead of demand for a long time
- Sales will not be lost
- There may be economies of scale
- An organization can gain an advantage over its competitors
- There are fewer disruptions

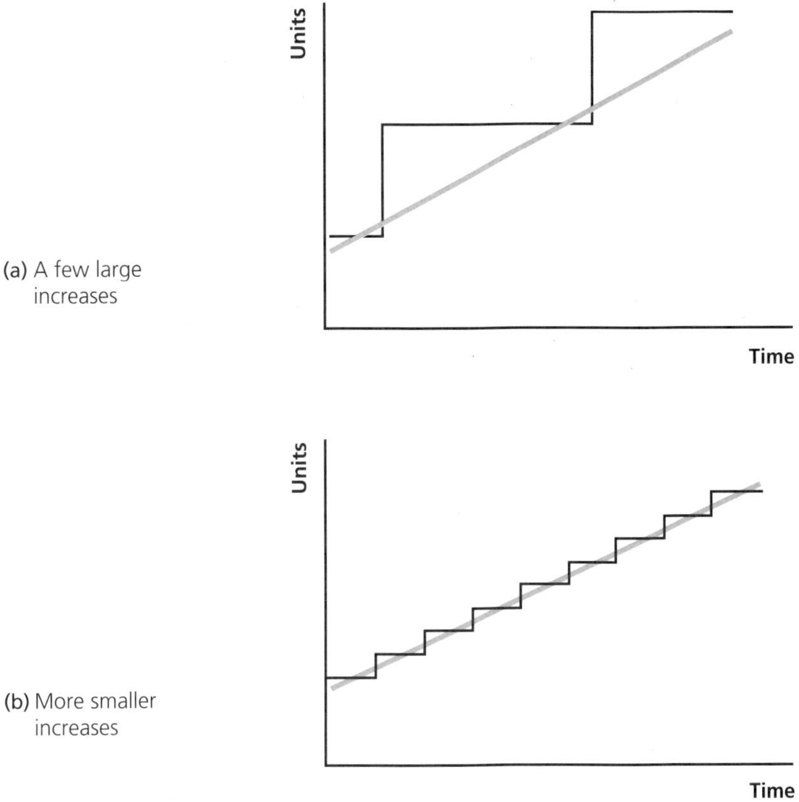

Figure 9.2 Alternatives for Increasing Capacity

The disadvantages include:

- Capacity does not closely match demand
- Disruptions may be more serious
- High capital costs
- Utilization of new capacity will be low
- High risk if demand changes
- The policy is less flexible

Example

The Barrett Corporation makes a range of snowploughs. It is planning production of one model over the next three years. The current capacity matches the demand of 100 units per year. But demand is rising by 50 units per year. The company can expand capacity now, or at the beginning of next year—but the machinery needed means that capacity can only be increased in discrete steps of 50 units. Each unit of spare capacity has notional costs of $400 per year, while each unit of shortage has a cost of $1,000 per year. What should the company do about its capacity?

Solution

The company has five alternatives.

Alternative 1. Do not increase capacity, but keep it at 100 units a year.

Year	Units of Demand	Sales	Spare	Shortage
0	100	100	0	0
1	150	100	0	50
2	200	100	0	100
Totals	450	300	0	150

This has total costs of 0 × 400 for spare capacity plus 150 × 1,000 for shortages, or $150,000 over the three years.

Alternatives 2 and 3. Increase capacity by either 50 or 100 units now, giving:

		50 Increase to 150			100 Increase to 200		
Year	Demand	Sales	Spare	Shortage	Sales	Spare	Shortage
0	100	100	50	0	100	100	0
1	150	150	0	0	150	50	0
2	200	150	0	50	200	0	0
Totals	450	400	50	50	450	150	0

Increasing capacity by 50 now has total costs of 50 × 400 + 50 × 1,000 = $70,000

Increasing capacity by 100 now has costs of 150 × 400 + 0 × 1,000 = $60,000

Alternatives 4 and 5. Increase capacity by 50 units or 100 units next year, giving:

		50 Increase to 150			100 Increase to 200		
Year	Demand	Sales	Spare	Shortage	Sales	Spare	Shortage
0	100	100	0	0	100	100	0
1	150	150	0	0	150	50	0
2	200	150	0	50	200	0	0
Totals	450	400	0	50	450	50	0

Increasing capacity by 50 next year has total costs of 0 × 400 + 50 × 1,000 = $50,000

Increasing capacity by 100 next year has costs of 50 × 400 + 0 × 1,000 = $20,000

The policy with the lowest costs is to increase capacity by 100 units next year.

Case Study – E-Z Office Products

E-Z Office Products makes a range of office supplies, including looseleaf ring binders. The long-term forecast demand for the binders is:

Year	Forecast Demand	Year	Forecast Demand
1	78,000	6	150,000
2	98,000	7	155,000
3	111,000	8	160,000
4	126,000	9	175,000
5	141,000	10	190,000

Current equipment can make 5,000 units per month. Extra capacity can be added in two ways.

1. Buying small machines which cost $10,000 and can produce 1,000 units per month
2. Buying larger machines which cost $100,000 and can produce 5,000 units per month

Questions

- Draw a graph of the forecast demand.
- Design a capacity plan to meet forecast demand if the company decides to buy smaller machines only. Calculate the annual utilization of equipment using this plan.
- Design a capacity plan if the company decides to buy larger machines only. Find the utilization of equipment with this plan.
- Discuss the benefits of each plan. Which of these two plans, or any other, would you prefer? What other information would you need to make a decision?

In Summary

One problem with capacity management is that capacity often comes in discrete units while demand is almost continuous. Managers must decide the best time and size for capacity changes.

Economies of Scale

Large increases in capacity can lead to **economies of scale**. These were discussed in the section on break-even analyses in Chapter 3. Bigger operations can produce units more cheaply than smaller operations. Mass-produced cars are much cheaper to make than specialized cars; colour supplements to newspapers are cheaper than limited edition prints; ordinary beer is cheaper than real ale.

These lower costs occur for three reasons:

1. Fixed costs are spread over more units
2. More efficient processes can be used, using larger batches and more automation
3. More experience with the product increases efficiency

Figure 9.3 shows how the unit cost may go down with various levels of designed capacity.

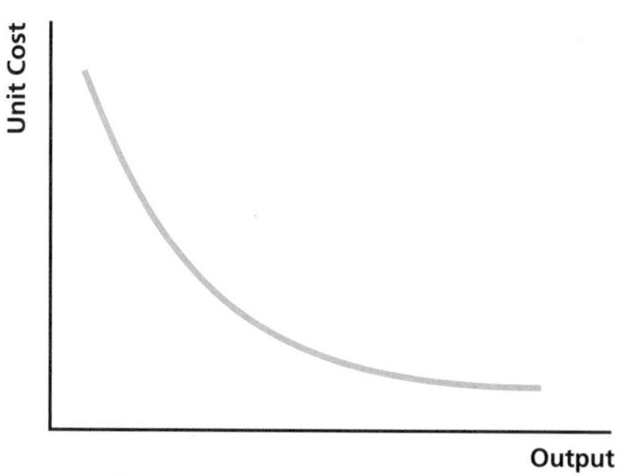

Figure 9.3 Economies of Scale Giving Lower Unit Costs

Example

The capacity of Belgrade Services is set by the number of staff employed. Total output is:

Staff	1	2	3	4	5	6	7
Output	25	60	110	150	180	205	220

The fixed cost of the operation is $50,000, and each staff member costs a total of $25,000 to employ. How would you compare the performance of different numbers of staff?

Solution

The spreadsheet in Figure 9.4 shows the costs in thousands of dollars.

The additional output per person is rising for the first three, showing economies of scale. But after this the output declines as diseconomies appear. The total cost per unit is found by adding the variable and fixed costs. This gives a minimum with five staff.

Figure 9.4 Spreadsheet of Calculations

Staff	Total Clients	Additional Clients per Staff Member	Average Clients per Staff Member	Variable Cost	Variable Cost per Client	Total Cost	Total Cost per Client
1	25	25	25.00	25.00	1.00	75.00	3.00
2	60	35	30.00	50.00	0.83	100.00	1.67
3	110	50	36.67	75.00	0.68	125.00	1.14
4	150	40	37.50	100.00	0.67	150.00	1.00
5	180	30	36.00	125.00	0.69	175.00	0.97
6	205	25	34.17	150.00	0.73	200.00	0.98
7	220	15	31.43	175.00	0.80	225.00	1.02

However, there are also what are known as diseconomies of scale. The communications, management, and organization needed by large facilities sometimes become so complex that they become less efficient and unit costs rise.

In Summary

Managers must consider economies of scale when planning capacity. These can make larger processes more attractive. In some circumstances there are also diseconomies of scale.

Review Questions

1. What are the two alternatives for dealing with short-term mismatches in capacity and demand?
2. What are the basic steps in capacity planning?
3. Why are discrete increases in capacity a problem?
4. What are the two basic questions for capacity expansion?
5. Give three reasons for falling unit cost with increasing output.

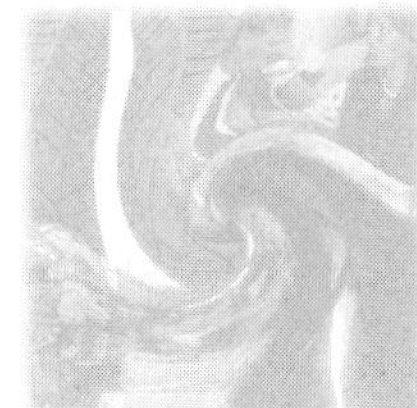

Changing Capacity over Time

Capacity planning tries to match available capacity as closely as possible to forecast demand. This is made difficult by factors such as discrete capacity and economies of scale. Another problem is that the capacity of an operation changes over time. Even if no major changes are made to the process, there are short-term variations due to operator illness, holidays, interruptions, and breakdowns. There are also longer-term changes in capacity. Two causes for these are learning curves and the declining performance of equipment.

Learning Curves

We all know that the more often we repeat something, the easier it becomes. Musicians and athletes, for example, spend a long time practising to become more skilful — they find it easier to reach a given level of performance. You can see this in almost all operations, where efficiency increases with the number of units made. In other words, the time needed for an operation falls as the number of units made rises. This effect is shown in Figure 9.5, and the graph is called a **learning curve**.

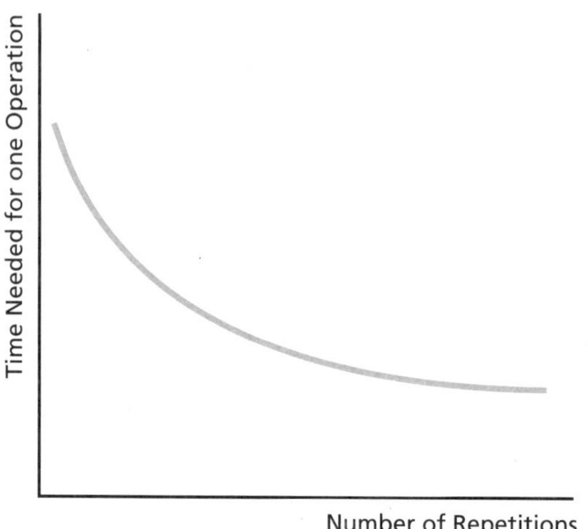

Figure 9.5 A Typical Learning Curve

With a common learning curve, the time taken to do an operation falls by some fixed proportion every time the number of repetitions is doubled. Typically this proportion is about 10 percent. If it takes 10 minutes the first time an operation is done, the second time it takes only 90 percent of this time or 9 minutes; the fourth time it takes 90 percent of the time needed for the second repetition or 8.1 minutes; the eighth time it takes 90 percent of the time needed for the fourth repetition or 7.29

Example

Jim delivers flyers to houses around his city. The first day he finished his round in two hours. How long would it take him to do the round on the second, fourth, eighth, and sixteenth days, with 90 percent, 80 percent and, 70 percent learning curves?

Solution

With a 90 percent learning curve, the second day will take 0.9 × 120 = 108 minutes, the fourth day 0.9 × 108 = 97.2 minutes, and so on. The results are given in the table to the right.

You can clearly see how different learning curves affect the time for Jim's round.

Day	Learning Curve 90%	80%	70%
1	120	120	120
2	108	196	84
4	97.2	76.8	58.8
8	87.5	61.4	41.2
16	78.7	49.2	28.8

minutes; the sixteenth time it takes 90 percent of the time needed for the eighth repetition or 6.561 minutes. This is described as a 90 percent learning curve. An 80 percent learning curve reduces the time faster, as you can see in the example on page 265.

The calculations for a learning curve can be done easily on a spreadsheet or from tables. Table 9.3 shows the cumulative time to make N units when the time to make the first unit is 1. To find the cumulative times when the first units takes T, simply multiply the result in the table by T. Thus, to make 8 units with an 80 percent learning curve and an initial time of 10 takes 10 × 5.35 = 53.5.

Table 9.3 *Learning Curve—Showing Cumulative Times*

N	75%	80%	85%	90%	95%
1	1.00	1.00	1.00	1.00	1.00
2	1.75	1.80	1.85	1.90	1.95
3	2.38	2.50	2.62	2.75	2.87
4	2.95	3.14	3.35	3.56	3.77
5	3.46	3.74	4.03	4.34	4.66
6	3.93	4.30	4.69	5.10	5.54
7	4.38	4.83	5.32	5.84	6.40
8	4.80	5.35	5.94	6.57	7.26
9	5.20	5.84	6.53	7.29	8.11
10	5.59	6.32	7.12	7.99	8.95
15	7.32	8.51	9.86	11.38	13.09
20	8.83	10.48	12.40	14.61	17.13
25	10.19	12.31	14.80	17.71	21.10
30	11.45	14.02	17.09	20.73	25.00
40	13.72	17.19	21.43	26.54	32.68
50	15.78	20.12	25.51	32.14	40.22
60	17.67	22.87	29.41	37.57	47.65
70	19.43	25.47	33.17	42.87	54.99
80	21.09	27.96	36.80	48.05	62.25
90	22.67	30.35	40.32	53.14	69.45
100	24.18	32.65	43.75	58.14	76.59
150	30.93	43.23	59.89	82.16	111.57
200	36.80	52.72	74.79	105.00	145.69
250	42.08	61.47	88.83	126.91	179.18
300	46.94	69.66	102.23	148.20	212.18
400	55.75	84.85	127.57	189.27	277.01
500	63.68	98.85	151.45	228.79	340.65

Example

Planned production of a new product in the next eight months is shown below. Trials suggest that the first unit will take 40 hours to make, and there is a 90 percent learning curve. How many employees are needed for the product, if each works an average of 200 hours per month?

Month	1	2	3	4	5	6	7	8
Production	4	6	20	30	40	50	100	50

Solution

The calculations for this are shown in Figure 9.6.

The cumulative time is found by multiplying the entry in the table above by 40, so the cumulative time to make 300 units with a 90 percent learning curve is 40 × 148.20 = 5,928 hours. The time needed in each month is the difference between consecutive cumulative times. When this figure is divided by 200, it shows the number of workers needed in a month.

Month	Production	Cumulative Production	Cumulative Time	Time in Months	Employees Needed
1	4	4	142.4	142.4	0.71
2	6	10	319.6	177.2	0.89
3	20	30	829.2	509.6	2.55
4	30	60	1502.8	673.6	3.37
5	40	100	2325.6	822.8	4.11
6	50	150	3286.4	960.8	4.80
7	100	250	5076.4	1790	8.95
8	50	300	5928	851.6	4.26

Figure 9.6 Calculations with Learning Curves

In Summary

The capacity of a process changes over time. There are several reasons for this. One reason is the effect of the learning curve, where repeating an operation reduces the time it takes.

Maintenance of Equipment

Learning curves make productivity rise over time, but there are some other factors that make productivity decrease. The most important of these is the aging of equipment.

New equipment is expected to work well, but as it gets older it breaks down more often, develops more faults, gives lower quality output, slows down, and generally wears out. If nothing is done to stop this, the performance of equipment will decline until it becomes unsatisfactory. Sometimes this change is slow, at other times the change is very fast, such as a bolt that suddenly breaks. A way of avoiding this decline is to introduce **routine maintenance** and **replacement**.

With routine maintenance, equipment is inspected and vulnerable parts are replaced at regular intervals. By replacing parts that are worn the equipment is restored to give continuing, satisfactory performance. How often should this maintenance be done? If it is done too frequently, the equipment will run efficiently but the maintenance costs will be very high. If it is not done frequently enough, the maintenance costs will be low but the system will still have breakdowns and failures.

The best policy for maintenance can be found by adding the two costs—from maintenance and expected failure. This gives a U-shaped curve which has a minimum. This minimum identifies the best time between maintenance periods, as shown in Figure 9.7.

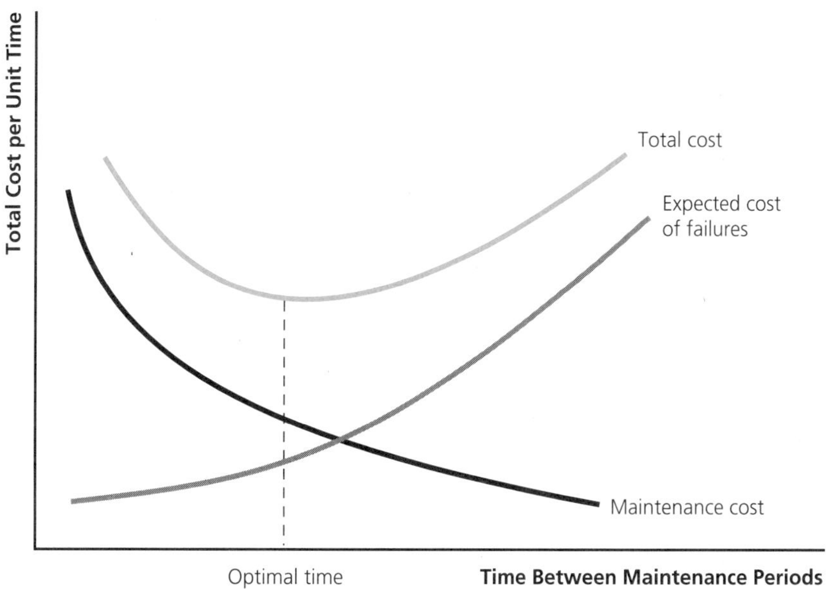

Figure 9.7 Finding the Best Time Between Maintenance Periods

Example

If a piece of equipment works continuously, the expected cost of failure rises each week as shown below. Routine maintenance can be done at a cost of $1,000, and this brings the equipment back up to new condition. What is the best time between maintenance periods?

Weeks Since Maintenance	0	1	2	3	4	5
Cost of Breakdowns in Week	$0	50	150	200	1,600	3,000

Solution

If the equipment is maintained every week, there is no cost for expected breakdowns; if maintenance is done every two weeks, the expected cost is $0 in the first week plus $50 in the second week; if maintenance is done every three weeks, the expected cost is $0 in the first week, $50 in the second week, and $150 in the third week. Adding the routine maintenance cost of $1,000 gives the following costs.

Weeks Between Maintenance	Maintenance Cost	Cost of Breakdowns in Week	Total cost of Breakdowns	Total Cost	Cost per Week
1	$1,000	$0	$0	$1,000	$1,000
2	1,000	50	50	1,050	525
3	1,000	150	200	1,200	400
4	1,000	200	400	1,400	350
5	1,000	1,600	2,000	3,000	600
6	1,000	3,000	5,000	6,000	1,000

If maintenance is done every four weeks, the cumulative cost of breakdowns is $400 and maintenance costs $1,000, to give a total cost of $1,400. This gives an average of $350 per week, which is the cheapest alternative.

Organizations do not have to use programs of routine or preventive maintenance, they can simply repair equipment when it breaks down. But this is not generally recommended, as breakdowns can occur at inconvenient times—preventive maintenance can be scheduled for quiet periods at night or weekends, but breakdowns can occur during busy times. A second option is to replace equipment when its performance declines to a specified level, but this results in very high capital costs. A third option is to have spare equipment waiting so that it can take over when there is a breakdown. Most organizations find the cheapest alternative is to use planned maintenance.

In Summary

The performance of equipment tends to decline with age. A program of routine maintenance can be used to keep it operating at a satisfactory level.

Replacing Equipment

Routine maintenance may keep equipment working efficiently, but there comes a point at which maintenance and repairs become too expensive and it is cheaper to buy new equipment. These replacement decisions can be expensive and need careful planning. There are, for example, many nuclear power stations around the world which are being phased out and need replacing. Nobody is really sure of the costs involved because there is still no way to dispose of nuclear waste. Other examples of expensive replacement decisions include office buildings, steel mills, ships, and airplanes.

A useful method of finding the best age of replacement is to add the cost of operating equipment over a number of years and divide this by the equipment's age to give an average annual cost. Repeating this calculation for several values of lifetime will show the age of replacement which gives the lowest annual cost. This is similar to the approach used for maintenance.

Example

Every year a company looks at the performance of its production machines so that any replacements can be delivered before the end of the financial year. The cost of replacing each machine is $150,000. Expected resale values at the end of each year and average annual operating costs are given in the following table. What is the best age to replace the machines?

Age of Machine	1	2	3	4	5
Resale Value	$75,000	$45,000	$22,500	$15,000	$ 7,500
Running Cost in Previous Year	$ 7,500	$13,500	$22,500	$61,500	$90,000

Solution

When a machine is sold, the total cost of use during its lifetime has two parts:

1. A capital cost equal to the difference between the price of a new machine and the resale value of the old one
2. A running cost, which is the cumulative running cost over the machine's life.

If a machine is sold after one year of use:

- Capital cost is 150,000 - 75,000 = $75,000
- Running cost is $7,500

The total cost of using the machine for one year is $82,500.

If the machine is sold after 2 years:

- Capital cost are 150,000 - 45,000 = $105,000
- Running cost are 7,500 in the first year plus $13,500 in the second year.

The total cost of using the machine for two years is $126,000, which is an average of $63,000 per year.

Repeating these calculations for other ages of replacement gives the following values.

Age of Replacement	1	2	3	4	5
Capital Cost	$75,000	$105,000	$127,500	$135,000	$142,500
Running Cost	7,500	21,000	43,500	105,000	195,000
Total Cost	82,500	126,000	171,000	240,000	337,500
Average Annual Cost	$82,500	$63,000	$57,000	$60,000	$67,500

You can see that replacement after three years gives the lowest average annual cost.

In Summary

Even with routine maintenance, there will come a time when equipment needs replacing. By considering the operating and replacement costs, an optimal replacement policy can be found.

Review Questions

1. What is meant by an 80 percent learning curve?
2. Why does the time taken to do an operation decline over time?
3. What is the purpose of routine maintenance?
4. Do you think it is likely or unlikely that maintenance costs for a machine will decline over time?
5. When do you think a machine should be replaced?

Chapter Review

- There are several measures for the performance of an organization. These include capacity, utilization, productivity, and efficiency.
- Productivity can be measured in several ways, the main ones being total and partial productivity. While most organizations want to improve productivity, the measures they use must be related to their overall objectives. Any single measure of productivity gives only one view of an organization's performance, so a range of measures must be used to give the overall view.
- Capacity measures the maximum output that can be achieved in a given time. Capacity is sometimes obvious, but generally needs some calculation or some agreed measure. The designed capacity is the maximum output of a process in ideal conditions, while the effective capacity is the maximum output under normal circumstances.
- The aim of capacity planning is to match available capacity to forecast demand. This is largely a strategic function but includes both tactical and operational decisions. Short-term mismatches between capacity and demand can be overcome by either demand management or capacity management.
- Important questions in capacity planning are when to change capacity and by how much. These decisions are complicated by factors such as discrete changes in capacity and economies of scale.

- The capacity of a process changes over time. Two specific causes of this are learning curves — which reduce the amount of time needed for an operation — and declining equipment performance with aging.

Key Terms

capacity *(p.243)*
capacity management *(p.254)*
capacity planning *(p.252)*
demand management *(p.254)*
designed capacity *(p.251)*
economies of scale *(p.261)*
effective capacity *(p.251)*
effectiveness *(p.244)*
efficiency *(p.244)*
learning curve *(p.263)*
partial productivity *(p.247)*
production *(p.244)*
productivity *(p.244)*
replacement *(p.267)*
resource requirement management *(p.255)*
routine maintenance *(p.267)*
total productivity *(p.246)*
utilization *(p.244)*

Problems

9.1 Coffee machines in a factory cafeteria are designed to serve up to 2,000 cups of coffee in a two-hour meal break. During a typical break, they were used for 90 minutes and served 1,000 cups. How could you measure their performance?

9.2 A family doctor sees patients for an average of ten minutes each. There is another five minutes of paper work for each visit, so appointments are made at 15-minute intervals. Her office is open for five hours each day, but during one session she was called away for an emergency which lasted one hour. Four patients who had appointments during this time were told to come back later. How could you measure the doctor's performance?

9.3 A ski lift has a pair of chairs pulled on a cable from the bottom of a ski run to the top. Ordinarily one pair of chairs arrives at the bottom of the slope every three seconds. If the lift works 10 hours per day for 100 days per year, what is its designed capacity? On a typical day, 10 percent of skiers need help getting on the lift, and they cause average delays of 10 seconds. A further 25 percent of skiers use the lift alone, and only one chair of the pair is used. What is the utilization of the lift?

9.4 In two consecutive years, a process had the following results.

	Year 1	Year 2
Number of Units Made	5,000	6,500
Raw Materials Used	15,000 kg	17,500 kg
Cost of Raw Materials	$40,000	$50,500
Hours Worked	1,200	1,500
Direct Labour Costs	$12,000	$18,000
Energy Used	20,000 kWh	24,000 kWh
Energy Cost	$2,000	$3,000

How has the productivity changed?

9.5 A service organization tries to deal with 100 customers per day. Each person in the organization can see three customers an hour, but has to do paper work which takes an average of 40 minutes per customer. Employees also lose 20 percent of their time when they do other tasks and cannot deal with customers' work. The standard working day in the organization is from 9:00 a.m. to 5:00 p.m. five days per week, with an hour off for lunch. How many employees should the organization hire? What is their utilization? One week the organization only dealt with 90 customers. What were the efficiency and utilization?

9.6 The fixed cost of a process is $110,000, and the capacity can be increased by using more machines at a cost of $55,000 each. The total output of the operation, measured in some consistent units, is:

Machines	1	2	3	4	5	6	7	8
Output	55	125	230	310	375	435	460	470

How many machines should be used to give the lowest unit cost?

9.7 It takes 25 minutes to make the first unit of a product. How long will it take to make each of the next nine units with a learning rate of 0.9?

9.8 New cars cost a company $24,000 each, with resale values and maintenance costs shown below. What is the best age of replacement?

Age of Car (years)	1	2	3	4	5	6
Resale Value	$16,000	$10,000	$6,000	$4,000	$2,400	$1,200
Annual Maintenance	$2,000	$2,400	$3,000	$4,000	$6,000	$17,500

Discussion Questions

9.1 Why do you think organizations are so eager to have quantitative measures of performance? How reliable are these likely to be? Does this reduce the importance of qualitative factors in performance?

9.2 Employees in a company say that productivity has risen by 20 percent, so they deserve a pay raise. Employers say that the amount of overtime worked has risen by 20 percent, raising the payroll by 30 percent, so employees should take a pay cut. What do you think of such arguments? Can you find other examples?

9.3 "There are so many different meanings of productivity that no one really knows what it describes." Do you think this is true? Explain.

9.4 It is generally said that 85 percent of productivity is set by the system, which is designed by managers. Only 15 percent is under the control of individual workers. Does this seem realistic? How should rewards for high productivity be shared? What should happen if an organization has low productivity?

9.5 Organizations are often tempted to find the easiest type of productivity to measure and then concentrate on improving this. What problems does this raise? Give any real examples of these problems.

9.6 How can routine maintenance and replacement programs help increase the efficiency of an organization? Is this equally valid in services and manufacturing?

9.7 Many of the calculations for maintenance and replacement decisions can be done using spreadsheets. Design a spreadsheet that will help in such decisions. How does this compare with standard software you have?

Chapter 10

PRODUCTION PLANNING

What plans are needed for production?

Contents

Introduction

The last chapter described capacity planning, which is a *strategic* function that ensures sufficient capacity of a process to meet forecast demand. Capacity planning forms part of the business strategy as shown in Figure 10.1. But capacity planning is only one stage in the planning. It leads to a series of *tactical* and *operational* plans that describe the details of a process.

This **hierarchy of plans** can be illustrated by an example of a manufacturing process. Suppose the capacity plan needs more capacity or space. This extra capacity can be found by building another factory—clearly a *strategic* decision. While the factory is being built, capacity might be increased by leasing additional space. This is a *tactical* decision. While the leased space is being prepared, overtime may be worked at weekends. This is an *operational* decision.

Thus, strategic decisions about capacity lead to a series of tactical decisions about resources. These in turn lead to a set of operational decisions about schedules.

Learning Objectives

After reading this chapter you should be able to answer questions such as:

- What are the different levels of planning?
- Why is planning so difficult?
- What is the purpose of aggregate planning?
- How are aggregate plans designed?
- What is the purpose of master schedules?
- How are master schedules designed?

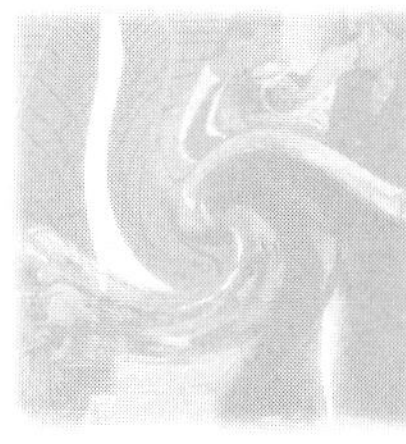

Hierarchy of Plans

All managers agree that there is a hierarchy of plans in every organization. Unfortunately, there is some disagreement about the terms used. We shall describe the steps in the planning process as follows:

- *Mission and business strategy* set the overall direction of the organization, as described in Chapter 2.
- *Capacity plans* ensure sufficient capacity to meet forecast demand, as discussed in Chapter 9.
- *Aggregate plans* show the overall production planned for families of products, typically by month for individual locations.
- *Master schedules* show a detailed schedule of production for individual products, typically by week.
- *Short-term schedules* show detailed schedules of jobs, equipment, and employees, typically by day.

Aggregate plans are sometimes called *aggregate production plans*, and master schedules are sometimes called *master production schedules*, but these terms may give the faulty impression that they are only used in manufacturing. Some also use the term a **business plan**, which is a broader view of a capacity plan that includes financial and other relevant information.

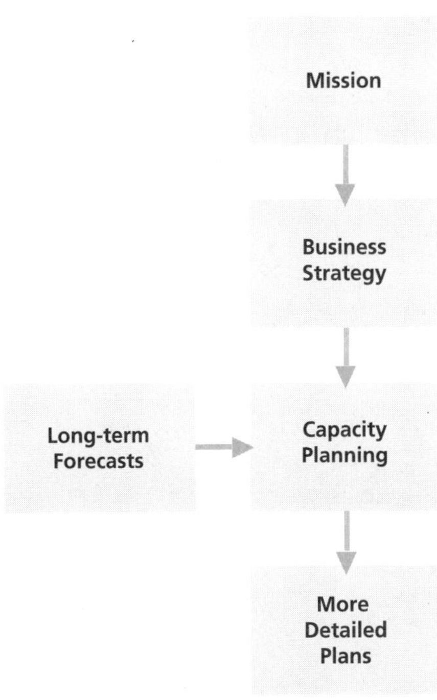

Figure 10.1 Levels of Planning

A typical planning process can be summarized as follows.

An organization's *mission* gives its overall purpose and aims. This leads to a *business strategy*, which includes decisions about what products to make, where to make them, how to make them, etc. *Long-term forecasts* show the likely demand for products over the next few years. These are used in *capacity plans*, which show how the demand can be met and determine the annual production for each location. The capacity plans are then broken down into *medium-term aggregate plans*. These show planned monthly production for families of products over the next year in each location. The aggregate plans take into account factors such as current stock, available manpower, and machines. The monthly aggregate plans are expanded to give *master schedules*, which show a timetable for the production of individual products, perhaps by week. The weekly master schedules are then expanded to give *short-term schedules*, or daily schedules of machines, operators, and other equipment for each day.

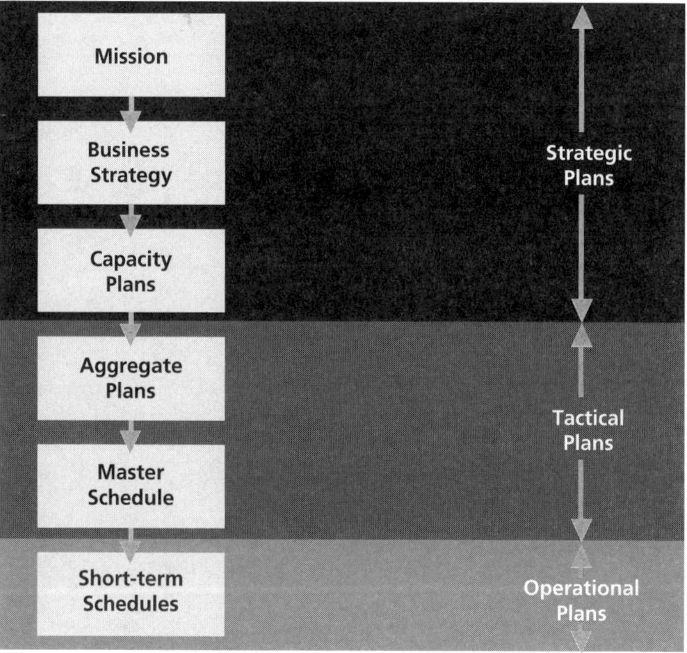

Figure 10.2 Outline of the Planning Process

In Summary

Every organization has a hierarchy of plans. These start with the mission and business strategy and move down into more detail. The operations strategy includes capacity planning. This leads to tactical aggregate plans and master schedules. These in turn lead to operational short-term schedules.

Review Questions

1. "Capacity planning is a purely strategic function." Do you agree or disagree with this?
2. What is the usual sequence of planning decisions?
3. What type of plans usually refer to:
   a) overall production at different locations
   b) individual products
   c) individual pieces of equipment
   d) equipment operators?

Case Study

Allenby Tools

Allenby Tools makes a variety of garden tools in three factories in Ontario. One run of their planning procedure is summarized as follows.

- *Business strategy*—concerns the organization's fundamental decisions.
  The company plans to continue making garden tools of high quality, using appropriate processes. They will continue operations in three factories at Thunder Bay, Sudbury, and Hamilton.

- *Capacity plans*—take long-term forecasts of demand and adjust capacity to match these.
  Long-term forecasts suggest sales of 50,000 garden tools next year. This leaves Allenby with a shortage in capacity of 10,000 tools for the year. A decision is made to overcome this shortage by increasing the staff in Hamilton and working two shifts at Sudbury. Then forecast demand can be met by Thunder Bay making 10,000 tools, Sudbury making 20,000 tools, and Hamilton making 20,000 tools.

- *Aggregate plans*—break down the capacity plans to create monthly plans for families of tools at each location.
  - Thunder Bay makes 1,000 tools in January. This requires a staff of 10 and results in 90 percent utilization of equipment.
  - Sudbury makes 2,500 tools in January. This requires 20 staff and gives 85 percent utilization of equipment.

- *Master schedules*—break down aggregate plans into weekly plans for individual products.
  - Thunder Bay. Week 1 of January. 100 spades
    50 forks
    100 rakes
    Week 2 of January. 50 spades
    250 rakes
    Week 3 of January. 100 spades
    100 rakes

- *Short-term schedules*—break down master schedules into daily timetables for individual batches of tools and equipment.
  - Thunder Bay. Week 1 of January.
    Monday morning shift
    10 spades on machines 1 to 4
    10 rakes on machines 5 to 8
    10 forks on machines 1 to 8
    Monday afternoon shift
    20 forks on machines 1 to 8
    Tuesday morning shift
    10 spades on machines 1 to 4
    10 forks on machines 5 to 8
    10 rakes on machines 1 to 8,
    etc.

Overall Planning Procedure

Chapter 9 described the steps in capacity planning as:

Step 1—forecast demand and use this to find the capacity needed
Step 2—calculate the capacity available with present facilities

Example

Silver Arrow Coach Lines operates in New Brunswick. Silver Arrow plans its capacity in terms of "bus-days." All business is classified as "full day," which are long-distance journeys, or "half day," which are shorter runs. Forecasts show expected annual demands for the next two years to average 400,000 full-day passengers and 750,000 half-day passengers. The company has 61 buses, each with an effective capacity of 40 passengers per day for 300 days per year. Breakdowns and other unexpected problems reduce efficiency to 90 percent. If there is a shortage of buses, the company can buy extra ones for $220,000 or rent them for $200 per day. How should the company approach its planning for the next two years?

Solution

Following the capacity planning steps listed:

- Step 1 starts by using the forecast demand to find the capacity needed. 400,000 full-day passengers are equivalent to 400,000/40 = 10,000 bus days per year, or 10,000/300 = 33.33 buses. 750,000 half-day passengers are equivalent to 750,000/(40 × 300 × 2) = 31.25 buses. So the total demand is 33.33 + 31.25 = 64.58 buses.
- Step 2 calculates the capacity of existing buses. The company has 61 buses, but the efficiency of 90 percent means that 61 × 0.9 = 54.9 buses are available.
- Step 3 compares the capacity needed and capacity available. There is a shortage of 64.58 - 54.9 = 9.68 buses.
- Step 4 lists alternative plans for overcoming any differences. In this case the alternatives are either to buy or rent buses.
- Step 5 looks at the alternatives and selects the best. To buy ten coaches would cost $2,200,000. To hire buses to make up the shortage would cost 9.68 × 300 × 200 = $580,800 per year. There are, of course, other alternatives of buying some coaches and renting a smaller number. A reasonable solution might be to buy eight coaches and make up any shortages by renting.

Step 3—identify any differences between the capacity needed and capacity available

Step 4—list alternative plans for overcoming these differences

Step 5—study the alternative plans and choose the best one

This same procedure can be used for other types of planning. It is a general procedure and is sometimes called **resource requirements planning**.

The example on page 280 shows the general approach to planning, but it does not give the whole picture. It can, for example, be very difficult to find alternative plans and to compare these. The problem is that plans are complicated and have many competing objectives. The difficulty of planning means that a more realistic view would replace the single procedure described above by an iterative procedure. This keeps modifying proposed plans until an acceptable one is found—so Steps 4 and 5 are repeated a number of times. The planning process then becomes:

General Planning Procedure

Step 1—find the production needed for the period

Step 2—find the resources available to make the products

Step 3—see if the available resources can meet the plans—and find any differences between resources needed and resources available

Step 4—suggest a production plan, with ways for overcoming these differences

Step 5—examine the plan to find any problems—perhaps constraints or objectives not met

Step 6—if the plan is not good enough, go back to Step 4

This procedure is illustrated in Figure 10.3 on page 282.

Figure 10.3 also shows that the planning process does not end, but is continuous. As plans for one period are finalized and implemented, planning moves on to the next period. It is difficult to generalize, but strategic plans might be updated annually, aggregate plans every three months, master schedules every month, and short-term schedules every week. Many companies adapt this process to planning cycles. So aggregate plans covering the next six months, say, might be produced every three months. The first half of these plans are more tentative, while the second half are more definite and form the basis of the master schedules. A typical timetable for this is shown in Figure 10.4 on page 283.

This iterative planning procedure is used because it is generally difficult if not impossible to find the "best" plans. Plans are judged by how well they compare with previous plans, how they balance conflicting objectives, how they include subjective views, and so on. There are always many factors to consider, including:

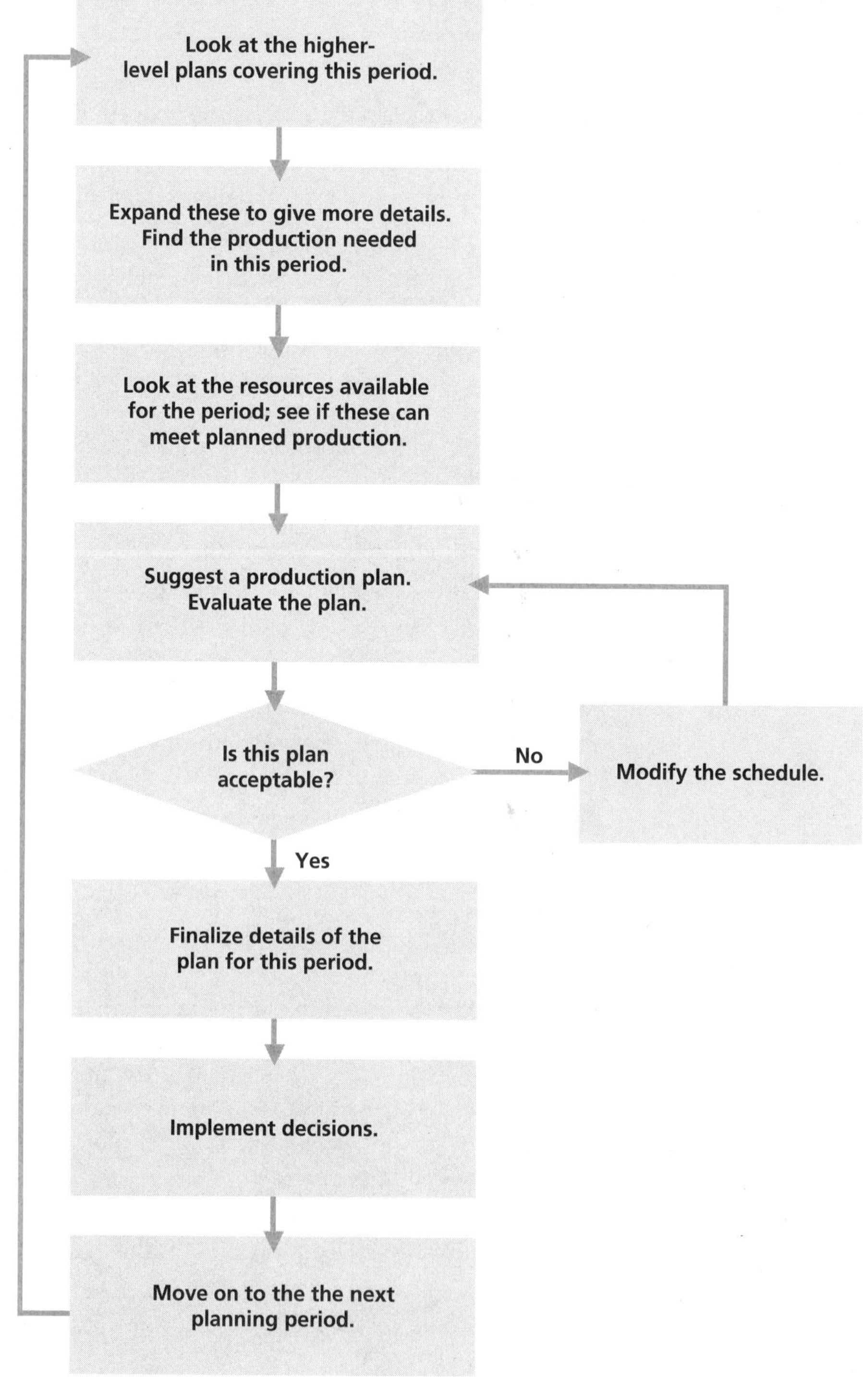

Figure 10.3 General Planning Procedure

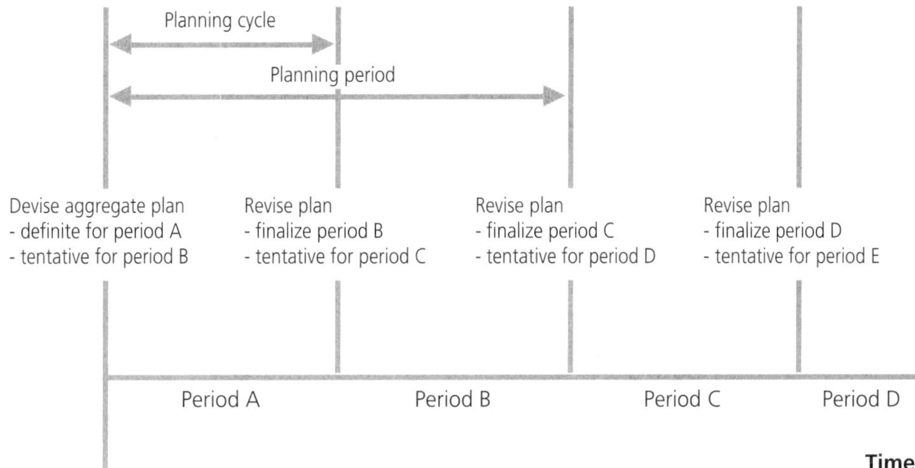

Figure 10.4 Continual Updating of Plans in Cycles

- *Demand*
  - forecast sales
  - sales already made
  - back orders
  - variation in demand
- *Operations*
  - machine capacity and utilization
  - aim of stable production
  - plans for new equipment
  - use of subcontractors
  - productivity targets
- *Materials*
  - availability of raw materials
  - inventory policies
  - current inventory levels
  - constraints on storage
- *Finance*
  - costs
  - cash flows
  - financing arrangements
  - exchange rates
  - general economic climate
- *Human Resources*
  - size of the workforce
  - levels of skills and productivity
  - unemployment rates
  - hiring and training policies

- *Marketing*
  - reliability of forecasts
  - competition
  - plans for new products
  - product substitution

In Summary

A general planning procedure takes the plans from the higher level and adds details to these. This is done by designing plans, assessing them, and then making adjustments until a good solution is found. In practice, these adjustments may be repeated many times.

Updating Plans

An important part of planning is updating. For every planning cycle, an organization does not try to produce entirely new plans but prefers to revise plans from the last cycle. This makes planning easier, and it also gives continuity to operations. We can illustrate this updating by looking at the stocks of products. Inventories of a product can give a buffer, so that production during a period need not exactly match demand in that period. In practice, demand during a period can be met from 1. stocks already held at the beginning of the period; 2. production during the period; 3. future production with late delivery.

The mix adopted should minimize the overall costs, maximize overall profit, or meet some other measure of performance.

Suppose we define S_t as the stock level at the end of period t, P_t as the production in period t, and D_t as the demand. You can see that:

Stock at end of this period = Stock at end of last period + Production during this period – Demand met during this period

or $$S_t = S_{t-1} + P_t - D_t$$

This assumes that there are no back orders, where some demand in one period is met by production from the following period. If we take this into account we have:

$$S_t = S_{t-1} + P_t - D_t - B_{t-1} + B_t$$

where B_t is the number of back orders in period t which are met from production in period t + 1.

The updating procedure in the example on page 285 can be used for planning other resources. You could, for example, replace inventory levels with number of employees:

Example

Nestor Services forecast demand for a product over the next eight months as follows:

Month	1	2	3	4	5	6	7	8
Demand	15	25	25	30	40	40	25	20

A minimum of 10 units is kept in stock, and no back orders are allowed. There are currently 35 units in stock and production is in batches of 50, with a very short lead time. Design a production plan to satisfy the demand.

Solution

You can do the calculations for this in the following table.

Month	1	2	3	4	5	6	7	8	9
Stock at Beginning	35	20	45	20	40	50	10	35	15
Demand	15	25	25	30	40	40	25	20	
Production	0	50	0	50	50	0	50	0	
Stock at End	20	45	20	40	50	10	35	15	

At the beginning of the first month, there are 35 units in stock and demand during the month is 15. No production is needed and the stock at the end of the month is 35 - 15 = 20. This stock of 20 is available at the beginning of the second month. Demand is 25 in the second month, so a batch must be made. Scheduling a batch of 50 units in month 2 gives stock at the end of the month of 20 + 50 - 25 = 45.

As there must be at least 10 units left in stock, a batch of 50 is made whenever the stock at the beginning of a month minus demand in that month is less than 10. Repeating this procedure gives a production plan for the following months. This plan is only one alternative; many others are possible, and managers should examine a range before making a final decision.

Number employed in current month = Number employed last month – Dismissals and resignations at end of last month + New hires at beginning of current month

In Summary

The amount of a resource available in a period can be found by updating the amount available in the previous period. This is particularly useful for looking at production where inventories are important.

Case Study

Kawasaki Heavy Industries

Kawasaki Heavy Industries is best known for its motorcycles, which are made in a number of plants around the world. Production planning at these plants has inputs from several sources, including local demands and needs of the main plant in Akashi, Japan. Kawasaki looks for continuous improvement in its operations, so its methods are always changing. Some standard elements of Kawasaki's planning are outlined below.

- The process begins with *a sales forecast,* which gives the monthly demand for each model of motorcycle for the next year. This is updated every three months.
- The forecasts are consolidated into a s*ales plan,* which shows the number of each model that must be available for sale each month for the next year. The plan is updated every three months, with the final three months considered firm.
- The sales plan is one input to the *production plan* at plants. This looks up to 18 months ahead and is used for capacity planning and budgeting. The plan is updated every three months, with the last three months fixed to agree with the sales plan. Scheduled deliveries of parts allow no changes in the last six weeks.
- The production plan is expanded to give a *daily production schedule,* which is the master schedule and shows the daily assembly program. Details of this are added four or five months in advance, and plans are updated every three months to fit into the cycles of the sales and production plans. The last six weeks of this plan are fixed by the production plan, but minor adjustments are made every week.
- The daily production schedule is expanded to produce *fabrication schedules,* which show the timetable for making components needed for final assembly.
- The fabrication schedules are used to find the *purchase orders* needed to get parts and materials from suppliers.

Review Questions

1. Where do the initial requirements for a planning period come from?
2. "A planning process starts off with general plans and adds more details at each stage." Do you think this is true?
3. How do updating procedures work with plans?

Aggregate Plans

Aims of Aggregate Plans

Aggregate plans and master schedules bridge the gap between strategic capacity plans and operational details. This section considers aggregate plans, and the following section discusses master schedules.

Aggregate planning takes the forecast demand and capacity and translates this into production plans for each family of products for, typically, each of the next few months. Aggregate planning looks only at production of families of products and is not concerned with individual products. A knitwear manufacturer, for example, may produce many different styles, colours, and sizes of sweaters and skirts. The aggregate plan only shows the total production of sweaters and the total production of skirts. It does not look in any more detail at the production of a particular style, colour, or size. Aggregate plans will consider the total number of barrels of chemicals to be produced or books to be printed, but will not consider the amount of each chemical or the copies of each title.

Aggregate planning starts when the long-term demand has been forecast, and when planned capacity can meet this demand. Now the forecast demand and capacity plan are transformed into an aggregate production plan, which considers questions such as:

- Should production be kept steady or should it change with demand?
- Should stocks be used to meet changing demand—producing for stock during periods of low demand and using stocks during periods of high demand?
- Should subcontractors be used for peak demands?
- Should the size of the workforce change with demand?
- How can employee work patterns be changed to meet changing demand?
- Should prices be changed?
- Are shortages allowed, perhaps with late delivery?
- Can demand be smoothed?

As you can see, an important question is how much variation is allowed in the aggregate plan—should production change with changing demand or should it be more steady? The usual answer is that aggregate production should vary as little as possible. There are many advantages to keeping production constant, including:

- Planning is easier
- Flow of products is smoother
- There are fewer problems because of changes
- There is no need to "hire-and-fire" employees
- Employees have regular work patterns
- Larger lot sizes reduce costs
- Inventories can be reduced as there is less variation
- Quality is more reliable
- Experience with a product reduces problems

The purpose of **aggregate planning** is to design medium-term production plans for families of products which:

- Allow all demand to be met
- Keep production relatively stable
- Keep costs low
- Keep within the constraints of the capacity plan
- Meet any other specific objectives and constraints

The final output from aggregate planning is a schedule of production for each family of products, typically for each of the next few months.

As already stated, production need not match demand exactly. But in practice there are three ways to meet uneven demand.

1. *Chase demand.* Here production exactly matches demand, and we produce exactly what we need every month. This gives no inventories, but we have to change production every period, hiring or firing workers, changing production levels, and so on. Production should be kept relatively stable, so this is not usually a good plan.

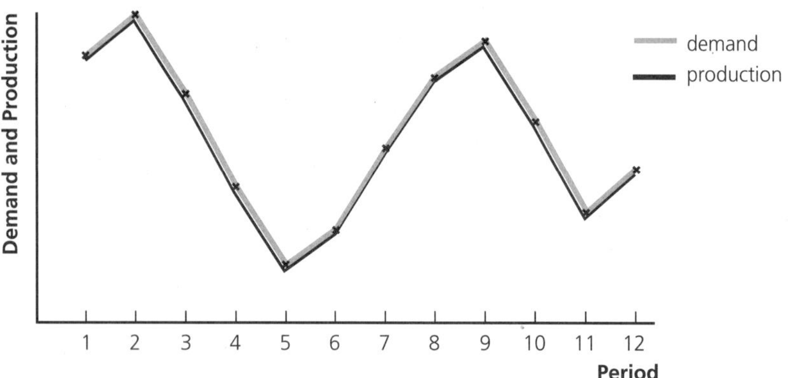

Figure 10.5 Chase Demand Policy for Production

2. *Produce at a constant production rate.* Here the organization produces at a constant rate equal to the average demand. Since the production rate is constant and demand is variable, the differences are met by building or using inventories. This means that there are always inventory holding costs and there may also be shortage costs. In general this is the best approach, but it can be difficult to achieve.

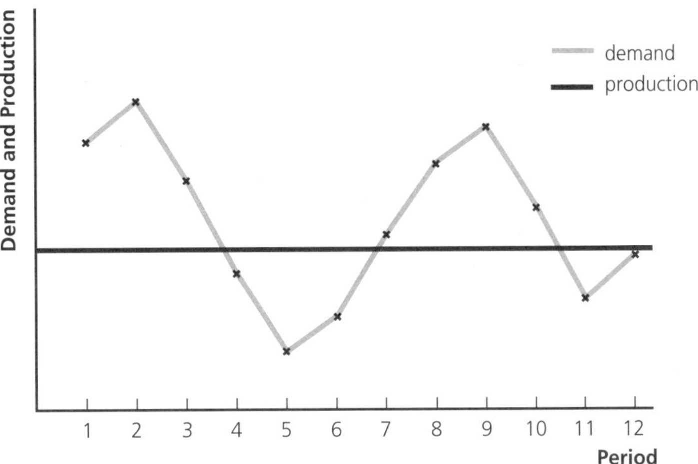

Figure 10.6 Constant Production Policy

3. *Mixed policy.* This is a combination of the first two policies. Here there are some changes in the production rate, but not every period. The policy tries to compromise by having a fairly stable production, but reduces the inventory costs by allowing some changes. In practice, this is probably the most commonly used strategy. In any circumstances there are many possible mixed strategies. Managers must look at a range of these until they find one that meets their objectives.

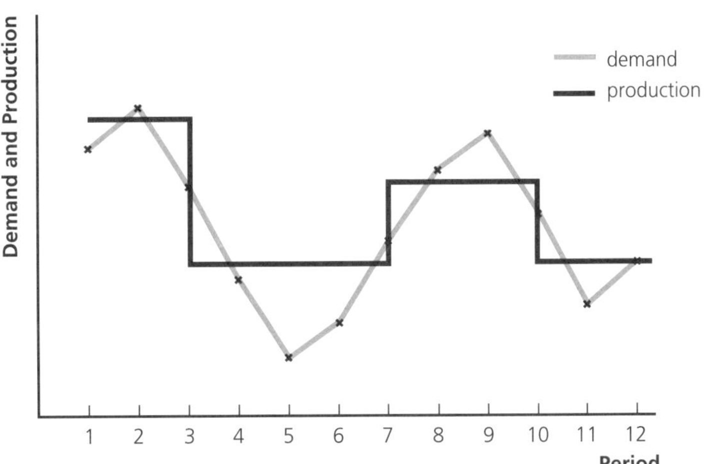

Figure 10.7 A Mixed Production Policy

In Summary

Aggregate planning takes the forecast demand and capacity plans and generates medium-term production plans for families of products. It designs plans which meet overall demand, while keeping stable production, and meeting any other specific conditions.

Case Study – Canadian Producers

Bob Jones, the Operations Manager of Canadian Producers, designs an aggregate plan every month. This plan covers the following 6 months. He has just started a planning cycle, and has the following data.

Period	1	2	3	4	5	6
Forecast Demand	1,600	2,000	2,500	2,600	3,000	1,500

Costs are as follows:

Inventory holding cost = $0.50 per unit held at the end of a month

Shortage/back-order cost = $5 per unit per month

Cost of moving an employee from other jobs to this product = $200 per employee

Cost of moving an employee from this product to other jobs = $150 per employee

Beginning inventory = 0

Beginning number of employees = 16

An average employee can produce 100 units per month.

Using these figures, Bob did the calculations shown in the following tables.

Chase Demand

No.	Period	1	2	3	4	5	6	Total
1	Aggregate Demand	1,600	2,000	2,500	2,600	3,000	1,500	13,200
2	Production Rate	1,600	2,000	2,500	2,600	3,000	1,500	13,200
3	Ending Inventory	0	0	0	0	0	0	
4	Stockout/Back Order	0	0	0	0	0	0	
5	Inventory Carrying Cost (Line 3 × 0.5)	0	0	0	0	0	0	0
6	Stockout Cost (Line 4 × 5.0)	0	0	0	0	0	0	0
7	No. of Employees	16	20	25	26	30	15	
8	Cost of Moving Employees	0	800	1,000	200	800	2,250	5,050
9	Total Cost (Line 5 + Line 6 + Line 8)	0	800	1,000	200	800	2,250	5,050

(Continued)

Case Study – Canadian Producers – *Continued*

Constant Production Rate

No.	Period	1	2	3	4	5	6	Total
1	Forecasted Demand	1,600	2,000	2,500	2,600	3,000	1,500	13,200
2	Production Rate	2,200	2,200	2,200	2,200	2,200	2,200	13,200
3	Ending Inventory	600	800	500	100	0	0	2,000
4	Stockout/Back Order	0	0	0	0	700	0	700
5	Inventory Carrying Cost (Line 3 × 0.5)	300	400	250	50	0	0	1,000
6	Stockout Cost (Line 4 × 5)	0	0	0	0	3,500	0	3,500
7	Number of Employees	22	22	22	22	22	22	–
8	Cost of Moving Employees	1,200	0	0	0	0	0	1,200
9	Total Cost (Line 5 + Line 6 + Line 8)	1,500	400	250	50	3,500	0	5,700

Mixed Policy—Initial Plan

No.	Period	1	2	3	4	5	6	Total
1	Forecasted Demand	1,600	2,000	2,500	2,600	3,000	1,500	13,200
2	Production Rate	1,800	1,800	2,600	2,600	2,600	1,800	13,200
3	Ending Inventory	200	0	100	100	0	0	400
4	Stockout/Back Order	0	0	0	0	300	0	300
5	Inventory Carrying Cost (Line 3 × 0.5)	100	0	50	50	0	0	200
6	Stockout Costs (Line 4 × 5)	0	0	0	0	1,500	0	1,500
7	Number of Employees	18	18	26	26	26	18	–
8	Cost of Moving Employees	400	0	1,600	0	0	1,200	3,200
9	Total Cost (Line 5 + Line 6 + Line 8)	500	0	1,650	50	1,500	1,200	4,900

Questions

- Are Bob's calculations correct?
- Which of these three policies is best?
- Can you suggest any other policies which would be better?

Most plans use a mixed policy, so we need some way of designing these. There are three main ways of designing aggregate plans, which are classified here as:

- Intuitive approach
- Graphical methods
- Matrix arithmetic

Intuitive Approach

Like most plans, aggregate plans are not usually designed from scratch but are variations of previous plans—so next month's production will be similar to last month's. The simplest approach to aggregate planning, then, is to use an experienced planner to look at the current situation and, in the light of experiences with similar plans, design updated plans. In practice, this is the most widely used method of planning.

Unfortunately, this intuitive approach can give results that have variable quality, the plans may take a long time to produce, and they may include bias. However, the intuitive approach is convenient and easy to use, the process is well understood, and experts can create good results which are trusted by the organization.

Example

The aggregate, monthly demand for a family of products is shown below. If this is the only information you have, what monthly production schedule would you suggest for the products?

Month	Jan	Feb	March	April	May	June	July
Aggregate Demand	80	70	60	120	180	150	110

Solution

You could, of course, suggest that production matches demand. However, most organizations prefer stable production. In the absence of any further information, you could suggest a steady production equal to the average demand of 110. During the first three months, the demand will be less than supply—so stocks will rise, but these will be used during the following months.

Month	Jan	Feb	March	April	May	June	July
Demand	80	70	60	120	180	150	110
Production	110	110	110	110	110	110	110
Stock at Month End	30	70	120	110	40	0	0

The stock at the end of each month is equal to the stock at the end of the previous month, plus the production in the current month, minus the demand in the current month.

Stock at month end = Stock at end of last month + Production in month − Demand in month

An obvious disadvantage of this plan is the high stock levels. If you had more information about the costs, stock-holding policies, materials supply, availability of workforce, and so on, you could look for some improvements to the plan.

In Summary

Intuitive methods of aggregate planning are widely used, and are based on planners' experience. They are easy to use, but can give poor and unreliable results.

Graphical Methods

The second approach to aggregate planning uses a graph. This is really just a convenient tool for the intuitive method. The most popular format uses a graph of cumulative demand over some time period. Then an aggregate plan is drawn as a line of cumulative supply. Planners aim to get the cumulative supply line nearly straight, giving constant production, and as close as possible to the cumulative demand line. The difference between the two lines shows the mismatch:

- When the cumulative demand line is below the cumulative supply line, production has been too high and the excess has accumulated as stock
- When the cumulative demand line is above the cumulative supply line, production has been too low and some demand has not been met

Graphical approaches have the advantages of being easy to use and to understand. Their limitations are that optimal solutions are not guaranteed, sometimes very poor results occur, the planning may take some time, and the method still relies on the skills of a planner.

Example

The forecast monthly demand for a family of products is shown below. At the end of every month the plans are examined and a holding cost of $10 is given for every unit held in stock. Any shortages are satisfied by back orders, but each unit of shortage is given a cost of $100 for lost profit, goodwill, and future sales. Each time the production rate is changed it costs $10,000. The effective capacity for the products is 300 units per month and the company wants to spend less than $1,900 per month on these activities. Design an aggregate plan for the products.

Month	1	2	3	4	5	6	7	8	9
Aggregate Demand	280	320	260	160	120	100	60	100	130

Solution

The company should aim for stable production as changes are very expensive. So a first step would suggest a constant production equal to the average demand of 170 per month. The cumulative demand and supply for this are shown in Figure 10.8.

(Continued)

Example - Continued

Unfortunately, the cumulative demand line is always above the cumulative supply and there are continuous shortages. The total cost of these shortages is calculated in the following table.

Month	1	2	3	4	5	6	7	8	9
Aggregate Demand	280	320	260	160	120	100	60	100	130
Cumulative Demand	280	600	860	1,020	1,140	1,240	1,300	1,400	1,530
Supply	170	170	170	170	170	170	170	170	170
Cumulative Supply	170	340	510	680	850	1,020	1,190	1,360	1,530
Shortage in Month	90	260	350	340	290	220	110	40	0

The shortage in each month is the amount by which cumulative demand is higher than cumulative supply. The total cost of this plan comes from shortages and is found by adding the shortages and multiplying this by $100; i.e., 1,700 × 100 = $170,000. This is considerably above the company target of $1,900 per month or a total of $17,100.

Although changing the production rate is expensive, it might be worthwhile to reduce the shortages found in the initial plan. As demand is heavy in the first three months, the process could be run at its maximum output of 300 units per month. Then the total demand to be met from production in the remaining six months is (1,530 – 3 × 300) = 630, for an average of 105 per month. So a reasonable production plan is 300 for the first three months and 105 for the next six months. The cumulative graph of supply and demand is shown in Figure 10.9. You can see that there is a close match, and therefore lower costs would be expected.

Month	1	2	3	4	5	6	7	8	9
Aggregate Demand	280	320	260	160	120	100	60	100	130
Cumulative Demand	280	600	860	1,020	1,140	1,240	1,300	1,400	1,530
Supply	300	300	300	105	105	105	105	105	105
Cumulative Supply	300	600	900	1,005	1,110	1,215	1,320	1,425	1,530
Stock at Month End	20	0	40	0	0	0	20	25	0
Shortage in Month	0	0	0	15	30	25	0	0	0

If cumulative supply is greater than cumulative demand, this shows up as a stock at the end of the month. If cumulative demand is greater than cumulative supply, this shows up as a shortage in the month. The cost of this plan is found from:

Stock Holding	105 × 10 = 1,050
Shortage	70 × 100 = 7,000
Production Change	1 × 10,000 = 10,000

(Continued)

Example - Continued

This gives a total cost of $18,050 or more than $2,000 per month. This is an improvement but still does not meet the company target, so the plan must be adjusted. Shortages still result in high costs, so the organization could try to maintain production at 300 units for another month. Then the average production in the remaining five months is (1,530 - 4 × 300)/5 = 66.

Month	1	2	3	4	5	6	7	8	9
Aggregate Demand	280	320	260	160	120	100	60	100	130
Cumulative Demand	280	600	860	1,020	1,140	1,240	1,300	1,400	1,530
Supply	300	300	300	300	66	66	66	66	66
Cumulative Supply	300	600	900	1,200	1,266	1,332	1,398	1,464	1,530
Stock at Month End	20	0	40	180	126	92	98	64	0

With this plan there are no shortages, so costs are:

Stock holding 620 × 10 = 6,200

Production change 1 × 10,000 = 10,000

This total of $16,200 (or $1,800 per month) is within the company target and could be the final aggregate plan. If necessary, the plan could be adjusted further until a better solution is found.

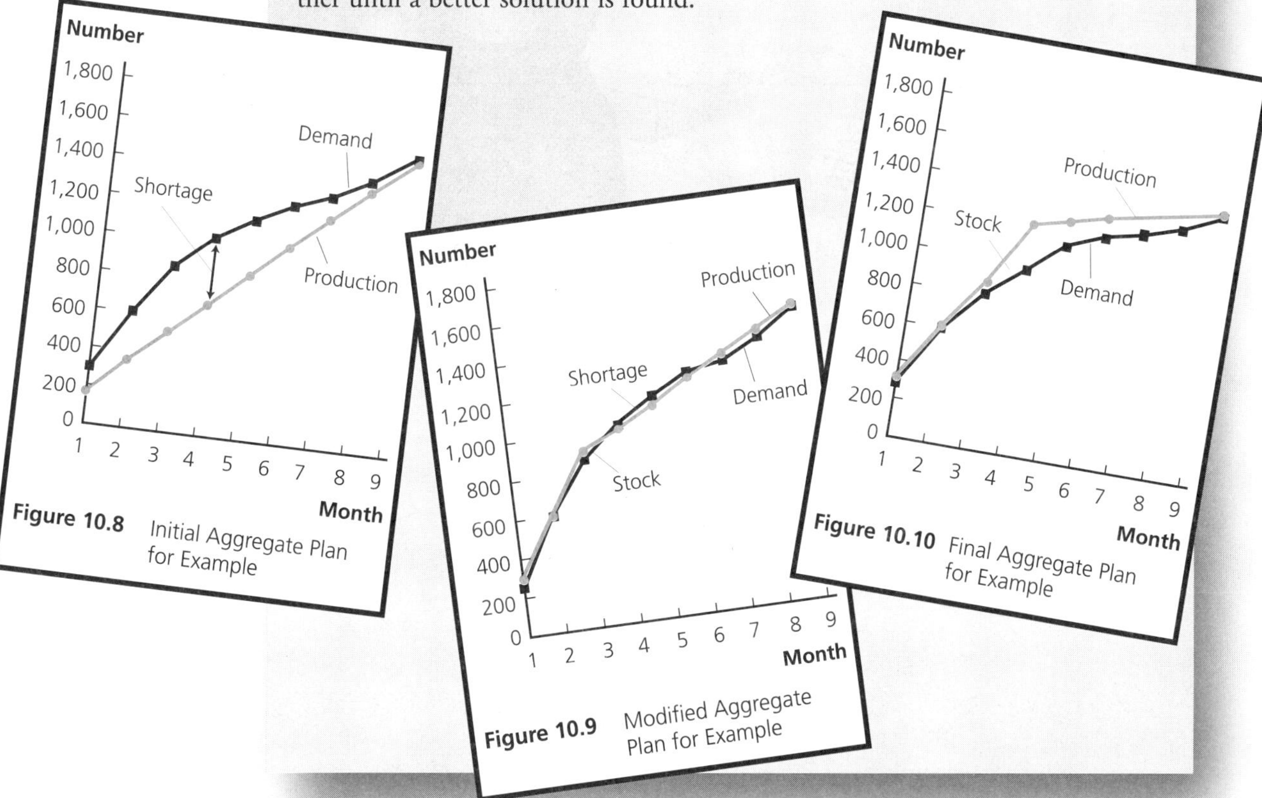

Figure 10.8 Initial Aggregate Plan for Example

Figure 10.9 Modified Aggregate Plan for Example

Figure 10.10 Final Aggregate Plan for Example

In Summary

Graphs can be used for aggregate planning, usually by plotting cumulative demand and supply. These still rely on experience, but can give useful results.

Matrix Calculations

Graphs can take a long time to draw—even with graphical packages—and they show overall patterns rather than details. If you want to compare a number of alternative plans, it is often easier to do some calculations using a matrix. This has the major advantage of using a computer spreadsheet.

The usual approach is to draw a matrix with the resources to be used down the left-hand side and the time periods across the top. The available capacity for each resource is shown down the right-hand side of the matrix, and the demand is shown across the bottom. The body of the matrix has two values: the cost of using resources, and the amount of resources used in a period. An example of this is shown in Figure 10.11.

Cost of using resource (value in the small box)
Amount of resource used (value beside the box)

		Period				Capacity
		1	2	3		
Resources	1	124 [16]	220 [14]	49 [9]		400
	2	240 [10]	40 [15]			360
	3	60 [15]	30 [13]			240
	4	120 [11]				240
	5	60 [10]				
	6					
Demand		1,820	1,430			Totals

Figure 10.11 Typical Matrix for Aggregate Planning

Often, the resources include the number of units that can be made in regular time, overtime, and by subcontractors in each period. Then, the cost entries are the costs of producing in one period for supply in another, and might include stock-holding or back-order costs. This leads to a simple method for designing an aggregate plan as follows.

Procedure for Aggregate Planning

1. Take the next time period.
2. Find the lowest cost in this column.
3. Assign as much production as possible to the cell with lowest cost—without exceeding either the supply of resources or the demand for products.
4. Subtract the amount assigned from the total capacity to give the spare capacity, and calculate the unmet demand.
5. If there is unmet demand, go to Step 2; if all demand has been met, move on to the next period in Step 1.

Example

Chen Suen is the Operations Manager for a small manufacturing company. He has forecast the aggregate demand for a family of products for the next four months as 130, 80, 180, and 140. Normal capacity is 100 units per month, overtime has a capacity of 20 per month, and subcontractors have a capacity of 60 units per month. The unit cost is $10 for normal capacity, $12 for overtime, and $15 for subcontractors. It costs $1 to stock a unit for a month, and no back orders or shortages are allowed. Use a matrix method to design an aggregate plan for the products.

Solution

The first step is to build a matrix with costs, capacities, and demand, as shown in Figure 10.12.

		Period				Capacity
		1	2	3	4	
Period 1	Normal work	10	11	12	13	100
	Overtime	12	13	14	15	20
	Subcontract	15	16	17	18	60
Period 2	Normal work	X	10	11	12	100
	Overtime	X	12	13	14	20
	Subcontract	X	15	16	17	60
Period 3	Normal work	X	X	10	11	100
	Overtime	X	X	12	13	20
	Subcontract	X	X	15	16	60
Period 4	Normal work	X	X	X	10	100
	Overtime	X	X	X	12	20
	Subcontract	X	X	X	15	60
	Demand	130	80	180	140	

Figure 10.12 Initial Matrix for Example

(Continued)

Example – Continued

The demands and capacities are given directly in the problem. The costs in each cell are a combination of production and stock-holding costs. It costs \$10 to make a unit in normal work hours, but if this is used in a later period holding costs are added—so the cost rises to \$10 + \$1 = \$11 in the following period, \$10 + \$2 × 1 = \$12 in the next period. No back orders are allowed, so you can cross out the cells for meeting demand in period 1 by producing in period 2, etc.

Using the procedure described above, the first step is to look down column 1 to find the smallest cost. This is the \$10 for normal work done in period 1, so you would make as much as possible there. The normal capacity is 100 units, so this leaves a shortage of 30 units. The next lowest cost is \$12 for overtime, which has a capacity of 20 units, so the shortage is still 10 units, which must be made by subcontracting. These amounts are subtracted from capacities.

Moving to period 2, the lowest cost is the \$10 for normal work done in period 2, which can meet all demand.

Moving to period 3, the lowest cost is the \$10 for normal work done in period 3, which can meet 100 of the demand. The next lowest cost is \$11 for normal work done in period 2. There is still capacity of 20 units here, so this leaves a shortage of 60 units. The next lowest cost with spare capacity is \$12 for overtime in period 3. This meets 20 units of demand, but there is still a shortage of 40 units. The next lowest cost is \$13 for overtime in period 2. This meets 20 units of demand, but there is still a shortage of 20 units, which can best be met from subcontracting in period 3.

This process is repeated for period 4, to give the results shown in Figure 10.13.

		Period 1		Period 2		Period 3		Period 4		Capacity
		Units	Cost	Units	Cost	Units	Cost	Units	Cost	
Period 1	Normal work	100	10	–	11	–	12	–	13	0
	Overtime	20	12	–	13	–	14	–	15	0
	Subcontract	10	15		16		17		18	50
Period 2	Normal work			80	10	20	11	–	12	0
	Overtime				12	20	13	–	14	0
	Subcontract				15		16		17	60
Period 3	Normal work					100	10	–	11	0
	Overtime					20	12	–	13	0
	Subcontract					20	15		16	40
Period 4	Normal work							100	10	0
	Overtime							20	12	0
	Subcontract							20	15	40
	Demand	130		80		180		140		

Figure 10.13 Final Solution for Example

The three approaches to aggregate planning described here all rely on the skills of the planner. There are more formal, mathematical approaches, but they are complex, difficult to understand, require a lot of data, and the models may take too simplified a view of real situations. These mathematical approaches are most useful in oil companies and other organizations where small variations from optimal plans give much higher costs.

In Summary

Calculations for aggregate planning can be done easily in a matrix. Then a spreadsheet can do the calculations. This is a very popular way of planning.

Review Questions

1. What period would a typical aggregate plan cover?
2. What are the main inputs for aggregate planning?
3. What is the main output of aggregate planning?
4. What are the benefits of intuitive aggregate planning?
5. How can a good aggregate plan be recognized from a graph?
6. What are the benefits of using a matrix method for aggregate planning?

Master Schedule

The aggregate plan shows overall production by families of products. Once this plan has been accepted, it is broken down to provide more details in a master schedule. So the master schedule "disaggregates" the aggregate plan and shows the number of individual products to be made in, typically, each week. It gives a detailed timetable of planned output for each product. An aggregate plan may show 1,000 radiators being made next month, while the master schedule gives details for each product with, say, 50 super radiators, 100 medium radiators, and 25 cheaper radiators in week 1, followed by 100 super radiators and 25 medium radiators in week 2. The master schedule is the first point where due dates are given to individual products—it is the first time that planned production is matched to actual orders.

The master schedule is constrained by the aggregate plan. In particular, the overall production in the master schedule must equal the production described in the aggregate plan. There may be some differences to allow for such things as short-term variations, errors in forecasts, and capacity constraints, but these should be small.

The aim of the **master schedule** is to give a detailed timetable for making individual products. This timetable should allow the aggregate plan to be achieved as efficiently as possible.

In principle, designing the master schedule is similar to designing an aggregate plan. But in some ways the master schedule is more difficult as it deals with more detail, often down to individual customer orders. Again, the usual methods of designing schedules are based on the skills of planners.

The design of a master schedule starts by looking at short-term demand as the larger of: 1. production specified in the aggregate plan; 2. actual customer orders booked for the period.

Forecasts are not totally accurate, so this gives the first opportunity to compare actual customer orders with forecast demand. Most organizations want to avoid shortages so the demand is set at the larger of these two figures. Some of this demand can be met from stocks, so schedulers must compare current inventory levels and production capacities, and then design a schedule to make up any differences. Designing these schedules again uses an iterative approach, as shown in Figure 10.14.

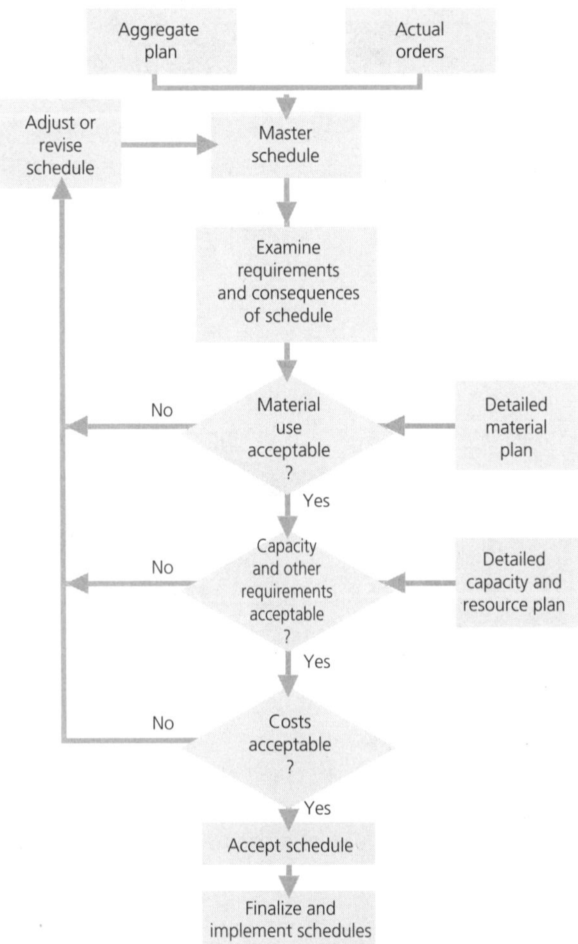

Figure 10.14 Procedure for Designing Master Schedule

At some point the master schedule is passed to production who actually implement the plans. So the plans must be fixed at some point, with no further changes allowed. This iterative procedure can, therefore, take place up to, say, three weeks before the master schedule is implemented. Beyond this, the plans are fixed.

Example

Comark Bicycles produce two bicycles — a women's model and a men's model. The aggregate plan has 8,000 bicycles made next month, and 6,400 the month after. Current stocks are 500 men's and 300 women's, and the factory has a capacity of 2,200 bicycles per week. Men's bicycles usually account for 60 percent of sales, and actual orders have been received for the following deliveries.

Week	1	2	3	4	5	6
Men's	1,400	1,200	1,000	700	300	-
Women's	2,000	800	400	100	-	-

Design a master schedule for the next eight weeks.

Solution

There is an unexpectedly high demand for women's bicycles in the first two weeks. As there are 300 in stock, 1,700 must be made to meet orders in the first week. This leaves only enough capacity for 500 men's bicycles. These, together with current stocks of 500, still leave a shortage of 400 men's bicycles which must be met by back orders.

In the second week, the back orders for 400 men's bicycles can be cleared together with the 1,200 actually ordered. This leaves only enough capacity for 600 women's bicycles, so 200 must be back ordered to meet the 800 orders.

The aggregate plan calls for 8,000 bicycles the first month. 4,400 were made in the first two weeks, so an additional 1,800 should be made in each of the last two weeks. In week 3, the back orders for 200 women's bicycles can be cleared, plus the 1,400 ordered (both men's and women's), and an additional 200 for stock (say 100 men's and 100 women's). In week 4, dividing the 1,800 into 1,080 men's and 720 women's (to match the expected 60:40 ratio) covers all orders and adds spare units to stock.

In weeks 5 to 8, the planned production of 6,400 can be divided into weekly production of 1,600 (960 men's and 640 women's). So far there are only orders for 300 units in this period, so the rest are added to stock.

The whole process gives the master schedule shown below.

Week	1	2	3	4	5	6	7	8
Men's								
Actual Orders	1,400	1,200	1,000	700	300	-	-	-
Opening Stock	500	-400	0	100	480	1,140	2,100	3,060
Production	500	1,600	1,100	1,080	960	960	960	960
Women's								
Actual Orders	2,000	800	400	100	-	-	-	-
Opening Stock	300	0	-200	100	720	1,360	2,000	2,640
Production	1,700	600	700	720	640	640	640	640
Total Production	2,200	2,200	1,800	1,800	1,600	1,600	1,600	1,600
Aggregate Plan	← 8,000 →				← 6,400 →			

The build-up of stock in later weeks shows that this production has not yet been allocated to customers, and shows the stock levels if no more orders are received. In practice, orders will be received and the stock level will be reduced by the amount sold.

This is, of course, only one of many feasible solutions. It has the advantages of meeting the aggregate plan and keeping production at a stable level. Iterative improvements can now be made to the initial plan.

You can see from this example that schedulers must possess a number of skills. They must be able to:

- Identify all known demands—forecasts, actual sales, internal transfers, etc.
- Keep within the aggregate plan
- Make sure existing customer orders are met
- Balance the needs of production, marketing, finance, and all other functions
- Identify problems and resolve them
- Communicate well with all functions

In Summary

A master schedule adds details to the aggregate plan to give a detailed timetable of production for each product. The methods of producing master schedules are similar to those of aggregate planning.

Review Questions

1. What is the main purpose of the master schedule?
2. What constraints are set on the master schedule?

Chapter Review

- Capacity planning is essentially a strategic function which matches available capacity to forecast demand. This is one step in a hierarchy of decisions about resource planning at tactical and operational levels. The steps in this hierarchy are capacity plans, aggregate plans, master schedules, and short-term schedules.
- Typically, capacity plans set the output at each location over the next few years; aggregate plans look at the output of families of products in each location for the next few months; master schedules break this down by individual products each week; short-term schedules look at operations each day.
- The general procedure for planning has a number of steps. These start by finding the requirements set by the previous level of planning. These requirements are broken down into more detail and alternative plans designed to meet them. Alternative plans are examined and the best is chosen.
- Creating an acceptable plan can be very difficult. In practice an iterative procedure is used to repeatedly adjust plans until a good one is found.

Case Study – Ontario Heritage Furniture

Ontario Heritage Furniture is a maker of fine furniture and has three product lines — tables, chairs, and other items. The company makes a number of products in each of these lines.

The following is an outline of their planning.

- The President of the company designs a business plan for the next 12 months. This gives an overall view of the company each month, as shown in the following table. The inputs to the business plan include the business strategy, long-term sales forecasts, financial performance, inflation rates, and economic figures.

Summarized Business Plan (in $)

	January	February	March	April	...	...	...	Dec.
Sales	1,000,500	1,050,000	1,100,000	...	...	...	..	
Cost of Sales	450,000	460,000	470,000	...	...	..		
Total Costs	900,000	940,000	993,000	...	..			
Profit	100,500	110,000	107,000	..				
Assets Employed	....	...	...	..				

- The Production Manager designs the aggregate plan with details of production over the next 12 months. The inputs to the aggregate plan include the business plan, machine capacities, workforce size, etc. These plans are updated monthly.

Summarized Aggregate Plan (in units)

Product Line	January	February	March	April	...	...	...	Dec.
1. Tables	1,000	1,100	1,800	...	..			
2. Chairs	6,900	7,500	4,000	...				
3. Others	850	850	600	..				

- The Master Scheduler produces the Master Production Schedule detailing production of each type of furniture over the next three months. The inputs to the master production schedule include the aggregate plan, customer orders, available machine capacities, etc. This schedule is updated weekly

Summarized Master Production Schedule (in units)

Product	Week 1	Week 2	Week 3	Week 4	5	6	7	8	9	10
Table A10	250									
Table B20		300	300							
Table C30				150						
Chair K11	2,500									
Chair L22		1,000	1,000							
Chair M33				2,400						
Quilt Stand X19		250								
Magazine Rack Y29			400							
Book Case Z39	200									

Questions

- Does this approach to planning seem reasonable? Would you suggest any changes? What other information would you need for this decision?
- Give examples of another company's planning.

Career Profile — A Production Planner

Name: Edwin Joseph
Title: Assistant Production Manager
Company: Caradon Indalex

Indalex is a world leader in manufacturing high-quality aluminum extrusion, finishing, and fabricating. There are four plants in Canada and two in the U.S.A., which service a wide range of customers in such areas as construction, transportation, electrical, residential, and nonresidential building products.

Education:
Edwin completed his three-year Production & Operations Management (POM) Diploma from Centennial College in 1990. "I chose the POM program because I was interested in a career where I would deal with people and at the same time be able to use my creative problem-solving abilities."

Work Experience:
"During my studies, I worked at the GM van plant for a semester. Upon graduation, I joined Indalex as a production planner. The job proved to be very interesting as I could put my problem-solving abilities to immediate use. The production planning and control and computer skills I had obtained during the course of my studies proved very useful.

Currently, as the assistant production manager, I supervise the production planning department consisting of four planners and a clerk. I find this position is a challenge to my communication skills, because I have to constantly deal with customer-service people, the production department, and engineers to meet the common company goals of satisfying the customers and improving the efficiency of the plant. My major functions are to set weekly production levels, forecast and order raw materials, oversee monthly physical inventory counts, monitor and report plant recovery and efficiency, and coordinate all shipments to the U.S.A. Customer contact, internal and external, is a key to my success.

I am constantly learning as I am also involved in various task forces such as re-engineering and TQM projects to help improve methods and quality and reduce costs. I assist in training other employees in these new problem-solving techniques.

Future Goals:
"I plan to obtain my CPIM designation and enrol in an Industrial Engineering program."

- Aggregate planning uses the forecast demand and capacity plans to create schedules for each family of products, typically for each of the next few months.
- Aggregate planning is usually done by intuition, a graphical method, or a matrix method. Mathematical models can be used, but these are too complicated for real problems.
- The next stage in planning is the master schedule. This "disaggregates" the aggregate plans and shows a detailed timetable for production of individual products. The methods of designing master schedules are similar in principle to the methods of designing aggregate plans.

Key Terms

aggregate planning *(p. 288)*
aggregate plans *(p. 287)*
business plan *(p. 277)*
hierarchy of plans *(p. 276)*
master schedule *(p. 300)*
resource requirements planning *(p. 281)*

Problems

10.1 A machine makes two different products: A and B. The machine works for 250 days per year, with two eight-hour shifts per day and a utilization of 95 percent. Other information is as follows.

	A	B
Forecast Annual Demand	2,100	5,600
Time to Make One Unit (hours)	2.0	1.5
Batch Size	50	100
Set-up Time per Batch (hours)	5	6

If the company currently has three identical machines, how could it start capacity planning?

10.2 The aggregate, monthly demand for a family of products is shown below. Use intuitive reasoning to suggest a monthly production schedule for the products.

Month	1	2	3	4	5	6	7
Aggregate Demand	90	120	100	120	180	270	225

10.3 The forecast monthly demand for a family of products is shown on page 306. At the end of each month, a holding cost of $20 is assigned to every unit held in stock. If there are shortages 20 percent of orders are lost at a cost of $200 per unit, and the rest are met by back orders, with a cost of $50 a unit. Each time the production rate is changed it costs $15,000. Designed capacity of the system is 400 units per month, but utilization seldom reaches 80 percent. Use a graphical method to design an aggregate plan for the products.

Month	1	2	3	4	5	6	7	8
Aggregate Demand	310	280	260	300	360	250	160	100

10.4 The aggregate demand for a family of products for the next five months is 190, 120, 270, 200, and 140. Normal capacity is 150 units per month, overtime has a capacity of 10 per month, and subcontractors can handle any amount of production. The unit cost is $100 for normal capacity, $125 for overtime, and $140 for subcontractors. It costs $15 to stock a unit for a month, while back orders have a penalty cost of $100 per month. Use a matrix method to design an aggregate plan for the products.

10.5 The aggregate plan of a manufacturer has 12,000, 10,000, and 10,000 units made in the next three months. A master schedule is needed for the two products, A and B. Current stocks are 700 of A and 500 of B, and the factory has a capacity of 3,000 units per week. Sales of A are usually twice as large as sales of B, and actual orders have been received for deliveries of:

Week	1	2	3	4	5	6	7
A	2,100	1,800	1,600	1,100	800	200	-
B	3,000	1,400	700	400	100	-	-

Design a master schedule for the next 12 weeks.

Discussion Questions

10.1 What exactly is the purpose of planning in an organization?

10.2 Where would you start the product planning process? Where would you end it?

10.3 What hierarchy of decisions are needed in product planning? Do you think this hierarchy exists in every organization?

10.4 How far ahead does each stage of planning look? Give specific examples to show the variation in this.

10.5 How frequently should aggregate plans and master schedules be updated? How do these times fit into planning cycles?

10.6 What costs should be considered in aggregate plans?

10.7 Why is planning so complicated?

10.8 Spreadsheets are widely used in planning. Why? Design a spreadsheet that is useful for master scheduling.

Chapter 11
SCHEDULING RESOURCES

Designing a schedule for operations

Contents

Introduction

The last two chapters discussed production planning, which begins with strategic decisions, such as the business strategy and capacity plans. Then aggregate plans and master schedules add more details to create schedules of production for each product, usually in each week. This chapter examines the last stage of planning, which is **short-term scheduling**.

Short-term scheduling uses the master schedules to design detailed plans for individual jobs, people, equipment, and other resources. These produce schedules for individual operations.

Learning Objectives

After reading this chapter you should be able to answer questions such as:

- What is the purpose of short-term scheduling?
- Why is scheduling so difficult?
- What are scheduling rules, and how are they used?
- How can these rules be used in flow shops?
- How can you schedule employees?
- How are schedules controlled?

What Is Scheduling?

Designing the very detailed timetables that show what each piece of equipment and employee is doing at any given time is called **scheduling**. There are three ways of doing this scheduling. This chapter describes short-term scheduling. Two related approaches are materials requirement planning and just-in-time. (These two are more directly related to materials management, and are covered in Chapters 16 and 17.)

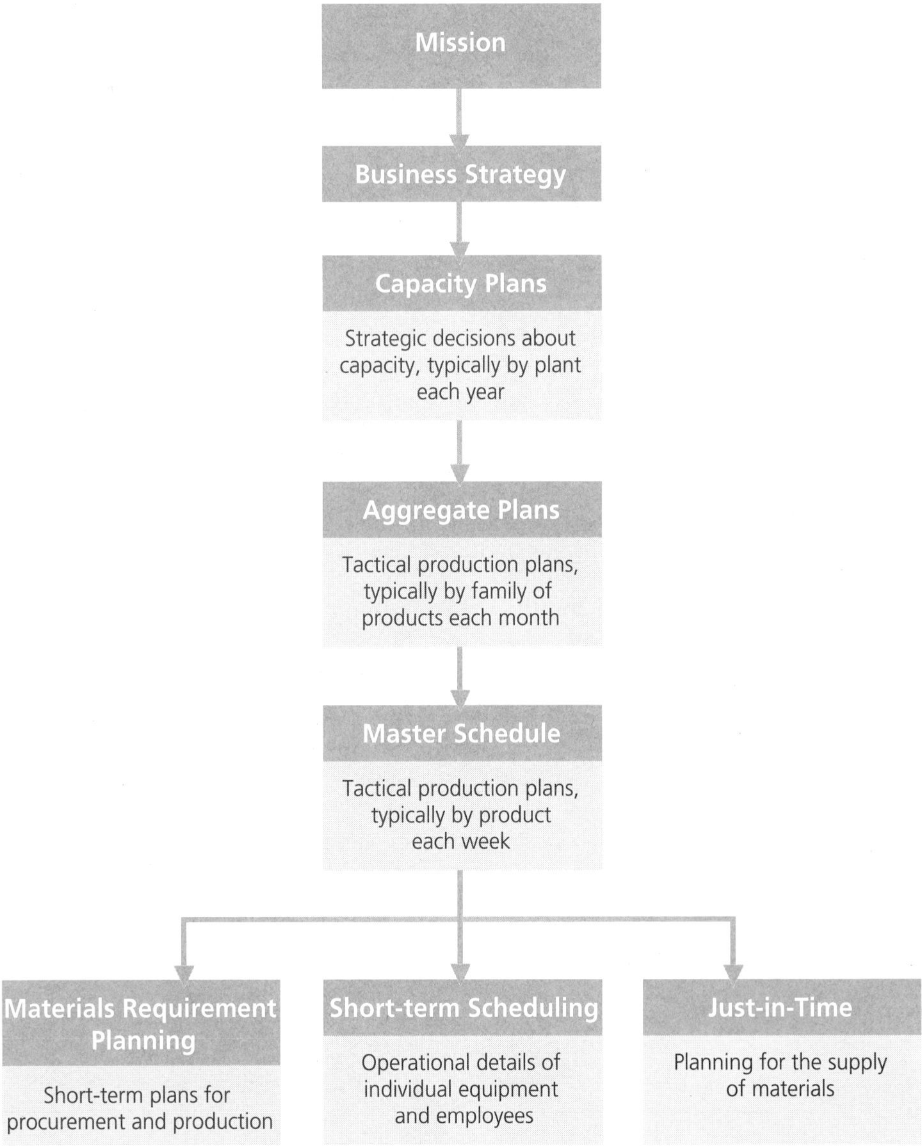

```mermaid
flowchart TD
    A["Mission"] --> B["Business Strategy"]
    B --> C["Capacity Plans<br>Strategic decisions about capacity, typically by plant each year"]
    C --> D["Aggregate Plans<br>Tactical production plans, typically by family of products each month"]
    D --> E["Master Schedule<br>Tactical production plans, typically by product each week"]
    E --> F["Materials Requirement Planning<br>Short-term plans for procurement and production"]
    E --> G["Short-term Scheduling<br>Operational details of individual equipment and employees"]
    E --> H["Just-in-Time<br>Planning for the supply of materials"]
```

Figure 11.1 Summary of the Planning Process

Some specific examples of short-term schedules are:

- College schedules for classes, rooms, instructors, and students
- Airline schedules for airplanes, pilots, flight attendants, and food
- Hospital schedules for patients, nurses, beds, and operating rooms
- Manufacturing schedules for customer orders, employees, machines, material purchases, and shipping of completed orders

Short-term schedules create detailed timetables for operations. They show what jobs, people, and equipment are doing at any given time.

The overall aim of a short-term schedule is to allow the master schedule to be achieved, while keeping costs low and maintaining high utilization of equipment.

There is a problem in describing short-term schedules. Many examples talk about "jobs" being processed on "machines." This is just for convenience. Scheduling is one of the most common problems in any organization. Buses and trains work to schedules, delivery vehicles are given schedules of customers to visit, classes are scheduled into rooms, and doctors have appointment books. When describing "jobs on machines," we are using one type of process to illustrate a very common problem.

Although it may seem easy, short-term scheduling is surprisingly difficult. Schedules have to balance many factors and compare different plans. In practice, short-term scheduling might involve:

- Allocating jobs to equipment
- Allocating staff and other resources to the equipment

Case Study – 3P Injection Moulding

3P Corporation uses an injection-moulding machine that can make 120 parts per hour. This machine currently works a single shift of 8 hours per day. So, the capacity of the injection moulding machine is 120 x 8 = 960 parts per day. If the forecast sales are 1,050 units per day, the capacity has to be adjusted upward to meet this increased demand. The company can do this in several ways.

1. It can schedule 3/4 hour of overtime per day on the machine. This will result in overtime costs.
2. It can work occasional extra shifts. Each extra shift would make 960 units that are put into stock and withdrawn as needed. This will give extra stock-holding costs.

Questions

- Will these two options meet the extra demand?
- What other plans could 3P use to meet the demand?
- What other information would you need before choosing the best plan?

- Setting the sequence of jobs on equipment
- Controlling the work, including checking progress and expediting late jobs
- Revising schedules for late changes

In Summary

After designing master schedules, an organization needs more detailed short-term schedules. These show a detailed schedule for every person, piece of equipment, materials, and other resources used in the process.

Review Questions

1. What is the purpose of short-term scheduling?
2. What factors must be considered in short-term scheduling?

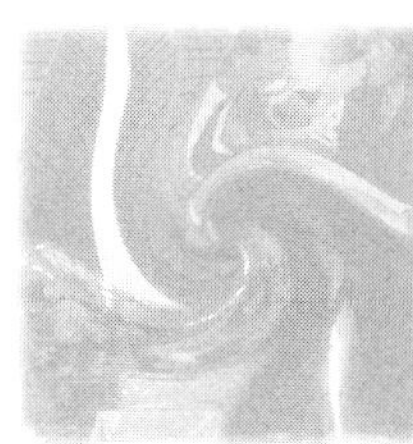

Job-shop Scheduling

Scheduling Rules

Chapter 4 described a job shop. This has different types of equipment, and each job goes through these in a different order. As you can imagine, it can be difficult to arrange jobs so that all equipment has high utilization. This section examines ways of scheduling a job shop.

Job-shop scheduling assumes that there are a number of jobs, or batches of products, waiting to use equipment. These jobs should be arranged so that the work is done as efficiently as possible—perhaps minimizing the waiting time, minimizing the total processing time, keeping inventories low, reducing the maximum lateness, achieving high utilization of equipment, or some other objective. Effectively, the problem is one of finding the best sequence of jobs on equipment.

In a job shop, jobs are often made for specific customer orders, so the scheduling has to take into account when the customer needs the product. There are two methods of doing this.

- *Forward scheduling,* where the scheduler knows the start date for the first operation. Then, by working through all operations needed for the job, the scheduler can calculate the date the job will be finished.
- *Backward scheduling,* where the customer gives a due date. This due date is the

finish date for the last operation, so the scheduler must work back through the operations to find the date when the job must be started.

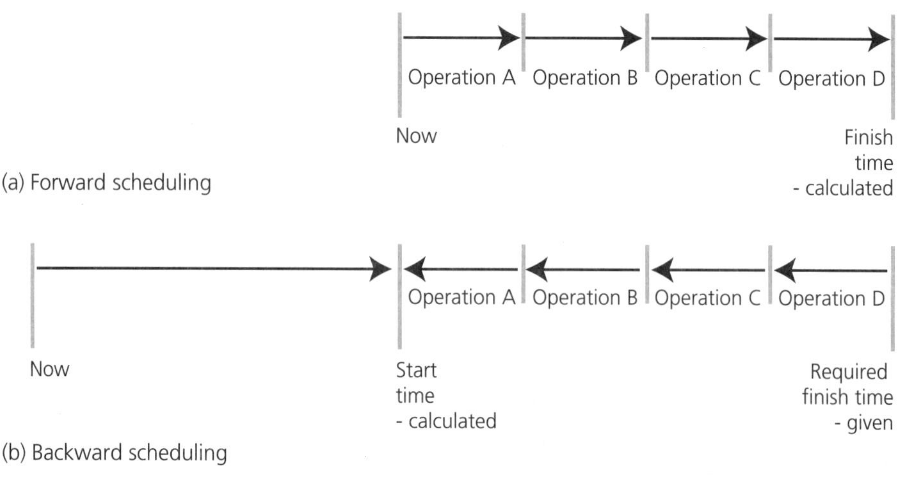

Figure 11.2 Setting Times in Schedules

You may think that sequencing problems are easy to solve, but in practice they are notoriously difficult and complicated.

Case Study – Marc's Auto Body Works

Marc's Auto Body Works is well known for high quality. Marc Thibodeau worked for a number of years in a local Ford dealer in Winnipeg. There he gained a lot of experience with auto body repairs. When he decided to open his own auto body shop, he knew that it would be difficult. Although he knew about cars, he did not have any experience of managing a business. Now he has to do his own planning. He knows that scheduling of customers' jobs is very important—as customers like their cars back quickly, and at the promised time.

At 8:00 a.m. one Monday morning, a customer brought in a car for repairs. It needed a lot of body repair work, including plastering, sanding, and painting. Marc estimated that it would take 1 hour for plastering, 2 hours for sanding, and 1.5 hours for painting. The customer wanted to pick up the car at 5:00 p.m. the same day.

Questions

- Design a forward schedule and a backward schedule for this car repair job. What are the differences between the two schedules?
- Suppose a second car arrives at 9:00 a.m. and it needs 1.5 hours of work in each of the three departments. Design a new forward schedule for Marc.
- What would happen if a third car arrived at 12.00 p.m. for one hour of emergency work in each department?

The variables include:

- Patterns of job arrivals
- Amount and type of equipment to be used
- Number and skills of operators
- Patterns of work flow through equipment
- Priority rules for jobs
- Disruptions caused by such things as customers changing orders and equipment breakdown
- Methods of evaluating schedules

Although people have looked for better methods, the most effective approach to job-shop scheduling is to follow simple rules. These **scheduling rules** are rules of thumb that usually give good results. Suppose that there are a number of jobs waiting to use a single machine. If we assume that the set-up time for each job is fixed, regardless of the job that was being worked on before, the total time for processing is the same for any sequence of jobs. The order of taking jobs does, however, change other measures of performance. This is illustrated by four standard scheduling rules.

1. *First come, first served.* This is the most obvious scheduling rule and simply takes jobs in the order they arrive. It assumes no priority, no urgency, nor any other measure of relative importance. The drawback to this rule is that urgent or important jobs may be delayed, while less urgent or important ones are being processed. The benefits are simplicity, and obvious fairness. Many lines are based on this system, and when we wait at a supermarket check-out line, for example, it seems only fair that everyone is treated the same.

2. *Most urgent job first.* This rule assigns an importance, or urgency, to each job; jobs are then processed in order of decreasing urgency. Emergency departments in hospitals, for example, will treat first those patients who are most seriously ill. There are many other applications of this rule. A manufacturer might determine when current stocks of parts will run out—then the most urgent job is the one that supplies parts that will run out first. The benefit of this rule is that more important jobs are given higher priority. Unfortunately, those jobs with low priority may get stuck at the end of a line for a very long time. Having partially completed jobs waiting a long time for processing is generally a sign of poor planning.

3. *Shortest job first.* A useful objective is to minimize the average time spent in the system. The time in the system is defined as:

$$\text{Time in the system} = \text{processing time} + \text{waiting time}$$

If a job needs two days of processing but it waits in line for three days, its time in the system is five days.

Taking jobs in order of increasing duration minimizes the average time spent in the system. It allows those jobs which can be done quickly to move on through the system, while longer jobs are left until later. The overall effect is that the average time in the system is minimized. The disadvantage is that long jobs can spend a long time waiting to be processed.

4. *Earliest due date first.* For this rule, the line of jobs is sorted into the order of delivery date. Those jobs that are needed first are processed first. This has the benefit of minimizing the maximum lateness of jobs, but again some jobs may have to wait a long time.

Each of these rules is useful in particular circumstances. Students doing course-work often use such rules. Some students do work in the order it is set, using first come, first served. A more common approach is to do course-work in the order it is due—most urgent first, which in this case is the same as earliest due date first. If students have a backlog of course-work, they may do the shortest first. This clears their desks quickly, but minimizing the time course-work is in the system may be a strange objective.

Example

The following six jobs are to be scheduled on a piece of equipment. Each job fully uses the equipment for the time given.

Job	A	B	C	D	E	F
Duration in Days	6	4	2	8	1	5

a) How long would it take to finish all jobs if they are scheduled in order of arrival?

b) What schedule would minimise average time in the system?

c) Suppose each job makes a batch of products that is put into stock. If the demand for these products and current stocks levels are as follows, what schedule would you suggest?

Job	A	B	C	D	E	F
Demand	10	15	40	2	5	80
Current Stock	260	195	880	20	75	1,280

d) Returning to the basic problem, suppose the jobs have been promised to customers by the following dates. What schedule would minimise maximum lateness?

Job	A	B	C	D	E	F
Due Date	6	20	22	24	2	10

(Continued)

Example – Continued

Solution

a) Using the first come, first served rule gives the sequence:

Job	Duration	Start	Finish
A	6	0	6
B	4	6	10
C	2	10	12
D	8	12	20
E	1	20	21
F	5	21	26

The start time for each job is the finish time for the previous job; the finish time is found by adding the duration to the start time. All jobs will be finished by day 26. The sequence of jobs does not change this overall duration, but different sequences can achieve different objectives.

b) The average time in the system is minimized by taking the shortest jobs first. This gives the following schedule:

Job	Duration	Start	Finish
E	1	0	1
C	2	1	3
B	4	3	7
F	5	7	12
A	6	12	18
D	8	18	26

The average time in the system is found from the average finishing date, which is (1+3+7+12+18+26)/6 = 67/6 = 11.2 (compared with 15.8 days for first-come-first-served). By day 18, we have finished five jobs in this case, while the previous schedule had only finished three.

c) It would be sensible to schedule the jobs in order of urgency, where urgency is measured by the number of days of stock remaining. This is found by dividing the current stock by the demand.

Job	A	B	C	D	E	F
Stock Remaining	260	195	880	20	75	1,280
Demand	10	15	40	2	5	80
Days Stock Remaining	26	13	22	10	15	16
Order of Urgency	6	2	5	1	3	4

This gives the following schedule:

Job	Days Stock Remaining	Duration	Start	Finish
D	10	8	0	8
B	13	4	8	12
E	15	1	12	13
F	16	5	13	18
C	22	2	18	20
A	26	6	20	26

All jobs are finished before the products are due to run out, except F, where stocks run out two days before the jobs is finished.

(Continued)

Example – Continued

d) Maximum lateness is minimized by taking jobs in order of due date. This results in the following schedule:

Job	Duration	Start	Finish	Due Date	Lateness
E	1	0	1	2	0
A	6	1	7	6	1
F	5	7	12	10	2
B	4	12	16	20	0
C	2	16	18	22	0
D	8	18	26	24	2

This has a maximum lateness of 2 days for jobs D and F, and an average lateness of 0.8 days.

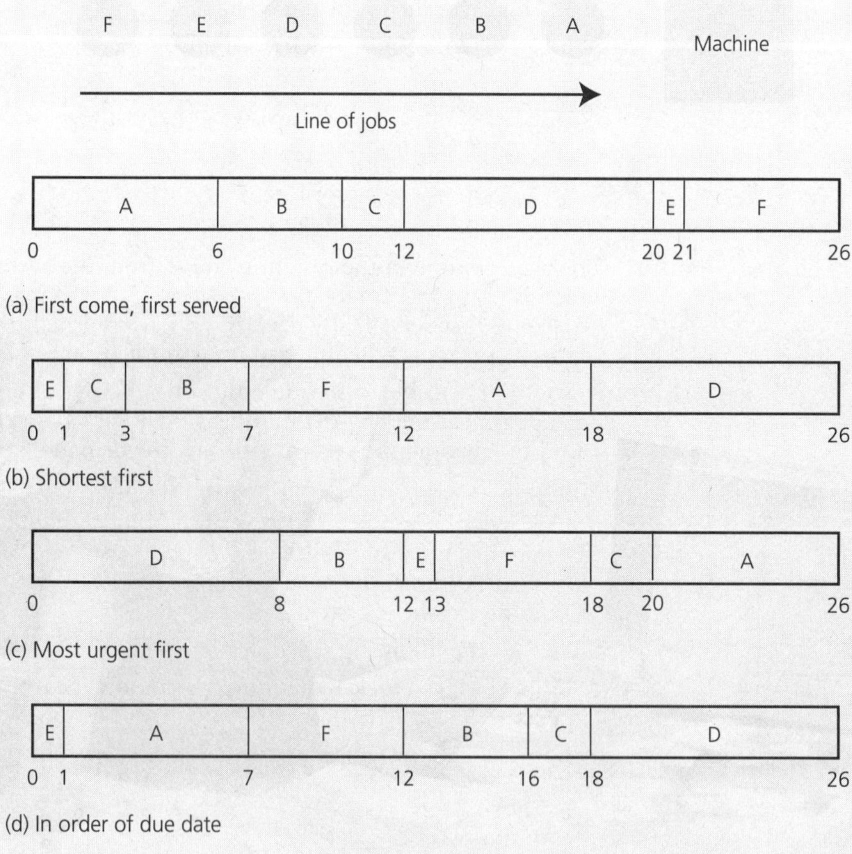

Figure 11.3 Results for Different Scheduling Rules

Although the discussion here has described four scheduling rules, there are many others used for different purposes. For example, jobs could be scheduled in order of least work remaining, or fewest operations remaining. Subsequent operations could be considered, and the combined times for two or three of these calculated—the slack could also be considered, which is the time remaining until the job is due minus the time needed for processing.

A particularly useful rule schedules jobs in order of the **critical ratio**. The critical ratio is the time remaining until the job is due divided by the time needed to complete it.

$$\text{Critical ratio} = \frac{(\text{due date} - \text{today's date})}{\text{time needed for the job}}$$

If this ratio is low, the time to finish the job is short compared with the time available and the job becomes urgent. If the ratio is high, there is plenty of time left and the job is less urgent. The critical ratio changes as jobs move through the process, so priorities also change.

Many other rules can be used, with common objectives of:

- Making sure the job is finished when the customer wants it
- Minimizing the time in the system
- Minimizing stocks of work in progress
- Minimizing the time equipment or operators are idle
- Minimizing costs

In Summary

Job-shop scheduling designs schedules for jobs on individual pieces of equipment. This is surprisingly difficult. The best results come from simple scheduling rules. There are many of these, including:

- First come, first served—which is easy and is obviously fair
- Most important first—which makes sure high priority jobs are done first
- Earliest due date first—which minimizes the maximum lateness of jobs
- Shortest job first—which minimizes the average time spent in the system

Scheduling services

Although scheduling services is essentially the same as scheduling manufacturing, there are some differences. First, the customer is directly involved in the process. This means that customers often form lines—so waiting times are particularly important. Second, services have to be provided when they are needed and cannot be held in inventory. This means that the capacity must be set to meet peak demands. Wide variations in demand give low utilization of resources and difficult scheduling problems.

Service organizations can deal with uneven demand in several ways.

1. *Appointment systems,* where the organization asks customers to set up appointments in advance. This is widely used by doctors, lawyers, counsellors, etc. This system tries to increase utilization of resources and improve customer service. But it has the drawbacks of making customers wait for a fixed—often long—time, and if they cancel an appointment, the time is wasted.
2. *Fixed schedule system,* where a service is given to many customers at the same, fixed time. Examples of this are a bus or airline schedule, or times of hockey games. The schedules are published and known to the customers some time in advance.
3. *Delayed delivery,* where the service is delayed so that an organization can balance its capacity and workload. This is used when delays may cause relatively little inconvenience to customers, such as repair shops. If you want your television set fixed, you take it to a repair shop and go back later to collect it.
4. *First come, first served,* which is the most common schedule in services. Customers are simply dealt with in the order in which they arrive. Examples of this are customers waiting in a bank, a fast-food restaurant, or in the check-out counter of a grocery store.

In Summary

Although scheduling services is the same in principle as scheduling in other organizations, there are some differences. The most important difference is that customers usually line up and wait for service. This makes the time spent in the line particularly important.

Review Questions

1. What is a scheduling rule?
2. Which scheduling rules might you use for:
   a) hospital admission b) selling ice cream bars
   c) telephone calls d) writing reports for consulting clients?

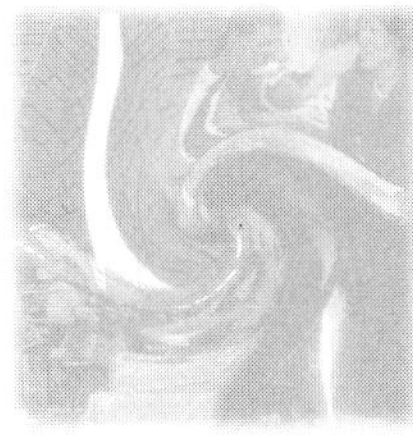

Flow-shop Scheduling

The previous section examined the problems that arise when a line-up of jobs has to be processed on a single machine. The discussion here centres on more complicated problems where, for example, different machines are in used. Unfortunately, when we go beyond simple problems it is almost impossible to find good, widely used scheduling rules. These problems have to be solved either by human experience or by using a good deal of computer time.

One problem that does have a useful scheduling rule is a **flow shop** with two machines. In a flow shop, all jobs are processed on the same set of machines in the same order. So, with two machines the situation is as shown in Figure 11.4—all jobs are processed on Machine 1 followed by Machine 2.

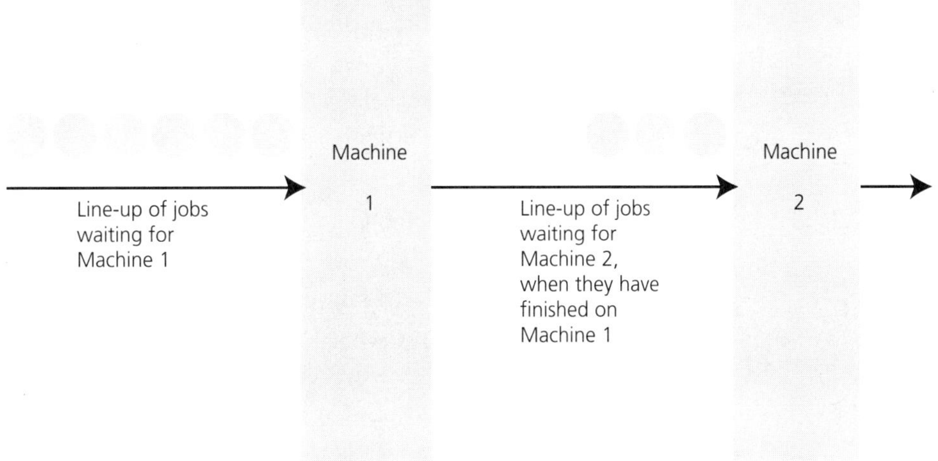

Figure 11.4 A Two-Machine Flow Shop

To solve this problem, we can use **Johnson's rule**. This finds the minimum **makespan**, which is the time between starting the first job and finishing the last job.

Johnson's rule has four steps.

1. List the jobs and their processing time on each machine.
2. Find the job with the next shortest processing time on either machine.
3. If this processing time is on Machine 1, schedule the job as early as possible without moving jobs already scheduled; if the processing time is on Machine 2, schedule the job as late as possible without moving jobs already scheduled.
4. Do not consider any job already scheduled, and repeat Steps 2 and 3 (working inward from the ends of the sequence) until all jobs have been scheduled.

Example

A series of four jobs is to be processed on a sanding machine followed by a painting machine. If the hours needed on each machine are as follows, design a schedule that minimizes the makespan.

Job	A	B	C	D
Time on Sanding Machine	30	20	60	80
Time on Painting Machine	50	40	10	70

Solution

- Step 1 of Johnson's rule has been done, and we have a list of jobs and their processing times.
- Step 2 finds the shortest processing time is Job C on the painting machine.
- Step 3 recognizes that this is on the second machine, so the job is scheduled as late as possible. This means the job is scheduled last to get a sequence which is currently:

  – – – C

- Step 4 now ignores Job C and returns to Step 2.
- Step 2 identifies the shortest remaining processing time (from Jobs A, B, and D) as Job B on the sanding machine.
- Step 3 recognizes this is on the first machine, so the job is scheduled as early as possible to give the sequence:

  B _ _ _ C

Now, repeating these steps, we find the shortest remaining processing time (from Jobs A and D). This is Job A on the sanding machine. This job is scheduled as early as possible to give the sequence:

B A _ _ _ C

Now, ignoring Job A, the shortest remaining processing time is Job D on the painting machine. This is scheduled as late as possible to give the final sequence:

B A D C

The finished schedule is:

	1st Operation Sanding Machine			2nd Operation Painting Machine		
Job	Duration	Start	Finish	Duration	Start	Finish
B	2	0	2	4	2	6
A	3	2	5	5	6	11
D	8	5	13	7	13	20
C	6	13	19	1	20	21

(Continued)

Example – Continued

You can see jobs can only start on the painting machine when they have finished on the sanding machine, and when the previous job on the painting machine has finished. So Job A has to wait until Job B is finished before it can start, while Job D is only held up by the time it takes on the sanding machine.

The makespan with this solution is 21 days. You can compare this with a makespan of 26 days for the first come, first served rule.

	1st Operation Sanding Machine			2nd Operation Painting Machine		
Job	Duration	Start	Finish	Duration	Start	Finish
A	2	0	2	4	2	6
B	3	2	5	5	6	11
C	6	5	11	1	11	12
D	8	11	19	7	19	26

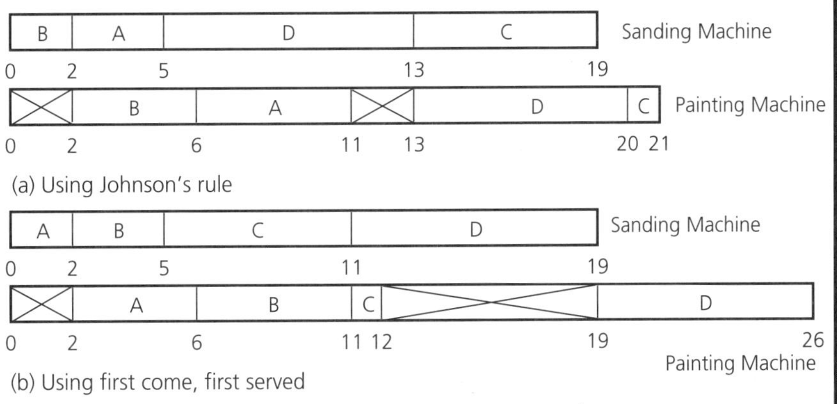

Figure 11.5 Bar Chart for the Schedule

In Summary

It is difficult to find good, general rules for complicated scheduling problems. One exception is Johnson's rule for flow shops with two machines.

Review Questions

1. What is a flow shop?
2. What is the makespan?
3. When is Johnson's rule used?

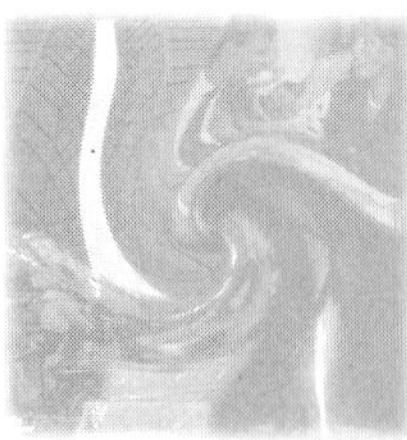

Scheduling Employees

Thus far our discussion has focused on methods for scheduling equipment. But another problem in short-term scheduling involves people—in other words, it designs staff schedules. If the same operators are always assigned to the same equipment, the equipment schedule effectively fixes the staff schedule. Usually this does not happen, however, and one operator can work on several pieces of equipment. An organization can then use some assignment rule that is similar to a scheduling rule, perhaps one of the following:

- Assigning operators to the equipment that has the most jobs waiting
- Assigning operators to work on the job with the earliest due date
- Assigning operators to work on the job that has been waiting longest
- Or some other simple rule

Again, these problems are surprisingly difficult to solve. But one simple rule designs an operator schedule that gives each person two consecutive days off per week.

Operator Scheduling—giving two consecutive days off:

1. Find the minimum number of operators needed each day of the week.
2. Find the two adjacent days needing the fewest operators. This means finding the day needing the fewest, then the day needing the next fewest, then the next fewest, and so on until two adjacent days have been found.
3. Give the next operator these two days off.
4. On the days when this operator works, reduce the number of operators needed by one.
5. If there are still more operators needed, go to Step 2, otherwise a schedule has been found.

In Summary

Scheduling employees is usually a separate problem from scheduling equipment. These problems are again difficult, but we can use assignment rules that are similar to scheduling rules.

Review Questions

1. When does scheduling operators become a problem?
2. "Most schedules for employees are designed using simple scheduling rules." Do you think this is true?

Example

Jane Schultz wants to find the smallest number of operators needed for a process. The numbers needed each day are shown below. Each operator has two consecutive days off. What schedule can Jane use?

Day	Mon	Tues	Wed	Thurs	Fri	Sat	Sun
Operators	1	2	3	3	4	4	0

Solution

Step 1 is already done with the data given.

Step 2 finds the two adjacent days with smallest numbers of operators. Assuming the schedule is continuous, this is Sunday and Monday.

Step 3 gives the first operator these two days off.

Step 4 reduces the operator needs for Tuesday to Saturday by one, and we return to Step 2.

Day	Mon	Tues	Wed	Thurs	Fri	Sat	Sun
Operators	1	1	2	2	3	3	0

The next cycle again finds Sunday and Monday as the adjacent days with lowest demand, so the second operator also works Tuesday to Saturday. Repeating this another three times gives the following results:

	Day	Mon	Tues	Wed	Thurs	Fri	Sat	Sun
Cycle 1		1	2	3	3	4	4	0
Cycle 2	Operators	1	1	2	2	3	3	0
Cycle 3	Operators	1	0	1	1	2	2	0
Cycle 4	Operators	0	0	1	0	1	1	0
Cycle 5	Operators	0	0	0	0	0	0	0

This completes the schedule, with all demand met by four operators, as follows:

Day	Mon	Tues	Wed	Thurs	Fri	Sat	Sun
Operators Needed	1	2	3	3	4	4	0
Operators Off	3	2	1	0	0	0	2
Operators Available	1	2	3	4	4	4	2
Spare Operators	0	0	0	1	0	0	2

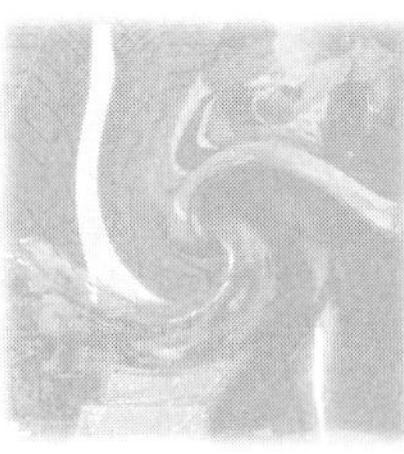

Control of Schedules

Short-term schedules give detailed plans that show what each job, piece of equipment, and person should be doing at any given time. But there is a difference between designing plans and making sure they are implemented properly. The control of schedules ensures that they are accurate, up-to-date, and show what is actually happening in the system. Controls check performance and report any differences between schedules and actual performance.

The control of schedules is in two parts.

- The first part records the progress of jobs and gives information back to managers. At regular intervals in the process, details of the jobs' progress are checked and times, efficiency, productivity, utilization, and other measures reported.
- The second part of the control occurs when circumstances change or when there are some problems which cause the schedules to be revised.

Both of these functions feed back information to managers so that they know how operations are going, and can take any necessary action. The purposes of a control system can be summarized as follows:

- To ensure that jobs are actually scheduled according to the plans
- To warn of problems with resources, delivery dates, etc.
- To ensure that materials, equipment, and operators are available for each job
- To assign jobs to specific orders, and set delivery times
- To check progress as jobs move through the process
- To make small adjustments to schedules as needed
- To allow rescheduling if there is a major disruption to plans
- To give information on current activities
- To give feedback on performance

Sometimes a **dispatch list** is prepared from the short-term schedules, which gives a daily list of jobs to be done, their order of importance, and how long each will take. This can be an important input to the control system. Other inputs might include inventory records, bills of materials, routing through machines, and orders for jobs. The main outputs from the control system are status and exception reports. Other outputs might include the release of job orders, dispatch of finished jobs, and schedule receipts.

Some organizations link the control system to an **input/output report**, which keeps a check on the units entering and leaving an operation. Obviously, these should match or there is an accumulation of work somewhere. Figure 11.6 shows a section from a typical input/output report. You can see that output is well below plans, and as the inputs are also below plans, there must be a hold up in some previous operation.

Assembly Operation 14			Manual Assembly	Week 17	Day 4	Operator	Tolerance ±10
Week	**11**	**12**	**13**	**14**	**15**	**16**	**17**
Inputs							
Planned	240	240	200	200	240	240	240
Actual	215	210	200	180	165	200	210
Difference	–25	–30	0	–20	–35	–40	–30
Cumulative Difference	–25	–55	–55	–75	–110	–150	–180
Outputs							
Planned	220	220	220	200	200	200	220
Actual	205	200	195	195	180	190	190
Difference	–15	–20	–25	–5	–20	–10	–30
Cumulative Difference	–15	–35	–60	–65	–85	–95	–125

Figure 11.6 A Section from an Input-Output Report

In Summary

Once schedules have been designed, there must be some controls for comparing actual performance with plans. Such systems may include a range of activities, and may be very complicated.

Review Questions

1. What is the main purpose of a control system for schedules?
2. "The control of schedules is only important when something goes wrong." Do you think this is true? Explain.

Case Study – Too Many Red Tags

Bill Wagner, the President of Ontario Heritage Furniture, likes to walk through his plant. This is his way of getting to know the employees and it helps maintain good working relations. Unfortunately, he has had to stop many of his regular tours because he is too busy. Over the last two years, the company's sales have doubled to 6,000 orders per year valued at $12 million. Bill now spends much more time in meetings.

Ontario Heritage Furniture's plant is organized into three departments: cutting and wood preparation, framing and assembly, and painting and varnishing. Each of these is managed by a supervisor who has been promoted from the shop floor. The supervisors are more craftsmen than managers in their outlook, so they control their departments informally and do not use rigid schedules. With the growth in sales, this informal approach is causing problems. Plans are not coordinated, orders are missing due dates, and employees are often idle because they have no work. There is more expediting of orders, with increased costs for overtime and transportation.

All of the production planning seems ineffective. For example, orders for large tables are given five weeks lead time, while orders for small tables are given four weeks. If the company does not have the materials needed in stock, customers are called and given a later delivery date. When a customer calls to ask about an overdue order, a supervisor tries to expedite it by putting a red tag on it. On average, 30 percent of the orders are shipped late.

During a recent walk through the plant, Bill Wagner noticed five red-tagged items at a cutting machine. He talked to the machine operator who said that there are too many red tags and it is confusing.

Questions

- What are some of the main problems faced by Ontario Heritage Furniture?
- How would you describe the short-term planning at the company?
- Design a scheduling system that would improve the performance of the company.

Chapter Review

- Strategic capacity planning is one step in a hierarchy of planning decisions. Later decisions give tactical aggregate plans and master schedules. These in turn lead to short-term schedules.
- Short-term scheduling expands the master schedule to give details of operations. It shows detailed timetables for jobs, people, materials, and equipment.
- It is deceptively difficult to design good schedules. The most common method uses simple scheduling rules. Many rules have been suggested for job-shop scheduling, ranging from first come, first served to more complex ones.
- The rules used in job-shop scheduling can be extended to deal with flow shops and staff schedules.
- A control system is needed to make sure planned production is actually achieved, and to report any differences.

Key Terms

critical ratio *(p. 317)*
dispatch list *(p. 324)*
flow shop *(p. 319)*
input/output report *(p. 324)*
job-shop scheduling *(p. 311)*
Johnson's rule *(p. 319)*
makespan *(p. 319)*
scheduling *(p. 309)*
scheduling rules *(p. 313)*
short-term scheduling *(p. 308)*
short-term schedules *(p. 310)*

Problems

11.1 Eight jobs are to be processed on a single machine, with the following times:

Job	A	B	C	D	E	F	G	H
Processing Time	2	5	3	8	4	7	2	3

Use a number of different scheduling rules, and compare the results.

11.2 In what order should the jobs in the last problem be scheduled if they have the following due dates?

Job	A	B	C	D	E	F	G	H
Due Date	13	7	8	30	14	20	2	36

11.3 Seven jobs are to be processed on Machine 1 followed by Machine 2. The time needed by each job on each machine is as follows. What sequence of jobs would maximize the machine utilization?

Job	A	B	C	D	E	F	G
Machine 1	4	10	20	16	8	24	18
Machine 2	28	14	6	20	10	12	12

11.4 Compucash Services has to prepare the payrolls of six factories at the end of each week. This needs the following times for computing and printing. What schedules would you recommend?

Factory	1	2	3	4	5	6
Computing Time	10	20	20	35	10	15
Printing Time	20	15	40	50	15	30

11.5 A small museum needs the following number of guides:

Day	Mon	Tues	Wed	Thurs	Fri	Sat	Sun
Guides	4	6	8	8	10	14	12

Design a schedule that gives each guide two consecutive days off.

Discussion Questions

11.1 What is short-term scheduling and when is it used? Describe some different approaches to short-term scheduling.

11.2 How does short-term scheduling fit in with other planning decisions?

11.3 Why is scheduling such a difficult problem?

11.4 What scheduling rules would be best for a fast-food restaurant? Would different rules be better for a doctor's office? What other examples can you give where different rules are used?

11.5 How do you think spreadsheets can help with short-term scheduling?

11.6 "The effects of different scheduling rules can be found using computer simulation." What does this mean?

11.7 Control systems can become complex, need access to large amounts of information, and yet need quick decisions. Do you think this type of problem could use expert systems?

Chapter 12

JOB DESIGN AND WORK MEASUREMENT

What is the best way of doing a job?

Contents

Introduction

The last three chapters have described the plans that are required in every organization. These start with strategic plans, move through tactical plans, and end with short-term schedules. But there is one more level of detail, which describes how each operation is actually done. This is the function of job design.

Job design must take into account the needs of both the organization and its employees—it therefore must consider a number of factors, ranging from employee motivation to salary-bonus schemes.

Having designed a job, the organization must determine how long it will take to do it. This is the function of work measurement.

Learning Objectives

After reading this chapter you should be able to answer questions such as:

- How is job design related to planning?
- What is the purpose of job design?
- How can an organization motivate and reward employees?
- What is work measurement?
- How long should it take to do a job?
- How can one determine standard times for jobs?

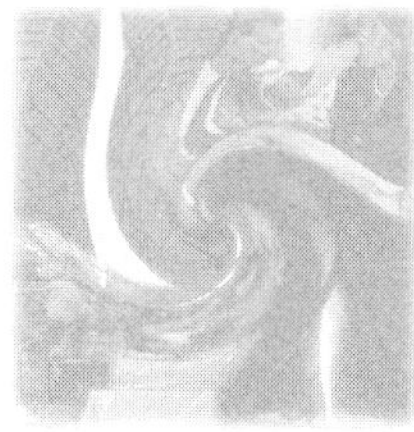

Job Design

Aims of Job Design

The last chapter discussed the scheduling of jobs, equipment, materials, and people. There was an assumption that each operation takes a fixed amount of time. But the time needed to do a job can be affected by many things such as the layout, process design, environment, convenience of tools and equipment, motivation, and rewards. This chapter examines in more detail the time needed to complete a job. In particular, it considers:

1. The best way of doing a job, which is known as *job design*
2. How long the job will take, which is known as *work measurement*

In this context a **job** is defined as the set of tasks an individual does during his or her work day. Most people repeat a basic job many times in their work. Perhaps they talk to customers and arrange insurance, or they drive trains, or make films, or assemble computers. As they repeat the same job many times, it is clearly best to use the most efficient method possible. Finding this best method is the purpose of job design.

Job design defines the specific tasks, responsibilities, environment, and methods used by individuals to do their work. The aim is to design jobs that satisfy the needs of both the organization and the individual doing the job.

There are two parties involved in a job—the employer and the employees. But their needs are different. Employers want their employees to make products at low cost while meeting quality and service targets. The needs of managers are basically economic and technical—their main concern is that the value added by workers is greater than the wages paid them.

However, the needs of workers are social and psychological. Humans are social animals. They have emotions, they like to interact with other people, and they want their efforts to be recognized and appreciated.

So you can see that there are two main factors to be considered in job design:

1. The economic, technical, productivity, quality, and other goals of the organization
2. Job safety, personal fulfilment, and reward for the individual

Until fairly recently the first of these was given far more attention than the second. Traditionally, managers did not give any weight to their workers' feelings and saw investment in their welfare as an extra cost that had no returns. More recently, managers have come to learn that this view is mistaken. Now we know that "a happy worker is a productive worker"—so any money spent in properly designing a job should be seen as an investment and not a cost.

Motivating and Rewarding Employees

Job design should consider both the management's economic and technical needs and the employees' behavioural, social, and psychological needs. It has become increasingly clear over the years that people are more productive when they get satisfaction from their jobs. So an organization can achieve high productivity not by treating people as part of the machinery, but by treating them as the most important part of the organization. This has concept led to trends in job design such as:

- Giving people broad training to do multiskilled jobs
- Broadening of work responsibilities
- Formation of worker councils and other means of participating in management
- Formation of work teams with authority to make decisions about operations
- Automation of dull or dangerous jobs
- Removal of artificial barriers between trades, levels, etc.
- Self-directed work teams

There have been many studies of the needs of employees. Two important ones were conducted by Maslow and Hertzberg.

Maslow's Hierarchy of Needs: According to Maslow, individuals have a hierarchy of needs. The first level is physiological or survival needs which include food, shelter, and clothing. The next level is the need for security, followed by the levels of social, esteem, and self-actualization needs. This hierarchy is shown in Figure 12.1. When each lower level of needs is met, employees look for ways of meeting their higher needs.

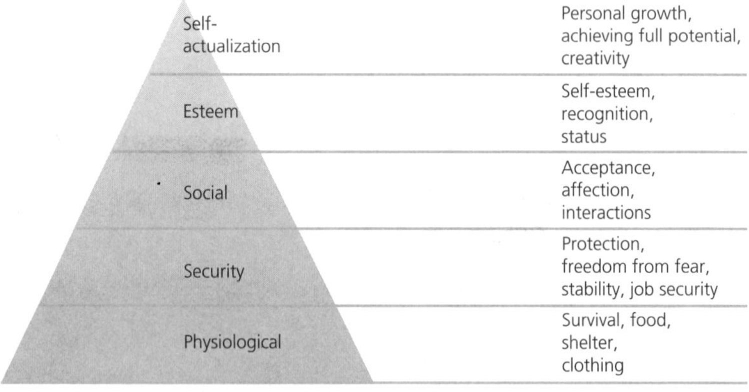

Figure 12.1 Maslow's Hierarchy of Needs

Hertzberg's Two-factor Theory: Hertzberg studied over 200 engineers and accountants to see what motivates people in their work place. He found two sets of factors:

- *Hygiene factors.* Without these, employees are dissatisfied. Examples are wages, job security, working conditions, relationship with supervisor, and company policies.
- *Motivators.* These motivate employees. Examples are recognition, promotion, responsibility, sense of achievement, the work itself, etc.

The work of Maslow and Hertzberg—and many others—suggests that fair and reasonable treatment of employees is important for achieving high labour productivity. One aspect of such fair treatment is reasonable payment. It is common for organizations to reward employees for the quality of their work. There are many different ways of doing this, but two main methods are **time-based** and **output-based remuneration.**

In time-based systems, employees are paid for the amount of time spent at work. This system is the most widely used, and includes all hourly paid and most salaried employees. It is simple to use and to control. Output-based systems are also called incentive plans. Here employees are paid for the amount they produce. There are many types of incentive plans, including the following:

- *Piece-rate plan.* Here an organization pays an employee an agreed amount for each unit of output. If an organization pays $1 per part, and an employee makes 50 parts in a particular day, then he or she is paid $50. In this scheme, each employee is paid directly for their efforts and they know how much they will earn.

  Piece-rate plans were more popular before the government introduced minimum-wage laws. With minimum wages, even if an employee's output is low, he or she still has to be paid at least the minimum wage. A more important criticism of piece-rate plans is that they do not take enough account of quality. An employee might try to earn more money by working faster, even if this means lower quality products. Finally, this plan does not encourage cooperation and teamwork. For these reasons, organizations do not use the piece-rate system as widely as they used to.

- *Standard-hour plans.* Here an organization sets a standard time to do a job and the worker is paid for this regardless of how long it actually takes. For example, suppose the standard time for a job is 6 minutes and an employee produced 88 units in a given day. His output in standard hours is (88 × 6) / 60 = 8.8 hours. If his pay rate is $10 per hour, he is paid $88 for the day. This is 10 percent more than what he would be paid by a simple hourly rate. In this system, workers are usually guaranteed a minimum wage irrespective of their output. Auto repair shops use this system to pay their mechanics.

There are many disadvantages of such individual incentive plans. They do not encourage cooperation among employees. Again, some people will try to make extra money by increasing output while ignoring quality. Since different people work at different paces, it is difficult to balance work flows.

- *Group incentive systems.* These share any gains among all employees. In some circumstances, such as assembly lines, no single worker can dramatically affect the output, so any bonuses should be shared among all the workers on the line. This encourages cooperation and teamwork. There are many different types of group plans. Some of the most popular are "Scanlon plans," where any profits from productivity gains are shared by the workers and the company.

A clear message that has come from studies of motivation and reward is that an organization's operations depend entirely on its employees. One way of using employees' skills and knowledge is **self-directed work teams**. These are groups of people who have day-to-day responsibility for managing themselves and the processes they work with. Instead of being instructed by supervisors, self-directed work teams take the work to be done, and then schedule their time to achieve this most effectively. This approach requires a variety of skills within the team, but many organizations have used this system both to increase productivity and to reduce costs. Perhaps the most obvious benefit is the increase in employee motivation and morale that comes from giving employees challenging work.

In Summary

Employees have a range of behavioural, social, and psychological needs. These needs must be satisfied before an organization can run efficiently. There are several ways of motivating employees.

Elements in Job Design

As stated, the needs of an organization are mainly technical and economic, and the needs of employees mainly social and psychological. A job should be designed to satisfy the needs of both. Three main elements should be considered:

1. *Physical environment,* or where the job is done
2. *Social environment,* which affects the worker's well-being
3. *Work methods,* which describe how the job is done

• *Physical Environment*

This concerns the place where the job is done, its layout, the tools used, equipment available, etc. If these are badly organized, the environment can be distracting, and it

Case Study

The Magna Employee's Charter

Magna International Inc. is a leading global supplier of high-technology systems, assemblies, and components. In 1994, it had sales of $3,569 million and a net profit of $234.4 million. Frank Stronach, the chairman of Magna, believes in fairness and concern for his employees. He has created The Magna Employee's Charter, which is as follows:

THE MAGNA EMPLOYEE'S CHARTER

Magna is committed to an operating philosophy which is based on fairness and concern for people. It includes these principles:

JOB SECURITY

Being competitive by making a better product for a better price way is the best way to enhance job security. Magna is committed to working together with you to help protect your job security. To assist you, Magna will provide:

• Job Counselling • Training • Employee Assistance Programs

A SAFE AND HEALTHFUL WORKPLACE

Magna strives to provide you with a working environment which is safe and healthful.

FAIR TREATMENT

Magna offers equal employment opportunities based on an individual's qualifications and performance, free from discrimination or favoritism.

COMPETITIVE WAGES AND BENEFITS

Magna will provide you with information which will enable you to compare your total compensation of total wages and total benefits with those earned by employees of your competitors, as well as with other plants in your community. If your total compensation is found not to be competitive, then your wages will be adjusted.

EMPLOYEE EQUITY AND PROFIT PARTICIPATION

Magna believes that every employee should own a portion of the company.

COMMUNICATION AND INFORMATION

Through regular monthly meetings between management and employees and through publications, Magna will provide you with information so that you will know what is going on in your company and within the industry.

THE HOTLINE*

Should you have a problem, or feel the above principles are not being met, we encourage you to call the Hotline or use the self-addressed *Hotline Envelopes* to register your complaints. *You do not have to give your name, but if you do, it will be held in strict confidence.* Hotline Counsellors, speaking several languages, will record your concern. Your concern will then be forwarded to the Magna Corporate Employee Relations Department. The Magna Corporate Employee Relations Department is committed to investigate and resolve all concerns or complaints and must report the outcome to the Employee Relations Advisory Board.

EMPLOYEE RELATIONS ADVISORY BOARD

The Employee Relations Advisory Board is a group of people who have proven recognition and credibility relating to humanitarian and social issues. This Board will monitor, advise and ensure that Magna operates within the spirit of the *Magna Employee's Charter* and the principles of *Magna's Corporate Constitution.*

*Magna employees can call a direct, toll-free number to reach a Hotline Counsellor at the Corporate Employee Relations Department if they are unable to resolve a concern with their supervisor, human resources representative or manager. This confidential 'Hotline' helps to ensure the fast and fair resolution of employee concerns.

Source: With permission from Magna International Inc.

Question

- What impact do you think the Magna Employee's Charter has on its employees' morale and productivity?

can make the work unpleasant, hard, or even dangerous. Designing the physical environment is part of **ergonomics**, which is the function that designs tools, machines, work places, layouts, etc. to take account of the physical capabilities of people.

Typical questions to be asked about the environment are:

- Who will use the work place?
- How will the work be done?
- What must the user see?
- What must the user hear?
- Where must the user reach?

Suppose, for example, a person has to lean forward repeatedly to adjust a lever. We know from standard data of body measurements that 75 percent of people can remain sitting and reach forward a distance of 53 cm or more. But this leaves 25 percent who cannot reach this far. The job design would have to ask whether the same persons will always be doing the job, whether they will be sitting, how much they will have to move, if there is anything in the way, how much time they have to make the adjustment, could the lever be moved, and is the adjustment necessary.

Many of the early studies of work place design looked at operators using manufacturing machines. Nowadays, more emphasis is put on white-collar jobs, particularly on "knowledge workers." Designers consider the layout of an office, the height of chairs and tables, the position and size of keyboards, and a series of other factors. You can see the effect of this with telephones, which have become lighter, easier to use, have more functions, and connect to computer systems.

Other aspects of the work environment concern:

- *Light*—in general jobs that require high speed and accuracy need more light. The type of light is also important, so the colour, contrast, and direction must be considered.
- *Temperature and humidity*—most people work at their best in temperatures around 20–24°C: if the temperature in an office is too high, people get sleepy and slow down; if the temperature is too low, people spend time trying to keep warm.
- *Noise and vibrations*—noise can be annoying, but it can also damage hearing. There are limits on the time a person can work with loud noise. As always, people must be protected from all possible danger in the work place.
- *Air pollution*—pollution or fumes can be irritating, but they can also be dangerous. Pollution can come from something as simple as dust or gasoline fumes.

• *Social Environment*

The design of a job must also take into account the well-being of the people doing it. An organization must start, then, by giving employees:

- Sufficient training for the job
- Sufficient supervision and help
- Knowledge of the organization's policies, rules, and regulations
- A clear statement of what is expected from each person
- Credit for good work

These factors are clearly linked to motivation. This is a complex subject which is still not fully understood. However, six important factors should be considered:

- *Task significance*—the extent to which employees feel the job has an effect on the organization or on the community
- *Task identity*—the extent to which employees can see the job as a whole, single piece of work from start to finish
- *Task variety*—the extent to which a job contains a variety of different tasks
- *Skill variety*—the extent to which employees use a variety of skills and talents
- *Autonomy*—the extent to which each employee has freedom, independence, and personal control over the work
- *Feedback from the job*—the extent to which clear, timely information about individual performance is available

A common, but misleading, view of motivation is that it depends on how much an organization pays its employees. There are many examples of organizations whose pay rates are high, but the workforce is unmotivated and relatively unproductive. Some people say that there are many examples of this in the civil service. But there are many examples of organizations with low salaries whose workforce is well-motivated and highly productive. This is often found in charities and nonprofit organizations such as health and education services.

• *Work Methods*

Work methods look at the details of how a job is actually done, or the design of individual tasks.

The usual approach of work methods starts by looking at the way a job is done at present. Then it breaks the job into very small parts. A barber, for example, spends a lot of time cutting hair. This involves a series of standard tasks such as washing hair, giving an initial cut with scissors, tidying loose ends, trimming with shears, and dry-ing hair. Each of these tasks can be broken down into **microelements**, such as reaching out, picking up a hairdryer, moving the hairdryer back to the customer's head, and so on. In other words, the whole job can be broken down into a series of very small microelements.

A number of diagrams can help describe the job's microelements. Process charts of the type described in Chapter 4 are often used for this. Multiple activity charts can look at a job in so much detail that an operator's left and right hands are taken as working separately. Slow-motion videos are widely used to pinpoint inefficient movements.

Operation: Assembly
Standard Time: 30 seconds
Equipment: Punch, die, press, holder

Left Hand	Right Hand
Reach for casing	Put last assembly into bin
Pick up casing	
Put casing into holder	Put casing into holder
Reach for washers	Reach for insert
Pick up washers	Pick up insert
	Fit insert to casing
Add washers to insert	Hold casing
Hold casing	Reach for punch
	Pick up punch
Adjust punch and press	Adjust punch and press
	Operate press
Remove assembly	Remove assembly

Figure 12.2 Example of an Activity Chart for Two Hands

The microelements can then be analyzed to find the most efficient way of doing the whole job. The barber, for example, might spend too much time reaching for implements, so the job could be improved by moving them closer to the customer. A series of questions is asked: Why is this done? How is it done? Could this step be eliminated? Could it be done at another time? Could it be done automatically? How could the layout of the work place be improved? Would different tools help? The answers to these questions lead to better ways of doing the job.

Such detailed analyses of jobs can be very important, but usually the detailed design is less important than the overall view of the job. Some broader views of work methods consider:

- *Job rotation*—each person's job is rotated, perhaps daily, to avoid boredom. Some organizations find this results in only a temporary improvement to morale, as people soon feel they are being switched around a series of equally boring jobs.
- *Job enlargement*—which combines several simple jobs into a larger one. Again, some organizations find this provides only temporary improvement as it replaces a short boring job with a longer boring job.
- *Job enrichment*—which adds more responsibility to the job, and makes it inherently more interesting. This has been used with quality management, where everyone becomes responsible for the quality of their own work.

In Summary

The three main elements in job design are:

- The physical environment, which is concerned with the surroundings in which the job is done
- The social environment, which is concerned with the welfare of the person doing the job
- Work methods, which look for the best way of doing the tasks in the job

Review Questions

1. How do the needs of employees and employers differ?
2. Who are the main people concerned with job design?
3. Why is job design important?
4. What are the main elements in job design?
5. What factors will generally improve morale in an organization?

Case Study – York Stamping Works

York Stamping Works is a medium-sized company supplying stamped parts for consumer appliance industries. Their process starts with coils of sheet metal. These coils are cut into smaller strips using shearing machines. The strips are passed to stamping presses which form the products. Other processes used at the shop are welding, painting, plating, and assembly.

The working conditions in the plant are far from pleasant. The plant is noisy and cluttered. Its heating and ventilation system needs improvement. Since York does not have a good production planning system, customer orders are always being expedited and rush work seems to be the norm. This puts a lot of pressure on workers. Sometimes the machines are operated in unsafe conditions and often by poorly trained workers. The company has had many inspections by Health and Safety inspectors from the Workers' Compensation Board.

There is poor communication between managers and workers. Tony Packard, one of the long-time employees, can remember no occasion when a manager has shown any appreciation of the job done by a worker. But, he noticed that managers are always complaining about increased costs and low profits. Tony is not surprised that the company has high employee turnover, poor quality, and a series of other problems.

Questions

- What are some of the problems facing the York Stamping Works?
- Will proper job design help the company? How?
- What should be done to improve the quality and profitability of the company?

Work Measurement

Purpose of Work Measurement

The last section discussed the design of jobs. This section examines how well jobs are actually done. But first, it must be determined how long it should take to do a job—that is its **standard time**, which is the purpose of **work measurement**.

Work measurement determines the standard time needed to do a job.

Work measurement can be used for a variety of purposes including:

- Capacity planning
- Estimating the size of workforce needed
- Finding the cost of operations
- Designing wage incentive schemes
- Monitoring employee performance
- Scheduling production

The basic question one must ask is, How long will it take to do a job? This is surprisingly difficult to answer. Different people take different amounts of time to do the same job. Also, if the same person does a job several times, he or she will take different amounts of time each repetition. These variations simply show that people have different abilities, and each individual has some inconsistency in their performance. The time required to complete a job also depends on how well it is designed and managed.

The basic work content of a job determines the minimum time needed to complete it. This is the time needed for the job if the design of the product is perfect, the ideal process is used, no time is lost, materials are delivered on time, and the workforce is motivated. The actual time taken to do the job will be greater than this basic time because of the following factors:

- *Work added by poor design of the product*
  - the product design may not allow the best process to be used
  - it may need complex or extra tasks
  - there is no standardization, so small batches are made
  - quality standards are not set properly
  - it uses too many materials

- *Work added by inefficient operations*
  - using the wrong type or size of machinery
  - operating the process improperly
  - having a poor layout
  - using poor methods that give extra work

- *Ineffective use of time caused by poor management*
  - making too wide a range of products
  - having too many design changes
  - poor flow of materials from suppliers to customers
  - poor maintenance of plant and equipment
  - poor working conditions, morale, etc.

- *Ineffective use of time within the control of the operator*
  - absenteeism, lateness, idleness
  - careless workmanship
  - unsafe behaviour causing accidents

This means that managers must look beyond the basic work content of a job. They must take into account all the factors that add to the basic time, and then find a realistic time that is needed for the job.

In Summary

Work measurement determines the standard time needed for a job. This can be used for a variety of management decisions. Unfortunately, it is surprisingly difficult to find standard times.

Standard Times

The International Labour Organization gives the following definition:

> **Work measurement** is the application of techniques designed to establish the time for a qualified operator to carry out a specific job at a defined level of performance.

This definition specifies a "qualified operator" and assumes that the operator is:

1. Properly prepared and qualified for the job
2. Properly trained and experienced to do the job
3. Physically and mentally capable of doing the job

The "specified job" must define both the method to be used, and the circumstances surrounding the job.

When both the operator and the job have been specified, there must still be some way of finding a standard time for the job. One could, of course, time someone doing the job—but any two individuals will do the same job in slightly different ways and take different times to do it. What is needed is a standard time that does not depend on the operator. For this we must define a standard rate of work.

Standard rate of work is the output that qualified workers will naturally achieve without overdue exertion as an average over the working day or shift, provided that they know and use the specified method, and provided that they apply themselves to the work.

A number of operators can be timed doing the same job, and at the same time their work rate can be compared to the standard rate. If a person works 10 percent faster than the standard rate, he would have a **rating** of 110 percent. If he works 10 percent slower than the standard rate, he would have a rating of 90 percent

This rating relies on judgement and experience. The person measuring the job must know what a standard rate means, and then compare the operator's performance to this rate. This may seem difficult, but we do it all the time. When you see someone walking down the street, you can easily tell if they are hurrying or strolling casually. With experience, work-measurement analysts can do the same thing for a wide range of operations.

There are three sorts of time in work measurement—actual time, normal time, and standard time.

- *Actual time.* This is the time an operator actually takes to do the essential parts of the job. This time excludes avoidable delays (such as dropping tools or looking for something that has been misplaced) and unavoidable delays (such as waiting for material, coffee breaks, and getting instructions from the supervisor).
- *Normal time.* This is the time an operator would normally take to do the job if they worked at standard rate. It is the time an average worker will need for the job. It follows that:

$$\text{Normal time} = \text{actual time} \times \text{rating}$$

Example

The times taken by five workers to complete the same job are 3.8, 5.2, 4.6, 4.1, and 4.3 minutes. What is the normal time for the job and the rating of each worker? How long will the job take someone working 5 percent faster than normal?

Solution

- The actual time is the average of the observations, which is (3.8 + 5.2 + 4.6 + 4.1 + 4.3)/5 = 4.4 minutes.
- Then the rating of the first worker is:

  Rating = normal time/actual time = 4.4/3.8 = 1.16 or 116 percent

  This shows the first worker is working 16 percent above normal time.

Similarly, the other workers have ratings of 84.6 percent, 95.7 percent, 107.3 percent, and 102.3 percent

- Someone working 5 percent faster than normal has a rating of 105 percent or 1.05, so they will take:

  Actual time = normal time/rating = 4.4/1.05 = 4.2 minutes

The actual time and normal time only consider the essential parts of a job. There is a range of other things that are not part of the job but which must be considered. These include coffee breaks, interruptions to supplies, accidents, and rest periods. We can classify these as:

- *Personal allowances*—the time allowances for normal human needs of the operator during the working day including coffee breaks, washroom visits, rest, and meals. The time for these varies widely. In an office, the personal allowances may be little more than coffee breaks and lunch hours, but in a steel mill or cold-storage depot, people may need frequent breaks. These may account for 20 minutes each hour.

- *Contingencies*—used to cover random events outside the control of the operator. These include getting instructions, filling in record sheets, in-process inspections, accidents, and any other interruptions.

Allowances are usually given as a percentage of normal time, say 10 percent, and lead to a third definition:

- *Standard time.* This is the total time that should be allowed for a job.

  Standard time = normal time × (1 + allowance factor)

Example

Time studies show that a job actually takes 5 minutes with a rating of 120 percent. An allowance factor of 10 percent is used. What does this tell you?

Solution

- Actual time = 5 minutes, which is the actual time a person took to do the job. The rating of 120 percent shows that the person worked hard, at 20 percent faster than the normal rate
- Normal time = actual time × rating = 5 × 1.2 = 6 minutes, which is the time taken for the basic job in ideal conditions
- Standard time = normal time × (1 + allowance factor) = 6 × (1 + 0.1) = 6.6 minutes. This is the time that should be allowed for the job.

Standard time is the basis of all planning, scheduling, and control decisions. Although this is based on judgements and opinions, it is the best measure we have.

In Summary

There are three different times for a job. The actual time taken to do the basic job, the normal time which allows for a rating, and the standard time which adds allowances. The standard time is the total time needed, and is used in all planning decisions.

Finding Normal Times

To find the standard time for a job, one must start with the normal time. Sometimes this can be found by direct observation, but this is not always possible. Direct observation cannot be used, for example, to find the time for a new job, or one that will be done only once. Some other method is needed. In general, there are three ways of finding normal times:

1. Historical data
2. Estimation
3. Time study

- *Historical data.* When a job has been done many times before, the easiest way to find how long it will take is to review how long it took in the past. But work conditions change, as do the quality of materials, skills of people, condition of equipment, and the environment. Although historical data can give quick findings, changes mean that they are, perhaps surprisingly, not very reliable.
- *Estimation.* This method is used when there are no historical data. It is based on the experience of an analyst, who estimates the time needed to do a job, based on his experience with similar jobs. This is often seen with tradesmen. When you take your car to a garage for repairs and ask for an estimate of costs, the garage will give an estimate based on its experience with similar repairs. This method has the usual drawbacks of personal opinions, but it is widely used in small organizations, it can be fairly reliable, and it is the only possible method for one-off jobs.
- *Time study.* This is the most common way of finding the normal time for a job. It is based on direct observation of the job, and usually breaks down the job into small parts. There are four ways of doing time studies:

  1. Stopwatch studies
  2. Internal standard data
  3. Predetermined motion-time standards
  4. Work sampling

1. *Stopwatch studies.* These use direct observation of a job. An analyst watches an operator and times a number of repetitions of the job. In more detail, the analyst must:
   - Gain the confidence and cooperation of operators and their supervisors. It must be made clear that the analyst is looking for a standard time and is not trying to judge the operator.
   - Be sure that the proper methods are being used
   - Set the number of repetitions that are needed and choose the operators to study
   - Break the job into tasks that have a distinct beginning and end, and that can be easily timed
   - Time each task and rate the operator's performance over the repetitions
   - Find the actual time for the whole job, usually from the average of repetitions
   - Adjust the actual time by the rating to give the normal time
   - Set allowances and calculate the standard time
2. *Internal standard data.* Results from stopwatch studies can be saved, and eventually the organization will have a databank of times for various operations. These can be used to set times for similar jobs, perhaps using regression to find relationships between types of jobs and times needed.

3. *Predetermined motion-time standards.* These are similar to internal standard data, except that the times for tasks are not found from the organization's own experience but from other sources. Experiments over many years has led to normal times for certain basic movements. These include activities such as reaching, grasping, turning and applying pressure, and releasing. These times can be combined to give an overall time for a job. The main problem with this approach is the large effort needed to get results. But computer programs can analyze video recordings and automatically calculate standard times.

4. *Work sampling.* Many jobs, like cooking meals, answering telephones, and interviewing customers are too variable for standard times to be used. But managers still need some way of finding the time people spend on each activity. This can be done by work sampling. This uses random visits to operators to record what they are doing. After many such visits, work sampling gives a picture of the operator's overall pattern of work. Work sampling is used mainly to find the proportion of time a person spends doing particular activities or the time a machine is actually busy. It depends on:

   - Clear definitions of the types of activities to be studied

Case Study – A Hasty Stopwatch Study

Workers in the welding department at Moncton Welding and Fabrication Co. are worried. They had heard through their supervisor, Karim Ahmed, that the new production manager is planning to implement time standards in the department. Cedric Paxton was recently hired as the production manager with instructions to reduce the company's costs and to make it more profitable.

Moncton makes a standard range of heat exchanger, for use in the chemical industry. There are five different models of heat exchanger, each of which requires a lot of welding. The welding department has seven experienced welders and a supervisor. The quality of their workmanship is very good, but Cedric is concerned that each welder has his or her own method of welding.

One morning, to the surprise of Karim and the welders, Cedric showed up in the welding department with a stopwatch. He started to time a welder working on the tubes of a model XL150 heat exchanger. Cedric had barely taken seven readings when he was interrupted by the supervisor from the cutting department who had some urgent business. Cedric stopped his study to take care of the matter.

Later in the day, Cedric mentioned to Karim the results of his stopwatch study and asked for his opinion. Cedric had set the standard time of 10.5 minutes for welding the tubes in the XL150 heat exchanger. He had calculated this from five "good readings" he had taken earlier in the day. Karim knew from experience that it was an unrealistic standard, and the welders would not accept it.

Questions

- What do you think of Cedric's stopwatch study?
- How could he do a proper stopwatch study?
- What should Karim tell Cedric?

Case Study

A Factory Learns to Survive

Honeywell Limited of Scarborough, Ontario is a wholly owned subsidiary of Honeywell Inc. It used to make 15 different lines of heating, cooling, and ventilation control units for the Canadian market. In 1988, Honeywell reduced its production to five key products for the world market. Honeywell decided to implement just-in-time manufacturing, total quality management, and self-directed work teams. Mandatory training in these areas was provided to employees during regular work hours.

This sudden change in direction put the spotlight on the workforce. Now the workers were expected to work in teams, solve problems, and make decisions. The average age of the workforce was 50; on average, they had less than grade 12 education, and they had worked at Honeywell for an average of 20 years. Eighty percent of them were women and 50 percent had English as a second language. But managers saw this as an opportunity to use proper training and education, and to build well-rounded work teams.

Honeywell also introduced a voluntary program called "Learning for Life." Employees were given the opportunity to take classes in English, mathematics, computer skills, communication, and many other subjects—all in the employees' own time. The response was more positive than anticipated. The first English class had 130 people sign up for the 30 places. Responses for other courses were equally enthusiastic. People on the night shift complained that they could not register for the evening courses, so the company added an afternoon session for them. The communication course was particularly popular, especially among the teams that had trouble working together. In some cases the entire team signed up for that course.

The budget for this education program is $300,000 per year, which the company feels is a good investment that has paid off in increased productivity. About 80 percent of the 450 employees have taken at least one course. Many have taken more than one, and they feel the education program has made them better communicators and has given them more confidence.

A view expressed by most workers, which is supported by their union, is that they had to change and adapt to new techniques, or the survival of the plant was in jeopardy.

Questions

- Why did Honeywell introduce self-directed work teams?
- What is the company's approach to training and education?
- Is the Honeywell employees' view of change unique or does it exist in other Canadian companies?

- Random visits to operations
- Visits over a period sufficiently long to allow for work cycles, etc.
- A large number of observations
- An analyst who is a skilful observer

In Summary

There are three ways of finding the actual time for a job: historical data, estimation, or time study. Time studies are most reliable, particularly when using stopwatch studies.

Review Questions

1. What is the purpose of work measurement?
2. What is the difference between actual, normal, and standard times?
3. How could you find the normal time for a job?
4. Which time would you use to schedule resources?

Chapter Review

- Job design and work measurement look in detail at the jobs actually done by employees. They can be viewed as the most detailed level of planning.
- Job design looks for the best way of doing a job. It usually breaks down jobs into very small tasks, analyses these, and sees how the tasks can be done more efficiently.
- There are two parties in job design—employers and employees. These have different aims, but both must be considered. Labour productivity is increased by treating employees fairly and reasonably.
- Three important elements in job design are the physical environment, the social environment, and work methods.
- Work measurement finds the time needed to do a job.
- There are three different times for a job—actual time, normal time, and standard time. The standard time is the allowed time for a job, and is used in all planning decisions.
- The times can be found from historical data, estimation, or time studies. Time studies are the most reliable of these.

Key Terms

ergonomics *(p. 336)*
Hertzberg's Two-factor Theory *(p. 333)*
job *(p. 331)*
job design *(p. 331)*
Maslow's Hierarchy of Needs *(p. 332)*
microelements *(p. 338)*
output-based remuneration *(p. 333)*
rating *(p. 342)*
self-directed work teams *(p. 334)*
standard rate *(p. 342)*
standard time *(p. 340)*
time-based remuneration *(p. 333)*
work measurement *(pp. 340, 341)*

Problem

12.1 An analyst times ten people doing a job. The times, in minutes, are:

14.3 12.8 13.9 16.2 14.8 15.2 13.6 15.8 14.4 14.0

What is the normal time for the job? What is the rating of each person? What is the standard time with allowances of 20 percent?

Discussion Questions

12.1 Why is job design important? What factors do you think are most important in designing a job?

12.2 Why is job design viewed as the most detailed level of planning?

12.3 How has the emphasis of job design changed over time?

12.4 What methods can be used to improve employee morale and motivation in an organization? Which of these methods work best in different types of organization?

12.5 How could one design a fair scheme for paying employees?

12.6 What is the purpose of work measurement?

12.7 Do you think work measurement is becoming less useful with increasing automation?

12.8 How realistic are the standard times used in work measurement? Are they accurate enough to be useful?

Career Profile

Name: Patricia Steger
Title: Manufacturing Supervisor
Company: Warner Lambert Canada, Adams Brand Division

I began my Production Operations studies at Centennial College in 1987. My first co-op work term was spent at Motorola, working in the Purchasing Department of the Custom Manufacturing section. My second work term was with Warner Lambert Canada as an Industrial Engineering Analyst. During this work term, I worked on material flow analysis and production floor layouts. At this time Warner Lambert had just installed an AutoCAD system, and part of my work-term assignment was to transfer all plant drawings to the system. I continued to work on a part-time basis through the next semester.

My third work term was spent in the Computer Integrated Manufacturing Department of Warner Lambert, and I joined the company on a full-time basis thereafter.

During my time in the C.I.M. Department, my role was expanded to include development of direct labour standards and co-ordination of plant cost of goods improvement projects. The next 18 months were spent developing and implementing independent cost improvement projects.

I was transferred to the Operations group and worked on simplification/analysis projects. I was promoted to Production Supervisor in December of 1993, responsible for processing and packaging of all compressed powder products. I also participated in evaluation and implementation of a new $1.4 million packaging line, and supported start-up of new export product.

During this time I was given the opportunity to receive training as an instructor for Natural Work Groups. The department I work in is presently participating in a Natural Work Group Pilot Project, which will be rolled out to the rest of the plant in 1995.

I am presently assigned for six months to an evaluation and implementation team for a new computer system, and will be returning to Operations at the end of the project.

In the future I am looking forward to contributing to the company's move towards Natural Work Groups by providing training in problem solving, communication skills, and project planning.

Chapter 13

MATERIAL REQUIREMENTS PLANNING

Using the master schedule to control materials

Contents

Introduction

Chapter 10 described an organization's planning down to the master schedule. As stated, there are several other stages in the planning process. Short-term scheduling was described in Chapter 11; the design of jobs was discussed in Chapter 12. This chapter looks at another aspect of scheduling, which considers the supply of materials. This is called *material requirements planning* (MRP). MRP expands the master schedule to give a timetable for the delivery of materials needed to support operations.

The master schedule gives details of the planned production. MRP uses this to find the demand for raw materials and parts. This is the basis of dependent-demand inventory systems.

MRP requires many calculations, so it always uses computers. It can only be used in certain circumstances, but it can bring a lot of benefits—particularly reduced stocks of materials and work-in-process.

Learning Objectives

After reading this chapter you should be able to answer questions such as:

- What is material requirements planning?
- When can MRP can be used?
- How does MRP schedule orders and operations?
- What are the advantages and disadvantages of MRP?
- How are lot sizing rules used for MRP orders?
- How can basic MRP systems be extended?

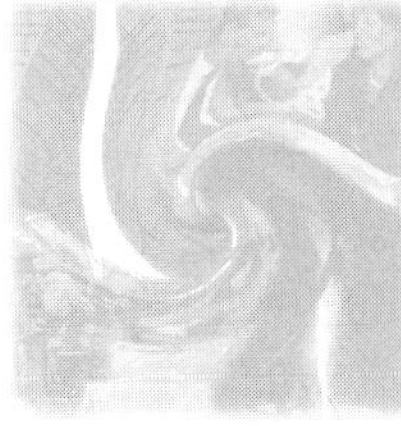

Elements of Material Requirements Planning

Material requirements planning uses the master schedule to plan the supply of materials. It expands the master schedule so that materials can be scheduled to arrive when they are needed.

MRP begins with the planned production described in the master schedule. It expands this to get a list of materials needed, then it develops a timetable for the delivery of these materials. The supply of materials—and therefore the stocks held—depends directly on the known demand. This kind of system is called a **dependent-demand inventory system**.

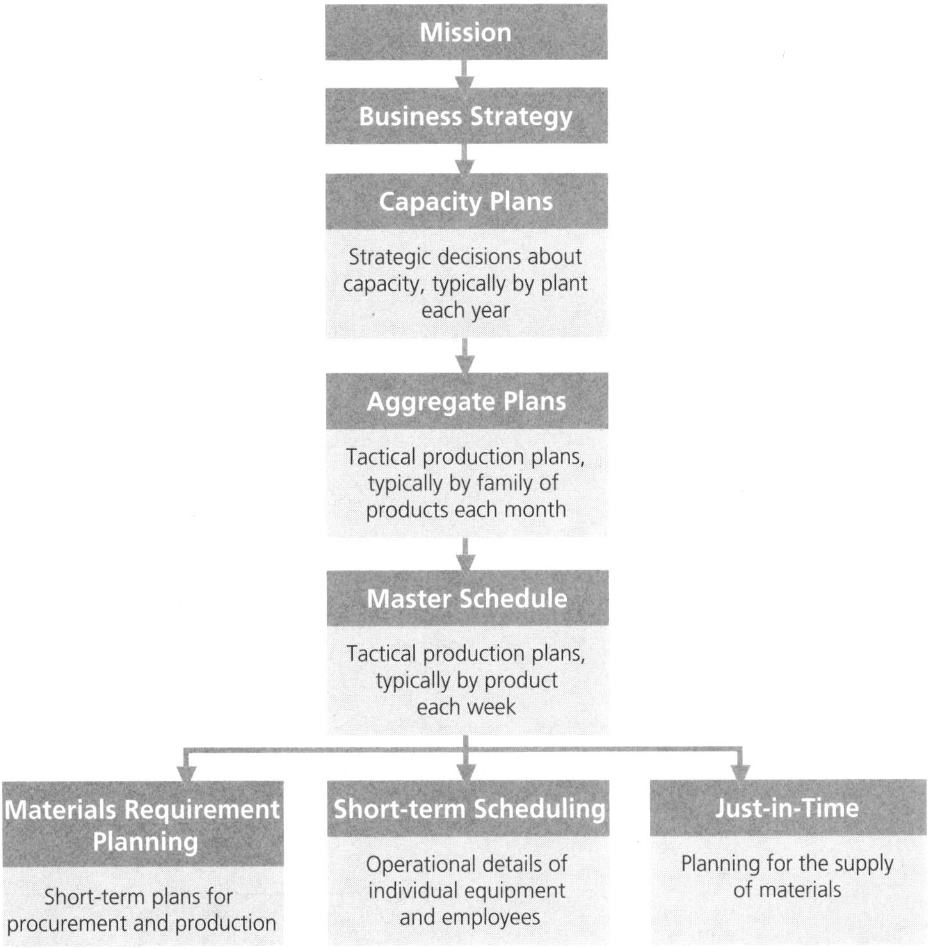

Mission
↓
Business Strategy
↓
Capacity Plans
Strategic decisions about capacity, typically by plant each year
↓
Aggregate Plans
Tactical production plans, typically by family of products each month
↓
Master Schedule
Tactical production plans, typically by product each week
↓

Materials Requirement Planning	Short-term Scheduling	Just-in-Time
Short-term plans for procurement and production	Operational details of individual equipment and employees	Planning for the supply of materials

Figure 13.1 Summary of the Planning Process

The alternative to a dependent-demand inventory system starts by forecasting demand for materials, and keeps stocks that are high enough to cover any likely demand. These stocks are not directly related to the demand specified in a master schedule and the result is an **independent-demand inventory system** (described in Chapter 17). An illustration of the differences is the way a chef plans the ingredients needed to cook a week's meals. The MRP approach would look at the meals to be cooked each day, find the ingredients needed, and then make sure that they are delivered in time. An independent-demand system looks at the ingredients that were used in previous weeks, forecasts demand for each, and makes sure there is enough in stock to cover likely demand.

An important difference between the two approaches is the pattern of material stocks. With MRP, stocks are generally low but rise as deliveries are made just before production starts. The stock is then used during production and declines to its normal, low level. This pattern is shown in Figure 13.2a. With independent-demand systems, the stocks are not related to production plans, so levels must be higher. These are reduced during production, but are replenished as soon as possible to give the pattern shown in Figure 13.2b.

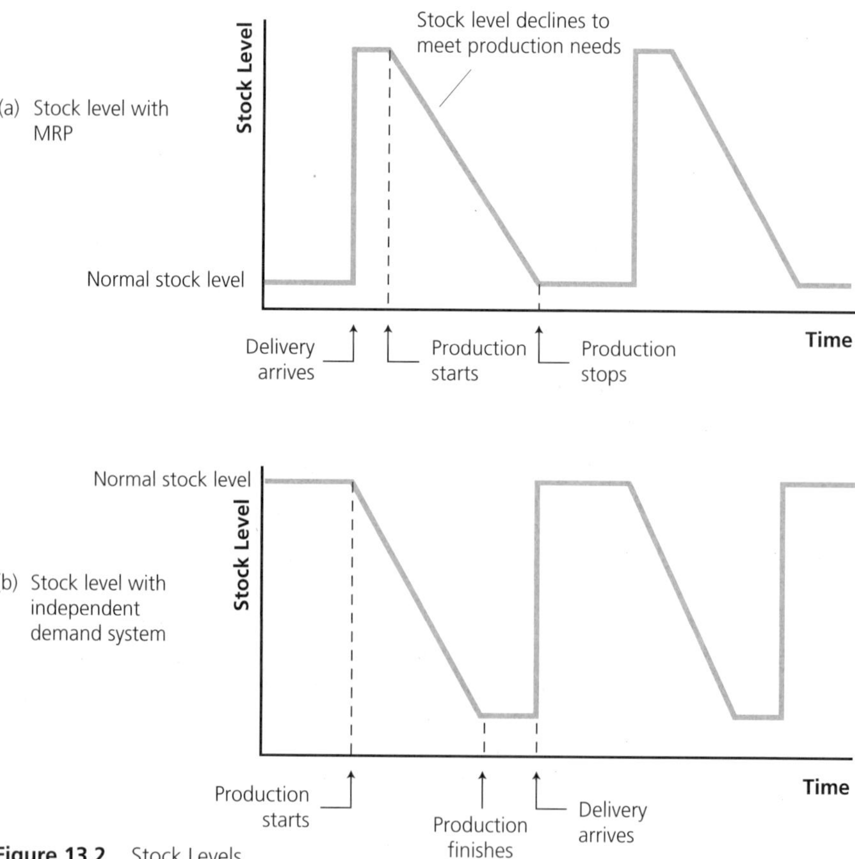

Figure 13.2 Stock Levels

In general, independent-demand inventory systems are used for finished goods. Dependent-demand inventory systems are used for raw materials. In the past, organizations tried to use independent-demand systems to control stocks of parts and raw materials—but results were mixed. For example, if a company makes bicycles, the number of pedals, seats, wheels, etc. it needs are directly related to the number of bicycles it makes. If it is to make 1,000 bicycles next month, it will need 2,000 pedals, 1,000 seats, 2,000 wheels, and so on. The demand for these parts clearly depends on the production of bicycles, so it should be found from the production schedule and not from forecasts.

The following questions illustrate exactly how MRP works.

Question 1: What products will be made, when, and in what quantity?
Answer: The answer to this comes from the master schedule. Chapter 10 described how this gives a detailed timetable for making each product.

Question 2: What materials do we need to make the products?
Answer: This depends on the product design. From the product design, a bill of materials is prepared. This lists all the parts and materials that are required to make the product.

Question 3: What materials do we have in stock?
Answer: Inventory records contain a list of all the stocks currently held. This is normally held in a computer **inventory record file**.

Question 4: What do we have on order?
Answer: Again, the inventory records will list all orders that have been placed, and their expected delivery date.

Question 5: What extra materials do we need?
Answer: Some calculations are required to answer this question. We know what materials we need. We also know what materials are in stock, and those due to be delivered. So the difference is the extra amount that must be ordered.

Question 6: When do we order these materials?
Answer: The materials are either bought or made within the organization. Inventory records will show the expected lead times. So, we place orders this lead time before the materials are needed.

You can see how these questions move from the master schedule to a schedule for materials supply. This is the basis of MRP.

MRP was originally designed for manufacturing industries. It is still most common in manufacturing but is now used in many other industries. For convenience's sake, the discussion will stick to the original terms used—components being delivered to make products.

In Summary

Material requirements planning is a dependent-demand inventory system. Demand for materials is found by expanding the master schedule. This gives a detailed timetable for purchases of materials.

Review Questions

1. What is meant by MRP?
2. What are the important differences between dependent-demand inventory systems and independent-demand systems?

The MRP Procedure

Information Needed

MRP requires a great deal of accurate information about a product. Because of this, and because of the number of calculations, MRP is always computerized. Its main inputs come from three data files:

1. Master schedule
2. Bill of materials
3. Inventory records

The master schedule gives details of the products to be made in each period. Then MRP "explodes" the master schedule using a bill of materials. This gives the details of all materials needed to support production.

A **bill of materials** is an ordered list of all materials, parts, components, subassemblies, etc. that are needed to make a product. All the parts for a product are not needed at the same time but are used in a specific sequence. So each item in this list is given a "level" number, which shows where it fits into the process. The finished product is at level 0; level 1 items are needed to make the level 0 item; level 2 items are needed to make level 1 items; and so on. Suppose, for example, a table is made from a top and four legs. The bill of materials is shown in Figure 13.3. The figures in parentheses show the number needed to make each unit.

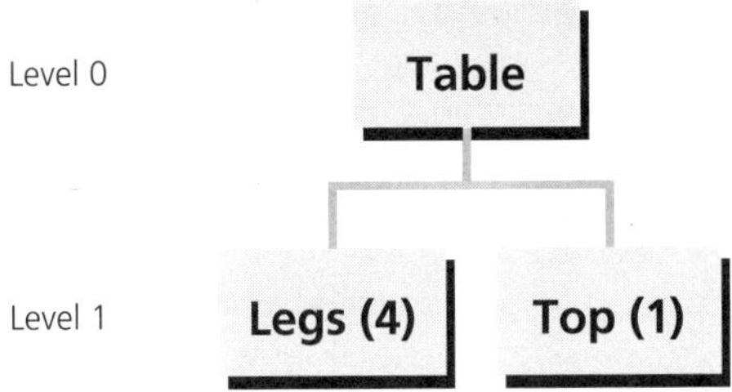

Figure 13.3 Single Level Bill of Materials for a Table

If you were to look at the table in more detail, you might see that each top is made from a wood kit and hardware, and that the wood kit consists of four oak planks which are 2 m long, and so on. Part of this more detailed bill of materials is shown in Figure 13.4.

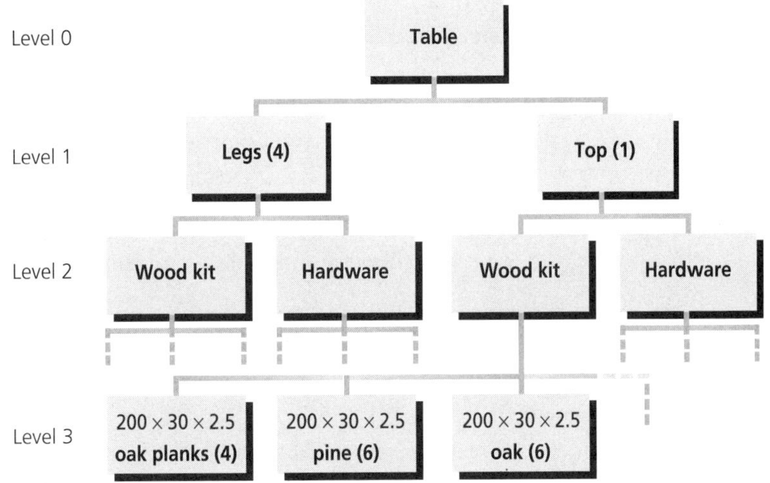

Figure 13.4 Partial Bill of Materials for a Table

Sometimes the bill of materials is simply given as an indented list, as follows:

Table
- Legs (4)
  - Wood kit (1)
  - Hardware (1)
- Top (1)
  - Wood kit (1)
    - oak planks 200 × 30 × 2.5 (4)
    - pine 200 × 30 × 2.5 (6)
    - oak 200 × 30 × 2.5 (6)
  - Hardware (1)

The next information we need is found in the inventory records. These contain details of each item held in stock: the amount on hand, quantities on order, lead time, costs, and suppliers. These records are used to determine whether there is enough stock on hand, whether more should be ordered, and when it should be ordered.

In Summary

MRP is always computerized. The information it needs is kept in three computer files—the master schedule, bill of materials, and inventory records.

Detailed Calculations

Now the example of a table can be used to illustrate the overall approach of MRP. Suppose the master schedule states that 10 tables are to be made in February. This means that 10 tops and 40 legs must be ready to be assembled at the beginning of February. This is the **gross requirements** for parts. Not all of these parts need to be ordered as there may be some materials already held in stock, or some orders that are due to arrive in the near future. Subtracting these from the gross requirements gives us the **net requirements** for materials.

Net requirements = gross requirements – current stock – stock on order

The quantities to order and when these orders should arrive have now been determined. The next step is to find when orders must be placed. For this the company needs to know the lead times so that orders can be placed this lead time before the materials are actually needed. If it buys the table tops and legs from suppliers who give a lead time of four weeks, it would need to place orders at the beginning of January. These orders will arrive by the end of January just before assembly is due to start. Determining when to place orders in this way is called **time shifting** or lead time offsetting.

Finally, other information about orders, such as minimum quantities and discounts, must be considered, and then the detailed timetable for orders can be designated. This process is summarized in Figure 13.5 and in Table 13.1.

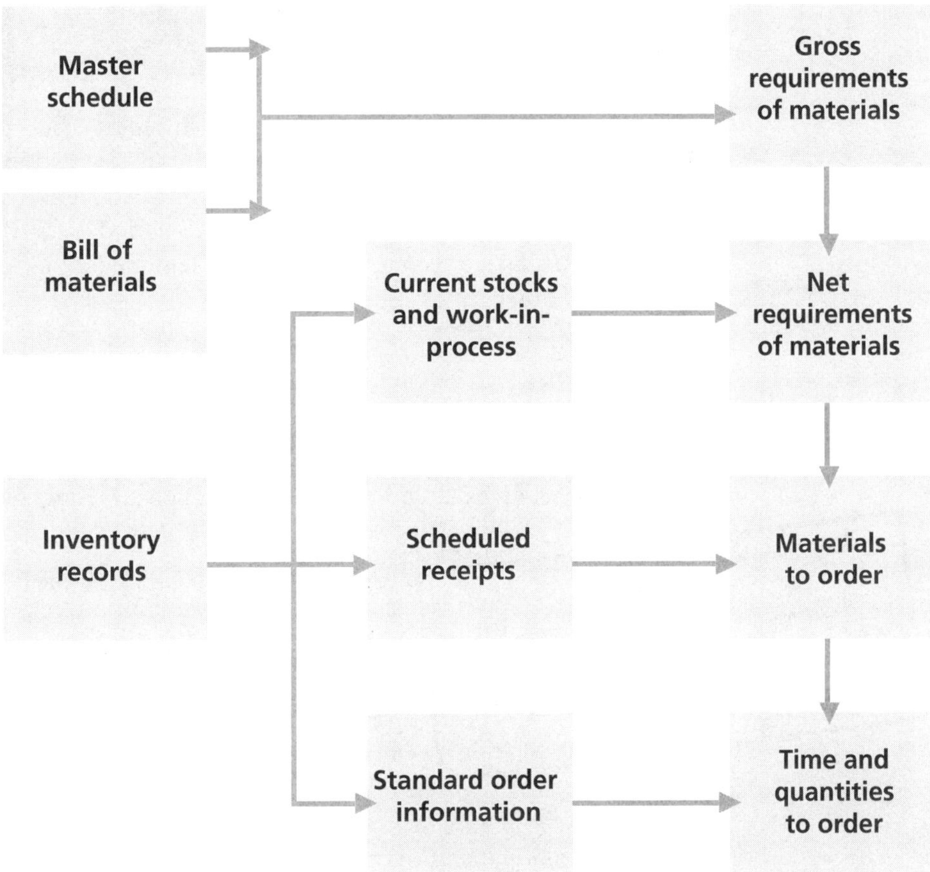

Figure 13.5 The MRP Procedure

Table 13.1 *The MRP Procedure*

1. Use the master schedule to find the gross requirements of level 0 items.
2. Subtract any stock on hand to give the net requirements of level 0 items. Schedule production to start so that these net requirements can be made in time.
3. If there are any more levels of materials, use the bill of materials to translate net requirements from the last level into gross requirements for the next level. If there are no more levels, go to Step 5.
4. Take each of the materials in turn and:
   - Subtract the stock on hand and scheduled deliveries to find the quantities of materials to order
   - Use the lead time and any other relevant information to find when to order

   Go to Step 3.
5. When there are no more levels of materials, finalize the schedule of events.

Example

Johnson Furniture assembles dining room tables using purchased parts of four legs and a top. These have lead times of two and three weeks respectively, and assembly takes a week. The company receives orders for 20 tables to be delivered in week 5 of a production period, and 40 tables in week 7. Current stocks are 2 complete tables, 40 legs, and 22 tops. When should the company order parts?

Solution

Johnson's production schedule for dining room tables is shown below. This gives the gross requirements for level 0 items. Subtracting the stocks of finished tables gives the net requirements. Then allowing a week for assembly gives the start times shown in the following plan.

Level 0 — Dining room tables

Week	**1**	**2**	**3**	**4**	**5**	**6**	**7**
Gross Requirements					20		40
Opening Stock	2	2	2	2	2		
Net Requirements					18		40
Start Assembly				18		40	
Scheduled Receipts					18		40

The "Scheduled Receipts" show the number of units that become available in a week, which is the number started the lead time earlier.

The bill of materials for this problem has already been shown in Figure 13.3. This can be used with the assembly plans to find gross requirements for level 1 items (legs and tops). In week 4, there is a net requirement of 18 tables, which gives a gross requirement of 72 legs and 18 tops. Similarly, the gross requirements for other parts are:

- Legs: $18 \times 4 = 72$ in week 4, and $40 \times 4 = 160$ in week 6
- Tops: 18 in week 4, and 40 in week 6

Subtracting stock on hand from these gross requirements gives the net requirements. To make sure the parts arrive on time, they must be ordered the lead time in advance (i.e., 2 weeks for legs and 3 weeks for tops).

Level 1 — Legs

Week	**1**	**2**	**3**	**4**	**5**	**6**	**7**
Gross Requirements				72		160	
Opening Stock	40	40	40	40			
Net Requirements				32		160	
Place Order		32		160			
Scheduled Receipts				32		160	

Level 1 — Tops

Week	**1**	**2**	**3**	**4**	**5**	**6**	**7**
Gross Requirements				18		40	
Opening Stock	22	22	22	22	4	4	
Net Requirements						36	
Place Order			36				
Scheduled Receipts						36	

There are no more levels of materials, so the timetable of events can be finalized:

- Week 2: order 32 legs
- Week 3: order 36 tops
- Week 4: order 160 legs and assemble 18 tables
- Week 6: assemble 40 tables

Number of Time Periods: 13
Bill of Materials

```
                                          End Irem
                                             |
         - - - - - - - - - - - - - - - - - - -
         |                     |
         X                     X
         |                     |
   - - - -                - - - -
   |    |                 |    |
   X    X                 X    X
```

Level 0 – End Item

Item Number : Part-0 — Beginning Inventory ; 10
Description: Product — Lead Time: 2
Safety Stock: 5
Lot Size: 1

	Week 6	Week 7	Week 8	Week 9	Week 10	Week 11	Week 12	Week 13
Gross Requirements :	0	0	0	45	60	0	0	40
Scheduled Receipts :	0	0	0	0	0	0	0	0
Available :	10	10	10	5	5	5	5	5
Net Requirements :	0	0	0	40	60	0	0	40
Receipts :	0	0	0	40	60	0	0	40
Requests :	0	40	60	0	0	40	0	0

Level 1 – Comp 1

Item Number : Part-1 — Beginning Inventory ; 50
Description: Part-B — Lead Time: 1
Bill of Materials: 2 — Safety Stock: 0
Lot Size: 1

	Week 6	Week 7	Week 8	Week 9	Week 10	Week 11	Week 12	Week 13
Gross Requirements :	0	80	120	0	0	80	0	0
Scheduled Receipts :	0	0	0	0	0	0	0	0
Available :	50	0	0	0	0	0	0	0
Net Requirements :	0	30	120	0	0	80	0	0
Receipts :	0	30	120	0	0	80	0	0
Requests :	30	120	0	0	80	0	0	0

	Week 6	Week 7	Week 8	Week 9	Week 10	Week 11	Week 12	Week 13
Gross Requirements :	30	120	0	0	80	0	0	0
Scheduled Receipts :	0	0	0	0	0	0	0	0
Available :	20	20	20	20	20	20	20	20
Net Requirements :	10	120	0	0	80	0	0	0
Receipts :	10	120	0	0	80	0	0	0
Requests :	120	0	0	80	0	0	0	0

Level 2 – Comp 1-2

Item Number : Part-3 — Beginning Inventory ; 150
Description: Material-E — Lead Time: 2
Bill of Materials: 3 — Safety Stock: 100
Lot Size: 300

	Week 6	Week 7	Week 8	Week 9	Week 10	Week 11	Week 12	Week 13
Gross Requirements :	90	360	0	0	240	0	0	0
Scheduled Receipts :	0	0	0	0	0	0	0	0
Available :	360	300	300	300	360	360	360	360
Net Requirements :	40	100	0	0	40	0	0	0
Receipts :	300	300	0	0	300	0	0	0
Requests :	0	0	300	0	0	0	0	0

Level 1 – Comp 2

Item Number : Part-4 — Beginning Inventory ; 100
Description: Part-C — Lead Time: 2
Bill of Materials: 3 — Safety Stock: 0
Lot Size: 1

	Week 6	Week 7	Week 8	Week 9	Week 10	Week 11	Week 12	Week 13
Gross Requirements :	0	120	180	0	0	120	0	0
Scheduled Receipts :	0	0	100	0	0	0	0	0
Available :	100	0	0	0	0	0	0	0
Net Requirements :	0	20	80	0	0	120	0	0
Receipts :	0	20	80	0	0	120	0	0
Requests :	80	0	0	120	0	0	0	0

Level 2 – Comp 2-1

Item Number : Part-5 — Beginning Inventory ; 100
Description: ComponentF — Lead Time: 3
Bill of Materials: 2 — Safety Stock: 50
Lot Size: 100

	Week 6	Week 7	Week 8	Week 9	Week 10	Week 11	Week 12	Week 13
Gross Requirements :	160	0	0	240	0	0	0	0
Scheduled Receipts :	0	0	0	0	0	0	0	0
Available :	100	100	100	60	60	60	60	60
Net Requirements :	150	0	0	190	0	0	0	0
Receipts :	200	0	0	200	0	0	0	0
Requests :	200	0	0	0	0	0	0	0

Figure 13.6 Computer Printout for Example

Example

A master schedule needs 45 units of a product in week 9 of a cycle, 60 units in week 10, and 40 units in week 13. There are currently 10 units of the product in stock, but the company always keeps 5 units in reserve to cover emergency orders. Each unit of the product takes 2 weeks to assemble from 2 units of part B and 3 units of part C. Each unit of part B is made in 1 week from 1 unit of material D and 3 units of material E. Part C is assembled in 2 weeks from 2 units of component F. Lead times for D, E, and F are 1, 2, and 3 weeks respectively. Current stocks are 50 units of B, 100 of C, 40 of D, 150 of E, and 100 of F. The company keeps minimum stocks of 20 units of D, 100 of E, and 50 of F. The minimum order size for E is 300 units, while F can only be ordered in discrete batches of 100 units. An order placed with a subcontractor for 100 units of C is expected to arrive in period 8. Design a timetable of activities for the company.

Solution

As you can see, even a simple MRP problem needs a lot of calculation and becomes quite complicated. In practice, a computer is always used. The following printout from a simple program shows the results for this problem.

(Continued)

Example – Continued

The program starts at level 0, with production of the final product, A. The company keeps a minimum stock of 5 units of A, so you must remember this reserved stock when calculating net requirements. Then it moves on to level 1 materials and expands the assembly plan for A into gross requirements for components B and C. The 40 units of A assembled in week 10 is expanded into gross requirements of 80 units of part B and 120 units of part C. The 60 units of A assembled in week 11 is expanded into gross requirements of 120 units of B and 180 units of C, and so on.

Gross requirements for B and C can be partly met from opening stocks, with the rest forming net requirements. We must also remember the planned delivery of 100 units of part C in week 5. This schedule for level 1 parts can now be expanded to give the timetable for level 2 items.

The gross requirements for materials D and E are found from the assembly plans for part B. 30 units of B are started in period 9 and this expands into gross requirements for 30 units of D, 90 units of E, and so on. One complication here is the minimum order size of 300 units of E. In week 9, there is a gross requirement of 90 for material E; 50 of these can be met from free stock, while keeping the reserve stock of 100. The net requirement is 40, but 300 have to be ordered with the spare 260 added to stock.

Finally, the gross requirements for component F can be found from the assembly plan for part C. 100 units of C are started in week 9 so this expands into a gross requirement of 200 units of F, and so on. Orders must be in discrete batches of 100 units, so they are rounded to the nearest hundred above net requirements.

The timetable of activities now becomes:

- Week 3: place order for 200 units of F
- Week 4: place order for 300 units of E
- Week 5: order for 100 units of C arrives
  place orders for 10 units of D and 300 units of E
- Week 6: start making 30 of B and 100 of C
  place orders for 120 units of D and 200 units of F
  orders arrive for 10 units of D, 300 units of E, and 200 units of F
- Week 7: start making 40 of A and 120 of B
  finish 30 units of B
  orders arrive for 120 units of D and 300 units of E
- Week 8: start making 60 of A
  finish 120 units of B and 100 units of C
  place order for 300 units of E
- Week 9: finish making 40 units of A
  start making 120 of C
  place order for 80 units of D
  order arrives for 200 units of F
- Week 10: finish 60 units of A
  start making 80 units of B
  orders arrive for 80 units of D and 300 units of E
- Week 11: start making 40 units of A
  finish 80 units of B and 120 units of C
- Week 12: finish 40 units of A

In Summary

MRP explodes the master schedule using a bill of materials. This gives the detailed needs for materials. Accurate information about current stocks, orders outstanding, and lead times are then used to schedule orders so that materials arrive when they are needed.

Case Study – MRP and Skateboards

Figure 13.7 shows the parts needed to make a skateboard.

The assembly of a skateboard is as follows. The boards and wheels are moulded using resin. All the metal parts such as rivets, plates, axle support, axle, and hubcaps are bought from outside suppliers, as are the brochures, decals, and cartons.

A roller subassembly is made using an axle support, an axle, a wheel, and two hubcaps. The roller subassembly is then welded to a plate. Next, the plate-roller subassembly is riveted to a board using four rivets. A decal is put on the bottom of the board. Then a finished board is put into a box along with an instruction brochure.

Questions

- Describe a bill of material for the skateboard.
- Describe this bill of materials as an indented list.

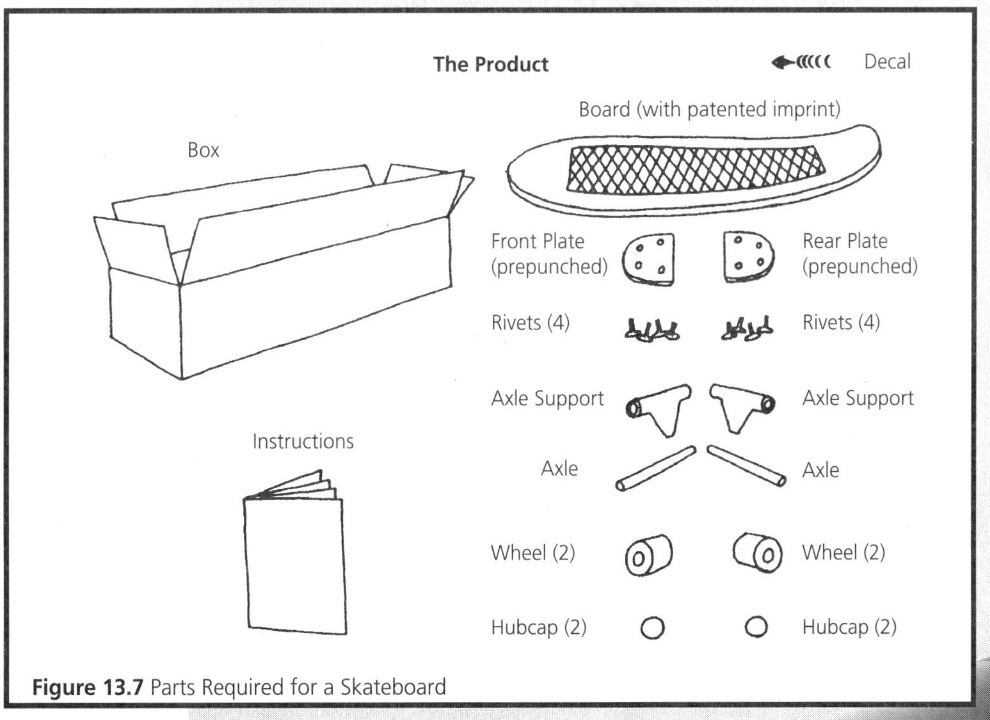

Figure 13.7 Parts Required for a Skateboard

Review Questions

1. What kinds of organizations can use MRP?
2. How is the net requirement for a material found in MRP?

Case Study – MRP Procedures

The Thompson Manufacturing Group has given you the following information:

- Product: LD 4720
- Bill of Materials

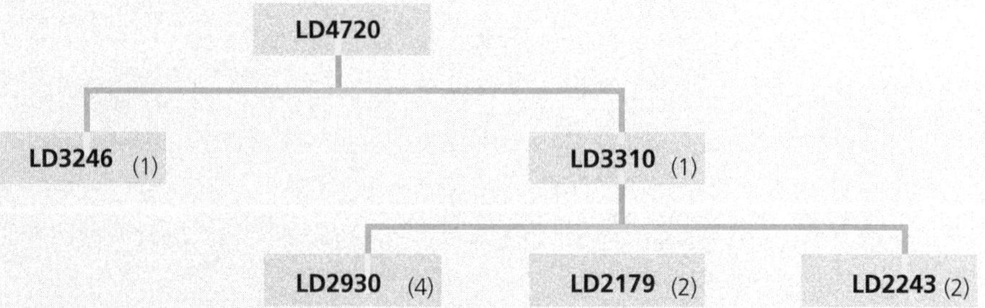

Figure 13.8 Bill of Materials for Case Study

- Master Production Schedule

Week Number	1	2	3	4	5	6	7	8	9
Production of LD 4720							1,000		

- Inventory Record File

Item	Stock on Hand	Lead Time (weeks)
LD 4720	0	1
LD 3246	100	2
LD 3310	0	2
LD 2930	500	2
LD 2179	50	3
LD 2243	100	1

Questions

- Design a material plan for the production of LD 4720.

Advantages and Disadvantages of MRP

Independent-demand inventory systems use forecasts to determine likely demand and then hold sufficient stocks to meet the demand. But forecasts almost always contain errors. Organizations therefore hold more stock than they really need as a safety net. The result is high stocks and high costs. MRP avoids these costs by relating the supply of materials directly to demand. There are many direct benefits of MRP, including:

- Lower stock levels, with savings of capital, space, warehousing, etc.
- Higher stock turnover
- Better customer service with fewer delays caused by shortages of materials
- More reliable and faster deliveries
- Better utilization of facilities, as materials are always available when needed
- Less time spent on expediting and emergency orders
- MRP schedules can be used for other short-term planning
- MRP can give priorities for jobs on the shop floor

As MRP is based on a master schedule, an organization may be more likely to design a reliable schedule and stick to it. The result is better planning. MRP can also give early warning of potential problems and shortages. If needed, deliveries can be expedited, or production plans changed. In other words, MRP can help with short-term scheduling decisions. So MRP improves the performance of an organization—which may be measured by such things as equipment utilization, productivity, customer service, and response to market conditions.

Another benefit of MRP comes from its process of detailed analysis. This can highlight problems that are usually hidden. With other systems, an unreliable supplier, for example, might not be noticed because the organization has high stock levels. This stock effectively hides any problems. MRP will reduce stocks, highlight the problems, and take steps to solve them—either by changing the supplier or by making the supplier more reliable.

There are also disadvantages of using MRP. The most obvious of these is the amount of information needed before MRP can be used. The procedure starts with a detailed master schedule, so MRP cannot be used if:

- There is no master schedule
- The master schedule is inaccurate
- Plans are frequently changed
- Plans are not made far enough in advance

As stated, MRP also needs information about the bill of materials, current stocks, orders outstanding, supplier reliability, lead times, and other relevant information about suppliers. In practice, MRP needs so much information that many people describe it as an information system rather than a planning system.

Many organizations lack the detailed information needed for MRP. Even those organizations that seem to have the information required often find it is not detailed enough, or in the right format, or reliable enough. MRP needs completely accurate data. If there are any errors in the information used, the schedules for materials will be wrong and the master schedule cannot be achieved.

You can see from the examples above that even simple problems require a lot of data manipulation. This means that MRP can only be used when all related systems are computerized. MRP is not a new idea, but it has only become practical with inexpensive computing. The elements of a computerized MRP system are summarized in Figure 13.9.

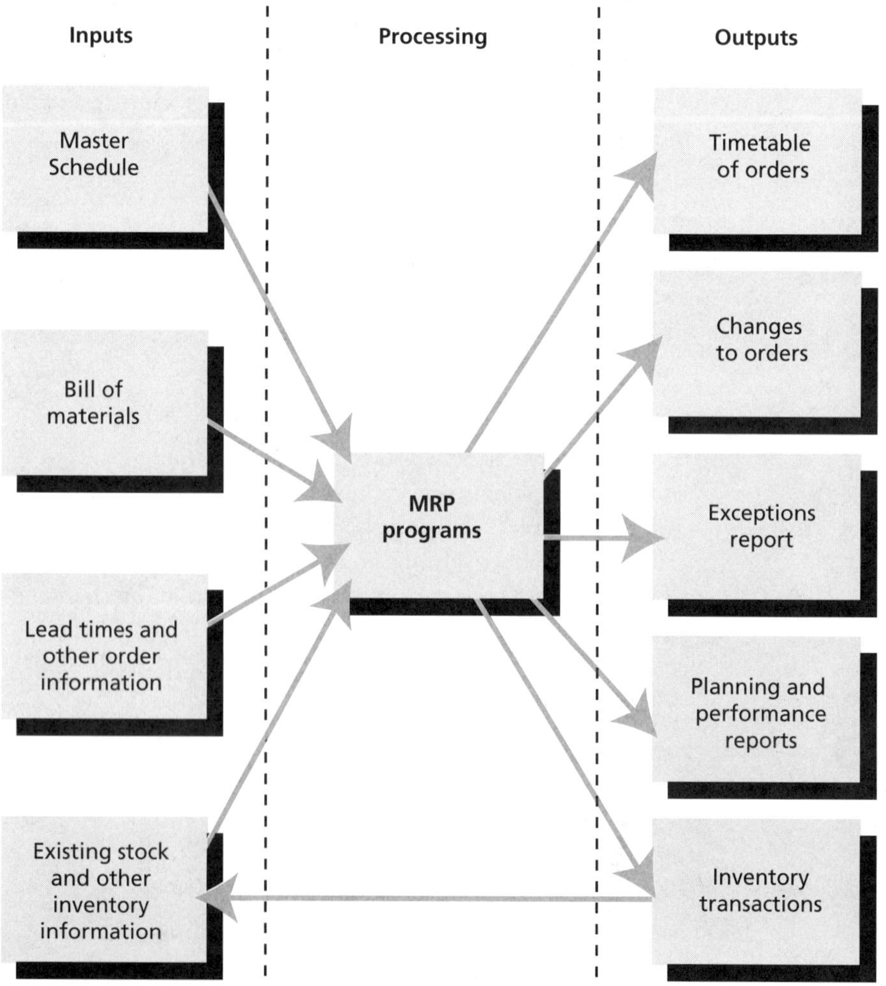

Figure 13.9 A Computerized MRP System

The outputs from a typical system, include:

- *Timetables*—of orders and other operations
- *Times of planned orders*—to implement the proposed timetable
- *Changes to previous plans*—whenever the master schedule is revised, or any other changes are made, the MRP schedules are updated. These can give changes to order quantities, cancelled or changed orders, and changes of due dates.
- *Exceptions*—the system may note exceptions that require management action, including late orders, too much scrap, requests for nonexistent parts, etc.
- *Performance reports*—which show how well the system is operating and might include measures for investment in stocks, inventory turnover, and number of stockouts.
- *Planning reports*—which can be used in longer-term planning decisions
- *Records of inventory transactions*—allow the system to maintain accurate records of current stock and to check progress

As you can see, one problem with MRP systems is that they can generate a huge amount of paper work.

The fact that MRP can only be used in certain situations, and even then requires a great deal of data manipulation, is its main disadvantage. But there are others. It might, for example, reduce an organization's flexibility to respond to changes. Stocks are expensive, but they allow plans to be changed at short notice. With MRP, the only materials available are those that are needed for the specified master schedule. Other disadvantages to MRP are that:

- MRP assumes lead times are constant and independent of the quantities ordered
- In practice, materials are made in a different order to that specified in the bill of materials
- If MRP is used to schedule the production of parts, this can result in poor schedules
- MRP may not recognize capacity and other constraints
- Management may recognize MRP as a way of scheduling materials but not its wider role as a planning tool
- It can be expensive and time-consuming to implement (typically 18–24 months)

Case Study

Alco Office Supplies

Alco Office Supplies make a range of desks, filing cabinets, and other office furniture. In 1979, the company introduced MRP for its standard filing cabinets. The manufacturing process was simple, and with the help of a consultant, a system was working in slightly less than a year, at a cost of $160,000. By the end of the second year, the system was judged a success and was extended to other products.

Alco's move to MRP illustrates the amount of information needed. Although the company had integrated computer systems, these had to be thoroughly checked and overhauled before they were reliable enough for MRP. The single biggest job was organizing data in a suitable form for MRP.

Alco's experience also shows the complexity of real MRP systems. Alco's standard four-drawer filing cabinet is assembled from 162 different parts. Many of these are small and duplicated, but exploding the master schedule requires a lot of calculations. Alco makes 24 variations on this basic filing cabinet.

On Alco's first trial run of the MRP system, the weekly report was over 5,000 pages long. Needless to say, when the system became operational this was trimmed, to 100 pages. The simplified printout is shown in Figure 13.10.

***** ALCO OFFICE SUPPLIES - MRP SYSTEM *****

TTILE : DEMONSTRATION
DATE : Sunday 09-03-1995
TIME : 10:36 PM

ANALYSIS REQUESTED - DEMONSTRATION

Product (488 available) - DR-45672 - Four Drawer Filing Cabinet
Product Options (24 available) - vertical, sizes, green, locks, fittings
Components (162 available) - all level 1, first 4 level 2
Weeks (104 available) - first 5
Continuity - no
Report Formats (34 available) - 1, 2, 3
Details (62 pages available) - Summary 2 pages
Options - off

Report 1 - Bill of Materials

```
Level 0   DR-45672
          |
Level 1   DR-46831    FN-53762    FN-62534    FN-26374    others
          |
Level 2   FN-63541    PR-3645     PR-7495     PR-1135
```

Report 2 - Inventory

NAME	# OF SUBCOMP	# PER PARENT	INVENTORY ON HAND	LEAD TIME	LOT SIZE
DR-45672	4	-	125	1	50
DR-46831	8	4	487	2	1250
FN-53762	16	4	257	2	1200
FN-62534	16	4	1253	2	2000
FN-26374	16	4	566	3	2000
FN-63541	8	4	124	4	1000
PR-3645	4	2	255	1	1500
PR-7495	4	2	458	1	1500
PR-1135	4	2	1087	1	2500

Report 3 - Master Production Schedule

PRODUCT NAME : DR-45672
NUMBER OF SUBCOMPONENTS ; 4
ON HAND INVENTORY ; 125
LEAD TIME (WEEKS) : 1

WEEK	REQUIRED QUANTITY
1	175
2	250
3	250
4	175
5	175

Item: DR-45672 Level : 0
Parent : NONE Lead Time : 1

Week	Gross Required	On hand Inventory	Net Required	Planned Receipts	Planned Releases
1	175	125	50	50	250
2	250	------	250	250	250
3	250	------	250	250	175
4	175	------	175	175	175
5	175	------	175	175	------

Item: DR-46831 Level : 1
Parent : 45672 Lead Time : 2

Week	Gross Required	On hand Inventory	Net Required	Planned Receipts	Planned Releases
1	1000	487	513	1250	-------
2	1000	737	263	1250	-------
3	700	987	------	-------	1250
4	700	287	413	1250	1250
5	-------	837	-------	-------	-------

Item: FN-53762 Level : 1
Parent : DR-45672 Lead Time : 2

Week	Gross Required	On hand Inventory	Net Required	Planned Receipts	Planned Releases
1	1000	257	743	1200	-------
2	1000	457	543	1200	-------
3	700	657	43	1200	1200
4	700	1157	------	-------	1200
5	-------	257	------	-------	1200

Figure 13.10
Example of a Simplified MRP Printout

In Summary

The main advantage of MRP is its ability to match demand for materials directly to the master schedule. This reduces stock levels and costs. The main disadvantages are the conditions that must be met before MRP can be used and the amount of data manipulation.

Review Questions

1. What are the main advantages of MRP?
2. What are the main problems with using MRP?
3. What are typical outputs from an MRP system?

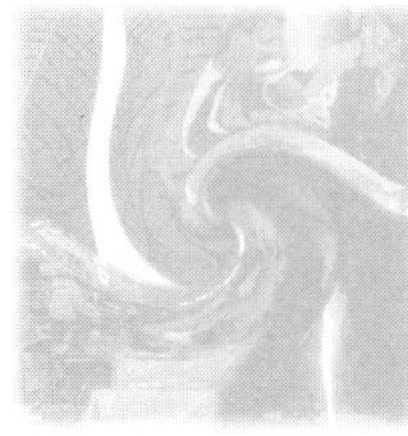

Lot Sizing with MRP

MRP provides a detailed schedule for ordering materials. But MRP may suggect a series of small orders that are placed every week or so. Such frequent orders are inconvenient and can have high administration and delivery costs. If several small orders are combined into fewer, larger batches, the costs may be reduced. This is called **lot sizing**. There are several ways of finding the best lot size, including the following:

- *Lot-for-lot method.* Here the organization would order exactly the net requirement for each period. This is a very simple method that minimizes inventory carrying costs but can result in large ordering or set-up costs.

- *Fixed-order quantity method.* Here the organization finds an order size that is convenient to use and always orders this same amount. This might, for example, be a truckload, a container load, or some other convenient quantity. The organization may calculate an economic order quantity (described in Chapter 17). This method ignores much of the planning of MRP, but it allows for other factors, such as price discounts on larger orders.

- *Period-order quantity.* This combines the net requirements of a few periods, so that the amount ordered is close to some convenient, fixed-order quantity. This tries to reduce both the ordering costs and carrying costs, and is often the most successful approach.

There are many other lot sizing methods. One method that generally gives good results looks for the best number of periods of demand that should be combined into a single order. If orders are placed more frequently than this, the administration and delivery charges rise; if orders are placed less frequently, stock levels rise, with higher costs. This means that there is a cost curve with a distinct minimum, as shown in Figure 13.11.

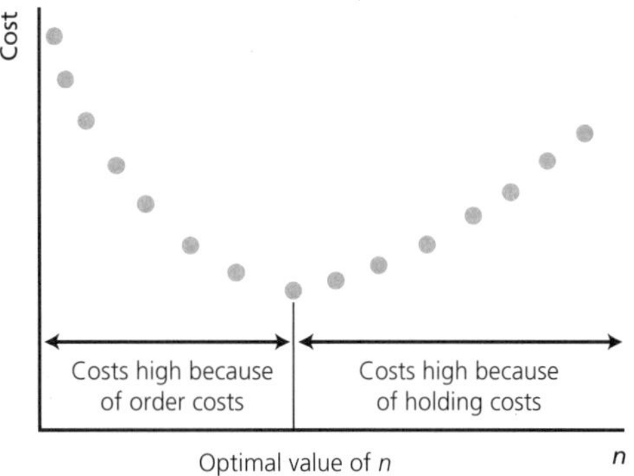

Figure 13.11 Variation of Costs with Number of Periods Combined into a Single Order

You can add all of the costs of placing and receiving an order into the single figure C_R, the re-order cost. We can add all of the costs of holding a unit of stock for a unit of time into the single figure C_H, the holding cost. Then, if we buy enough stock to cover all orders for the next n periods, we can use these to calculate a total cost. The aim is to find the value of n that minimizes this total cost.

One way to find the best value for n is to start with short stock cycles at the left-hand side of the graph in Figure 13.11. Then increasing n will follow the graph downward until costs start to rise, at which point the optimal cost is found. The formal procedure for this is as follows:

- First calculate the cost of buying for a single period and compare this with the cost of buying for two periods. If it is cheaper to buy for two periods than for one, we are moving down the left-hand side of the graph in Figure 13.11 and the cost is reducing as the value of n is increasing.
- Next compare the cost of buying for two periods with the cost of buying for three periods. If it is cheaper to buy for three periods, we are still on the declining part of the graph and have not yet reached the point of minimum cost.
- Continue this procedure, comparing the cost of buying for three periods with the cost of buying for four periods, and so on. In general, we will always compare the cost of buying for the next n periods with the cost of buying for the next n + 1 periods.
- The procedure is continued until at some point it becomes cheaper to buy for n periods than for n + 1 periods. At this point we have reached the bottom of the graph and found the lowest cost. Any further increases in n would raise costs as we climb up the right-hand side of the graph.

Fortunately, there is a shortcut to the arithmetic, which removes most of the work. We will not bother with the derivation of this, but the result is:

$$n(n + 1)\ D_{n+1} > 2C_R / C_H$$

where: C_R = cost of placing an order

C_H = cost of holding a unit in stock for a period

D_{n+1} = demand in the $n + 1^{th}$ period

If this inequality is *not true*, it is cheaper to order for n+1 periods than for n, so we are on the left-hand side of the graph of costs in Figure 13.11. If we increase n until the inequality becomes *true*, it is cheaper to order for n periods than n + 1, and we are on the right-hand side of the cost graph. This suggests a procedure where n is set to 1 and the inequality is checked. If it is not true, we increase n to 2 and the inequality is checked again. Then we keep on increasing n, until eventually the inequality will become true. This means that we are at the bottom of the cost curve and have found an optimal value for n. The process then stops. A flow diagram of this procedure is shown in Figure 13.12.

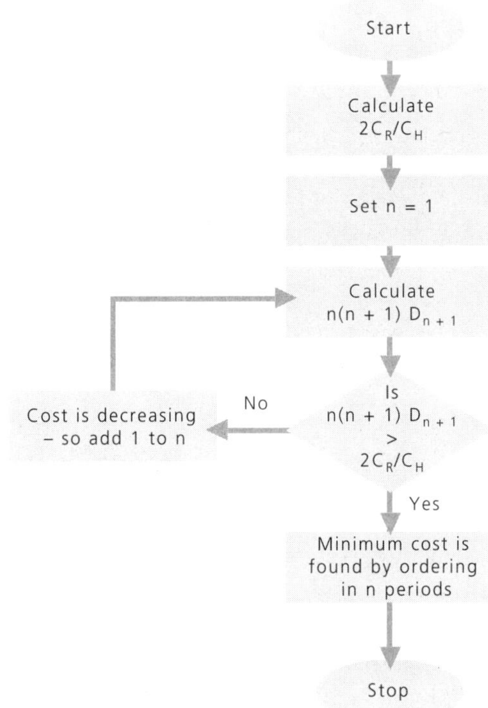

Figure 13.12 Procedure for Lot Sizing

Although it seems a little complicated, the procedure is quite straightforward and can be done easily using a spreadsheet.

Example

A procurement manager knows the total cost of placing an order is \$90, and the holding costs are \$4 per month. If an MRP analysis of demand for the item is given below, find an ordering policy that will give reasonable costs.

Month	1	2	3	4	5	6	7	8	9	10	11	12
Demand	1	3	5	8	8	5	2	1	1	5	7	9

Solution

Following the procedure shown in Figure 13.10, with $C_R = 90$ and $C_H = 4$:

$$2C_R / C_H = 2 \times 90/4 = 45$$

- Then, starting with n = 1, n + 1 = 2, and $D_2 = 3$ we calculate:

  $$n(n + 1)D_{n+1} = 1 \times 2 \times 3 = 6$$

  As this is less than 45, the inequality is not true and we have not reached the minimum.

- Next, taking n = 2, n + 1 = 3, and $D_3 = 5$, we calculate:

  $$n(n + 1)D_{n+1} = 2 \times 3 \times 5 = 30$$

  This is less than 45, so the inequality is still not true and we have not reached the minimum.

- Next, taking n = 3, n + 1 = 4, and $D_4 = 8$, we calculate:

  $$n(n + 1)D_{n+1} = 3 \times 4 \times 8 = 96$$

  This is more than 45, so the inequality is true and we have found the minimum cost with n = 3.

This means we would order enough at the beginning of month 1 to last for the first three months, i.e., we would place an order for 1 + 3 + 5 = 9 and arrange for this to arrive before the beginning of month 1.

It is easier to do these calculations in a table, as shown below:

Month, i	1	2	3	4
Demand, D_i	1	3	5	8
n	1	2	3	
$n(n + 1)D_{n+1}$	6	30	96	
Delivery	9			

We can now continue the analysis for subsequent months. Remember that every time a new calculation is started, the value of n returns to 1.

Month, i	1	2	3	4	5	6	7	8	9	10	11	12
Demand, D_i	1	3	5	8	8	5	2	1	1	5	7	9
n	1	2	3	1	2	3	4	5	6	1	2	1
$n(n + 1)D_{n+1}$	6	30	96	16	30	24	20	30	210	14	54	
Delivery	9			25						12		

This results in an ordering policy that ensures 9 units arrive by month 1, 25 by month 4, and 12 by month 10.

In Summary

MRP often suggests small, frequent orders. Costs can be reduced by combining several of these orders into larger batches. A lot-sizing rule can be used to find the order sizes that minimize costs.

Review Questions

1. Why might several small orders be combined into a single larger one?
2. What is a lot-sizing rule?
3. Why does the lot-sizing rule described not really give an optimal solution?

Case Study – Canadian Heritage Furniture

Canadian Heritage Furniture is a medium-size job shop that makes pine furniture to customers' specifications. Its main customers are small, independent furniture stores and large, specialty home-furnishing stores.

Lately the company has been having problems. It has missed a lot of delivery dates and has very high overtime costs. Its planning seems generally weak. Last month, for example, it scheduled overtime to make an order of tables, but found it could not finish the tables because there were no stocks of brackets. Even with $10 million in inventories, there were frequent stockouts.

Victor Samuel, Vice-president of Operations, sent the memo below to Joanne Ash, Manager, Production Planning and Inventory Control.

Question

- Prepare the report on MRP that Joanne Ash could submit to Victor Samuel.

Memorandum

To: Joanne Ash, Manager PP&IC

From: Victor Samuel, VP Operations

Our customer service level, measured as on-time shipments of customer orders, has been showing a steady downward trend. Our objective is 95 percent, but, for the last six months, we have been averaging 85 percent.

I have talked to the president about an MRP system to solve our production planning and stockout problems. He likes the idea but would like some more details.

Please prepare a brief report about MRP, explain what it is, what it will do for us, and how you would go about implementing it. I will take up your report in the next management committee.

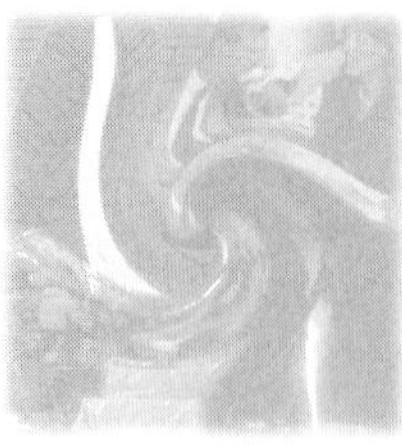

Extensions to MRP

Because of its dependence on computers and the need to link several systems, MRP has only really been used in organizations since the early 1970s. Since then, it has been widely adopted in the manufacturing industry. But services also need schedules for materials, labour, and other resources, so the first extensions of MRP used it in service organizations. It is more difficult to use MRP for services because of its need for detailed and accurate master schedules, but some organizations, such as hospitals, restaurants, and colleges, have successfully used it.

In a college, the finished product is graduating students. The master schedule shows the number of students who will be graduating from each program in each semester. The bill of materials is the courses the students must take in a semester, based on their program. Then MRP is used to find the materials needed—which are the number of teachers, classrooms, laboratories, etc.

A hospital can use MRP to schedule surgical procedures and to ensure that supplies and equipment are ready when needed. The master schedule states the planned surgical procedures in any period. The bill of materials contains information about the equipment and resources needed for each type of surgery. The inventory file will contain information about such things as surgical instruments, disposable materials, reusable instruments, sterilized materials, and so on.

A restaurant can use MRP to schedule its food and equipment. The master schedule states the meals the restaurant plans to prepare each mealtime. The recipes for each meal are in the bill of materials.

MRP is used sucessfully in many organizations. So it is not surprising that the basic system has been extended in several ways. Some of these extensions improved the procedures for dealing with variable supply, supplier reliability, wastage, defective quality, variable demand, and variable lead times. Several different lot-sizing rules were also developed.

Other extensions to MRP added feedback to help with larger planning decisions. Two important types of feedback are:

1. If the proposed master schedule needs more capacity for parts than is available, this is detected by the MRP system, which allows early rescheduling—so MRP is linked to capacity decisions

2. If operations are interrupted for some reason—such as equipment breakdowns—the master schedule can be revised quickly with inputs from the MRP system

Systems that include this type of feedback are called **closed-loop MRP**. They allow MRP results to be used more widely in planning decisions.

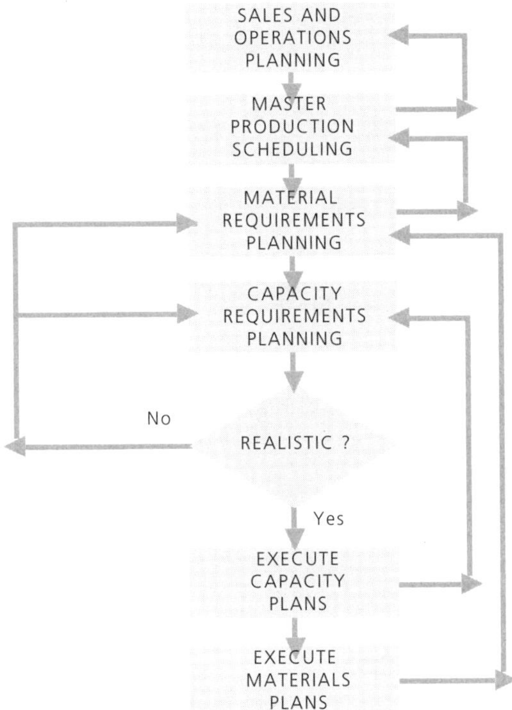

Figure 13.13 Closed-Loop Map Diagram

The next important extension is known as **manufacturing resources planning**, or **MRP II**. In the early 1980s, organizations realized that they could extend the MRP approach of exploding a master schedule to provide a timetable for materials; they could use the same procedures for scheduling other functions. Ordering and purchasing are included in MRP, but why not extend the analyses to dispatching, distribution, production processes, and even to marketing and finance? A master schedule can, for example, be used to determine the amount of machinery and equipment needed in each period. This in turn can set the number of operators needed, etc. The use of these resources can determine cash flows, business plans, and long-term capacity plans. Eventually, the master schedule can form the basis for planning most of the resources used in a process.

The original aim of MRP II was to create an integrated system, with all parts linked to a master schedule. But this complete integration was usually impractical. The systems became so complex, with so much data needed, that most organizations could not use a full MRP II system. But they could use parts of a system, often with different names, such as:

- *Distribution resources planning* schedules transport and other logistics functions

- *Capacity requirements planning* uses the master schedule to make sure there is enough capacity available to meet planned production
- *Resource requirements planning* is sometimes used as another name for MRP II, and sometimes used in a wider sense to include all planning decisions

All such systems rely heavily on computing, and the installation of working systems can be very complicated and expensive.

In Summary

Since MRP was introduced in the early 1970s, there have been continuous improvements and extensions. MRP II is the most important of these. This gives an integrated approach to planning based on the master schedule.

Review Questions

1. What is MRP II?
2. "Distribution resources planning needs a lot of computer processing." Do you think this is true? Explain.

Chapter Review

- The master schedule can be used to design short-term schedules for equipment and operators. Sometimes it can also be used for planning the supply of materials. This is the basis of material requirements planning (MRP).
- MRP is a dependent-demand inventory system, where stocks are matched directly to production plans.
- MRP "explodes" a master schedule using a bill of materials to create detailed materials requirements. Orders for materials and operations are then timetabled so that the master schedule can be achieved.
- MRP requires a great deal of information and computer processing before it can be used. It is therefore most widely used in manufacturing, but it is now being used more widely in services and other organizations.
- The main benefit of MRP is its ability to match the supply of materials to known demands. This reduces stock levels and costs.

Duties and Responsibilities of a Material Planner/Analyst

Name: Jim Giantsopoulos

Position: Material Planner/Analyst

Company: Invotronics Manufacturing

Reports to: Materials Manager

Jim is a 1992 graduate of a three-year Production and Operations Management (POM) program from Centennial College. His duties and responsibilities as a material planner/analyst are:

1. **Ensure availability of raw materials:** to ensure production has raw materials based on customer demand. The Material Planner is responsible for making sure that all the necessary steps have been completed to run the MRP program and generate the MRP reports. He is also responsible for planning the vendor release quantities, based on the Master Production Schedule (MPS), and releases the orders to the vendors via a PC.
2. **Expedite materials:** arrange for the materials to be shipped to Invotronics to meet production requirements, deal with vendors, freight companies, and customs to ensure timely arrival of material.
3. **Inventory control:** maintain an optimum level of raw materials using ABC classification of materials, and develop proper lot sizes.
4. **Ensure inventory accuracy on the system:** this requires reconciliation of over- and undershipments from vendors, coordination of receipts, and issuing of materials for "hot" items, verification of inventory accuracy by cycle counting, etc.
5. **Coordination of engineering changes:** work closely with engineering department, communicate any material specification and tooling changes to vendors, pull old tooling from vendors, etc.

What do I like about my job?

"I am glad I chose to pursue my career in the operations field. There is never a dull moment in my job as production is a very dynamic environment and customers' requirements change frequently. My job requires good planning, analytical, and coordination skills. It is challenging since I have to frequently update my plans based on customers' requirements, communicate these changes to suppliers and others, and make sure materials arrive on time.

The knowledge that I had gained during my POM studies such as how to do ABC analysis, managing inventories, MRP, computer, etc., is helping me a lot in doing my current job. That makes me confident that I can make a significant contribution to my company. I see a good career path for me in the production department at Invotronics and its parent company."

- The basic MRP approach suggests frequent, small orders. These would be difficult and expensive to administer. Costs can be reduced by combining several small orders into a single larger one. This is known as lot sizing.
- Several extensions to MRP have been designed, the most important of which is MRP II.

Key Terms

bill of materials *(p. 356)*
closed-loop MRP *(p. 374)*
dependent-demand inventory system *(p. 353)*
gross requirements *(p. 358)*
independent-demand inventory systems *(p. 353)*
inventory record file *(p. 355)*
lot sizing *(p. 369)*
manufacturing resources planning (MRP II) *(p. 375)*
material requirements planning *(p. 353)*
net requirements *(p. 358)*
time shifting *(p. 358)*

Problems

13.1 A company makes a final product A. Forty units of A are ordered for delivery in week 16 of a production cycle, 60 units in week 13, and 50 units in week 12. It takes 1 unit of component B and 2 units of component C to make each unit of A, and assembly takes two weeks. Components of B and C are bought from suppliers, and have lead times of three and two weeks respectively. Current stocks of A, B, and C are 5, 10, and 20 units respectively, and an order for 40 units of C is due to arrive in week 7. Design a production and order plan for the company.

13.2 Each unit of product AF43 is made from 12 units of BL19, 10 units of CX23, and 20 units of DY33. Each unit of BL19 is made from 2 units of EM08, 2 units of FF87, and 2 units of GO95. Each unit of both EM08 and DY33 is made from 6 units of HX22. A master schedule needs 60 units of AF43 to be ready by week 8 of a planning cycle and 50 units by week 10. There are minimum order sizes of 2,000 units for HX22, and 500 units of both FF87 and GO95. Information about stocks and lead times in weeks (either for assembly or orders) is as follows:

	Current Stocks	Minimum Stocks	Lead Time (weeks)
AF43	20	10	2
BL19	230	50	3
CX23	340	100	1
DY33	410	100	3
EM08	360	200	2
FF87	620	200	2
GO95	830	200	2
HX22	1,200	200	4

Design an order schedule for the materials.

13.3 It costs $0.125 to store a unit of an item for one month. The total cost of placing an order for the item, including delivery, is $100. MRP has found the following demands for the item.

Month	1	2	3	4	5	6	7	8	9	10	11	12	13
Demand	100	50	60	60	100	100	80	60	40	70	80	100	140

Find a good ordering policy for the item.

13.4 It costs $1 to hold one unit of an item in stock for one month, and each order costs a total of $60. There are currently no stocks of the item, but MRP has suggested the following demands. Find a good ordering policy for the item.

Month	1	2	3	4	5	6	7	8	9	10	11	12
Demand	40	39	60	81	238	722	998	1,096	921	161	0	40

Do you think this is the best ordering policy available?

Discussion Questions

13.1 When can MRP be used most effectively? What happens when it cannot be used?

13.2 Why do you think that MRP has only been widely used in the past few years? In what types of organization is it most widely used? Why?

13.3 How can MRP be used in services? Give some specific examples to support your views.

13.4 What extensions can be made to basic MRP systems?

13.5 What features would you expect to see in a commercial MRP computer package?

13.6 MRP is often placed at the end of the planning process. Is this the best place for it? Could it play a more active part in planning?

13.7 MRP is said to be difficult to implement and many failures have been reported. Why is this?

Chapter 14

JUST-IN-TIME

Performing operations just as they are needed

Contents

Introduction

The last chapter examined material requirements planning, which uses a master schedule to design a timetable for the materials needed to support production. But there is another view of materials management which states that if planning is done properly, there is no need for complicated MRP systems. This approach uses simple methods to make sure materials arrive just as they are needed. These are **just-in-time** (JIT) operations.

Just-in-time methods were developed in Japan, particularly by Toyota. These methods are difficult to introduce, but they can result in considerable cost reductions. But just-in-time has many benefits beyond cost savings. It introduces a different kind of thinking to an organization, and can result in improvements ranging from better relations with suppliers to more motivated employees. Not surprisingly, many organizations now use just-in-time principles.

Learning Objectives

After reading this chapter you should be able to answer questions such as:

- What are just-in-time operations?
- When can just-in-time systems be used?
- What are the key elements of just-in-time?
- How can an organization control just-in-time operations?
- How does just-in-time change an organization's relationships with suppliers and employees?
- What are the advantages and disadvantages of just-in-time?

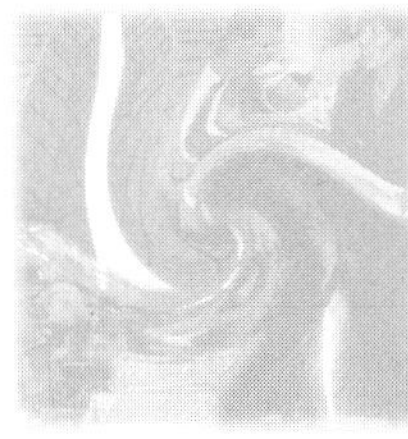

Principles of Just-in-Time

Definition

In essence, JIT is a system of production in which all operations occur just as they are needed. This means, for example, that materials needed for production are not purchased in advance and kept in stock but are delivered directly to the production process when they are needed. The result is that stocks of materials are virtually eliminated.

One reason so much attention has been given to JIT is the success of Japanese manufacturing. Since the 1950s, Japan has continuously increased its share of world trade; many Japanese manufacturers now dominate world markets. Organizations outside of Japan came to realize that if JIT had played even a small part in the success of Japanese companies, it could bring benefits to other organizations.

Many organizations around the world have improved their performance dramatically with JIT. The main problem with JIT is that, like MRP, it can only be used in certain circumstances. Even when it can be used, there may be practical difficulties, and the benefits only come after much effort.

JIT is not a new idea. In the 1920s, iron ore arriving at Ford plants in Detroit was turned into steel within a day, and into finished cars a few days later. This was a very efficient way of using resources and reducing inventories of work-in-process—but few organizations followed Ford's lead. Even today, many organizations feel they need large stocks of work-in-process. Organizations use these stocks to make sure operations continue smoothly when problems arise, such as equipment breakdown or materials arriving late.

This view, that inventories are essential to smooth operations, prompted managers to ask the question: How can we provide inventories at the lowest cost? But during the past few years, some organizations have changed their view, and have begun asking another question: How can stocks be eliminated? The answer to this has laid the foundations of just-in-time.

In Summary

Just-in-time operations were largely developed in Japan. They try to arrange operations so they occur just as they are needed. For example, by arranging for materials to arrive just as they are needed, managers can eliminate many inventories.

Effects of JIT Operations

We can start describing JIT by looking at its effect on inventories. The main purpose of stock is to allow for short-term mismatches between supply and demand. Independent-demand inventory systems (described in Chapter 17) allow for this mismatch by holding enough stock to cover expected demand. Sometimes, particularly with the lumpy demand of batch production, independent-demand systems give very high stock levels. MRP overcomes this problem by using the master schedule to match the supply of materials more closely to demand. The closer supply can be matched to demand, the smaller the stocks needed to cover any differences. It follows, then, that if the mismatch can be eliminated, so too can stocks. This is the basis of just-in-time systems (see Figure 14.1).

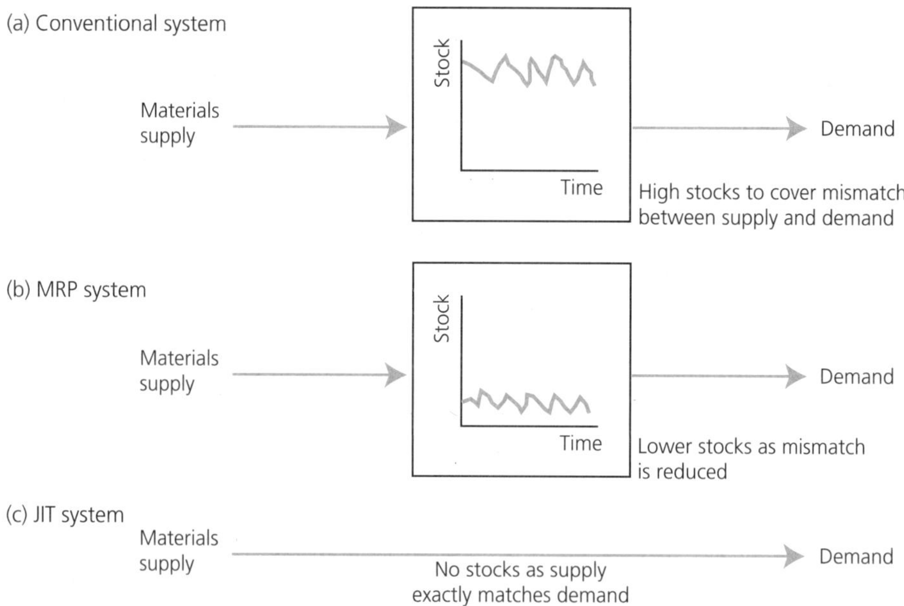

Figure 14.1 Stock Levels with Different Materials Planning Methods

The JIT process can be illustrated with the example of a lawnmower. If your lawnmower has a gas engine, there is a mismatch between fuel supply, which is bought from a gas station, and demand when the lawn is being mowed. This means that you need stocks of fuel in the mower's tank and the spare can. If your lawnmower has an electric motor, the supply of electricity is exactly matched to demand and you do not need any fuel stocks. The gasoline engine uses an independent-demand inventory system, while the electric motor uses a JIT system.

Just-in-time systems organize operations so that they occur just as they are needed.

Another example of JIT in practice is a car assembly line. Just as the chassis moves down the line to a work station, an engine arrives at the same point and is fitted. As the car body arrives at another work station, four doors also arrive and are added. All the way down the line, materials arrive just at the time they are needed, so the car is assembled in one smooth process.

JIT is a simple idea, and its main argument about inventories can be summarized as follows:

1. Inventories are held in an organization to cover short-term variation and uncertainty in supply and demand
2. JIT systems assume these stocks serve no useful purpose—they only exist because poor coordination does not match the supply of materials to demand
3. As long as stocks are held, organizations will continue to be poorly managed and many problems will be hidden
4. An organization should improve its management, find the reasons for differences between supply and demand, and then take corrective action

JIT, then, is more than an inventory control system; JIT requires a change in the way an organization views its operations. It has been described as "a way of eliminating waste," and as "a way of enforced problem solving." This change starts with a desire to eliminate all waste from an organization.

The JIT view is that any organization that needs inventories of work-in-progress has a series of problems that interrupt the smooth flow of materials. These problems include lengthy equipment set-up times, unbalanced operations, constrained capacity, machine breakdowns, defective materials, interrupted operations, unreliable suppliers, poor quality, too much paper work, and too many changes. Stock is only held to avoid the effects of these problems and effectively hide them from sight. A better approach would be to identify the hidden problems, and then solve them.

This approach leads to a number of changes in viewpoint.

- *Reliability.* When equipment in a process breaks down, production is usually transferred to another process or to another product. JIT does not allow this flexibility. It is based on continuous, uninterrupted production, so managers are forced to recognize problems with the reliability of equipment. The reason for the breakdown is found and actions taken to ensure that it does not break down in the future.
- *Quality.* Organizations have traditionally used acceptable levels of quality for their products, such as 2 defective units in 100. JIT holds that all defects have costs, so it is really cheaper to prevent these from ever happening than to correct them later. This clearly reinforces the principles of total quality management.

- *Suppliers.* It is often assumed that suppliers and customers are in some sort of conflict, where one can only benefit at the expense of the other. JIT systems rely totally on their suppliers, so this attitude will not work. Instead, it sees customers and suppliers as partners with a common objective.
- *Employees.* Sometimes there is friction between "managers" and "workers." JIT realizes that this distinction is meaningless. The welfare of all employees depends on the success of the organization, so all employees are treated with equal respect.

The overall aim of JIT is to minimize waste by identifying and solving any problems. This view of operations is known by different names, including "zero inventory," "stockless production," "Toyota system," "Japanese manufacturing," "world-class manufacturing," and "continuous flow manufacturing."

In Summary

Just-in-time systems aim for a smooth flow of product through operations, with materials arriving just as they are needed. To achieve this, an organization must change the way it looks at operations. In particular, the organization must eliminate all waste. This means that problems are identified and solved rather than hidden.

Simplicity in JIT Systems

A key element of JIT is its view that the effort put into administration is an overhead that is largely wasted. JIT tries to simplify operations so that they are controlled by manual systems with very little paper work, and most decisions are made on the shop floor. This is in marked contrast to MRP, which is computerized, expensive to administer, and involves decisions made by planners some distance from operations.

The aim of simplicity means that JIT's methods are all practical and based largely on common sense. Therefore, plant layouts are simplified; routine maintenance of equipment is scheduled to avoid breakdowns; everyone is trained in quality control to reduce the number of defects; simpler designs are used to reduce processing time; equipment set-ups are changed to reduce their time; re-order costs are reduced to allow smaller deliveries; and suppliers are encouraged to make more frequent deliveries. These changes have major effects on operations—so they cannot be introduced in one go. Instead, they evolve with small, continuous improvements over a long period of time. It is said that Toyota made continuous improvements in its operations for 25 years before it used JIT properly. Now that other organizations can use Toyota's experience, they can introduce JIT much faster.

Case Study

Just-in-Time Is More Than Cosmetic at Avon Canada

Avon Canada is a leading direct seller of beauty products such as cosmetics, toiletries, and jewellery. It has a production plant to the west of Montreal with 900 employees.

In an effort to maintain its market share and to meet the challenges of changing customer demands, Avon is now emphasizing product variety. This requires smaller batches and shorter production runs at Avon's plant. To deal with this, Avon is adopting just-in-time manufacturing. The company sees many benefits in JIT. There will be smaller batch sizes, less inventory, better service, and fast response to changing customer tastes. For instance, customers are less likely to get stale perfume that has been sitting on a shelf.

Avon has many examples of production-run reductions: Skin-So-Soft bath oil has changed from a production run of 60,000 units every 30 days to 10,000 units every 5 days; the run of 200,000 units of lipstick every 65 days has changed to 60,000 units every 20 days. With an inventory holding cost of 25 percent, the $1 million reduction of lipstick inventory will save the company $250,000 per year.

The conversion to JIT is supported and liked by Avon employees. It has made every worker multiskilled, and workers now work in teams rather than as individuals. Shortening the length of production runs from 2 days to 2–3 hours means that set-up changes must be fast, and the work is therefore more interesting.

Source: "Ding-Dong, Avon Calling," *The Globe and Mail*, August 18, 1992.

You can now see one reason that there is often misunderstanding about JIT: it is based on simple ideas, but these simple ideas are very difficult to implement. Getting materials to arrive just as they are needed is a simple idea—but it is very difficult to achieve. Avoiding disruptions by having perfect quality is a simple idea but it, too, is very difficult to achieve. Perhaps the key element to JIT is employee involvement and support; without it, JIT will not work.

In Summary

Just-in-time tries to simplify operations. It assumes that any complexity is a waste, and looks for manual control systems near to operations. Although it is a simple idea, JIT can be very difficult to implement.

Key Elements of JIT

JIT can only work in particular types of organization. While MRP is really only effective in batch manufacturing industries, JIT is even more specialized and really only works in large-scale assembly. At present, the most successful users of JIT are car assembly plants that make large numbers of identical products in a repetitive process.

The operations in an organization must have several characteristics before JIT can be considered.

- Every time production is changed from one item to another, there are delays, disruptions, and costs. JIT says that these changes waste resources and should be eliminated. This means that JIT needs a stable environment where production of an item remains at a fixed level for some time. Standard products are made with few variations.
- This stable environment allows costs to be reduced by using specialized automation. The fixed costs of this can be recovered with high production volumes. This means that JIT works best with high volume, mass-production operations.
- The specified production level must allow a smooth and continuous flow of products through the process. Each part of the process, and all resources, must be fully used. In other words, careful planning is required to ensure that the assembly line is balanced.
- Materials are delivered just as they are needed. Suppliers must be able to adapt to this kind of operation. It is not practical to bring individual units from suppliers, but the next best thing is very small batches.
- If small batches of materials are bought, re-order costs must be reduced as much as possible or the frequent deliveries will be too expensive. Unlike JIT,

Case Study

Japanese Motorcycles

In the 1960s, many countries had local manufacturers of motorcycles that met most of the domestic demand. These included Harley-Davidson in America, BSA in Britain, and BMW in Germany. But the industry changed dramatically, and many well-established companies went bankrupt. The problem was the sudden, new competition from the Japanese companies of Honda, Yamaha, Suzuki, and Kawasaki.

These four companies could supply motorcycles anywhere in the world of higher quality and lower cost than competitors' brands. In 1978, Harley-Davidson in America tried, but failed, to prove that the Japanese companies were dumping motorcycles on the market at less than the cost of manufacture. During these hearings, it was shown that the Japanese companies had operating costs 30 percent lower than Harley-Davidson's. One of the main reasons for this was their use of JIT manufacturing.

Harley-Davidson recognized that it could only compete by using the same methods, and adopted JIT in 1982. Despite initial problems, it stuck to its "materials as needed" program and is now once again successful in a very competitive market. In a five-year period, Harley-Davidson reduced machine set-up times by 75 percent, warranty and scrap costs by 60 percent, and work-in-process stocks by $22 million. At the same time productivity rose by 30 percent.

other inventory-control systems assume the re-order cost is fixed. One way to reduce such costs may be flexible manufacturing.

- Lead times and set-up times must be short or the delay in answering a request for materials is too long. Again, traditional inventory-control systems assume fixed lead times. JIT views long lead times as a problem that must be solved. This means working closely with suppliers, and often having them build facilities, perhaps focused factories, nearby.
- Because materials arrive just as they are needed, there is no stock to cover any defects that would disrupt production. Suppliers must, therefore, be totally reliable and provide materials that are free from defects.
- If something goes wrong and there is an interruption to the process, the workforce must be able to find out what went wrong. Then they must take any action needed to correct the fault, and make sure that it does not happen again. This requires a skilled and flexible workforce that is committed to the success of the organization.

Table 14.1 *Key Elements in JIT Operations*

- A stable environment
- Standard products with few variations
- Continuous production at fixed levels
- Automated, high-volume operations
- A balanced process that uses resources fully
- Reliable production equipment
- Minimum stocks
- Small batches of materials
- Short lead times for materials
- Low set-up and delivery costs
- Efficient materials handling
- Reliable suppliers
- Materials of consistently high quality
- Flexible workforce
- Fair treatment and rewards for employees
- Ability to solve any problems
- An efficient method of control

Although it is a simple idea, it is clear that JIT has a wide effect on an organization. Everything is changed, from the way that materials are ordered to the role of people working on the process. It is, therefore, a step that requires total commitment from the workforce at all levels.

Case Study

GM Decides to Buy Car Seat JIT

In 1985, GM awarded a contract to supply seats for its Ste-Thérèse assembly plant to Woodbridge Foam Corp. of Mississauga, Ontario. Woodbridge had six months to gear up its production from scratch, and it had to introduce just-in-time operations.

Woodbridge decided to build a plant in St-Jérome, Quebec, 20 miles from Ste-Thérèse. A task force of senior managers organized the move. Their objective was to build a plant that could make and ship seats for about 120,000 cars in a year.

Woodbridge successfully set up a state-of-the-art seat-manufacturing plant. Very small stocks of raw material and work-in-process are carried, while finished goods have been virtually eliminated. GM sends its demands for seats electronically to the Woodbridge plant, specifying the order in which they will be needed on the assembly line. The plant can start producing seats as soon as 10 minutes after receiving an order. The seats can be completed and sent out to the Ste-Thérèse plant, loaded on trucks to come off in the sequence specified by GM, in just over 3 hours.

Source: "Inventory: Taking Stock," *Canadian Business*, April 1991.

In Summary

Not every organization can use just-in-time operations. There are many conditions that must be met before JIT is possible. Even when these conditions are met, JIT needs commitment from all employees to make the fundamental changes needed.

Review Questions

1. How are the basic questions posed by JIT systems different from those posed by other inventory control systems?
2. What is the main characteristic of a JIT system?
3. How does JIT view stocks?
4. To what type of process is JIT best suited?

Achieving Just-in-Time Operations

Controlling Operations

Just-in-time systems try to eliminate all waste from an organization. Their aim is to meet production targets using the minimum amount of materials, with the minimum amount of equipment, and the smallest number of operators. They do this by making sure all operations are done at just the time they are needed.

One approach of ensuring that materials arrive as they are needed uses **Kanbans**. *Kanban* is Japanese for visible record, or card. Operations are controlled by having kanbans "pull" materials through a process.

In traditional operations, each work station is given a timetable of work that it must finish in a given time. Finished items are then "pushed" through the process to form a stock of work-in-process in front of the next work station. This ignores what the next station is actually doing—it might be working on something completely different or be waiting for a different item to arrive. At best, the second work station must finish its current job before it can start working on the new material just passed to it. The result is delays and increased stock of work-in-process.

JIT uses a "pull" approach, where a work station finishes its operations, and then requests materials from the preceding work station. In theory, the preceding work station only starts making the requested materials when it gets this request, so there are no stocks of work-in-process. In practice, there must be some lead time, so requests for materials are passed backward just before they are actually needed. Materials are delivered in small batches rather than continuous amounts. So JIT still has some stocks of work-in-process, but these are much lower than for "push" systems. It would be fairer to say that JIT minimizes stocks rather than eliminates them.

One obvious problem with JIT is that all operations must be perfectly balanced—the output from each work station must exactly match the needs of following stations. If there is any imbalance, productivity of some equipment will be low. In practice, this problem occurs in all operations and is not limited to JIT systems. But JIT would consider any imbalance to be a waste, and would find ways of eliminating it.

In Summary

Just-in-time systems need some means of control. Kanbans are a convenient way of giving a simple, manual control mechanism. These organize a "pull" of materials between work stations.

Kanban Systems

Kanban control systems use cards to coordinate the movement and production of materials. There are several ways of using Kanbans, with the simplest system as follows:

1. All material is stored and moved in standard containers. A container can only be moved when it has a Kanban attached to it.
2. When a work station needs more materials—i.e., when its stock of materials falls to a re-order level—a Kanban is put on an empty container and this is taken to the preceding work station. The Kanban is then attached to a full container, which is returned to the work station.
3. The empty container is a signal for the preceding work station to start work on this material, and it produces just enough to refill the container.

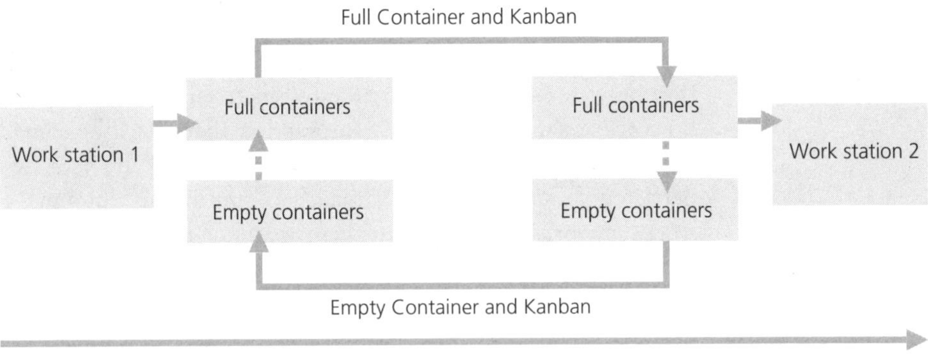

Figure 14.2 Simple Kanban System

You can see that the main features of this single Kanban system are as follows:

- A message is passed *backwards* to the preceding work station to start production, and it only makes enough to fill a container.
- Standard containers are used that hold a specific amount. This amount is usually quite small, and is typically 10 percent of a day's needs.
- The size of each container is the smallest reasonable batch that can be made, and there are usually only one or two full containers at any point.
- A specific number of containers and/or Kanbans is used.
- The stock of work-in-process is controlled by limiting the size of containers and the number of Kanbans.
- Materials can only be moved in containers, and containers can only be moved when they have a Kanban attached. This provides a rigid means of controlling the amount of materials produced and the time they are moved.
- This system makes sure stocks of work-in-process do not accumulate.

A more common Kanban system is slightly more complicated and uses two distinct types of cards: a production Kanban and a movement Kanban.

- When a work station needs more materials, a movement Kanban is put on an empty container. This gives permission for the operator to take the container to the area where stocks of work-in-process are kept.
- A full container is then found, which has a production Kanban attached.
- The production Kanban is removed and put on a post. This gives permission for the preceding work station to produce enough to replace the container of materials.
- A movement Kanban is put on the full container, giving permission to take it back to the work station.

This process is shown in Figure 14.3.

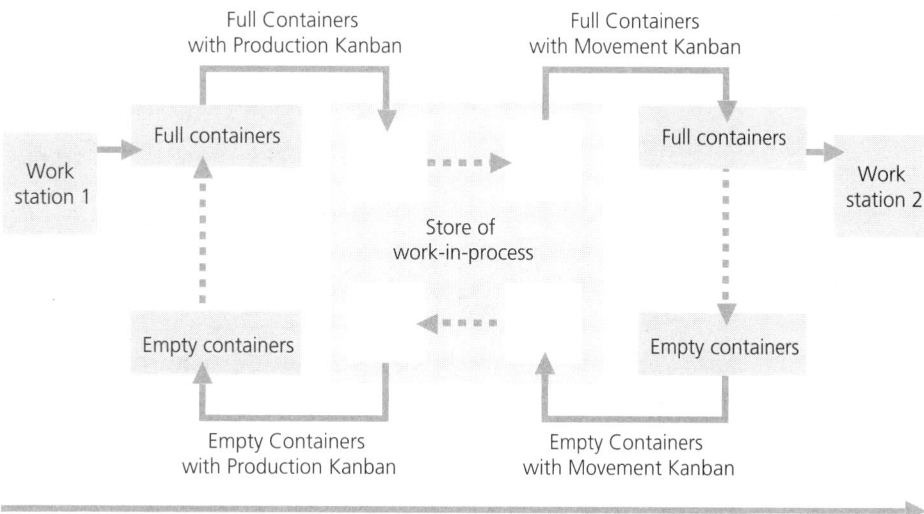

Figure 14.3 A Common Two-Card Kanban System

This system has a stock of work-in-process, but the stock is very small. When a full container is removed, it is usually the only container in stock—and the parts are not replaced until the previous work station makes them. The description of "moving" to the store of work-in-process is also misleading. JIT operations almost always use a product layout, such as an assembly line, so that movements of materials are minimized. Then the small stocks of work-in-process are kept as part of the line, and there is no actual movement.

As each container has a Kanban attached to it, the number of Kanbans sets the amount of work-in-process. Suppose, for example, that there is only one production Kanban. Then the stock of work-in-process is limited to one container of items. However, if there is a large number of Kanbans, stocks may be quite high. When a new JIT system is installed, an organization may keep some flexibility by having a fairly large number of Kanbans. But, the organization will look for continuous improvements, and will reduce the number of Kanbans. When the process is working properly, the number of Kanbans should be as small as possible.

There are many different Kanban systems. Some use varying Kanbans for emergency requests, such as high-priority needs, materials requested from suppliers, and signals for batch processes to start. Whatever the differences in detail, each system uses a signal between one stage in a process and the previous stage to show when it is time to start making a part.

Another control element appears when something goes wrong. JIT often uses a system called **Andon**. This has three signals, often coloured lights, above each work station:

- A green signal shows that the station is working as planned
- An amber signal shows the work station is falling a bit behind
- A red signal shows serious problems

This allows everyone to see where problems are growing, and to look for ways of solving them.

In Summary

Kanbans are cards that are used for controlling JIT systems. They give signals for something to happen. When a Kanban is put on a container, it gives a signal for movement or production. This allows a very simple, manual way of controlling operations.

Relationships with Suppliers

There is always potential for some friction between suppliers and customers. Many people think that one can only benefit at the expense of the other. Suppliers are often rigid in their conditions, and, as there is often little customer loyalty, they try to make as much profit as possible from each sale. Customers, on the other hand, shop around to make sure they get the best deal, and remind suppliers of the competition. They are concerned with their own objectives and will, when it is convenient for themselves, change specifications and conditions on short notice. The result is uncertainty among suppliers about items being ordered, the size of likely orders, the time orders will be placed, and the possibility of repeat orders.

JIT recognizes that customers and suppliers have the same objective—which is a mutually beneficial trading arrangement. The best approach, then, is for an organization to find a single supplier for each part or service who can meet their conditions—and develop a long-term relationship with that supplier. The trading conditions are quite demanding and include items of perfect quality, small frequent deliveries, short lead times, and reasonable costs. In return for meeting these conditions, organizations with JIT use **single sourcing**. This means that they buy each item exclusively from one supplier with whom they have a long-term contract. At one time when Toyota was using JIT, it had 250 suppliers, while General Motors, who had not yet introduced JIT, had 4,000.

JIT recognizes the importance of stability to a supplier. It knows that suppliers are geared to work with present operations and that any changes will cause disruptions. But each supplier has its own suppliers who are in turn affected by changes, and so on down the supply chain. A small change in the finished product may have many effects on earlier suppliers. JIT sees such changes as inefficient, so it makes a product that does not change during long production runs.

The stability of these long production runs are of benefit to suppliers. They can specialize in one type of item, and may reduce their product range and number of customers. Many suppliers to JIT operations build focused factories. As we saw in Chapter 4, a focused factory is a small plant which concentrates almost entirely on making one product, but aims to make this very well and very efficiently.

JIT aims for closer cooperation between a customer and its suppliers. This cooperation can help suppliers adapt to JIT, and even install JIT in their own operations. It also allows suppliers to make suggestions for improvements to customers, without the fear that their future profits will be reduced. Ideally, suppliers become a part of an extended JIT system.

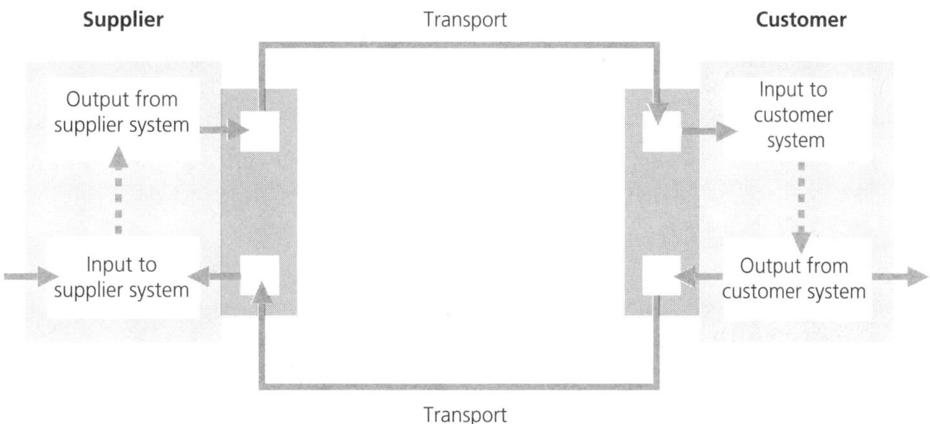

Figure 14.4 Integrating Supplier and Customer Kanban Systems

This means that whenever the customer needs some material, it sends a vehicle with containers and Kanbans to the supplier. The vehicle exchanges empty containers for full ones from the supplier's stock of finished goods. The Kanbans are then transferred to the full containers, which are delivered to the customer. The supplier now has empty containers, which are a signal that it is time to replace the contents.

In Summary

JIT recognizes that organizations and their suppliers want a mutually beneficial trading relationship. They should cooperate to achieve this. This contrasts with the traditional view, which often leads to conflicts between an organization and its suppliers.

Jidoka—Quality at Source

JIT can only work if materials are delivered with perfect quality. As materials are only delivered when they are needed, any defect will disrupt the process. There are two ways of avoiding this:

- The first is for the organization to accept that defects are possible and to check the quality of all items as they arrive. This is, however, wasteful, and it destroys many of the benefits JIT is aiming for.
- The second alternative is to make sure that all items arriving are of perfect quality. This is clearly better, as we saw when discussing total quality management in Chapter 5.

Even low defective rates are not good enough for JIT operations, so total quality management is essential.

In Summary

JIT needs supplies of materials with perfect quality. This means the total quality management must be used.

Respect for Employees

Japanese companies generally offer their employees a job for life. In return, employees are expected to stay with the same organization for their entire working lives. This is typical of Japanese organizations, which view employees as the most important part of their operations.

The respect for employees is particularly relevant to JIT, where it has a number of effects. There has traditionally been some friction between "managers" and "workers" in organizations. This is largely caused by their different aims. Managers are judged by the performance of the organization, and this performance is often measured by profit. However, often workers are not rewarded for performance, and their wages are seen as a drain on profits. JIT states that all employees are concerned with the success of the organization. They should, therefore, all be treated equally. One result of this is that all employees are rewarded for the organization's performance by having a share of profits.

Another aspect of JIT's respect for employees is its approach to improving a process. In many organizations, managers look for improvements while they work in isolation, away from the details of the process. Sometimes they employ consultants who do not know that much about the operations. JIT suggests that the best people to find improvements are those who actually work on the process. So JIT inevitably has suggestion boxes, with rewards for good ideas. A more formal approach for prompting suggestions is to use quality circles. As discussed in Chapter 6, a quality circle is an informal group who are involved in a particular operation. They meet once or twice a month to discuss ways of improving their operations.

JIT's use of automation can also be seen as a sign of respect for employees—although there is some disagreement about this. One view says that JIT uses automation because it is more reliable and cheaper for the high-volume processes used. Another view is that some jobs are so boring, repetitive, and unsatisfying that they should not be done by humans if there is any alternative. Robots and computer-controlled machines can do most of the tedious work in assembly lines, and this should be automated as a matter of principle.

In return for their respect, organizations using JIT demand more from their employees. When, for example, operators are given authority to stop a process, it means they must then solve the problem that led to the stoppage. As stated, quality at source gives everyone responsibility for the quality of their own work. So JIT passes some responsibility from managers to people working on the shop floor. Employees must also have the flexibility to do a variety of jobs, the willingness to adapt to new practices, relevant skills and knowledge, active participation in the running of the organization, and interest in its continuing success.

One problem with JIT that has only recently received attention is the increased stress it can put on the workforce. There is some evidence that employees who work on JIT assembly lines have higher levels of stress than those who work on traditional lines. More work is needed in this area, but even a suggestion of dissatisfaction in the workforce runs counter to JIT principles.

In Summary

Just-in-time operations assume that people are the most important resource in the organization. Everyone should work for the good of the organization, and be rewarded accordingly. This has many effects on the way an organization treats its employees.

Review Questions

1. What is the purpose of Kanbans?
2. How do Kanbans limit the amount of work-in-process?
3. Why might JIT systems be supplied from focused factories?
4. What is JIT's view of the relationship between an organization and its suppliers?

Implementing Continuous Improvement

Most managers realize that continuous improvement (CI) is a good idea for improving quality and reducing costs. But many say they lack the resources to implement CI. They ignore the most important resource that is readily available and obvious: the people who are involved in the operations. To implement CI, an organization does not need a team of experts. It can get good results from the local experts—the people who actually work on the process.

A good place to start continuous improvement is to train the operators to set-up their own equipment. This has many benefits:

- It expands operators' jobs and makes the jobs more interesting
- It gives operators new skills
- Operators can be trained to do simple tasks such as cleaning and lubricating the machines—they can then learn preventive maintenance, set-ups, and so on
- This frees technicians' time, so they can move to other work, perhaps looking for improvements to the process or designs
- Operators are made members of quality improvement teams

With these changes, management will quickly see quality improvement and cost reduction.

Source: "Continuous Improvement in Manufacturing," *Business Quarterly*, Spring 1994.

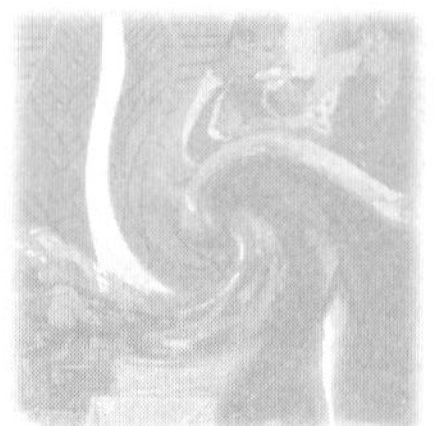

Advantages and Disadvantages of JIT

In the discussion of JIT as a means of controlling stocks, we saw that the major advantage was a dramatic reduction of stocks of raw materials and work-in-process. Organizations can typically reduce these stocks by more than 75 percent with JIT. This leads to a number of other advantages, such as reductions in space needed, lower warehousing costs, and less investment in stocks. Other benefits of JIT arise from the reorganization necessary to get a working system. Several of these are listed in Table 14.2.

Table 14.2 *Advantages of JIT*

- Reduced lead times
- Shorter time needed to make a product
- Increased productivity
- Increased equipment utilization
- Simplified planning and scheduling
- Reduced paper work
- Improved quality of materials and products
- Reduction in scrap and wastage
- Improved morale in the workforce
- Improved relations with suppliers
- Emphasis on problem solving in production

Some of these benefits increase costs. Making high-quality products with few interruptions caused by breakdowns means that better equipment must be used. Reduced set-up times usually need more sophisticated equipment. This equipment must respond quickly to changing demands, so there must be more capacity. The result is that JIT can only work if organizations buy better equipment with higher capacity. Many smaller organizations have found this costs too much, especially if the costs of training all employees are added. Although the long-term rewards may be high, the short-term costs of JIT can be prohibitive for many organizations.

There are, of course, some disadvantages to JIT. It can be expensive to implement and can involve many years of slow progress. Its inflexibility is another weakness. It is difficult to change product design, mix, or demand levels—so it does not work well with small production numbers or specially ordered material. There are also problems with seasonal variations in demand. There are four ways of overcoming these.

- Stocks of finished goods can be built up when demand is low and used when demand is high. This option does, of course, go against JIT principles.
- Production can be changed to match demand. Again, such changes go against JIT principles.
- Demand can be smoothed by pricing policies. In particular, discounts or other offers can be given during periods of low demands.
- The delivery time promised to customers can be adjusted. Customers can be asked to wait longer for deliveries when demand is high, with the backlog cleared when demand falls.

None of these options is entirely satisfactory, so JIT operations must be flexible enough to deal with some variation in demand.

Some of the benefits of JIT may also be seen as disadvantages. Having frequent set-ups and small batches, for example, is essential to JIT. But unless an organization is careful, this can create high re-order costs. Similarly, JIT requires decisions to be made on the shop floor. This responsibility given to lower levels in the workforce may be considered an advantage or a disadvantage, depending on your viewpoint. Some specific problems cited by JIT users are listed in Table 14.3.

Table 14.3 *Disadvantages of JIT*

- The initial investment and cost of implementation
- The time needed to get improvements in the system
- Reliance on perfect quality of materials from suppliers
- Problems with product quality
- Inability of suppliers to adapt to JIT methods
- The need for stable production
- Changing customer schedules
- Variable demand from customers
- Demand for a range of options with products
- The reduction in flexibility to change products
- Difficulty of reducing set-up times
- Lack of commitment within the organization
- Lack of cooperation and trust among employees
- Problems with linking JIT existing information systems
- Need to change the layout of facilities
- Increased stress in the workforce

Perhaps one disadvantage of JIT is its deceptive simplicity. This has led many organizations to try to use it without understanding its underlying principles. Some organizations have tried to apply only some principles of JIT to an existing process. In extreme cases, a note has been circulated simply stating that "The company is adopting JIT principles by eliminating stocks of work-in-process over the next two months—so please change your practices accordingly." You must remember that JIT is an approach that needs a complete change of attitudes and operations within an organization. It is likely to take several years of careful planning and controlled implementation to introduce it successfully.

In Summary

Just-in-time systems can give many advantages. Some of these come directly from the procedures used. Others come indirectly from the overall approach of eliminating waste. A successful system needs careful planning and implementation. JIT can also have disadvantages.

Comparisons with MRP Systems

There are some obvious similarities between JIT and MRP systems. They are, for example, both dependent-demand systems, where demand for materials is found directly from production schedules. But there are a number of contrasts, as shown in Table 14.4.

Table 14.4 *Differences Between JIT and MRP*

- JIT is a manual system—while MRP relies on computers
- JIT is purely a "pull" system—MRP allows a "push" system on the shop floor
- JIT emphasizes physical operations—MRP is largely an information system
- JIT allows the actual process to control work using Kanbans—MRP uses predetermined schedules
- JIT puts overall control of the process on the shop floor—MRP gives control to planners
- JIT works with a minimum amount of data—MRP tries to collect all possible data
- JIT reduces the amount of clerical effort—MRP increases it
- JIT needs a constant rate of production—MRP can work with varying production
- JIT makes a priority of reducing set-up costs—MRP considers these to be fixed
- JIT can be easily understood by everyone using it—MRP is more difficult to understand
- MRP uses batching rules to set batch sizes—JIT does not
- JIT typically carries hours stock of materials—MRP typically carries days stock

Review Questions

1. What are the three main advantages of JIT?
2. Would it be a good idea to introduce JIT to part of a process to see how it works?

Chapter Review

- Just-in-time systems aim at eliminating waste from an organization. They do this by organizing the operations to occur just as they are needed. This requires the organization to adopt a new way of thinking, which solves problems rather than hides them.
- JIT can only be used in certain types of organizations. In particular, it needs a stable environment, small batches, short lead times, and total quality.

- JIT matches the supply of materials to the demand, by "pulling" materials through the process, rather than "pushing" them.
- In practice, JIT needs a simple control system. This is supplied by Kanbans.
- An important part of JIT is its emphasis on good relations with suppliers and employees. It recognizes that cooperation is more productive than conflict, and any differences should be resolved.
- JIT systems can bring a lot of benefits to an organization, but there can also be disadvantages.

Key terms

Andon *(p. 395)*
just-in-time (JIT) *(pp. 382, 384)*
Kanban *(p. 392)*
single sourcing *(p. 396)*

Discussion Questions

14.1 Is JIT really just an extension of MRP?

14.2 Describe some applications of JIT to services.

14.3 What happens if an organization finds its suppliers cannot cope with JIT principles?

14.4 JIT reduces waste in an organization. What is meant by waste in this sense, and how can it occur?

14.5 Suppose a manufacturer only has enough demand to work for 7 hours in an 8-hour shift. Would it be more wasteful to leave all operations idle for an hour, or to make extra units and put them into stock?

14.6 What factors are important for the successful implementation of JIT?

14.7 JIT reduces the amount of paper work for operations. Does this have any consequences for accounting procedures? How can costs be found for operations?

14.8 To what extent is JIT dependent on high technology, such as focused factories, work cells, and flexible manufacturing systems?

Case Study

Self-directed Work Teams at Honeywell

Honeywell makes heating, cooling, and ventilation controls in Scarborough, Ontario. It sells these worldwide, and 80 percent of its production is exported.

Honeywell used to have an assembly line to make the products, with workers doing narrowly defined repetitive jobs. But in early 1990, management decided to break up the traditional assembly line and form smaller manufacturing cells. John MacMillan, director of manufacturing, does not like the term "cells" and prefers to use the more people-oriented term "self-directed work teams." Honeywell formed 35 such teams. Each team had 2–19 people, with the average size around 7. The team members were trained to do several jobs, and became responsible for their own quality.

Self-directed work teams do not need the traditional organization structure. The organization is much flatter—and supervisors became facilitators or coaches. The teams make many of their own decisions about work assignments, ordering materials, maintaining equipment, and training new staff. One aim of a team is to find ways of increasing productivity, improving quality, and reducing costs. To facilitate this, the teams can ask for help from any managers or support staff, such as engineers, designers, and material planners.

Implementing this new team approach in a diverse workforce was not without challenges. As John MacMillan stated, "You can naturally expect some problems." The trick is to educate and train workers, to discuss the issues, and to resolve any problems that arise.

The self-directed team approach has helped Honeywell to increase productivity by 40 percent, cut management staff by 30 percent, and reduce work-in-process inventory by 60 percent.

Sources: "Now Everyone Can Be a Boss," *Canadian Business*, May 1994; "People Programs Pay Dividends," *Plant*, Monday, May 2, 1994.

Career Profile – Manufaturing Director

Name: John M. MacMillan, CPIM, P.Eng.

Position: Director, Manufacturing,
Scarborough Operations

Company: Home & Building Control
Honeywell Limited, Scarborough, Ontario

John MacMillan is currently the Director of Manufacturing at Honeywell Ltd., where he is engaged in activities leading to manufacturing excellence, including total quality management, just-in-time, self-directed work teams, and the education process that supports manufacturing excellence.

John has been employed by Honeywell for the last 16 years and previously worked for Northern Telecom and Rolls Royce. He has managerial experience in several functional areas including production engineering, production and inventory, customer service, quality, and distribution.

John is a member of the Association of Professional Engineers of Ontario and is certified in production and inventory management, and integrated resource management.

Chapter 15

PROJECT MANAGEMENT

How to plan one-of-a-kind operations

Contents

Introduction

Chapter 4 described the different types of process as project, job shop, batch, mass production, and continuous flow. *Projects* are used for making one-of-a-kind products, and can range from preparing a meal to organizing the World Series. The planning needed for projects is so important, and so different from the planning of other processes, that it requires a different approach. This chapter describes the most common methods of project planning.

Learning Objectives

After reading this chapter you should be able to answer questions such as:

- Why is the planning of projects so important?
- What do project managers do?
- How can projects be drawn as networks of activities and events?
- How are the completion times found for a project?
- What are critical paths?
- What are PERT networks?
- Can the times of activities be changed?
- What are Gantt charts?
- How can one schedule activities to level the resource needs?

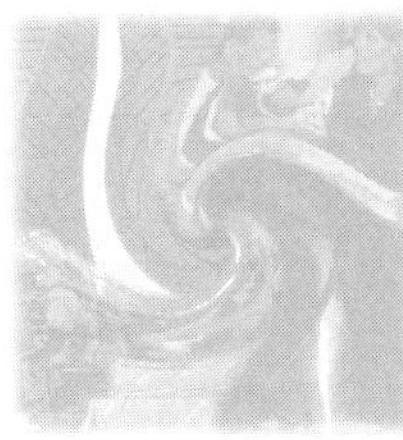

Projects and Their Management

Definitions

A **project** is a unique job that makes a one-of-a-kind product. It has a clear start and a clear finish, and all operations have to be coordinated within this fixed time frame. Projects often use considerable amounts of resources.

You can see from this definition that a project is any job that is done once to make a unique product. So each of us may do a number of small projects every day — such as doing the laundry, writing a report, painting a fence, or organizing a party. We can do these small projects without any formal planning, and a bit of thought is usually enough to make sure they run smoothly. But some projects are very large and involve a lot of money. Installing a new computer system, building a nuclear power station, organizing the Olympic Games, and building an oil refinery are examples of large projects which can cost millions of dollars. We would only expect such large projects to be successful if much planning had been done. This is the function of project management.

Project management deals with all aspects of planning, organizing, staffing, and controlling a project. The operations manager in this case is called a **project manager.**

In Summary

A project is a unique job that has a clear start and finish, and an aim of making a unique product. Projects are often large and need a lot of detailed planning.

Approach of Project Management

Any project has two phases:

1. *The planning phase* during which the project is defined, feasibility is tested, goals are set, detailed design work is done, resources are allocated, times are agreed on, management and work are organized, and so on
2. *The execution phase* during which materials are purchased and delivered, work is actually done, finished products are handed over to customers, initial operations are tested

These two phases can be illustrated in the construction of a house. In the planning phase, an architect draws plans, a site is found, a construction company is chosen, finances are arranged, etc. In the execution phase, the construction company prepares the site, lays the foundation, builds the walls, workers install windows and doors, electricians and plumbers add wiring and fixtures, etc. Projects bring together people with a range of knowledge and skills. Most of these people work on the project for a time, and then move on to other jobs.

Project mangers are central figures in these operations. They are responsible for making the project happen. This is a notoriously difficult job. Project managers have to work with different kinds of people, in situations where there is a lot of uncertainty, they must use many resources, and keep within tight budgets and time frames—and still provide a product that satisfies the customer. Project managers are often generalists rather than specialists, and they need wide experience in different operations. Their job is not necessarily to supervise and direct but to make sure conditions are right for other people to do their jobs effectively. This means that they must ensure that there are good relationships among the project team, the rest of the organization, the customers, and anyone else involved in the project. Generally, then, a project manager needs skills in four areas—getting jobs finished, administration, interpersonal relations, and leadership.

Thus, the choice of a project manager is a key factor in a project's success. The management of a large project is done by a team under the control of the project manager. Choosing the people for this team is often the most important part of a project.

When the team has been chosen, it usually has a **matrix organization**. With this, staff from different functions are brought together to form a team for a specific project. Each person remains within his or her functional area, but each has another responsibility to the project manager.

	Sales/ Marketing	Accounting/ Finance	Design	Planning	Procurement
Project 1 Manager	Sales/ marketing for project 1	Accounting/ finance for project 1	Design for project 1	Planning for project 1	Procurement for project 1
Project 2 Manager	Sales/ marketing for project 2	Accounting/ finance for project 2	Design for project 2	Planning for project 2	Procurement for project 2
Project 3 Manager	Sales/ marketing for project 3	Accounting/ finance for project 3	Design for project 3	Planning for project 3	Procurement for project 3

Figure 15.1 A Matrix Organization Structure

The aim of project management is to complete the project successfully—giving the customers the product they want, keeping within the specified time frame, and within the budget. A project can take many years to complete and use many resources, so timing is very important. The project completion date actually becomes part of the product. A construction company that builds a bridge within 18 months provides a better product than one that builds the same bridge at the same price in two years. Of course, decisions are not always this easy and the company that takes longer will usually offer a lower price. Then some compromise is needed between price and time considerations.

Project managers must always balance a number of factors, particularly cost, resources needed, and time available. If, for example, a project gets behind schedule, is it better to increase costs by using more resources? If a project gets ahead of schedule, is it better to finish it quickly and free up all the resources early, or slow down and transfer some resources to other projects? If some resources are not available when they are needed, should the manager pay more for alternatives, or should the project be allowed to fall behind schedule?

The key functions of the project management team are shown in Table 15.1.

Table 15.1 *Functions of the Project Management Team*

1. Identify all of the activities in the project, and the order in which these activities must be done
2. Estimate the length of each activity, the total length of the project, and the time at which each activity must be finished
3. Find if there is flexibility in the timing of activities, and determine which activities are most critical to the completion time
4. Estimate costs, and schedule activities so that the overall cost is minimized
5. Allocate resources and schedule these so that the project can be done as efficiently as possible
6. Keep a check on the progress of the project, react quickly to any deviations from plans, and adjust the schedules as necessary
7. Anticipate problems and take any actions needed to avoid them
8. Give regular reports on progress

The first five of these steps are concerned with the project schedule and are done in the planning phase. The last three are concerned with control of the project in the execution phase. The rest of this chapter describes some methods of planning projects.

An example of a construction project is the Skydome in Toronto. This huge sports and entertainment facility had the world's first retractable roof. The stadium was designed by Roderick Robbie and Michael Allen, it took three years to build, and it had an initial estimated cost of $240 million. It has 50,000 seats, and in 1993 hosted 256 events attracting over 6 million visitors, many for the home baseball team—the Toronto Blue Jays. You can imagine the difficulty of building this facility. It required the coordination of hundreds of activities, many contractors and subcontractors, and hundreds of workers. Without good project management, it would have been impossible to complete the project within a reasonable time and cost. Even with good project planning and control, the Skydome was over budget by $350 million.

By definition, each project is unique. Therefore, there may be little prior experience with such a project and no chance to use such things as a learning curve. There is also a lot of uncertainty in projects—inflation raises costs, difficult conditions are met, activities take longer than expected. As a result, major projects often overrun their schedule and budget. The Hibernia project of building an oil platform off the coast of Newfoundland had an initial budget of $1 billion, and finally cost over $5 billion. The Channel Tunnel between Britain and France (the Chunnel) had original cost estimates of $9 billion, but eventually cost well over $20 billion. Denver International Airport had original cost estimates of less than $2 billion, and finally cost more than $5 billion.

In Summary

Projects consist of planning and execution phases. The management team, headed by a project manager, is concerned with all aspects of scheduling and control of activities.

Review Questions

1. What is a project?
2. What is the purpose of project management?
3. What are the two main phases of a project?

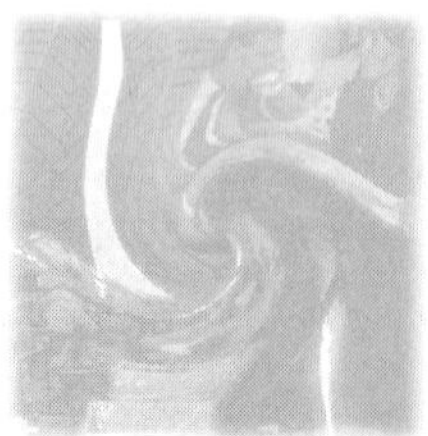

Project Networks

The management of a project begins with a **statement of work**. This is a description of the aims of the projects, the work to be done, the proposed start and finish dates, the budget, and a list of milestones to check progress.

The overall project can then be broken down into smaller parts. This is done in a **work breakdown structure**. This clearly defines different parts of the project to be finished by different times. After the work breakdown, the project is described as a series of **activities**. Project managers must determine the best time to do each of these activities. To help with this, they can use **project network analysis**.

Project network analysis was developed by two groups working independently in the late 1950s. The first group worked on the Polaris missile project for the United States Department of Defense. At that time, the U.S. government was concerned that its missile systems were being developed too slowly. The Polaris project involved over 3,000 contractors, and to help with control they developed a technique called **PERT—project evaluation and review technique**. This reduced the overall length of the project by two years.

The second group worked for Du Pont and developed **CPM—critical path method**—for planning maintenance programs in chemical plants. PERT and CPM were always very similar, and any minor differences in the original ideas have disappeared over time. The one remaining difference is that PERT stresses probabilistic durations of activities while CPM assumes fixed durations.

In Summary

An important stage in planning a project is to break down the whole project into a series of activities. Then network analysis, particularly PERT and CPM, can be used for planning.

Drawing Networks

Drawing a project network begins with a list of **activities** that make up the project. Then the project can be seen as a network of these activities. A project network consists of a series of circles, or nodes, connected by arrows. Each activity is represented by an arrow and each node shows the point when activities start and finish. The nodes are called **events,** and a network consists of alternating activities and events.

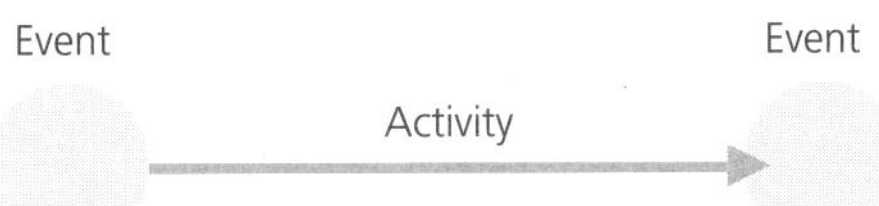

Figure 15.2 Activity and Events

Figure 15.3 shows part of a project network. This has two activities, A and B, and three events. Event 1 is the start of activity A, event 2 is the finish of activity A and the start of activity B, and event 3 is the finish of activity B.

Figure 15.3 Part of a Network

Example

A gardener is building a greenhouse from a kit. The instructions make it clear that this is a project with three parts:

- A, preparing the base (which will take 3 days)
- B, building the frame (which will take 2 days)
- C, fixing the glass (which will take 1 day)

Draw a network for the project.

Solution

The project has three activities which must be done in a fixed order; building the frame must be done after preparing the base and before fixing the glass. This order can be described by a **dependence table,** where each activity is listed along with those activities which immediately precede it, for example:

Activity	Duration (days)	Description	Immediate Predecessor
A	3	Prepare base	-
B	2	Build frame	A
C	1	Fix glass	B

Labelling the activities A, B, and C saves time as we can refer to activity B having activity A as its immediate predecessor—this is usually stated as "B depends on A." In this table, only *immediate* predecessors are given. That C depends on A as well as B need not be shown separately—it follows from the other dependencies. Activity A has no immediate predecessors and can be started whenever convenient.

Now we can draw a network from the dependence table, as shown in Figure 15.4.

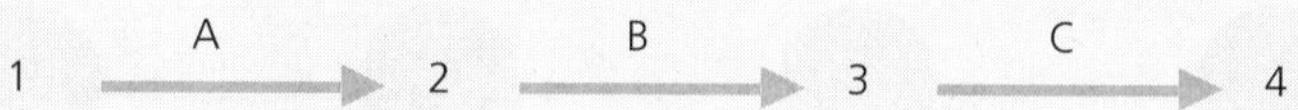

Figure 15.4 Network for Building a Greenhouse

The directions of the arrows in a project network show precedence. Each preceding activity must be finished before the following one is started—and following activities can start as soon as preceding ones are finished. In the greenhouse example, preparing the base must be done first, and as soon as this is finished the frame can be built. The glass can then be fixed as soon as the frame is built. After drawing the basic network for the project, we can look at its timing. For this, we normally assume a notional starting time of 0, and then calculate the start and finish times of each activity.

Example

Find the times for each activity in the greenhouse example. What happens if the base takes more than 3 days or the glass is delayed? What happens if the frame takes less than 2 days?

Solution

If we take a starting time of 0, we can finish preparing the base by the end of day 3. Then we can start building the frame. As this takes 2 days, we can finish by the end of day 5. Then, we can start fixing the glass. As this takes 1 day, we can finish by the end of day 6.

If the concrete of the base takes more than 3 days to set, or if the glass is not delivered by day 5, the project will be delayed. If building the frame takes less than 2 days, the project will be finished early.

We now have a timetable for the project showing when each activity starts and finishes, and can use this for scheduling resources. This quick illustration shows the major stages of project network analysis. We can summarize these as:

1. List the separate activities
2. Find the dependence and duration of each activity
3. Draw a network
4. Analyze the timing of the project
5. Schedule resources

In Summary

Project network analysis helps with the management of projects. It divides the project into a number of distinct activities and draws these on a network of alternating activities and events. After the network is drawn we can calculate the timing of activities and allocate resources.

Larger Networks

We can draw larger networks in exactly the same way as for the greenhouse example. Drawing networks from dependence tables is a matter of practice. A useful approach is to start drawing on the left-hand side of the network with those activities that do not depend on any others. Then activities that only depend on these first activities can be added, then those that only depend on the latest activities added, etc. The network is expanded systematically, working from left to right, until all activities are included, and the network is complete.

When drawing networks, you must remember two main rules and two minor rules.

Two main rules:

- Before an activity can begin, all preceding activities must be finished
- The arrows representing activities show precedence only, and neither the length nor orientation is important

Example

Allied Commercial is opening a new office. This is a project with the following activities and dependencies:

Activity	Description	Depends On
A	Find office location	-
B	Recruit new staff	-
C	Make office alterations	A
D	Order equipment needed	A
E	Install new equipment	D
F	Train staff	B
G	Start operations	C,E,F

Draw a network of this project.

Solution

Activities A and B have no predecessors and can start as soon as is convenient for the company. As soon as activity A is finished, both C and D can start; E can start as soon as D is finished; and F can start as soon as B is finished. G can only start when C, E, and F have all finished. The resulting network is shown in Figure 15.5.

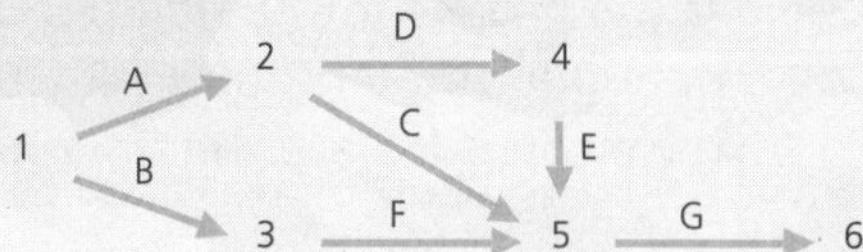

Figure 15.5 Network for Example

You can see from the network that this project can start with activities A and B, but this does not mean that these *must* start at the same time—only that they can start as soon as convenient and must be finished before any following activity can start. However, event 5 is the point where C, E, and F are finished, again this does not mean that these must finish at the same time—only that they must all be finished before G can start.

Two minor rules:

- A network has only one starting and finishing event
- Any two events can only be connected by one activity

The last of these rules is only for convenience, so we can talk about "the activity between events i and j" and know exactly which one we are talking about. Networks of any size can be drawn using these rules.

In Summary

Networks of almost any size can be drawn from a dependence table. The general approach is to draw the first activities, then systematically add all following ones.

Dummy Activities

When drawing networks, there are two situations where we must take care. The first is illustrated by the following dependence table.

Activity	Depends On
A	-
B	A
C	A
D	B,C

You might be tempted to draw this as shown in Figure 15.6a—but this breaks the rule that any two events can only be connected by one activity. The way around this is to use a **dummy activity**. This is not a part of the project, has zero duration, and uses no resources—it is simply there to give a proper network. In this case, the dummy ensures that only one activity goes between two events. This is known as a **uniqueness dummy**. In Fig 15.6b, the dummy activity is shown as the broken line, X.

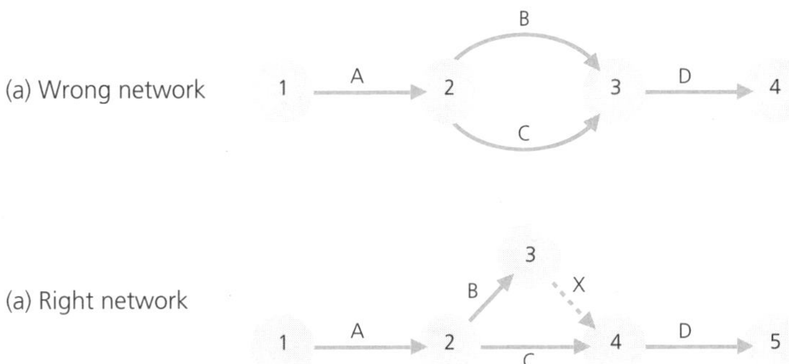

Figure 15.6 Uniqueness Dummy, X

A second situation that needs a dummy activity is shown in the part of the dependence table shown below.

Activity	Depends On
D	not given
E	not given
F	D,E
G	D

You might be tempted to draw this part of the network as shown in Figure 15.7a—but the dependence would clearly be wrong. Activity F is shown as depending on D and E, which is correct, but G is also shown as depending on D and E. The dependence table shows that G can start as soon as D is finished, but in the network it also has to wait for E to finish. The way around this is to separate the dependencies using a dummy activity, as shown in Figure 15.7b. The dependence of F on D is shown through the dummy activity X. In effect, the dummy cannot start until D has finished, and then F cannot start until the dummy and E are finished; as the dummy activity has zero duration this does not add any time to the project. This type of dummy is called a **logical dummy**.

(a) Wrong network

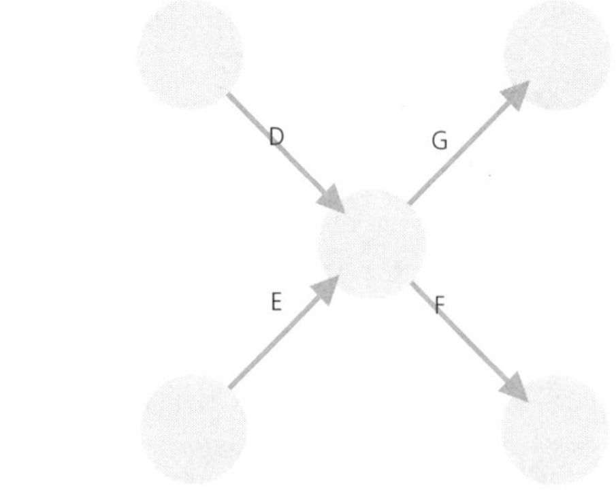

(b) Right network

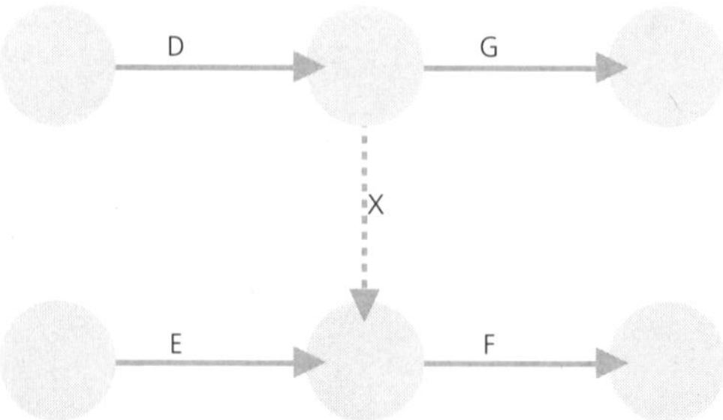

Figure 15.7 Logical Dummy, X

Example

A project is described by the following dependence table. Draw a network of the project.

Activity	Depends On	Activity	Depends On
A	J	I	J
B	C,G	J	-
C	A	K	B
D	F,K,N	L	I
E	J	M	I
F	B,H,L	N	M
G	A,E,I	O	M
H	G	P	O

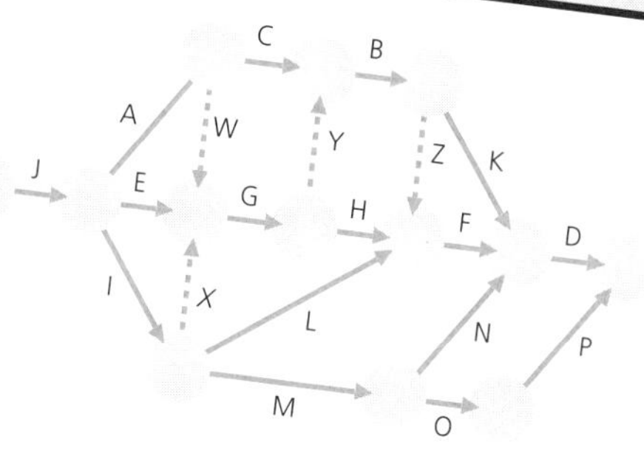

Figure 15.8 Network for Example

Solution

This may seem a complicated network, but the steps are fairly straightforward. Activity J is the only one that does not depend on anything else, so this starts the network. Then you can add activities A, E, and I, which only depend on J. Then you can add activities that depend on A, E, and I. Continuing this systematic addition of activities creates the network shown in Figure 15.8. As you can see, this includes four dummy activities.

You can see from this example that networks with many activities can take quite a long time to draw. In the initial example of building a greenhouse, the project was divided into three activities. It could have been divided into a lot more—such as finding the best location, clearing the ground, levelling and preparing the ground, digging foundations, mixing concrete, and laying a concrete base. This would result in a much more complicated network, and the importance of each activity would decrease. We have to strike a balance between using too few activities —so the network is of little use for planning—and using too many activities—so the network is too complicated.

If there are more than about 20 activities, it is best to use a computer package. If there are even more activities, the network will be very complicated, cover many pages, and will be difficult to follow. Then it is useful to start with a general, master network showing the major activities of the project. Each of these major activities can be expanded into a separate, more detailed network. For very large projects, each of the activities in the more detailed networks can be expanded into even more detailed networks. This approach is particularly useful when there are a number of contractors and subcontractors on a project. The owner of the project can draw a master network, each contractor can have a network covering their own work, and any major subcontractors can have separate networks of their parts of the work. At each stage, the networks cover less of the overall project but show more detail.

Example

The managers of Loch Moraigh whisky distillery examined their inventory control system to see how stock levels could be set to meet forecast demand. They concluded that an expanded computer system was needed to extrapolate past demand patterns and, based on these, set appropriate stock levels. These stock levels are then passed to a production control module that varies the quantities bottled.

The first part of this proposed system was called DFS (Demand Forecasting System), while the second part was ICS (Inventory Control System). The introduction of these systems took about 18 months, including linking to the production control module which was already working. The introduction of DFS and ICS was a self-contained project with the following activities.

Activity	Description
A	Examine existing system and environment of ICS
B	Collect costs and other data relevant to ICS
C	Construct and test models for ICS
D	Write and test computer programs for ICS models
E	Design and print data input forms for ICS data
F	Document ICS programs and monitoring procedures
G	Examine sources of demand data and its collection
H	Construct and test models for DFS
I	Organize past demand data
J	Write and test computer programs for DFS models
K	Design and print data input forms for DFS data
L	Document DFS programs and monitoring procedures
M	Train staff in the use of DFS and ICS
N	Initialize data for ICS programs (ICS staff)
P	Initialize data for DFS programs (DFS staff)
Q	Create base files for DFS
R	Run system for trial period
S	Implement final system

A computer program was used, with the results shown in Figure 15.9

PROBLEM: DISTILLERY　　Date: 09-09-1996

ORIGINAL NETWORK DATA

No.	Letter Code	Name	Expected Completion Time	Letter Code for Immediately Preceding Activities 1	2	3	4	5	6	7
1	A	Examine system	2.00							
2	B	Collect ICS data	1.00	A						
3	C	Test ICS models	2.00	A						
4	D	Program ICS	4.00	C						
5	E	Design ICS forms	1.00	C						
6	F	Document ICS	2.00	D	E					
7	G	Examine demand	2.00							
8	H	Test DES models	4.00	A	G					
9	I	Organize data	2.00	G						
10	J	Program DFS	6.00	H	K					
11	K	Design DFS forms	2.00	A	G					
12	L	Document DFS	3.00	J						
13	M	Train staff	2.00	F	L					
14	N	Initialize ICS	1.00	B	M					
15	P	Initialize DFS	1.00	I	M					
16	Q	Create DFS files	1.00	P						
17	R	Trial period	4.00	N	Q					
18	S	Implement	2.00	R						
19	D*1	Dummy--1	0.00							
20	D*2	Dummy--2	0.00							
21	D*3	Dummy--3	0.00							
22	D*4	Dummy--4	0.00							
23	D*5	Dummy--5	0.00							
24	D*6	Dummy--6	0.00							

ACTIVITY REPORT

Activity No.	Code	Name	Event Beg.	End..	Planning Times Exp.t	ES	LS	EF	LF	Slack
1	A	Examine system	1	2	2.00	0.0	0.0	2.0	2.0	0.0
2	B	Collect ICS data	2	12	1.00	2.0	17.0	3.0	18.0	15.0
3	C	Test ICS models	2	4	2.00	2.0	7.0	4.0	9.0	5.0
4	D	Program ICS	4	5	4.00	4.0	9.0	8.0	13.0	5.0
5	E	Design ICS forms	4	5	1.00	4.0	12.0	5.0	13.0	8.0
6	F	Document ICS	5	10	2.00	8.0	13.0	10.0	15.0	5.0
7	G	Examine demand	1	3	2.00	0.0	0.0	2.0	2.0	0.0
8	H	Test DES models	6	8	4.00	2.0	2.0	6.0	6.0	0.0
9	I	Organize data	3	13	2.00	2.0	15.0	4.0	17.0	13.0
10	J	Program DFS	8	9	6.00	6.0	6.0	12.0	12.0	0.0
11	K	Design DFS forms	7	8	2.00	2.0	4.0	4.0	6.0	2.0
12	L	Document DFS	9	10	3.00	12.0	12.0	15.0	15.0	0.0
13	M	Train staff	10	11	2.00	15.0	15.0	17.0	17.0	0.0
14	N	Initialize ICS	12	15	1.00	17.0	18.0	18.0	19.0	1.0
15	P	Initialize DFS	13	14	1.00	17.0	17.0	18.0	18.0	0.0
16	Q	Create DFS files	14	15	1.00	18.0	18.0	19.0	19.0	0.0
17	R	Trial period	15	16	4.00	19.0	19.0	23.0	23.0	0.0
18	S	Implement	16	17	2.00	23.0	23.0	25.0	25.0	0.0
19	D*1	Dummy--1	3	6	0.00	2.0	2.0	2.0	2.0	0.0
20	D*2	Dummy--2	2	6	0.00	2.0	2.0	2.0	2.0	0.0
21	D*3	Dummy--3	2	7	0.00	2.0	4.0	2.0	4.0	2.0
22	D*4	Dummy--4	3	7	0.00	2.0	4.0	2.0	4.0	2.0
23	D*5	Dummy--5	11	13	0.00	17.0	17.0	17.0	17.0	0.0
24	D*6	Dummy--6	11	12	0.00	17.0	18.0	17.0	18.0	1.0

Expected Project Duration : 25

The following path(s) are critical.

A D*2 H J L M D*5 P Q R S
G D*1 H J L M D*5 P Q R S

NETWORK EVENT MILESTONE REPORT

No.	Event Connections: Predecessors	Successors	Times: TE	TL	Slack	Activity Connections: Ending	Starting
1	none	2 3 --	0.0	0.0	0.0	none	A G
2	1 -- --	12 4 6	2.0	2.0	0.0	A ----	B C
		7 -- --					D*2 D*3
3	1 -- --	13 6 7	2.0	2.0	0.0	G ----	I D*1
							D*4 ----
4	2 -- --	5 5 --	4.0	9.0	5.0	C ----	D e
5	4 4 --	10 -- --	8.0	13.0	5.0	D E	F ----
6	3 2 --	8 -- --	2.0	2.0	0.0	D*1 D*2	H ----
7	2 3 --	8 -- --	2.0	4.0	2.0	D*3 D*4	K ----
8	6 7 --	9 -- --	6.0	6.0	0.0	H K	J ----
9	8 -- --	10 -- --	12.0	12.0	0.0	J ----	L ----
10	5 9 --	11 -- --	15.0	15.0	0.0	F L	M ----
11	10 -- --	13 12 --	17.0	17.0	0.0	M ----	D*5 D*6
12	2 11 --	15 -- --	17.0	18.0	1.0	B D*6	N ----
13	3 11 --	14 -- --	17.0	17.0	0.0	I D*5	P ----
14	13 -- --	15 -- --	18.0	18.0	0.0	P ----	Q ----
15	12 14 --	16 -- --	19.0	19.0	0.0	N Q	R ----
16	15 -- --	17 -- --	23.0	23.0	0.0	R ----	S ----
17	16 -- --	none --	25.0	25.0	0.0	S ----	none

Expected Project Duration : 25

The following path(s) are critical.

1 2 6 8 9 10 11 13 14 15 16 17
1 3 6 8 9 10 11 13 14 15 16 17

Figure 15.9 Printout for Distillery Example

Review Questions

1. What information is needed to draw a project network?
2. What are the main rules of drawing a project network?
3. When are dummy activities used?

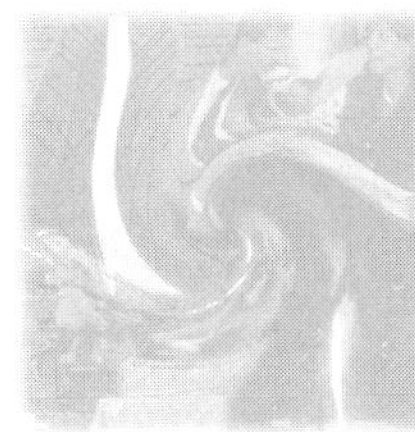

Timing of Projects

As stated, the only real difference between the Critical path method (CPM) and the project evaluation and review technique (PERT) is in the timing of activities. In particular, CPM assumes that each activity has a fixed duration which is known exactly, while PERT assumes the duration is less certain and may vary. The basic analyses are identical for each of these methods, so the discussion here will illustrate them by CPM and then move on to PERT.

Event Analysis

When looking at the timing of events, an organization wants to find the earliest and latest times these can occur. It is easiest to show the calculations for this in an example. Suppose a project has the following dependence table, where a duration (in weeks) has been added.

Activity	Duration	Depends On
A	3	-
B	2	-
C	2	A
D	4	A
E	1	C
F	3	D
G	3	B
H	4	G
I	5	E,F

The network for this project is shown in Figure 15.10, where durations have been added under the activities.

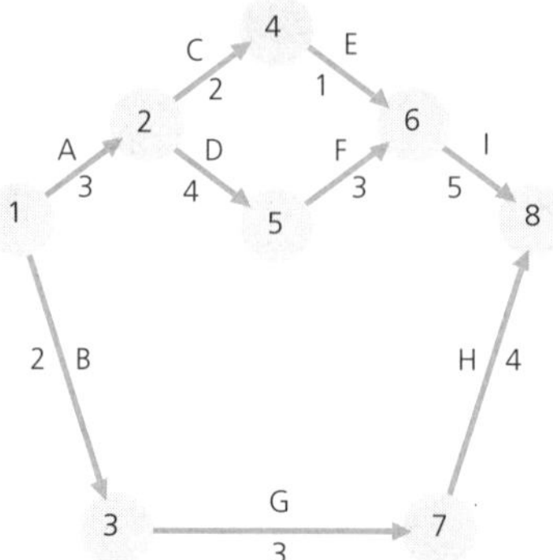

Figure 15.10 Network for Example

The analysis of times starts by finding the earliest possible time for each event, assuming a notional start time of 0 for the project as a whole. The earliest time for event 1 is clearly 0. The earliest time for event 2 is when A finishes, which is 3 weeks after its earliest start at 0; the earliest time for event 4 is the time when C finishes, which is 2 weeks after its earliest start at 3 (i.e., week 5). Similarly, the earliest time for event 5 is 4 + 3 = 7, for event 3 is 2, and for event 7 is 2 + 3 = 5.

When several activities must finish before a given event, the earliest time for the event is the earliest time by which *all* preceding activities can be finished. The earliest time for event 6 is when both E and F are finished. E can finish 1 week after its earliest start at 5 (i.e., week 6); F can finish 3 weeks after its earliest start at 7 (i.e., week 10). Then the earliest time at which both of these can be finished is week 10. Similarly, event 8 must wait until both activities H and I are finished. Activity H can be finished by week 5 + 4 = 9, while activity I can be finished by week 10 + 5 = 15. The earliest time for event 8 is the later of these, which is week 15. This gives the overall duration of the project as 15 weeks. Figure 15.11 shows the earliest times for each event added to the network.

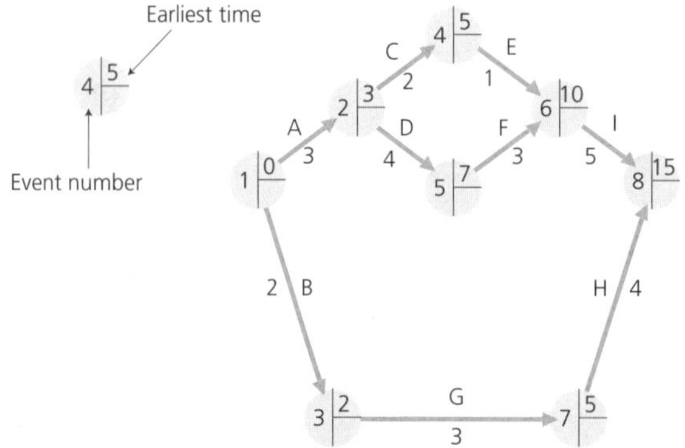

Figure 15.11 Network with Earliest Event Times

Now that we have gone through the network and found the earliest time for each event, we can do a similar analysis to find the latest time for each. Then we can use these times to find the events which need strict control and those which have some slack.

The procedure for finding the latest times is almost the reverse of the procedure for finding the earliest times. Starting at the end of the project with event 8, this has a latest time for completion of week 15. To allow activity I to be finished by week 15, it must be started 5 weeks before this, so the latest time for event 6 is week 15 - 5 = 10. The latest H can finish is week 15, so the latest time it can start is 4 weeks before this, and the latest time for event 7 is week 15 - 4 = 11. Similarly, the latest time for event 3 is 11 - 3 = 8, for event 5 is 10 - 3 = 7, and for event 4 is 10 - 1 = 9.

For events that have more than one following activity, the latest time must allow all following activities to be completed on time. Event 2 is followed by activities C and D; C must be finished by week 9, so it must be started 2 weeks before this (i.e., week 7); while D must be finished by week 7, so it must be started 4 weeks before this (i.e., week 3). The latest time for event 2 which allows both C and D to start on time is the earlier of these, which is week 3.

Similarly, the latest time for event 1 must allow both A and B to finish on time. The latest start time for B is 8 - 2 = 6, and the latest start time for A is 3 - 3=0. The latest time for event 1 must allow both of these to start on time and this means a latest time of 0. Figure 15.12 shows the network with latest times added for each event.

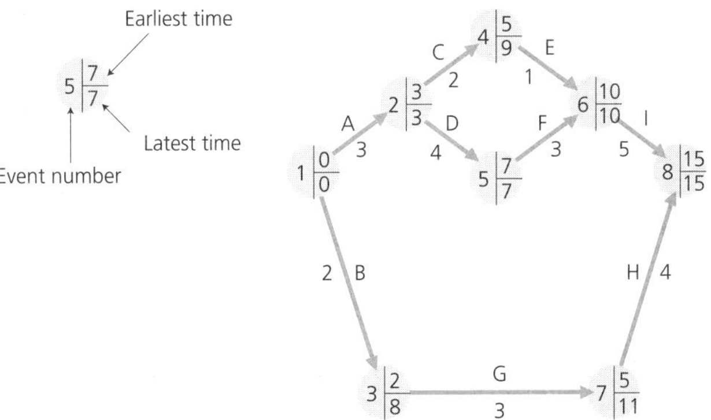

Figure 15.12 Network with Earliest and Latest Event Times

In Summary

Finding the earliest and latest time for each event is an important part of project planning. These can be found by a simple procedure, working through the network to find earliest times, and then backwards to find latest times.

Activity Analysis

The analysis of project times can be extended to activities by finding the earliest and latest start times (and corresponding earliest and latest finish times) for activities.

The earliest start time for an activity is the earliest time of the preceding event. The earliest finish time is the earliest start time plus the duration. Looking at one specific activity in Figure 15.12, say G, the earliest start time is week 2 and the earliest finish time is, therefore, week 2 + 3 = 5.

Figure 15.13 Finding Activity Times

The latest start and finish time for an activity can be found using similar reasoning, but working backwards. The latest finish time for each activity is the latest time of the following event; the latest start time is the latest finish time minus the duration. For activity G, the latest finish is week 11 and the latest start is week 11-3 = 8. Repeating these calculations for all activities in the project gives the following results.

Activity	Duration	Earliest Start	Earliest Finish	Latest Start	Latest Finish
A	3	0	3	0	3
B	2	0	2	6	8
C	2	3	5	7	9
D	4	3	7	3	7
E	1	5	6	9	10
F	3	7	10	7	10
G	3	2	5	8	11
H	4	5	9	11	15
I	5	10	15	10	15

You can see from this table that some activities have flexibility in timing; activity G, as we have seen, can start as early as day 2 or as late as day 8, while activity C can start as early as day 3 or as late as day 7. However, there are other activities that have no flexibility; activities A, D, F, and I cannot move as their latest start time is the same as their earliest start time. Those activities, like A, D, F, and I, that have to be done at a fixed time are called the *critical activities.*

Activities that must be done at a fixed time are called the **critical activities.** They form a continuous path through the network, called the **critical path.**

The length of the critical path sets the overall project duration. If one of the critical activities is extended by a certain amount, the overall project duration is extended by this amount; if one of the critical activities is delayed by some time, the overall project duration is again extended by the time of the delay. However, if one of the critical activities is made shorter, the overall project duration may be reduced by this amount.

The activities which have some flexibility in timing are the **noncritical activities**. These can be delayed or extended without necessarily affecting the overall project duration. But there is a limit to the expansion, and this is measured by the float. The **total float** is the difference between the maximum amount of time available for an activity and the time actually used.

Total float = latest finish time - earliest start time - duration

Total float is always zero for critical activities and has some positive value for noncritical activities. It shows the maximum amount the duration of an activity can increase without affecting the completion date of the project.

The total float for activity G in the previous example has:

- Earliest start = earliest time of preceding event = 2
- Latest finish = latest time of following event = 11
- Duration = 3
- Total float = latest finish time - earliest start time - duration = 11 - 2 - 3 = 6

Repeating this calculation for other activities in the example gives the following results.

Activity	Duration	Earliest Times		Latest Times		Total
		Start	Finish	Start	Finish	Float
A	3	0	3	0	3	0
B	2	0	2	6	8	6
C	2	3	5	7	9	4
D	4	3	7	3	7	0
E	1	5	6	9	10	4
F	3	7	10	7	10	0
G	3	2	5	8	11	6
H	4	5	9	11	15	6
I	5	10	15	10	15	0

Activity E, for example, can expand by up to 4 weeks without affecting the duration of the project.

Example

A small telephone exchange is planned as a project with ten main activities. The estimated durations (in days) and dependencies are shown in the following table. Draw the network for this project, find its duration, and calculate the floats of each activity.

Activity	Description	Duration	Depends On
A	Design internal equipment	10	-
B	Design exchange building	5	A
C	Order parts for equipment	3	A
D	Order material for building	2	B
E	Wait for equipment parts	15	C
F	Wait for building material	10	D
G	Employ equipment assemblers	5	A
H	Employ building workers	4	B
I	Install equipment	20	E,G,J
J	Complete building	30	F,H

Solution

The network for this is shown in Figure 15.14, and repeating the calculations described above gives the following results.

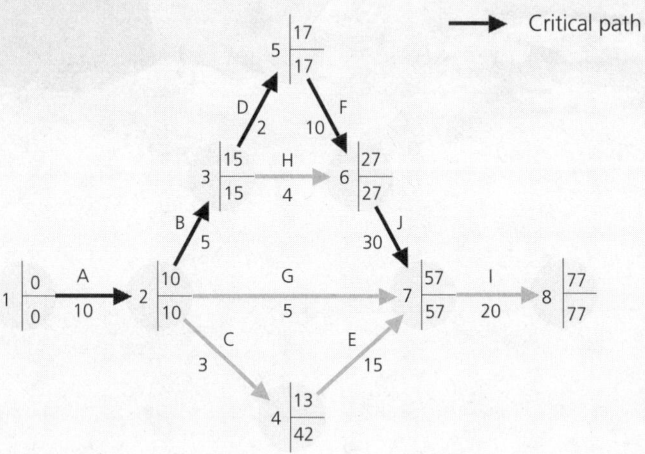

Figure 15.14 Network for Telephone Exchange

(Continued)

Example - Continued

Activity	Duration	Earliest Times Start	Earliest Times Finish	Latest Times Start	Latest Times Finish	Total Float
A	10	0	10	0	10	0*
B	5	10	15	10	15	0*
C	3	10	13	39	42	29
D	2	15	17	15	17	0*
E	15	13	28	42	57	29
F	10	17	27	17	27	0*
G	5	10	15	52	57	42
H	4	15	19	23	27	8
I	20	57	77	57	77	0*
J	30	27	57	27	57	0*

As you can see, the duration of the project is 77 days, defined by the critical path A, B, D, F, I, and J.

In Summary

An earliest and latest start and finish time can be found for each activity. The amount of flexibility in these times is measured by the total float. Critical activities have no float and form the critical path. This sets the overall duration of the project.

Review Questions

1. How are the earliest and latest times for an event calculated?
2. What is meant by the total float of an activity?
3. How big is the total float of a critical activity?
4. Why is the critical path so important?

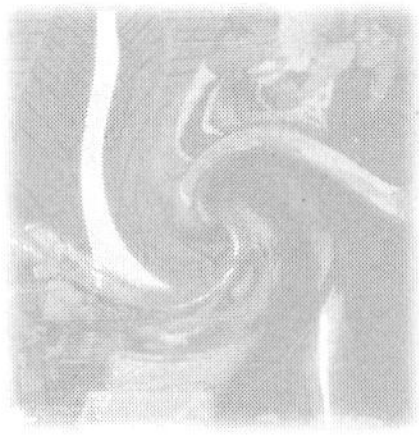

Project Evaluation and Review Technique

The method used here so far is the critical path method (CPM), in which each activity is given a single estimate for duration. But, of course, the time needed for any job can vary widely. So a useful extension to CPM adds some uncertainty to activity durations. This extension is the main difference between CPM and PERT (project evaluation and review technique).

Experience has shown that the duration of an activity can usually be described by a Beta distribution. This looks something like a skewed Normal distribution and has one very useful property—the mean and variance can be found from three estimates of duration. In particular it needs:

- *An optimistic duration (O),* which is the shortest time an activity will take if everything goes smoothly, without any difficulties
- *A most likely duration (M),* which is the duration of the activity under normal conditions
- *A pessimistic duration (P),* which is the time needed if there are significant problems and delays

The expected activity duration and variance are then calculated from the **rule of sixths**:

Rule of Sixths

$$\text{Expected druation} = \frac{O + 4M + P}{6}$$

$$\text{Variance} = \frac{(P - O)^2}{36}$$

Suppose an activity will optimistically take 4 days, will most likely take 5 days, and will pessimistically take 12 days. Using a Beta distribution for duration:

$$\text{Expected duration} = (O + 4M + P)/6 = (4 + 4 \times 5 + 12)/6 = 6$$

$$\text{Variance} = (P - O)^2 /36 = (12 - 4)^2/36 = 1.78$$

Now these expected durations can be used for analyzing project timing in the same way as the single estimate of CPM.

Example

A project has nine activities with dependencies and durations shown in the following table. Draw a network for the project, find the critical path, and estimate the overall duration of the project.

Activity	Depends On	Duration Optimistic	Duration Most Likely	Duration Pessimistic
A	-	2	3	10
B	-	4	5	12
C	-	8	10	12
D	A,G	4	4	4
E	B	3	6	15
F	B	2	5	8
G	B	6	6	6
H	C,F	5	7	15
I	D,E	6	8	10

Solution

Using the rule of sixths for the duration of activity A:

Expected duration $= (2 + 4 \times 3+10)/6 = 4$

Variance $= (10 - 2)^2/36 = 1.78$

Repeating these calculations for the other activities gives the following results.

Activity	Expected Duration	Variance
A	4	1.78
B	6	1.78
C	10	0.44
D	4	0
E	7	4.00
F	5	1.00
G	6	0
H	8	2.78
I	8	0.44

(Continued)

Example – Continued

The network for this problem is shown in Figure 15.15. The critical path for the project is B, G, D, and I, with an expected duration of 24.

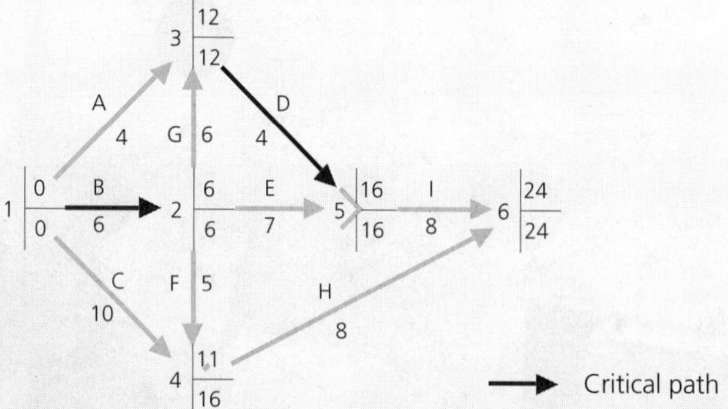

Figure 15.15 Network for Example

The analysis of activity times gives:

Activity	Expected Duration	Earliest Times Start	Earliest Times Finish	Latest Times Start	Latest Times Finish	Total Float
A	4	0	4	8	12	8
B	6	0	6	0	6	0 *
C	10	0	10	6	16	6
D	4	12	16	12	16	0 *
E	7	6	13	9	16	3
F	5	6	11	11	16	5
G	6	6	12	6	12	0 *
H	8	11	19	16	24	5
I	8	16	24	16	24	0 *

The duration of the critical path is the sum of the durations of activities making up that path. If there is a large number of activities on the path, the overall duration of the project is Normally distributed with:

- *Mean* equal to the sum of the expected durations of activities on the critical path
- *Variance* equal to the sum of the variances of activities on the critical path

These values can be used to find the probability that a project will be finished by any particular time.

Example

What are the probabilities that the project described in the last example will be finished before a) day 26; b) day 20?

Solution

The critical path is made up of activities B, G, D, and I, with expected durations of 6, 6, 4, and 8, respectively and variances of 1.78, 0, 0, and 0.44 respectively. Although the number of activities on the critical path is small, we can assume the overall duration of the project is Normally distributed. Then the expected duration has mean 6 + 6 + 4 + 8 = 24. The variance is 1.78 + 0 + 0 + 0.44 = 2.22, so the standard deviation is $\sqrt{2.22}$ = 1.49.

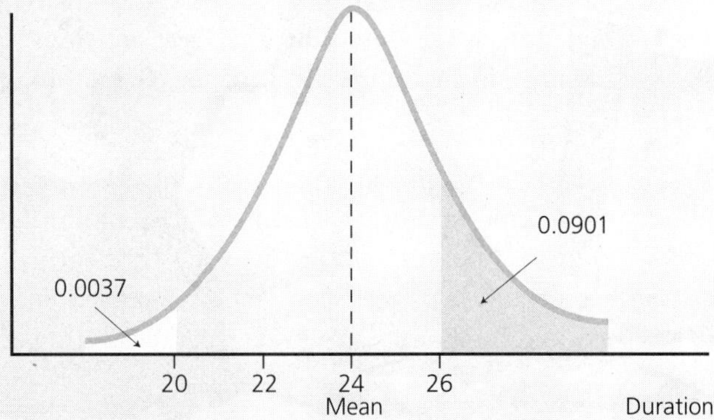

Figure 15.16 Normal Distribution of the Project Duration

a) The probability that the project will not be finished before 26 is found from Normal tables. Z is the number of standard deviations away from the mean, so:

$Z = (26 - 24)/1.49 = 1.34$ standard deviations

Tables (in Appendix A) show this to correspond to a probability of = 0.0901.

b) Similarly the probability it will be finished before 20 is:

$Z = (24 - 20)/1.49 = 2.68$

Probability = 0.0037

Review Questions

1. What is the "rule of sixths" and when is it used?
2. How could one calculate the expected duration of a project and its variance?

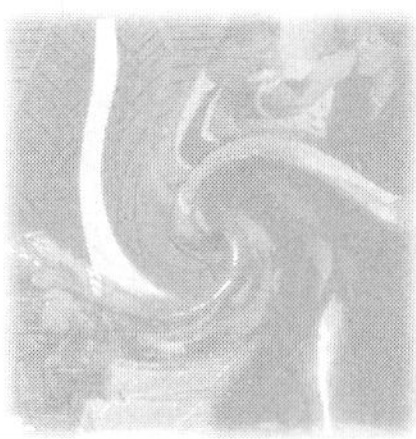

Resource Planning

This section discusses ways of adjusting the project plans, beginning with an examination of ways of changing project durations. There are two main reasons project durations may need changing:

1. When a network is analyzed the timing is found to be unacceptable—it may, for example, take more time than the organization has available
2. During the execution of a project, an activity might take shorter or longer than originally planned

Reducing the Length of a Project

Suppose that the initial plans for a project show that it will take too long. Then one must look for ways of reducing the length. The first thing to remember is that the duration of a project is set by the critical path, so the project can only be shortened by reducing the durations of critical activities. Reducing the duration of noncritical activities will have no effect on the overall project duration.

One must also consider what happens when a critical path is shortened. Small reductions will be acceptable, but if the critical path is reduced again and again, there must come a point when some other path through the network becomes critical. This point can be found from the total float on paths parallel to the critical path. Each activity on a parallel path has the same total float, and when the critical path is reduced by more than this, the parallel path itself becomes critical.

Example

The project network shown in Figure 15.17 has a duration of 14 with A, B, and C as the critical path.

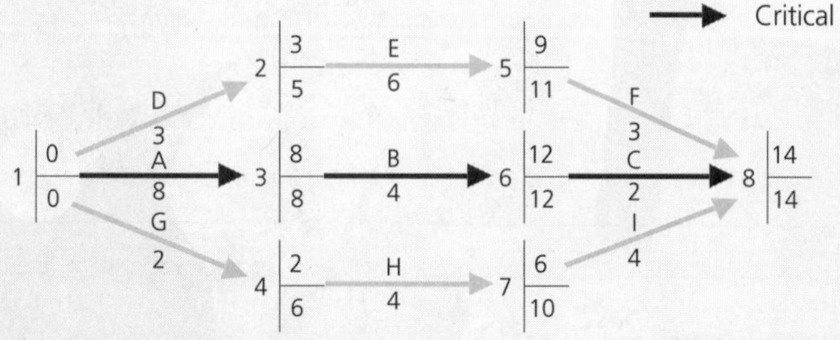

Figure 15.17 Critical Network for Example

If each activity can be reduced by up to 50 percent of the original duration, how would you reduce the overall duration to a) 13 weeks; b) 11 weeks; c) 9 weeks?

(Continued)

Example – Continued

If reductions cost an average of $1,000 a week, what would be the cost of finishing the project by week 9?

Solution

The analysis of activity times for this project is as follows.

Activity	Expected Duration	Earliest Times Start	Earliest Times Finish	Latest Times Start	Latest Times Finish	Total Float
A	8	0	8	0	8	0*
B	4	8	12	8	12	0*
C	2	12	14	12	14	0*
D	3	0	3	2	5	2
E	6	3	9	5	11	2
F	3	9	12	11	14	2
G	2	0	2	4	6	4
H	4	2	6	6	10	4
I	4	6	10	10	14	4

You can find the amount by which the critical path can be reduced without affecting any parallel path from the total float in parallel paths. In this network there are three parallel paths, A-B-C, D-E-F, and G-H-I. The total float of activities on these paths are 0, 2, and 4 respectively. This means the critical path A-B-C can be reduced by up to 2, but if reduced by more than this, the path D-E-F, becomes critical. If the critical path is reduced by more than 4, the path G-H-I also becomes critical.

a) We need a reduction of 1 week in the critical path. Reducing the longest activity—as it is usually easier to find savings in longer activities — gives A a duration of 7 weeks and the project is finished by week 13.

b) To finish in 11 weeks, we need a further reduction of 2 weeks in the critical path. This can also be removed from A. Unfortunately, the path D-E-F has now become critical, with a duration of 12 weeks. A week must be removed from E —again chosen as the longest activity in the critical path.

c) To finish in 9 weeks, we need 5 weeks removed from the path A-B-C (say 4 from A and 1 from B), 3 weeks removed from the path D-E-F (say from E), and 1 week removed from the path G-H-I (say from H).

To reduce the duration of the project by 5 weeks, we must reduce individual activity durations by a total of 5 + 3 + 1 = 9 weeks. The cost of this is $1,000 per week, or $9,000 total.

In Summary

The duration of a project can only be reduced by making critical activities shorter. The critical path can only be reduced by a certain amount before another parallel path becomes critical. This reduction is given by the total float of parallel paths.

Minimizing Costs

The total cost of a project is made up of direct costs, such as labour and materials; indirect costs, such as management and financing; and penalty costs if the project is not finished by a specified date.

$$\text{Total cost} = \text{direct costs} + \text{indirect costs} + \text{penalty costs}$$

All of these are affected by the duration of the project. There are no penalty costs if the project is finished on time, but this might need more resources and therefore increase the direct costs. Sometimes a bonus is paid if a project is finished early, but this may require more workers, which again increases direct costs. Overall, some kind of balance is needed between project duration and total cost. Useful calculations for this can be done using two figures:

1. **Normal Time** is the expected time to complete the activity, and this has associated **normal costs**
2. **Crashed Time** is the shortest possible time to complete the activity, and this has the higher **crashed costs**

To make the calculations easier, we shall assume that the cost of completing an activity in any particular time is a linear combination of these costs. Then, the cost of crashing an activity by a unit of time is:

$$\text{Cost of crashing by one unit of time} = \frac{\text{crashed cost} - \text{normal cost}}{\text{normal time} - \text{crashed time}}$$

An approach to minimizing the costs starts by analyzing a project with all activities done at their normal time and cost. Then the duration of critical activities is systematically reduced. Initially, the cost of the project may decline as its duration is reduced, but there comes a point when the cost starts to rise. When this happens, the minimum cost has been reached. The procedure for this is as follows.

1. Draw a project network—analyze cost and timings assuming all activities take their normal times.
2. Find the critical activity with the lowest cost of crashing. If there are more than one critical paths, they must all be considered at the same time.

3. Reduce the time for this activity until:
   - it cannot be reduced any further;
   - another path becomes critical; or
   - the cost of the project begins to rise
4. Repeat Steps 2 and 3 until the cost of the project begins to rise.

Example

A project is described by the following table, where times are in weeks and costs are in thousands of dollars.

Activity	Depends On	Normal Time	Normal Cost	Crashed Time	Crashed Cost
A	-	3	13	2	15
B	A	7	25	4	28
C	B	5	16	4	19
D	C	5	12	3	24
E	-	8	32	5	38
F	E	6	20	4	30
G	F	8	30	6	35
H	-	12	41	7	45
I	H	6	25	3	30
J	D,G,I	2	7	1	14

There is a penalty cost of $3,500 for every week the project finishes after week 18. By what time should the project be completed?

Solution

Following the procedure described above:

Step 1. The network for this project is shown in Figure 15.18, with times based on normal durations.

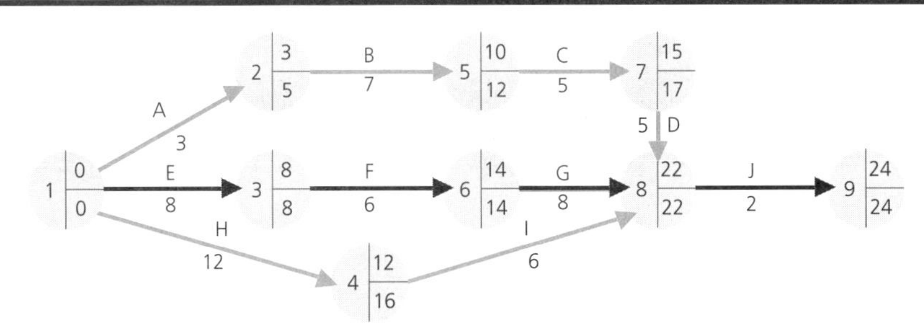

Figure 15.18 Network for Crashing Example

(Continued)

Example – Continued

The critical path is E-F-G-J, which has a duration of 24 weeks. The total cost is found by adding the normal costs of each activity ($221,000) to the 24 – 18 = 6 days of penalty costs ($21,000) to give a total of $242,000.

The cost of crashing each activity (in $'000 a week) is as follows:

Activity	A	B	C	D	E	F	G	H	I	J
Normal Time	3	7	5	5	8	6	8	12	6	2
Crashed Time	2	4	4	3	5	4	6	7	3	1
Reduction in Weeks	1	3	1	2	3	2	2	5	3	1
Crashed Cost	15	28	19	24	38	30	35	45	30	14
Normal Cost	13	25	16	12	32	20	30	41	25	7
Cost of Reduction	2	3	3	12	6	10	5	4	5	7
Cost per Week	2	1	3	6	2	5	2.5	0.8	1.7	7

The total float of activities on the parallel path A-B-C-D is 2; so if the critical path is reduced by this amount, A-B-C-D becomes critical.

- Step 2 finds the activity on the critical path (E-F-G-J) with the lowest cost of crashing. This is E at $2,000 per week.
- Step 3 reduces the time for activity E by 2 weeks—as any further reduction makes path A-B-C-D-J critical.

  Total cost of crashing by 2 weeks = 2 × 2,000 = $4,000
  Total savings = 2 × $3,500 = $7,000

  This step has reduced the penalty cost by more than the crashing cost, so we look for more savings.

- Step 2 identifies the lowest costs in the critical paths as E in E-F-G-J, and B in A-B-C-D-J.
  Step 3 reduces the time of these activities by 1 week, as E is then reduced by the maximum allowed.

  Total cost of crashing by 1 week = $2,000 + $1,000 = $3,000
  Total savings = $3,500

  Again, the overall cost has been reduced, so we look for more savings.

  Step 2 identifies the lowest costs in the critical paths as B in A-B-C-D-J, and G in E-F-G-J.

  Total cost of crashing by 1 week = $1,000 + $2,500 = $3,500
  Total savings = $3,500

(Continued)

Example – Continued

At this point, the savings exactly match the cost, and a minimum total cost has been found. If any more activities were crashed, the cost would be more than the savings from reduced penalties.

The overall duration of the project is now 20 days, with costs of $221,000 for normal activities, $10,500 for crashing, and $7,000 for penalties for a total of $238,500.

In Summary

A project has direct, indirect, and penalty costs. These all vary with the project duration. Project managers should look for the duration which minimizes the total cost.

Review Questions

1. By how much can a critical path be usefully shortened?
2. By how much can a noncritical activity be expanded without affecting the project duration?
3. What is the crashed time of an activity?
4. "As penalty costs, labour costs, financing costs, etc. all decrease with time, the total cost of a project is bound to decrease as the project gets shorter." Do you think this is true?

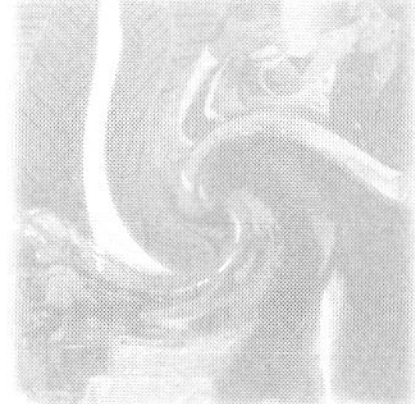

Gantt Charts

When a project is in the execution phase—the work is actually being done—project managers must monitor progress to make sure the activities are done at the right times. But the timing is not always clear from a network. It is much easier to monitor progress using a **Gantt chart**.

A Gantt chart is simply another way of showing a project, which emphasizes the timing of activities. It is a bar chart; it has a time scale across the bottom, activities are listed down the left-hand side, and times when activities should be done are blocked off in the body of the chart.

Example

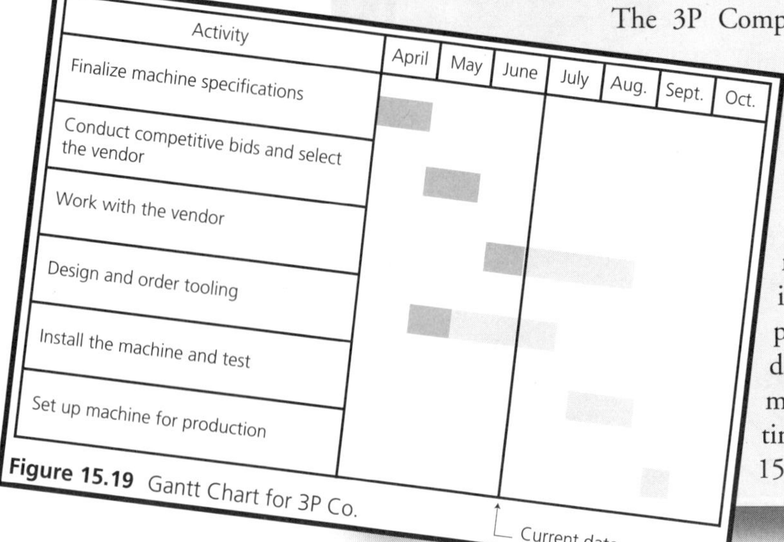

Figure 15.19 Gantt Chart for 3P Co.

The 3P Company is buying a specialized injection-moulding machine. The production manager sent in a purchasing proposal last year, but the Finance Department did not approve it. Finally, in March of this year the request was approved and $500,000 was set aside to buy the machine. The Finance Department insisted that a Gantt Chart be used to plan and control the purchase. The production manager estimated that the new machine would be working in six months time. He drew the chart shown in Figure 15.19 for his June progress report.

You can see from the 3P example that a Gantt chart clearly shows the project plan and the progress to date. A vertical line shows the current date, so all activities to the left of this should be complete. In this case, the proportion of each activity actually complete is shown as darker bars, while the lighter bars show the work still to be done.

Example

Draw a Gantt chart for the original data of the example on page 432 assuming each activity starts as early as possible.

Solution

The activity analysis for this example gives the following times.

Activity	Duration	Earliest Times		Latest Times		Total
		Start	Finish	Start	Finish	Float
A	8	0	8	0	8	0*
B	4	8	12	8	12	0*
C	2	12	14	12	14	0*
D	3	0	3	2	5	2
E	6	3	9	5	11	2
F	3	9	12	11	14	2
G	2	0	2	4	6	4
H	4	2	6	6	10	4
I	4	6	10	10	14	4

(Continued)

Example – Continued

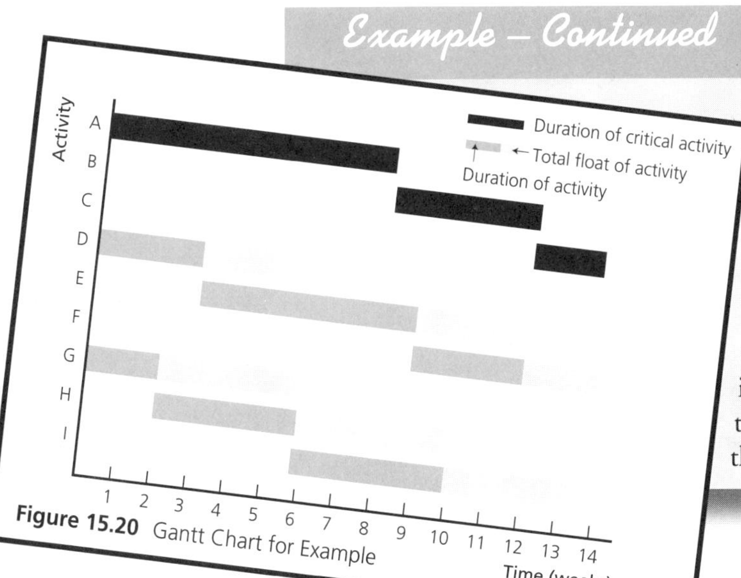

Figure 15.20 Gantt Chart for Example

If each activity starts as early as possible, the time needed is shown by the blocked-off areas in Figure 15.20. The total float of each activity is added afterward as a broken line. The total float is the maximum amount an activity can expand without delaying the project; so provided an activity is finished before the end of the broken line, there should be no problem keeping to the planned schedule.

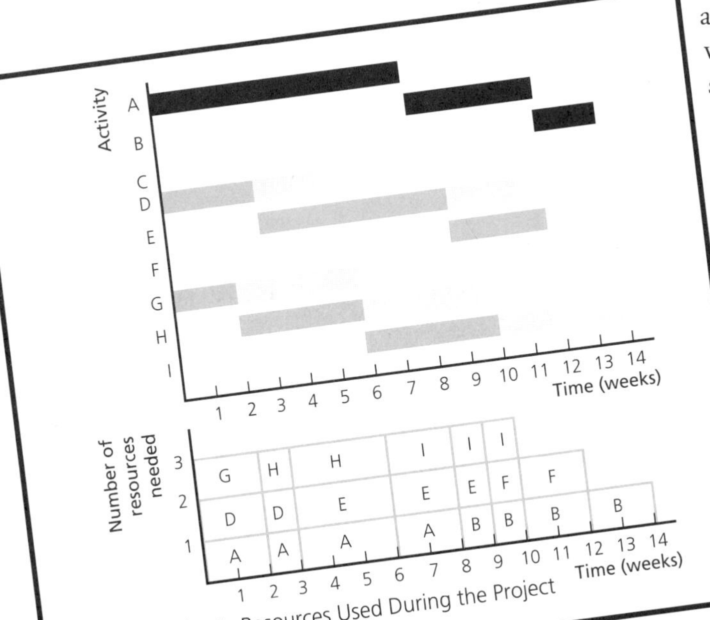

Figure 15.21 Resources Used During the Project

Gantt charts clearly show the state of each activity at any point in the project. They show which activities should be in hand, which should be finished, and which are about to start. Gantt charts are also useful for planning and allocating resources. Look at the Gantt chart in Figure 15.21 and assume, for simplicity, that each activity uses one unit of a particular resource—perhaps one team of workers. If all activities start as soon as possible, we can draw a vertical bar chart to show the resources used at any time. The project starts with activities A, D, and G, so three teams are used. At the end of week 2, one team can move from G to H, but three teams are still needed. Continuing this allocation produces the graph of resources shown in Figure 15.21.

In this example, the use of resources is steady for most of the project and only begins to fall near the end. It is unusual to achieve such a smooth pattern of resource use, and more often there are a series of peaks and troughs which should be levelled. As critical activities are fixed at certain times, this levelling must be done by rescheduling noncritical activities, and in particular by delaying those activities with large total floats.

Example

The network shown in Figure 15.22 shows a project with 11 activities over a period of 19 months. If each activity uses one work team, how many teams will be needed at each stage of the project? Would it be possible to schedule the activities so that a maximum of three work teams are used at any time?

Figure 15.22 Network for Example

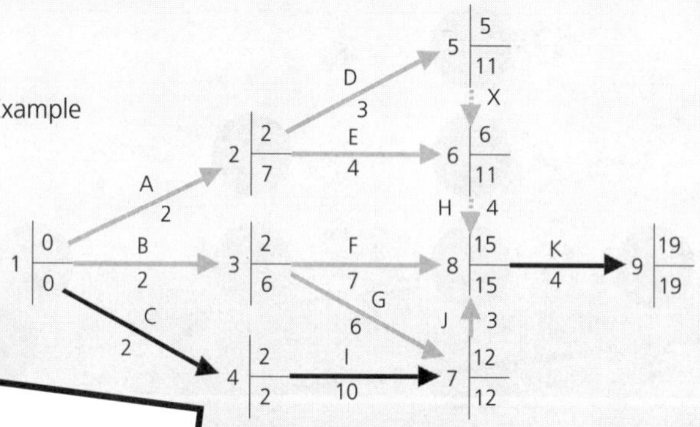

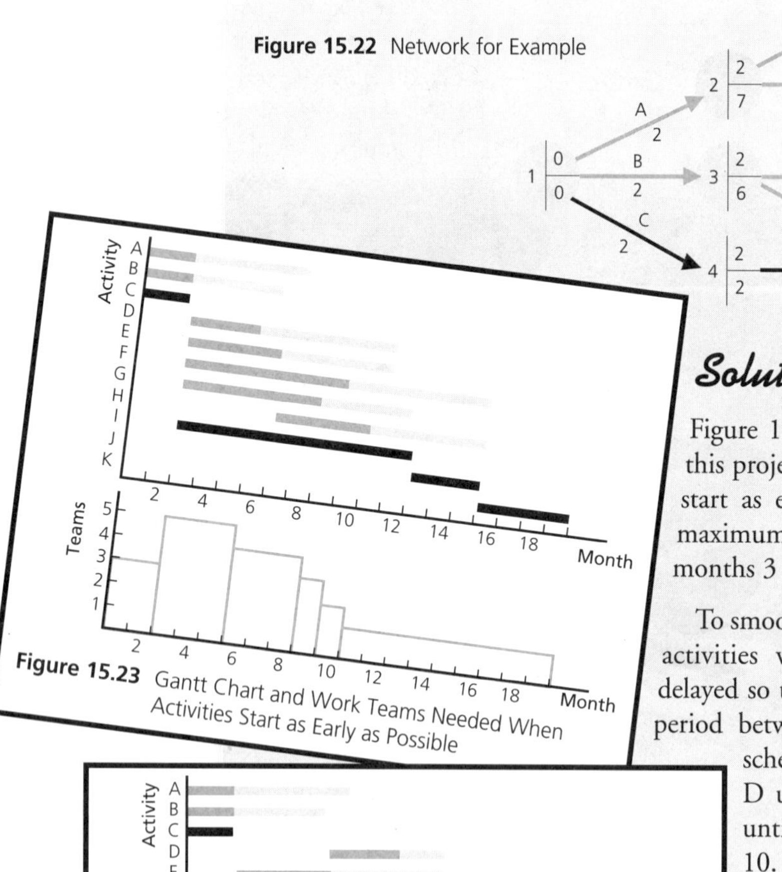

Figure 15.23 Gantt Chart and Work Teams Needed When Activities Start as Early as Possible

Solution

Figure 15.23 shows a Gantt chart for this project, assuming that all activities start as early as possible. This uses a maximum of five work teams during months 3 to 5.

To smooth the number of work teams, activities with large floats should be delayed so they do not occur in the busy period between months 3 and 5. One schedule would delay the start of D until month 7, the start of F until 9, and the start of H until 10. This rescheduling reduces the maximum number of work teams to 3 and gives a smoother workload, as shown in Figure 15.24.

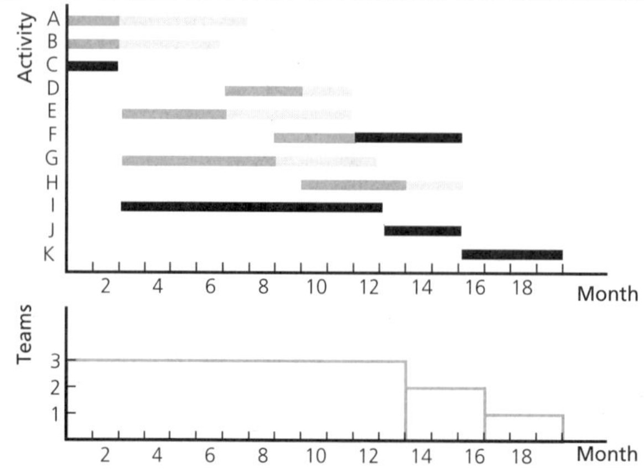

Figure 15.24 Gantt Chart and Work Teams Needed with Revised Schedule

In Summary

Gantt Charts give another view of projects, emphasizing the timing. They are used mainly in the planning of resources, and to monitor progress during the execution of a project.

Review Questions

1. What are the main benefits of Gantt charts?
2. How can the use of resources be smoothed during a project?

Case Study – Planning and Controlling a Term Project

Students are often assigned term projects in their courses. Many of these are group projects, which teach students how to work in groups, the importance of team work, how to handle large jobs, and a range of planning and organizational skills. But many students find it difficult to coordinate the work needed by the group. Proper planning and coordination of all tasks is very important if the term project is to be finished on time.

Imagine that you have been assigned a term project for one of your current courses. It is a group project where four of you will work together to do a literature search, conduct interviews and surveys, and write a report on your findings. The final report should be typewritten and is due 10 weeks from today.

Questions

- List the main activities needed for the project.
- Draw a Gantt chart of the project.
- Describe how you would monitor the progress of the project.

Chapter Review

- A project is a unique piece of work with a distinct start and finish. It consists of the activities needed to make a one-of-a-kind product. Projects often use many resources and take a long time, so their management is particularly important.
- Because projects are different in several ways from other processes, a different approach is needed for their planning.
- An important factor in the success of a project is the choice of a good project manager and management team.
- Project networks are widely used for managing projects. The relationships between activities can be shown in a dependence table. This can be translated into a network of alternating activities and events.
- When the network is complete, the timing of the project can be analyzed. A critical path identifies those activities which set the duration of the project and need particular attention. Event analyses find the earliest and latest times for events; activity analyses find the earliest and latest start and finish times for activities. The total float measures the amount an activity can expand without affecting the overall project duration.
- Critical path method (CPM) assumes a fixed duration for each activity, while project evaluation and review technique (PERT) includes some uncertainty.
- A project can be finished earlier by reducing the durations of critical activities, but if these reductions are too big, parallel paths become critical.
- The costs of a project change with its duration.
- Gantt charts allow the progress of a project to be monitored and can also be used for resource planning.

Key Terms

Problems

15.1 A project has the activities shown in the following dependence table. Draw the network of the project.

Activity	Depends On	Activity	Depends On
A	-	G	B
B	-	H	G
C	A	I	E,F
D	A	J	H,I
E	C	K	E,F
F	B,D	L	K

15.2 a) An amateur dramatic society is planning its annual production and is interested in using a network to coordinate the various activities. What activities should be included in the network?

b) If discussions lead to the following activities, what would the network look like?

- Assess resources and select play
- Prepare scripts
- Hold auditions
- Cast actors
- Rehearse
- Design and organize advertisements
- Prepare stage, lights, and sound
- Build scenery
- Sell tickets
- Conduct final arrangements for opening

15.3 Draw a network for the following dependence table.

Activity	Depends On	Activity	Depends On
A	H	I	F
B	H	J	I
C	K	K	L
D	I,M,N	L	F
E	F	M	O
F	-	N	H
G	E,L	O	A,B
H	E	P	N

15.4 If each activity in Problem 15.3 has a duration of 1 week, find the earliest and latest times for each event. Calculate the earliest and latest start and finish times for each activity and the total floats.

15.5 Draw the network represented by the following dependence table and calculate the floats for each activity.

Activity	Duration (weeks)	Depends On
A	5	-
B	3	-
C	3	B
D	7	A
E	10	B
F	14	A,C
G	7	D,E
H	4	E
I	5	D

If each activity can be reduced by up to 2 weeks, what is the shortest duration of the project and which activities are reduced?

15.6 A project is represented by the following table, which shows the dependency of activities and three estimates of durations.

a) What is the probability that the project will be completed before 17?

b) By what time is there a probability of 0.95 that the project will be finished?

Activity	Depends On	Duration		
		Optimistic	Most Likely	Pessimistic
A	-	1	2	3
B	A	1	3	6
C	B	4	6	10
D	A	1	1	1
E	D	1	2	2
F	E	3	4	8
G	F	2	3	5
H	D	7	9	11
I	A	0	1	4
J	I	2	3	4
K	H,J	3	4	7
L	C,G,K	1	2	7

15.7 A project consists of ten activities with estimated durations (in weeks) and dependencies shown in the following table. What are the estimated duration of the project and the earliest and latest times for activities?

Activity	Depends On	Duration	Activity	Depends On	Duration
A	-	8	F	C,D	10
B	A	6	G	B,E,F	5
C	-	10	H	F	8
D	-	6	I	G,H,J	6
E	C	2	J	A	4

If activity B needs special equipment, when should this be scheduled? A check on the project at week 12 shows that activity F is running 2 weeks late, that activity J will now take 6 weeks, and that the equipment for B would not arrive until week 18. What effects will this have on the overall project duration?

15.8 Draw a Gantt chart for the project described in Problem 15.5. If each activity uses one team of men, draw a graph of manpower needs assuming each activity starts as soon as possible. How can these manpower needs be smoothed?

15.9 Analyze the times and resource needs of the project described by the following data.

Activity	Depends On	Duration	Resources
A	-	4	1
B	A	4	2
C	A	3	4
D	B	5	4
E	C	2	2
F	D,E	6	3
G	-	3	3
H	G	7	1
I	G	6	5
J	H	2	3
K	I	4	4
L	J,K	8	2

15.10 In the project described in Problem 15.9, it costs $1,000 to reduce the duration of an activity by 1 unit. If there is $12,000 available to reduce the overall duration of the project, how should this be allocated, and what is the shortest duration of the project? What are the minimum resources needed by the revised schedule?

Discussion Questions

15.1 What are the main functions of project management?

15.2 Why is the management of projects so difficult? Illustrate your answer with examples of projects that have had difficulties.

15.3 Describe the matrix management structure usually found in a project. What are the advantages and drawbacks of this?

15.4 What specific skills should a project manager have?

15.5 What information is needed for project network analysis? What can you do if this information is not available?

15.6 How can the timing of activities be found? How accurate are these timings likely to be?

15.7 How is the control of a project linked to the planning stages?

15.8 Computers are always used for project network analysis. What feature would you expect to see in a good project-management package?

Chapter 16
LOGISTICS MANAGEMENT

Moving materials from suppliers, through operations, and to customers

Contents

Introduction

Logistics is responsible for the physical flow of goods through an organization. This flow starts when raw materials are moved from suppliers into an organization. It continues as goods are moved through operations, and ends when finished products are delivered to customers. The aim of logistics is to make this flow of materials as efficient as possible.

Several different functions make up logistics. These include procurement, transport, inventory control, warehousing, and distribution. Although these are often separated in an organization, it is best if they are integrated into a single function.

Procurement is responsible for obtaining materials from suppliers and aims to have the right materials available when they are needed. Most of the work in procurement is centred on a purchasing cycle.

Physical distribution moves finished products from an organization to its customers. This is the final link in the supply chain.

Learning Objectives

After reading this chapter you should be able to answer questions such as:

- What are logistics?
- What is a supply chain, and how is it managed?
- What are the aims of logistics?
- What is procurement?
- How is purchasing done?
- What is a purchasing cycle?
- What does a physical distribution system look like?

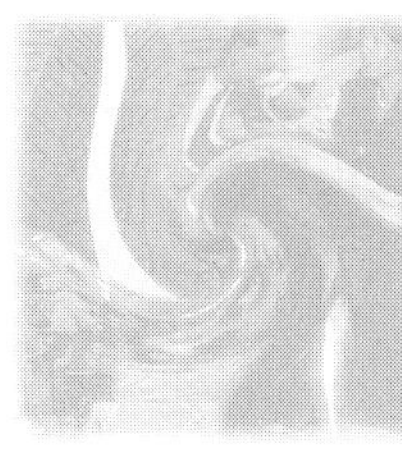

What Are Logistics?

Definitions

Chapter 1 discussed how **materials** are one of the inputs to a process. Materials are the physical items needed to make goods and services. These can be raw materials, parts, components, subassemblies, tools, consumables, services, or any other type of item. This chapter deals with the movement of these materials.

> **Logistics** is responsible for the physical movement of all materials through an organization.

Logistics really looks at three types of movement.

1. *Movement of raw materials*—where materials are moved from supplies *into* the organization. Here logistics is concerned with purchasing, inward transport, receiving, storage, and retrieval of goods.
2. *Movement of work-in-process*—where materials are used *within* the organization. Logistics deals with handling, movement, and storage of goods during operations.
3. *Movement of finished goods*—where materials are moved from the organization *out* to customers. Here logistics deals with packaging, storage, retrieval from warehouses, shipping, and distribution to customers.

The whole logistics function can be broken down into two parts. **Materials management** is responsible for the movement of materials into and within the organization. **Physical distribution** is responsible for the movement of finished goods out to customers.

As stated, logistics control the flow of materials through an organization, on their journey from suppliers, through operations, and on to customers. But the final product of one organization is the raw material of another. Gasoline, for example, is a final product of PetroCanada, but a raw material for Greyhound buses. So materials are actually moved through a series of organizations. This is called a **supply chain**, as shown in Figure 16.1.

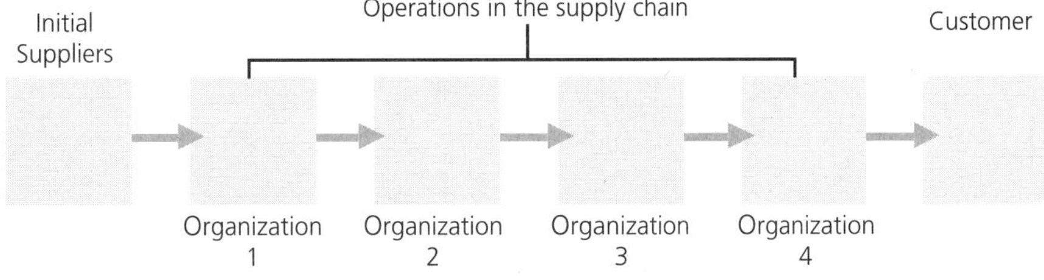

Figure 16.1 Elements in a Supply Chain

Organizing the movement of materials can be very difficult. Consider a simple product, such as a cotton shirt. This has a long and complicated journey from the farm growing cotton to the customer. Even the supply chain for a sheet of paper can involve many organizations. These include loggers, chemical companies, paper makers, transport operators, wholesalers, retailers, and many others.

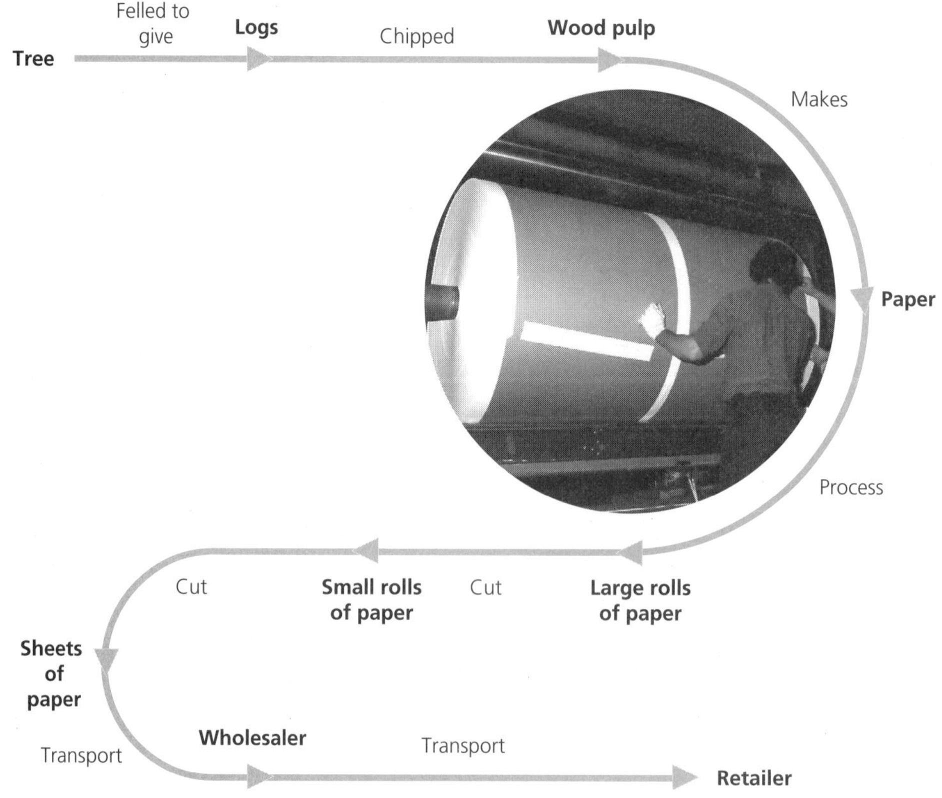

Figure 16.2 Outline of the Supply Chain for Paper

Such supply chains do not work by chance, but need careful planning and coordination. This is the function of logistics.

In Summary

Logistics is responsible for the movement of goods into, through and out of an organization. This function can be considered in two parts. Materials management is responsible for the movement of materials into and through the organization. Physical distribution is responsible for the movement of finished goods out to customers.

Aims of Logistics

Materials account for approximately 60 percent of costs in a typical Canadian manufacturing company. As you can imagine, there is no part of an organization that is not affected in some way by the movement of materials. The material flow for a simple manufacturing company is shown in Figure 16.3.

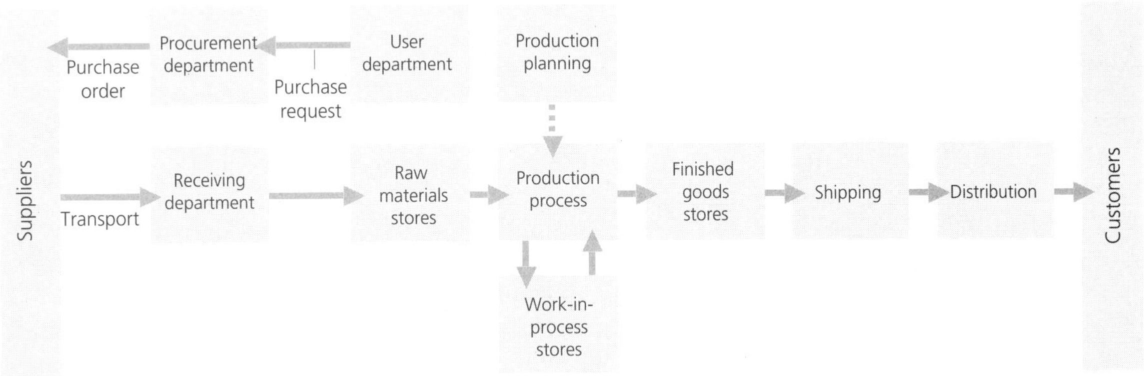

Figure 16.3 Material Flow in a Manufacturing Company

The flow of materials starts with production plans, which fix the raw materials that are needed. User departments describe the materials needed in a purchase request. The purchasing department actually buys the materials by issuing purchase orders. The materials move into the organization, through receiving, and into storage. As they are needed, the materials are removed from storage and used in the production process. Finally, finished goods are sent out to customers.

In principle, logistics is responsible for all these movements. But in most organizations, different functions control different parts of the materials flow. Typically, the purchasing department organizes the storage of raw materials moving into the organization, the production department looks after its own inventory of work-in-process, and the marketing department controls the inventory of finished goods. This gives three separate departments doing the single job of storing materials, which can lead to real inefficiencies. Each department builds its own administration for logistics, and there is much duplication. More importantly, the separate views of logistics have different objectives, and this can lead to conflicts. We might find, for example:

- **Marketing wants:**
  - high stocks of finished goods to satisfy customer demands quickly
  - a wide variety of finished goods always held in stock close to customers
  - an extensive distribution network so products can be moved quickly to customers
  - production to respond to orders from marketing

- **Production wants:**
  - little variety of products to create long production runs
  - high stocks of raw materials and work-in-process
  - efficient movement of materials through operations
  - marketing to respond to output from operations
- **Finance wants:**
  - low stocks everywhere
  - few warehouses and other facilities
  - large production quantities to reduce costs in long production runs
  - make-to-order operations

Each function tries to satisfy its own needs, often ignoring the aims of the whole organization. The best way of overcoming this is to have one function in charge of all the material movement. Then logistics becomes a single, integrated function with the aim of moving all materials into, through, and out of an organization while making the best use of resources and guaranteeing customer service. This aim leads to more detailed objectives, including:

- Organizing an uninterrupted flow of materials into the organization
- Finding and developing reliable suppliers
- Making purchases at lowest long-term cost
- Efficient movement of work-in-process
- Efficient movement of finished goods out to customers
- Minimizing costs of holding inventory
- Maintaining acceptable quality
- Maintaining good relations with suppliers and customers

In Summary

Logistics aims to have a smooth flow of materials through the supply chain. This function is often broken into parts, but best results come with a single, integrated function.

Functions of Logistics

While logistics is primarily concerned with movement of materials through an organization, it includes a number of other functions, as shown in Table 16.1.

Table 16.1 *Functions of Logistics*

- *Procurement or purchasing* is responsible for buying the raw materials from suppliers
- *Traffic and transport* moves the raw materials from suppliers to the organization's receiving area
- *Receiving* unloads the trucks bringing in raw materials, inspects the goods for any damage, and checks that the goods delivered are the same as those ordered
- *Warehousing or stores* holds materials until they are needed, and takes care of them
- *Inventory control* deals with the replenishment of stocks and controls inventory levels
- *Material handling* moves the materials needed for operations during the process.
- *Shipping* takes finished products, checks them, and loads them onto trucks for delivery to customers
- *Distribution* delivers finished products to customers
- *Location* decides how many warehouses should be built, and where they should be located
- *Communication* keeps all records for the logistics system

To reduce the materials cost, we must look at all of these functions. If we try to reduce each cost separately, the total logistics cost might actually rise. This is because many of the costs need a balance. Purchasing, for example, might reduce the unit price of a raw material by buying large quantities, but this increases the cost of inventories.

In Summary

Logistics consists of a number of related functions. These should all be considered together as an integrated function.

Review Questions

1. What is the primary aim of logistics?
2. "Managing materials is best left to the people most closely involved with them." Do you agree with this? Explain.
3. What jobs are usually considered part of logistics?

Case Study – Wise & Co.

Sam Wise is concerned that his company has been late delivering some important orders. The marketing manager is also upset that promised deliveries to customers have not been made.

When Sam asked the production manager for an explanation, he found that the shipments were late because stockouts of raw materials had interrupted operations. "But that is impossible," said Sam. "Inventory levels have been climbing for the past six months, and they were at an all-time high last month."

The inventory controller, Arif Ahmed, had a good explanation for this. Inventory levels were high because purchasing had been buying in large quantities. Although most inventories were high, there were shortages of other materials. Sam then checked with the purchasing manager, Nick Swarosky, who reminded Sam that four months ago he was instructed to reduce the materials costs. So Nick said, "I am taking advantage of the quantity discounts offered by suppliers." Buying these large volumes of raw materials — together with the express shipping services used to bring in stocked-out raw materials — had made shipping and warehousing supervisor Ed Espasito exceed his freight budget last month.

Just when Sam thought he knew all the problems facing the company, controller Chandra Krishnan came to Sam's office. "The company's inventory costs are so high that we will have to borrow money to pay the suppliers next month," she said. Later that day, Sam found that the late customer deliveries that had started his investigation were actually caused by poor sales forecasts by the marketing department.

Sam knew that all his employees were trying to do their best, but somehow things were going wrong.

Questions

- Why did the inventory levels rise?
- What caused Ed Espasito to go over his freight budget?
- What else went wrong in the company?
- How could forming a single logistics function help?

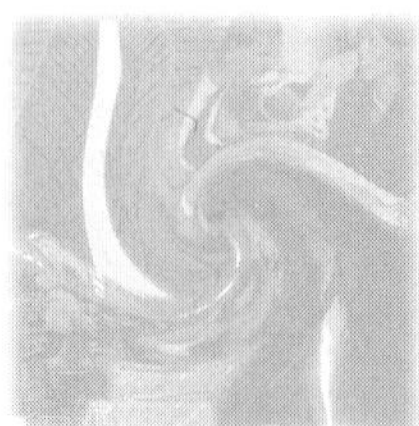

Procurement

Aims of Procurement

Procurement describes the range of activities that are responsible for buying the materials needed by an organization. It is generally responsible for getting materials from suppliers into the organization, and for ensuring that materials needed to support operations are available when needed.

Many organizations use the terms **purchasing** and **procurement** to mean the same thing. Purchasing is concerned with the actual buying of materials. Procurement is a broader term which includes a number of related activities, such as:

1. Buying the materials needed for operations
2. Making sure these materials are of reliably high quality
3. Finding good suppliers, working closely with and developing good relations with them
4. Negotiating good prices from suppliers
5. Keeping inventory levels low by buying standard materials, etc.
6. Working closely with the user department, understanding its needs, and getting the materials it needs at the right times
7. Keeping management informed about price increases, scarcities, etc.

These aims are often abbreviated to *getting the right materials, with the right quality, at the right time, to the right place, from the right source, at the right price.* If any one of these aims is not met, the organization cannot function efficiently. Operations may be interrupted, customer demand not met, costs too high, deliveries delayed, or productivity reduced.

In Summary

Procurement is responsible for getting materials from suppliers into the organization. It includes purchasing and related functions. It has the aim of delivering the right materials, with the right quality, at the right time, to the right place, from the right source, at the right price.

How Procurement Works

When you buy something expensive, such as a car, you generally go through a number of steps. You might start by looking at different kinds of cars, comparing companies, costs, options, warranties, etc. The procurement function in an organization follows these same steps. The procurement function can be seen in more detail with the **purchasing cycle**, which describes the procedures needed to buy materials. It typically has the following steps.

1. *User department*:
   a) the person needing the materials makes a request to the department head;
   b) this is checked against budgets within the department;
   c) a purchase request is prepared and sent to procurement.

Case Study – Buying at Harrington Industries

Linda Owens has been the Purchasing Manager at Harrington Industries for the last five years. The purchasing department also has a buyer, an expeditor, and a clerk. Because of the increasing workload, Linda and her staff have been very busy for the past year. Three months ago, she asked to hire a junior buyer. This request was recently approved and she wrote the following job description.

Position: Junior Buyer

Reports to: Purchasing Manager, who is responsible for $1.5 million of annual purchases

Responsibilities: The person is responsible for buying office supplies, plant supplies (MRO items), and office furniture. The person should have effective working relationships with engineering, production, accounting, and sales departments. The person should be able to interpret specifications, suggest changes to specifications, locate suppliers, and negotiate prices. He/she must develop and maintain good supplier relationships to assist in getting good quality material at low prices.

The person should be able to follow the existing purchasing policies and procedures. He/she has the authority to make purchasing decisions up to $5,000 on his/her own judgement.

Qualifications: The person should possess good analytical abilities and communications skills. He/she should have a minimum of a college diploma, preferably in a business/management subject.

Salary: The salary range is $24,000 – $36,000 per year.

Questions

- Do you think this junior buyer would be an interesting job? Explain your answer.
- Why do you think the job calls for good communications skills?
- If you could save 2 percent of the total material budget, what would be the savings to the company?

2. *Then procurement:*
   a) receives and analyzes the purchase request;
   b) verifies and checks the request;
   c) checks current stocks, alternative products, etc.;
   d) makes a short list of possible suppliers;
   e) sends a request for price quotation to this short list of suppliers.

3. *Then suppliers:*
   a) examine the request for quotation;
   b) see how it could best satisfy such an order;
   c) send an offer back to the organization, with prices, conditions, etc.

4. *Then procurement:*
   a) selects the best supplier, based on its product, delivery, price, etc.;
   b) discusses and finalizes any details with the supplier;
   c) issues a purchase order.

5. *Then the supplier:*
   a) receives and processes the purchase order;
   b) makes or assembles the order;
   c) ships the order to the organization, and sends an invoice.

6. *Then procurement:*
   a) does any necessary follow-up to make sure the materials are delivered;
   b) receives, inspects, and accepts the items;
   c) updates inventory records, notifies the purchasing department;
   d) approves the supplier's invoice for payment.

Example

Last year Zetafile Limited had a total income from sales of $108 million. Its direct costs were $58 million for materials, $27 million for employees, and $12 million for other overheads. What would have been the effects on profits if the cost of materials had dropped by 1 percent?

Solution

Zetafile's profit last year was 108 – (58 + 27 + 12) = $11 million. This was 10.19 percent of sales value. If the cost of materials had dropped by 1 percent, to $57.42 million, the profit would have risen to $11.58 million. This is 10.72 percent of sales value. A 1 percent decrease in materials costs would have increased profits by 5.2 percent.

In Summary

There are several stages in procurement. These can be described by a purchasing cycle. A small reduction in material costs can have a major effect on profits.

Trends in Procurement

The role of the procurement manager has changed significantly in recent years. Procurement used to be little more than a clerical job, buying materials as they were requested. Now it is a profession, and procurement managers take an active part in planning. General Motors, for example, spends over $50 billion a year in purchasing materials, so it is not surprising that purchasing is a very important function.

One development in procurement is **value analysis**. This is a way of improving product quality and performance, while reducing material cost. In effect, value analysis finds substitutes for materials that are cheaper to buy but of equally good quality as the original. Value analysis uses a team of people from different functional areas, including suppliers, to critically review a product design and suggest improvements. With value analysis, both purchasing departments and their suppliers are involved early in product design. The organization and its suppliers then become partners. Their common aim is to develop a long-term business relationship that is profitable for both sides.

Such partnerships have encouraged **single sourcing**. In the past, purchasing departments had little loyalty to suppliers, and companies used competitive bidding to choose their suppliers. Contracts were awarded for the short term—typically up to a year. Organizations thought this system gave them good prices as suppliers would compete fiercely to get business. With single sourcing, companies use a single supplier for a given item, with a long contract—typically 3–5 years. This creates good will with the suppliers, who are then encouraged to look for improvements to product design.

In Summary

The role of procurement has changed in recent years. It is now a profession. The old ideas of conflicts with suppliers have been replaced by partnerships.

Case Study

Purchasing and Materials Management at Ontario Hydro

In this modern world, we are highly dependent on electricity. It is difficult to imagine what our lives would be like without electricity. Ontario Hydro makes sure that Ontario residents and businesses get an uninterrupted supply of electricity. It is one of the largest electric utilities in North America, with a generating capacity of 34,000 megawatts (MW) in 1993. It had $8.363 billion in revenue in 1993, and employed 22,590 people at the end of 1993.

The Purchasing and Materials Division (PMMD) is responsible for buying and providing functional direction for all products and services except for the fuels. It is headed by Mr. Vipin Suri, who is the director of the division. He reports to the Vice-president, Business Services. PMMD is respected as one of Canada's largest purchasers of equipment and materials. In 1993, PMMD purchased close to $1 billion in goods and services from more than 10,000 suppliers worldwide. "Currently, Ontario Hydro is in a maintenance mode, so our material purchases are lower than they were when we were building new power plants," says Mr. Suri.

PMMD's vision statement is "to be the supplier of choice by providing purchasing and materials management services which contribute to the success of our customers." Since assuming the directorship in 1993, Mr. Suri has been involved in re-engineering the procurement process. He has decentralized the purchasing function to make it more responsive to customer needs. His responsibilities include providing procurement strategy, policies and procedures, satellite purchasing services, purchasing corporate commodities, quality surveillance and inspection, meter and relay services, investment recovery, and updating management. Ontario Hydro has 175 people who do the purchasing function, and 729 people who are involved in doing the materials management function. Of the total of 904 purchasing and material management staff, 250 are located at the corporate head office in Toronto, and the others are located in business units and field sites, which bring them closer to the customers, that is, generating stations.

Ontario Hydro has embarked on many innovative procurement practices in recent years. Some of them are:

1. Focus on total life cycle cost: Here the idea is to minimize the total cost of using the product over the life cycle of the requirements. The total life cycle costs consist of purchase price, transportation costs, maintenance costs, operating costs, etc. This approach means working closely with capable suppliers on a long-term basis.
2. Developing the joint purchasing arrangements with electric utilities and government agencies. This will help them to standardize the products, increase procurement power, lower costs, etc.
3. Reducing administration costs through use of the Corporate Procurement Card.

Ontario Hydro is committed to the principles of sustainable energy development and is very environmently conscious. A "Buy Green" program has been introduced and Ontario Hydro is adopting the Three Rs—Reduce, Reuse, Recycle—as an alternative to buying new products.

Source: Ontario Hydro Annual Report 1993, PMMD brochures, and an interview with Mr. Vipin Suri.

Case Study

Accounts Payable at Ford

In 1988, Ford of America was seeking ways to increase productivity in its Accounts Payable Department. The department employed 500 people who used a standard accounting system, in which:

- The purchasing department sent a purchase order to the vendor and a copy to Accounts Payable
- The vendor shipped the goods ordered
- When the goods arrived at Ford, a clerk in the receiving area checked the goods, completed a form describing the goods, and sent the form to Accounts Payable
- The vendor sent an invoice to Accounts Payable
- Accounts Payable now had three descriptions of the goods — from the purchase order, the receiving area, and the invoice. If these matched, the invoice was paid, but in a few cases there were discrepancies. These often took weeks to trace and sort out.

Ford estimated that they could save up to 25 percent of staffing costs by redesigning the system. They looked at Mazda, who was running its Accounts Payable with a fraction of the Ford staff. In the end, Ford radically redesigned the system. In the revised system:

- The purchase department sends a purchase order to a vendor, and enters details on a database
- The vendor ships the goods
- When the goods arrive at Ford, a clerk at the receiving dock uses the database to check the goods to see if they correspond to an outstanding order. If they do, the clerk updates the database to show that the goods have arrived and the computer automatically sends a cheque to the supplier. If there are discrepancies, the clerk will refuse to accept the delivery and send it back to the supplier.

Ford's "We pay when we receive the invoice" has changed to "We pay when we receive the goods." The new system takes 125 people to operate, resulting in a 400 percent increase in productivity.

Review Questions

1. What is the main aim of procurement?
2. Is there any difference between procurement and purchasing?
3. What are the stages in a typical purchasing cycle?

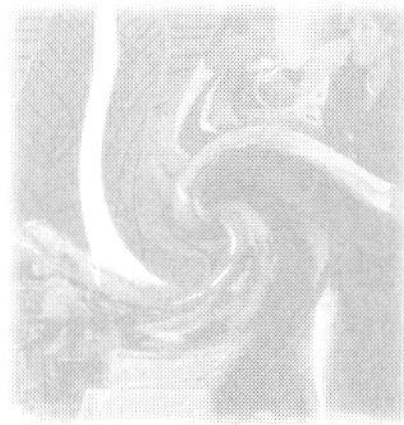

Physical Distribution

Procurement is concerned with moving materials from suppliers into the organization. At the other end of the operations is **physical distribution** which is concerned with moving finished goods from the organization and out to customers. Some describe distribution as the final link in a supply cycle, as shown in Figure 16.4.

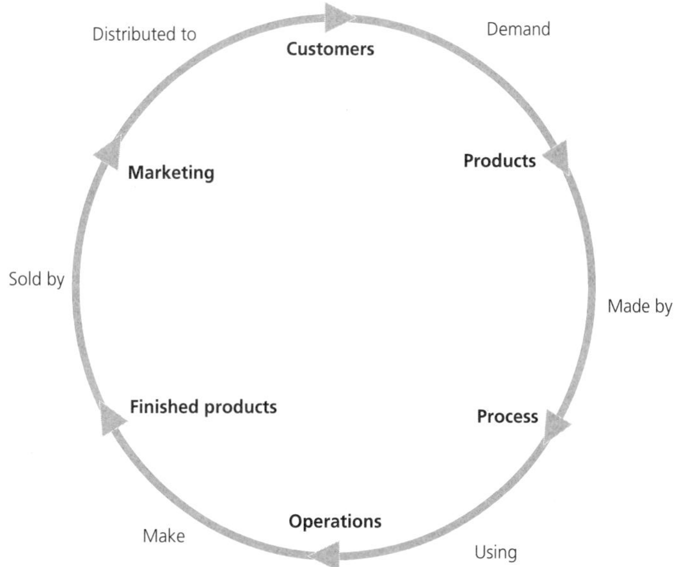

Figure 16.4 Distribution in a Supply Cycle

Finished goods are typically moved from operations and stored in warehouses until they are distributed to customers, as shown in Figure 16.5. These systems have developed because many operations are best done in locations that are some distance from both customers and suppliers. The best location for power stations, for example, is some distance from cities, and may also be away from fuel supplies.

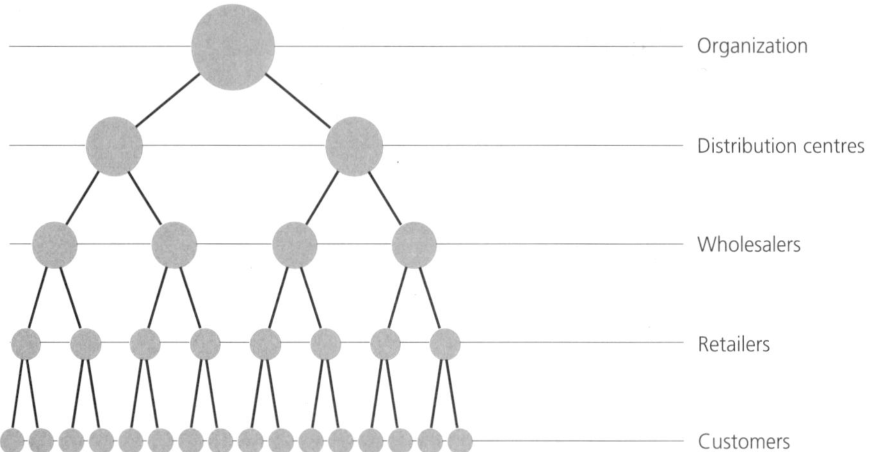

Figure 16.5 A Typical Distribution System

There are several advantages to this type of distribution system, including:

- Possible economies of scale by concentrating operations in central locations
- Production facilities need not keep large stocks of finished goods
- Wholesalers are close to retailers and therefore have short lead times
- Wholesalers can place large orders and therefore reduce unit prices
- Wholesalers keep stocks from many suppliers, allowing retailers a choice of goods
- Retailers can carry less stock as wholesalers offer reliable delivery times
- Distribution costs are reduced as large orders are moved from production facilities to wholesalers, rather than moving small orders directly to retailers or customers

You can probably imagine this kind of distribution system used by manufacturers, but it is also used by services. Air Canada uses a similar system for moving passengers from major "hub" airports, through feeder services, and on to smaller local airports; banks collect all cheques in central clearing houses before sending them back to branches and customers; blood banks have regional centres which act as wholesalers.

Physical distribution has several objectives, including:

- Developing an efficient system of distribution to customers
- Making sure deliveries to customers are reliable
- Using appropriate and cost-effective transport
- Having low-cost storage and high inventory turnover in warehouses
- Maintaining high quality of distribution
- Low administration costs
- Keeping accurate records

Case Study

Wal-Mart

Sam Walton founded Wal-Mart in Bentonville, Arkansas, in 1962. In 1993, Wal-Mart had 2,100 stores and sales of $67 billion. The whole organization is considered a model of efficient operations. For its logistics, it uses road transport almost exclusively.

The company operates 18 regional distribution centres, with another 15 speciality centres for clothes and hobbies. The largest of these centres covers more than 100,000 square metres and can handle 200 truck deliveries and 250,000 cartons each day. Wal-Mart employs 2,500 drivers and runs 2,100 articulated tractors and 13,000 trailers. Each store is within 250 miles of its nearest distribution centre, and the allocation of stores to centres is checked twice a year to look for improvement.

In 1988, Wal-Mart opened a chain of Sam's warehouse outlets, and needed more flexibility than it had with its existing distribution network. It decided to use third-party operators, and 14 of its 16 centres are now run by third-party operators. In 1994, when Wal-Mart bought a large part of Woolco in Canada, it decided to expand its third-party contacts and use Tibbett & Britten for distribution in Canada.

Each of these objectives leads to a range of other decisions. For example, when you consider transportation, you have to consider the *mode of transport.* There are essentially five modes of transport: road, rail, air, water, and pipeline. The best choice in any particular circumstance depends on the type of goods to be moved, the distance, value, and a whole range of other things. Road transport is the most flexible, as it can move goods from door to door. But it is not as good for long distances or high volumes. Rail is better with high volumes, but it can be slower and needs transfers at rail terminals. Air transport is fastest, but it is expensive and can only take limited weights. Ships can carry big loads but can only work between ports. Pipelines can carry large quantities cheaply, but can only carry gas, liquid, or slurry over certain areas. The best transport may use more than one mode, perhaps road to a rail terminal, then train to a port.

All organizations rely on the movement of finished goods to customers. This is an expensive function, and one where considerable savings can be found. Thus, distribution is important to an organizations because it:

- Directly affects profits
- Provides a link between the organization and its customers
- Effects lead times, service levels, etc.
- Provides public exposure for the organization, with trucks, etc.
- Determines the size and location of facilities
- Can encourage the development of other organizations—such as transport operators
- Is expensive
- Can be risky, with safety considerations
- May prohibit some operations—such as moving very heavy loads

In Summary

Physical distribution is concerned with moving finished products from an organization to its customers. It is an important function which makes a series of decisions about location, transport, inventory control, warehousing, communications, and so on.

Review Questions

1. What is the difference between logistics, physical distribution, and materials management?
2. What functions does physical distribution include?
3. What modes of transport are there?

Chapter Review

- Logistics is responsible for the movement of materials from suppliers, through operations, and on to final customers. The aim of logistics is to have a smooth flow of materials through the supply chain.
- Logistics interact with every other function in an organization. For this reason it is often considered in several parts. But there are real benefits in having a single, integrated logistics function to organize the movement of all materials.
- The complete function of logistics consists of a number of related jobs, such as procurement, materials management, warehousing, transport, and inventory control.
- Procurement ensures that an organization has the materials it needs for its operations. It aims to get the right materials, with the right quality, at the right time, to the right place, from the right supplier, at the right price.
- There are several steps in procurement. These centre on a purchasing cycle.
- Physical distribution is concerned with moving finished products from operations out to final customers. This is the final link in the supply chain.

Key Terms

logistics *(p. 449)*
materials *(p. 449)*
materials management *(p. 449)*
physical distribution *(pp. 449, 461)*
procurement *(pp. 454–455)*
purchasing *(p. 455)*
purchasing cycle *(p. 455)*
single sourcing *(p. 458)*
supply chain *(p. 449)*
value analysis *(p. 458)*

Discussion Questions

16.1 Describe an actual supply chain and show how it is used to get products from initial suppliers to final customers.

16.2 What activities are part of logistics? What new issues are facing the function?

16.3 Describe the material flow in an organization with which you are familiar. How could this flow be improved?

16.4 What are the benefits of an integrated logistics function? Are these inevitable? Would it be better to separate logistics into several smaller units?

16.5 What are the main objectives of procurement? How can these be achieved?

16.6 What recent trends have there been in procurement? What has encouraged these?

16.7 Do you think an organization should always negotiate aggressively with suppliers to get the cheapest prices and best conditions?

16.8 Why is it that the amount of goods travelling by rail has been steadily decreasing in recent years?

16.9 How much does logistics cost a typical organization? Do you think this is too much? Explain your reasoning.

Chapter 17

MANAGING INDEPENDENT DEMAND INVENTORY

How to organize inventories and control their costs

Contents

Introduction

All organizations hold inventories, or stocks of materials that are stored until they are needed. These inventories can be very costly, so they need careful management. Just about everything is held as stock somewhere, at some point in time, whether raw materials in a factory, finished goods in a retail store, or canned goods in a pantry. Stocks can be classified as raw materials, work-in-process, and finished goods.

The main purpose of holding inventories is to provide a buffer between supply and demand. This chapter discusses the management of independent demand inventory systems.

Learning Objectives

After reading this chapter you should be able to answer questions such as:

- Why are inventories held?
- How much do they cost?
- How much should we order?
- When should we place orders?
- How do we control production inventories?
- What happens if demand varies?
- What are periodic review systems?
- Which items are most important?

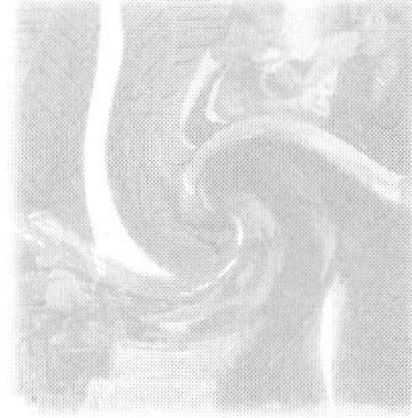

What Are Inventories?

Inventories are supplies of goods and materials that are held by an organization. They are created whenever the organization's inputs or outputs are not used at the time they become available.

All organizations have inventories. These always involve costs for warehousing, tied-up capital, insurance, and deterioration. An obvious question then, is, Why hold stocks? There are several answers to this, but the most common is, *To form a buffer between supply and demand.*

When a gas station gets a delivery of gasoline, it is held as inventory until it is sold to a customer; when a factory moves finished goods to a warehouse, they are put into inventory. Inventories are also called **stocks** or **stock holdings.**

There are three types of stocks:

1. **Raw materials** are the materials, parts, and components that have been delivered to an organization, but are not yet being used
2. **Work-in-process** are materials that have started, but have not yet finished, their journey through the production process
3. **Finished goods** are the goods that have finished the production process and are waiting to be shipped out to customers

Consider the raw materials being delivered to a factory. These are usually delivered in large quantities, perhaps a truckload at a time. But they are used in smaller quantities. The result is a stock of raw materials that is replenished with every delivery, and is reduced over time to meet demand. The stock of raw materials provides the organization with a cushion against unexpected variations in supply—it allows operations to continue when delivery vehicles are delayed, poor quality materials are rejected, or some disruption occurs at the supplier.

At the other end of production are stocks of finished goods. These accumulate at the end of the process until there is enough to meet an order, or to form a load for sending to a distribution centre. These stocks of finished goods allow an organization to meet unexpected demand from customers.

A third type of stock is work-in-process. This separates the stages in a production process so that each can work at its most efficient rate. If two consecutive operations in a process work most efficiently at different rates, they can be separated or "decoupled" by having a stock of work-in-process between them. This grows when the first process works faster than the second, and is reduced when the second process catches up.

So you can see from these examples that the main purpose of inventories is to form a buffer between supply and demand.

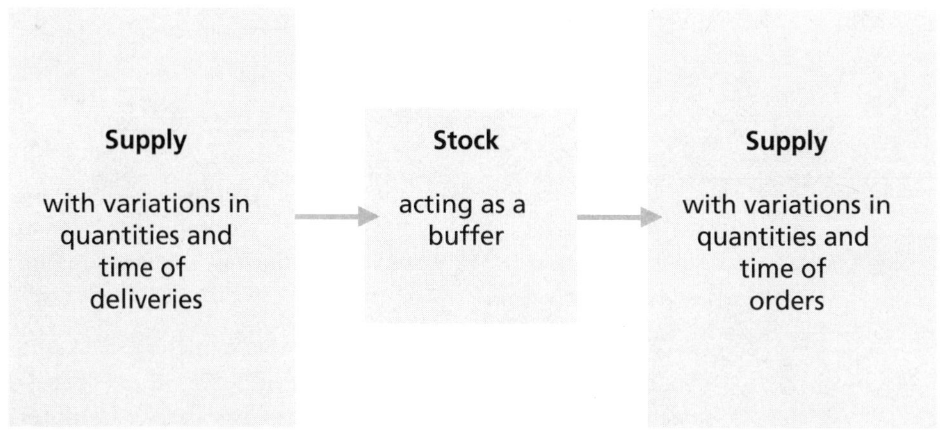

Figure 17.1 Stock Acts as a Buffer Between Variable Supply and Demand

A more detailed list of reasons for holding stock is given in Table 17.1.

Table 17.1 *Reasons for Holding Stock*

- To create a buffer between different operations
- To allow for demands that are larger than expected, or that occur unexpectedly
- To allow for deliveries that are delayed or that are too small
- To take advantage of price discounts on large orders
- To buy items when the price is low and is expected to rise in the future
- To buy items that are going out of production or that are difficult to find
- To make full loads and reduce transport costs
- To provide cover for emergencies

Of course, one company's finished goods are another company's raw materials. Aviation fuel, for example, is a finished product for Petro Canada but a raw material for Air Canada. This means that the same materials can appear in different categories. In Canadian industries, around 30 percent of stocks are raw materials, 40 percent work-in-process, and 30 percent finished goods.

Some items do not fall easily into any of these categories. Another classification then is called **maintenance, repair, and operating supplies (MRO)**. These include spare parts for machinery, equipment, etc. and consumables such as lubricants, paper, cleaning supplies, and tools.

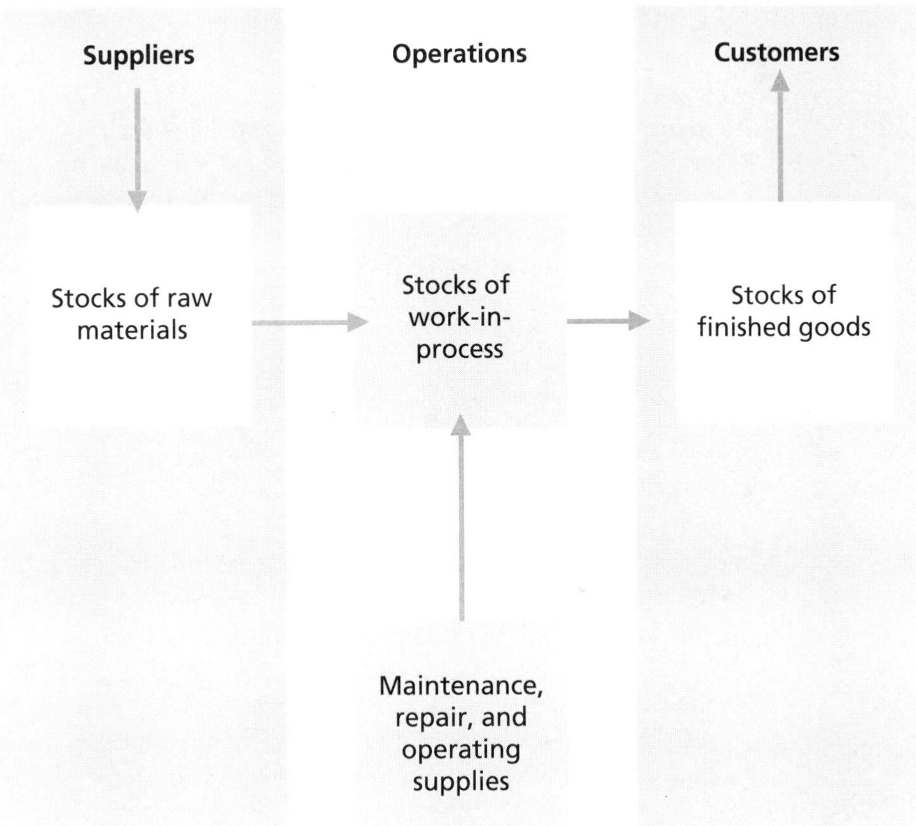

Figure 17.2 Types of Inventory

In Summary

All organizations hold stocks of various kinds. Their main purpose is to provide a buffer between supply and demand. Stocks allow normal operations to continue through variable and uncertain supply and demand.

Review Questions

1. What is the main reason for holding stock?
2. What types of things are held in stock?
3. Can you give an example of an organization that does not hold any stocks?

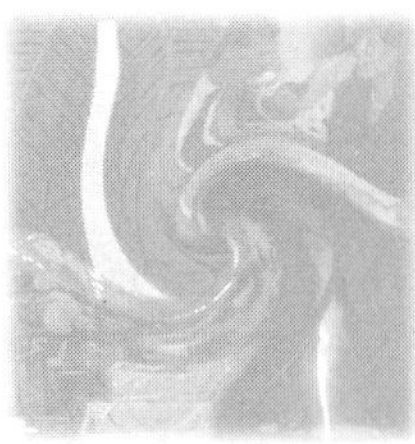

Costs of Inventories

The cost of holding stock is typically around 25 percent of amount held a year. This means that Sears Canada spends over $150 million per year keeping its stock of goods valued at $628 million on the shelves. Not surprisingly, with such high costs, organizations are always looking for ways to save money in this area. Some people think that costs can be minimized by reducing inventories, but this is not true. If a shop holds no stock, it certainly has no inventory costs, but it also has no sales. Costs associated with inventories can be classified as follows:

1. Unit cost
2. Re-order cost
3. Holding or carrying cost
4. Shortage or stockout cost

Unit Cost

This is the price of the item charged by the supplier, or the cost of obtaining one unit of the item. This cost may be easy to determine with quotations or recent invoices from suppliers. Sometimes it is more difficult to determine because various suppliers offer slightly different products, or set different purchasing conditions. If a company makes the item itself, it may be difficult to give a reliable production cost or to set a transfer price.

Often, when an organization buys large quantities of a certain material, the supplier will give the organization a discount that lowers the unit cost.

Re-order Cost

This is the cost of placing a repeat order for an item. It includes the cost of drawing up an order (checking the order, clearance, distribution, and filing), computer costs, correspondence and telephone costs, receiving the goods (unloading, checking, and testing), supervision, use of equipment, and follow-up. Sometimes, costs such as quality control, transport charges, sorting, and movement of delivered goods are included in the re-order cost.

The re-order cost is for repeat orders only. First orders might have additional costs of searching for suitable suppliers, checking the reliability and quality of the product, negotiating with alternative suppliers. In practice, the best estimate for an order cost is often found by dividing the annual cost of running the purchasing department by the number of orders it sends out.

A different kind of re-order cost occurs when the company makes the item itself. Here the re-order cost is a batch set-up cost and might include production planning and documentation costs, allowance for lost production while resetting machines, idle time of operators, material spoiled in test runs, and time spent by specialist tool setters. This is also called a set-up cost.

Holding or Carrying Cost

This is the cost of holding one unit of an item in stock for a given period of time. It might, for example, be the cost of holding a spare engine in stock for a year. The obvious cost is the money tied up. This money is either borrowed—in which case interest is paid—or it is cash, which the organization could have put to other use—in which case there are opportunity costs. Other holding costs are due to storage space (supplying a warehouse, rent, heat, light, taxes, etc.), loss (due to damage, deterioration, obsolescence, and pilferage), handling (including special packaging, refrigeration, putting on pallets, etc.), administration (stock checks, computer updates, etc.), and insurance. Typical values for these, as annual percentages of unit cost, are:

	Percent of Unit Cost
Cost of money	10–20
Storage space	2–5
Loss	4–6
Handling	1–2
Administration	1–2
Insurance	1–5
Total	19–40

Shortage or Stockout Cost

This cost occurs when an item is needed to meet customer demand but cannot be supplied from stock. In the simplest case, a retailer may lose direct profit from a sale. But the effects of shortages are usually much more widespread and include lost good will, loss of reputation, and lost future sales. Shortages of raw materials for a production process can cause disruptions and force production to be rescheduled, maintenance periods to be changed, and employees to be laid off.

Shortage costs might also include payments for action to remedy the shortage, such as sending out emergency orders, paying for special deliveries, storing partly finished goods, or using alternative, more expensive suppliers. Shortage costs are usually difficult to determine, but there is general agreement that they can be very high.

Case Study

Sears Canada

Sears Canada is a leading Canadian retailer which prides itself on providing high-quality products, value, and service. Its 1992 Annual Report cited the following figures:

Total revenue	$ 3,958	million
Accounts receivable	$ 906	million
Inventories	$ 628	million
Total assets	$ 2,431	million
Number of retail stores	109	
Catalogue selling units	1,470	

Case Study

TSC Shannock Corporation

TSC Shannock is a fast-growing supplier of home entertainment goods, including video- and audiocassettes, compact and laser discs, and similar items. From its distribution centres in Vancouver, Calgary, and four other locations, it supplies to customers across Canada. Its 1991 Annual Report cited the following figures:

Sales	$34.7 million
Accounts receivable	$ 4.1 million
Inventory	$ 3.4 million
Total assets	$ 8.1 million

As you can see, these organizations hold large stocks. At Sears, the inventory accounts for 15 percent of revenue, and at TSC Shannock, it accounts for 10 percent. Manufacturers can have even higher inventories, and it is not unusual for these to be over 25 percent of sales.

Example

At the Standard Time Corporation, an order clerk earns $24,000 a year. She places an average of 100 orders each month. Her departmental budget for telephone, stationery, and postage is $9,600. Inspections of raw material cost $30 per order. The cost of borrowing money is 15 percent, the obsolescence rate is 5 percent, and insurance and property taxes average 3 percent. What are the re-order and holding costs for the company?

Solution

The total number of orders per year is 12 × 100 = 1,200 orders.

The re-order cost includes all costs that occur for an order. These are:

- Salary = $24,000/1,200 = $20 per order
- Expenses = $9,600/1,200 = $8 per order
- Inspection = $30 an order

Thus, the re-order cost is $20 + 8 + 30 = $58 per order.

Holding costs include all costs that occur for holding stock. These are:

- Borrowing = 15 percent
- Obsolescence = 5 percent
- Insurance and taxes = 3 percent

Thus, the holding cost is 23 percent of inventory value per year.

An important point to remember about inventory costs is that some rise with the amount of stock, and others fall. The holding cost will be higher when there is more stock, but the shortage cost will be lower. Inventory control must balance these competing costs and suggest policies that result in the lowest overall costs. To do this, it must answer three basic questions.

1. *What items should we stock?*

   No item, however inexpensive, should be stocked without considering the costs and benefits of holding the stock. An organization should make careful checks to ensure that unnecessary items are not added to inventory, and it should make regular searches to remove obsolete or "dead" stock.

2. *When should an order be placed?*

   This depends on the inventory control system used; the type of demand (high or low, steady or erratic, known exactly or estimated); value of the item; lead time between placing an order and receiving it into stock; and supplier reliability.

3. *How much should be ordered?*

   If frequent, small orders are placed, average stock levels are low, but the costs of placing and administering orders is high. If large, infrequent orders are placed, average stock levels are high, but the costs of placing and administering orders is low. This question is discussed in more detail in the following sections.

In Summary

Inventories are expensive, typically costing 25 percent of value per year. Their costs can be classified as unit, re-order, holding, or shortage. Organizations control their inventories to minimize the overall cost. They have to find what items to stock, when to place orders, and how much to order.

Review Questions

1. What are the four types of cost associated with inventories?
2. How do these costs vary with stock holdings?
3. What are the basic questions of inventory control systems?

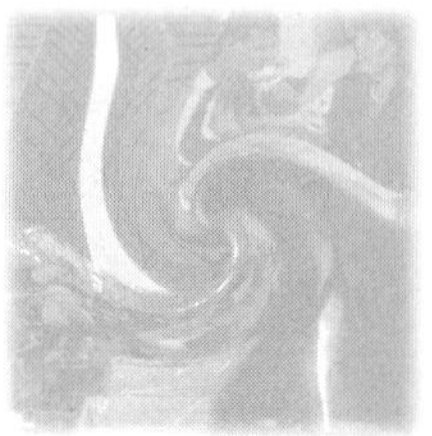

Economic Order Quantity

The **economic order quantity** (EOQ) is the basic analysis of **scientific inventory control**. First described in the 1920s, it finds the order quantity that minimizes total inventory costs. The results are widely used and form the basis of most inventory control systems.

For the basic model, we will assume a single item, where the demand is known to be constant at exactly D per unit time. Then the amount of stock falls at a uniform rate, as shown in Figure 17.3.

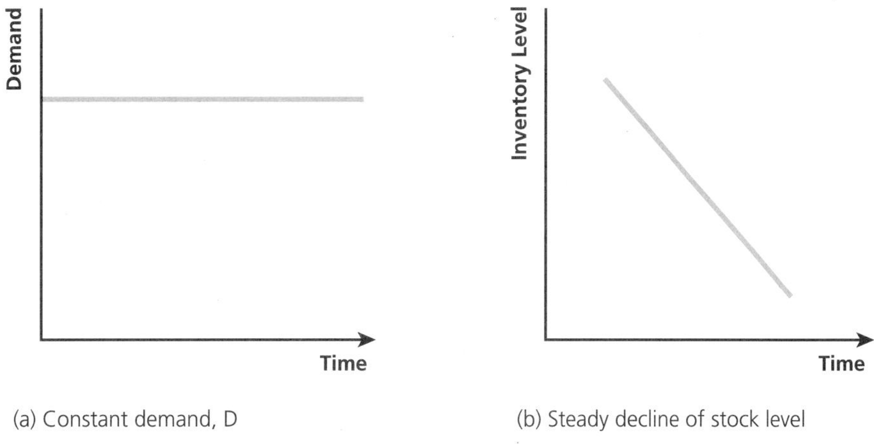

(a) Constant demand, D

(b) Steady decline of stock level

Figure 17.3 Demand and Stock Level for the Economic Order Quantity

The item is bought in batches from a supplier, and when an order arrives it is all available for use immediately. We assume that we know the unit cost (C_U), re-order cost (C_R), and holding cost (C_H), while the shortage cost (C_S) is so big that all demands must be met and no shortages are allowed.

We want to find the best order size, so that orders are always placed for the same quantity, Q. Then, as units are removed from stock to meet the demand, the stock level follows the saw-tooth pattern shown in Figure 17.4.

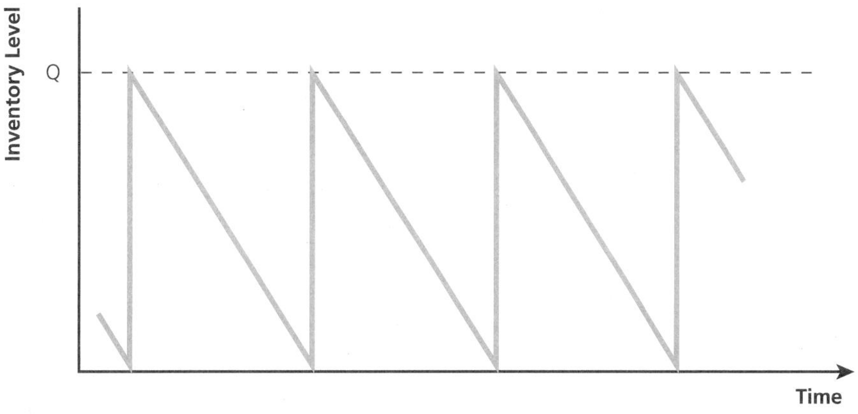

Figure 17.4 Pattern of Inventory Level

For this model, our overall approach is to find costs for a single stock cycle, then divide this by the cycle length to give a cost per unit time. Minimizing this cost per unit time gives an optimal order quantity.

Consider one cycle of the saw-tooth pattern shown in Figure 17.5.

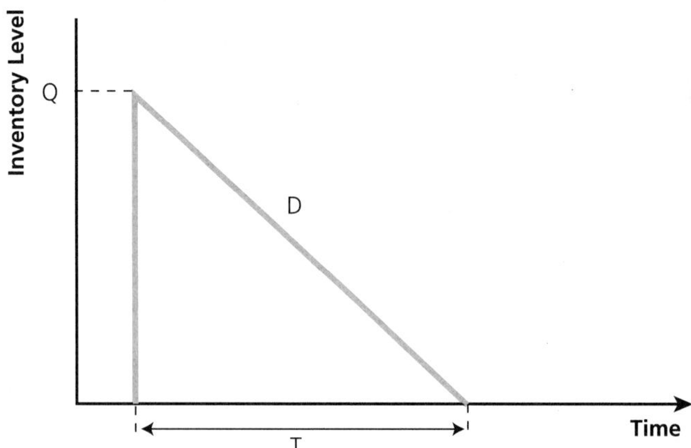

Figure 17.5 A Single Stock Cycle

At some point an order of size Q arrives. This is used at a constant rate, D, until no stock is left. The resulting stock cycle has length T. We know that in this single cycle:

Amount entering stock in the cycle = amount leaving stock in the cycle

$$Q = DT.$$

We also know that the stock level varies between Q and 0, so the average stock level is

$$(Q + 0)/2 = Q/2.$$

Example

The demand for an item is 10 units per week and regular orders are placed for 100 units. What are the stock cycle length and the average stock level?

Solution

We know that:

$Q = 100$ units

$D = 10$ units a week

We can find the stock cycle length from:

$Q = DT$, so $100 = 10 \times T$ or $T = 10$ weeks

The average stock level is:

Average stock = $Q/2 = 100/2 = 50$ units

We can find the total cost for the cycle by adding the three components of cost—unit, re-order, and holding—remembering that no shortages are allowed, so there are no shortage costs. We can save some effort here because the amount paid for the materials does not change with order size. If we buy 100 units a month, the total price paid is the same whether we buy in quantities of 10 or 100. This means that we really only need look at the total re-order cost and the total holding cost.

Total Cost for Cycle:

- Total re-order cost = number of orders (1) × re-order cost (CR)

  $= C_R$
- Total holding cost = average stock level(Q/2) × time held(T) × holding cost (C_H)

  $$= \frac{C_H QT}{2}$$

Adding these two gives the total cost per cycle as :

$$C_R + \frac{C_H QT}{2}$$

If we divide this by the cylce length, T, we get the total cost per unit time, C_T.

$$C_T = \frac{C_R}{T} + \frac{C_H Q}{2}$$

Then, substituting Q = DT, which we found above, gives :

$$C_T = \frac{C_R D}{Q} + \frac{C_H Q}{2}$$

We now have the cost per unit time. All we have to do is find a way of minimizing this. If we plot the two parts on the right of this equation separately against Q, we get the results shown in Figure 17.6.

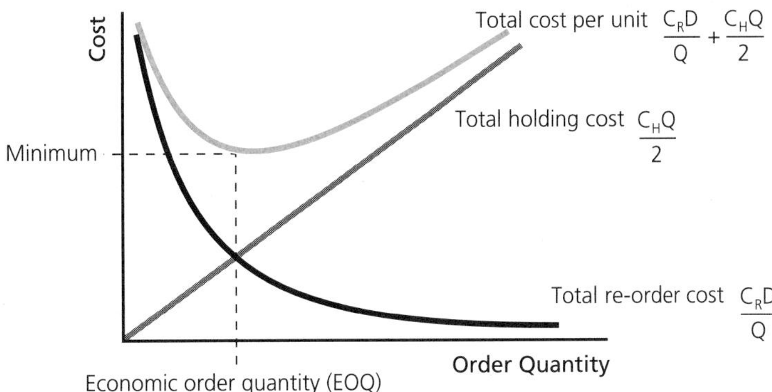

Figure 17.6 Variation of Costs with Order Quantity

This graph illustrates the following:

- The total holding cost, C_H Q/2, rises linearly with Q.
- The total re-order cost, C_R D/Q, falls as Q increases.
- Large infrequent orders (to the right of the graph) result in high total holding costs and low total re-order costs; small frequent orders (to the left of the graph) result in low total holding costs and high total re-order costs.
- Adding the two costs results in a total cost curve, which is an asymmetric "U" shape with a distinct minimum. This minimum corresponds to the optimal order size.

The example on page 481confirms the result of Figure 17.6, that there is an optimal order size that minimizes costs. This is the *economic order quantity,* EOQ. To find the value of EOQ, we differentiate the equation for the total cost with respect to Q, and set this to equal zero. (Do not worry if you cannot do this—we are really interested in the result, not how to get it!)

$$0 = -\frac{C_R D}{Q^2} + \frac{C_H}{2}$$

This can be rearranged to find the economic order quantity:

$$EOQ = \sqrt{\frac{2C_R D}{C_H}} = \text{Economic Order Quantity}$$

Looking at Bill Wong's problem in the example on page 481, C_R = \$16 an order, C_H = \$10 per unit per year, and D = 500 units per year, therefore:

$$EOQ = \sqrt{\frac{2C_R D}{C_H}} = \sqrt{\frac{2 \times 16 \times 500}{10}} = 40 \text{ units}$$

This confirms our previous results.

Example

Bill Wong buys office supplies for a B.C. lumber company. He buys 10 boxes of plain photocopying paper each week. A box costs $50 and the re-order cost is $16. The holding cost is 20 percent of the paper's value per year. Should Bill change his ordering pattern?

Solution

Bill should use the buying pattern that minimizes his total cost. Since the price of a box is fixed at $50 per box, Bill should minimize the total re-ordering and holding costs.

For the sake of simplicity, let us assume that there are 50 working weeks per year. Then the annual demand for paper, D, is 50 × 10 = 500 boxes. The re-order cost, C_R, is $16. The holding cost, C_H, is 20 percent of $50, or $10 per box per year. Now we can find the total costs for varying order sizes, as shown in the following table.

Order Quantity Q	Re-order Cost $C_R\ D/Q$	Holding Cost $C_H\ Q/2$	Total Cost
10	800	50	850
20	400	100	500
40	200	200	400
50	160	250	410
100	80	500	580

As you can see, this table shows that Bill Wong should order 40 boxes of paper at a time. This will reduce his total cost from $850 to $400 a year.

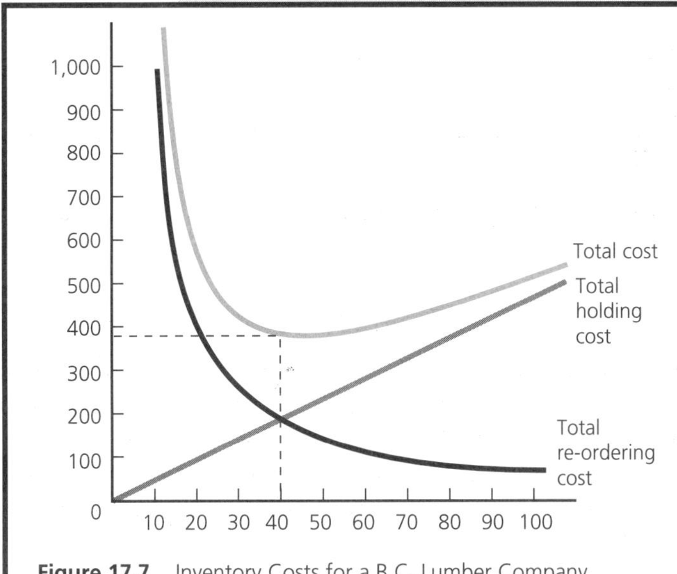

Figure 17.7 Inventory Costs for a B.C. Lumber Company

Example

The demand for an item is constant at 80 units per month. Unit cost is \$50, the cost of processing an order and arranging delivery is \$60, and the holding cost is \$18 per unit per year. What is the economic order quantity? What are the corresponding cycle length and costs?

Solution

List the known values, making sure the units are consistent:

$D = 80 \times 12 = 960$ units per year

$C_U = \$50$ per unit

$C_R = \$60$ per order

$C_H = \$18$ per unit per year

Then put these values into the equation for EOQ:

$$EOQ = \sqrt{\frac{2C_R D}{C_H}} = \sqrt{\frac{2 \times 60 \times 960}{18}} = 80 \text{ units}$$

Then find the cycle length, by seeing how long an order of 80 units will last. This comes from:

$Q = DT$, therefore $80 = 960 \times T$, or $T = 0.083$ years or 1 month.

The optimal policy is to order 80 units every month. The cost of this policy can be found from:

$$C_T = \frac{C_R D}{Q} + \frac{C_H Q}{2}$$

$$= \frac{60 \times 960}{80} + \frac{18 \times 80}{2} = 720 + 720 = \$1,440 \text{ per year}$$

There is also the fixed cost of buying the units $= C_U D = 50 \times 960 = \$48{,}000$ per year.

One problem with the economic order quantity is that it can give awkward order quantities. It might, for example, suggest buying 127.6 kg of cement, when cement is only available in 50 kg bags. The EOQ might suggest buying 88.39 tires. This could automatically be rounded to 88 tires, but a company might prefer to order 90 or even 100. We really need to know whether this rounding has much effect on overall costs.

We know that the EOQ gives the lowest cost. In practice, if we were to order quantities a bit away from EOQ the costs would rise, but only by a small amount. The amount ordered can increase to 156 percent of the EOQ, or can reduce to 64 percent, and only raise the inventory costs, C_T, by 10 percent. This is one reason the EOQ is so widely used. Although it makes a series of assumptions and approximations, the total cost rises slowly with small changes around the optimal.

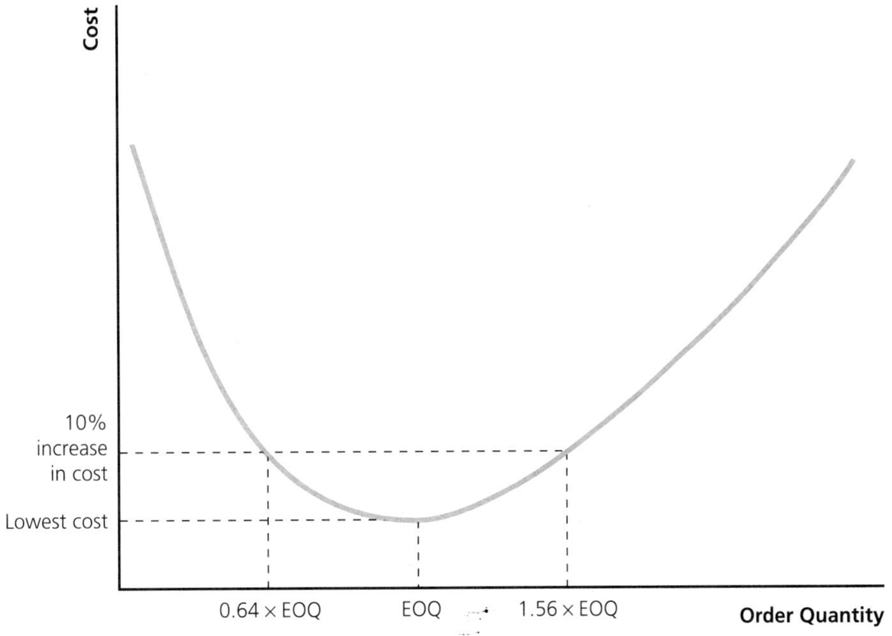

Figure 17.8 Small Increases in Cost Close to the EOQ

In Summary

The economic order quantity is the order size that minimizes inventory costs. The calculations are based on a number of assumptions, but the results are widely used. One reason for this use is that costs rise slowly around the economic order quantity.

Review Questions

1. What are the main assumptions when calculating the economic order quantity?
2. What exactly is the economic order quantity?
3. How does placing small, frequent orders (rather than large, infrequent ones) affect inventory costs?

Case Study – McTeague Electrical Engineering

McTeague Electrical Engineering (MEE) is a small electric-motor manufacturer with annual sales of $15 million. As John Smith, the inventory controller, entered his office one day, he noticed the monthly inventory report. He was anxious to read this as the company accountant had recently expressed some concern. Looking at the report, John found, to his surprise, that total inventory had jumped from $4.5 million to $5 million in the past month.

John noticed that there were very high stocks of part number RB101, a 3-cm diameter ball bearing. MEE used 10,000 of these last year, at a steady rate throughout the year. The ball bearings cost $10 per unit and John has been buying 2,500 units at a time. There were many such items in the report, and John realized that he had been ordering parts without any consideration of inventory costs.

John is studying for an Operations Management certificate at a community college and has recently come across the idea of the economic order quantity. Now he wondered if he could use this at MEE. He remembered that MEE's accountant had calculated the cost of inventory as 30 percent per year and the ordering costs were about $25 per order.

Questions

- Does MEE have problems with its inventories?
- What are the costs of inventory at MEE?
- What is the EOQ for part number RB101?
- What should John Smith do to reduce inventory costs?

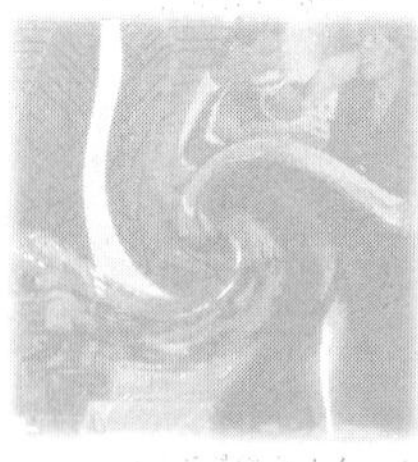

Re-order Level

The economic order quantity answers the question of how much to order, but it still leaves the question of *when* to place an order. This can be determined from the **re-order level**.

When buying goods, there is a **lead time** between placing the order and the goods arriving in stock. This is the time taken for an organization to prepare an order and send it to the supplier, for the supplier to assemble the goods and prepare them for shipment, to ship the goods back to the customer, and for the customer to receive and check the goods, and to put them into stock. Depending on circumstances, this lead time can vary from a few days to months.

Figure 17.4 showed an inventory level, rising when a delivery is made and falling slowly back to zero to meet demand. Suppose the lead time for an item is constant at L. To make sure a delivery arrives just as stock is running out, an order must be placed a time L earlier. The easiest way of finding this point is to look at the stock on hand and place an order when there is just enough left to last the lead time. This means that with a demand, D, an order must be placed when the stock level falls to LD. This point is called the *re-order level.*

Re-order level = lead time demand

Re-order level = L × D = LD

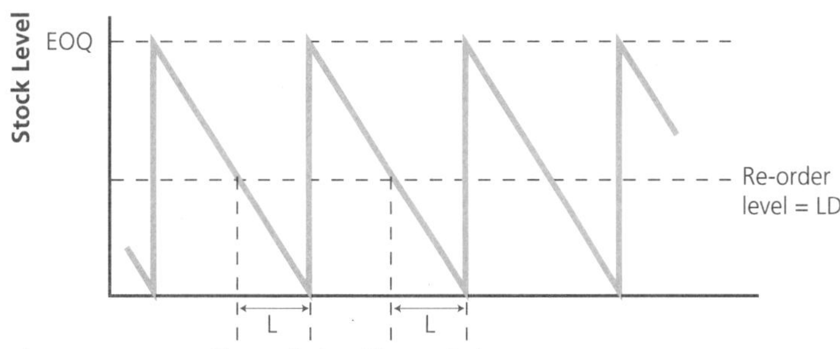

Figure 17.9
Orders Are Placed When Stock Falls to the Re-order Level

One way to find when stock falls to the re-order level is to keep a continuous record of the stock level. This has traditionally been done using stock cards of the type shown in Figure 17.10, but is now almost always computerized. The computer keeps a record of all transactions and signals when it is time to place an order.

STOCK RECORD	
Description:	Maximum stock:
Location:	Minimum stock:
Item Number:	Re-order Level:
Unit of Issue:	Re-order Quantity:
Comments:	

RECEIVED:			ISSUED:			BALANCE
Date	Order Number	Quantity	Date	Requisition Number	Quantity	

Figure 17.10 Typical Stock Record Card

Sometimes, it is easier to use a simple **two-bin system** to see when stock falls to the re-order level. In this system, stock is kept in two bins, one of which holds the re-order level, while the second holds all remaining stock. Demand is met from the second bin until it is empty. At this point the stock level has fallen to the re-order level and it is time to place an order. When an order arrives, the first bin is filled to the re-order level, and all the rest of the delivery is put in the second bin.

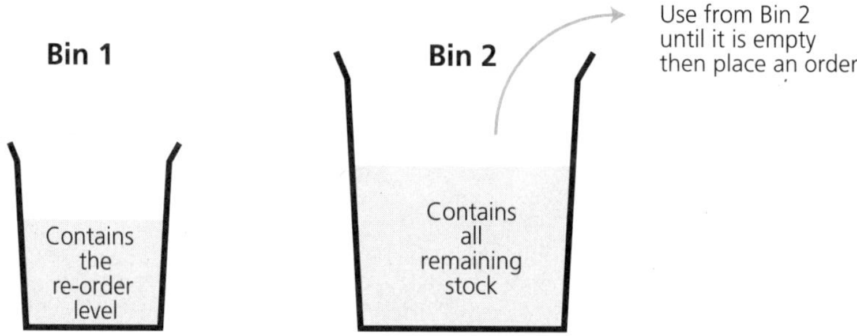

Figure 17.11 A Two-bin System

Example

Demand for an item is constant at 20 units per week, the re-order cost is $125, and the holding cost is $2 per unit per week. If suppliers guarantee delivery within 2 weeks, what would be the best ordering policy for the item?

Solution

Listing the variables in consistent units:

D = 20 units per week
C_R = $125 per order
C_H = $2 per unit per week
L = 2 weeks

We can substitute these values to find the optimal order size, EOQ:

$$EOQ = \sqrt{\frac{2C_RD}{C_H}} = \sqrt{\frac{2 \times 125 \times 20}{2}} = 50 \text{ units}$$

The re-order level is found by:

Re-order level = LD = 2×20 = 40 units

The best policy is to place an order for 50 units whenever stock declines to 40 units.

The calculation shown works well when the lead time is less than the length of a stock cycle. In the last example, the lead time was 2 weeks and the stock cycle was 2.5 weeks. Suppose the lead time is raised to 3 weeks. The calculation for re-order level then becomes:

$$\text{Re-order level} = LD = 3 \times 20 = 60 \text{ units}$$

The problem with this is that the stock level never actually rises to 60 units, but varies between 0 and 50 units.

A way around this problem is to recognize that the calculated re-order level refers to both stock on hand and stock on order. Then the re-order level equals lead time demand minus any stock that is already on order.

$$\text{Re-order level} = \text{lead time demand} - \text{stock on order}$$

In the previous example, the order quantity is 50 units, so a lead time of 3 weeks would have one order of 50 units outstanding when it is time to place another order. Then:

$$\text{Re-order level} = 3 \times 20 - 50 = 10 \text{ units}$$

An order for 50 units should be placed whenever actual stock declines to 10 units.

In Summary

The time to place an order is found from the re-order level. This is the point where there is just enough stock left to last through the lead time. For constant lead time and demand, the re-order level equals lead time demand minus any stock on order.

Review Questions

1. What exactly is the re-order level?
2. How is the re-order level calculated?

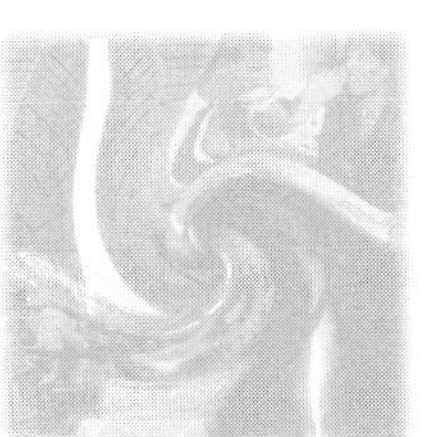

Economic Production Batch Size

There are many extensions to the basic EOQ model. This section considers one of these which is used in production systems—it calculates an economic production batch size by adding a finite production rate. If an item is manufactured at a steady rate of 10 units per hour, the output will pass into stocks of finished goods at this rate.

Assuming that none are used, the stocks will rise steadily by 10 units per hour. The basic EOQ model assumes large batches arrive at one time, but this model can be adjusted by allowing units to move into stock at a finite rate, P. This is shown in Figure 17.12.

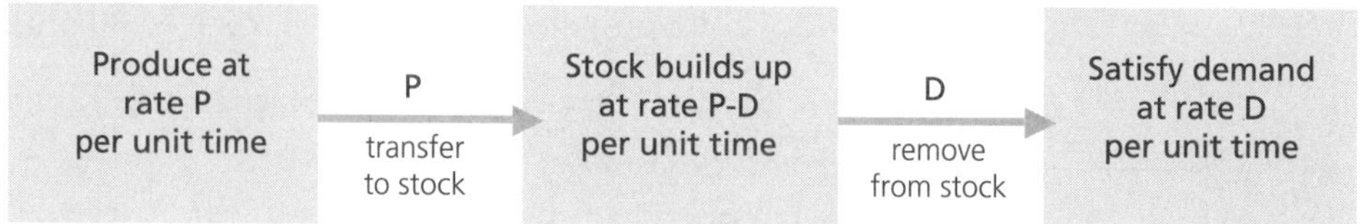

Figure 17.12 Stock Movements with a Finite Production Rate

If the rate of production is less than the rate of demand—so that P is less than D—there is no problem with stock holding. Supply is not keeping up with demand; as soon as a unit is made it is sent straight out to customers. Inventory problems only arise when the rate of production is higher than the demand—so P is greater than D. Then stock builds up at a rate of P - D for as long as production continues.

Production is stopped when a large enough batch of the item has been made, and the process is changed to work on other products. When production is stopped, demand from customers continues at a rate D, and is met from the accumulated stock. At some point, the stock runs out and production must restart. The resulting stock level is shown in Figure 17.13.

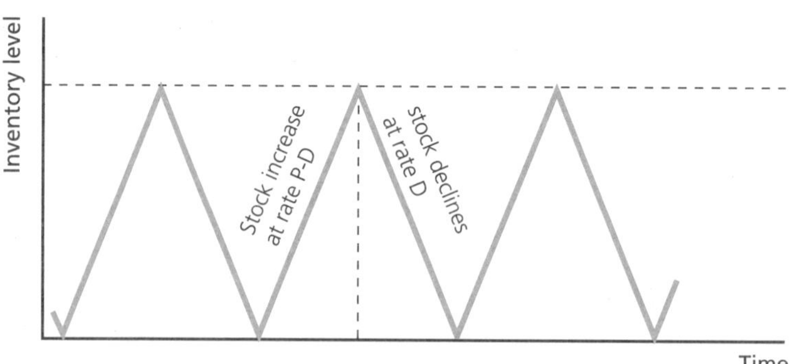

Figure 17.13 Inventory Level with a Finite Production Rate

Again, we want to find an optimal batch size. The method is very similar to the basic EOQ, and involves finding the total cost for a single stock cycle, dividing this by the cycle length to find a cost per unit time, and then minimizing this cost. If we repeated these calculations, the only difference would be a factor (P - D)/P. We shall not bother repeating the arithmetic, but will simply quote the result.

$$\text{Economic production lot size } Q = \sqrt{\frac{2C_R D}{C_H}} \times \sqrt{\frac{P_r}{P - D}}$$

Again there is a compromise between large, infrequent batches—which result in high holding costs but low set-up costs—and small frequent batches—which result in low holding costs but high set-up costs.

Example

Demand for an item is 600 units per month. Costs have been estimated as:

- Unit production cost of \$40 per unit
- Production set-up cost of \$128 per order
- Shop order preparation of \$100 per order
- Scheduling of shop order at \$22 per order
- Insurance of 1 percent of unit cost per year
- Obsolescence, deterioration, and depreciation allowance of 2 percent of unit cost per year
- Capital costs of 20 percent of unit cost per year
- Storage space at \$10 per unit per year
- Handling costs of \$12 per unit per year
- Shortage costs are so large that no shortages are allowed

The rate of production is 1,200 units per month. What is the optimal batch size?

Solution

Some figures are known:

$$D = 600 \times 12 = 7{,}200 \text{ units per year}$$
$$P = 1{,}200 \times 12 = 14{,}400 \text{ units per year}$$
$$C_U = \$40 \text{ per unit}$$

Now we need to look at the costs. Every cost must be classified as unit, re-order, or holding, as no shortages are allowed. Combining all costs that come from an order results in:

$$C_R = 128 + 100 + 22 = \$250 \text{ per order}$$

There are two types of holding costs:

1. a percentage (1 percent, 2 percent, and 20 percent) of unit cost; and
2. a fixed amount (\$10 + \$12) per unit per year.

Then, $C_H = (10 + 12) + (0.01 + 0.02 + 0.2) \times 40 = \$31.20$ per unit per year

Now we can substitute these values in the equation to find the optimal production quantity:

$$Q = \sqrt{\frac{2C_RD}{C_H}} \times \sqrt{\frac{P}{P-D}} \times \sqrt{\frac{2 \times 250 \times 7{,}200}{31.20}} \times \sqrt{\frac{14{,}400}{14{,}400 - 7{,}200}}$$
$$= 480 \text{ units}$$

In Summary

The EOQ model can be extended in many ways. One extension is used in production systems. This calculates an economic production batch size by adding a finite production rate. This adds a factor $\sqrt{P/(P - D)}$ to the EOQ.

Review Questions

1. Are inventories more difficult to control when
   a) production rate is greater than demand, or b) production rate is less than demand?
2. When compared with the EOQ, does a finite production rate lead to
   a) larger batches, b) smaller batches, or c) same size batches?

Uncertain Demand and Safety Stock

The models described so far assume that demand is constant. In practice, demand can vary widely, with much uncertainty. A company producing a new CD, for example, does not know in advance how many copies will sell, or how sales will vary over time. When the variation is small, the basic EOQ model still gives useful results. But results are not as good when the demand varies more widely; then another approach must be used.

We shall look at one approach where demand is Normally distributed. (There is a short review of the Normal distribution in Appendix A.) When demand is Normally distributed, you can easily see why assuming that it is constant will provide poor results. The re-order level is the mean lead time demand, LD. When demand in the lead time is greater than average, stock will run out and there will be shortages. Unfortunately, when demand is Normally distributed, the lead time demand is above the average in 50 percent of cycles, as shown in Figure 17.14. This means that 50 percent of stock cycles will have shortages. This clearly results in a very poor level of performance.

An alternative approach for variable demand balances shortage costs and holding costs. It is difficult to find accurate costs for shortages, but they are usually high in comparison to holding costs. This means that organizations are willing to hold additional stocks, above their forecast needs, to add a margin of safety. These **safety stocks** are available if all the normal working stock has been used.

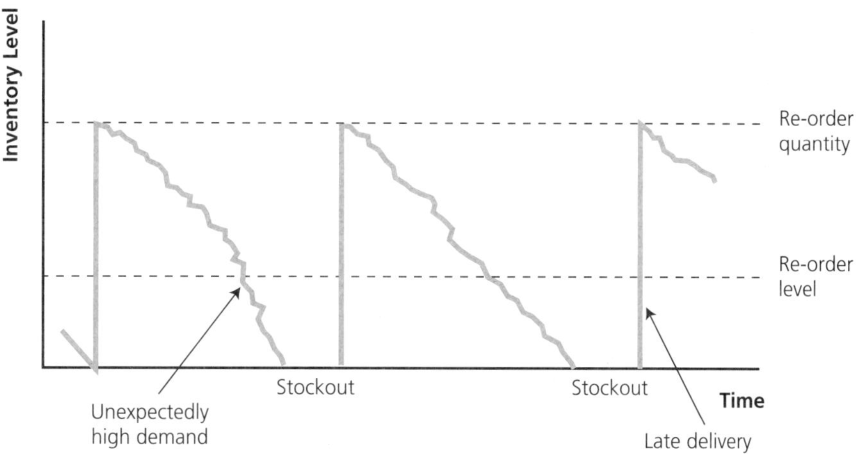

(a) Unexpectedly high demand or late deliveries gives stockouts

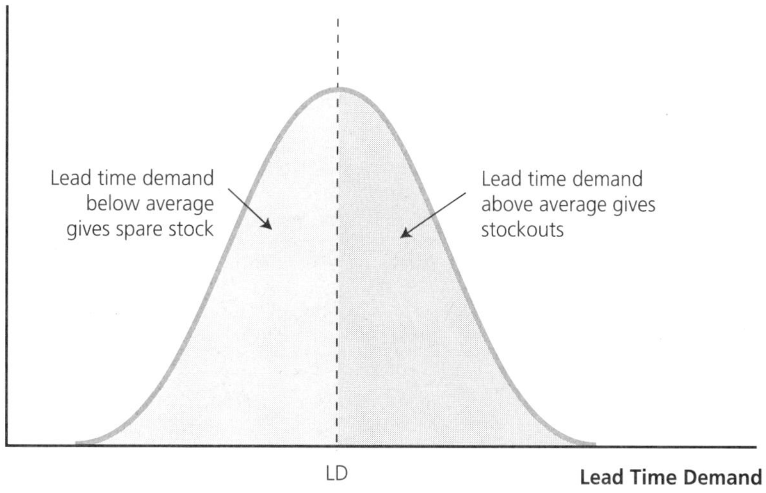

(b) Normal distribution of lead time demand

Figure 17.14 Without Safety Stock, Normally Distributed Demand Gives Stockouts in 50% of Stock Cycles

Suppose a computer supplier sells an average of 10 machines per week, and places an order for 20 machines every two weeks. With our previous analyses, we would assume that the stocks of computers will decline to zero at the end of the second week, and at this point a new delivery will arrive. But the supplier may keep an extra five units as a safety stock. Then with the expected demand, these units will not be used. But if there is a sudden increase in demand, it can be met from the safety stock.

The safety stock has no effect on the re-order quantity, which is still defined by the EOQ. But it does affect the time an order is placed. In particular, the re-order level is raised by the amount of the safety stock.

$$\text{Re-order level} = \text{lead time demand} + \text{safety stock}$$

$$\text{Re-order level} = LD + \text{safety stock}$$

Of course, the larger the safety stock, the greater the cushion against unexpectedly high demand, and the greater the level of customer service. But the costs of holding larger stocks are also higher. The question to ask now is, How much safety stock should we hold?

To answer this question, we must define a **service level**. This determines the probability that a demand will be met directly from stock. An organization will typically provide a service level of 95 percent, which means that it meets 95 percent of orders from stock—and accepts that 5 percent of orders cannot be met from stock. The service level must be set by managers, based on their experience and knowledge of customer expectations.

Suppose that demand for an item is Normally distributed with a mean of D per unit time and standard deviation of σ. If the lead time is constant at L, the lead time demand is Normally distributed with mean of LD, as before. However, this time there is a known variance of $\sigma^2 L$ and standard deviation of $\sigma\sqrt{L}$. This results from the fact that variances can be added but standard deviations cannot.

If • demand in a single period has mean D and variance σ^2,

then • demand in two periods has mean 2D and variance $2\sigma^2$;

• demand in three periods has mean 3D and variance $3\sigma^2$, etc.

so that • demand in L periods has mean LD and variance $L\sigma^2$.

The size of the safety stock depends on the service level. If an organization has a high service level, the safety stock must also be high. To be specific, when lead time demand is Normally distributed, the calculation of safety stock becomes:

$$\text{Safety stock} = Z \times \text{standard deviation of lead time demand} = Z\sigma^2\sqrt{L}$$

Here, Z is the number of standard deviations away from the mean. Some specific values of Z and the corresponding service level are:

- $Z = 1$ gives a service level of 84.1 percent
- $Z = 1.64$ gives a service level of 95 percent
- $Z = 1.88$ gives a service level of 97 percent
- $Z = 2$ gives a service level of 97.7 percent
- $Z = 3$ gives a service level of 99.9 percent

The effects of safety stocks are shown in Figure 17.15.

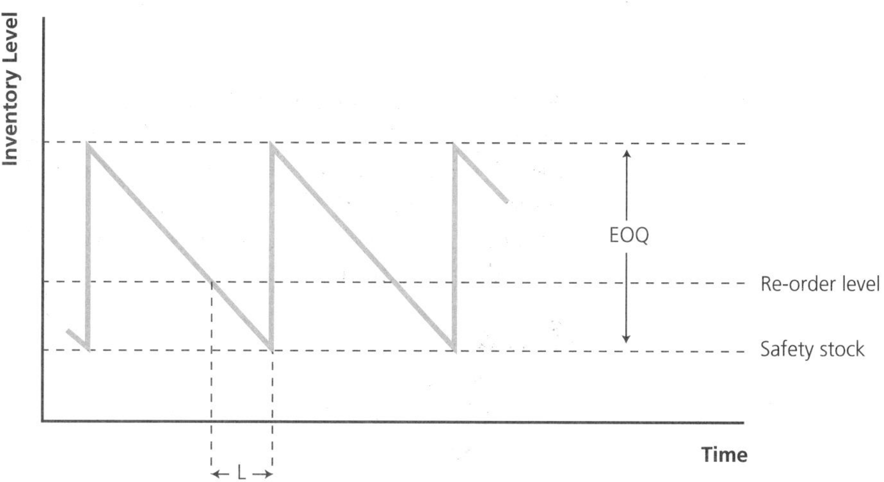

(a) Stock cycles with safety stock

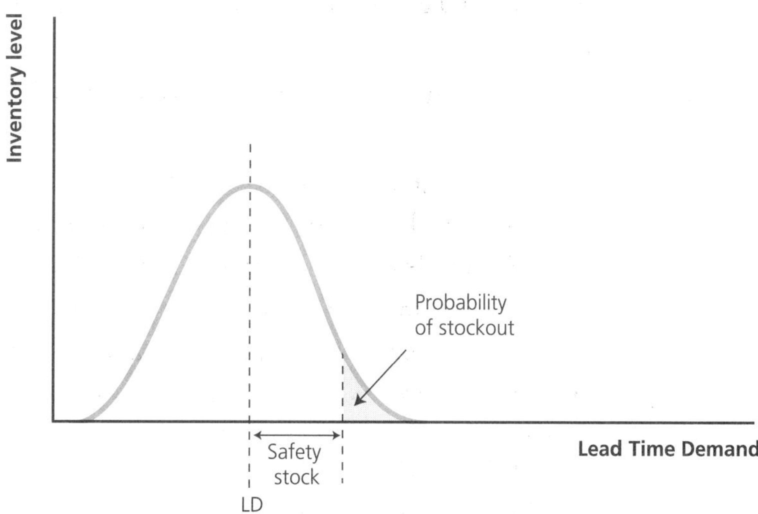

(b) Probability of stockout with safety stock

Figure 17.15 Effects of Adding a Safety Stock

If demand varies widely, the standard deviation of lead time demand will be high, which means that very high safety stocks are needed to provide a service level close to 100 percent. This can be too expensive and companies will usually set a lower level, typically around 95 percent. Sometimes it is useful to give items different service levels depending on their importance. Very important items may be given levels close to 100 percent, while less important ones are set around 85 percent.

Example

Demand for an item is Normally distributed with a mean of 150 units per week and a standard deviation of 30 units. The re-order cost includes transport and is $600, holding cost is $20 per unit per year, and lead time is fixed at 3 weeks. Describe an ordering policy that will give a 95 percent service level. What is the cost of holding the safety stock? How much will the costs rise if the service level is raised to 97 percent?

Solution

The values given are:

$D = 150 \times 52 = 7{,}800$ units per year

$\sigma = 30$ units

$C_R = \$600$ per order

$C_H = \$20$ per unit per year

$L = 3$ weeks

- The EOQ can be found from the usual equation:

$$EOQ = \sqrt{\frac{2C_R D}{C_H}} = \sqrt{\frac{2 \times 600 \times 7800}{20}} = 684 \text{ units}$$

- The re-order level is found from:

  Re-order level = lead time demand + safety stock

  Re-order level = LD + safety stock = 3×150 + safety stock = 450 + safety stock

- The safety stock depends on the service level:

  Safety stock = $Z \times$ standard deviation of lead time demand $= Z\sigma\sqrt{L}$

- For a 95 percent service level, $Z = 1.64$ standard deviations from the mean. Then:

  Safety stock $= Z\sigma\sqrt{L} = 1.64 \times 30 \times \sqrt{3} = 85$ units (to the nearest integer)

- The best policy is to order 684 units whenever stock falls to 450 + 85 = 535 units. On average, orders should arrive when there are 85 units remaining.
- The safety stock is not usually used, so its cost is simply:

  Cost of safety stock = safety stock × holding cost = 85×20 = $1,700 per year

- If the service level is raised to 97 percent, Z becomes 1.88, and:

  Safety stock $= Z\sigma\sqrt{L} = 1.88 \times 30 \times \sqrt{3} = 98$ units, so that

  Re-order level = LD + safety stock = 450 + 98 = 548 units

This means that 684 units are ordered when stock falls to 548 units. The cost of holding the safety stock is:

Cost of safety stock = safety stock × holding cost = 98×20 = $1,960 per year

In Summary

When there is variation in demand, the basic EOQ models do not give reliable results. When the lead time demand is Normally distributed, an alternative approach should be used. This uses the same re-order quantity, but adds a safety stock to give a higher service level. The safety stock increases stock holdings, and is related to the variation in demand.

Review Questions

1. Define service level.
2. What is the purpose of safety stock?
3. How might the service level be increased?

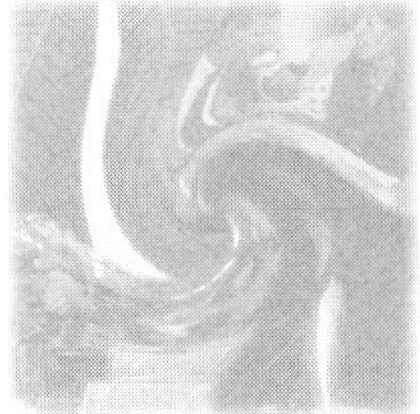

Periodic Review Systems

Thus far the models described for inventory control are **fixed order quantity systems.** These place an order of fixed size whenever stock falls to a certain level. An alternative is called a **periodic review system**. This places orders of varying size at regular intervals to raise the stock to a given level.

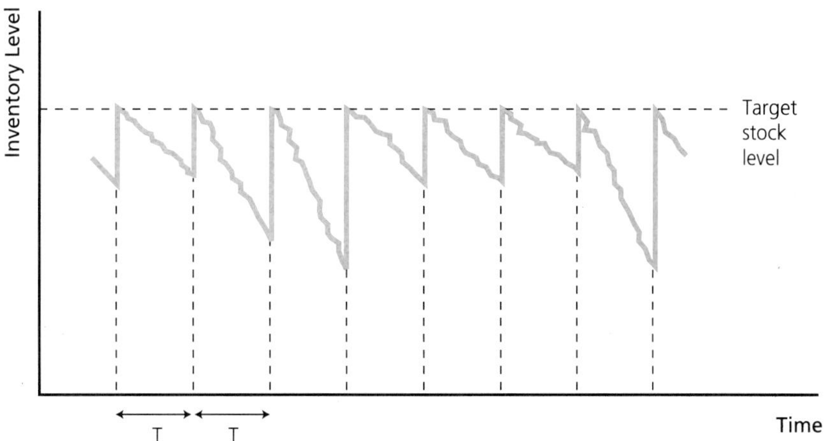

Figure 17.16 Inventory Level with a Periodic Review System

If the demand is constant, these two systems are the same. Differences only appear when demand varies. The last analysis can be extended to look at a periodic review system where demand is Normally distributed. Then there are two basic questions:

1. How long should be the interval between orders?
2. What should be the target stock level?

The order interval, T, can be any convenient period. It might, for example, be easiest to place an order every morning, at the end of each week, or at the end of each month. If there is no obvious cycle, the aim might be for a certain number of orders per year or some average order size. One approach would be to calculate an economic order quantity, and then find the period that gave orders of about this size. The final decision must be a matter for management judgement.

Whatever interval is chosen, a **target stock level** must be found. The system works by looking at the amount of stock on hand when an order is placed, and ordering the amount that would bring this up to the target stock level.

For a periodic review system:

Order quantity = target stock level - stock on hand

Suppose the lead time is constant at L. When an order is placed, the stock on hand plus this order must be enough to last until the next order arrives, which is T + L away (as shown in Figure 17.17).

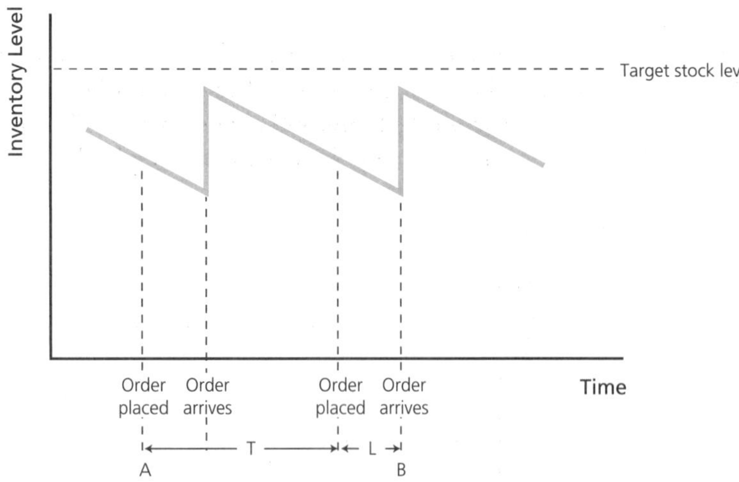

Figure 17.17 An Order Placed at Time A Must Cover All Demand Up to Time B

The target stock level must be high enough to cover mean demand over this period, so it must be at least D(T + L). As demand is Normally distributed, some safety stock is needed to allow for the 50 percent of cycles when demand is above average. Assuming that both the cycle length and lead time are constant, the demand over T + L is Normally distributed with mean of D(T + L), variance of σ^2(T + L) and standard deviation of $\sigma\sqrt{(T + L)}$. A safety stock can then be defined as:

$$\text{Safety stock} = Z \times \text{standard deviation of demand over } (T + L) = Z\sigma\sqrt{(T + L)},$$

$$\text{Then, target stock level} = \text{demand over } (T + L) + \text{safety stock}$$

$$= D(T + L) + Z\sigma\sqrt{(T + L)}$$

Example

Demand for an item has a mean of 200 units per week and standard deviation of 40 units. Stock is checked every four weeks, and the lead time is constant at two weeks. Describe a policy that will give a 95 percent service level. If the holding cost is $2 per unit per week, what is the cost of the safety stock with this policy? What would be the effect of a 98 percent service level?

Solution

The variables given are:

D = 200 units
σ = 40 units
H_C = $2 per unit per week
T = 4 weeks
L = 2 weeks

For a 95 percent safety stock, Z is 1.64. Then:

Safety stock = $Z\sigma\sqrt{(T + L)} = 1.64 \times 40 \times \sqrt{6} = 161$ (to the nearest integer)

Target stock level = $D(T + L)$ + safety stock = $200 \times (6) + 161 = 1{,}361$.

When it is time to place an order, the policy is to find the stock on hand, and place an order for:

Order size = 1,361 – stock on hand.

If, for example, there were 200 units in stock the order would be for 1,161 units.

The cost of holding the safety stock is 161×2 = $322 per week.

If the service level is increased to 98 percent, Z = 2.05, and

Safety stock = $2.05 \times 40 \times \sqrt{6} = 201$.

The target stock level is then 1,401 units and the cost of the safety stock is 201×2 = $402 per week.

Review Questions

1. How is the order size calculated for a periodic review system?
2. Will the safety stock be higher for a fixed order quantity system or a periodic review system?

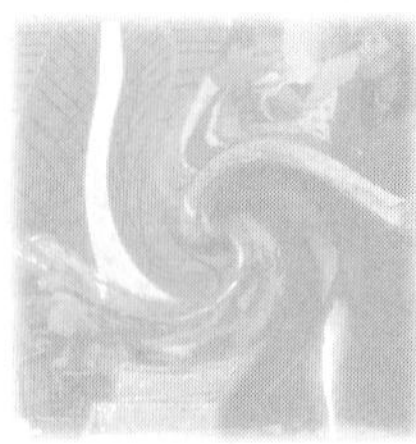

ABC Analysis of Inventories

Controlling inventories can involve a great deal of effort. A typical inventory consists of thousands of items, so even finding the EOQs requires a lot of calculations. Almost all inventory control is done by computer, but it still requires human effort to input data, check values, update supplier details, and confirm orders. For some items, especially inexpensive ones, this effort is not worthwhile. Very few organizations, for example, include routine office supplies in their computerized inventory control.

At the other end of the scale are very expensive items that need special care above the routine calculations. An aircraft engine, for example, can cost several million dollars, so airlines look very carefully at their stocks of spare engines.

An **ABC analysis** puts items into categories which show the amount of effort worth spending on inventory control. This kind of analysis is sometimes called a **Pareto analysis** or the "rule of 80/20." This suggests that 20 percent of inventory items need 80 percent of the attention, while the remaining 80 percent of items need only 20 percent of the attention. ABC analyses define:

- A items as expensive or have high special care $ usage and need
- B items as ordinary ones needing standard care
- C items as inexpensive or have low $ usage and need little care

Typically an organization might use an automated system to deal with all B items. The computer system might make some suggestions for A items, but final decisions are made by managers. C items are the inexpensive ones that are left out of the automatic system or are controlled very informally.

Table 17.2 *ABC Analysis*

A Items	B Items	C Items
Require tight control	Require moderate control	Require little control
Require accurate records of use	Have reasonable records of use	Have few checks on use
Review all changes in demand	Review major changes in demand	Need few reviews
Frequently need expediting	Occasionally need expediting	Little or no expediting
Low or no safety stock	Moderate safety stock	Large safety stock
Aim for fast turnover of inventory	Slower turnover of inventory	Slow turnover

An ABC analysis begins with calculating the total annual use of each item, in terms of $ value. This is found by multiplying the number of units used in a year by the unit cost. Usually, a few expensive items account for a lot of use, while many inexpensive ones account for little use. Then, the items are listed in order of decreasing annual use by $ value. A items are at the top of this list, B items are in the middle, and C items are at the bottom. For example:

Category	% of Items	Cumulative % of Items	% of Use by $ Value	Cumulative % of Use by $ Value
A	10	10	70	70
B	30	40	20	90
C	60	100	10	100

Plotting the cumulative percentage of use by value against the cumulative percentage of items gives a graph with the shape shown in Figure 17.18.

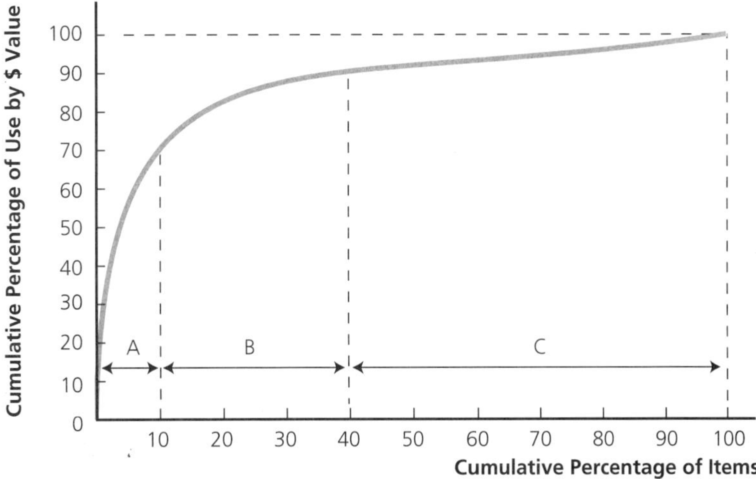

Figure 17.18 ABC Analysis of Inventories

Example

A small store has ten types of item with the following costs and annual demands.

Item	P1	P2	P3	P4	P5	P6	P7	P8	P9	P0
Unit Cost ($)	20	10	20	50	10	50	5	20	100	1
Annual Demand ('00s)	2.5	50	20	66	15	6	10	5	1	50

Do an ABC analysis of these items. If resources for inventory control are limited, which items should be given the least attention?

Solution

The annual use of P1 in terms of value is 20 × 250 = $5,000. As there are ten items, each item accounts for 10 percent of the total. If these calculations are repeated for the other items, the following are the results.

Item	P1	P2	P3	P4	P5	P6	P7	P8	P9	P0
% of Items	10	10	10	10	10	10	10	10	10	10
Annual Use ($'000s)	5	50	40	330	15	30	5	10	10	5

When the items are sorted in order of decreasing annual use, the results are as follows.

Item	P4	P2	P3	P6	P5	P8	P9	P1	P7	P0
Cumulative % of Items	10	20	30	40	50	60	70	80	90	100
Annual Use ($'000s)	330	50	40	30	15	10	10	5	5	5
Cumulative Annual Use	330	380	420	450	465	475	485	490	495	500
Cumulative % Annual Use	66	76	84	90	93	95	97	98	99	100

Category <A><——B——><————C————>

The boundaries between different categories are sometimes unclear, but in this case P4 is clearly an A item; P2, P3, and P6 are B items; and the rest are C items. The C items account for only 10 percent of annual use by value. If resources are limited, these should be given the least attention.

In Summary

ABC analyses categorized items according to their importance. This allows available resources to be sensibly shared out. Typically, 20 percent of items account for 80 percent of use by $ value (A items), while the bulk of items account for very little use (C items).

Case Study – Peterson Pulley Inc.

Peterson Pulley Inc. is a small job shop with a good reputation for quality and service. The company started making belt pulleys, but now makes precision machine parts, particularly different types of gears.

Tom Peterson, the founder and president, takes a keen interest in operations. He is very conscious of inventory levels, and often comments that, "In our business it is dangerous to keep inventory. We make quality precision parts according to customers' specifications—so we should only buy the raw materials after we receive an order." At the same time, if a supplier gives a good price discount, Tom does not hesitate to buy large quantities. Often these materials are discontinued or obsolete, with little future demand.

Business is booming for Peterson Pulley, and it has recently won a large contract from a national hardware chain. But customer service has been getting worse and lead times are getting longer. Ravi Tandon, the production manager, is worried by these poor results.

At present, the company receives orders and processes them to find the materials needed. Then it orders these materials, which arrive 2 to 5 weeks later. Customers often make changes to specifications after the materials have been ordered. This creates a lot of problems for Ravi. He often has to shut down operations or change production because he does not have the materials to deal with changes.

Ravi told Tom that customer service could be improved, lead times shortened, and inventory reduced, if they use ABC analyses. Tom looked puzzled and asked Ravi to prepare a report. Ravi collected the following information about 20 raw materials.

Material Type	Last Year's Usage ($000)
MA	26
MB	58
MC	8
MD	130
ME	38
MF	14
MG	42
MH	19
MI	90
MJ	52
all other	62

Questions

- What are some of the problems facing Peterson Pulley Inc.?
- What should Ravi's proposal to Tom contain?
- What average level of inventory do you think the company should carry?

Review Questions

1. What is the purpose of doing ABC analyses of inventories?
2. Which items can best be dealt with by routine, automated control procedures?

Chapter Review

- The main purpose of inventories is to provide a buffer between supply and demand. There are often uncertainties in both supply and demand, and stocks are the only way of allowing operations to continue smoothly.
- There are many kinds of stock including finished goods, raw materials, work-in-process, spare parts, and consumables. These stocks have associated costs that can be very high.
- Inventory control systems try to minimize costs by answering three fundamental questions: what to stock, when to place orders, and how much to order.
- The economic order quantity is the order size that minimizes inventory costs for a simple system. The re-order level shows when it is time to place an order.
- The EOQ model can be extended in many ways. One extension adds a finite replenishment rate for production systems.
- If demand varies widely, another approach should be used. This may use a safety stock to set a customer service level. This is useful when, say, demand is Normally distributed.
- A different approach to inventory control uses a periodic review system, where orders are placed at regular intervals.
- ABC analyses show the effort worth spending to control different types of items.

Key Terms

ABC analysis *(p. 498)*
economic order quantity (EOQ) *(p. 476)*
finished goods *(p. 469)*
fixed order quantity system *(p. 495)*
holding costs *(p. 473)*
inventories *(p. 469)*
lead time *(p. 484)*
maintenance, repair, and operating supplies (MRO) *(p. 470)*
Pareto analysis *(p. 498)*
periodic review system *(p. 495)*
raw materials *(p. 469)*
re-order cost *(p. 472)*
re-order level *(p. 484)*
safety stock *(p. 490)*
scientific inventory control *(p. 476)*
service level *(p. 492)*
shortage cost *(p. 473)*
stock holdings *(p. 492)*
stocks *(p. 469)*
target stock level *(p. 496)*
two-bin system *(p. 486)*
unit cost *(p. 472)*
work-in-process *(p. 469)*

Problems

17.1 The demand for an item is constant at 100 units per year. Unit cost is $50, the cost of processing an order is $20, and the holding cost is $10 per unit per year. What are the economic order quantity, cycle length, and costs?

17.2 A company works 50 weeks per year and has demand for an item which is constant at 100 units per week. The cost of each unit is $20, and the company aims for a return of 20 percent on capital invested. Annual warehouse costs are 5 percent of the value of goods stored. The purchasing department of the company costs $45,000 per year and sends out an average of 2,000 orders. Find the optimal order quantity for the item, the time between orders, and the cost of stocking the item.

17.3 Demand for an item is steady at 20 units per week and the economic order quantity has been calculated at 50 units. What is the re-order level when the lead time is:

a) 1 week, b) 3 weeks, c) 5 weeks?

17.4 How would the results for Problem 17.1 change if the item could only be supplied at a finite rate of 10 units per week?

17.5 A manufacturer forecasts its demand for components to average 18 per day over a 200-day working year. If there are any shortages, production will be disrupted at a very high cost. The holding cost for the component is $40 per unit per year and the cost of placing an order is $80. Find the economic order quantity and the optimal number of orders per year. What is the effect on the inventory system if the components are made internally and can only be supplied at a finite rate of 80 units per day?

17.6 A company advertises a 95 percent cycle-service level for all stock items. Stock is replenished from a single supplier who guarantees a lead time of 4 weeks. What re-order level should the company use for an item that has a Normally distributed demand with mean 1,000 units per week and standard deviation of 100 units? What would the re-order level be if a 98 percent service level is used?

17.7 An item of inventory has a unit cost of $40, re-order cost of $50, and holding cost of $1 per unit per week. Demand for the item has a mean of 100 per week with standard deviation of 10. Lead time is constant at 3 weeks. Design an inventory policy for the item to provide a service level of 95 percent. How would this be changed to achieve a 90 percent service level? What are the costs of these two policies?

17.8 Describe a periodic review system with an interval of two weeks for the company in Problem 17.7.

17.9 A small store consists of ten categories of product with the following costs and annual demands:

Product	X1	X2	X3	Y1	Y2	Y3	Z1	Z2	Z3	Z4
Unit Cost ($s)	20	25	30	1	4	6	10	15	20	22
Annual Demand ('00s)	3	2	2	10	8	7	30	20	6	4

Do an ABC analysis of these items.

Discussion Questions

17.1 Why do organizations hold stock?

17.2 Why is that minimizing inventory does not necessarily minimize costs? Give some specific examples to support your answer.

17.3 What are the costs of holding stock? Are these generally difficult to find?

17.4 What assumptions are made in the calculation of the economic order quantity? Do these seem realistic?

17.5 How can the basic EOQ model be extended? How could shortage costs be included? Would more complex models give better results?

17.6 How do inventories affect customer service? Provide examples of ways to measure customer service.

17.7 What is a safety stock, and what is its purpose?

17.8 What functions would a computerized inventory control system have? Give examples of actual systems.

17.9 What does the printout in Figure 17.19 show?

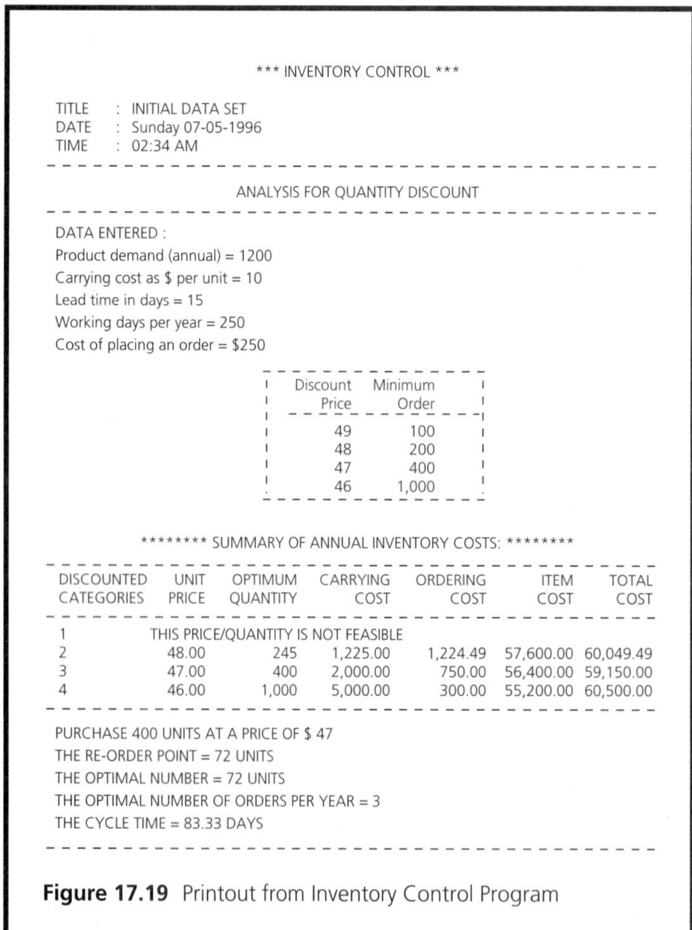

*** INVENTORY CONTROL ***

TITLE : INITIAL DATA SET
DATE : Sunday 07-05-1996
TIME : 02:34 AM

ANALYSIS FOR QUANTITY DISCOUNT

DATA ENTERED :
Product demand (annual) = 1200
Carrying cost as $ per unit = 10
Lead time in days = 15
Working days per year = 250
Cost of placing an order = $250

Discount Price	Minimum Order
49	100
48	200
47	400
46	1,000

******** SUMMARY OF ANNUAL INVENTORY COSTS: ********

DISCOUNTED CATEGORIES	UNIT PRICE	OPTIMUM QUANTITY	CARRYING COST	ORDERING COST	ITEM COST	TOTAL COST
1	THIS PRICE/QUANTITY IS NOT FEASIBLE					
2	48.00	245	1,225.00	1,224.49	57,600.00	60,049.49
3	47.00	400	2,000.00	750.00	56,400.00	59,150.00
4	46.00	1,000	5,000.00	300.00	55,200.00	60,500.00

PURCHASE 400 UNITS AT A PRICE OF $ 47
THE RE-ORDER POINT = 72 UNITS
THE OPTIMAL NUMBER = 72 UNITS
THE OPTIMAL NUMBER OF ORDERS PER YEAR = 3
THE CYCLE TIME = 83.33 DAYS

Figure 17.19 Printout from Inventory Control Program

Chapter 18

FACILITIES LOCATION

Finding the best locations for operations

Contents

Introduction

Whenever an organization wants to set up a new factory, warehouse, shop, office block, or other facility, it must make a decision about the location. This is an important decision that can affect the organization's performance for many years.

The aim of location decisions is to find the best geographical area for operations. This requires a series of decisions about the best country, region, city, and site within a city. These decisions must consider a range of factors, some of which can be measured quantitatively, while others require decisions based on judgement.

There are several ways of tackling location problems. This chapter gives a summary of the most widely used methods. These include costing models, scoring models, and geometric models.

Learning Objectives

After reading this chapter you should be able to answer questions such as:

- Why are location decisions important?
- What factors affect location decisions?
- How are costing models used?
- How do scoring models help with location decisions?
- What are geometric models?

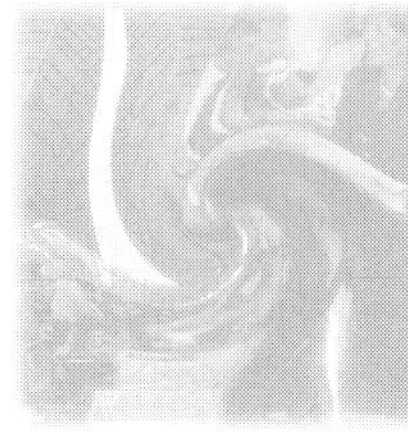

Decisions about Location

When Are Location Decisions Required?

Whenever General Motors Canada builds a new factory, Eaton's opens a new store, or Tim Horton's opens a new donut shop, they must make an important decision about the best location. This decision can affect the organization's performance for many years. If General Motors Canada opened a factory in a poor location, it might find that the productivity of the workforce is low, but it could not simply close down the factory and move. It costs hundreds of millions of dollars to open a new factory, and the costs of moving could be prohibitive. If Eaton's or Tim Horton's opened facilities in the wrong location, they would have low sales and would not make a profit.

Facilities location aims at finding the best possible geographic location for an organization's operations.

There are many reasons for an organization to find a new location for its facilities. These include:

- Expiry of a lease on existing premises
- A desire to expand into a new geographic area
- A change in location of customers or suppliers
- Major changes in operations that require a different type of location—such as a company changing from coal generators to hydroelectric generators
- Improving facilities, perhaps to introduce new technology
- Changes to the logistics system—such as changing from rail transport to road transport
- Changes in the transport system—such as the bridge to Prince Edward Island that makes travel easier

Commercial realtors often say that the three most important things for a successful business are location, location, location. A night club, for example, will not fare well in an area where most people are retired; art galleries and museums are often found at the centre of large cities rather than in suburbs; small shops cluster around large shopping centres. Location decisions often determine an organization's success or failure, and there are many examples of organizations that have made the wrong location decision and have gone out of business.

Location decisions are strategic, with consequences felt over a long period. If an organization chooses a poor location for, say, a factory, it must remain there for years or even decades. Even if warehouse or shop space is rented, it is a major undertaking to close down one facility and move to another area.

Case Study

Canary Wharf

Olympia and York is a Canadian property company with large office developments in many cities. In the late 1980s, it decided to build one of Europe's largest developments at Canary Wharf in London, England.

Canary Wharf had obvious attractions for Olympia and York. It is located in the Isle of Dogs in East London, which is the old dock area. When the docks closed, London was left with a large, run-down area. The government gave companies incentives to encourage development of this important area. Unfortunately, there were also drawbacks with the location and the timing of the development.

Canary Wharf tried to attract companies that wanted office space in the centre of London. But Canary Wharf was not actually in the City—which is the main financial district. Canary Wharf found that it was difficult to attract companies away from the City to a more distant, less convenient site, with poor transportation and few facilities. Competing developers opened less prestigious—but more convenient—buildings closer to the City, and the office vacancy rate rose to 17 percent. This had an effect on average rents, which fell by 30 percent. At the same time, Britain was struggling through its worst recession since the 1930s, and most companies were aiming for survival rather than expansion into new premises. The Canary Wharf site drained huge amounts of money from Olympia and York. By March 1992, it had serious financial difficulties, with reported debts of $20 billion.

Questions

- Was Canary Wharf a good choice for location?
- What could Olympia and York have done differently?

Location decisions can be very complicated. If you think about buying a house, for example, you may find it difficult to choose the best location — but this is relatively simple compared with a decision about where to open a new factory, distribution centre, hospital, college, amusement park, or any other major facility. Before making its decision, an organization must consider a range of factors such as operating costs, wage rates, taxes, international exchange rates and regulations, competition, current locations, availability of government grants, and reliability of supplies. Most of these can be measured in some quantitative way, but the organization must also consider a range of less tangible factors. These include attitude of the workforce, political stability, international relations, the legal system, and potential developments of the economy. These factors are discussed later in the chapter, but first we will ask if there are alternatives to finding new locations.

In Summary

Location decisions are needed in a variety of circumstances. These decisions are among the most important an organization has to make, as the effects can be felt for a long time. Location decisions can be complex and involve many factors.

Alternatives to Locating New Facilities

Any organization must make location decisions whenever it expands or contracts. It also must review its location when there is some other major change in its operations, such as a new process, changing customers, or new products. New facilities are always expensive and many organizations prefer to look for alternatives. Suppose, for example, a company decides to sell its goods in a new market. It has five options, which are listed below in order of increasing investment.

- *Licensing/franchising:* local operators make and supply the company's products in return for a share of the profits
- *Exporting:* the company makes the product in its existing facilities and sells it to a distributor operating in the new market
- *Local warehousing and sales:* the company makes the product in its existing facilities, but sets up its own warehouses and sales force to handle distribution in the new market
- *Local assembly/finishing:* the company makes most of the product in existing facilities, but opens limited facilities in the new market to finish or assemble the final product
- *Full local production:* the company opens complete facilities in the new market

An organization's choice depends on many factors, such as the capital available, the risk the organization will accept, the target return on investment, its local knowledge, existing operations, timeframe for the move, transport costs, local tariffs, trade restrictions, and available workers. The advantages of having local facilities as opposed to exporting include greater control over products, higher profits, avoidance of import tariffs and quotas, easier transportation, reduced costs, and closer links with local customers. These must be balanced against the more complex and uncertain operations.

You might think that a way to avoid a decision about locating new facilities is to simply alter existing ones. But this is still a location decision—as it suggests that the current site is the best available. In practice, when an organization wants to change its facilities, it has three alternatives:

1. Expand, or change, existing facilities
2. Open new facilities at another site, while keeping all existing facilities
3. Close down existing operations and relocate

Surveys suggest that around 45 percent of companies choose onsite expansion, a similar proportion open additional, new facilities, and 10 percent close down existing operations and relocate.

Case Study

Hudson's Bay Company

Hudson's Bay Company (HBC) is Canada's oldest and largest chain of retail stores. In February 1994, it was considering various options for expansion. These included opening a different style of retail shop such as warehouses, opening specialty retail stores, diversification into non-retail businesses, expansion into the U.S., and opening businesses outside North America. It eventually decided to look at the opportunities for opening department stores in China. The plan was to open a store in Beijing or Shanghai in early 1996.

The reasons for this decision were China's large market of 1.2 billion consumers, China's economic growth, which had averaged 9 percent per year throughout the 1980s, the increased disposable income and savings of its citizens, their enthusiasm for foreign products, and the lack of competition from North American retailers. HBC had existing trade links in the area, as it had bought goods from China since the early 1980s. It now bought 25 percent of its goods from Asia, and opened an office in Hong Kong in 1988.

There were several drawbacks to the plan. These included the need to form a joint venture with a large Asian company, possibly based in Hong Kong, the difficulty of finding a suitable location for a large retail development, the distance from current operations in Canada, the difficulty of repatriating profits, and the need to develop relationships with new customers. There were also some cultural differences that would necessitate training for Canadian executives about the Chinese market—and for Chinese employees about HBC's operations.

Questions

- Should HBC expand into China? Explain your views.
- Discuss the possible benefits and difficulties of this expansion.

Economies of scale are important in such decisions as bigger facilities are usually more efficient than smaller ones. This encourages organizations to expand existing facilities. But if you look more closely at the costs, you get a different view. Consider, for example, the costs of running a warehouse. These costs can be classified as operating, inventory, inward transport, and outward transport. Some of these costs go down with fewer, large warehouses, while other costs rise.

- *Operating costs.* Larger warehouses are usually more efficient than smaller ones. This means that the operating cost is minimized with a few, large warehouses, and it rises with an increase in smaller warehouses.
- *Inventory costs.* With fewer warehouses there is little duplication of inventory, so these costs are low. As the number of warehouses increases, the amount of stock duplication rises. This gives higher inventories and higher carrying costs.
- *Inward transport costs.* These are the costs of moving goods in from suppliers to warehouses. If there are few warehouses, large deliveries are made to a few locations and costs are low. As the number of warehouses rises, smaller deliveries are made to more destinations and the inward transport costs rise.
- *Outward transport costs.* These are the costs of moving goods out from warehouses to customers. If there are many warehouses they will, on average, be close to customers so the local delivery costs are low. However, if there are few warehouses customers will, on average, be farther away and the costs of delivery are high.

Plotting these four costs gives the graph shown in Figure 18.1. This shows that the total cost has a distinct minimum, which gives the optimal number of warehouses. In practice, before an organization makes a final decision, many other factors should be considered, including management costs, communications, fixed costs, employment effects, customer service, and data processing.

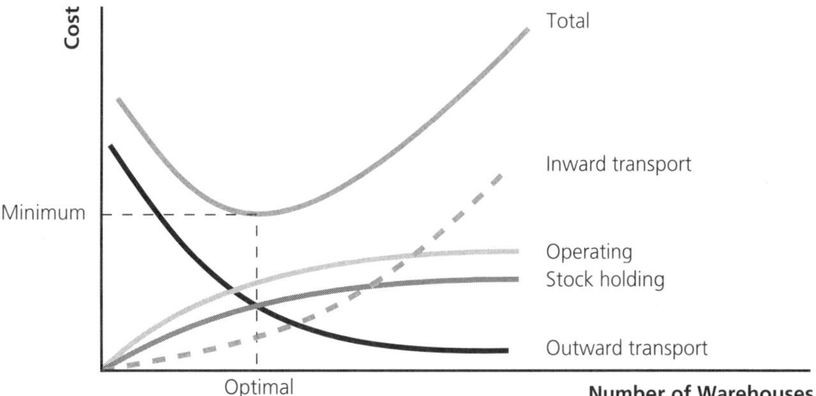

Figure 18.1 Variation in Costs with Number of Warehouses

Example

Semantic Services is reviewing five options for expansion. Each of these has a fixed annual payment (for rent, electricity, and other overheads) and a variable cost that depends on production (handling, depreciation, staffing, etc.).

Alternative	Fixed Cost	Variable Cost
A. Open new medium-sized facility	$80,000	$90
B. Open two new small facilities	$240,000	$70
C. Expand current facility	$900,000	$52
D. Build large new facility and close old one	$800,000	$36
E. Build large new facility and keep old one	$1,200,000	$44

Over what range of production would each alternative be most attractive?

Solution

This is an extension of the break-even analysis. Alternatives C and E will always be more expensive than D, semantic Services will not choose alternatives C and E. This leaves a choice between alternatives A, B, and D. The costs for various production levels are shown in Figure 18.2.

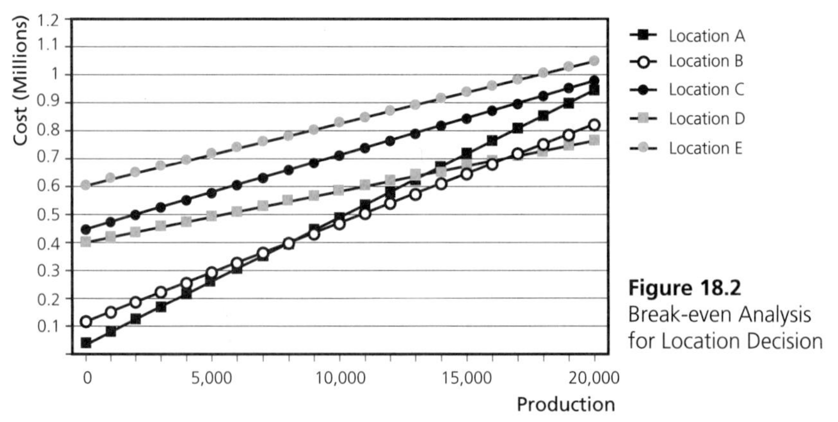

Figure 18.2 Break-even Analysis for Location Decision

- Alternative A is the least expensive for production, X, from 0 until:

  80,000 + 90X = 240,000 + 70X or X = 8,000

- After this, alternative B is least expensive until:

  240,000 + 70X = 800,000 + 36X or X = 16,471

- After this point, D remains the cheapest.

In Summary

There are several alternatives to opening new facilities. Expanding existing facilities can give economies of scale, but a detailed analysis is needed to find the best number of locations.

Review Questions

1. Why are location decisions important?
2. What are the three alternatives if an organization wants to expand its facilities?
3. "Economies of scale mean that it is always cheaper to operate a single large warehouse than a number of smaller ones." Do you think this is true? Explain.

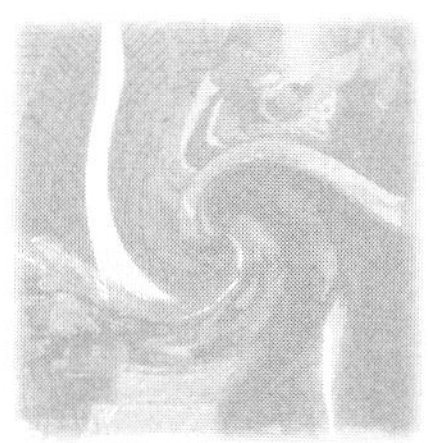

Selecting the Geographic Area

As stated, when an organization decides it must look for a new location, it must make a series of decisions. These begin with the "big picture," examining the attractions of different countries or geographic regions and move to a consideration of alternative areas within this region. Then they look at towns and cities within this area, and, finally, the organization looks at different locations within a preferred district.

If the organization's long-term forecasts show continuing demand for a product in a particular country, it may decide to open facilities there. As discussed, this can be avoided by exporting or licensing, but the organization then may lose control over its products.

In recent years, many organizations have opened facilities in other countries not to be close to their customers but to take advantage of lower costs. Low wage rates in developing countries have encouraged many manufacturers to open factories in the Far East, South America, and Eastern Europe. Often these facilities provide a convenient base for international trade; therefore, a Japanese company might open a factory in Taiwan to supply goods to Europe. Sometimes the trade is more focused, when, for example, an American company moves one of its plants to Mexico, and then imports the products back to the United States. Such arrangements involve high transport costs, but reduced operating costs can more than compensate for these.

But you should not assume that low wage rates automatically mean low costs. In many parts of the world, low wage rates are accompanied by very low productivity. Perhaps more importantly, manufacturing processes have changed over the years so that labour costs often form a very small part of overall costs. Most organizations now prefer to locate in areas that are close to their market, that have reliable suppliers, a good infrastructure, a high rate of productivity, a quality and skilled workforce—even if these areas also have high labour costs.

Case Study

McDonald's in Moscow

The world's busiest McDonald's restaurant is in Moscow. This is operated jointly by McDonald's of Canada, who own 49 percent, and the Food Service Administration of the Moscow City Government, who own 51 percent. McDonald's has opened branches throughout the world, but this was one of their most difficult to set up. Negotiations began with the Soviet Union 12 years before the restaurant finally opened.

The inside of the restaurant is exactly as you would expect with everything follows the standard McDonald's pattern: menu, colour scheme, decor, staff training, levels of cleanliness, and cooking. But this was only achieved with considerable effort and could only be done when conditions in Russia changed. As well as the obvious political problems, there were tremendous practical problems. There is often a shortage of beef in Moscow and the quality is poor. McDonald's has built a food-processing complex that supplies Moscow McDonald's with locally sourced food products. Potatoes are plentiful, but they are the wrong type to make McDonald's fries. Seed potatoes were imported and grown. Russian cheese was not suitable for cheeseburgers, so a dairy line was started at the food-processing complex. As well, restaurant staff had to be extensively trained in McDonald's procedures.

Questions

- Why did McDonald's open in Moscow?
- What problems did they face?

In 1980, Tandy Corporation moved production of its latest computer from the United States to South Korea. But rising shipping costs, the long sea voyage to the United States, the changing value of the dollar, and a redesign of the product to allow more automated production made this location increasingly less attractive. In 1987, Tandy moved its production back to Fort Worth, Texas, and reduced costs by 7.5 percent.

The location of sites in international markets depends on a number of factors. Some of these are commercial, but experience suggests three other factors are important.

- *Culture.* It is easier for an organization to expand into an area that has a similar language, culture, laws, and costs than to expand into a completely foreign area. So, a company operating in Canada would find it easier to expand into the United States than into, say, Korea.
- *Organization.* If operations expand overseas, there are really two ways they can be organized. A company may choose to operate internationally or multinationally. An international organization keeps its headquarters in the "home" country and runs its worldwide activities from there; a multinational organization opens subsidiary headquarters around the world so that each area is largely independent.
- *Operations.* Another concern is whether it is better to use the same operations around the world or to adapt to the local environment. McDonald's hamburger restaurants have almost identical operations in every country where they operate. Other organizations blend into the local environment and adapt their operations so that they are more familiar to their host countries.

In Summary

The starting point for location decisions is to define the best country or region for operations. There may be several reasons for the best choice here, including closeness to markets and operating costs.

Review Questions

1. Name three noneconomic factors that play an important part in the success of an international expansion.
2. "If jobs are created in one country, they must inevitably be lost in another." Do you think this is true? Explain, with examples.

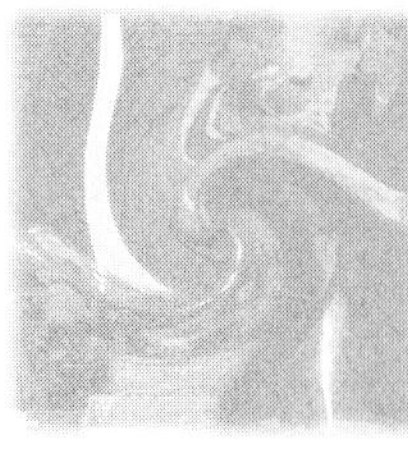

Costing Alternative Locations

Once a decision has been made about the particular country or geographic region, more detailed decisions are needed about cities, districts, and specific sites. There are several ways an organization can approach these decisions, and the best approach depends on the specific circumstances. One approach that is *not* recommended is personal preference. There are many examples of poor locations where a decision-maker simply chose a site he or she liked—perhaps in the town they grew up in, or in the area they spent their holidays.

We can classify **costing models** for location decisions as follows:

1. **Feasible set approach:** where there are only a small number of feasible sites from which to choose
2. **Infinite set approach:** which uses geometric arguments to determine the best site if there were no restrictions on site availability

A feasible set approach compares sites that are currently vacant and chooses the best, while an infinite set approach finds the best location in principle and then looks for a site nearby.

We shall start by looking at feasible set approaches. An obvious way of comparing locations is to look at the total costs involved. Many costs can be included, but the calculations can be simplified by considering only transport costs—both inward and outward—and operating costs.

- **Inward transport cost:** the cost of moving goods and services into the facility from suppliers—typically this includes the cost of transporting raw materials and components
- **Outward transport cost:** the cost of moving finished goods and services out to customers
- **Operating cost:** the total cost of running the facility

These costs will vary with location. In particular, sites close to suppliers have low costs for inward transport but high costs for outward transport. However, sites located close to customers have low costs for outward transport but high costs for inward transport, as shown in Figure 18.3.

A direct comparison of sites can be determined by adding these three costs.

$$\text{Total cost of facility} = \text{operating cost} + \text{inward transport cost} + \text{outward transport cost}$$

Operating costs depend on a number of factors such as wage rates, local taxes, reliability of local suppliers, and weather conditions. In practice, there is often little difference in operating costs between nearby locations, so these can be removed from the equation.

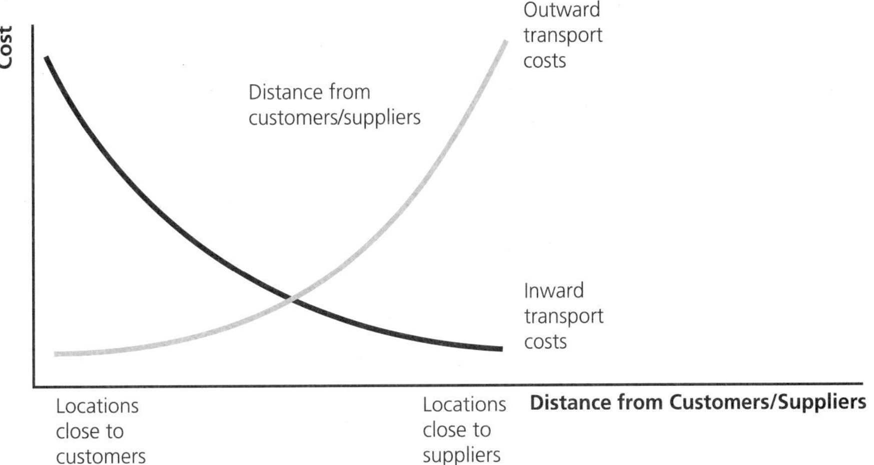

Figure 18.3 Transport Costs and Location

The obvious problem with the feasible set approach is that exact costs are not known in advance. How, for example, can an organization determine the costs for outward transport when the precise demand and customers are not known before opening? Even if the costs were known, they are likely to change and comparisons will become outdated. So, the calculated costs are useful for the purposes of comparison, but they are not necessarily the costs that will actually be incurred.

If the costs only give comparisons rather than actual values, we can simplify the calculations further. For example, it may be difficult to determine the exact cost of delivering products to particular customers, but it can be assumed that transport costs are proportional to the rectilinear distance from the facility to the customer. Here rectilinear distance is used simply because it is easy to find on a map. The rectilinear distance between two points is the difference in their x coordinates plus the difference in their y coordinates. Then the transport cost can be approximated as follows:

Transport cost = dFWP

where: d = rectilinear map distance between facility and customer

F = a constant factor to convert the rectilinear map distance into an actual road distance

W = the expected weight of goods to be transported between the facility and the customer

P = the price of moving a unit weight a unit distance

This equation provides a measure of the cost of delivering to one customer, so repeating the calculation for all potential customers and adding the results provides an overall cost for outward transport. A similar calculation provides the total cost for inward transport from suppliers.

Example

A warehouse, located at coordinates 12 and 16, makes regular deliveries to a customer located at coordinates 15 and 20. Experience suggests that a rectilinear map distance of 1 unit corresponds to 12 kilometres of actual road distance. It costs an average of 20 cents per tonne-kilometre to move goods. What is the cost of outward transport if forecast demand from the customer is 8 tonnes per week?

Solution

The rectilinear map distance between the warehouse and the customer is the difference in x coordinates plus the difference in y coordinates:

Rectilinear distance = (15 - 12) + (20 - 16) = 7 units

We know that the factor, F, = 12, and price, P, = 0.2. Then the expected weekly cost of transport to the customer is:

$$\text{COST} = \text{dFWP} = 7 \times 12 \times 8 \times 0.2 = \$134.40 \text{ per week}$$

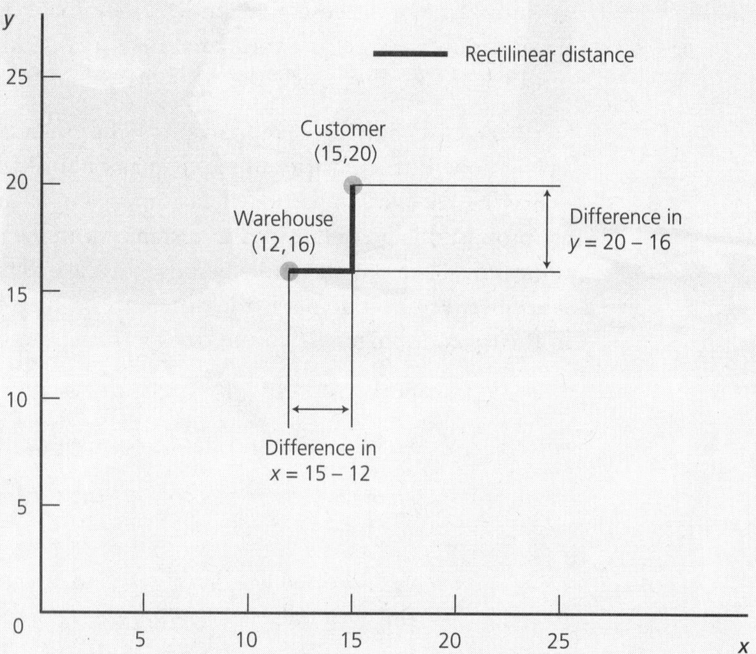

Figure 18.4 Rectilinear Distance

Example

Rondacorp Industries wants to build a depot to serve five major customers located at coordinates 120,120; 220,120; 180,180; 140,160; and 180,120. Average weekly demands, in vehicle loads, are 20, 5, 8, 12, and 8 respectively. Two alternative locations are available at 140,120, and 180,140. Which of these is better if operating costs and inward transport costs are the same for each location?

Solution

A map for this problem is shown in Figure 18.5.

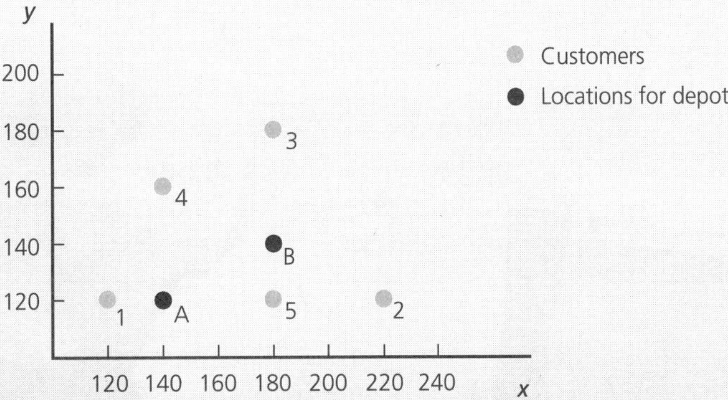

Figure 18.5 Map of Locations

As operating costs and inward transport costs are the same for both locations, we need only compare outward transport costs with each location, A and B. For this we can use the rectilinear distance, d. To make the calculations easier we can set the factor, F, as 1. Then the distance from A to customer 1 is:

$$\text{Difference in X coordinate} + \text{difference in Y coordinate}$$
$$= (140 - 120) + (120 - 120) = 20$$

All of the calculations for this problem are given in the following spreadsheet, which shows that location A is clearly better.

Figure 18.6 Calculations for Rondacorp Industries

				Location A		Location B	
Customer	**X**	**Y**	**Load**	**Distance**	**Distance*Load**	**Distance**	**Distance*Load**
1	120	120	20	20	400	80	1,600
2	220	120	5	80	400	60	300
3	180	180	8	100	800	40	320
4	140	160	12	40	480	60	720
5	180	120	8	40	320	20	160
Totals					**2,400**		**3,100**

Costing models can provide useful comparisons, but they have some weaknesses, including the following:

- It is difficult to find accurate costs
- Data depend on the accounting conventions
- Costs will vary over time
- Customer locations may not be known in advance
- Customer demands may not be known exactly
- There are many factors that cannot be costed

Because of these weaknesses, other methods, particularly scoring models, are often used to get another viewpoint.

In Summary

There are two approaches to location problems: feasible set and infinite set. The first of these compares alternative sites and can be illustrated by costing methods. These compare some measures of the cost of operating in different locations.

Review Questions

1. What is the difference between a feasible set approach and an infinite set approach to facility location?
2. What costs might be included in a costing model?
3. What is the difference between inward transport and outward transport?

Scoring Models

Costing models cannot deal with some factors that may be important in a location decision. How, for example, can you put a cost to a high quality of life? Other factors that may be important, but that are difficult to quantify, include the following:

Country and Region

- Availability and quality of workforce
- Climate
- Local and national government policies

- Availability of development grants
- Attractiveness of locations
- Quality of life—including health, education, welfare, and culture
- Reliability of local suppliers
- Infrastructure—particularly transport and communications
- Economic stability of an area

City or Location

- Proximity to customers and suppliers
- Location of competitors
- Potential for expansion
- Local restrictions on operations
- Community feelings

One way of considering such nonquantifiable factors is to use **scoring models**. These were described in Chapter 3 to compare different products, and the procedure for location decisions is the same:

- Decide the relevant factors in a decision
- Give each factor a maximum possible score that shows its importance
- Consider each location in turn and give it an actual score for each factor
- Add the total score for each location and find the highest
- discuss the result and make a final decision.

Obviously, the importance of these factors will change with circumstances. Decisions about the location of a new factory, for instance, are dominated by factors such as:

- Availability of a labour force with appropriate skills
- Labour relations and community attitudes
- Environment and quality of life for employees
- Closeness of suppliers and services
- Quality of infrastructure
- Government policies toward industry

However, decisions about the location of a service put more weight on factors such as:

- Population density
- Characteristics of nearby population
- Location of competitors and other services
- Location of retail stores and other attractions

- Convenience for passing traffic and public transport
- Ease of access and convenient parking
- Visibility of site

These lists reinforce the obvious point that manufacturers have different needs from service industries in their location decisions. In general, manufacturers try to gain economies of scale by building large facilities that may be close to raw materials. They will typically look for a site where costs are low, there is a skilled workforce, and suppliers are nearby. But services must be close to their customers. This difference is the reason city centres have stores but no factories, and why industrial areas have factories but no retail stores.

Example

Jim Bowen is considering four alternative locations for a new electronics warehouse. After much discussion with colleagues, he makes a list of important factors, their relative weights, and scores for each site. What is the relative importance of each factor? Which site would you recommend?

Factor	Maximum Score	A	B	C	D
Climate	10	8	6	9	7
Infrastructure	20	12	16	15	8
Accessibility	10	6	8	7	9
Construction Cost	5	3	1	4	2
Community Attitude	10	6	8	7	4
Government Views	5	2	2	3	4
Closeness to Suppliers	15	10	10	13	13
Closeness to Customers	20	12	10	15	17
Availability of Workers	5	1	2	4	5

Solution

The most important factors are the infrastructure and closeness to customers. Jim has assigned up to 20 points for each of these. Closeness of suppliers is a bit less important with up to 15 points, followed by climate, accessibility, and community attitude with up to 10 points each. Construction cost, government views, and availability of workers are least important.

Adding the scores for each location results in:

Location	A	B	C	D
Total Scores	60	63	77	69

These scores suggest that location C is the best. Jim must now consider all other relevant information before coming to a final decision.

Case Study – The Brownsville Blunder

Fastcut Abrasives Corporation is a world leader in manufacturing abrasive products, such as grinding wheels and sandpapers. It is based in Smalltown, Pennsylvania, where it operates separate divisions for coated abrasives and bonded abrasives.

Coated abrasives—such as sandpapers—are made using "wide web" technology. This takes wide rolls of paper, cloth, or fibre and coats them with adhesive. Then a layer of abrasive particles are added using electrostatic coating, followed by another layer of adhesive. The web is then cured in an oven. This first part of the process is capital-intensive, using giant machines called "makers."

The second part of the process is finishing. This cuts the web into various shapes and sizes for belts, discs, etc. Finishing uses less automation and is labour-intensive.

In 1970, the coated abrasive plant was plagued with labour problems. These came to a head with a long strike by workers. After the strike was settled, the average wage rate at Fastcut was $6.00 per hour, while the minimum wage rate in 1970 was $1.90 per hour. Fastcut had now become a high-cost operation and was therefore much less competitive. It lost its market leadership to its closest rival, 3M Co.

Fastcut then conducted a study to see how it could reduce its costs and regain its market share. One of the recommendations of this study was to move the finishing operations to a less developed region, which would have much lower wage rates. After a long search, largely in the Southern states, the company picked the town of Brownsville, Texas, as a site for a new finishing plant. The two main reasons for selecting Brownsville were:

1. The State of Texas and the local municipal government gave generous tax breaks and incentives to industry;
2. Brownsville had a lot of cheap, unskilled labour. It was close to the border with Mexico, and an agreement between the Mexican government and the U.S. Immigration and Naturalization Services allowed workers from Mexico to commute and work in Brownsville.

The study showed that Fastcut would save $10 million per year with this move.

The company began preparing for the move. This meant moving all the finishing machines from Smalltown to Brownsville. Fastcut had estimated this move would take six months to complete, with another six months to iron out any production problems.

The company lost most of its experienced employees when they accepted an early retirement package rather than move. Of the remaining 100 managers and supervisors, only 25 moved to Brownsville. All the hourly paid workers in the Smalltown finishing plant were terminated.

Fastcut hired 500 employees in Brownsville at $2.50 per hour. Most of these unskilled workers spoke only Spanish. The company's instructions and procedure manuals were all in English. The resulting language barrier created serious problems with supervision, training, and creating efficient operations. These problems reduced productivity and caused labour costs to rise.

There were also technical problems, as some of the finishing machines were damaged in the move. Rather than risk more damage, the last phase of transfer from Smalltown was stopped. The cost of transporting coated rolls from the making plant in Smalltown to the finishing plant in Brownsville was also higher than expected because of an increase in gasoline prices.

Two years after the start of the relocation project, there was still no end in sight to the company's problems. Costs seemed to be rising. The marketing department was concerned because market share was again declining.

Paul Moore, the general manager of the coating division, was very concerned. A meeting of the board of directors was scheduled for the next week and he was not sure what to tell them about the problems.

Questions

- Why did the company have so many production problems at Brownsville?
- What should Paul Moore do now?

In Summary

Many location decisions include subjective factors that cannot be used in costing models. The easiest way to consider such factors is to use scoring models.

Review Questions

1. What are the benefits of using scoring models for location decisions?
2. Are some factors important for locating a factory and locating a retail store?
3. What factors might be important in locating a professional service, such as a doctor's office?

Geometric Models

The last two sections described cost and scoring models, which are examples of feasible set approaches for comparing alternative locations. In this section, the discussion concerns **geometric models**, or how an infinite set approach works.

Many location models are based on the geographic layout of customers and suppliers. These models assume that facilities should be located near the centre of potential demands and supplies. One way of finding the centre is to calculate the **centre of gravity** of demand. This uses an analogy from engineering, with the demand at each customer replacing the weight.

The coordinates of the centre of gravity are:

$$X_0 = \frac{\sum X_i W_i}{\sum W_i} \qquad Y_0 = \frac{\sum Y_i W_i}{\sum W_i}$$

where: X_0, Y_0 are the coordinates of the centre of gravity—that is the facility location;

X_i, Y_i are the coordinates of each customer and supplier, i;

W_i is the expected demand at customer i, or expected supply from source i.

As usual, you should not worry too much about the details of these calculations as they are best done with a computer.

Example

Amstead Industries is planning an assembly plant to take components from three suppliers, and to send finished goods to six regional warehouses. The locations of these and the amounts supplied or demanded are shown in the following table. Where would you begin looking for a site for the assembly plant?

Location	X,Y coordinates	Supply/Demand
Supplier 1	91,8	40
Supplier 2	93,35	60
Supplier 3	3,86	80
Warehouse 1	83,26	24
Warehouse 2	89,54	16
Warehouse 3	63,87	22
Warehouse 4	11,85	38
Warehouse 5	9,16	52
Warehouse 6	44,48	28

Figure 18.7 Calculation of Centre of Gravity

Supplier	X	Y	Weight	X*Weight	Y*Weight
1	91	8	40	3,640	320
2	93	35	60	5,580	2,100
3	3	86	80	240	6,880
Warehouse					
1	83	26	24	1,992	624
2	89	54	16	1,424	864
3	63	87	22	1,386	1,914
4	11	85	38	418	3,230
5	9	16	52	468	832
6	44	48	28	1,232	1,344
Totals			**360**	**16,380**	**18,108**
Centre of Gravity	X = 45.5		Y = 50.3		

Solution

The calculations for this are shown in the spreadsheet in Figure 18.7.

As you can see, the centre of gravity is $X_0 = 45.5$, and $Y_0 = 50.3$. This is found from:

$$X_0 = \frac{\sum X_i W_i}{\sum W_i} = \frac{16,380}{360} = 45.5 \qquad Y_0 = \frac{\sum Y_i W_i}{\sum W_i} = \frac{18,110}{360} = 50.3$$

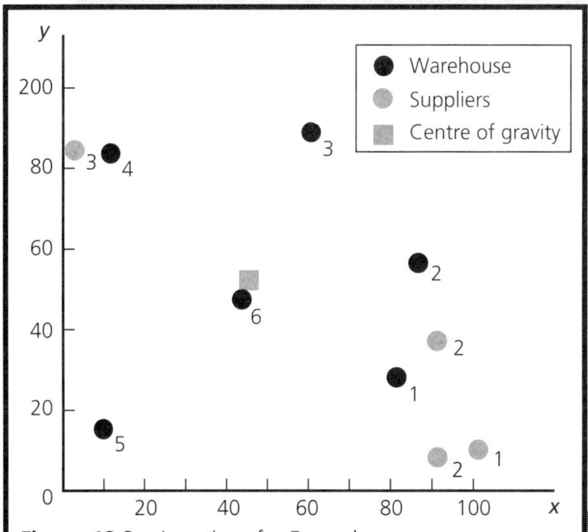

A good place to start looking for locations is around (45.5,50.3) as shown in Figure 18.8. As this is very close to warehouse 6, it might be better to expand this site rather than to look for an entirely new location.

Figure 18.8 Locations for Example

The centre of gravity can give a reasonably good location, but it is only a starting point. There may be no site available anywhere near the centre of gravity, or available sites may be too expensive; it might be a long way from roads, in an area with no workforce, or even in a river. For these reasons, the centre of gravity is most useful for cutting down the area of search for a location. Then the organization can use a finite set approach for comparing locations within this smaller area.

We now have a useful approach to location decisions, which:

- Uses the centre of gravity to find a reasonable location for facilities
- Searches near the centre of gravity to find alternative sites
- Uses a costing method to compare these alternatives

Case Study – Locating a Health Care Business

Danielle Miscampbell sounds enthusiastic and upbeat about her new business venture. She has just embarked on a new career in holistic health care counselling and education. "People want to be healthy," remarks the Registered Nutritional Consultant. Danielle owns and operates the Richmond Hill Natural Health Centre. Her one-year lease for the 1,500 sq.ft. office is about to expire, and she is contemplating moving to a new location.

The present office location has served her well, and it has helped her to establish her business. But she feels that the current facility will not be able to meet her future needs. She plans to focus more on the education side of her business rather than the counselling side. For this, she will need a classroom large enough to hold 15–20 students. The existing facility lacks such a large classroom.

Danielle described her requirements for a new office location as follows. She would like her new office to be on Yonge Street in Richmond Hill. According to Danielle, having the Yonge Street address is a definite advantage to a business. Also, she has the established practice in Richmond Hill, so she would not like to move from this community. The floor area of the new office should be 1,500–1,800 sq.ft. For a service business like hers, the aesthetics of the office building are very important. The building should be clean and well maintained, and have a large parking area which is well lit during the night for safety purposes. The location should be easily accessible through the public transit system. And, most of all, the rent should be reasonable. "I would like to spend less time on the facility maintenance issues, so I would prefer an all-inclusive lease, whereby the landlord is responsible for the maintenance, utilities, etc.," comments Danielle.

In a service business, the location of the business is important. Fortunately for her, Danielle has found a new facility that appears to meet most of her requirements. She hopes to sign a long-term lease this time so that she does not have to move again.

Questions

1. Why is Danielle Miscampbell looking for a new office?
2. What are some of her qualitative requirements for the location of her new office?
3. How are location requirements for a service business different from a manufacturing business? Discuss.

- Adds costs and other information to a scoring model
- Discusses all available information and comes to a final decision

In Summary

The centre of gravity method is an example of an infinite set approach to facility location. It gives a reasonable starting point for locations, and can be used to cut down the area of search for a feasible set.

Review Questions

1. What exactly is the centre of gravity of customer demand?
2. "The centre of gravity finds the optimal location for a facility." Do you think this is true? Explain.

Chapter Review

- Organizations often face decisions about the best locations for facilities. These are important, strategic decisions that can affect the organization for years to come.
- A location decision is needed whenever an organization expands, contracts, or makes major changes to operations. Organizations often make such changes by opening new facilities, but there are several alternatives such as licensing and exporting.
- Location involves a series of decisions. These start with a decision about the region or country to locate in, then move through decisions about the best geographic area, city, and specific site.
- There are two approaches to location decisions. The first compares a limited number of feasible locations and chooses the best. The second uses geometric arguments to suggest where the best location would be in principle—then it looks for a site in this area.
- The feasible set approaches were illustrated by costing and scoring models, followed by a discussion of infeasible set approaches by the centre of gravity method. Often these methods can be used together, so that a centre of gravity method provides a starting point for finding a feasible set of locations.

Case Study

Toronto SkyDome

The Stadium Study Committee, established in mid-1983 by Premier William Davis and chaired by Mr. Hugh Macaulay, discovered quickly that the most important and difficult issue confronting it was the location of the new stadium. Observing that the Metropolitan Toronto area contained several attractive sites, the committee found no shortage of debate on the subject:

"There is no site known to us in the Metropolitan Toronto area that does not have shortcomings. Every site worthy of consideration has rational, sincere, and passionate supporters and detractors. Moreover, several important factors relating to site are quite subjective. For example, does one's vision of Toronto dictate a downtown, suburban, or greenfield location; is it more important to provide relatively more convenient access for automobile passengers or transit passengers? Consequently, it is extremely difficult, if not impossible, to prove on the basis of empirical evidence the superiority of one site over another."

"Furthermore, it has become clear to us that there is no site in the Metropolitan Toronto area where, to use the words of the author of the B.C. Place Report, 'In excess of 60,000 people can expect to arrive and depart within one hour time periods without a significant degree of disruption. It is a question of relative advantage.'"

Ultimately, the Committee set the following criteria as a guide to rating site options:

- Located centrally
- Served by at least one existing major expressway and several arterial roads
- So situated that it would not impact unreasonably on its immediate neighbours and neighbourhood
- Available and be capable of quick development
- A location that would enable the stadium to be readily marketed for the various uses contemplated
- A large enough site to accommodate ancillary uses
- Served by a transportation system that would work well on opening day and into the foreseeable future at an acceptable cost

After seven months of considering some 34 site possibilities, the Committee recommended, in February of 1984, that the stadium be located on part of the Downsview Airport lands in North York. (This property is owned by the Federal Government and, based on discussions during the study, was considered to be available. Ultimately, it was not)

In considering that turn of events, it is well to review the comments made by the Committee concerning the railway lands as a possible site:

"As our work progressed, increasingly we became intrigued by the idea of a site within walking distance of the amenities of downtown Toronto, well served by public transportation yet accessible by automobile, and with adequate parking available. After visiting Vancouver and Seattle, we realized that, just as underutilized railway lands in Vancouver and Seattle had become sites for B.C. Place and the Kingdome respectively, perhaps there was an opportunity to build our new stadium somewhere on the lands own by CN/CP railways west of University Avenue on the edge of Toronto's downtown core."

Indeed, during the Committee's study, the railway land owners were, for a variety of reasons, hesitant to advance the concept of the lands as a stadium site. The Committee therefore reluctantly ruled out this possibility while allowing that the owners could yet come forward with a workable proposal.

That is exactly what transpired in the weeks immediately following the Committee's report, when CN Real Estate presented a conceptual plan to Mr. Davis. By late summer of 1984, the Stadium Corporation of Ontario, headed by Mr. Charles J. Magwood, had been established to advance the recommendations of the Committee, including finalization of site selection.

As events unfolded, it became clear to all who were involved in the project that the financial arrangements and the choice of stadium site were closely related. Eventually, it came down to two sites, both of which met the criteria:

1. The railway lands in downtown Toronto where CN Real Estate would be the developer
2. The lands adjacent to the Jockey Club site at Woodbine, where Cadillac-Fairview would be the developer

After full consideration of both proposals, it was decided that the CN land should be the location of the new facility.

Key Terms

centre of gravity *(p.524)*
costing models *(p.516)*
facilities location *(p.507)*
feasible set approach *(p.516)*
geometric models *(p.524)*
infinite set approach *(p.516)*
inward transport cost *(p.516)*
operating cost *(p.516)*
outward transport cost *(p.516)*
scoring models *(p.521)*

Problems

18.1 A company manufactures a total of 60 tonnes of goods per week in factory A, and 40 tonnes a week in factory B. The map coordinates of these factories are 8,9, and 52,47 respectively. These goods are delivered to 12 major customers whose average weekly demands and coordinates are shown below. The company wants to improve its customer service and decides to open a distribution centre. There are four possible locations, each with the same operating costs, located at 20,8; 61,19; 29,32, and 50,22. Which of these locations is the best?

Customer	Average	Coordinates	Customer	Demand	Coordinates
1	4	11,16	7	16	12,69
2	11	30,9	8	2	27,38
3	8	43,27	9	4	51,6
4	7	54,52	10	6	43,16
5	17	29,62	11	3	54,16
6	10	11,51	12	12	12,60

18.2 A new electronics factory is planned in an area that is encouraging industrial growth. There are five alternative sites. A management team is considering these sites, and has suggested the important factors and relative weights shown below. The team also gave scores to each of the sites. What is the relative importance of each factor? Which site seems best?

Factor	Maximum Score	Scores for Sites				
		A	B	C	D	E
Government Grants	10	2	4	8	8	5
Community Attitude	12	8	7	5	10	5
Availability of Engineers	15	10	8	8	10	5
Experienced Workforce	20	20	15	15	10	15
Nearby Suppliers	8	4	3	6	3	2
Education Centres	5	5	4	1	1	5
Housing	5	2	3	5	3	2

18.3 Find the centre of gravity of the data in Question 18.1. What is the cost of transport for a distribution centre located there?

18.4 An assembly plant is planned to take components from four suppliers and send finished goods to eight regional warehouses. The locations of these and the amounts supplied or demanded are shown in the following table. Where would you start looking for a site for the assembly plant?

Location	X,Y Coordinates	Supply/Demand
Supplier 1	7,80	140
Supplier 2	85,35	80
Supplier 3	9,81	120
Supplier 4	11,62	70
Warehouse 1	12,42	45
Warehouse 2	60,9	65
Warehouse 3	92,94	25
Warehouse 4	8,79	45
Warehouse 5	10,83	60
Warehouse 6	59,91	35
Warehouse 7	83,49	50
Warehouse 8	85,30	85

Discussion Question

18.1 Do you think an organization should consider its location as a strategic issue? Give examples to support your view.

18.2 Which areas of the world do you think will develop most quickly over the next decade or so? What effects will this have on the world economy?

18.3 What costs do you think should be considered in a location decision? What other factors should be considered?

18.4 What factors are most likely to affect a manufacturer's decision to locate a factory? What are the different factors for a service?

18.5 Give some examples of location decisions you are familiar with. How successful have these been?

18.6 Compare the location of facilities for a typical manufacturer and for an airline. What are the main differences?

CONCLUSION

This book offers readers an introduction to the important study of operations management. Our discussion began with an explanation of how and why operations management is a central function in all organizations. The discussion then centred on how to make decisions in a series of areas that are critical to the success of the organization.

In several ways, the book has balanced different viewpoints. It has emphasized that "operations management" is not the same as "production management." Operations are not limited to manufacturing, but are used in every organization. About 75 percent of us work in services; another 5 percent work in primary industries; the remaining 20 percent work in manufacturing. Almost half of the population does not work in the formal sense—usually because they are too young to work, are retired, are ill, work from home, or care for relatives. About 10 percent of the potential workforce is unemployed. But we are all concerned with operations in our day-to-day lives. We all belong to, and use, organizations that have different types of operations—whether they be businesses, governments, charities, sports teams, recreational clubs, or families.

This book is based on the idea that decisions are needed for all of these operations. If good decisions are made, resources are used effectively and there is little waste of resources. If poor decisions are made, resources are wasted. This could mean that too many materials are used, people work inefficiently, money is spent unwisely, and so on. You have probably passed a construction site and noticed the amount of materials that is thrown away; or been asked to fill in a form with information that seems to have no possible use; or have had to wait a long time to be served in a store; or have visited an office and been passed from one person to another; or have bought something that broke as soon as you started using it. These are examples of bad operations and you can see other examples every day. Have a look around and see how often you can find organizations that could easily improve their operations.

Operations management looks for ways of running an organization well. Often a little thought and common sense are all it takes. How often have you looked at an operation and thought, Why do they do it this way—and not that way?

Sometimes, problems facing operations managers are more complicated and need some rational analyses. This is the job of managers—to analyze situations and make decisions. This might involve some quantitative analysis, but such analyses are usually done by computer. There is no point in a manager doing arithmetic by hand—it just wastes time and is inaccurate.

All organizations face similar problems. They all have to employ people, design products, forecast demand, make products, find customers, pay bills, and so on. There are therefore common ideas that are important to operations managers in all organizations. In this book we have met a number of different types of such problems.

By now you should have some clear and useful ideas about the way an organization should manage its operations. The performance of any organization depends on its operations. This means its continued success and its long-term survival depend on operations management.

On a wider front, the wealth, standard of living, and quality of life in Canada depend on the success of our organizations. When you practise good operations management, you will have a direct effect on your organization. You will contribute to its ultimate success—and we shall all benefit from this success.

APPENDIX A

The Normal Distribution

The Normal distribution has been mentioned several times in this book. The Normal distribution is the most widely used statistical distribution. It describes many variables — such as people's heights, the weight of candy bars, student exam marks, output of chemical works, etc.

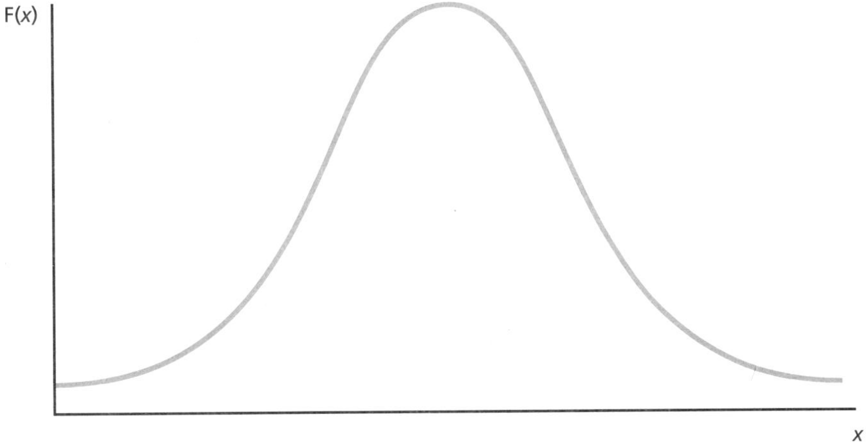

Figure A1 General Shape of the Normal Distribution

Suppose a machine is making sticks of chalk. The length of each stick of chalk is not exactly the same but will vary a little. The variation is random and we cannot say exactly how long any particular stick will be. But we can determine an average length of sticks—that is, the *mean.* We can also say how much the variation is, that is, the *variance* and *standard deviation.* If the length of each stick is x, and the number of sticks we measure is n:

$$\text{Mean} = m = \frac{\sum x}{n}$$

$$\text{Variance} = \frac{\sum (x - m)^2}{n}$$

$$\text{Standard deviation} = s = \sqrt{\text{variance}}$$

Although the Normal curve does, in theory, stretch from plus infinity to minus infinity, most values are close to the mean:

- 68.26 percent are within one standard deviation of the mean
- 95.45 percent are within two standard deviations of the mean
- 99.73 percent are within three standard deviations of the mean

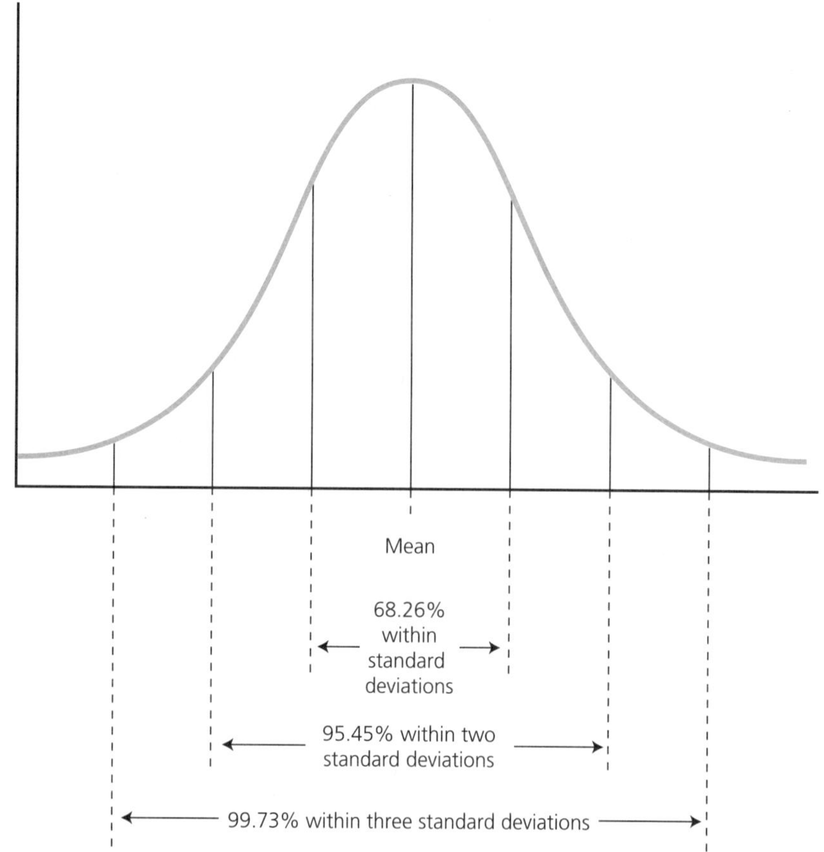

Figure A2 Probabilities with Normal Distributions

This means that we can use standard tables to find the probabilities. All we need do is find how many standard deviations a point is away from the mean. Then we can look up this figure—which is called Z—in standard tables, and they will show the proportion of observations that are this close to the mean.

The table on page 536 is a standard Normal table. Be careful when you use such tables, as there are several different formats they can use. The ones given show the area that is in one tail of the distribution.

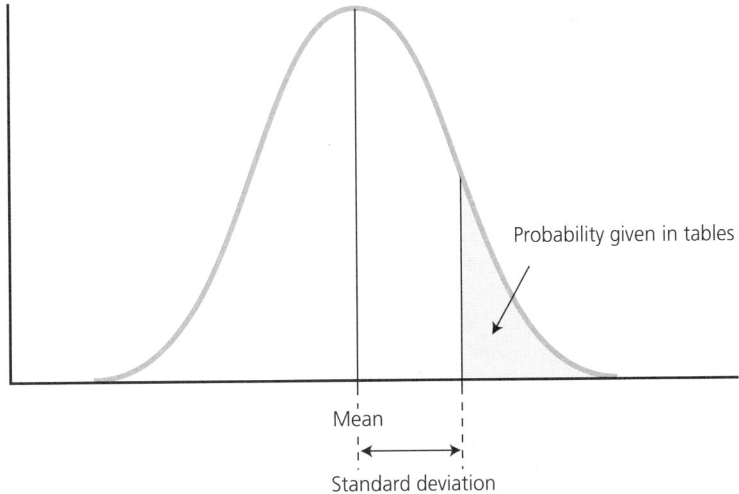

Figure A3 The Area Given in Tables

If you look up 1.0 in the table, the entry is 0.1587. This shows that the area in *each* tail of the distribution more than one standard deviation away from the mean is 0.1587. So, the total proportion of observations more than one standard deviation away is $2 \times 0.1587 = 0.3174$. Or, $1 - 0.3174 = 0.6826$ of observations are within 1 standard deviation of the mean, which is the result we quoted above.

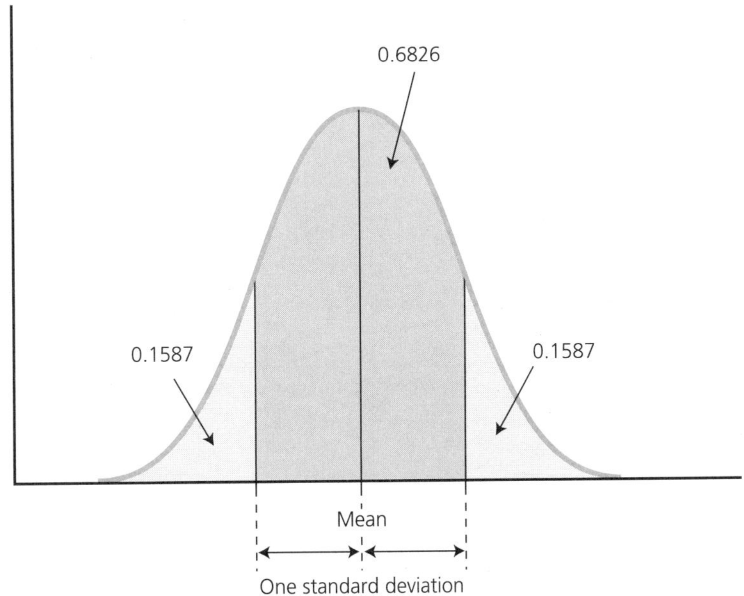

Figure A4 Probabilities One Standard Deviation from the Mean

Suppose the machine producing sticks of chalk mentioned above makes 10,000 sticks in one shift. The average length is 100 mm, with a standard deviation of 2 mm. How many sticks will be shorter then 95 mm?

The point we are interested in is 95 mm, and this is (100 – 95)/2 = 2.5 standard deviations from the mean. Looking up 2.5 in the Normal tables shows 0.0062. This shows that 0.0062 or 0.62 percent of sticks are shorter than 95 mm. As the machine makes 10,000 sticks in a shift, 10,000 × 0.0062 = 62 sticks will be less than 95 mm long.

The Normal Distribution

Normal Deviate z	.00	.01	.02	.03	.04	.05	.06	.07	.08	.09
0.0	.5000	.4960	.4920	.4880	.4840	.4801	.4761	.4721	.4681	.4641
0.1	.4602	.4562	.4522	.4483	.4443	.4404	.4364	.4325	.4286	.4247
0.2	.4207	.4168	.4129	.4090	.4052	.4013	.3974	.3936	.3897	.3859
0.3	.3821	.3783	.3745	.3707	.3669	.3632	.3594	.3557	.3520	.3483
0.4	.3446	.3409	.3372	.3336	.3300	.3264	.3228	.3192	.3156	.3121
0.5	.3085	.3050	.3015	.2981	.2946	.2912	.2877	.2843	.2810	.2776
0.6	.2743	.2709	.2676	.2643	.2611	.2578	.2546	.2514	.2483	.2451
0.7	.2420	.2389	.2358	.2327	.2296	.2266	.2236	.2206	.2177	.2148
0.8	.2119	.2090	.2061	.2033	.2005	.1977	.1949	.1922	.1894	.1867
0.9	.1841	.1814	.1788	.1762	.1736	.1711	.1685	.1660	.1635	.1611
1.0	.1587	.1562	.1539	.1515	.1492	.1469	.1446	.1423	.1401	.1379
1.1	.1357	.1335	.1314	.1292	.1271	.1251	.1230	.1210	.1190	.1170
1.2	.1151	.1131	.1112	.1093	.1075	.1056	.1038	.1020	.1003	.0985
1.3	.0968	.0951	.0934	.0918	.0901	.0885	.0869	.0853	.0838	.0823
1.4	.0808	.0793	.0778	.0764	.0749	.0735	.0721	.0708	.0694	.0681
1.5	.0668	.0655	.0643	.0630	.0618	.0606	.0594	.0582	.0571	.0559
1.6	.0548	.0537	.0526	.0516	.0505	.0495	.0485	.0475	.0465	.0455
1.7	.0446	.0436	.0427	.0418	.0409	.0401	.0392	.0384	.0375	.0367
1.8	.0359	.0351	.0344	.0336	.0329	.0322	.0314	.0307	.0301	.0294
1.9	.0287	.0281	.0274	.0268	.0262	.0256	.0250	.0244	.0239	.0233
2.0	.0228	.0222	.0217	.0212	.0207	.0202	.0197	.0192	.0188	.0183
2.1	.0179	.0174	.0170	.0166	.0162	.0158	.0154	.0150	.0146	.0143
2.2	.0139	.0136	.0132	.0129	.0125	.0122	.0119	.0116	.0113	.0110
2.3	.0107	.0104	.0102	.0099	.0096	.0094	.0091	.0089	.0087	.0084
2.4	.0082	.0080	.0078	.0075	.0073	.0071	.0069	.0068	.0066	.0064
2.5	.0062	.0060	.0059	.0057	.0055	.0054	.0052	.0051	.0049	.0048
2.6	.0047	.0045	.0044	.0043	.0041	.0040	.0039	.0038	.0037	.0036
2.7	.0035	.0034	.0033	.0032	.0031	.0030	.0029	.0028	.0027	.0026
2.8	.0026	.0025	.0024	.0023	.0023	.0022	.0021	.0021	.0020	.0019
2.9	.0019	.0018	.0018	.0017	.0016	.0016	.0015	.0015	.0014	.0014
3.0	.0013	.0013	.0013	.0012	.0012	.0011	.0011	.0011	.0010	.0010

APPENDIX B

Solutions to Review Questions

Chapter 1—What Is Operations Management?

Page 5

1. Many factors affect an organization's productivity, but the most important is the quality of its management.
2. It does not perform well and loses out to competitors. There are many examples where this has happened.

Page 9

1. All the activities that are directly concerned with making a product.
2. The managment function that is responsible for all aspects of operations.
3. You can give many examples here.

Page 11

1. You can give many examples here.
2. Personnel management is not *directly* concerned with making the product—and when it is, it becomes part of operations management.

Page 14

1. They are not fundamentally different in any way.
2. Public services, retail and wholesale stores, distribution services, nonprofit services, other services for industry, and other services for individuals.
3. No—it is a broader function and specifically includes services.

Page 15

1. False—most of them work in services.
2. There are several reasons for this, but the most important is probably increased competition.

Page 17

1. There are many possible titles, some of which are given in the chapter.
2. They need a number of skills—both technical and behavioural.

Chapter 2—Operations Management Decisions

Page 31

1. Strategic, tactical, and operational.
2. No; operational decisions concern day-to-day operations. All decisions are important.
3. a) strategic; b) operational; c) strategic; d) tactical.

Page 38

1. A statement of its fundamental beliefs and aims.
2. Strategic decisions about the organization as a whole.
3. The organization's environment and its specific competence.
4. What is our industry like, what are the future prospects, what are our strengths, who are the competitors, what are the competitors' strengths?

Page 43

1. No—they make decisions at all levels.
2. Business strategy concerns the whole organization; competitive strategy is the part of business strategy concerned with how the organization competes; operations strategy is within the operations function.
3. Strategic ones. Because these give the context for more detailed decisions.

Chapter 3—Product Planning and Design

Page 51

1. Any goods or services that satisfy customer demand.
2. To make sure that an organization continues to supply products that satisfy customer demand.
3. Because customers have different needs.
4. Because they are experts in producing one type of product, they know the market, can use common materials and resources, and use common designs and processes, etc.

Page 56

1. Generation of ideas, initial screening of ideas, initial design, development and testing, market and economic analysis, final product development, launch of product.
2. There are many possible criteria, based on how well the product meets customer expectations and how well it fits into existing operations.
3. No.

Page 57

1. No.
2. Three common factors are that the product is functional, attractive, and easy to make.

Page 64

1. To compare alternatives when there is a combination of qualitative and quantitative information.
2. Yes—this only gives one view.

3. Number of units produced.
4. Overheads, administration, marketing, research, development, testing, tooling, and any other cost that does not depend on the number of units produced.
5. The product is making a profit.

Page 73
1. Introduction, growth, maturity, decline, and withdrawal.
2. Reasonable values are about a) 1 year; b) 5 years; c) 10 years; d) 1 day.
3. No.
4. Costs are higher near the beginning of the life cycle and decline over time. Revenue is highest around the maturity stage. High profits can be made in the growth stage, but these generally peak with maturity.
5. No—few organizations work in this way
6. Research-driven, new product exploiters, cost reducers.

Chapter 4—Process Design

Page 80
1. The operations used to make a product. You can describe any process here.
2. Process planning makes the decisions about a process—it makes sure each product uses the best process. It is needed whenever a new product is introduced or when there is a change to an existing product.

Page 90
1. Many factors can be important, including demand pattern, flexibility needed, customer involvement, product quality, and vertical integration.
2. Project, job shop, batch, mass production, and continuous flow.
3. Reasonable answers a) mass production; b) continuous flow; c) batch; d) project; e) job shop; f) project.
4. Continuous flow and mass production. The processes have no time lost for set-ups, they are largely automated, use more advanced technology and specialized equipment, planning is easier, etc.
5. There are several ways, including reorganizing operators, group technology, and flexible automation.

Page 97
1. Manual, mechanized, and automated.
2. Numerically controlled machines, robots, flexible manufacturing systems, automated factories, computer-aided design, etc.
3. a) numerically controlled; b) computerized numerically controlled; c) computer-aided manufacturing; d) computer-aided design; e) flexible manufacturing system; f) computer-integrated manufacturing.
4. To improve productivity, reduce costs, and achieve consistently high quality.
5. Generally, NC, CNC, CAM, FMS, and CIM.

Page 99

1. The same as manufacturing—project, job shop, batch, mass production, and continuous flow.
2. No—many services are not expensive and some have a lot of automation.

Page 109

1. They describe the details of a process and highlight the areas where improvements might be made.
2. They are a type of process chart that shows the relationships between individual operations.
3. Operation A must be finished before operation B starts, and B can start as soon as A is finished.
4. When you want to describe the actions of all the participants in a process.

Chapter 5—Layout of Facilities

Page 116

1. The physical arrangement of facilities in a process. A well laid-out process will work smoothly and efficiently—a poor layout will give poor efficiency, productivity, utilization, and general performance.
2. To make sure the process works as well as possible.
3. There may be many of these including the product design, capacity, process used, materials handling, building, capital available, safety, etc.

Page 127

1. No—job shops do not use product layouts.
2. Yes—often this is true.
3. Because such measures may not be available, the data may be too difficult to collect, or there may be other factors that are more important, such as safety, noise, and security.
4. A—Absolutely essential; E—Especially important; I—Important; O—Ordinary importance; U— Unimportant; X—Undesirable.

Page 134

1. Yes—they are more like assembly lines.
2. To separate work stations so that a short disruption to one does not interfere with the others.
3. The smallest output of any work station along the line.
4. A line where all work stations are working at 100 percent utilization. No—it is very difficult.
5. The maximum time a work station can work on a unit of product. If more time is used, there is a bottleneck and the line cannot meet its output target.

Page 137

1. A layout that is neither totally product nor process. There are many possible examples.
2. An arrangement with a dominant process layout, but with some operations taken aside in a product layout. They aim for the high utilizations of a product layout in a process environment.

Page 143

1. No—the product is in a fixed location, not the equipment.
2. All materials, parts, and people must be moved to the site, there may be limited space, scheduling is difficult, the intensity of work varies, external factors affect operations.
3. No—customers should be encouraged to stay in the shop for longer.
4. There are many different layouts—we have looked at the most important types.
5. Reasonable answers are a) product; b) hybrid; c) fixed position; d) product; e) process; f) fixed position.

Chapter 6—Quality Management

Page 156

1. No—customers will not buy poor quality products at any price.
2. Because it affects the reputation, marketing effort needed, market share, prices charged, profits, costs, liability for defects, and almost every other aspect of an organization's products.
3. Because there are so many different opinions, viewpoints, judgements, and possible measures.

Page 162

1. No—higher quality can reduce costs.
2. The cost of all aspects of quality including design, appraisal, and internal and external failure.
3. Because fewer defects are produced and these are detected earlier.
4. By finding the quality with lowest total cost—this is often "perfect" quality.

Page 170

1. Quality management is a broad term that looks after all aspects of quality. Quality control describes the sampling and statistical analyses that make sure designed quality is actually being achieved.
2. A scheme in which everyone is responsible for passing on products of perfect quality to following operations.
3. A small group working in an area that meets informally to discuss ways of improving quality.
4. There are many of these, ranging from long-term survival, through lower costs, to higher morale.

Page 175

1. Not really. The quality of services usually needs more subjective judgements, but there are many similarities.
2. By asking customers how satisfied they are.

Chapter 7—Quality Control

Page 179

1. No—it is less expensive and more effective not to produce faults in the first place.

2. Quality management is a broad term that looks after all aspects of quality. Quality control describes the sampling and statistical analyses that make sure designed quality is actually being achieved.

Page 188

1. As early as possible—preferably at the product design stage and with suppliers.
2. Acceptance sampling makes sure the products are reaching designed quality; process control makes sure that the process is working properly.
3. Because inspecting all the products may be expensive, destructive, or infeasible.
4. No—because there are always random variations.
5. The distribution of means found in samples from the population.

Page 195

1. Sampling by attribute classifies units as either acceptable or defective; sampling by variable measures some continuous value.
2. AQL is the acceptance quality level; LTPD is the lot tolerance percent defective.

Page 203

1. Farther away.
2. The process is out of control and needs adjusting (but also check for random fluctuations).
3. A single reading outside the control limits, a clear trend, several consecutive readings near to a control limit, a sudden change, very erratic observations, or several consecutive readings on the same side of the mean.
4. Because $\bar{x}$ charts give mean values, but they do not show the variations from these means.

Chapter 8—Forecasting Demand

Page 213

1. All plans and decisions are effective at some point in the future. So they need information about future circumstances—and this must be forecast.
2. No—it need not be mathematical and should not be specialized.
3. Judgemental, projective, and causal forecasting.

Page 216

1. Subjective views, based on opinions and intuition, rather than quantitative analysis.
2. Personal insight, panel consensus, market surveys, historic analogy, and the Delphi method.
3. Unreliability, conflicting views of experts, cost of data collection, lack of available expertise.

Page 224

1. Forecasting methods look at the underlying pattern, but they cannot deal with short-term, random noise.
2. Linear regression finds the line of best fit through a set of points—that is, the equation relating a dependent variable to an independent one.
3. How well the regression line fits the data.

Page 238

1. Because older data tend to swamp more recent and more relevant data.
2. By using a lower value of n.
3. By choosing a value of n equal to the cycle length.
4. Because the weight given to the data declines exponentially with its age, and the method smooths the effects of noise.
5. By choosing a higher value of α.
6. The amount by which a deseasonalized value must be multiplied to allow for seasonal variations.

Chapter 9—Capacity Planning

Page 246

1. Capacity, productivity, utilization, efficiency, etc.
2. Capacity is the maximum amount of a product that can be made in a specified time; utilization is the proportion of available capacity that is actually used; productivity is the amount produced in relation to one or more of the resources used; efficiency is the ratio of actual output to effective capacity.
3. Yes, if the efficiency decreases.

Page 249

1. Total productivity is the ratio of total output to total input; partial productivity measures the output for a single input.
2. Yes—because they measure different types of performance.
3. Disagree—it gives only one narrow view of performance.

Page 252

1. Because the capacity measure the rate of output—the output has no meaning unless it is related to a period of time.
2. Designed capacity is the maximum output in ideal circumstances; effective capacity is the maximum output that can be expected under normal circumstances.
3. a) passengers per trip; b) customers per performance; c) games per hour; d) cases per week; e) call-outs per year.
4. In decreasing order, they are designed capacity, effective capacity, and actual output.

Page 263

1. Demand management and capacity management.
2. Examine forecast demand and translate this into a capacity requirement; calculate available capacity; identify mismatches between capacity required and capacity available, generate alternative plans for overcoming the mismatch; evaluate these plans and select the best.
3. Capacity must be closely matched to demand to give high utilization. This cannot be done when demand is continuous but capacity is discrete.
4. When to expand and how much to expand.
5. Fixed costs are spread over more units, more efficient processes can be used, and there is more experience with the product.

Page 271

1. If the first operation takes T, the second takes 0.8T, the fourth takes 0.8^2T, the eighth takes 0.8^3T, etc.
2. Experience and practice make jobs easier, shortcuts are found, skills increase, routines are known, etc.
3. To stop the performance of equipment falling below an acceptable level.
4. No.
5. After the period that minimizes the total cost per unit time.

Chapter 10—Production Planning

Page 278

1. Disagree—it is largely strategic, but there are both tactical and operational decisions.
2. Strategic plans lead to capacity plans, then aggregate plans, master schedules, and short-term schedules.
3. a) aggregate plans; b) master schedule; c) short-term schedule; d) short-term schedule.

Page 287

1. A number of places, including forecasts, plans for previous periods, decisions at higher levels of planning, etc.
2. Yes.
3. They find the resources available this period, by taking the resources last period, adding any new arrivals, and subtracting any deletions.

Page 299

1. Monthly production over the next few months.
2. Forecast demand, available capacity, higher level decisions, and any other relevant information.
3. A schedule of monthly production for each family of products.
4. It is easy to use, convenient, the results can be good, the process is well understood and trusted, and an experienced planner has credibility in the organization.
5. The cumulative supply line should be close to the cumulative demand line, and it should not change gradient often.
6. It is easy to understand and use, it is convenient, and it can be done on a spreadsheet.

Page 302

1. To add details to the aggregate plan, and to create a timetable for making individual products.
2. These mainly come from the aggregate plan, available capacity, actual customer orders, and available resources.

Chapter 11—Scheduling Resources

Page 311

1. To give detailed timetables for jobs, equipment, and people.
2. Resources needed and available, the master schedule, costs, etc.

Page 318

1. A simple heuristic rule that experience has found to give good results.
2. Useful rules would be a) most urgent first; b) first come, first served; c) shortest first; d) earliest due date first.

Page 321

1. A process where jobs use the same machines in the same order.
2. The time between starting the first job and finishing the last.
3. To minimize the makespan in a flow shop with two machines.

Page 322

1. When operators are not permanently assigned to a piece of equipment, and when they are in short supply.
2. Yes.

Page 325

1. To monitor progress, make sure planned schedules are actually being achieved, warning of problems, making minor adjustments to schedules, giving feedback, etc.
2. No.

Chapter 12—Job Design and Work Measurement

Page 339

1. Employers want to meet the economic, technical, productivity, quality, and other goals of the organization; individuals want a job that is safe, satisfying, and rewarding to meet their social and psychological needs.
2. Employers and employees.
3. Because it affects the way operations are done and, hence, the performance of the organization.
4. The physical environment, the social environment, and the work methods.
5. Morale, and motivation, are improved by significant, identifiable, and varied tasks, needing a variety of skills, and giving workers autonomy and feedback.

Page 348

1. To find the time needed to do a job—its standard time.
2. Actual time is the time an operator actually takes to do the essential parts of the job; normal time is the time an operator would normally take to do the job if he or she worked at a standard rate; standard time is the total time that should be allowed for a job, including allowances.
3. Using historical data, estimation, or a time study.
4. Standard time.

Chapter 13—Material Requirements Planning

Page 356

1. Material requirements planning—a procedure in which the master schedule is used to

plan the arrival of materials, components, parts, etc.
2. Dependent-demand systems find requirements from known production plans; independent-demand systems forecast demand, usually from historic figures.

Page 364
1. Any organization that can meet the requirements of MRP can use it.
2. By subtracting current stock and scheduled receipts from gross requirements.

Page 369
1. It relates demand for materials directly to a master schedule.
2. The requirements that limit its use, and the amount of data manipulation.
3. Timetable of orders, changes to orders, exception reports, planning and performance reports, and inventory transactions.

Page 373
1. Because small orders have high administration and delivery costs.
2. A rule to suggest how many separate orders should be combined into a single larger order.
3. Because it uses approximations for the average stock level and costs, demands are assumed to be discrete and occurring at fixed points, and we have assumed that an optimal solution occurs as soon as cost begins to rise.

Page 376
1. Manufacturing Resources Planning—which extends the MRP approach to a wide range of functions.
2. Yes—in common with all approaches of this type.

Chapter 14—Just-in-Time

Page 392
1. Other systems assume that stocks are essential and ask: How can costs be minimized?; JIT assumes that stocks are not necessary and asks the question: How can stocks be eliminated?
2. Operations are organized so that they occur just as they are needed—with materials delivered just as they are to be used.
3. They are a waste of resources and should be eliminated; they hide problems which should be tackled and solved.
4. An organization with a stable environment, standard products with few variations, a balanced process that uses resources fully, reliable production equipment, small batches of materials, short lead times for materials, efficient materials handling, reliable suppliers, etc.

Page 399
1. To control the flow of materials in a JIT system.
2. Each container has a Kanban, so the number of Kanbans sets the number of containers and hence the amount of work-in-process.
3. Focused factories specialize in making one item very efficiently. They can use specialized equipment in the long production runs guaranteed by JIT systems.

4. They are long-term partners who cooperate and have a mutually beneficial trading arrangement.

Page 403

1. There are many advantages to choose from including reduced stocks, easier planning, higher quality, better control, lower costs.
2. No—just-in-time needs a change of attitudes, plans, procedures, and operations. It cannot be tried as a small experiment.

Chapter 15—Project Planning

Page 412

1. A self-contained piece of work with a clear start and finish aimed at making a unique product.
2. To plan, schedule, and control the activities in a project—and to make sure specifications are met within budget and time.
3. Planning and execution.

Page 421

1. A list of all activities in the project with their immediate predecessors. Durations, resources, and other information can be added, but these are not essential for drawing the network.
2. Before an activity can start, all preceding activities must be finished; the arrows simply show precedence and their length and orientation have no significance. There are also some secondary rules.
3. Uniqueness dummies make sure only two activities go between two nodes; logical dummies make sure the network shows the proper dependence.

Page 427

1. The earliest time for an event is the latest time by which all preceding activities can be finished; the latest time for an event is the latest time that allows all following activities to be started on time.
2. The total amount the duration of the activity can expand without affecting the length of the project—it is the difference between the time available for an activity and the time actually used.
3. Zero.
4. The critical path is the chain of activities that set the length of the project. If any critical activity is extended or delayed, the whole project is delayed.

Page 431

1. The rule of sixths uses three estimates of activity time to give the expected duration and variance; it is used in PERT networks.
2. The project duration is assumed to be Normally distributed with mean equal to the sum of the expected durations of the critical path, and variance equal to the sum of the variances.

Page 437
1. By the amount of the total float of activities on a parallel path.
2. By its total float.
3. The shortest time to finish an activity if more resources are used.
4. No.

Page 441
1. They show clearly what stage each activity in a project should have reached at any given time. This highlights any expediting, rescheduling, and preparation needed.
2. By delaying noncritical activities to times when fewer resources are needed.

Chapter 16—Logistics Management

Page 453
1. Logistics is responsible for the physical movement of all materials and products from initial suppliers through operations and on to final customers.
2. No. Efficient logistics needs an overview of material movements.
3. Procurement or purchasing, traffic and transport, receiving, warehousing or stores, inventory control, material handling, shipping, distribution, location, and communications.

Page 461
1. To make sure that materials needed to support operations are available at the time they are needed.
2. Purchasing is concerned with the actual buying of materials; procurement is a broader term that includes a number of related activities.
3. The cycle begins with the person who needs an item making a request for it, moves through the work done in the procurement area, and suppliers, and finishes when the item is delivered to the person.

Page 464
1. Logistics is the overall function concerned with all movements of product; physical distribution is primarily concerned with movements out to customers; materials management is primarily concerned with movements in from suppliers.
2. Location, transport, inventory control, warehousing, communications, etc.
3. Road, rail, air, water, and pipeline.

Chapter 17—Managing Independent Demand Inventory

Page 471
1. To act as a buffer between supply and demand.
2. All types of goods, classified as raw materials, work-in-process, finished goods, spare parts, and consumables.
3. No—all organizations hold stocks of some kind.

Page 476
1. Unit, re-order, holding, and shortage costs.

2. The holding cost rises with higher stocks, while the others fall.
3. What items to stock, when to place orders, how much to order.

Page 483
1. A single item is considered, demand is known exactly, demand is constant, costs are known exactly, and no shortages are allowed.
2. The order quantity that minimizes inventory costs.
3. Holding costs are reduced, but other costs rise.

Page 487
1. The amount of an item that is in stock when it is time to place an order.
2. It is the lead time demand minus any stock already on order.

Page 490
1. a) Production rate is greater than demand.
2. a) Larger batches.

Page 495
1. The probability that a demand can be met from stock.
2. To reduce the probability of shortages and to increase service levels.
3. By increasing the amount of safety stock.

Page 498
1. Order quantity = target stock level - current stocks (- any orders outstanding).
2. For a periodic review system—as there is more uncertainty over a longer period.

Page 501
1. They show which items are most important so that appropriate effort can be spent on controlling their stocks.
2. B items.

Chapter 18—Facilities Location

Page 513
1. Because they have long-term effects, are expensive, have serious consequences for mistakes, affect all operations, etc.
2. It can expand the current site, open additional facilities, or close existing facilities and relocate.
3. No. Some costs rise with increasing warehouse size.

Page 515
1. Culture, type of operation, organization.
2. No—developments can expand overall demand.

Page 520
1. A feasible set approach compares a small number of feasible sites and chooses the best; an infinite set approach uses geometric arguments to show where the best site would be if

there were no restrictions on site availability.

2. Many costs could be included, but the most important are inward transport, outward transport, and operating costs.
3. Inward transport moves materials in from suppliers; outward transport moves products out to customers.

Page 524

1. They allow a range of factors, both quantitative and qualitative, to be considered.
2. No—factories look for locations that give economies of scale—perhaps near to supplies. Services locate near to their customers.
3. These might include population size and age, incomes, locations of hospitals and other doctors, public transport, roads, parking, security, location of other businesses such as pharmacies, etc.

Page 527

1. A measure for the centre of customer demand.
2. No—it gives a reasonable place to start looking for a location.

INDEX

Pages on which key terms are defined appear in **boldface.**

Q

PLANT MANAGER

to lead our operations in Brantford, Ontario. Reporting to the V.P. Operations, the incumbent will take charge of manufacturing and maintenance of our largest plant. We envison the candidate as a "hands on" mechanical or metallurgical engineer with several years experience in a manufacturing environment. Individuals ...ground would also be considered.

...lary and benefit package commensurate ...d individuals should apply in writing by

Manager, Corporate Purchasing/Transportation

A diverse and challenging role, you will be responsible for both the purchasing and supplying actions as well as the transportation functions of the organization. In this capacity, your mandate will include negotiating contract prices on all plant materials and ensuring all plants are properly supplied, maintaining high quality standards and co-ordinating all complaints relating to quality and

VICE-PRESIDENT OPERATIONS

Kumtor Operating Company, a subsidiary of Cameco Corporation, requires a Vice-President, Operations.

This is a challenging opportunity to become a key member of Kumtor's senior management team to ensure th... meets its objective of becoming a leading gold p...

Reporting directly to the President of Kumtor, yo... candidate will be the startup and subsequent opera... remarkable Kumtor gold project in Kyrgyzstan in C... You will be directly responsible for the planni... ordinating and commissioning of a large open pit ... You will play a leadership role in selecting pe... establishing operating procedures and subsequent ... managing the operations leading to planned annual production of 500,000 ounces of gold.

A seasoned mining professional with 20 or more ye... progressively responsible experience, including inter... assignments, you also possess superior organization... managerial and communications skills. Experience in ... developing countries and fluency in Russian are defini...

These senior-level responsibilities in a unique environ... offer the right executive the opportunity for promotion ... two to three years. In addition, you will ... development opportunities with Came... company with worldwide activities. ... an excellent base salary, premiums ... performance incentive plan. Relocati... of Kyrgyzstan, and a housing allowa...

Forward your curriculum vitae no l... 1995, in complete confidence to:

Operations Director - Shipping

A senior, Hong Kong based appointment with an international company

Management of shipping projects. Shipowning, Time Charter operations. Commercial and financial ship management. These are the core activities of our client - a substantial and fast expanding publicly listed international shipping company, with its Operations Department based in Hong Kong.

The company's rapid growth now creates the new position of Operations Director, responsible for all day-to-day operations of the company and its fleet of approximately 40 dry bulk carriers/tankers on period, trip and voyage charter.

An interesting challenge of the role will be direct responsibility for ship management together with ...

At least in your 30's, your ten year plus background must include considerable experience in bulk shipping at general management level.

Experience in Asia would be useful, and a long term commitment to remain in Hong Kong is important. This is a high level appointment requiring the stature and confidence to operate at senior levels with both Asian and European clients and colleagues, as well as an attention to detail, flexibility and commitment to contribute to a young and dynamic team.

For the right person a substantial basic salary will form part of an attractive overall package.

Please forward full career details by fax or mail, in complete confidence, to the Managing Director, Ref: 95109, Robert Friend Associates Ltd, 618 Prince's Building, Central, ... Fax (852) 2521 8657

Senior Quality Assurance Manager

You will be responsible for the administration of our Quality Program and Transport Canada manufacturing and distributions approval. You will also establish and maintain quality policy and procedures, auditing, and program plans. Your B.Sc., P. Eng., or equivalent, is complemented by extensive, hands-on experience in a related area, ideally in the aerospace field. Engineering and/or operation experience is essential, as is knowledge of quality assurance concepts, TC AM 561 563 etc., ISO 9000, MIL-Q-9858, FAA regulations, and SPC.

Supervisor, Work & Material Planning

Responsible for the effective management of unionized and salaried personnel, you will ensure usage of, and compliance to, the Master Production Schedule (MPS) and other production and inventory systems. You will also make certain that inventory and service levels and order accuracy meet with departmental guidelines. Your several years of experience in a manufacturing environment is enhanced by previous management ...

PROJECT MANAGER

...responsibility for directing an industrial R&D ... successful commercial implementation of a new ...

...of R&D for production, Precision mechanics ... Paper engineering, Industrial electronics ... Engineering, Surface Engineering, Electrochemistry

A LEADERSHIP ROLE IN EASTERN ONTARIO

Our client is a Canadian leader in the printing industry and is a major force in North America, with more than 6,000 employees at offices and plants across the continent. Technological innovation, a constant broadening of products and services, and a progressive, dynamic operating style have all contributed to a solid track record of profitable growth.

This organization provides ample career mobility for talented individuals and due to a promotion is seeking a proactive leader capable of sustaining the current momentum of achievement at one of its key manufacturing facilities.

Plant Manager

...is a high-profile manufacturing role with ...nsibility for all aspects of a high-speed ...tion that includes pre-press, press, main... and shipping functions. Top priorities ...cus on identifying and implementing ...ctivity improvements, with continued ...asis on reducing changeover and setup ... improving throughput, effective plan... and scheduling, and strengthening ongo... ...ste-/cost-control initiatives. Overseeing ...ionized employees through a team of ...rs and supervisors, you will demon... ...our commitment to open communica... ...participative management.

...ee/diploma or equivalent in Mechanical, ...al or Industrial Engineering ... ...logy is preferred. The success... ...didate will bring 10+ years of ...cturing experience including ...management credentials in a

high-speed environment. Equally relevant are your success in team-building and employee relations and your ability to develop a highly focused, aligned workforce within a fast-paced, unionized environment. Strong project management, budget control and administrative skills are also required.

If you're looking for room to grow with a diversified Canadian company that offers excellent career prospects reflective of your performance and abilities, please forward your resumé, in confidence, to: **File #1089, The Bedford Consulting Group Inc., Bedford House, 60 Bedford Road, Toronto, Ontario, M5R 2K2. Fax: (416) 963-9998**

New Horizons New Opportunities

At deHavilland Inc., we have maintained our position of leadership through the manufacture of sophisticated commercial transport aircraft and products for markets around the world. Continued success has led to these opportunities for accomplished professionals.

Senior Quality Assurance Manager

...will be responsible for the administration of our ...ity Program and Transport Canada manufacturing ...distributions approval. You will also establish and ...tain quality policy and procedures, auditing, and ...ram plans. Your B.Sc., P. Eng., or equivalent, is ...mented by extensive, hands-on experience in a ... area, ideally in the aerospace field. Engineering ...operation experience is essential, as is knowledge ...ity assurance concepts, TC AM 561 563 etc., ISO ...MIL-Q-9858, FAA regulations, and SPC.

Supervisor, Work & Material Planning

...for the effective management of unionized ...personnel, you will ensure usage of, and ...to, the Master Production Schedule (MPS) ...oduction and inventory systems. You will ...tain that inventory and service levels and ...meet with departmental guidelines. Your ...of experience in a manufacturing ...enhanced by previous management ...uivalent community coll... ...a strong team orienta... ...ledge of operations ...uling and inventory co... ...and the ability to deal ... ...nel are essential.

...itive compensation pac... ...to apply your skills with a reco... ...your resume, clearly indicating ...are applying for, in confidence, to: Office N14-03, deHavilland Inc., Garratt Blv... Ontario M3K 1Y6.

Process ... Windsor... the

Poised for ISO and QS 9000 certification, this $80MM C... demanding, critical few customer base internationally from a... and ensure the quality of an ultra sensitive manufacturing pr... thinking. Customer excellence is absolute. Take on the lead...

Operati...

and provide the vision and spark in demonstrating an unrestricted ... asset and people resource leadership to this 200 employee site. ... management to the test. You'll secure the "buy in" across this hi... in a fast paced, deadline driven environment. You'll develop yo... the boardroom, you'll partner with employees at all levels and ... ensure commitment to delivering the performance standards.

You're a builder... you've learned how to balance corporate disc... traditional box." You not only have proven how to inspire initiative ... MRP, SPC and SQC information can become the working tools ...

The lifestyle is family centred with gorgeous recreational opportuniti... include an executive base and a meaningful bonu... in complete confidence to Mr. R.C.P. Ward by fa... 3W9. We sincerely appreciate your inter...

Distribution Manager
(Montreal)

The Bedford ... EXECUTIVE RECRU...

Member, TRANSEARC... INTERNATIONAL ASSOCIATION

Our client, a leading national fashion retailer, re... expertise of a progressive distribution managem... fessional to join their dynamic and growing organ... Vision and entrepreneurial leadership have positioned **Rogers** at the pinnacle of its industry. We now need a resourceful and enthusiastic professional to ensure our top position.

Distribution and Transportation Manager

Reporting to the Director of Customer Service and working closely with our Production and Sales staff, you are a "take charge" team leader who will ensure the efficient and economical integration of warehousing, distribution and telesales functions. Demonstrating your expertise, you will provide leadership in the continuing development of our newly created team of Customer Distribution Representatives. Monitoring inventory quantity and quality and developing a departmental budget round out your mandate.

You possess at least 6 years' warehouse/distribution experience, preferably within a Food/Foodservice environment, 3 years of which have been at a managerial level. A degree in a related business field is essential. ... conversant with warehousing techniques, related systems applications ... customer service functions, you demonstrate excellent organizational ... communication skills. Proven knowledge and practical implementation ... service principles are essential, while a sound understanding of ... a focus on Health and Safety issues related to material ha...

...forward their resume, by May 10, to: ... Nestlé Foodservice, 25 Sh...

Supervisor, Stores (Warehouse) and Fleet

Responsible for all receiving and shipping to & from the warehouse, you will ensure that all proper tracking and control procedures are in place at all times, that appropriate stock levels are tracked and maintained, and that staff development is provided ...unter and dock service. You ... the safe operating conditions ... leased vehicles, maintenan... ...s, and all budget...

Ryder Dedicated Logistics is a leading provider of Third Party Logistics services which include dedicated contract carriage, contract warehousing and fully managed logistics programs. We are currently seeking candidates for the position of:

MANAGER - OPERATIONS

As a qualified Manager - Operations, you will be responsible for the overall development and operations of an area in our product line, including daily operations management, development, analysis and customer service.

You have a minimum of five years' senior management experience in a transportation related field and are skilled in general management functions. A degree in Logistics or Business and some development background would ...

...forward your resume, to: **Human Resources, Ryder ... Minnesota Court, Suite 120, Mississauga, ...**

CONTINUOUS IMPROVEMENT MANAGER

CCL Custom Manufacturing, Liquid Division, specializes in the manufacturing of household and personal care liquid based products and has an immediate opening for a Continuous Improvement Manager.

DUTIES:

To continue the implementation of the C.I. culture change within the division. To train and facilitate as required, specifically, in the areas of Total Quality Management and Continuous Improvement practices. Research and develop innovative and progressive concepts at all levels of the division. Provide leadership and guidance to C.I. teams as required. Sponsor presentations to all levels regarding C.I. developments.

REQUIREMENTS:

Practical experience in C.I. Management and/or T.Q.M. Good understanding of business requirements of the 1990's. Managerial Experience preferred. Excellent training and facilitation skills. Strong communication skills with particular emphasis on presentations. Proficient computer skills (Word Processing and Presentation software). Motivated self-starter with the ability to work ...

The Ford St. Thomas Assembly Plant is currently recruiting highly skilled individuals who can motivate their staff to achieve high production standards. Positions are available for

Production Supervisors

The position of **Production Supervisor** requires the hands-on supervision of assembly line operations at our high-volume, two-shift production plant. Potential candidates must possess a Degree or Diploma preferably in the area of Science or Technology. Additionally, candidates require prior experience in an assembly or manufacturing operation with demonstrated abilities in administration, effective communication skills, and the achievement of organizational objectives. Proficiency with quality control methodologies and ... would be an asset. Individuals able to excel in a results-oriented and demanding environment are encouraged to respond.

...offer excellent remuneration and a comprehensive company-paid benefits ...m. Interested candidates should apply in writing, quoting File #TS-1000, ...Salaried Personnel Supervisor, Ford Motor Company of C... Box 2005, St. Thomas, Ontario N5P 3W1

PRODUCTION SUPERVISION

As the successful candidate, you have well developed planning, organizational and leadership skills acquired through at least three years supervisory experience in a unionized manufacturing environment. Knowledge of SPC and a post-secondary education in a technical discipline are desirable.

A competitive salary and a comprehensive ...

Millan Bathurst is a recognized leader in the corrugated ...ing industry, bringing together over 109 years of Canadian ...ss traditions. We are now seeking a highly responsible ...ofessional self-starter.

Manager, Corporate Purchasing/Transportation

...d challenging role, you will be responsible for both the ...and supplying actions as well as the transportation ...the organization. In this capacity, your mandate will ...iating contract prices on all plant materials and en... ...s are properly supplied, maintaining high quality ...co-ordinating all complaints relating ...

PLANT MANAGER

to lead our operations in Brantford, Ontario. Reporting to the V.P. Operations, the incumbent will take charge of manufacturing and maintenance of our largest plant. We envison the candidate as a "hands on" mechanical or metallurgical engineer with several years experience in a manufacturing environment. Individuals

Materials M...

...responsible for purch... departments. You wil... improve inventory m... growth. The successful ... years' experience in el...

Buyer... In this ... deliveries for designa... functions. You will ev... Reporting to the Purch... experience as a buye... manufacturing enviro...

Quality En...

...stem to ensure tha... requirements. You ... yield, product quali... be required to imple... in electronics eng... experience in a ... Experience in comp... assurance is essent... ASQC certification ...